Register Now for Online Access to Your Book!

S0-CUD-525

SPRINGER PUBLISHING COMPANY
C⏻NNECT™

Your print purchase of *Management and Leadership in Social Work* **includes online access to the contents of your book**—increasing accessibility, portability, and searchability!

Access today at:

http://connect.springerpub.com/content/book/978-0-8261-3068-6 or scan the QR code at the right with your smartphone and enter the access code below.

NWKA5BN7

Scan here for quick access.

If you are experiencing problems accessing the digital component of this product, please contact our customer service department at cs@springerpub.com

The online access with your print purchase is available at the publisher's discretion and may be removed at any time without notice.

Publisher's Note: New and used products purchased from third-party sellers are not guaranteed for quality, authenticity, or access to any included digital components.

SPC

SPRINGER PUBLISHING COMPANY
View all our products at springerpub.com

Todd W. Rofuth, DSW, LMSW, has been at Southern Connecticut State University (SCSU) for 28 years, where he was the chairperson of the Social Work Department for 18 years, and the former director of the Urban Studies Program for 10 years. He has taught at both the graduate and undergraduate level, including many courses in social service management, research, social welfare policy, ethnic realities, and the thesis practicum seminar. His most recent accomplishment was the creation of a Doctor of Social Work Program for SCSU which commenced operation in June 2018. He has presented at more than 50 national and regional conferences and workshops and several international meetings. Dr. Rofuth holds a Master of Social Work degree from the University of Minnesota, Duluth, and a Doctor of Social Work from the University of Pennsylvania. In 2013 he completed two 3-year terms as vice president of the National Association of Deans and Directors (NADD) for Graduate Social Work programs. He served on the Board of NADD for 11 years. From 2000 to 2002 he was the co-coordinator of SCSU's 10-year reaccreditation self-study for the New England Association of Schools and Colleges. He has had 35 years of post MSW social work practice experience, primarily in social welfare policy analysis, research, and supervisory positions in federal and state government and private consulting. While attending the doctoral program at the University of Pennsylvania, Dr. Rofuth worked at the Wharton School as a senior research associate directing the Economic Development and Jobs project. He served as a policy analyst in the General Service Administration Office of the Administrator during the Jimmy Carter administration and evaluated the Labor Surplus Set-Aside Program and designed a contract proposal for the President's Report to Congress. He also served as the director of the Maryland Department of Human Resources, Office of Welfare Employment and Policy.

He has obtained over 60 grants in a variety of areas, including child welfare, drug courts, community housing, Ryan White, child care, and welfare reform. Since 2006 Dr. Rofuth has served on the editorial board of the *Journal of Family Social Work*. Dr. Rofuth is a site visitor chairperson for the Council on Social Work Education (CSWE) and has conducted eight site visits. He also has served as an external promotion and tenure reviewer for five universities. He is active in the New Haven community, serving on the board of the New Haven Farms and the board of the New Haven Occupational Industrial Corporation.

Julie M. Piepenbring, PhD, LCSW, has taught in the Social Work Department at Southern Connecticut State University (SCSU) for over 6 years as an adjunct professor, and is currently an assistant professor in the Social Work Department at the College of Saint Rose. She has extensive leadership and management experience working in nonprofit social service organizations, and as a chief clinical officer and executive vice president, she applied her social work knowledge and skills in the administrative arena to successfully lead large teams and expand programs. During her tenure as an executive leader in a large nonprofit organization, she also taught in the SCSU graduate social work program and provided clinical therapy to children and adults in private practice for more than 10 years. She has experience working in a variety of settings that required managing challenging clinical administrative issues, educating other clinicians and students, and troubleshooting in complex administrative hierarchies.

Dr. Piepenbring obtained her MSW from Southern Connecticut State University and her doctorate in social work from Fordham University. Her research and academic interests have focused on autism and the impact of autism spectrum disorder (ASD) on families, culturally competent clinical practice, and organizational leadership. Dr. Piepenbring has presented on ASD-related topics at national and local conferences and was an invited panelist at Autism Speaks, Connecticut chapter. She has presented on "Strategic Planning" and the "It Factors of Leadership" at the National Network for Social Work Management.

Dr. Piepenbring strongly believes in the practice principles of empowerment, modeling, collaboration, and coaching when working with teams. Additionally, she is the type of professor who supportively challenges students to become critical thinkers and aim to instill the value of continuous growth by encouraging and expecting them to work to their full potential. Dr. Piepenbring is incredibly passionate about and committed to the social work profession and takes great pride in educating future leaders in the field.

MANAGEMENT AND LEADERSHIP IN SOCIAL WORK

A Competency-Based Approach

Todd W. Rofuth, DSW, LMSW
and
Julie M. Piepenbring, PhD, LCSW

SPRINGER PUBLISHING COMPANY

Springer Publishing Company, LLC
11 West 42nd Street
New York, NY 10036
www.springerpub.com
http://connect.springerpub.com

Acquisitions Editor: Kate Dimock
Compositor: diacriTech, Chennai

ISBN: 9780826130679
ebook ISBN: 9780826130686
DOI: 10.1891/9780826130686

Instructor's Materials: Qualified instructors may request supplements by emailing textbook@springerpub.com
Instructor's Manual: 9780826135247
Instructor's PowerPoints: 9780826135032

19 20 21 22 / 5 4 3 2 1

The author and the publisher of this Work have made every effort to use sources believed to be reliable to provide information that is accurate and compatible with the standards generally accepted at the time of publication. The author and publisher shall not be liable for any special, consequential, or exemplary damages resulting, in whole or in part, from the readers' use of, or reliance on, the information contained in this book. The publisher has no responsibility for the persistence or accuracy of URLs for external or third-party Internet websites referred to in this publication and does not guarantee that any content on such websites is, or will remain, accurate or appropriate.

Library of Congress Cataloging-in-Publication Data

Names: Rofuth, Todd W., author. | Piepenbring, Julie M., author.
Title: Management and leadership in social work : a competency based approach
    / Todd W. Rofuth and Julie M. Piepenbring.
Description: New York, NY : Springer Publishing Company, LLC, [2019] |
    Includes bibliographical references and index.
Identifiers: LCCN 2019015621| ISBN 9780826130679 | ISBN 9780826130686
    (e-book) | ISBN 9780826135247 (Instructors manual)
Subjects: | MESH: Social Work–organization & administration | Leadership |
    Professional Competence | Personnel Management–methods | Efficiency, Organizational
Classification: LCC HV40 | NLM HV 40 | DDC 361.3068–dc23 LC record available at
https://lccn.loc.gov/2019015621

Contact us to receive discount rates on bulk purchases.
We can also customize our books to meet your needs.
For more information please contact: sales@springerpub.com

Todd Rofuth: https://orcid.org/0000-0002-1719-7765
Julie Piepenbring: https://orcid.org/0000-0001-5951-3415

Publisher's Note: New and used products purchased from third-party sellers are not guaranteed for quality, authenticity, or access to any included digital components.

Printed in the United States of America.

CONTENTS

Foreword   William Rowe, DSW   *vii*
Preface   *ix*

Part 1: Executive Leadership in Social Work

1. Leadership and Management Theory in Social Work   3

2. Best Leadership and Management Practices in Social Work   33

3. Effective Communication and Marketing the Organization for Social Workers   55

4. Making Meetings Productive and Working With Groups for Social Workers   89

5. Problem Solving and Decision Making in Social Work   119

6. Developing and Motivating Staff in Social Work   163

7. Professional Development in Leadership and Management in Social Work   191

8. Managing the Organizational Functions for Social Workers   221

Part 2: Resource Management Practices in Social Work

9. Accountability in Social Work   239

10. Human Resource Functions in a Social Work Environment   263

11. Supervising Staff in a Social Work Environment   319

12. Management Information Systems and Managing Technology for Social Work Environments   349

13. Financial Management in Social Work   367

Part 3: Strategic Management and Administrative Skills for Organizational Growth and Success in a Social Work Environment

14. Strategic Planning in a Social Work Environment   389

15. Designing and Assessing Programs for Social Work   427

16. Strategic Resource Development in a Social Work Environment   441

Part 4: Community Collaboration

17. Community Collaboration for Social Workers   477

Part 5: Supplemental Material

18. Book Outline by Parts and Domains From the NSWM and the CSWE Competencies and Practice Behaviors by Chapters   493

19. The Network for Social Work Management Human Services Management Competencies and Practice Behaviors   511

20. The Council on Social Work Education Competencies   519

Index   525

FOREWORD

Management and Leadership in Social Work: A Competency-Based Approach by Rofuth and Piepenbring is a long-awaited work that will help to fill a gap that has been a concern for educators, administrators, and practitioners for decades. For some time most of the topics addressed in this book were based on materials that have been adapted from knowledge and skills originally developed in schools of business and organizational behavior. This effort by Rofuth and Piepenbring will help to change that as it is written by social workers for social workers.

The authors themselves are two highly accomplished leaders/managers who have lived and mastered the competencies and skills detailed in this work. By incorporating the competencies and practice behaviors identified by both the Network on Social Work Management and the Council on Social Work Education, the work will be eagerly adopted as a text and teaching resource in accredited schools of social work. The comprehensive nature of the book, which is filled with exercises and case examples in settings familiar to social workers, makes the materials more accessible and ready for implementation. These features are critical to the graduate student exploring leadership and administration in social work settings as well as those practitioners who are considering shifting their focus from frontline to supervision and administration. For those already in management, the detailed competency-based practices and the skills needed to implement them are especially useful for those who are reviewing or wish to refresh and advance their management techniques.

The authors have expertly woven together well-tested evidence-based practices with numerous exciting innovations and tied them directly to the kinds of challenges that face us in a wide variety of social work settings. The design of the book itself is a testament to the authors' organizational skills. One clear example of this is using the supplemental materials in Chapters 18–20 to link the competencies and practice behaviors to the exercises and examples in each chapter, which is exactly what is needed when doing program evaluations or writing annual reports.

This book is particularly timely given the recent proliferation of social work practice doctorates (DSW). The express purpose of most DSW programs is to prepare graduates to advance their clinical practice, enter university teaching positions, and assume leadership in agencies, communities, and the profession. The number of DSW programs is set to double in the next 5 years and the Council on Social Work Education is moving toward accreditation of these programs. *Management and Leadership in Social Work: A Competency-Based Approach* will be a welcome text for the students and instructors in those courses and a valuable reference for social workers already in leadership and management positions.

William Rowe, DSW
Professor
Social Work Department
Southern Connecticut State University
New Haven, Connecticut

PREFACE

WHY DID WE WRITE THIS BOOK?

Dr. Todd Rofuth and Dr. Julie Piepenbring have had many years of leadership and management experience in a variety of settings (federal government, state government, large healthcare settings, public nonprofits, and state universities) and have discovered that there are few books that cover the majority of topics related to leadership and management specifically for social work education and practice. Most books on leadership and management are highly specialized for a particular field, and few are designed for social work educators and the nonprofit and for-profit agency sectors.

Leading and managing others can be an extremely rewarding, challenging, stressful, and invigorating experience. Many leaders and managers, at one point or another, will find themselves eagerly turning to the literature as well as seasoned professionals or educators not only in search of answers for how to handle difficult and unanticipated situations but also—and perhaps importantly—because they are seeking ways to enhance their abilities to lead or manage others authentically, judiciously, and confidently. Whether you are an educator, a student, or a current or aspiring leader or manager in any of the vast arenas in which social workers find themselves making a difference, we believe this book has much to offer all.

Each chapter offers case examples that cover a wide variety of topics that blend both the art and science of leadership and management, such as understanding different leadership styles, practicing self-reflection and self-care, understanding methods to motivate teams and mentor others, developing strategic plans, understanding financial management, marketing, fundraising, human resources, program evaluations, community collaboration, and much more. Besides discussing theoretical approaches to management and leadership, this book offers a wide variety of strategies that can be practically applied using knowledge and skill development through competency-based cases, exercises, and questions. Furthermore, this book illustrates the parallels between social work practice skills, knowledge, and ethics and leadership and management competencies, knowledge, skills, and practice behaviors. As you will learn throughout the pages of this text, leading and managing others requires a perpetual state of reflection (much like social work practice) to continuously improve one's ability to successfully lead and manage others. We encourage the readers through case examples and chapter activities to actively engage in both technical and self-reflective exercises to develop and improve both the stylistic and methodical skills that will impact and inspire those you lead and manage.

HOW IS THIS BOOK UNIQUE?

This book covers all the main areas of expertise required in a typical social work leadership and management experience. We have incorporated all 21 competencies and 126 practice behaviors from the Network on Social Work Management and nine competencies and 29 practice behaviors espoused by the Council on Social Work Education (CSWE). The chapters in which all these competencies and practice behaviors appear are listed in Chapter 18. Since the publication of this textbook the Network for Social Work Management has made some updates and revisions to the competencies and behaviors, and these changes can be found at: https://socialworkmanager.org/wp-content/uploads/2018/12/HSMC-Guidebook-December-2018.pdf

For academic settings, this book can serve as a textbook for social work programs at the graduate level. That said, it can serve as a text for any graduate program including those in public policy management, health policy management, and business schools that focus on social service management. For those in agency settings, the material in this book provides information on how to lead and manage your agency so it survives, improves, and accomplishes its mission and goals.

Social work graduate students typically land leadership roles soon after graduation and most have had little, if any, education or experiences in leadership and management. This book provides information, knowledge, and skills that will be of value in managing and leading agencies for neophytes starting out in the job. Nonprofits are frequently led by non–social workers, who may bring technical expertise to the job, but can also lack a background in social work values along with a strong social justice emphasis. Reading and mastering the techniques and practices in this book will allow social workers to better counter this trend in leading social service organizations.

This book also provides a focused opportunity to learn how to analyze and apply leadership skills in a variety of settings, including academic leadership roles. Faculty frequently ascend to leadership roles as deans, directors, and chairpersons, sometimes with little formal management education and leadership practice experience. This book will show them the way!

Finally, reading cases and examples and participating in activities will help students, managers, and academic leaders discover how they may evaluate various leadership situations and use a variety of strategic methods to address issues.

UNIQUE FEATURES

This book has many unique features. They include the following:

- A comprehensive list of leadership and management competencies from the Network for Social Work Management (NSWM) and the CSWE are provided in Chapters 18–20, along with a list of competencies and practice behaviors that are located in each chapter.
- Leadership and management competencies and practice behaviors are presented in each chapter along with cases, examples, and activities of how to use them in practice situations.
- Each chapter has case examples and discussion questions that focus on the challenges of management and leadership and are competency-based.
- Each chapter can stand alone so that some chapters can be used in other courses and different levels of programs (undergraduate—master's—doctoral). For example, the chapter on supervising staff could be used in any supervision course.
- The differences between management and leadership are discussed in detail along with best management and leadership practices.
- Examples of how to motive and successfully work with different age cohorts are provided.
- This book presents effective communication and marketing strategies.
- We discuss in detail how to effectively work with groups and give examples of how to make meetings productive.
- We exhibit specific problem-solving and decision-making strategies along with examples.

- We discuss ideas on supervising, developing, and motivating staff in addition to one's own professional development.

- This book summarizes how to manage a range of organizational functions.

- We provide tips on recruitment and hiring, particularly for diversity.

- This book discusses understanding the challenges of financial management and management information, along with examples from both the academic and public sector.

- We provide examples of how to effectively raise funds through fundraising, creating research centers, and writing grants.

- We discuss how to incorporate a process to design a long and short version of a strategic plan, along with how to successfully implement the plan.

- This book discusses how to design programs that meet the needs in the community.

- We discuss the importance of collaborating with community groups and other stakeholders to succeed in making a difference.

INSTRUCTOR RESOURCES

As an aid for using the book in class, qualified instructors may obtain access to instructor resources (Instructor's Manual, sample course syllabi, and PowerPoints) by emailing *textbook@springerpub.com*. The PowerPoint slides highlight the most significant points in each chapter along with practice exercises and questions.

INTENDED AUDIENCE

The intended market for the book includes all social work programs at every level, although it is more suited for graduate education. In addition, the book discusses and provides information on how to apply best management and leadership practices in both the social service agency sector and university administration.

A national review of graduate social work programs at both the MSW and DSW level uncovered a number of different types of courses that are offered; these programs may find this book useful. These types of courses include the following titles and/or cover the following content:

• Program design • Strategic planning • Program implementation • Program administration • Leadership in today's environment, including decision making in uncertain times, conflict management put to good use, and the power of collaboration • Leadership and social change, including teamwork • Managing people through communication skills, personnel management, and leadership	• Group work, including running meetings effectively • General and clinical supervision, including mentoring and evaluating performance • Financial management and resource development • Grant writing for success • Managing money through financial management strategies and fiscal responsibilities of administrators • Information system design and management • Human resource management

CONTENTS

This book contains five parts that replicate the NSWM's four domains of leadership: (1) Executive Leadership in Social Work, (2) Resources Management Practices, (3) Strategic Management and Administrative Skills for Organizational Growth and Success, (4) Community Collaboration, and (5) Supplemental Materials.

▨ Part 1: Executive Leadership in Social Work

This part of the book provides information on leadership and management theory and practices with the intent of developing effective leaders in social work, social work higher education, and human and social service organizations. Readers are provided the opportunity to both learn about different leadership and management styles, including their own, and then to practice specific leadership and management skills. In addition, readers will learn about promoting organizational vision, employing effective cross-cultural and multigenerational practices, facilitating innovative changes, advocating for social justice, effectively communicating, employing best time management practices, making meetings productive, using problem-solving and decision-making techniques, managing the organizational functions, developing and motivating staff, and promoting lifelong learning practices.

The NSWM *Executive Leadership* domain suggests that the following knowledge and skills are important and should be covered in any curricula on leadership and management (Network competency numbers are in parentheses).

The following competencies are covered in Part 1:

• Promotes vision, goals, and objectives (Competency 1) • Interpersonal skills (Competency 2) • Analytical and critical thinking skills (Competency 3) • Professional behavior (Competency 4) • Cross-cultural understanding (Competency 5) • Maintains stakeholder relationships (Competency 6) • Facilitates innovate changes (Competency 7)	• Advocates for social justice (Competency 8) • Communication skills (Competency 9) • Decision making (Competency 10) • Promotes lifelong learning practices (Competency 11) • Marketing and public relations (Competency 17)

According to the NSWM, these interpersonal skills are necessary to motivate others to successfully communicate the organizational mission and vision at all levels of management.

▨ Part 2: Resource Management Practices in Social Work

This part of the book covers how to effectively manage human resources, the budget and other financial resources, and information technology and social media. In addition, organizational accountability is discussed, including transparency, governance, and fiduciary responsibility.

The NSWM *Resources Management* domain suggests that the following knowledge and skills are important and should be covered in any curricula on leadership and management (Network competency numbers are in parentheses).

The following competencies are covered in Part 2:

• Analytical and critical thinking skills (Competency 3) • Cross-cultural understanding (Competency 5) • Advocates for social justice (Competency 8) • Communication skills (Competency 9) • Promotes lifelong learning practices (Competency 11) • Effectively manages human resources (Competency 12)	• Effectively manages and oversees the budget and other financial resources (Competency 13) • Ensures transparency, protection, and accountability (Competency 14) • Manages all aspects of information technology (Competency 15) • Manages risk and legal affairs (Competency 19)

According to the Network for Social Work Management, the competencies delineated under the domain of Resource Management list the intellectual skills that provide a clear perspective on the organization in its environment and are essential to possessing the capacity to think and act strategically.

Part 3: Strategic Management and Administrative Skills for Organizational Growth and Success in a Social Work Environment

This part of the book provides the knowledge base and theory from which to develop advanced administrative skills that are critical to organizational growth and survival. These skills include fundraising, designing and developing effective programs, and strategic planning.

The NSWM *Strategic Management* domain suggests that the following knowledge and skills are important and should be covered in any curricula on leadership and management (Network competency numbers are in parentheses).

The following competencies are covered in Part 3:

• Promotes vision, goals, and objectives (Competency 1) • Fundraising (Competency 16)	• Designs and develops effective programs (Competency 18) • Ensures strategic planning (Competency 20)

According to the NSWM, the competencies delineated under the domain of Strategic Management provide a selection of technical skills that are essential to successfully managing organizational functions such as budget and finance, human resources, and technology.

Part 4: Community Collaboration

This part of the book covers the final domain from the NSWM: Community Collaboration. Topics include building relationships to enhance program resources and service delivery, improving the likelihood in achieving organizational mission and better client well-being, and how to effectively manage policy advocacy coalitions to improve organizational function and client well-being.

The NSWM *Community Collaboration* domain suggests that the following knowledge and skills are important and should be covered in any curricula on leadership and management (Network competency numbers are in parentheses).

The following competencies are covered in Part 4:

- Analytical and critical thinking skills (Competency 3)
- Maintains stakeholder relationships (Competency 6)
- Builds relationships with complementary agencies, institutions, and community groups to enhance the delivery of services (Competency 21)

Part 5: Supplemental Material

In conclusion, Chapters 18–20 provide

- Information on where the NSWM and the CSWE Competencies and Practice Behaviors appear in each chapter (Chapter 18).
- A list of the NSWM Human Services Management Competencies and Practice Behaviors (Chapter 19).
- A list of the CSWE Competencies and Practice Behaviors (Chapter 20).

A final unique feature of this book is the linking of NSWM and CSWE competencies and practice behaviors to specific knowledge and skills that could be used for accreditation purposes. For social work programs to be accredited by the CSWE they must document how they are meeting the nine CSWE competencies. The behaviors that accompany each competency are provided by CSWE as examples of behaviors that programs can use to meet the competencies; however, programs are not required to use these behaviors, although most do and some programs modify them slightly or create totally different behaviors to meet the competencies. Programs could add the NSWM practice behaviors identified in this book to the CSWE practice behaviors used for program assessment. By doing so, programs could expand the use of macro-practice behaviors in their curricula and their program assessment process.

ACKNOWLEDGMENTS

As we discuss throughout this book, you can go further as a team than you can individually. This book would not have happened without the support and encouragement of each other. We challenged one another's ideas, writing, and philosophies . . . and deadlines! This book would also not be possible without the help from our graduate assistant Natalie R. Schriefer who put in endless hours of editing and dedicated her time to overseeing the many details that went into our manuscript. We also want to thank Dr. Stephen Monroe Tomczak for contributing two chapters (Chapters 15 and 17) and also sharing insights and ideas on several other chapters (Dr. Tomczak is an Associate Professor of Social Welfare Policy and Community Organization, Department of Social Work, at Southern Connecticut State University, New Haven, Connecticut). Finally, we would like to thank our Southern Connecticut State University (SCSU) colleagues for their thoughtful inquiries about our progress and book content, and for providing honest and constructive feedback.

PART 1

EXECUTIVE LEADERSHIP IN SOCIAL WORK

CHAPTER 1

LEADERSHIP AND MANAGEMENT THEORY IN SOCIAL WORK

CHAPTER OBJECTIVES

- Understanding leadership and management theories and styles.
- Identifying and assuming various leaderships styles that can be situationally adapted.
- Learning to inspire confidence in others and form positive relationships.
- Demonstrating commitment to and knowledge about the agency.
- Applying emotional intelligence, including self-awareness, self-management, social awareness, and relationship management in leadership and management.
- Understanding the distinctions between leadership and management.
- Identifying ways to align and inspire individuals to work collaboratively toward envisioned goals.

INTRODUCTION

Throughout this text we explore the concepts of leadership and management, specifically as these constructs relate to the Network for Social Work Management (NSWM) and Council on Social Work Education (CSWE) competencies, to illustrate how various leadership and management paradigms can translate to practice behaviors. Across diverse professions there is growing interest in gaining comprehensive understanding of the various traits, styles, and philosophies that successful leaders and managers employ. Within social work literature there has been a burgeoning focus on supervision, management, and administration. Much of the research on leadership is culled from different fields, particularly business markets, but empirical information has also been gathered from the related healthcare and human service industries that similarly seek to understand how one effectively leads and manages others within their respected fields. The phenomenon of leadership and management talents recognizes a melding of both art and science to succeed (Weinbach & Taylor, 2015). As this book is designed to be a how-to on leadership and management in organizational and academic arenas of social work, throughout this text we offer scenarios that one may encounter in the field and dismantle the dual scientific (theory) and artistic (application) nature of leadership and management while purposefully overlaying the constructs with the CSWE and NSWM competencies. This approach allows you, as the reader, to consider how particular competencies can be met in a variety of situations, which you will likely be exposed to, in varying ways. The competencies are outlined in the beginning of each chapter to orient the reader to the practice behaviors, and are discussed throughout. Practice and reflection questions are also presented so that the reader can begin to think about ways to critically appraise leadership and management behaviors as they align with the CSWE and NSWM competencies.

There are copious studies and writings on leadership and management, far too many to be all-inclusive within the pages that are bound in this book; but the wealth of such teachings will prove ineffectual if you are not paying mind to understanding, or knowing, oneself first. What are your ways of relating to others in the myriad situations that can evoke a passel of emotional and cognitive reactions that subsequently govern the behavioral response? How do you handle different personalities, manage adversity, tackle and resolve complex issues? What are your communication strengths and weaknesses? Whenever seeking answers to the burning questions that give impetus to knowledge quests, particularly knowledge quests of the how-to nature, be mindful that the zeal for "knowing" should never shroud the *process* of discovery. Give pause to the questions themselves along the journey of reflecting on how to develop, and, moreover, *continuously* develop, your style and the philosophical underpinnings that impel practice behaviors as leaders and managers in the field. Excellent leaders and managers have an insatiable hunger for knowledge and an eagerness to perpetually grow and the confidence and wisdom to know that they have never simply "arrived" at greatness, but instead steadfastly build on strengths and learn from failures to refine their skills and knowledge that translate to practice behaviors.

In this chapter, we introduce the types of leadership styles and traits to provide an overview of the various methods and guiding principles, to help the reader begin to identify their own style, and to consider what may be influential about adopting or modifying certain traits for certain scenarios. Interpersonal skills are discussed as they impact organizational functions and tie to how one engages with individuals, groups, and organizational culture. The competencies and practice behaviors addressed in this chapter are shown in Box 1.1.

BOX 1.1

COMPETENCIES AND PRACTICE BEHAVIORS ADDRESSED IN THIS CHAPTER

Possesses interpersonal skills that support viability and positive functioning of the organization (Network for Social Work Management Competencies 2). Practice Behaviors:

- Demonstrates the ability to assume different leadership styles as appropriate to the situation (2.3).
- Possesses strong skills in emotional intelligence, self-awareness, self-mastery, etc. (2.4).
- Is able to find common ground with others and form positive relationships easily (2.5).
- Is able to inspire confidence in others, both internally and externally (2.6).
- Demonstrates commitment to the work of the agency (2.7).

(continued)

BOX 1.1 *(Continued)*

▨ Demonstrates and communicates deep knowledge about the work of the agency, using current performance data to discuss successes and challenges (2.8).

Advocates for public policy change and social justice at national, state, and local levels (Network for Social Work Management Competencies 8). Practice Behaviors:

▨ Strategically disseminates information about unmet needs and program accomplishments (8.1).

▨ Participates in professional organizations and industry groups that advocate for client social justice, equity, and fairness (8.2).

CSWE Competency 1—Demonstrate Ethical and Professional Behavior

▨ 1.2 Use reflection and self-regulation to manage personal values and maintain professionalism in practice situations.

CSWE Competency 2—Engage Diversity and Difference in Practice

▨ 2.1 Apply and communicate understanding of the importance of diversity and difference in shaping life experiences in practice at the micro, mezzo, and macro levels.

▨ 2.2 Present themselves as learners and engage clients and constituencies as experts of their own experiences.

▨ 2.3 Apply self-awareness and self-regulation to manage the influence of personal biases and values in working with diverse clients and constituencies.

CSWE Competency 6—Engage With Individuals, Groups, Organizations, and Communities

▨ 6.1 Apply knowledge of human behavior and the social environment, person-in-environment, and other multidisciplinary theoretical frameworks to engage with clients and constituencies.

▨ 6.2 Use empathy, reflection, and interpersonal skills to effectively engage diverse clients and constituencies.

CSWE, Council Social Work Education.

LEADERSHIP: TRAITS, STYLES, AND PHILOSOPHIES

Box 1.2 displays the competencies/behaviors in this section.

BOX 1.2

NETWORK FOR SOCIAL WORK MANAGEMENT COMPETENCY AND PRACTICE BEHAVIOR 2

In the following section we explore the following competency and practice behavior:
Possess interpersonal skills that support viability and positive functioning of the organization (Network for Social Work Management Competencies 2). Practice Behaviors:

▨ Demonstrates the ability to assume different leadership styles as appropriate to the situation (2.3).

Leadership styles have been explored across a multitude of disciplines, and as immeasurable as the possibilities of professions exist so too are the unbounded personalities and styles that develop into venerated leaders. Many scholars have explored the construct of leadership and sought to distill the key ingredients that make individuals successful. Before dismantling the technical application of these leadership theories, we proffer one key term to encourage current and emerging social work leaders and managers to contemplate as these constructs are unpacked: *parallel process*.

We, of course, understand the implications of the parallel processes related to social work practice, but consider how social workers turned social work leaders have utilized skill sets from direct practice experiences and unwittingly applied them to management tasks as well as the use of self to develop their leadership style. For instance, the valued tenant in clinical practice of *authenticity* is largely perceived as a key attribute of leadership (HBR, 2011). Just as the clinician uses authenticity to build trust and establish a working rapport with the client, leaders build trust with their teams, on individual and collective levels, which in turn invokes a sense of confidence that the work—no matter how painful—can be done. There is an array of practice principles combined with tacit wisdom that run parallel to leadership and management principles, which have assumably helped social workers organically transition from practice roles to leadership and management positions well before scholars attempted to operationalize what it is and how it is done. In the chapters ahead, we aim to draw parallels where applicable to the myriad of practice skills in an effort to consider how the repertoire can be transferred to one's professional leadership or management development as it aligns with the CSWE and NSWM competencies and practice behaviors.

The age-old question of whether or not one was "born to lead" has stimulated intrigue about the innate leadership traits one possesses and competent behaviors and thought patterns that can be developed and refined. We propose that the effective leaders have both innate and developed attributes. Before discussing the various traits, styles, and philosophies of leaders, it is important to note that these attributes are not one-dimensional and many leaders do, and should, adopt different features from each axiom to apply in different situations, as contextually indicated by the environmental aspects at play including, though not limited to, the audience of followers, the task/project at hand, and the available resources.

Distinguishing Leadership and Management

Leadership and management are considered two distinct practices, albeit within organizations and academic institutions these practices tessellate. The terms "management" and "leadership" are often used interchangeably, and perhaps for good reason, as there are times when good leaders must manage and times when good managers must lead; and a combination of both must be present in successful organizations and academic institutions. It is important, however, to understand from the onset that leadership does not supplant management, and management is certainly not void of leadership, that is, the traits, styles, and philosophies on how to lead others into action. However, it is worthwhile for us to define these individual terms as separate roles within an organizational structure. In brief, management is focused on maintaining the systems, subsystems, and structures that are in place and designed to help people successfully complete the tasks expected of them and ensure that the operations within the organization run smoothly. A strong manager must know that there is little room for abstractions in instructions and must always be unmistakably clear in the written and oral communications that outline said expectations.

Managing often requires skills for implementing processes and regulatory mechanisms for tasks such as planning, budgeting, organizing and staffing, providing structure, and problem solving. A key ingredient for managing effectively often comes down to effective communication and, as the saying goes, "the biggest problem with communication is believing that happened in the first place." See Box 1.3 for an example about the importance of communication.

BOX 1.3

WATERING THE TOMATOES

When mentoring a novice manager, I often advise them to be cognizant of when they have to "water the tomatoes." They, of course, respond with a perplexing stare before I go on to explain this seemingly absurd advice through the story of my 4-year-old nephew, Cole, who proudly watered the tomatoes. One summer day while skipping around the garden, my father asked if he would be his "big helper" and water the tomatoes, to which Cole eagerly obliged. He walked over with his pail of water that half spilt along his journey through the garden and confidently poured water over every single tomato growing on the vine. He proudly announced, "PaPa! I watered the tomatoes!" My father soaked in his innocence and then chuckled at himself as he realized that he had not quite explained that tomatoes should be watered at the roots. The moral of the story: be clear in giving directions, learn from and take ownership of your missteps in directing others, laugh at yourself when you can, share your story to help others learn from your mistakes, and model the importance of being human.

Management has been defined as a collection of action-oriented behaviors that, in accordance with Lewis et al. (2017), include the following:

(a) Making a plan to achieve some end, (b) organizing the people and resources needed to carry out the plan, (c) encouraging the helping workers who will be asked to perform the component tasks, (d) evaluating the results, and then, (e) revising plans based on this evaluation (p. 4).

Similarly, Lewis et al. (2017) assert that the terms "management" and "administration" are also used interchangeably. The authors encapsulated the definition of management by delineating the various categories of management activities that have been identified throughout the literature, which include (a) planning, organizing, staffing, leading, and controlling; (b) planning, organizing, and controlling; (c) organizing, coordinating, leading, and controlling; and (d) planning, organizing, leading, and controlling (p. 4).

Whereas management activities tend to focus on the direct oversight of production and the daily action steps that ensure an organization's viability, leadership tends to focus on inspiring a team of individuals to energize and propel the work forward and demonstrate confidence in members' application of skill sets and creative energies to collectively achieve a common goal. Kotter (2011) focused his definition of management on control mechanisms, noting that the centrality of control renders motivation or inspiration as irrelevant to the process.

The term control may have a negative association for some at first glance, and it is important that we contextualize its use here. Control in relation to management is not meant to imply that there should be any oppressive or dictatorship qualities, but rather that the systems for assuring the quality of services delivered are such a well-oiled, or well-controlled, machine that there is little to no room for error—that is, the roots will get watered and not the tomatoes. It is control in the sense that the processes of oversight are so factitious that the subordinates establish a routine. For example, the manager of a group home who starts each shift reviewing the shift reports from the most recent shifts and collects data on staff who have also reviewed the shifts reports, and then immediately follows up with staff who have not adhered to the expectation, is demonstrating good managerial control. Likewise, the supervisor who puts procedures in place that monitor when staff have treatment plans due, and sets alerts through an electronic health record system or other platform, has developed good mechanisms of control. Controls are put in place to be the procedural guides that help staff perform their duties in a predictable, quality-assured manner. Leaders, on the other hand, infuse vision, emotional intelligence (EI), and motivation to gain buy-in from performers to collaboratively achieve a goal. Kotter (2011) noted that managers "organize to create human systems that can implement plans as precisely and efficiently as possible" (p. 47). He differentiates managing from leadership, explaining that whereas managers organize, leaders "align" people, which always involves the complex art of communication, simplified ever slightly by one's ability to read and relate to others. EI is central to effective leadership as it contains the key ingredients for knowing the audience, knowing oneself, and, thus, how to tailor communication to inspire confidence and motivation among, what should ideally be, a diverse team of skilled individuals. Lewis et al. (2017) cited Northouse's (2010) definition of leadership as "a process whereby an individual influences a group of individuals to achieve a common goal" (p. 235). Cashman (2012) explained that "the art of management is consistently, efficiently achieving results; the art of leadership is growing people to produce enduring value" (p. 82).

The synergic relationship between management and leadership is webbed by *style* and *impact*. A clinical social worker may relate this webbing to the art of connecting—*the style*—with the client, relying on one's clinical instincts, and fostering a strong therapeutic alliance for engaging in the work, which will be measured at various intervals throughout treatment to evaluate the application and efficacy of the intervention—*the impact*. Style and impact move interdependently through management and leadership undertakings to achieve results. Emotional intelligence, being attuned with teams and stakeholders, provides insight to how one can use their authentic style and charisma to stimulate others into action—*the style*—while also remaining attentive to details and assessing progress over the course of the project in order to maximize outcomes—*the impact*. Thus, it is a dexterous ebbing and flowing between the abstract and the concrete that produces dynamic and sustainable outcomes. See Box 1.4 for an example of the blending of leadership and management.

BOX 1.4

BLENDING LEADERSHIP AND MANAGEMENT

Elle was assigned to lead the implementation of an electronic health records system at a large social service agency, after three project mangers had left the agency. At the time it was assigned to Elle, it had been through many iterations of change and many staff had given up on the idea that the project would ever come to fruition.

The agency culture was entrenched in an archaic style of doing paperwork—there was no electronic record keeping for any data, the billing department still mailed out typed invoices, and a large portion of the employees still had never even set up their email accounts. Elle quickly realized that the project would need both aligning and organizing. She understood that launching a project of this magnitude would require that she create an "A-team" of staff who could first and foremost help to align others and increase the buy-in for this project. After all, everyone was already stretched way too thin and asking them to commit what little time they had to learn the system and create the technological functionality to be tailored to the agency's needs and regulations would be a big ask. Once she obtained buy-in from a select group of individuals working in diverse roles to represent all levels of the organization, she was confident that they could promote the changes by modeling their commitment, knowledge and enthusiasm for the much needed change.

Elle organized weekly meetings and collaborated with the team to set achievable tasks in order to slowly build the team's confidence in their competencies and skills (leave them hungry to keep growing, she figured). She even worked with IT consultants to help translate the tech jargon that was so foreign to the team. The team had gelled and reached a point where they were truly excited to launch the electronic health record system; all members had proven their dedication to the agency, the team, and the progressive nature of the work. On the day of the go-live training, the company that had sold the electronic health record system reported that vital forms such as assessments, treatment plans, and progress notes were not ready for deployment, meaning the agency could not use them. Over the next few weeks, Elle and the team of IT consultants pressed for the product completion, but to no avail. Elle's A-team was

(continued)

BOX 1.4 *(Continued)*

told by the company that they had "outpaced" the company, which meant they could not quality test their own product in stride with the completion of tasks the A-team finished. The team's enthusiasm was rapidly deflating. The weekly meetings seemed to lose purpose and energy. Elle now had to rebuild, and regain, their confidence while also managing her own feelings of frustration and dissatisfaction with the company they were working with.

Question

1. What EI skills can Elle employ to manage this situation?

Leadership

We all have an idea of what leadership is and perhaps an even more lucid idea about what it is not. Take a moment to consider someone in your life—a coach, teacher, supervisor, colleague—that you consider to be a leader. What characteristics come to mind when you think of that person? How do/did they lead? What were you drawn to about their leadership style? And now, how about yourself? Maybe you have been in a leadership role historically, or presently hold a position of leadership. How do people view you as a leader? How would you like them to view you as a leader? Chances are that in doing a brief self-appraisal you perhaps overlooked some of your strengths as well as your blind spots. Maybe you even had difficulty articulating what defines a leader, whether considering someone else or yourself, which can be a signal that it is time to pause and take inventory. Taking time to reflect deeply, to be purposeful in seeing ourselves as leaders and others as future leaders with greater clarity, can be a formidable task when one considers the quotidian crisis-oriented nature of our field, especially against the backdrop of austere climates fraught with diminished funding streams and resources—really, who has the time or energy left for that? But it is incumbent upon us to create the time and space needed to crystalize our thinking on this very matter. Why? Well, for one thing, new social workers entering the labor force deserve leaders that will stimulate environments that match the values and mission of the profession. And it is overwhelming enough for the novice social worker to begin to navigate the "real world" that can often present drastically different from idealized textbook cases, classroom role-plays, and internship caseloads versus professional caseloads. The demands of social work are difficult even for the seasoned social worker, and an influential force in how professionals do their jobs many times comes down to how they are managed and led. See Box 1.5 for a competency-based exercise on leadership.

BOX 1.5

COMPETENCY-BASED READER QUESTIONS

Before reading further, take a moment to list 10 leadership qualities that immediately come to mind for you.
Examples:

- Motivator
- Innovator
- Role Model
- Change Agent
- ——

(continued)

BOX 1.5 *(Continued)*

- Look at your list of leadership qualities and answer the following:
  1. What are the top three qualities that you value most in leaders?
  2. What are your top three strengths as a leader?
  3. What are three qualities that you would like to improve as a leader?

Additional Resource: For further reading on strengths-based leadership we recommend *The Strengths Finder 2.0 Strengths Based Leadership* by Rath and Conchie. The text includes access to an online StrengthsFinder 2.0 assessment.

LEADERSHIP STYLES

Transactional Leadership Style

As the name suggests, transactional leadership style is marked by mutually accepted and expected exchanges, thus there are anticipated transactions between the leader/organization and the follower, or subordinate. Transactional leadership suffuses the principles of contingent rewards and management by exception.

A contingency rewards system embraces a quid pro quo philosophy that fuels both parties to provide expected tasks, skills, or resources to meet each other's needs (Lewis et al., 2017). Essentially both parties understand the value of the rewards that will be provided in exchange for performing the desired task. An example of this may be that an executive asks his or her team to complete additional responsibilities for an upcoming regulatory evaluation, and upon receiving passing scores the team is rewarded with an additional day off for the upcoming year as a sign of appreciation for providing additional hours of work to successfully complete the site evaluation.

Management by exception assumes that the leader will provide little supervisory intervention or oversight under normal, or expected, circumstances; however, should unexpected circumstance arise then the supervisory oversight may shift to a substyle of either active or passive. Again, true to term, active transactional leaders tend to be more actively involved in the oversight of the subordinates' actions and behaviors to troubleshoot problems before they reach a level of severity that is difficult to remedy. Contrastingly, passive transactional leaders, often referred to as laissez-faire leaders, are less involved in the oversight of subordinates' actions and tend to wait until the problems reach a grave level of concern before they actively engage in troubleshooting or taking corrective action steps (Murray & Chau, 2014). Murray and Chau (2014) further identified an avoidant leadership style marked by the leader demonstrating an indifference, or passivity, to both her or his role as leader and the role of their subordinates.

Transformational Leadership Style

Transformational leadership style embodies four domains of leadership behaviors: idealized influence, inspirational motivation, intellectual stimulation, and individualized consideration. Each component is imbued in transformational leaders' behaviors and philosophies. *Idealized influence* is the notion that the leader is perceived by the follower, or subordinate, to be made of strong moral fiber and have the unwavering ability to demonstrate high ethical standards. When the leader is trusted by subordinates to do the right thing, the subordinates will mirror this behavior as well. *Inspirational motivation* is employed by the transformational leader to motivate, encourage, and inspire subordinates to work toward achieving the goal or vision. The transformational leader will inspire confidence in others by welcoming ideas and creative suggestions and will provide encouragement by demonstrating genuine enthusiasm for the vision, all of which helps to unite and inspire the team to collaboratively engage in the process of goal attainment. Transformational leaders foster creative thinking and value input about new ways of doing things and encourage curiosity that challenges assumptions, to provide *intellectual stimulation* for their subordinates. The transformational leader aims to listen to the ideas of subordinates and provides opportunities for intellectual stimulation and growth. Finally, transformational leaders provide individualized consideration when coaching and mentoring subordinates. The leader takes an interest in the subordinate to understand what his or her professional aspirations are and continuously seeks opportunities to help the subordinate reach individual goals. While these growth opportunities, or stretch goals, may be beneficial to the individual, they are also beneficial to the team and entire organization.

Charismatic Leadership Style

The charismatic leader is focused on interactions with subordinates, and the connections such leaders develop can be powerful motivators for their subordinates. One who leads with a charismatic style often portrays a strong sense of confidence and competence, and communicates high expectations (Lewis et al., 2017). The strengths of charismatic leaders are found in their relationally focused energy and drive to enhance the self-esteem of their subordinates. Enhancing the self-esteem of subordinates will subsequently increase subordinates' expended energy and efforts to achieve the organization's vision and goals. Additionally, charismatic leaders have a keen ability to cultivate an internalization of their goals among subordinates and advance the moral commitment to the goals that transcends self-interest and focuses on the shared interest of the organization (Lopez & Ensari, 2014). While followers may gravitate to the charismatic leader, Lewis et al. (2017) warned of the potential drawbacks of charismatic leadership, explaining that subordinates may become dependent on the charismatic leader, and there can be misuses of power by the leader. They further note the need to be aware of the paradoxes that are found with charismatic leadership, citing Collins (2001), who highlighted that "charisma can be as much a liability as an asset, as the strength of your leadership personality can deter people from bringing you the brutal facts" (as cited by Lewis et al. [2017, p. 239]). Hence the subordinates' draw to the charismatic leader can potentially de-emphasize the tie to the organization at large.

Exemplary Leadership Style

Lewis et al. (2017) note that exemplary leaders demonstrate some of the top characteristics people look for in leaders including honesty, forward thinking, competency and ability to inspire. Leaders prove themselves to be trustworthy, model the ability to apply strategic thinking and forecasting to analyze and plan for future developments, have a proven history of goal attainment, and have an energizing demeanor that encourages forward thinking. Exemplary leaders show appreciation to individuals, but also commend commitment to organizational values through collective acknowledgement. See Box 1.6 for a competency-based case example.

BOX 1.6

COMPETENCY-BASED CASE EXAMPLE

A COO of a 24-7 operation received a call from a concerned staff, Lisa, that a fellow staff member was speaking down to peers and clients. As the COO attempted to gather more information from Lisa, she could hear in the background that the other staff, Rob, was escalating and threatened to leave shift. The COO decided to drive out to the home to assess the situation. When she arrived she determined that it

(continued)

BOX 1.6 (Continued)

was necessary to send Rob home, as he had become emotionally dysregulated and she was concerned about the impact this would have on the clients and fellow teammates. Rather than simply sending the staff off shift, she remained on shift to help get the residents prepared for dinner and later for bed. She felt a sense of responsibility to restore a feeling of harmony in the home and ensure that both staff and clients resumed their evening without further difficulty.

The staff was grateful for her commitment to them, and the work. But the following week the COO received another call afterhours from the manager of the same home wondering if she could help to find coverage. While the COO always sought to lead by example, she was beginning to wonder if there were some unforeseen consequences of this and contemplated how she should modify her style in this particular situation.

Questions

1. How should the COO address the request of the house manager? And what are the potential outcomes if she does address it in the manner you suggest?

2. What do you think needs to be communicated to the staff, and how would you go about doing so?

COO, chief operating officer.

Servant Leadership Style

The servant leader is concerned with the leader–follower relationship. The style of behaviors that the servant leader exhibits has been developed by the former executive of AT&T, Robert Greenleaf (Lewis et al., 2017), and have gained increasing interest in recent years. Lewis et al. (2017, p. 242) noted that servant leadership is composed of the following 10 behaviors:

1. Listening
2. Empathy
3. Healing "broken spirits" and "emotional hurts"
4. General and self-awareness
5. Persuasion, not positional authority
6. Broad conceptual thinking and visioning
7. Learning from past and foreseeing future outcomes
8. Stewardship
9. Commitment to the growth of the people
10. Building community

The previously mentioned behaviors are closely aligned with the values and ethics of social workers and can be closely tied to a number of the CSWE and NSWM competencies. See Box 1.7 for a competency-based question.

BOX 1.7

COMPETENCY-BASED QUESTIONS FOR THE READER

Take a moment to describe how the style of servant leader can be applied using two CSWE competencies and concomitant practice behaviors outlined for this chapter.

CSWE, Council on Social Work Education.

See Box 1.8 which displays the competencies/behaviors in this section.

BOX 1.8

COMPETENCIES ADDRESSED IN THIS CHAPTER

Possesses interpersonal skills that support viability and positive functioning of the organization (Network for Social Work Management Competencies 2). Practice Behaviors:

- Demonstrates the ability to assume different leadership styles as appropriate to the situation (2.3).
- Possesses strong skills in emotional intelligence, self-awareness, self-mastery, etc. (2.4).
- Is able to find common ground with others and form positive relationships easily (2.5).
- Is able to inspire confidence in others, both internally and externally (2.6).
- Demonstrates commitment to the work of the agency (2.7).
- Demonstrates and communicates deep knowledge about the work of the agency, using current performance data to discuss successes and challenges (2.8).

Advocates for public policy change and social justice at national, state, and local levels
(Network for Social Work Management Competencies 8). Practice Behaviors:

- Strategically disseminates information about unmet needs and program accomplishments (8.1).
- Participates in professional organizations and industry groups that advocate for client social justice, equity, and fairness (8.2).

CSWE Competency 1—Demonstrate Ethical and Professional Behavior

- 1.2 Use reflection and self-regulation to manage personal values and maintain professionalism in practice situations.

CSWE Competency 2—Engage Diversity and Difference in Practice

- 2.1 Apply and communicate understanding of the importance of diversity and difference in shaping life experiences in practice at the micro, mezzo, and macro levels.
- 2.2 Present themselves as learners and engage clients and constituencies as experts of their own experiences.
- 2.3 Apply self-awareness and self-regulation to manage the influence of personal biases and values in working with diverse clients and constituencies.

CSWE Competency 6—Engage With Individuals, Groups, Organizations, and Communities

- 6.1 Apply knowledge of human behavior and the social environment, person-in-environment, and other multidisciplinary theoretical frameworks to engage with clients and constituencies.
- 6.2 Use empathy, reflection, and interpersonal skills to effectively engage diverse clients and constituencies.

CSWE, Council Social Work Education.

Autocratic Leadership Style

Autocratic leaders are described as being highly focused on goal attainment and are mainly interested in the information that is needed to accomplish the goal. To that end, autocratic leaders will often offer rewards for compliance and goal-oriented activities, have low tolerance for subordinates who do not comply with the rules, and have even been referred to by Bass (2009) as "punitive" and "closed-minded" (p. 439). This leadership style uses positions of power to set the trajectory of the project and gain group compliance with directives; leaders provide scarce information, or what they determine to be only necessary to complete the task, and do not seek input or ideas from subordinates (Lopez & Ensuri, 2014). The autocratic style constrains self-determination and subdues independent and creative thinking among subordinates, who become disempowered and therefore have a diminished drive toward goals. As you might imagine, there is little to no reciprocal trust between the employees and managers, as autocratic leaders make the decisions which then get passed down through the hierarchy.

Other Leadership Styles

Goleman (2000) identified six leadership styles: *authoritative, affiliative, coercive, democratic, pacesetting*, and *coaching*. Several of these styles (authoritative and coercive) contain some aspects of the autocratic leadership style. He asserts that while executives use six styles of leadership, only four of them are consistently used, and all are governed by various aspects of one's EI. The *authoritative leadership style* is described as one that is flexible in nature and allows for people to provide input, which reinforces values of innovation and helps people feel that their work and ideas are equally valued. The authoritative leader regards individuals' abilities to design their own tasks, which do not fit for every situation, as Goleman warns against using this approach when working with experts in the field.

Affiliative leadership style is concerned with building loyalty and trust. Affiliative leaders emphasize that the individuals they lead matter and primarily focus on praising the individuals. The benefit of this approach is the ability to develop cohesive teams, albeit the shortcoming of this style is that a strength-based approach focused primarily on praise fails to provide advice and feedback about what areas of weakness need to be addressed.

The *democratic leadership style* is concerned with providing followers with opportunities to have a say in the decisions that are being made. The democratic leader is typically looking to empower others and solicit ideas about how to improve and grow, which can foster a sense of commitment and ownership. However, there are times when this approach can prove ineffective, for instance, during crisis situations that frequently require active decision making. Additionally, leaders attempting to adopt the democratic style should be mindful of the potential pitfall of "overprocessing" the decisions as that can become overly drawn out and leave members of the team feeling frustrated by too little action and too much time and energy spent on attempting to reach consensus. One final word of caution is that there are times when followers will look for leaders to be more assertive and proactive in the process, and overreliance on democratic leadership style can potentially shake the confidence of followers who are looking to be more actively led. See Box 1.9 for an activity on the democratic leadership style.

BOX 1.9

COMPETENCY-BASED CASE EXAMPLE

Molly was recently promoted to a director position which now required her to facilitate meetings with her team. She was full of energy, eager to bring about change, and was committed to fostering a new culture where staff felt that they had a say. There were several issues that were in need of her immediate attention and resolution in the first few months of her new leadership role. She decided that she would bring these to the team and allow the team to decide how to manage these issues. At first this seemed to work well, but after a few meetings she started to notice that the group was teetering between seemingly

(continued)

BOX 1.9 *(Continued)*

frustrated and utterly disinterested. She could not understand how people could seem so frustrated and indifferent—after all she was giving them a voice in these matters. She started to reflect on how these meetings were being conducted and was able to recognize that she had perhaps allowed too much of a say by some, but had failed to facilitate the meeting in such a way as to ensure that there was input from all. Additionally, in reviewing her agenda notes she realized that so much time was consumed by getting input from folks that the meetings often ended without a definitive resolution, and without hitting all of the agenda items. She pondered if she had created a culture of paralysis by overanalysis in her well-intended desire to lead democratically.

Questions

1. How could Molly modify her use of the democratic style?
2. What are the potential risks and benefits of continuing to employ the democratic style?
3. In addition to the democratic style, what other style might she try to integrate at times?
4. What are the potential risks and benefits of trying to incorporate other styles?

The *coercive leadership style* is paradoxically different than democratic leadership. The coercive leader employs a top-down decision-making process and reigns with an attitude of "do what I say" in an effort to gain immediate compliance (Goleman, 2000, p. 4). As you can imagine, this style has the potential to thwart creativity and innovation as followers may feel guarded and reluctant to reveal their ideas out of fear of how the coercive leader will react. In spite of the coercive leadership style being the least favored, there are times when this approach is not only necessary, but effective. For example, coercive leadership may be useful when managing some personnel matters, particularly the difficult employee that regardless of the coaching, support, and resources provided will not follow through with directives, or when the organization is facing a particular crisis and there is a need for strong and directive leadership. This is a style that, as you may have already imagined, should not be used perpetually, but rather is short doses when absolutely needed.

The *pacesetting leadership style* is typically exemplified by leaders that are high performers and set the tone for others who are highly competent and intrinsically motivated. As you may assume, there is an overlap here with the exemplary leadership style in the sense that the desired behavior is modeled by the leader for the followers. A noble approach, this style, however, this must also be balanced with one's ability to be attuned with followers and recognize when the pace may be too prodigious. Overwhelming followers with too high of pacesetting standards can result in decreased pace and performance endurance of others, and moreover, can impact the morale if others feel they cannot keep pace with the leader. See Box 1.10 for a case example on leadership styles.

BOX 1.10

COMPETENCY-BASED CASE EXAMPLE

During a monthly meeting, a top executive reported to the executive team and director the barriers he was facing in completing a project. The majority of the team was well aware of impediments the external system posed and had believed that the executive had exhausted every possible troubleshooting method before bringing the problem to the entire executive team during their monthly meeting in search of guidance. The executive director became overtly frustrated by the lack of progress that had been

(continued)

BOX 1.10 *(Continued)*

made, and did not offer ideas to overcome the identified barriers but rather demanded that the project be completed within the next week. The executive again tried to ask for clarification on how to manage the problems; however, the executive director tangentially spoke in a raised voice about how overdue the project was and how crucial it is that it is done and that if the executive could not figure it out, then he would be forced to find someone else who could.

Questions

1. What do you think was the impact of using this approach on the individual executive member, and on the executive team?
2. How might this approach influence the organizational culture?

The *coaching leadership style* takes a mentoring approach with followers. The coaching leader is one that makes a commitment to the follower's professional development and growth. It may go without saying that this style fares best with followers who have insight to their underdeveloped skills and awareness of their areas of weakness that they need to improve upon. The coaching leader is able to tap into the follower's self-awareness and create goals, and stretch goals, that expand the follower's skills repertoire.

Wilcox et al. (2017) discussed how Theory X and Theory Y, first introduced in 1960 by Douglas McGregor, are differentiated by the types of assumptions made about what motivates followers. Theory X postulates that followers lack motivation and will seek opportunities to avoid the work when possible, whereas Theory Y views followers as intrinsically motivated to seek opportunities to apply creativity and take pride in accomplishing work tasks. Under this set of assumptions, a coercive and autocratic approach is most likely applied by leaders who view their followers as inherently unmotivated (Theory X), using rigidity and incentives to ensure the completion of tasks. In contrast, the leader who views subordinates as being internally driven to complete tasks (Theory Y) is more apt to apply a transformative and coaching style of leadership. Note that neither Theory X or Theory Y are superior to the other, and we caution readers not to discount the need to apply both frameworks to varying situations. There will be times when leaders who take a more transformational, coaching, or democratic style find themselves in situations that challenge the assumptions of Theory Y–they may feel as though their subordinates are not inherently motivated. Similarly, there will be times when leaders (recall that leaders seek to align people and managers seek to organize) have to be flexible in their approach and shift to operate in a more pacesetting or coercive manner, for instance, in managing an organizational crisis.

William Ouchi introduced a third theory, Theory Z (Wilcox et al., 2017), which incorporated the viewpoints of both the leader and follower. Theory Z assumes that the follower is dedicated to the employer, team, and mission and is seeking guidance from leadership to enhance his or her skills and give support for maintaining work–life balance. Theory Z has been seen in the Japanese culture that views workers as disciplined and committed to organizational success and anticipates that the organization will in return show commitment to helping workers maintain family commitments and uphold cultural traditions. This approach can enhance loyalty from followers and is closely aligned with affiliative and transactional leadership styles.

Social Role Theory and Differences in Leadership Styles

In this section we discuss the gender and cultural differences in leadership styles. Culture is applied in a very broad sense here to encompass ethnicity, race, sexual orientation and identity, age, and religion. While there is far too much to explore and discuss in terms of cultural and gender differences to be captured here, our hope is to illustrate that we have a human and professional responsibility to continuously ask how differences shape our environments. As you continue to read through the chapters ahead and consider the competencies and behavior practices, we encourage you to contemplate how cultural competence is applied in management and leadership.

The empirical data have established that women are overrepresented in the human service industry (Gardella & Haynes, 2004) as well as the public and nonprofit sectors of the workforce (Lanfranchi & Narcy, 2015). Understanding how leadership styles are applied, modified, and, moreover, perceived by others—as it relates to gender and culture—is critical, especially given the large representation of women in the field and the significantly disproportionate number of women in management and leadership positions as compared to men. Men working in the social service industry tend to enter management positions at much earlier stages in their careers than women do, are more quickly promoted in their positions than women, and earn significantly more than women at every level (Gardella & Haynes, 2004). In fact, Gardella and Haynes (2004) cited Gibelman's findings that men earn approximately $5,000 more than women do annually, even when controlling for "education, age, and field practice" (p. 7). While women and underrepresented individuals have made great strides throughout history to gain employment equality, there are remnants of cultural and gender biases that prevail, and as such may influence how leaders and managers are perceived by others. Additionally, women and underrepresented individuals may experience discrimination, particularly in regard to higher standards of performance (Gardella & Haynes, 2004; Lopez & Ensari, 2014).

Cuadrado, Navas, Ferrer, Molero, and Morales (2012) asserted that women's barriers to leadership and management positions have been attributed to psychological factors that include lack of interest, skill, or ambition; and they emphasize that none of these factors have been empirically supported but instead are socially constructed. Efforts to gain deeper understanding of the disproportionate number of women in management and leadership positions across a variety of professions have explored the difference in leadership styles. The rationale for examining the differences in leadership styles is that employers seeking candidates for management and leadership positions pay careful attention to the attributes that can hint at leadership styles (Cuadrado et al., 2012). However, examination of gender differences in leadership styles cannot discount the influence of social role theory which impacts the way males and females behave based on the social norms and structural pressures, such as expectations of communities and organizations (Hutchison, 2015). Accordingly, "men are perceived as being achievement oriented and acting in an aggressive or instrumental way, a phenomenon often referred to as agency or being agentic, whereas women are more often seen as social and service oriented, or communal" (Lopez & Ensari, 2014, p. 23). In a study examining the effects of leadership styles and gender attributional bias, Lopez and Ensari (2014) explained that characteristics of being communal, relational, and empathic are traits more often socially ascribed to women, and that leader stereotypes are more often described as being masculine. Lopez and Ensari (2014) found that women who were perceived by their subordinates as employing an autocratic leadership style experienced attributional bias, especially when accounting for failures. Attributional bias refers to the ways that individuals evaluate their own and others' behaviors in their social environments, essentially leading to causal judgments or attributional errors (Lopez & Ensari, 2014). Lopez & Ensari (2014) further explain attributional errors in stating that:

> Clearly, there is incongruity between stereotypes of women as communal and the perceptions of leaders as agentic (Eagly & Karau, 2002). According to the role incongruity theory (Eagly & Karau, 2002), prejudice can arise as a result of these incongruent perceptions between the predominantly communal qualities ascribed to women and the predominantly agentic characteristics ascribed to men. Women struggle to overcome preconceptions that they are not qualified to lead. Even when they become a leader, they continue to struggle to fulfill dual roles: the role of an agentic leader and the communal role of the female gender (Cialdini & Trost, 1998; Eagly & Karau, 2002; Eagly, Wood & Diekman, 2000). (Lopez & Ensari, 2014, p. 23)

Expanding on the concepts of social role theory, it can be further conjectured that men are more likely to be perceived, or expected, to exude more the autocratic, coercive, and pacesetting leadership styles because of the "instrumental dimension of gender stereotypes (e.g., aggressive, enterprising, independent, self-sufficient, dominant, competent, or rational" [Cuadrado et al., 2012]). Conversely, the perceptions or expectations set for women are that they demonstrate the communal dimension of "being concerned about others, generous, sensitive, understanding, affectionate, or compassionate" (p. 23), which would more closely align with the charismatic, transformational, democratic, affiliative, or coaching leadership styles. By extension, women of color and underrepresented individuals may experience strong community and familial ties that may also be viewed as being communal and as a result experience attributional bias.

Goffee and Jones (2000) also integrated social psychology concepts pertaining to women in management positions, adding that the representation of women in management positions is under 20% in any given society and explaining that women are cast as helpers, nurturers, or seductresses. Giving women these typecasts may encumber the development of their own identities, or styles. Goffee and Jones (2000) further noted that women are likely to react to such labels in one of three ways: (a) by making themselves invisible, or blending in; (b) collective resistance, that is, campaigning for change; or (c) playing into and playing up the role, to wittingly and skillfully use it to their benefit. The harm, Goffee and Jones (2000) added, is that it "continues to limit opportunities for other women to communicate their genuine personal differences" (p. 91). Whether female or member of an underrepresented group, the challenge is to remain true to oneself in a world that has not always embraced differences. Throughout the literature on leadership there is an overlapping theme that challenges leaders to be *authentic*, even if that means being different, and so we end this section by encouraging you to consider how you embrace the differences you see in yourself and others, and use them to challenge the status quos.

Social Work Skills and Leadership Styles

Leadership styles culled from the literature illustrate a number of overarching approaches that successful leaders may take. Leaders, and aspiring leaders, are encouraged to consider how these diverse styles of leadership can be applied in different situations, and tailored for the teams and individuals they lead. So how do effective leaders know when and how to modify their styles to achieve the vision and goals? Let us return briefly to the idea of parallel process. Social workers are constantly employing interpersonal, communication, and analytic skills, and are adaptive in their approaches to meet the diverse and complex needs of clients, groups, students, and communities. Social work leaders can employ self-efficacy garnered from experiences of direct practice work, and transfer analytic paradigms, practice behaviors, and competencies to lead teams through innovative changes within organizations. The application of social work skills is oftentimes in concert with the traits of effective leaders, and thus there are many similarities that social work practitioners can draw upon as they transition to leadership roles. Aspects of EI are paramount principles distilled from the copious literature on effective leadership. EI is the equivalent of the term "clinician's hunch." It is social work jargon for expressing that the clinician integrates self-awareness, empathy, ability to read and engage others—even the "resistant" clients—to establish trust, effectively convey messages in a manner that the client will relate to and understand, empowering clients, and more.

Modifying one's leadership style must always be expressed with authenticity, and thus it is prudent practice for leaders to identify the organic and exceptional attributes they hold in order to lead with their strengths in a genuine fashion. Cashman (2012) asserted that leaders demonstrate self-awareness, self-regulation, empathy, and self-management. In concert with these themes, Austin, Regan, Gothard, and Carnochan (2013) suggested that leadership requires self-awareness, self-directed learning, and dedicating time to reflect, practice, and learn. The consonance among the factors that comprise our understanding of successful leadership reveals an essence of EI.

Goleman (2011) proposed that effective leaders possess high EI, which encases self-awareness, self-regulation, motivation, empathy, and social skill. The amalgamation of components that constitute EI is the foundation for leaders to demonstrate the NSWM practice behavior 2.3 of assuming different leadership styles as appropriate to the situation. In addition to knowing how to modify one's own leadership style, the effective leader is also adept at recognizing the stylistic strengths of leaders around them. Having social awareness of the team dynamics and skills increases the likelihood that the leader can identify the type of leadership styles that must be used among the team to enhance collaboration and ensure that knowledge, skill, and motivation levels will complement team members in a productive manner. Here again, the emotionally intelligent leader will be attuned to the diverse needs and skills of the workers as well as the environmental aspects that may propel or thwart change.

Box 1.11 displays the competencies/behaviors in this section.

BOX 1.11

NETWORK FOR SOCIAL WORK MANAGEMENT AND COUNCIL ON SOCIAL WORK EDUCATION COMPETENCIES

Possesses interpersonal skills that support viability and positive functioning of the organization (Network for Social Work Management Competencies 2). Practice Behaviors:

- Possesses strong skills in emotional intelligence, self-awareness, self-mastery, etc. (2.4).
- Demonstrates commitment to the work of the agency (2.7).

CSWE Competency 1—Demonstrate Ethical and Professional Behavior

- 1.2 Use reflection and self-regulation to manage personal values and maintain professionalism in practice situations.

CSWE Competency 2—Engage Diversity and Difference in Practice

- 2.1 Apply and communicate understanding of the importance of diversity and difference in shaping life experiences in practice at the micro, mezzo, and macro levels.
- 2.2 Present themselves as learners and engage clients and constituencies as experts of their own experiences.
- 2.3 Apply self-awareness and self-regulation to manage the influence of personal biases and values in working with diverse clients and constituencies.

CSWE Competency 6—Engage With Individuals, Groups, Organizations, and Communities

- 6.1 Apply knowledge of human behavior and the social environment, person-in-environment, and other multidisciplinary theoretical frameworks to engage with clients and constituencies
- 6.2 Use empathy, reflection, and interpersonal skills to effectively engage diverse clients and constituencies.

CSWE, Council Social Work Education.

The Role of EI in Leadership and Management Practice

Goleman (2000) identified four domains of EI (self-awareness, self-management, social awareness, and social skills) and explored the relationship between EI and leadership qualities. EI, at its core, is having the ability to employ the awareness one has of both one's own and others' emotions to effectively navigate human interactions. It requires reflection, observation, flexibility, a willingness to understand others and oneself, and to effectively manage emotions, both for oneself and others. Similar to Goleman's (2000) construct of EI, Bradberry and Greaves (2005) propose that EI is the result of two main skills: personal and social competence. The axiom of personal competence focuses on self-awareness and self-management, whereas social competence focuses on social awareness and relationship management, or how one behaves with others.

In Box 1.12, there are excerpts from an interview about leadership with President Joe of Southern Connecticut State University in New Haven, Connecticut.

BOX 1.12

SOUTHERN CONNECTICUT STATE UNIVERSITY INTERVIEW

Interviewer: How can leaders use emotional intelligence to adjust leadership styles to various circumstance?

President Joe: You are constantly shifting, from one circumstance to the next. I don't think I have a choice; I need to do that to lead the institution. One needs to be able to segregate what they are doing and shift and be flexible. I can be in one meeting, put on a smile, and then in another meeting be firm.

It is important to understand style and have good mentors of different styles, to be comfortable and to be uncomfortable. And you have to feel okay being around people with other styles. A previous institution hired an academic leader and we had similar styles; in the end it was a disaster. I needed to regroup— and to own the decision I made, and say this was a mistake. Later I had to think carefully about whom I would ask to step into a key administrative role. I picked a scientist. It was the best decision I made; we complemented each other well (President Joe Bertalino, Interview on Leadership Style from March 5, 2018, SCSU, New Haven, Connecticut).
SCSU, Southern Connecticut State University.

◼ Personal Competence: Self-Awareness and Self-Management

Self-awareness is an idiom commonly encouraged throughout social work education and practice experiences. As such, there is a general understanding of its relevancy to generalist and clinical practice, which is also applicable to leadership and management in the field. To know oneself is to know how one will impact others and be impacted by others. Self-awareness inherently compels us to embrace our individual strengths and lends insight to know when our strengths may actually be functioning as a weakness, and to understand our belief systems and what drives us. Achieving and maintaining self-wisdom beckons one to reflect—often, honestly, gently, and hopefully humorously at times as well.

Goleman (2011) noted that those "with a strong self-awareness are neither overly critical nor unrealistically hopeful" but instead are "honest—with themselves and with others" (p. 7). Thus, self-awareness is having a balanced perception of the self and capacity to build authentic experiences and expectations. For example, the social worker with self-awareness of how frustrated she or he feels by a client's tendency for splitting can still foster a secure holding environment. Because of her or his awareness of her or his internal triggers, she or he has developed an ability to both anticipate and manage her or his intrinsic reaction and channel this to engage the client in decreasing the pervasive behavior of splitting. Similarly, the leader with the self-awareness that becomes stressed over the anticipation of a quarterly budget analysis might instead review monthly budget reports. Likewise, the manager who knows that she or he values strong work ethics anticipates managing her or his feelings of frustration when meeting with a staff who has been inattentive during shifts. Leaders also use self-awareness to capitalize on their own and others' strengths; a skill comparable to helping clients identify and build upon their strengths.

Leading with our strengths is something that may seem so natural, or almost too obvious, that we inadvertently minimize the art and power of inventorying our strengths. Here again, consider the impactful process of exploring clients' strengths and facilitating their ability to identify and employ them in a given context. Transferring this practice principle to the idea of leading with our strengths requires the art of reflecting in order to "know thyself" better, which can be an empowering exercise that contributes to both personal and professional growth. Rath and Conchie (2008) identify four leadership domains of leading with one's unique strengths: *executing, influencing, relationship building,* and *strategic thinking.* Each domain contains indicators that are informed based on individual characteristics and general preferences, such as one-on-one or group conversations. Not surprisingly, the relationship building domain consists of qualities of empathy, harmony, individualization, relationally focused, and others. Strategic thinking includes attributes of analytical, intellection, and learner. The influencing domain covers communication, wooing, and self-assurance. Lastly, the executing domain includes achiever, focus, responsibility, belief, and other like traits. The primary illustration of this particular self-assessment tool is that it explores the leaders' natural tendencies, which reinforces a leadership imperative—that leaders must be their authentic selves.

Empathy in leadership is a component of EI that is obvious to others; and just as it is apparent to clients and necessary for forging a therapeutic relationship, it is vital for leading teams and retaining staff. Empathic leaders, like empathic clinicians, do not take on the emotions of others but are able to consider the people's experiences and intuitively identify their emotional states (Goleman, 2011). Being attuned allows leaders to demonstrate that they take genuine interest and are invested in team members both individually and collectively, which steers the confident leader toward gaining consensus. Those who are inquisitive and take a sincere interest in others may be more likely to seek information from within and outside the organization to inform change efforts (Drucker, 2017). Information gathering is used to identify growth opportunities and guide strategic planning processes. Cuadrado et al. (2012) noted that task-oriented leaders are focused on achieving outcomes, while relationship-oriented leaders are focused on the quality of relationships with others and the overall well-being and satisfaction of staff. Not surprisingly, they suggested that effective leaders embrace both task- and relationship-oriented styles synchronously (impact and style).

Good leaders are able to foster environments that are both stimulating and safe. Deschamps, Rinfret, Lagace, and Prive (2015) explored how nonprofit organizations (NPO) can, and should, create a climate of justice. The authors describe three types of justice: organizational, distributive, and procedural. Organizational justice is marked by perceptions of fairness at every level of decision making, distributive justice recognizes the importance of parity in distributing outcomes and tasks, and procedural justice manifests in fair processes such as procedures for candidate selection. Transformational leaders are keenly aware of the diverse needs of supervisees and use their EI and charismatic social skills to take an authentic interest and display respect and concern for all subordinates. It is difficult to get a pulse of an agency from behind one's desk, and although the daily demands placed on leaders can make it seem difficult to get out and engage with staff, a leader who carves out the time to do so is exemplifying interactional justice.

Interactional justice is the simple act of treating others with dignity and respect (Deschamps et al., 2015). Hopefully the idea of dignity and respect feels like a no-brainer, but some well-intended leaders overlook the value and impact of frequent walks through the organization. Leaders can become so caught up in meetings, oversaturated in projects, and inundated by emails that they unknowingly neglect the most valued capital the organization has—the human capital. Thus, building time into one's schedule to connect with people at all levels of an organization exudes the empathy needed to promote interactional justice. Additionally, when leaders are able to make these connections they are more likely to use collective intelligence to sway adaptive organizational change.

An inherent aspect of EI that is imbued in components of self-awareness and regulation, empathy, and even motivation is the capacity for mindfulness. Marturano (2014) defined the mindful leader as focused, creative, and compassionate, with an ability to practice "nonjudgmental attention in the present moment" (p. 11). It is not enough for leaders to apply such qualities solely to development of their leadership tasks and style and regard for others, but one must be committed to caring for oneself in an open-minded, compassionate, creative, and focused manner as well.

Self-management is a skill social workers often address in clinical treatment to aid clients in enhancing their ability to control how their internal reactions manifest and influence their relationships, work, and overall well-being. It is the ability to manage and channel our emotional responses in a manner that is productive, and not destructive. When we consistently execute the skill of self-regulation, we garner the trust of the people that we lead, and we lead with integrity (Goleman, 2011). A mercurial temperament can evoke feelings of uncertainty, and uncertainty can quickly erode trust. Therefore, it is not enough to employ self-regulation skills, but to do so with consistency to promote an environment that permeates a sense of predictability and security.

The ability to show self-management engenders trust from followers and can also elevate conscientiousness and achievement orientation by motivating, or inspiring others. As the saying goes: "The uninspired cannot inspire." In order to motivate others, one has to first demonstrate that one is self-motivated, always eager to learn, consistently raising the bar of self-expectations, and committed to personal and professional growth. Self-motivation is sometimes perceived as one's passion for the work, which seemingly fuels an unrelenting dedication to the mission and, by extension, awakens visionary leadership. The motivated leader uses setbacks and failures as opportunities to transcend. The capacity for transcendence beyond setbacks is linked to one's curiosity, reception to feedback, and emotional stamina.

Self-determination theory undergirds the paradox between autonomous and nonautonomous motivation among nonprofit employees. Whereas autonomous motivation is driven by people's interest and sense of satisfaction because they perceive it to be enjoyable or rewarding, nonautonomous motivation is propelled by external forces that create a sense of pressure to act and performance is driven by pay or recognition (Goleman, 2011). From a social psychology perspective, sufficient rewards will be reciprocated with better support and production (Cuadrado et al., 2012). Understanding the two types of motivation is salient because emotionally attuned and intelligent leaders can utilize this knowledge to leverage commitment to tasks and influence outcomes. For instance, being able to offer formal and informal acknowledgements for performance can keep people engaged in the mission and work.

Informal recognition includes sending a note or verbally acknowledging efforts in a meeting, and formal mechanisms may include things like employee of the quarter (note: it is beneficial to nominate small task teams), an additional float holiday, and when, indicated and possible, a stipend (e.g., covering responsibilities of a vacant position). From the broadest perspective, this recognition sometimes requires leaders to be advocates for change in pay, which can be an onerous undertaking for human service organizations and academic institutions and oftentimes necessitates a change in organizational culture. For example, an NPO that has rich benefits, albeit low hourly wages might consider shifting the contribution from benefits to wages. Strategic planning would require an analysis that includes understanding the demographics of the staff, such as age cohort, amount of single and dependent enrollees, and gaining a firm grasp on where the majority of the staff place value (in fringe benefits or wages). For those that are governed by autonomous motivation, it is important to recognize and nurture that quality. Leaders can do so by discussing with the person what they enjoy about work in general and if there is a specific project that engages and motivates them. Expressing respect and appreciation of the drive they bring to the team can also keep the person motivated. Ideally, internally motivated individuals should be continuously challenged and intellectually stimulated by leaders.

BOX 1.13

NETWORK FOR SOCIAL WORK MANAGEMENT COMPETENCIES AND PRACTICE BEHAVIORS 2

Possesses interpersonal skills that support viability and positive functioning of the organization (Network for Social Work Management Competencies 2). Practice Behaviors:

- Is able to find common ground with others and form positive relationships easily (2.5).
- Is able to inspire confidence in others, both internally and externally (2.6).

Box 1.13 displays the competencies/behaviors in this section.

Social Competence: Social Awareness and Relationship Management

Social awareness is simply the ability to accurately read the emotions of others to understand what they are experiencing (Bradberry & Greaves, 2005). The human brain is constantly taking in nuanced messages in social exchanges, at times too many to mentally or verbally articulate in the moment, but messages that may nonetheless tug at our intuition and are mentally shelved to be processed at a later time. While some people are able to use the material in the moment, others may replay the social exchange in their minds and return to the emotional clues they discovered in future conversations. While we may not be able to process everything the other is emotionally experiencing in that moment, if one is attuned to another's feelings, of frustration or disappointment for instance, it can lead one to ask questions that get to the heart of the matter. The mere act of being in tune with the other, is demonstrating empathy—an ingredient that is commonly venerated whether one is a practicing social worker, teacher, manager, or leader.

Relationship management is akin to social skills, or having the ability to use one's self-awareness, self-management, and social awareness to engage and successfully handle social interactions. To successfully manage relationships, one has to ensure that communication is clear and straightforward. Goleman (2000) asserted that the visionary leader is marked by the ability to influence others, to resolve conflicts, and to de-escalate tension, while developing others through feedback and coaching and fostering bonds of teamwork and collaboration.

EI essentially involves the ability to be cognizant, or mindful, of what is happening in the moment to better understand the spoken and unspoken information revealed by others while simultaneously being aware of one's internal experiences. When leaders are able to reflect on how they are integrating EI with their leadership styles, they are more likely to demonstrate competencies of self-regard and acceptance, assertiveness, social responsibility, impulse control, and flexibility. These may seem like no-brainers, but as our watering the tomatoes example alluded to earlier in this chapter, it is sometimes necessary to state what you suspect is obvious, as it is not always so obvious to all.

BOX 1.14

NETWORK FOR SOCIAL WORK MANAGEMENT COMPETENCIES AND PRACTICE BEHAVIORS 8

Advocates for public policy change and social justice at national, state, and local levels (Network for Social Work Management Competencies 8). Practice Behaviors:

(continued)

BOX 1.14 *(Continued)*

▦ Strategically disseminates information about unmet needs and program accomplishments (8.1).

▦ Participates in professional organizations and industry groups that advocate for client social justice, equity, and fairness (8.2).

Possesses interpersonal skills that support viability and positive functioning of the organization (Network for Social Work Management Competencies 2). Practice Behaviors:

▦ Demonstrates and communicates deep knowledge about the work of the agency, using current performance data to discuss successes and challenges (2.8).

Box 1.14 displays the competencies/behaviors in this section. Good leaders and good managers are able to put things in context and are able to evaluate what the person's experiences in their environments are and respond accordingly. They soak in observations about what kind of challenges people are facing, and how they react to the orbiting barriers. For instance, they have a pulse on whether social workers are mired down by paperwork or overwhelmed thinking about how their rapport might be affected by a newly mandated group modality of treatment for the clients they have been working with individually. Do they appear deplete of energy to advocate for clients, or have diminished interest in creating changes? In the wake of decreased funding combined with increased regulations, community-based agencies work diligently to modify service delivery systems. Academic institutions are challenged with enrollment issues and must find new ways to market cutting-edge educational experiences to students. Social work as a profession has been oriented to quotas and business principles because of the cascading effects of the economic tides, service delivery systems, regulations governing the frequency and duration of treatments, client contact quotas, performance outcomes, ability to retain competent and sufficient staffing, and resources to provide continuing education and training, just to name a few. Todd and Schwartz (2009) noted that the vast impact of a neoliberal economy has pushed the globalization model of doing business onto social work practice "in which workers are expected to do more with less" (p. 381).

Well before Carol Meyer (1970) crafted her ecosystems perspective, she predicted that "as social policy and agency structures become more reconciled with practices and skills as part of the total approach to social work, it will become evident that policies and structures themselves are *part* of the cases and the problems being served" (p. 102). Expanding upon her construct, it seems that conceptualizing a "social worker-in-environment" as the "case" at hand needs to be ensconced in the ecosystems perspective as well. The breadth of social work practice has expanded exponentially in response to the rise in the complexities of client problems and dwindling of human and community-based resources, and the brunt of such paradoxical compression impinges on social workers that make up organizations. Therefore, how the leaders and managers in the field demonstrate empathy for the high demands while supportively challenging workers to adapt to ecological demands can have a mediating effect on professionals. In essence, the leaders and managers must be attuned with the ecosystem and how workers view the internal and external systems they work in. They must also use the information they have available to promote organizational justice and advocate for changes that create parity within the workplace. See Boxes 1.15 and 1.16 which each have a case example on leadership.

BOX 1.15

COMPETENCY-BASED CASE EXAMPLE

A petition has been circulating in a community agency stating that there is a lack of diversity among the top leaders of the organization. The lack of diversity has caused an uproar among middle level managers and direct staff, who perceive that they are treated unfairly and state the organization only hires minorities to "do the dirty work."

Questions

1. What does this suggest about the organizational culture? How should this be addressed?
2. How can leaders and mangers incorporate cultural competence in their skills repertoire?
3. Why is it important to demonstrate cultural competence and awareness in leading others?

BOX 1.16

COMPETENCY-BASED CASE EXAMPLE

A professor of 30 years has assigned a reading that quotes racial slurs. One day in class the professor was reading a passage aloud which included the racial slurs about African Americans. An African American student became angered at the professor for reading these racial slurs aloud, and, at the same she was expressing her anger over this, another student video-recorded both the professor reading the passage aloud and the upset student. This, as you may have already guessed, went viral immediately.

Question

1. How should the president of the university address this issue?

SUMMARY

In this chapter, we differentiated between leadership and management. Management is primarily concerned with organizing, staffing, and performing quality control tasks that contribute to organizations operating as well-oiled machines. Leadership is concerned with aligning and inspiring individuals to work collaboratively toward the envisioned goals.

There has been much written on how to effectively lead and manage others, but the core ingredients distill down to exercising EI. In this chapter, we discussed the four domains of EI: self-awareness, self-management, social awareness, and relationship management. There are a variety of leadership styles and social work leaders and managers must be flexible in their use of the diverse styles, as different situations call for modification of leadership styles. These leadership styles are listed in context in Table 1.1.

TABLE 1.1 **Leadership Styles in Context**

LEADERSHIP STYLE	KEY ATTRIBUTES	SITUATIONAL CUES/ WHEN TO USE	RELATED EI TRAITS
TRANSACTIONAL LEADERSHIP STYLE	Rewards and punishment to motivate. Clearly defines the roles and expectations from the leader. Organizational culture is maintained; behavioral norms are followed.	Performance improvement plans. Setting goals connected to contingent rewards (e.g., if census doubles, there will be a stipend).	*Self-management:* Achievement oriented; initiative. *Social awareness:* Service orientation. *Social skills:* Visionary leadership (take charge and inspire).
TRANSFORMATIONAL LEADERSHIP STYLE	The exchange value is the passion for the work. Inspire confidence in others by welcoming ideas and creative suggestions. Inspire the team to collaboratively engage in the process of goal attainment. Individualized consideration when coaching and mentoring subordinates.	Leading organization culture changes; major projects. Individual and team supervision. Individualizing goals and objectives.	*Self-awareness:* Self-confidence and accurate self-assessment. *Self-management:* Trustworthiness, conscientiousness. *Social awareness:* Empathy, organizational awareness. *Social skills:* Developing others, building bonds, conflict management.
CHARISMATIC LEADERSHIP STYLE	Relationally focused on the interactions with subordinates. Portrays a strong sense of confidence and competence, and communicates high expectations. Cultivates an internalization of goals among subordinates and advances the moral commitment to the goals that transcends self-interest.	Day-to-day operations, taking interest in subordinates to inspire trust. Leading through organization change (i.e., quality improvement plans and setting programmatic goals that have buy-in and accountability).	*Self-awareness:* Accurate self-assessment, emotional self-awareness. *Self-management:* Trustworthiness, initiative, self-control. *Social awareness:* Empathy, organizational awareness. *Social skills:* Influence, teamwork, and collaboration.

(continued)

TABLE 1.1 **Leadership Styles in Context** *(Continued)*

LEADERSHIP STYLE	KEY ATTRIBUTES	SITUATIONAL CUES/ WHEN TO USE	RELATED EI TRAITS
EXEMPLARY LEADERSHIP STYLE	Prove themselves to be trustworthy. Model the ability to apply strategic thinking and forecasting to analyze and plan for future developments. Have a proven history of goal attainment. Have an energizing demeanor that encourages forward thinking.	Project management: complete tasks in a way that demonstrates ability and commitment. Leader/manager may thoughtfully assign tasks to self to model and encourage the abilities of others, while also showing commitment to the vision and goals.	*Self-awareness:* Self-confidence. *Self-management:* Self-control, achievement, orientation. *Social awareness:* Empathy, organizational awareness, service orientation. *Social skill:* Developing others, change catalyst, cultivate relationships, conflict management.
SERVANT LEADERSHIP STYLE	Listening. Empathy. Healing "broken spirits" and "emotional hurts." General and self-awareness. Persuasion, not positional, authority. Broad conceptual thinking and visioning. Learning from past and foreseeing future outcomes. Stewardship. Commitment to the growth of the people. Building community.	Useful in all human service agencies and is seen as the underpinning values of most social services. Particularly emphasized by intuitions that are committed to community engagement and advocacy.	*Self-awareness:* Emotional. *Self-management:* Trustworthiness, conscientiousness, initiative. *Social awareness:* Service orientation, empathy, organizational awareness. *Social skill:* Visionary leadership, influence, cultivate relationships, conflict management.

(continued)

TABLE 1.1 **Leadership Styles in Context** *(Continued)*

LEADERSHIP STYLE	KEY ATTRIBUTES	SITUATIONAL CUES/ WHEN TO USE	RELATED EI TRAITS
AUTOCRATIC LEADERSHIP STYLE	Highly focused on goal attainment and mainly interested in the information that is needed to accomplish the goal. Offer rewards for compliance and goal-oriented activities. Gain group compliance with directives. Provide scarce information, or what is determined to only be necessary to complete the task. Do not seek input or ideas from subordinates.	Similar to transactional, often needed during times of crisis management. Useful in restoring baseline functioning of organizations and realigning focus toward quality improvement when abrupt change is needed.	*Self-awareness:* Self-confidence. *Self-management:* Achievement, orientation, initiative. *Social awareness:* Service orientation. *Social skill:* Visionary leadership, influence.
AUTHORITATIVE LEADERSHIP STYLE	People understand that what they do matters. Individualized tasks (fit with grand vision). Flexible (people are allowed to innovate).	Useful when organizational structure (hierarchy) has leader fairly removed from day-to-day tasks, but is able to communicate appreciation and hear from staff when possible about how to move the vision forward. Work with directors and leaders at various levels to help ensure that flexibility is imbued.	*Self-awareness:* Emotional self-awareness. *Self-management:* Self-control, conscientiousness,initiative. *Social awareness:* Organizational awareness, empa-thy, service orientation. *Social skill:* Change catalyst, developing others, influence, conflict management.
AFFILIATIVE LEADERSHIP STYLE	Loyalty: Build a sense of belonging. Trust allows for innovation and risks.	Useful for building or restoring team morale.	*Self-awareness:* Emotional self-awareness. *Self-management* Trustworthiness, self-control. *Social awareness:* Empathy, organizational awareness.

(continued)

TABLE 1.1 **Leadership Styles in Context** *(Continued)*

LEADERSHIP STYLE	KEY ATTRIBUTES	SITUATIONAL CUES/ WHEN TO USE	RELATED EI TRAITS
COERCIVE LEADERSHIP STYLE	Demands immediate compliance. Directive.	Useful when implementing corrective action plans, or program improvement plans, as well as individual performance improvement plans.	*Self-awareness*: Self-confidence. *Self-management*: Achievement orientation. *Social awareness*: Service orientation. *Social skills*: Change catalyst, influence, visionary.
DEMOCRATIC LEADERSHIP STYLE	Spend time to get others' ideas, gives a voice to others. Flexible. Builds organizational responsibility.	Useful when there is ample time to process and strategically plan changes. Can also be applied in direct supervision, asking for input and ideas about possible ways to handle the issue at hand.	*Self-awareness*: Emotional self-awareness, self-confidence. *Self-management*: Self-control, trustworthiness, initiative. *Social awareness*: Empathy, service orientation, organizational awareness. *Social skill*: Visionary, developing others, building bonds, teamwork and collaboration, conflict management.
PACESETTING LEADERSHIP STYLE	High performance. High achievement. Able to motivate others who are also highly self-motivated through demonstrated achievements.	Useful for short-term projects that need to be completed efficiently. Teams should be balanced with pacesetters to help propel project completion.	*Self-awareness*: Self-confidence. *Self-management*: Self-control, achievement orientation, initiative. *Social awareness*: Service orientation. *Social skill*: Visionary.
COACHING LEADERSHIP STYLE	Mentor approach. Concerned with personal and professional growth.	Useful at individual and collective levels, e.g., setting individually tailored goals to help advance professional skills. At the collective level, providing resources/trainings to larger teams.	*Self-awareness*: Accurate self-assessment. *Self-management*: Trustworthiness, conscientiousness. *Social awareness*: Empathy, organizational awareness, service orientation. *Social skill*: Developing others, change catalyst, influence.

EI, emotional intelligence.

ACTIVITIES

Review the following case scenarios and describe the type of leadership style that may best fit with the given situation. Note how you would adapt certain leadership styles (perhaps taking some, but not all, aspects of a particular style) to lead the team through the presented situation.

1. A social work department at a public university is faced with extreme budget cuts which require that professors teach one class more than has historically been required. The dean has also underscored that the department must finds ways to grow the program in order to sustain the department in the long run. The chair suggests that the department explore expanding the programs to include a DSW program, in addition to the established BSW and MSW programs. With the dean's approval, the chair brings this proposal to the team of faculty who are overwhelmed by their current workloads; many are stressed over their tenure applications, and a few do not see the value in spending the already limited resources to design a new program.

2. A nonprofit residential agency is faced with drastic cuts to its funding. This cut is a direct result of a philosophy change made by the state (i.e., funding) agency that recently hired a new commissioner. The new commissioner has developed a strategic plan to reduce the amount of residential placements by 50% in the next year. If the state achieves its placement goal, the nonprofit residential treatment facility will be forced to close down.

3. A state agency that provides inpatient care to adults has been exposed by the local media for mistreating clients, including being verbally and physically abusive toward them. The media has reported that staff that mistreated and abused the clients had worked a copious amount of overtime, and that concerns had previously been brought to the supervisor and director of the program.

4. A team of administrators has been noticing that the attire worn by direct care and professional staff is often inappropriate and does not adhere to the current dress code. Some members of the administrative team feel strongly that staff are not paid enough to purchase new clothing. Others suggest that the agency provide staff with a clothing voucher to purchase uniforms; still others believe that if staff can afford the latest cell phones then they should be able to afford basic articles of clothing that complies with the dress code.

5. The department of social work at a university has had a hiring freeze due to a lack of funds. Simultaneously, there has been an increase in enrollment at the undergraduate level which has created the need for more student advisors. The department has traditionally assigned professors for student advising based on the program they work in (either undergraduate or graduate), but there is now a significant imbalance of students assigned to undergraduate professors, while the graduate professors advisement loads have remained unchanged. This situation has created a divide and disputes about how to handle it have arisen in the department.

6. List your top five EI abilities and connect them with your top five leadership styles.

    a. Which EI traits are most comfortable for you?

    b. Which leadership styles feel most authentic for you, and why?

    c. What are the possible strengths and weaknesses of the list you created?

TABLE 1.2 **Table for Question 6**

EI STRENGTHS	LEADERSHIP STYLE

EI, emotional intelligence.

REFERENCES

Austin, M. J., Regan, K., Gothard, S., & Carnochan, S. (2013). Becoming a manager in nonprofit human service organizations: Making the transition from specialist to generalist. *Administration in Social Work, 37*, 372–385. doi:10.1080/03643107.2012.715116

Bass, B. M. (2009). *The Bass handbook of leadership: Theory, research and managerial applications* (4th ed.). New York, NY: The Free Press.

Bradberry, T., & Greaves, J. (2005). *The emotional intelligence quick book: Everything you need to know to put your EQ to work.* New York, NY: Simon & Schuster.

Cashman, K. (2012). *The pause principle: Step back to lead forward.* San Francisco, CA: Berrett-Koehler.

Cuadrado, I., Navas, M., Ferrer, E., Molero, F., & Morales, J. F. (2012). Gender differences in leadership styles as a function of leader and subordinates' sex and type of organization. *Journal of Applied Psychology, 42*, 3083–3113.

Deschamps, C., Rinfret, N., Lagace, M. C., & Prive, C. (2015). Transformational leadership and change: How leaders influence their followers' motivation through organizational justice. *Journal of Healthcare Management, 61*, 194–213. doi:10.1097/00115514-201605000-00007

Drucker, P. (2017). *The Peter F. Drucker reader: Selected articles from the father of modern management thinking.* Boston, MA: Harvard Business Review Press.

Eagly, A., & Karau, S. J. (2002). Role congruity theory of prejudice toward female leaders. *Psychological Review, 109*, 573–598. doi:10.1037//0033-295X.109.3.573

Gardella, L. G., & Haynes, K. S. (2004). *A dream and a plan: A woman's path to leadership in human services.* Baltimore, MD: NASW Press.

Goffee, R., & Jones, G. (2000). *Why should anyone be led by you?* Boston, MA: Harvard Business Review. September-October 2000.

Goleman, D. (2000). Leadership that gets results. *Harvard Business Review.* Retrieved from www.hbr.org

Goleman, D. (2011). What makes a leader? In *On leadership: HBR's 10 must reads.* Boston, MA: Harvard Business Review Press.

Hutchison, E. D. (2015). *Dimensions of human behavior: Person and environment* (5th ed.). London: Sage Publications.

Kotter, P. (2011). What leaders really do. In *On leadership: HBR's 10 must reads.* Boston, MA: Harvard Business Review Press.

Lewis, J. A., Packard, T. R., & Lewis, M. D. (2017). *Management of human service programs* (5th ed.). Belmont: Brooks/Cole.

Lanfranchi, J., & Narcy, M. (2015). Female overrepresentation in public and nonprofit sector jobs: Evidence from a French national survey. *Nonprofit and Voluntary Sector Quarterly, 44*, 47–74. doi:10.1177/0899764013502579

Lopez, E. S., & Ensari, N. (2014). The effects of leadership style, organizational outcomes, and gender on attributional bias toward leaders. *Journal of Leadership Studies, 8*(2), 19–37. doi:10.1002/jls.21326

Marturano, J. (2014). *Finding the space to lead: A practice guide to mindful leadership.* New York, NY: Bloomsbury Press.

Meyer, C. H. (1970). *Social work practice* (2nd ed.). New York, NY: The Free Press.

Murray, D., & Chau, S. (2014). Differences in leadership styles and motives in men and women: How generational theory informs gender role congruity. *Proceedings of the European Conference on Management, Leadership,* 192.

Rath, T., & Conche, B. (2008). *Strengths finder 2.0 strengths based leadership: Great leaders, teams, and why people follow.* New York, NY: Gallup Press.

Todd, S., & Schwartz, K. (2009). Thinking through quality in field education: Integrating alternative and traditional learning opportunities. *Social Work Education, 28*(4), 380–395. doi:10.1080/02615470902808326

Weinbach, R. T., & Taylor, L. M. (2015). *The social worker as manager: A practical guide to success* (7th ed.). Upper Saddle River, NJ: Pearson Education Inc.

Wilcox, J., Kersh, B. C., & Jenkins, E. (2017). *Motivational interviewing for leadership: MI-LEAD.* Tampa: FL: Gray Publishing LLC.

CHAPTER 2

BEST LEADERSHIP AND MANAGEMENT PRACTICES IN SOCIAL WORK

CHAPTER OBJECTIVES

- Managing ambiguous and complex organizational situations.
- Understanding appropriate professional behavior.
- Recognizing how to promote and manage diversity and cross-cultural competence.
- Identifying ways to initiate and facilitate innovative change processes.
- Understanding performance-based leadership and how to perform multiple roles.
- Describing moral leadership.
- Knowing the importance of team building, coalition building, and facilitating successful processes.
- Fostering relationships with staff.

INTRODUCTION

This chapter provides an overview of best practices that managers and leaders exemplify. Analyzing practice behaviors of leaders and managers is valuable because behaviors are actions that contribute to the overall culture of an organization or academic institution. Leaders and managers are responsible for demonstrating an ability to facilitate innovative visions, cultural competence, moral behaviors, and team building. Although both roles have trenchant agendas, the commensalism between leaders and managers is how they build relationships with staff to promote viable changes and enrich organizational cultures. In clinical practice, a social worker knows how to distinguish *process* from *content*; the content is, of course, the "what," or the topic, themes, and goals being discussed, while the process is "how" the content is discussed and gives meaning to the interpersonal relationship. Leaders and managers must similarly attend to both process and content to collaborate and build rapports with their followers. There are strategic ways to mobilize innovation and navigate systemic and political shifts, which are explored in detail in later chapters, but throughout this chapter we focus on the tacit skills of building working rapports with employees. A clinician working directly with clients understands that carefully selected, empirically supported intervention techniques will be a futile effort aimed toward a client's change behaviors if there is not a solid alliance or therapeutic rapport to serve as the foundation for this change work. As social workers, we are naturally driven to build relationships and connections with people, and these are the cornerstone of change work. Leadership and management are not dissimilar. Relationships must be fostered, trust needs to be established, cultural awareness must be imbued, behaviors should be modeled, and people are empowered through our valued belief that change is possible, and collaboration is an essential part of the change process.

We begin this chapter by revisiting the differences between leadership and management roles to better understand how the symbiotic nature of these roles is foundational for facilitative changes within service agencies and academia. In Chapter 1, we briefly discussed some of the distinctions between leadership and management and provided an overview of the individual styles that leaders, and managers by extension, can adopt and modify as situationally indicated. In this chapter we further dismantle the leader/manager distinctions and focus our attention on the best practices of both leaders and managers.

Recall from Chapter 1 that managers organize and leaders inspire. Analogous to this notion is the idea that "Managers do things right. Leaders do the right thing" (Fitch & Van Brunt, 2016, p. 34). Others have referred to leadership and management distinctions as "push/pull" forces, wherein managers often need to rely on their authority to *push* their teams to maintain compliance and efficiency, and leaders *pull* their teams by inspiring them to take an active role to contribute to successful organizational outcomes. The reality is that both good leadership and good management are essential for healthy organizations, and thus both the *push* and the *pull* are vital to an organization's success. Moreover, when the push and the pull are driven by compatible values, in other words the skill sets are diverse yet complementary, and are instilled with social change perspectives, they can augment outcomes and improve the workplace environment. Hence, "the sum is greater than its equal parts." In the sections that follow we will traverse through the manager/leader distinctions and consider how managers and leaders accomplish the tasks that are relevant to their roles through professional behaviors, cultural humility, innovation, and effective communication skills.

LEADERSHIP VERSUS MANAGEMENT

Boxes 2.1 and 2.2 display the competencies/behaviors in this section.

BOX 2.1

COMPETENCIES AND PRACTICE BEHAVIORS ADDRESSED IN THIS CHAPTER

Possesses analytical and critical thinking skills that promote organizational growth (Network for Social Work Management Competencies 3). Practice Behaviors:

■   Manages ambiguous and complex organizational situations (3.7).

Advocates for public policy change and social justice at national, state, and local levels (Network for Social Work Management Competencies 8). Practice Behaviors:

(continued)

BOX 2.1 *(Continued)*

- Advocates for an organizational culture that recognizes and rewards professionalism, quality customer service; employee engagement and empowerment, programs, and policies that further social justice; and efforts to achieve diversity in customers, employees, and ideas (8.6).

Models appropriate professional behavior and encourages other staff members to act in a professional manner (Network for Social Work Management Competencies 4). Practice Behaviors:

- Engages in and promotes ethical conduct (4.1).
- Protects the integrity and reputation of the organization (4.2).
- Creates and supports an organizational culture that values professionalism, service, and ethical conduct (4.3)
- Displays the ability to carry on effectively in the face of adversity, ambiguity, uncertainty, and anxiety (4.5).
- Demonstrates the ability not to be "consumed" by executive responsibilities and helps others to achieve the balance and maintain a sense of humor and perspective (4.7).

Initiates and facilitates innovative change processes (Network for Social Work Management Competencies 7). Practice Behaviors:

- Remains current on trends and identifies shifts that require an innovative response (7.1).
- Presents innovations to appropriate decision makers and stakeholders and makes decisions that are aligned with their feedback (7.2).
- Assists staff with implementing positive change and supports risk taking (7.3).
- Supports innovative practices to improve program-related issues and services (7.4).

CSWE Competency 1—Demonstrate Ethical and Professional Behavior

- 1.2 Use reflection and self-regulation to manage personal values and maintain professionalism in practice situations.
- 1.3 Demonstrate professional demeanor in behavior; appearance; and oral, written, and electronic communication.

CSWE Competency 2—Engage Diversity and Difference in Practice

- 2.1 Apply and communicate understanding of the importance of diversity and difference in shaping life experiences in practice at the micro, mezzo, and macro levels.
- 2.2 Present themselves as learners and engage clients and constituencies as experts of their own experiences.
- 2.3 Apply self-awareness and self-regulation to manage the influence of personal biases and values in working with diverse clients and constituencies.

CSWE Competency 6—Engage with Individuals, Families, Groups, Organizations, and Communities

- 6.2 Use empathy, reflection, and interpersonal skills to effectively engage diverse clients and constituencies.

CSWE, Council on Social Work Education.

BOX 2.2

NETWORK FOR SOCIAL WORK MANAGEMENT COMPETENCY AND PRACTICE BEHAVIOR 8.6

Advocates for public policy change and social justice at national, state, and local levels (Network for Social Work Management Competencies 8). Practice Behaviors:

- Advocates for an organizational culture that recognizes and rewards professionalism, quality customer service; employee engagement and empowerment, programs, and policies that further social justice; and efforts to achieve diversity in customers, employees, and ideas (8.6).

Leadership

Leaders maintain a focus on the larger, long-term vision, goals, and strategic plans and are able to use their interpersonal qualities to enthuse others to remain focused on and working toward the envisioned goals. Fitch and Van Brunt (2016) asserted that remaining focused on long-term goal attainment requires leaders to have a sense of delayed gratification and stamina to constantly inspire and mobilize teams in the desired direction of change. This practice often means that leaders do not get too deep into the weeds, or "micro-manage," the daily tasks that must be undertaken to assure that the ship is running smoothly, but that they nonetheless remain informed about the daily operations. Staying informed often occurs through collaboration with managers and directors at various levels of the organizational hierarchy. Creating an atmosphere of trust is paramount because it sets the tone for how your subordinates will be supported in doing the work, provides them with an understanding of how they are contributing to the outcomes, shows that they can rely on honest coaching, and can be assured in their belief that their work not only matters but is appreciated. Good leadership creates a trustworthy atmosphere through modeling reciprocity of trust and unwaveringly following through with actions. There is a saying, "Don't trust words, but don't trust actions either. Instead, trust patterns."

Leaders Focus on Organizational Culture

Leaders focus on organizational culture and the spirit of teams to ensure that morale and motivation are strong. Leaders are able to identify new directions that an organization or institution must take, and to do this successfully leaders must also have a good pulse on the psyche of the team. How are they collaborating? Are they showing up with passion, or feeling complacent? What are the perceived barriers that are possibly getting in the way of the changes envisioned? How do the individuals and collective teams that comprise the organizational structure need to be better supported? Leaders who are relationally focused, and take a genuine interest in listening to the ideas and concerns of followers, will have a good sense of what is needed by actively listening.

In Box 2.3 there are excerpts taken from an interview about leadership with President Joe of Southern Connecticut State University in New Haven, Connecticut.

BOX 2.3

SCSU INTERVIEW

The president of the university first explains why it was important to him that he be known by faculty and students as President Joe. He explained, "I'm a relationship-oriented kind of guy, and I thought calling me by my first name would break down barriers and formality. I wanted to be approachable."

When asked: *What leadership qualities do you feel are essential as the president of the university?* President Joe answered:

Everything is all about relationships. I follow a relational leadership model. Everything we do is about relationships: building good and strong relationships, confronting and dealing with challenging relationships. When you ask people about important things in their lives, it is all about relationships. Also depends on where an institution is at during a particular place in time. I may need to do a different style at a different point.

(President Joe Bertalino, Interview on Leadership Style from March 5, 2018, SCSU New Haven, Connecticut)

SCSU, Southern Connecticut State University.

The leader who is relationally driven, actively listening (i.e., listening to understand), and genuinely engaged with others will be at an advantage when it comes to motivating staff or leading them through turbulent times precisely because they already have a gauge on the perspective and emotions of those they are leading. Leaders must also work closely with managers, who are often overseeing the granular details of organizing and carrying out tasks that keep the operation running efficiently. Thus, leaders must know how to effectively communicate and what questions to ask.

Leaders Need to Exude Transparent Communication

Leaders need to communicate transparently with key players and offer regular feedback and direction toward the stated goals, as this transparency can have an infectious quality on how mangers communicate with their staff. When communicating with teams, managers must be able to trust that the leader is being authentic with them and that the leader has demonstrated a genuine understanding of the daily challenges and realities that may be deterring the team from achieving the vision and goals. The leader must always validate the valid, or objective, challenges and barriers, respond empathically, allocate time to collaboratively process how the team might overcome the stated obstacles, and rejuvenate staff with inspiration to continue to pull in the right direction. Conversely, leaders must also be cautious not to validate the invalid, or the subjective material that is sometimes more emotionally driven. Hence, leaders need to be cognizant of when subjective information is clouding the real issues that need to be addressed and tune into the factual, objective points laid out for them. Just as a clinician is skilled at detecting what is, and what is not, being said and uncovering insights that must come into more direct focus, leaders need to hone in on the core issues that are in need of direct and productive dialoguing.

Leaders are not coy about what needs to be said (and that applies to themselves too) and are able to couch information and feedback in a manner that is respectful and solution-focused. Conversations about problem areas should be discussed in a way that enables the other person to better understand the issue(s) and how individual performance outcomes have rippling effects on teams and populations served. Ideally, the conversation should generate ideas *from the individual*, rather than the leader, about how to make adjustments and improvements, although the leader can help process by facilitating the dialogue. Hence, leaders *pull* followers to greater insights and ownership. Similar to motivational interviewing skills, the adept leader will ask the right questions at the right moments to help the individual gain insight and take accountability for both previous and future outcomes. Leaders can consider themselves soundboards in the process of identifying solutions for individuals to adopt, because just as with clients, when people are able to determine the problem and corresponding solution(s), they have a greater investment in the change process. There will likely be times, however, when a leader is not able to employ a motivational interviewing approach, either due to the magnitude of the situation or recurrence of a pattern that simply no longer lends itself to this process. In these situations, the leader must take a more directive stance and concisely address the issues at hand and outline expectations for remedying the problem(s).

Leaders Must Be Strong Communicators

Leaders must be strong communicators, which, of course, includes written and spoken communication, as well as how they nonverbally communicate and engage. It is important that the leader tailor messages in a way that a *particular* audience will best understand and receive the message; you must know your audience. It is equally important that *leaders provide constructive feedback* along with praise. Remember, leaders are focused on continuous improvements and a lack of constructive feedback offers little to no room for growth. One example of how to suffuse this principle is by asking questions such as "What went well?" and "What can be better?" during project management. Such questions can be asked at certain benchmarks of the project and upon completing the project. Asking such questions shows that the leader is capable of being reflective and able to facilitate dialogues that constructively inspire followers to strive for improvement. Moreover, leaders must be open to receiving constructive feedback and not personalizing any feedback they do solicit, but instead using that information to make their own improvements.

Good communication requires that the leader does not talk with vagaries, nor do they talk "above" their audience; that is, the audience must be able to understand and relate with what is being said. Effective communicators are able to speak directly about what is happening, what needs to happen, and, when applicable, use metaphors, quotes, or stories that will evoke of spirit of "yes, we can!" and accomplish the stated goals and vision. (An example of this, and personal favorite of both authors, is the Wayne Gretzky quote: "I skate to where the puck is going to be, not where it has been.") Leaders will only evoke the "yes, we can" feeling from teams if they are also able to support them by providing the resources and coaching necessary, hearing out concerns and ideas from team members, and allowing others to also lead (themselves and others) in order to demonstrate trust in others' leadership abilities.

Leaders Must Be in a Perpetual State of Reflection

Leaders must be in a perpetual state of reflection to effectively heighten their self-awareness; to do so they must be present in all social, cerebral, and emotional exchanges with others. Good leaders will be aware of how they present in posing questions, providing feedback, facilitating meetings, and so on, meaning that they are able to observe their tone and nonverbal cues as well as spoken style of relating with others. It should go without saying that good leaders do not come across as punitive, condescending, righteous, or indifferent; they understand that their followers need to trust how they will process the content with and among them. Do followers feel that they are heard, understood, that their input—even when not feasible—is appreciated and valued? Is the conversation rushed? Conversely, can the leader redirect a tangential member during a time-limited meeting in a respectful and successful manner? As a leader, one must ask: How did I deal with that? What should I do differently next time? What did I miss in the moment that I can see more clearly now? What should I do about that now that I see it?

In summary, leaders are constantly seeking improvements. It is the active engagement in the process of reflection that propels leaders to become more visionary thinkers, effective communicators, relationally focused coaches or mentors, and emotionally intelligent leaders. The combination of the previously mentioned further enhances leaders' more technical skills connected with strategic planning, problem solving, and decision making, which are explored in detail in later chapters. The important point here is that the technical skills must be scaffolded from the tacit skills of relating to and modeling for others first, and to establish trust and confidence in the technical methods that are integrated in the processes for both short- and long-term aims.

Management

This section covers the managerial flow, manager in "flow", tasking assignments, organizing, and engaging staff.

Whereas leaders are charged with inspiring others and setting their sights on the long-term aims, managers are accountable for overseeing and organizing the minutia of daily tasks. To manage is to organize, plan, control, and coordinate, and often under what are crisis-oriented conditions, with deficient funding, and at unrelenting paces (Mintzberg, 1990). Managers must be comfortable with the repetitive nature that is required to help teams develop and maintain good habits, especially those related to programmatic compliance and quality assurance of services delivered. Managers control the outcomes by setting the expectations of staff, planning assignments accordingly, and coordinating and organizing the daily, weekly, and monthly operations. Managers' tasks in direct service organizations are frequently geared toward brief and varied activities. However, whether managing in direct service or academic arenas, managers, like leaders, must exude stamina and resiliency to best plan, organize, coordinate, and control. As Kotter (2011) explained, "Managers promote stability while leaders press for change, and the organizations that embrace both sides of that contradiction can thrive in turbulent times" (p. 25). There are many similarities between how managers and leaders meritoriously lead their designated teams. One such likeness is how they adapt to situations and utilize emotional intelligence to play "the game of chess," as Buckingham (2005) referred to it. Understanding the game of chess is similar to a good coach knowing when a player has a unique ability or skill that can be transferred, built upon, and sometimes better utilized, in a different position on the field.

Manager in "Flow"

Managers can use their social awareness and relationally focused skills to recognize the talents and strengths of their individual players and position them accordingly in an effort to capitalize on their skills for the betterment of the team and to champion the individual's growth as well. Godstick and Elton (2018) referred to the phenomena of being so immersed in work that one loses track of time as they are in a "flow"; this occurs when individuals are deeply satisfied with the work they are doing. Managers are encouraged to intentionally look and plan for the "flow" moments among their supervisees, as they are typically connected to individuals' strengths and innate talents and they are therefore more likely to gain greater satisfaction from tasks that provide that "flow" and be more intrinsically motivated to master their flow tasks. Managers can plan how they delegate tasks that offer a "flow" for workers and coordinate the assignment of tasks that may promote a cohesive "flow" among teammates at a particular time.

Tasking Assignments

Capitalizing on individuals' skills sets further requires the ability to discern how to avoid building teams that are fraught with personality clashes (Buckingham, 2005, p. 3) and, instead, optimizing the complement of staffing among a team, based on skills, knowledge, and, yes, interpersonal abilities. Importantly, being able to manage from an employee-centered perspective requires that the manager understands how to make the most of individuals and teams; and in making the most of teams the manager will be able to generate greater productivity through people. Since a major task of managers is to coordinate, the manager requires a team of people who can work in concert to accomplish individually designated and collective responsibilities. Thus, managers must coordinate tasks among varied personalities to get the job done.

Although assigning tasks to match individuals' unique strengths may initially appear as though it could prevent the manager from attending to many other seemingly pressing demands, Buckingham (2005) explained why puissant managers do capitalize on individuals' strengths. First, capitalizing on individual strengths saves time over the long run. For instance, the manager is able to tap into the person's natural strengths, which can save time on additional training. Second, by individualizing tasks to fit the person's strengths there is greater accountability. When assignments are delegated to the individuals based on their talents, and they are offered consistent feedback and are informed about the reasons why the assignment was carefully selected for them, there is a greater likelihood that they will feel a sense of ownership over what they are contributing to the larger goal. Third, when managers are able to judiciously match task-to-person assignments, they can create stronger comradery within teams because there is an inherent interdependence among them. Each person has an identified skill set and each member learns to rely on others' skills that she or he may lack and then reciprocate with her or his own skills in return. Finally, Buckingham (2005) offered that "when you capitalize on what is unique about each person, you introduce a healthy degree of disruption" and challenge the "existing beliefs about where the expertise lies" (p. 3). Challenging beliefs about who holds the expertise is especially critical for teams that may be experiencing a lack of cohesion. Evoking a healthy degree of disruption is beneficial for teams to become more adaptable, creative, and, ultimately, productive.

It should be noted that it is common that human resource agents encourage leaders to have tasks fit positions rather than people. There is good reason for this position orientation, of course, which stems from retention, meaning that if the individual were to leave the position where he or she was tasked with assignments tailored to play off of his or her strengths, then how does that role, which organically morphed into something that in reality now differs from how the job description reads, get filled? Again, this is a valid point that leaders must consider and attend to by documenting such changes as they evolve, either with amendments to job descriptions or redrafted job descriptions, or performance goals.

Organizing

Productivity through people is not only about knowing how to position people within their teams (i.e., organizing assignments tailored to their strengths to increase self-efficacy and by extension commitment to the work), it is also about the manager's ability to relate with those they manage. Organizing is not telescoped to the notion of organizing schedules, meetings, financial records, trainings, and so on, but rather includes the more delicate, often more time-consuming, but perhaps most omnipotent task of organizing personalities to work cohesively and productively. Some managers find themselves mired in what seems to be superficial employee relations complaints among coworkers, which more often than not compromise the quality of client or student services and consume a great deal of time and resources to ameliorate. Personality clashes are as inevitable as paying taxes; it will happen at some point and managers can fare best when they are able to identify this potentiality early, adjust accordingly, and develop and maintain solid rapports with all supervisees, as this can be impactful when the inevitable occurs and needs to be addressed. Mintzberg (1990) underscored that a primary role of a manager is to monitor the environment and seek information from others. In order to attain information one must develop a rapport and be entrusted with that information, and managers can reciprocate this rapport by appropriately disseminating information to subordinates as circumstantially appropriate.

Engaging Staff

Much like leaders, managers engage their staff by taking a genuine interest and observing what unique, and perhaps untapped, strengths and talents the individual has to offer. Managers must be able to identify with the individuals they manage and, to do so, they must employ strong social skills and be good communicators; take interest in the persons they supervise; provide supervision regularly; facilitate growth; and build relationships that are reciprocal (i.e., you can depend on me, and I can also depend on you). Buckingham (2005) talked about the "three levers" of management: (a) how to identify strengths, (b) understanding what exactly triggers those strengths, and (c) recognizing how one best learns. Managers must avail themselves to their workers' strengths by first availing themselves to the opportunities to observe their strengths firsthand, that is, being among the people and not always behind a desk. By being among the people on the frontlines they are able to stay curious and engage the individuals in conversations that can reveal what excites and what frustrates them about the work. They are also able to better glean what activates the individual's strengths. For instance, does the individual work better during a certain time of day, working with a particular subset of the population served, with more frequent check-in from the manager, or attending to particular tasks (Buckingham, 2005)? The attuned manager is able to pick up on what empowers the worker, or what gives the worker a greater sense of self-efficacy, and uses this information to further activate the individual's strengths to advance the individual and entire team.

In summary, managers pull their teams toward desired outcomes by planning, organizing, coordinating, and controlling the varied tasks of the larger operations. They are able to identify and build upon individuals' strengths and foster teamwork that enable the collective employees to successfully deliver services and duties that contribute to the organization's or institution's vision, mission, and goals. There are many commonalities interwoven with leadership and management, and a healthy organization establishes processes and relationships that allow both to complement, depend on, and advance the other (Box 2.4).

BOX 2.4

COUNCIL ON SOCIAL WORK EDUCATION COMPETENCIES 1 AND 6

CSWE Competency 1—Demonstrate Ethical and Professional Behavior

- 1.2 Use reflection and self-regulation to manage personal values and maintain professionalism in practice situations.
- 1.3 Demonstrate professional demeanor in behavior; appearance; and oral, written, and electronic communication.

CSWE Competency 6—Engage with Individuals, Families, Groups, Organizations, and Communities

- 6.2 Use empathy, reflection, and interpersonal skills to effectively engage diverse clients and constituencies.

CSWE, Council on Social Work Education.

Leadership and Management Overlays

There are many overlays of leading and managing people. Leaders and managers are constantly being observed by their followers and have a responsibility to always conduct themselves in a composed fashion. Nobody expects a leader or manager to be perfect. In fact acknowledging imperfections and shortcomings can serve to enhance one's ability to lead and manage others authentically. Leaders and managers who are uncomfortable and guarded about revealing their vulnerabilities can quickly lose trust, confidence, and commitment from their followers, and essentially create a closed system where sharing new ideas and feedback are perceived as unwelcoming, and worse yet—threatening to their job security. Additionally, leaders who do not allow themselves to be vulnerable can produce a sense of anxiety among those they lead, as their followers may have trepidations that their shortcomings will not be acceptable and anything less than perfection will put them at risk of being viewed as insufficient in the eyes of the beholder.

Leadership Communication

Effective communicators never let the substance of their message get lost in the style of how they deliver it. People can easily miss the crux of what is being said if the way in which it is being said overpowers its essence. For instance, being mindful of your tone of voice (Is it overly stern, or too meek, too loud and potentially perceived as aggressive? Is it sarcastic or cynical?), your facial expressions (Is there a scowl, or eyebrow raising? Is there even eye contact?), and your overall demeanor (Are you in control of your emotions? Can the listener sense you are overly frustrated, disappointed, angered, or indifferent toward them? What does your body language say?). As discussed in Chapter 1, employing emotional intelligence means that one is able to read the situation and use social skills, social awareness, and self-awareness to adjust one's leadership style as situationally indicated, while also employing self-regulation skills. Buckingham (2005) reminds us that "there is no one best way to lead and that instead, the most effective leadership style depends on the circumstance" (p. 4). As such, leaders' and managers' communication styles need to adjust to the individuals and groups in a given environment, under a specific set of circumstances, to carefully craft the content of the information and also effectively process the information. Although the stylistic approach may vary as the situation implies, one's ability to use self-regulation and self-reflection should not waver.

Given that communication among colleagues primarily occurs through electronic means, managers and leaders must develop written communication skills. While electronic communication has enhanced productivity and connectedness, a lack of face-to-face interactions does pose some limitations, mainly that messages without nonverbal cues to provide context can, at times, be misconstrued. Today's managers and leaders must embrace the fact that we work in an industry of feelings—and people have a lot of them! Emails, text messages, and other social media correspondences need to be worded so that they are not inadvertently coming across as short (which can be perceived as feelings of mad, frustrated, annoyed, indifferent, etc.). Additionally, whenever communicating directives or seeking clarification on matters clarity is key. It is good practice to proofread electronic messages through the lens of either an attorney or someone who is just stepping in to catch up on the subject matter. In other words, would a professional be able to (a) understand the directive or question(s) outlined in the communiqué, and (b) detect a tone that is exemplifying professionalism and sound ethics? (What leadership style does it suggest?)

Self-Reflection and Self-Regulation

Skills that social workers are taught to recognize both in themselves and in their clients are self-reflection and self-regulation. As social workers, we are educated about the tools and approaches for enriching ideas and deepening insights, for improving both the intra and the interpersonal realms of one's life. Whether you are an educator, practicing clinician, student, budding leader, or one in full bloom, you undoubtedly have already contemplated how practicing both self-reflection and self-regulation is necessary, helpful, and, at times, perhaps even a difficult part of the work.

Reflecting on one's leadership or management skills is an intricate process that can engender feelings of vulnerability, as any honest self-appraisal does. The additional strain that accompanies the practice of self-reflection as a leader or manager is that you are accountable to larger, dynamic groups of people both within your immediate professional setting and the larger external community collaborators. "If I see my flaws, so must they—so, it's best not to look!" is not a helpful approach to take. In actuality, people tend to value and respect leaders and managers that are comfortable enough in their own skin to model their reflective practices and speak honestly about their own shortcomings, provided it is done in a way that does not erode others' confidence in the leader or manager. Identifying one's shortcomings can be considered similar to the "limitations" section outlined in a research study; there will always be some limitations no matter how well the study is designed and executed, therefore compensatory strategies are implemented to help mitigate the limitations, and the researcher can outline these in a transparent yet productive manner.

Leaders and managers are unfailingly subject to estimations from those they lead. Whether these estimations are good, bad, or indifferent, we suspect that many would agree that it is a daunting responsibility, and privilege, to perpetually be in the hot seat. Leadership and management requires a certain amount of ego tenacity and level headedness. Reflections of the self as a professional appear to have higher stakes for some than do self-reflections in one's personal realm. And, let us be honest, if you are at all passionate about the work, then appraising your professional being is inevitably, at the very least loosely, entwined with your personal being. We all need to wake up in the morning believing we are good at what we are setting off to do. The process of self-reflecting on how we are doing what we are doing can expose vulnerabilities and weaknesses that may be less than pleasant to sit with, but that is okay; know that is great if you let it be. Why? Because it can serve as fuel to become better. If you can be open and balanced in self-appraisals, that is, accepting of what is identified as a skill, knowledge, interpersonal or communication deficit, then you are equally capable of developing ways to improve and grow, assuming that you then commit to the actions steps toward your desired change. Sometimes it is helpful to ask paradoxical questions such as: What leadership/management tasks do I feel least confident in doing? Followed by What leadership/management tasks do I feel most confident in doing? Asking the opposing question can help crystalize your strengths or weaknesses, and also keep your self-evaluations balanced.

Regardless of how cohesive a team is, it is human nature for a percentage of people to focus on what is wrong rather than what is going well. There may be truth to whatever it is that *is* actually going wrong, and that can be a bitter pill to swallow. But committing ourselves to reflect on how we can do better, choose our words wiser, attend to details more carefully, consider the range of emotional reactions one seemingly innocuous decision can elicit from teammates, or the rippling effects an "off" day can have, is a responsibility that leaders and managers must carry. Research shows that leaders who permit themselves to be vulnerable fare better than those who do not (George, Sims, McLean, & Mayer, 2007). Brené Brown (2010) talked about "the power of vulnerability" in a TED Talk that underscored the social work tenant of "leaning into the discomfort" and asking, "Is there something about me that people will see that causes a disconnection?" A question that is ripe with potential discoveries about weakness and corresponding vulnerability. However, in order for connections to happen we must allow ourselves to be vulnerable.

Engaging Staff

Connection, no matter what realm of social work you practice in, is at the core of everything we do. Some may presume that vulnerability and leadership are a contraindicative pairing; after all, many attribute qualities such as confidence and strength to leadership. However, it is erroneous to think that any leader is void of vulnerability; rather it is more a matter of how one attends to the vulnerability as they lead others which can provide greater confidence and strength.

Emotional Regulation

Aside from practicing self-reflection, leaders and managers need to attend to the ways they regulate and convey their emotions. Emotional regulation, as with many things, happens on a continuum. There are leaders that present so regulated that they can almost seem robotic and unapproachable, and there are leaders that can be so dysregulated that people walk on eggshells around them. The golden mean, it seems, is to be authentic enough that you are able to reveal appropriate emotions in a controlled fashion. That is to say that it is healthy for followers to see the spark of excitement and passion at times, and is equally healthy for leaders to unveil feelings of disappointment or frustration, assuming the following occurs: (a) the expression of either positive or negative emotions is not shared in a bombastic fashion and the range of emotion is not overly expressed in either direction of the continuum; (b) the emotion is congruent to the situation (i.e., it is a reasonable, even predictable response); (c) the emotional expression will not adversely affect those you share it with; and (d) you are modeling appropriate passion for the work and professional behavior in the way you are sharing your emotional response to the given situation (Box 2.5).

BOX 2.5

COMPETENCY-BASED EXERCISE: COUNCIL ON SOCIAL WORK EDUCATION 1.2 AND 1.3

Brandon's Unapologetic Boss

I once had a boss who never said "I'm sorry." I worked for someone for several years, he had a wealth of experience in the field, but had a very pugnacious style. He was the kind of boss that reminded people that he was boss ... literally. When he did not like some of the ideas that were offered or ways to solve a problem, even if a team would try to provide information as to why his idea may not be the best, the words "I'm the boss and I say that we do this" would actually leave his lips. People would get uncomfortably quiet and there was a feeling of demoralization and frustration that permeated the air in the room. But by then, people would just let it go. What choice did they have? They worried about job security and not being in the boss' good graces anymore. I mean, this guy would actually yell at people in front of their coworkers! I guess he thought that would get the message across. And it did! We quickly learned that the best way to survive was to just "yes" to him. Sure, we would still try to share our points from time to time, but the overall feeling was that he was feared and we all knew that he knew best. And he never, ever would apologize for the public humiliation, or the fact that the team may have had a better idea. We all just put our heads down, showed up for work, and tried not to rock the boat.

The example of Brandon's boss depicts a leader that lacks both self-regulation and self-reflection; for we hope if he had employed those qualities, he would have been able to see why his team was no longer as productive as he had hoped. By creating a system that forces employees to shy away from providing input, the leader in this case scenario has stifled innovation. We venture to guess that it also created workplace chatter that probably was very negative and perpetuated poor morale among those that felt shutdown by the "unapologetic boss." Consider the following questions:

1. How would you respond to a leader that did not consider your ideas?
2. How does power come into play in this example? What can the worker(s) do to feel empowered to contribute their ideas?
   a. Reflect on an experience where you felt that you did not have power. How did you handle this?
   b. Reflect on a time that you felt you did have power. How did you handle having power? What was this experience like for you?

CSWE, Council on Social Work Education.

LEADERSHIP AND MANAGEMENT OVERLAYS

The complexity and emotional strain of social work leaves many susceptible to burnout, compassion fatigue, stress, and vicarious traumatization. Many will be changed by the work we do (not just in direct client practice but also in leading and managing others), and while this change can often be for the better, there are times when certain realities raise questions ranging from basic safety concerns to existential crises about the very purpose of one's work, human civility, and core values. Just as clients act out misplaced emotions or deep-seated feelings and subconscious thoughts, there are times when professionals misdirect their feelings, too. They may erupt with feelings that can seem disconnected from the content, or "out of left field." We often first think of burnout when we see or directly experience it. Kottler (2012) explained that burnout is an insidious process, and mental health professionals should therefore be aware of how it begins to creep in and understand that it provides subtle warnings. As a manager or leader, it behooves you to develop ways to identify when and how burnout signals manifest, both for yourself and for your staff. Self-care is frequently paid discursive tribute in social work lectures, conferences, and workplace conversations, but, more often than not, the word does not consistently materialize. It is rather ironic that self-care is not considered as highly or, for that matter, required of professionals as continuing education credits are. Self-care is vital to maintain the stamina to continuously be effective and thrive in the wake of adversity, uncertainty, and anxiety. Thus, when leaders and managers are able to attend to their own self-care, they are also able to demonstrate that they are not consumed by the work and can effectively navigate the uncertain times that will inevitably be faced (Box 2.6).

BOX 2.6

NETWORK FOR SOCIAL WORK MANAGEMENT COMPETENCIES AND PRACTICE BEHAVIORS 3 AND 4

Possesses analytical and critical thinking skills that promote organizational growth (Network for Social Work Management Competencies 3). Practice Behaviors:

- Manages ambiguous and complex organizational situations (3.7).

Models appropriate professional behavior and encourages other staff members to act in a professional manner (Network for Social Work Management Competencies 4).

- Engages in and promotes ethical conduct (4.1).
- Protects the integrity and reputation of the organization (4.2).
- Displays the ability to carry on effectively in the face of adversity, ambiguity, uncertainty, and anxiety (4.5).
- Demonstrates the ability not to be "consumed" by executive responsibilities and helps others to achieve the balance and maintain a sense of humor and perspective (4.7).

NSWM, Network for Social Work Management.

Change Management

Change is ubiquitous and the fluidity of change can be understood as a microcosm of the rapid global shifts in markets, products, politics, and economics. Just think of your cell phone—a new and improved model is advertised shortly after your latest update. We have more expedient capabilities for our communication with people and more immediate access to goods and services than ever before. In the social work profession, the contemporary expectations for immediate change can sometimes seem counterintuitive to our appreciation that change happens through process rather than in an instant.

For social service agencies and academic institutions, the demands for services and supply of resources are frequently linked to financial pressures that impinge upon the system; but how the system navigates such demands is more often influenced by how the leaders and managers at the helm respond to the challenges, and formulate the organizational vision, goals, and values. How do they set the tone for difficult work to be done?

If an essential task of leadership requires innovation, then it follows that leaders must always be open to change. This ideal may befit many leaders who will embrace and pull others toward the ideas and actions of change, but change—no matter how necessary and beneficial it may be—will evoke some resistance, anxiety, and uncertainty from team members (even the leader at times). It is not uncommon to hear the phrase, "We've always done it like this," which is likely followed by a stream of unsolicited information to help further support the plea for sameness. Or rumblings from some who are eager to share their convictions about why the new way is not going to work. Leaders must be particularly cautious of this typology of change resistance and concentrate on ways to deter such people from influencing and fulfilling the prophecy that aims to disprove the benefits of change. As for managers, remember they are responsible for coordinating and organizing how changes may take shape on the frontlines. Leaders need to spend ample time with managers to ensure that they are sufficiently inspired, engaged, and understand the rationale and new approach to see that the needed change(s) come to fruition. Leaders need managers to help push the new visions forward.

Hopkins, Meyer, Shera, and Peters (2014) noted that 87% of the nonprofit sector is composed of healthcare, education, and social services, and was the fastest growing segment of the U.S. economy over the last decade. At first glance this is rather encouraging, albeit Hopkins et al. (2014) went on to elucidate that "while the demand for nonprofits to provide more services and accountability is increasing, there is also a thinner spread of funding that forces organizations to provide more services with less money" (p. 419). The confluence of an increased demand for services and decreased funding during an economic downturn has resulted in many leaders and managers having to make arduous decisions about staffing and services, as many are faced with dilemmas about how to handle "insufficient financial, human, and technical resources for responding to the growing need and demands for service in the face of government and foundation cutbacks, tightly defines contracts, high rates of underfunded infrastructure and overhead, and even higher expectations for accountability" (Hopkins et al., 2014, p. 419). The culmination of factors as outlined by Hopkins et al. can gravely influence how an organization operates and can also directly impact the organizational culture. When systems are chronically strained, the workforce can become overburdened, overworked, overwhelmed, and undermotivated. Lawlor (2005) explained that the commodification of social work has resulted in the "demise of intrinsic motivation for social workers" (p. 128).

Managing Organizational Culture

Bloom and Farragher (2011) highlighted that there is often copious attention paid (both in the empirical literature and through anecdotal discourse) about what spawns an unhealthy organizational culture, while there is less attention devoted to the factors that help increase abilities that promote healthy organizations. Lawlor (2005) revealed the contemporary debate about whether or not leadership is a function of the organizational culture or the individual, noting that researchers have turned their gaze toward leadership and management practices.

The social service sector has a pervasive reputation for being stress provoking, which is frequently attributed to the complexity of needs and human conditions that social workers are exposed to, especially when combined with limited resources and swelling demands. To disentangle the worker from stressors all together is simply unrealistic. However, leaders, in collaboration with managers, can promote an organizational culture that offers opulent guidance by providing a clear understanding of the vision and goals and supports individuals and collective teams to help promote a positive workplace culture and contribute to both the short- and long-term aims. To accomplish this end, the symbiotic relationship between management and leadership is essential for creating an optimal environment that facilitates positive organizational changes. For example, much of the research on workplace bullying in the social service arena has recognized that teams led by laissez-faire leaders experience greater instances of workplace bullying that contribute to poor morale and greater turnover, when compared with those whose leaders employ a transformational leadership style (Allen, Smith, & Da Silva, 2013). Hence, how leaders exemplify how to treat others as well as how they "walk the walk," particularly during times of adversity and uncertainty, can intensely influence the organizational culture. It is up to the leaders and managers to model appropriate professional behavior and provide unwavering encouragement to individual and collective staff members, always but especially during difficult times. During difficult times managers and leaders should not be so engrossed in their own emotions that they are blind to the needs of those they manage and lead. Being consumed by the work, or frenzied by feelings about the work, can become a form of team abandonment—at the precise time when the team most needs guidance and encouragement. It is prudent to walk the walk and take all changes, innovations, and work feelings in stride (Box 2.7).

BOX 2.7

COMPETENCY-BASED EXAMPLE: NETWORK FOR SOCIAL WORK MANAGEMENT 4.5

HOW DO YOU EAT AN ELEPHANT?

Brenda was sitting with Grace and two of the chief executives at a nonprofit agency one afternoon, listening to Grace describe her detailed plan for helping to get the organization "back on track." It had quickly grown from serving a relatively small amount of clients to a large census that was geographically stretched beyond the bounds that were originally envisioned. A great problem to have, but it did come at the cost of losing sight of the systems of compliance that needed to be put in place. To the organization's credit, it was extremely client focused and spent much time ensuring that the quality of services delivered was superior. However, the downside was that the organization had been so client focused that it neglected to adapt and update policies and procedures for the employees. The organization did not have systems in place for communicating with staff who were now bouncing between various program locations, and different trainings for employees and managers were needed. It started to appear that the people at the top were not committed to keeping frontline staff informed as new changes accompanying the rapid organizational expansion occurred. Grace had a long list of thoughtfully selected tasks that she was planning on working on, many of them had multifaceted parts and required some complex technological changes. As soon as Grace finished outlining her brilliant plan, she gave a deep sigh and then started to infectiously chuckle as she asked, "How do you eat an elephant?" After a brief pause and a smile as if anticipating the punchline, she cut straight to the answer: "One bite at a time!"

Grace always had a wonderful way of bringing levity to situations that felt overwhelming and daunting, and this time was no different. She was absolutely right. The changes needed to occur one step, or "one bite," at a time, and it was important that the executives committed themselves to showing their team of followers how to prioritize, be steadfast in their change efforts, and bring a little humor to the situation.

Grace could have become overwhelmed by the amount and complexity of tasks she had laid out for herself, but instead she is a wonderful, nonfactious example of someone who does not allow herself to be consumed by the work. You have, we assume, heard the saying "Never let them see you sweat," and there is great wisdom to be culled from it. Leaders can do a variety of things that help to prevent themselves from becoming consumed by the work, and ultimately prevent public perspiration (Box 2.8).

BOX 2.8

COMPETENCY-BASED EXAMPLE: NETWORK FOR SOCIAL WORK MANAGEMENT 4.3

THE SCREAMING ER PHYSICIAN

Sam tells his leaders a sage and comical story about maintaining composure, for the sake of keeping staff steady. The story goes: Imagine that you are a patient in the ER and have just suffered a compound fracture to your leg. You are nervous about if you will be able to take your annual ski trips and ever glide down the mountain the same again. You are in pain, you are in fear, and you are eager for the doctor to make it better. After waiting for what of course felt like an eternity in the bustling ER, the doctor finally makes his rounds to you, and as he pulls the curtain back and sees your bloody leg, with the bone poking out, he starts to panic and screams, "Oh my god!!!! Look at all of that blood!!! Ahhhhh, and the BONE!! The bone is sticking straight out of your leg!"

A tall tale, of course, which always gets a rise out of people when he tells it, but the point of it is not missed on anyone. People expect certain people, given their role and area of expertise, to stay calm and in control, to not be consumed by their own emotional reactions about how treacherous the situation may appear. No, in fact, just the opposite—people need to see that leaders are able to not only attend to their unique tasks but also take interest in how others are handling theirs.

ER, emergency room.

Not allowing oneself to be consumed by the tasks at hand and balancing the multitude of assignments manifests in many ways. The following are examples, poor examples, of how some leaders become so consumed, so overwhelmed in their roles, that they overlook the impact their behavior has on others (Boxes 2.9, 2.10, and 2.11).

BOX 2.9

COMPETENCY-BASED EXERCISE

Jack was a young, polite, and very smart man who recently accepted a position in a for-profit agency that specializes in macro practice, shortly after graduating college. He was motivated and eager to excel in his new role, and he was friendly and always willing to help his coworkers out. Everyone quickly took a liking to him and he was doing very well in his new position. His cubical was located close to the department task supervisor's, who had always proclaimed to staff that she had an "open door policy." She was also the type of task supervisor who would sometimes want to know the finite details of a project and at other times would want only the broad overview. Since nobody ever knew which way she would want material presented to her on a given day, they always prepared to give both the tedious details and the 50-yard view. Jack had been given an assignment directly from the task supervisor to complete an annual report, and when he finished (well before the assigned deadline), he emailed it to the her and, knowing that she preferred to read hard copies, also printed a copy of the drafted report. Jack walked enthusiastically down the hall to leave the printed copy for her, and when he arrived her door was open. Jack knocked and was greeted with a "yes?!" and peeked in the office and cordially and briefly explained that he just wanted to drop off a hard copy of the report he had just completed.

(continued)

BOX 2.9 *(Continued)*

As prepared as Jack was for his work-related tasks, he was completely unprepared for the wrath he was about to receive. The task supervisor darted her eyes as she turned to him abruptly to exclaim, "Can't you see I'm busy?! I'm trying to get something done here and don't have time for this right now!" Jack was so shocked by the intensity of the reaction that he could not find words, but eventually uttered an apology before he shuffled out of the room feeling embarrassed and completely shocked by the exchange. That evening, Jack ruminated about the interaction and feared that it would not be long before he was fired. The next morning, he went to his HR director to explain what had happened. As the HR director listened to his recount of their exchange he could not help but feel torn about how to respond to this. On the one hand, this was his (the HR director's) direct boss and he felt he should tread carefully in how he conveyed the concern, not only to protect himself but because he worried for Jack. By the end of the conversation, the HR director had grown angry toward his boss, Jack's task supervisor, not only for speaking to him that way but for causing him to feel responsible for such a negative interaction. He felt it was incredulous that the task supervisor, who was constantly demanding more from her supervisees and expecting them to be able to handle it, should provide such poor role modeling. How hard would be to just say, "Thank you. I'm in the middle of something now but will take a look at it when I can"? She knew that Jack was astute enough to get the point and would have just as quickly been on his way. The HR director brooded over whether or not Jack would soon leave for his own self-presevation and tried to reassure Jack that he had done nothing wrong. Jack left the HR director's office feeling somewhat more at ease by his feedback, but nonetheless dreaded returning to his cubicle.

Questions

1. How should the task supervisor have handled this differently? Assuming that the task supervisor reflected on her behaviors, what should she do next? How should she do it? What should she say?

2. If you were the HR director, how would you handle this situation? What would you do first, second, and so on?

3. If you were the HR director hearing this story about Jack, how might you feel? What are the internal and external factors that might influence how you address this situation?

4. How does this exchange influence the organizational culture? What kind of culture do you suspect it is?

HR, human resources.

BOX 2.10

COMPETENCY-BASED EXERCISE: NETWORK FOR SOCIAL WORK MANAGEMENT 4.5

Amanda is always on the move.

Amanda is the supervisor of five social workers that work in two different units in a hospital setting; three work on the child and adolescent unit, and two work on the adult unit. Amanda was promoted to a director position and charged with the task of expanding the census for the newly opened senior unit that specializes in geriatric psychiatric inpatient care. She collaborates with a team of nurses and doctors and, once a week, is expected to meet with her supervisees individually and hold a monthly staff

(continued)

BOX 2.10 *(Continued)*

meeting. About 3 months after the opening of the geriatric unit, Amanda began canceling supervision with her supervisor on a fairly regular basis and was not returning emails for days, and sometimes not at all. Additionally, she soon began canceling, at the last minute, supervision meetings with her supervisees, and staff meetings also seemed to halt. Amanda could often be seen walking quickly throughout the halls as if she were always late. When colleagues would politely inquire how she was doing she hurriedly replied, "Crazy busy!" and continued to rush past them. When she met with her supervisor after three canceled meetings that she claimed could not be rescheduled for any time sooner, her supervisor asked how things were going. Amanda explained that she was too busy to get tasks done and could not seem to keep her head above water. She felt that her supervisees did not understand the pressure she was under and the reasons why she had had to cancel individual supervision meetings.

Questions

1. As Amanda's supervisor, what are your primary concerns? How would you process these?
2. As Amanda's supervisor, what action steps are needed and how would you prioritize them?

BOX 2.11

NETWORK FOR SOCIAL WORK MANAGEMENT COMPETENCIES AND PRACTICE BEHAVIORS 7

Initiates and facilitates innovative change processes (Network for Social Work Management Competencies 7). Practice Behaviors:

- Remains current on trends and identifies shifts that require an innovative response (7.1).
- Presents innovations to appropriate decision makers and stakeholders and makes decisions that are aligned with their feedback (7.2).
- Assists staff with implementing positive change and supports risk taking (7.3).
- Supports innovative practices to improve program-related issues and services (7.4).

In this section, we broaden our view of leadership to encompass principles of distributive leadership that are embedded in the social work profession, including the importance of collaboration with and empowerment of others to promote social change. Distributive leadership does not assume that leadership resides with one key person, but is instead seen as the collective functions and responsibilities that are shared among a group of people (Iachini, Cross, & Freedman, 2015; King Keenan, Sandoval, & Limone, 2018). Conceptualizing leadership as a distributive process that is focused on a group of individuals interacting and influencing one another (Iachini et al., 2015; King Keenan et al., 2018) and distributing expertise for a shared purpose results in a number of individuals acting as leaders.

Iachini et al. (2015) proposed the supposition that the social change model (SCM) of leadership is infused with the value of empowerment. Iachini et al. defined the SCM as a framework that highlights a collaborative group process that "recognizes the importance of all individuals being able to grow, develop, and serve as leaders" (2015, p. 652). It is further explained that the model supports learning experiences that are geared toward social change, and analogous with distributive leadership, may provide a foundation for more than one individual to develop and emerge as a leader. Three core values are encased in the SCM. See Table 2.1.

TABLE 2.1 **Individual, Group, and Community Values**

Individual values • Consciousness of self • Congruence • Commitment	Being conscious of the beliefs, values, and temperament that motivate one's actions. Conducts oneself so that one's actions and convictions are in accord, which helps to foster trust when working with others. The passion and investment that motivates the individual toward the collective effort.
Group values • Collaboration • Common purpose • Controversy with civility	Working with others toward a common goal while building on the strengths of others. Working with shared aims, goals, vision, and values. Recognizing that conflict is inevitable but can be handled respectfully, openly, and with restraint.
Community • Citizenship	Connecting to the community, and working for change on behalf of others.

SOURCE: Adapted from Iachini, A. L., Cross, T. P., and Freedman, D. A. (2015). Leadership in social work education and the social change model of leadership. *Social Work Education, 34*(6), 653. doi:10.1080/02615479.2015.1025738

Leaders and managers need to understand the individual and group values that influence the qualities of engagement and decision making. Moreover, leaders and managers should be aware of how individual and groups value, promote, or prevent the inclusion of diverse persons from participating in impactful ways at the trilevels of social work intervention (micro, mezzo, and macro). As a leader or manager, you need to be aware of people's backgrounds and cultures when working with different constituencies and staff in order to empower others toward social changes and leadership opportunities. Leaders and managers need to develop meaningful understandings of different ways of relating, communicating, and applying cultural awareness to coworkers/teams, in addition to clients (Box 2.12).

BOX 2.12

COUNCIL ON SOCIAL WORK EDUCATION COMPETENCY 2

CSWE Competency 2—Engage Diversity and Difference in Practice

- 2.1 Apply and communicate understanding of the importance of diversity and difference in shaping life experiences in practice at the micro, mezzo, and macro levels.

- 2.2 Present themselves as learners and engage clients and constituencies as experts of their own experiences.

- 2.3 Apply self-awareness and self-regulation to manage the influence of personal biases and values in working with diverse clients and constituencies.

CSWE, Council on Social Work Education.

Developing a better understanding of our own biases that are barriers to talking about cultural differences among teammates/coworkers stands to benefit clients, organizations, and ourselves as individuals. It is, however, interesting that, as social workers, we profess to support cultural humility and competence—we discuss this in classrooms and case conferences, but consider this: When was the last time that you had a conversation with a coworker about the cultural differences that exist between you? Teaching about cultural biases and helping a supervisee recognize the impact of culture in their client, group, or community work are sometimes referred to as "safe zones" that can partially demonstrate awareness of differences. But at what level of depth is this happening? Why does it sometimes seem so taboo to strike up sincere, deep, meaningful, albeit sometimes uncomfortable, yet incredibly important conversations with coworkers about their background and beliefs? Some administrators shy away from such personal conversations with those they supervise out of fear that it will be misconstrued, or in some way eventually turned against them should they ever have to address performance concerns at a later date. Yes, we live in a litigious society, and that may scare some off from engaging in such dialogues in their professional relationships. But what is the real cost if these conversations are ultimately avoided? There are also different schools of thought about this: Why would I bring up your culture? If the conversation is avoided altogether it can be considered offensive because it minimizes the historic and present challenges that affront marginalized groups. It is important to reflect on the way diversity and differences are viewed and approached, and acknowledge how they either align with or run counter to the individual and group values that inspire the work we do, the ways we promote social change and empowerment.

SUMMARY

As we suggested in Chapter 1, the topic of leadership has vastly captured the attention of many curious persons from the neophytes to seasoned leaders and scholars across diverse fields. Why are we so driven to know what makes a leader great? What are we hoping to distill from the overwhelming knowledge and wisdom so many have offered on this remarkable topic? What do we seek to validate? How do we then apply it, whatever the "it" is, and make it fit with who we are, and what we believe in? How can we teach others to apply it? So many questions about leadership, and seemingly so fewer absolute answers.

The grey area that orbits any meaningful question has the powerful potential to awaken new insights and dislodge murky ideas, but at first such questions can deceivingly drive one to states of frustration and confusion. This dilemma is sometimes seen in social work students who search for conclusive answers to hypothetical case vignettes only to find themselves disappointed by the answer that there is no *one* best answer in social work (in spite of how one prepares for licensure exams). Some students are even surprised to learn of the experienced clinician's prior failures and mistakes, as if the years of practice wisdom and refined skills should make the clinician infallible to ruptures in rapport or void of any regrets in their facilitative change methods. This belief could not be further from the realities of direct social work practice, or leadership. In fact, we relish the term "practice" *because* we are all in perpetual need of just that—practice. Clinical practice constantly presents new situations, people, dynamics, problems, strengths, resources, and much more, all of which social workers are continuously learning how to engage with. Hence, we are constantly practicing our skills, constantly self-reflecting, and, yes, the adage that "the more we know, the less we *really* know" bears a striking resemblance between direct practice and leadership.

Whether an emerging or a seasoned leader or manager, we encourage you to never strive to *really know* (think of all that you could possibly miss if you ever reach the place of fully knowing). That is not to say that you should lack confidence in your decisions, and it also not to suggest that you should not know yourself well, but it is to say that you should constantly evaluate your decisions—understand how you came to make them, what factors influenced them, how you felt in making them, what impact it made, and how did it influence others? Embrace the reality that everything in life evolves, and also be open to the process that allows yourself to emotionally evolve in time as well, through experiences and excogitation. We reach for emotional evolution through consistent reflective practices.

ACTIVITIES

1. Are your agency's managers and staff representative of the client population? (a) How could your agency create greater diversity among managers? (b) What forms of discrimination occur at your agency?

2. Understanding your management style. Answer each of the following questions (make sure you answer the many components of each question):

   a. Which of the leadership styles do I think makes the most sense to me? How comfortable am I with participative management approaches that allow others to share decision making?

   b. Would I prefer to use planning methods such as rules that allow for little discretion in staff decision making or would I rather use methods such as policies that offer more staff autonomy and encourage the use of professional discretion? How important is contingency planning for me?

   c. Am I comfortable with a variety of types of staff and their unique contributions, as well as the potential problems that they bring? Do I prefer general job descriptions or carefully defined ones? How important do I think it is to "professionalize" a human service organization?

   d. What are my attitudes about the relative importance of supervision and continuing education for employee growth? Do I see the professional career development of staff as more the responsibility of managers or of individuals themselves? Would I rather work with locals or cosmopolitans?

   e. What is my attitude toward staff performance evaluations and personnel actions? Do I think that they are more useful for helping individual staff to improve their performance or for protecting the organization and its clients?

   f. Can I accept and appreciate staff who approaches their jobs differently from the way that I approach mine, or do I work to shape staff into people who are more like me?

   g. How comfortable am I with group cohesiveness among subordinates and the presence of an informal organizational structure? What is my attitude about conflict within the organization? What do I see as the most important purpose of communication, and what methods do I prefer?

   h. How comfortable am I with delegating tasks and authority to others? If I were to delegate, would I prefer to delegate staff or functional authority to a subordinate?

   i. Do I prefer to exercise a considerable amount of direct control through use of such methods as directives or do I prefer to control by using methods such as advice and information? How do I perceive the relative importance of support and structure as components of good leadership?

REFERENCES

Allen, S. L., Smith, J. E., & Da Silva, N. (2013). Leadership style in relation to organizational change and organizational creativity. Perceptions from nonprofit organizational members. *Nonprofit Management & Leadership, 24*(1), 23–42. doi:10.1002/nml.21078

Bloom, S. L., & Farragher, B. (2011). *Destroying sanctuary: The crisis in human service delivery systems.* New York, NY: Oxford University Press.

Brown, B. (2010). *The power of vulnerability.* TEDxHouston [Video file]. Retrieved from https://www.ted.com/talks/brene_brown_on_vulnerability?utm_campaign=tedspread&utm_medium=referral&utm_source=tedcomshare

Buckingham, M. (2005). What great managers do. *Harvard Business Review.* Retrieved from https://hbr.org/2005/03/what-great-managers-do

Fitch, P., & Van Brunt, B. (2016). *A guide to leadership and management in higher education.* New York, NY: Routledge.

George, B., Sims, O., McLean, A. N., & Mayer, D. (2007). Discovering your authentic leadership. *Harvard Business Review.* Retrieved from https://hbr.org/2007/02/discovering-your-authentic-leadership

Godstick, A., & Elton, C. (2018). *The best team wins.* New York, NY: Simon & Schuster.

Hopkins, K., Meyer, M., Shera, W., & Peters, S. C. (2014). Leadership challenges facing nonprofit human service organizations in a post-recession era. *Human Service Organizations: Management, Leadership & Governance, 38*(5), 419–422. doi:10.1080/233303131.2014.977208

Iachini, A. L., Cross, T. P., & Freedman, D. A. (2015). Leadership in social work education and the social change model of leadership. *Social Work Education, 34*(6), 650–665. doi:10.1080/02615479.2015.1025738

King Keenan, E., Sandoval, S., & Limone, C. (2018). Realizing the potential for leadership in social work. *Journal of Social Work, 0*(0), 1–19. doi:10.1177/1468017318766821

Kotter, P. (2011). What leaders really do. In *On leadership: HBR's 10 must reads.* Boston, MA: Harvard Business Review Press.

Kottler, J. A. (2012). *On being a therapist* [Audiobook]. Retrieved from Amazon.com

Lawlor, J. (2005). Leadership in social work: A case of caveat emptor? *British Journal of Social Work, 37,* 123–141. doi:10.1093/bjsw/bch404

Mintzberg, H. (1990). The manager's job: Folklore and fact. *Harvard Business Review.* Retrieved from https://hbr.org/1990/03/the-managers-job-folklore-and-fact

CHAPTER 3

EFFECTIVE COMMUNICATION AND MARKETING THE ORGANIZATION FOR SOCIAL WORKERS

CHAPTER OBJECTIVES

Demonstrates effective interpersonal and communication skills

- Developing public relations skills.
- Engaging in persuasive communication.
- Facilitating internal and external communication.
- Understanding how to communicate in conflict and crisis situations.

Marketing and public relations

- Creating and marketing an organizational brand.
- Developing and implementing a marketing plan in conjunction with fundraising activities.
- Discovering how to successfully manage the media and press.

INTRODUCTION

Effective communication skills, both oral and written, are considered to be important proficiencies in the social work field. Successful leaders understand how vital it is to master the art of communication. Communication that is well paced, worded, toned, and delivered to the intended audience increases the likelihood that the message can be well received, understood, and perhaps even appreciated. Effective communication skills are always important for social workers to demonstrate, but this is exceptionally true for social work leaders and managers. There will be times when leaders and managers have to facilitate difficult conversations with staff and tell people things that they may not want to hear. *How* a leader delivers information can be the difference between a good versus a bad outcome, a motivated versus unmotivated staff, or respect and appreciation for your coaching and guidance versus frustration, discouragement, and disregard for you as a leader.

Aside from its use to effectively motivate, build cohesive teams, and enhance productivity and performance, good communication is also needed to effectively market your organization. Effective marketing for nonprofit organizations (NPO) and academia moves people (much like effective communication with staff does); it makes them want to learn more about your organization and want to find a way to become a part of it to contribute to its successful outcomes. Good marketing strategies, like good communication strategies, understand the target audience and speak to that audience in a way that impresses and persuades people. Throughout this chapter we examine the many facets of communication in leadership, conflict resolution, and marketing strategies. See Box 3.1 which displays the competencies/behaviors in this chapter.

BOX 3.1

COMPETENCIES AND PRACTICE BEHAVIORS ADDRESSED IN THIS CHAPTER

Develops and manages both internal and external stakeholder relationships (Network for Social Work Management Competencies 6). Practice Behaviors:

- Communicates effectively to multiple constituencies, through various means and media, the mission, vision, and values of the organization along with organizational programs, policies, and performance so as to promote organizational transparency and enhance support and understanding from internal and external constituencies (6.2).

Advocates for public policy change and social justice at national, state, and local levels (Network for Social Work Management Competencies 8). Practice Behaviors:

- When appropriate and in line with organizational mission, promotes their organization as a well-recognized advocate on public policy issues (8.4).

Demonstrates effective interpersonal and communication skills (Network for Social Work Management Competencies 9). Practice Behaviors:

- Is able to articulate the mission and vision of the organization both orally and in writing to staff of the agency (9.1).
- Is able to articulate the mission and vision of the agency to those outside the agency to ensure understanding of the work of the organization (9.2).
- Ensures that all written and oral communication in the agency is carefully planned and articulated so that it is clear in its message and sensitive to the various audiences that receive it (9.3).
- Manages communication in conflict and crisis situations in a competent and sensitive manner (9.4).
- Engages in emotionally intelligent communications with all stakeholders (9.5).

Marketing and public relations: engages in proactive communication about the agency's products and services (Network for Social Work Management Competencies 17). Practice Behaviors:

- Consistently establishes and maintains positive external relationships with key organizational constituencies such as the media, public governance bodies, actual and potential donors, the business community, professional and service organizations, and the public at large (17.1).

(continued)

BOX 3.1 *(Continued)*

- Builds and conveys to multiple constituencies an organizational brand that reflects competence, integrity, and superior client/customer and community service (17.2).

- Develops and implements a successful marketing plan that dovetails with the fundraising activities of the organization (17.3).

- Ensures that the work of the agency is featured in various public relations venues to build and maintain visibility, access, and credibility and to ensure maximum usage of program resources (17.4).

- Develops clear guidelines for managing interactions with the press to ensure client confidentiality and accurate representation of agency performance (17.5).

- Maximizes the use of electronic media to communicate the work of the organization and deepens the public's understanding of the mission (17.6).

DEMONSTRATES EFFECTIVE INTERPERSONAL AND COMMUNICATION SKILLS

Effective interpersonal and communications skills require mastering a number of techniques, including the strategy statement, effective communication with individuals, basic communication style concepts, managing communication in crisis situations, managing communication in conflict situations, strategies for managing conflict in general and in the department, basic communication skills, leadership communication strategies for working with groups, and communicating with superiors and vice versa.

To begin this section, a university president (Box 3.2) shares his ideas about the value of communications for those in leadership positions.

BOX 3.2

EXCERPT OF INTERVIEW WITH PRESIDENT JOE

Which social work skills do you particularly employ as a president that you find useful?

Social work skills come into play, most of my time listening. Communication and listening is key. Relationships and listening combined help show value, feel heard, feel safe. Reinforces that I care about them as human beings. Important when an institution faces challenges you need the community around you to help with challenges. If you have not formed the relationships, and learned the culture, when the university needs to come together, it won't happen. Given where we are with the budget and race issues would not be able to navigate those issues without having set up a good communication link with students.

What is the biggest challenge facing leaders today?

Communication always the challenge, and has particularly become more difficult with advent of social media. Hard to have any control of a message. Finance and enrollment will always be a challenge but right now communication is at the top of the list, trying to get individuals to be on the same page. Trying to provide opportunities for accessibility is also important. Technology is always a challenge. And the academy is struggling. People are questioning the value of higher ed. Academy has always moved very slowly and cannot respond quickly to current issues. (President Joe Bertalino, Interview on Leadership Style from March 5, 2018, SCSU, New Haven, Connecticut).

SCSU, Southern Connecticut State University.

Box 3.3 displays the competencies/behaviors in this section.

BOX 3.3

NETWORK FOR SOCIAL WORK MANAGEMENT COMPETENCIES AND PRACTICE BEHAVIORS 6 AND 9

Develops and manages both internal and external stakeholder relationships (Network for Social Work Management Competencies 6). Practice Behaviors:

- Communicates effectively to multiple constituencies, through various means and media, the mission, vision, and values of the organization along with organizational programs, policies, and performance so as to promote organizational transparency and enhance support and understanding from internal and external constituencies (6.2).

Demonstrates effective interpersonal and communication skills (Network for Social Work Management Competencies 9). Practice Behaviors:

- Is able to articulate the mission and vision of the organization both orally and in writing to staff of the agency (9.1).
- Is able to articulate the mission and vision of the agency to those outside the agency to ensure understanding of the work of the organization (9.2).

Organizations need to be able to effectively communicate the mission, vision, values, and goals. It is important for staff to know what the mission, vision, values, and goals of the organization are because their job responsibilities are directly connected to these critical elements. Staff are the ones on the frontline who are charged with executing the mission, demonstrating the values, striving toward the vision and goals. By communicating orally on a regular basis to staff about the mission, vision, values, and goals, they will be better equipped to act upon these and verbalize these to other internal and external figures.

One way to communicate the mission, vision, values, and goals is to post them on your web page, in your building, and in other documents such as brochures and business cards. Repeating them in various meetings over time is also a good idea to help illustrate how the mission, vision, values, and goals manifest in the day-to-day operations of staff.

Mastering the Strategy Statement

To communicate to the outside world your organizational purpose, all directors should be able to describe the organization's Mission (why we exist), Values (what we believe in and how we behave), Vision (what we want to do), Strategy (what our competitive game plan will be), and Balanced Scorecard (how we will monitor and implement that plan). Mastering a strategy statement is the best way to achieve the strategy. The key elements of the strategy statement are Objective (Ends), Scope (Domain), and Advantage (Means). To create an actionable strategic statement, select one strategic objective that is specific, measurable, and time-bound. An example in academia is to attain top 10 national status in applications, and one in the nonprofit sector is to provide a bed for up to a week to any homeless person who comes in. Defining the scope requires identifying who the clients are (e.g., students) and what the geographic domain is or boundaries are (e.g., in academia for student recruitment and internship placements). The final component of the scope, or domain, is a vertical integration on how the organization deals with clients (e.g., students). Defining the advantage of the organization is the final component of the strategy statement. "Clarity about what makes the ... (organization) ... distinctive is what most helps employees understand how they can contribute to successful execution of strategy" (Collis & Rukstad, 2008, p.7). The strategy statement must explain why clients use your program, and differentiating your program from others is a good plan. The strategy statement should also identify the unique characteristics of your program that, once again, differentiates your program from others.

Use community engagement to articulate the organization vision and mission to outside agencies such as the local chamber of commerce and different nonprofit alliances. Using blogs and newsletters sent to other organizations and universities with a statement from the director is also a good strategy. Use your organization's media relations office and marketing directors and staff to get your message out. Staff participation in media relations can be very influential. For one, it brings a human touch to the marketing, as those professionals can enthusiastically share with the public how the mission and values make a difference in the lives of others. Oftentimes they can speak about the programs and offer information about how clients can access programs, while also sharing success stories and providing hope about how the program can enrich the lives of others.

Elevator speeches are also an excellent way to communicate your organization's vision, mission, and goals. Try to create an elevator speech about your organization in only 12 words. If you have a few drafts, try them all out on others and ask for feedback about what captured their attention. What word(s) did they cue in to? Elevator speeches are an important way to capture the attention of others because they are short and thus present your point concisely. Public speaking is typically judged by

- 70%—Facial expression and body movements
- 20%—Voice (spacing and emphasis are important—where you stop and pause are important). Shortest and slowest speeches are the most successful speeches, go as slow as possible, and use your personality or presence to support your position.
- 10%—Content

During most speeches, interacting with the audience takes up about 60% of the time compared to only 40% of the time actually speaking. What people remember also puts into perspective the importance of a good short speech. People remember

- 10% of what they read
- 30% of what they hear
- 50% of what they see
- 70% of what they share and discuss

There are several key points to take into consideration when developing an elevator speech:

1. Identify what the problem is you are trying to solve, for example, the program needs more secure funding.
2. Provide a value proposition or how you plan to solve the problem.
3. State your organization's position of why you are the right person or program to solve the problem.
4. State a call to action or what you need or want from your audience.

TABLE 3.1 **Target Audience and Goals for an Elevator Speech**

TARGET AUDIENCE	GOALS
Funders	Raise money
Students	Recruitment and retention
Faculty	Recruitment and retention
Agency	Partnerships
Press	Coverage
Colleagues	Personal branding
Legislature	Do not cut funding—why we need funding

Table 3.1 provides examples of possible target audiences, and also the goals of the elevator speech for each target audience.

The purpose of an elevator speech is to open the door to opportunities, and the presenter should remember that less is more while making the speech powerful enough to capture their interest.

Communications to various audiences should be carefully developed and screened for accuracy and appropriateness. Most organizations establish a chain of command as to who is allowed to communicate to the public and higher-ups in the organization, so make sure everyone in the organization understands the communication policy.

Emails should be short and specific—do not send long emails with multiple parts containing different information. Be sensitive to your clients and other key audiences and take into consideration any impact the statements may have on the audience. Get input from key teammates on developing the program message and make sure everyone understands it and can articulate it. Box 3.4 displays the competencies/behaviors in this section.

BOX 3.4

NETWORK FOR SOCIAL WORK MANAGEMENT COMPETENCY AND PRACTICE BEHAVIOR 9.3

Demonstrates effective interpersonal and communication skills (Network for Social Work Management Competencies 9). Practice Behaviors:

- Ensures that all written and oral communication in the agency is carefully planned and articulated so that it is clear in its message and sensitive to the various audiences that receive it (9.3).

Effective Presentations

One of the key communication methods is to present to an audience. Presentations in front of audiences can be challenging and stressful. A successful presentation will convey your message so that everyone understands it and pays attention for at least most of the presentation. Box 3.5 provides 11 steps that if followed will help make your presentation a success.

BOX 3.5

STEPS TO TAKE FOR A SUCCESSFUL PRESENTATION

- Step 1: Know your audience (recognize the way to learn, learn about your audience).

- Step 2: Determine your goal (develop objectives, brainstorm main ideas).

- Step 3: Collect ideas, notions, and all materials that may relate in any way to your talk. Organize your thoughts (organize main ideas for the body of the presentation, develop the introduction, and write the closing).

- Step 4: Phrase your message (illustrate with examples, use simple dynamic language).

- Step 5: Design visual aids (choose your medium, develop an effective design, prepare slide presentations, videos, and handouts).

- Step 6: Prepare notes for delivery (select a medium for notes, mark your text for delivery, and practice).

- Step 7: Prepare the presentation environment (plan your room arrangements, check your arrangements),

- Step 8: Get yourself in gear (dress for success and address your anxiety). Jitters are normal. When managed, they can add an undercurrent of energy to a talk. Take a few deep breaths, and believe—really believe—that you will do well.

- Step 9: Present with style (manage your voice, communicate through gestures and expression). Assess your body language. Are your gestures natural and helpful? Do you appear open, receptive, patient, and caring? Are you aware of your facial expressions? Monitor how fast you talk, and notice the length of your pauses. Pay attention to your posture and facial expressions.

- Step 10: Engage the audience (build rapport, stay in tune, manage the question-and-answer). Are you projecting the dynamic, sincere, caring self that you envision? Always take the higher road, conveying a positive, hopeful tone. Use the power of transformational reasoning: a problem is a challenge that may also be seen as an opportunity. Is the audience getting bored? If so make changes in how and what you are presenting to reengage them.

- Step 11: Be prepared to answer questions. If you are blindsided by a question or comment on an unfamiliar topic be candid: "I will look into that and get back to you." If you are heckled, "stay in character." Ignore brief catcalls. If a heckler persists, sometimes turning toward him or her silently, holding a pause, then continuing your talk will be sufficient.

Source: Adapted from International City/County Management Association. 2013. Career compass number 34: Making presentations like a pro, Retrieved from https://icma.org/articles/article/career-compass-no-34-making-presentations-pro

Ground Rules for Effective Communication With Individuals

When communicating with individuals, there are many things that should be taken into consideration; think of them as ground rules. Box 3.6 identifies what form of communication should be taken into account, depending on the content and context of the message, the role that relationships might have, the best way to accommodate the listener, and the importance of active listening.

BOX 3.6

GROUND RULES FOR EFFECTIVE COMMUNICATION WITH INDIVIDUALS

1. The form of the communication should match the message content.
   Consider

   a. The seriousness (weight) of the issue—such as in one-on-one meetings for personnel matters.

   b. The purpose or goal for the communication—send a text or email if you need to get the message out quickly.

2. The form of the communication should accommodate the listener.
   Consider

   a. The listener's perspective—what is salient for the listener?

   b. The listener's personality and communication style—the listener may need a communication in writing first.

3. The form of the communication should consider the context.
   Consider

   a. The listener's initial understanding of the issue—different listeners may have a different understanding of the issue, so structure the communication method to accommodate their understanding.

   b. The listener's perception of the context and timing—the listener may have a different perception of the context and timing of the communication; it is important to keep people in the loop while events are unfolding.

4. The form of communication should consider the role relationship.
   Consider

   a. Your rapport with the listener. Use different communication styles to fit the relationship. If the person is a friend, you will present differently than if the person does not like you.

   b. The listener's expectations for communication from you—the person may want to be in the loop or may not.

5. Practice active listening.
   Consider

   a. You often have more influence by how you listen than by what you say. Hear the person out; you might learn something about the situation.

▨ Basic Communication Style Concepts

People interpret communication differently depending on whether they are a sensing or an intuitive person. *Sensing people* pay close attention to what is experienced by their senses. They are interested in the immediate experience, literal facts, and concrete realities. Action is what drives them. And they want things to happen as soon as possible. People who prefer sensing develop differently and are motivated by needs differently than people who prefer intuitive perceptions. *Intuitive people* need to find associations or connections among things and are interested in theories and imagined possibilities. Meaning is what drives them. Intuitive people tend to wait until they are clear about WHY.

As we will discuss in Chapter 6, our minds are wired to make meaning, to connect the dots, and to draw conclusions; it is what helps humans feel like they can predict and make sense of their world. People draw conclusions about what they perceive and there are two ways to come to conclusions: (a) thinking judgement, which is an impersonal process and is logical, orderly, analytical, and more structured and (b) feeling judgment or appreciation, which is a more personal, subjective process. Feeling people tend to be interested in human values and harmony and to be motivated by caring, while thinking judgement people tend to be interested in the rationale for decisions and place little emphasis on the feelings related to the decision. To summarize the four basic styles, as in the case of perception, each person starts to prefer one kind of judging over the other, and this mode of decision making tends to become dominant. Because each individual may prefer either of two kinds of perception and either of two kinds of judging, all individuals can be classified under one of four categories:

1. Sensing thinkers—need action and meaning
2. Sensing feelers—need action and caring
3. Intuitive thinkers—need meaning and structure
4. Intuitive feelers—need meaning and caring

How do you communicate with each type of person? After interacting with a person over time you can begin to understand how they might react to your communication style with them.

Cullen (2013) has proposed the following styles for inspiring people through communication processes.

> *Inviting engagement:* Social workers described their approaches to patients and other service users in terms of issuing an invitation that respected each as a unique individual, allowing them to engage on their own terms. *Individualizing the medium of communication:* Social worker interviewees gave a number of examples of cases in which they had taken particular efforts to adopt a medium of communication that was responsive to the needs of an individual patient … . *Persuasive congruence:* The data included examples of how social workers consciously adapted their method of communication to fit the particular purpose in hand (p. 1534).

Box 3.7 displays the competencies/behaviors in this section.

BOX 3.7

NETWORK FOR SOCIAL WORK MANAGEMENT COMPETENCIES AND PRACTICE BEHAVIORS 9.4

Demonstrates effective interpersonal and communication skills (Network for Social Work Management Competencies 9). Practice Behaviors:

- Manages communication in conflict and crisis situations in a competent and sensitive manner (9.4).

Manage Communication in Crisis Situations

Social work leaders may find themselves in situations where they need to publicly communicate about a crisis situation. In dealing with crisis situations, focus on what went right, and take ownership of what went wrong, what actions steps are addressing it (i.e., launching a full investigation, cooperating and working collaboratively with other official parties), and provide a general statement about plans to remedy the situation. When situations arise that you know need to be dealt with immediately, do not delay in taking action; otherwise it will come back to haunt you. You may not be exactly clear on how to proceed, but it is important that you consult key members that may include board members, attorneys, compliance officers, and so on. It is important that you develop a plan to deal with the situation and that you do not protect people who have violated rules and regulations. A good rule of thumb when weighing decisions is to consider what the headlines would say when making any kind of decisions. When you do not know how to proceed, seek advice from your superiors. Or seek out others that have been through it and/or reach out to your social network. Once the issue is reported, and you have reported the issue to your chain of command, be sure to follow up on the issue and make sure action has been taken to resolve the situation.

When you need to make public comment to media sources, be concise and articulate how you are addressing the situation (briefly). The statement should not only contain accountability but also have a message that will instill confidence that the issue will be addressed, and promptly. Certain situations may also call for you to note that certain alleged behaviors go against agency policy and are taken very seriously by the organization.

One final note on communication during crisis: Leaders should not forget to communicate with their teams. That is to say that you do not want your teams to learn about the issue from the press, but instead want you to communicate directly with them that (a) there is an issue; (b) it is being addressed, and how it is being addressed; and (c) agency policy dictates who communicates with the press (i.e., only the CEO or designee by the CEO can publically comment). Additionally, it is important that teams have the opportunity to ask questions about how to respond if they are approached by the press or questioned by clients or other constituents, and develop a response that can be applied in a united fashion. Finally, staff will likely have their own emotional and cognitive reactions to the news. Providing them a supportive atmosphere to process their concerns may help to contain the situation and prevent them from discussing the situation in venues that are less, or not at all, appropriate. Box 3.8 discusses how leaders make decisions.

BOX 3.8

EXCERPT OF INTERVIEW WITH PRESIDENT JOE

Question: *What are the most important decisions you make as a leader of your organization? And how are these decisions made?*

Two issues, personnel and dealing with crisis. Most of my time is spent dealing with people. That is what I do. It is a revolving door, people want to talk and be heard, they want support. Decisions about people and leadership of the institution are critical to what is happening day to day. Decisions about investments relate to people, what positons to fill in what area, what is the most impact. Second most important decisions center around the handling of the unexpected, they may not rise to a crisis level, but ensuring that they do not rise to crisis level. Staff may question why we are bringing together all these people to meet. Being proactive. We have already done the work up front so we can deal with things in a cool, calm way.

Another important decision is about positioning the university. I have to ask: What is the message, what is the public relations, what are the priorities? (President Joe Bertalino, Interview on Leadership Style from March 5, 2018, SCSU, New Haven, Connecticut).
SCSU, Southern Connecticut State University.

Managing Communication in Conflict Situations

Facts About Conflict

Conflicts among colleagues and a perceived lack of time are strong causes of stress for administrators.

1. *Conflict is inevitable*—It is a natural outcome of human interaction. People think differently, have differences in attitudes, beliefs, and expectations. As a head of a program, you will be thinking differently about the way things happen and the various angles that must be thought through than the people that you lead. Perceptions may be different, particularly about the way things are or should be done differently. It is important to be aware of these differences, and to acknowledge where others are coming from, while helping them understand the critical thought process (i.e., the various angles you must consider) that needs to be factored in to how the situation is approached or resolved.

2. *Conflict can be positive*—Conflict can be desirable. Only through conflict can you begin to do true problem solving and actually view the situation through multiple lenses. Being open to discussing the differences that are experienced can unlock great potential. You can increase a person's involvement and commitment through positive conflict. You can empower persons and demonstrate that you value gaining an understanding of where they are coming from. And you model how to address conflict in a positive and productive manner. Conversely, if the conflict is avoided, the conflict is likely to manifest in other ways or simply continue to be heightened, which can ultimately foster a work atmosphere of distrust, disrespect, and pessimism. Most changes that result in meaningful and sustained improvement grow out of some conflict.

3. *Conflict can be managed*—How you manage or respond to the conflict will impact it. If two people are feuding, if you stay out of their conflict that will affect it, or if you get involved in their conflict, that will also affect it. You are never purely neutral when managing conflict, as you will likely see one side as more or less correct. However, you will need to help the parties to understand the other's position and facilitate their ability to move forward as part of the team, because resolving the issue is in the best interest of the client/organization/team.

4. *Conflict resolution is not always the goal*—If your goal is to get rid of conflict, you will deny diverse perspectives and you will fail to truly resolve the issue. However, your goal should be to minimize or eliminate destructive conflict and facilitate productive conflict. We have been teaching the same way for 30 years, should we look at it? You are using the same lecture notes over many years? But we have always done it like that. The changes to this new program are not working. These are conflict statements.

A director's objective is to maximize constructive conflict and minimize destructive conflict. There is no single recipe for doing this since every individual is different. What is always a core ingredient though is understanding your audience—that is, knowing how members communicate best, what they usually listen for in communication from others, how they relate, and what they value. Having an understanding of these elements that make up a person's uniqueness means that you as the leader are able to adapt your style of communication to your target audience to increase the likeliness that the communication will be effectively received, understood, and reciprocated. Adapting your communication style does not mean that you turn into a chameleon. On the contrary, you must stay true to who you are, what you value and believe in (while being open-minded to others' perspectives as well, of course), while tailoring how you deliver your points to the person(s) thoughtfully and empathically. If you are considerate of another, and can empathize with others on their position on a matter, even if they see it differently than you, then you can use the art of communication to increase collaboration, unification, and capitalize on differences. Essentially, you must employ emotional intelligence, particularly self-awareness and social skills, to maximize construction conflict.

Box 3.9 provides an example of how one might interact with a superior in a challenging situation.

BOX 3.9

COMPETENCY-BASED CASE: COMMUNICATING WITH DEAN ON ENROLLMENT ISSUES

In a meeting with the dean, Social Work Program X has been asked to increase enrollments in both its undergraduate and graduate programs as there are four applications for every one acceptance and the overall university's enrollments are down. As director of the program, you have been asked to take in 18 more students in each program, bringing both programs up to approximately 90 students each. You have 6 months to act on this request. In the meeting with the dean, you stated in an annoyed tone that you have been asked to do this in the past and, when you increased enrollments, there was no corresponding increase in the program's budget to accommodate the new students.

How should you respond to conflict in meeting with the dean?

Conflict in "meeting"

1. Perception of enrollment increase: Dean—good news, budget increase as a result of enrollment increase. Director—bad news, greater workload.

2. Perception of adding five new sections: Dean—essential to success and department's obligation. Director—last straw, this is unfair to the faculty.

3. Perception of director's resistance: Dean—uncooperative, director is ineffective and will jeopardize the institution. Director—it is necessary to protect faculty.

What are the possible statements and actions the director should take?

- Would it be okay to hire adjuncts to teach additional sections of courses?

- Can we talk about this in person after I have consulted with faculty?

- What can I do to help (before saying, "Does that mean you will restore our budget?")?

- Terminate the conversation and the faculty will come up with ideas.

- Let us get together and evaluate options.

- How can we work together to solve this problem?

- Ask for positive incentives from the dean, such as a 15% increase in tuition and revenue, with program receiving some of this revenue.

- Remind the dean of your department's situation (that everyone is already teaching in an overload).

- Should you turn the situation into a long-term fix? We will Band-Aid the issue now, but for the long term we need more staff.

- Your decisions on how to continue to communicate with the dean depend on the personality of the dean. Can you work better with dean in person or through email?

- The university has the right to increase class size by 10%. How do you respond to this action once it is taken?

Remember two things when communicating with the dean: (a) When you get really angry, your IQ drops by 25 points—so do not get angry; and (b) by fulfilling your role responsibilities (as director or dean), you will inevitably have conflict.

(continued)

BOX 3.9 (Continued)

Possible solutions to this situation

- Send an email to the dean and ask for a meeting.

- What if you call and she or he does not want to take the call? Always leave conversations open so you can get back to the dean.

- As you are unable to hire full-time faculty quickly, the hiring of adjuncts is the quickest solution, so how do you request approval for this action?

- Apologize to the dean for your announced statement.

- Increase class size just a little. How do you obtain faculty permission to do so?

- If you have doctoral students to possibly teach new students, determine what each doctoral student can teach and find out a way to hire them.

- If faculty are required to teach more than required, give them overload compensation, but first, communicate this request to the faculty.

- If you increase course cap size, obtain faculty approval first.

- Find out from the dean or higher-ups the likelihood that increasing student enrollments must take place.

- Meet with the dean and bring data, such as the number of sections and number of students faculty teach compared to other departments.

- Determine if tuition revenue can be used to hire people.

Tips: You should assume success in how you are going to manage this situation. The more heated the disagreement, the sooner you go back to work with the person, but focus on solutions that you agree on. You do not want one issue to define the relationship. You can disagree with people, but if you have respect for them you will learn.

Finally, write down what happened in this situation from your perspective and what you think is the dean's perspective to then identify wiggle room.

Strategies for Managing Conflict

1. *Establish and maintain a healthy work environment*
   Differences of opinion should be aired in a constructive manner. Ideally you want people with little job security, i.e., non-tenure or lower-ranking positions, to be comfortable to speak up. The goal is to establish a climate of mutual trust. Climate is unit specific, so do not let people complain about the poor climate within the larger institution, and if they do complain, that does not mean that your unit cannot have a good climate that is positive, respectiveful, and tolerates different views. When running a department meeting, encourage all to speak. Demonstrate that you want to hear equally from everyone.

2. *Be clear in communicating your goals and expectations for your unit*
   Help people know what is rewarded and valued. If in a university setting the requirement is that everyone must be involved in service on committees, you as the leader must help the faculty understand what this means and what type of committees would fit best for them. Help them know what counts. Be consistent in how you do this. Look to your university promotion and tenure committee to see how its set standards, which may not be written down but still exist. For example, how many research publications do faculty have to produce before going up for tenure? The number may

not be listed in writing but you may be able to determine a rough number, and then this number needs to be communicated. You need to set performance goals: tell staff what the university expects of them to be successful, and help guide them about ways to be successful. If you are clear, you defuse potential for conflict, and concurrently act as a coach, guiding their path to success.

3. *Establish ground rules for disagreement*
    Establish ground rules for disagreement that keep you on the issues of conflict but keeps you away from personalities. Establishing ground rules simply means that if and when the discussion goes off track, members quickly recognize that and refocus on the issue(s) at hand. Because emotions are sometimes difficult to untangle from the conflict, one member may have to step up to model the ground rules, which will eventually help the other to do the same. The ground rules for airing disagreements will vary with the style of the department head and the culture of the department, but can be adjusted at any time.
    The following is a suggested list of ground rules:

    - Abusive language will not be tolerated.

    - Derogatory comments that represent personal attacks will not be tolerated.

    - Differences of opinion will be discussed and everyone will be heard.

    - Individuals can express their views without interruption or fear of retaliation.

    - Unsubstantiated assertions will not influence the vote or outcome.

    - Issues and not personalities are subject to debate.

    - Tears or emotional outbursts do not derail discussion or substantive issues.

    - Faculty will discuss and decide important issues at department meetings, and not subgroups.
      One strategy to keep rules enforced is to give everyone a white handkerchief during meetings and have them wave it when people are not following the rules.

4. *Anticipate conflict areas and be ready to intervene when needed*
    Intervention does not need to wait for conflict to erupt. (a) Anytime you make a nontraditional hire, there is the potential for conflict. An example of a nontraditional hire in an academic setting could be a person who has no full-time teaching experience, but has extensive clinical or management experience. An example of a nontraditional hire in an organization could be a person without any human or social service experiences, but has management experience and an advanced degree in business management. During meetings make sure this new person's voice is heard. (b) Anytime restructuring is about to take place people will have questions. So make sure everyone understands their value in the restructuring. Also to intervene early you have to be able to see situations as others see them.
    Three general communication cues: (a) Any change in behavior, such as when a person who usually participates in meetings becomes silent, can be an indication that something is affecting the person. Sometimes these changes are triggered by work conditions, for instance, switching shared electronic programs, changing the core requirements for undergraduate degrees. Also sometimes changes in a person's personal life can affect how they work. (b) Any change in policy, no matter who imposed, it even if faculty and/or staff helped write it. (c) Any change in the department, such as a new faculty and/or staff hire, a retirement, increase or decrease in enrollment, office renovation, office relocation, a new leader. Personnel search committees have a lot of potential for conflict. Any change, no matter how subtle, is ground for conflict.

5. *Know when and how to confront conflict*
   Timing—Conflict does not need to be when voices are raised. But do not ignore shouting matches or inappropriate behavior.
   Know the facts—Be as objective as possible. Perception is not always reality. A student or client complaint about a faculty member and/or staff may not be the reality.
   Depersonalize the conflict—State to the person what exactly is needed of them to bring about a desired behavior. Give some thought about how language you are using is interpreted by the other person. Take the time to view the situation from the other person's perspective. If you are working on a performance review with a senior member of the faculty and/or staff who are about to retire, do not say you have much potential to be a good faculty and/or staff. Use the word legacy to describe them instead.
   Do not prolong confrontation—Do not carry a grudge and let one issue of disagreement define the relationship. Address it, resolve it, and move on; do not dwell on it.

6. *Know when and how to initiate action to deal with conflict—Examples of two times to initiate actions:*

   a. When offender does not realize his or her behavior is a problem—Meet with the person; try to understand what is bothering him or her that may be contributing to the problematic behavior.

   b. To help facilitate decision making—With an underperforming faculty and/or staff member, provide a clear explanation of expectations, for example, "Here is what you have to do in the next two years to get tenure." Help the underperforming staff consider all of her or his options and facilitate dialogues about what she or he values and feels she or he needs. It is important to mentor staff's careers, not just their current positions. Although it may not be ideal, it may be helpful for the staff to process that not all schools are the same, and thus may thrive and be happier somewhere else.

7. *Recognize which conflicts are not yours to resolve*—Only deal with issues if conflict is the business of your program. If the conflict is about something external to your program, it is not your role to get involved. Unless this conflict seeps into other areas related to work and performance that can impact the organization, and unless the individual is seeking advice about how to employ conflict resolution skills, you do not need to actually get involved in mediating the conflict, unless a coworker is seeking guidance and mentoring about how to effectively adopt conflict resolution skills.

Box 3.10 provides a case example of how to deal with a disgruntled faculty member who has success in some areas but not others.

BOX 3.10

COMPETENCY-BASED CASE: DEALING WITH THE SELF-CENTERED TEAM MEMBER

Dr. Jones case study—The self-centered team member

Facts of case: He is a prolific scholar and edits a journal in his area of expertise, but does not obtain grants. He developed a specialization that is widely used by other schools. However, his classes are underenrolled and students drop out of his class after a session or two. The university has a minimum enrollment policy that the head can override occasionally, and you have done so a number of times for his classes. As a result, your department has taken some budget hits for running the underenrolled class that professor Jones teaches. He chastises his students. He does not like his colleagues, does not attend department social gatherings, and does not approve of any changes in policy and curriculum and anyone going for

(continued)

BOX 3.10 *(Continued)*

tenure and promotion. This university has no requirement for a formal review of tenured professors. Dr. Jones is in his mid-50s. He sends his accomplishments to the administration regularly.

What can you do as a chair?

- Start steps to implementing a post tenure review.
- Try to get him to work on some projects for the department.
- Talk to the dean and VP about what is going on.
- Could make his life miserable. Move him around, change his office and phone.
- Find out what the rules are on firing people.
- Fire him due to financial exigencies.
- Document his pattern of behavior.

Where would you start with him?

Sit down with him. Clarify expectations and the impacts of his behavior. Have a conversation with the administration; make sure they will support whatever you do. Tell them they have been taking away budgets because of him (his low enrollments); therefore, the administration should support the chairperson's efforts to get the faculty to change his behavior.

Have a conversation with him but involve HR. He is setting up a hostile work environment. If you do not have in-house consul, go to an outside attorney of the university. Many universities have a harassment policy. Check guidelines for dismissal and termination of a tenured appointment. It depends on the campus culture as well as the policy.

Try to find out what motivates this person, or how to get this person some help. One-fifth of people are affected by some kind of chemical imbalance that affects their mood, emotional state, and so on. Look for employee assistance programs via the HR director. Difficult people can be threatening to others.

Write him up. Here is what I have noticed and I am seriously worried about this behavior.

What leverage points do you have with this person? What would happen if he lost teaching his favorite sections? Took away his dissertation students? How could we show him his legacy is in danger?

How would you actually have the discussion with Dr. Jones? What would you say to him first, second? Can you usually predict what he will say?

Role-play

Chair

- I am really worried about saving your underenrolled classes.
- Need to convince the person that I am the key to getting what they want.
- Should not reward problem behavior.
- Be reasonable, business-like. You the person is not upset; you the chairperson is upset.

Handling Conflict in the Department

"Conflict occurs when two people or two parties want the same thing but they have to settle for different things or when people want different things but have to settle for the same things" (Lucas, 2004).

Conflict can result from many causes. Examples of some causes of conflict include the following:

- Disagreement on a policy.
- Changes in policy.

- Differences between people's perspectives.
- Incompatible goals.
- Intolerance of others' views.
- Differences of opinions.
- Perceptions of scarce resources.
- Differences in needs.
- Lack of trust.
- Personal dislike of the other person.

Box 3.11 provides examples of typical conflict experiences and the differing opinions people have about conflict.

BOX 3.11

COMPETENCY-BASED CASE: PERSONAL CONFLICT EXPERIENCE

People have differing opinions about conflict. For example:

- Most people hate it (although a few people live for conflict; it makes their life interesting).
- Most people consider it is part of the job.
- It is fine until it gets personal.
- It is very time-consuming and can take away from productivity; it is so draining, it keeps you awake at night, and can create psychosomatic problems.
- It can expand to take on a life of its own.

How do you feel about conflict?

List how you feel about conflict. But first think about the conflict experiences you have had and then list how these experiences made you feel.

Examples of types of conflict experiences include the following:

- Substantive and personal.
- Differences in work ethic or work orientation.
- Over power and resources (academics fight so much because there is so little to fight about).
- Gossip and rumor.
- Conflict between generations (the university now wants more research).
- Elevated egos and intellectual property.
- Windows—some offices do not have them. How do you allocate office space (by productivity or seniority)?
- Long-standing many-years grudge that no one even understands the original problem (embedded conflict). Anytime a decision has to be made they emerge again.
- Lack of respect for a colleague's background and training.
- Student issues, such as when students complain about instructors or you cancelled the class that they need.

Box 3.12 allows leaders to create a list of conflicts that typically occur in their organization, and then practice solutions to resolve the conflicts.

BOX 3.12

COMPETENCY-BASED CASE: IDENTIFY KEY AREAS OF CONFLICT AND PRACTICE SOLUTIONS

Ask individuals in the department for a list of key areas of conflict in the department. Then attempt to come up with ways of dealing with it. Try one for 3 months. For example, if backstabbing occurs often, tell the backstabbers that if they have a problem with someone, do not go to a third party. If someone comes to you about a problem, ask them if they have talked to the person; if not, do not get involved.

Table 3.2 provides an exercise on identifying conflicts and possible solutions.

TABLE 3.2 **Competency-Based Exercise: Identify Conflicts and Possible Solutions**

CONFLICT	POSSIBLE SOLUTIONS	AGREE? OR ALTERNATIVES
1. Former chair was voted out and is now back on the faculty. He is disruptive, backstabbing, a lousy teacher, etc.	Take out of the loop. Find him something to keep busy. Could do a special assessment. Address him when he is acting unprofessionally.	
2. Most graduate faculty want to eliminate specializations but some are strongly opposed.	Maintain specializations in areas that are strong. Allow choice for students in courses and let them pick field of practice.	
3. Graduate coordinator does not do work in a timely fashion and is too process-oriented with an action-oriented chair.	Follow guidelines of progressive discipline. For missed deadlines, document pattern of missed deadlines or problems. Then meet with the coordinator and discuss the problem; coordinator may eventually do the job.	
4. Two faculty members really do not like each other and disagree on most things.	Have a meeting with the two of them and help them iron out their differences. It may be about something not even related to the job. Try to get them to see why they disagree on so many things.	
5. One faculty member is not fulfilling her job assignments and does not realize that she has a problem in not being available to students.	Meet with faculty and discuss issue. Then act by documenting performance.	

(continued)

TABLE 3.2 **Competency-Based Exercise: Identify Conflicts and Possible Solutions**
(Continued)

CONFLICT	POSSIBLE SOLUTIONS	AGREE? OR ALTERNATIVES
6. Some faculty do not follow the minimal job standards and you cannot do anything about it unless they are going for tenure and/or promotion.	Do an annual review of faculty according to standards, include your narrative and documentation on their performance.	
7. The average age of faculty is about 55. Some faculty are burned out or are troublesome. Some do not feel valued.	Do something that will make them feel valued. Do not alternate valuing and punishing. Value instead of punish.	
8. Curmudgeons are no longer active in the department. They frequently raise objections because they had once given the other department members sage advice that they did not take seriously, so therefore the curmudgeons will not be involved in a positive way. Most want back into the department but they do not know how to do it.	Ask them what happened, how can I help you, what do you want me to do?	
9. Had lots of student complaints about a sexist and capricious faculty member.	Encourage students to come forth and request written statements from them.	
10. Faculty want to produce but are unproductive.	Meet with faculty members and determine what type of help they need to make them more productive.	
11. Some faculty are struggling in the classroom.	Have a session on teaching effectiveness. Have each faculty identify an effective teaching moment or technique, and then ask what they noticed as a central theme for teaching effectively. Or invite several members to observe a class and evaluate the teaching. Then tell the department that you got good teaching tips that worked. Schedule workshops on effective teaching in the building where faculty work so faculty will more likely attend. Circulate a good book on teaching. Have several people read different chapters and then present to the faculty.	

(continued)

TABLE 3.2 **Competency-Based Exercise: Identify Conflicts and Possible Solutions** *(Continued)*

CONFLICT	POSSIBLE SOLUTIONS	AGREE? OR ALTERNATIVES
12. Problematic behavior at meetings.	Make the most of using group membership to collectively and cohesively address a problem. For an abrasive person, one might say: "I had this feeling when you were talking; how many other people feel the same way?" When a person makes disruptive statements, ask him or her how it is related to the agenda. Create a policies committee that develops criteria on behavior, performance, etc. Then do a gap analysis and give the person feedback on how to improve performance. When you document acts, make sure you send a copy to the person in question.	

Other tips on dealing with problematic faculty and conflict situations:

- Value faculty, try to be imaginative. Determine what areas you want to get involved in. Use an ombudsman for difficult faculty members. Do not be disrespectful and denigrate a faculty.

- Use punishment only when the person is incorrigible, because once you go down this road, it is very difficult to go back to trying positive reinforcement.

Box 3.13 displays the competencies/behaviors in this section.

BOX 3.13

NETWORK FOR SOCIAL WORK MANAGEMENT COMPETENCIES AND PRACTICE BEHAVIOR 9.5

Demonstrates effective interpersonal and communication skills (Network for Social Work Management Competencies 9). Practice Behaviors:

- Engages in emotionally intelligent communications with all stakeholders (9.5).

Basic Communication Skills

One good communication skill to always remember is to know what to say, when to say it, and who to say it to. There are a variety of basic communication skills for interacting successfully with individuals and groups. Box 3.14 includes a description of perception, listening, interpersonal, message construction, persuasion, negotiation, conflict management, team building, and consensus building skills.

BOX 3.14

BASIC COMMUNICATION SKILLS

Perception: Although we know about perceptions—everyone we talk to will have perceptions—but we do not always consciously acknowledge our perceptions.

Listening: Separate active listening. Really listen to a person to try to understand what they are saying; you want to gain understanding. Understand what the most challenging or difficult person in the organization is saying.

Interpersonal: The trust factor is most important. If staff trust you, you can lead change. Credibility is very important. It is easier to lose it than to gain it. Do not have temper tantrums in a meeting—one slip and you have a lot to recover. How do you help an individual staff member retain their credibility?

Message construction: The organization of the message and the timing as well as the medium comprise its construction. In an email message the recipient cannot read your intonation. Be careful about how and what kind of humor you use in an email. For a grievance issue, do not send an email; send a letter instead. Some staff prefer face-to-face meetings to help them understand issues, so even if you send an email to everyone, make sure you still meet with the staff who prefer in-person explanations. It is always a good idea to proofread any text or email messages, as there are likely to be some errors. Always focus on the content of the message, your objective, and what is the best available.

Persuasion: Advocate for change and cooperation. Explain the importance of the organization to external constituents.

Negotiation: Help everyone understand when the organization is well served, every idea is worth hearing.

Conflict management: Try and maximize constructive conflict and minimize destructive conflict.

Team building: Build shared ownership around common ideas. Team building is about a common purpose.

Consensus building: Consensus building, on the other hand, is getting agreement on the future or what should happen next. Consensus building allows for everyone to have a greater tolerance about different views and may create a greater understanding of the issues.

Leadership Communication Strategies for Working With Groups

Working with groups can be more challenging than working with individuals mainly due to the simple fact that multiple people are interacting. Box 3.15 provides a number of strategies and detailed explanations on why these strategies might work.

BOX 3.15

LEADERSHIP COMMUNICATION STRATEGIES FOR WORKING WITH GROUPS

- Help the group identify the tough questions—Groups typically struggle with identifying the underlying problem and the true issue(s).

- Keep the group focused on key issues—Allow the group to discuss member concerns but help the group members agree on understanding the underlying problem.

- Keep the group informed about the larger context—Some group members may not understand the larger context, such as shifts in organizational policy and goals.

(continued)

BOX 3.15 *(Continued)*

- Cultivate a collective identity and purpose—Move the group forward by working as a team to solve the problem(s).

- Be inclusive and participatory—Listen to each person's comments and suggestions. Make sure they are heard. Ask people who have not contributed what they think.

- Be consistent in applying organizational group rules—Do not let people interrupt others while speaking.

- Cultivate a climate conducive to airing differences constructively—Summarize the key points made and how they might impact the issue(s).

- Be responsive to group concerns—If the group wants to listen to everyone's comments or arguments, make sure that happens.

- Recognize individual contributions that support the group's purpose—Tell people that their contribution is really on point.

How Do You Deal With the Two Divergent Groups?

Faculty retreats can provide opportunities for teams to come together, share ideas, and collectively develop future goals and objectives. There are many reasons that give impetus to orchestrating a retreat, which can include identifying future directions; enhancing group cohesion, performance, and productivity; developing strategic plans; reviewing annual outcomes and future goals; and many others. If the budget allows, bringing in an outside consultant can be helpful. Gather all data and involve the faculty in gathering the data. You do not want camps to form that are uninformed. To prevent groups of staff that are uniformed, teaming up with one another and creating a uniformed chain reaction, it is critical to get faculty focused on what is known and what still needs to be known. Then what should be the framework or criteria of what you should select? You want to have good choices. Work with the group as a whole so they all hear the same information. Look at a timetable when dealing with specific issues, such as a cut in funding, and create a timeline upfront on what information still needs to be obtained.

How Can You as a Director Encourage Staff to Listen to You?

You must demonstrate that you are willing to really listen to them, process with them, and they need to trust that you will be supportive and straightforward with them. Give them the right facts, and they will appreciate it. In many ways, encouraging your staff to listen begins with gaining their trust and confidence that you are in fact capable of leading.

Have meetings with individual members and provide coaching on ways to improve their participation in group activities and functions. When people are discussing or proposing things, think about what motivates the person. Try not to rush into solving the problem or issue, or overcorrecting it for them, but rather ask questions to help them (a) gain more clarity about what the real issue is, and (b) think more critically about the process of problem solving. When a person really gets off track, bring her or him back to focus. How does this discussion relate to the issue, for example, the department discussion on where we are going with the curriculum? Create parking lots, or separate concerns, in the course of a meeting. For example, you can state, "This is a great idea but it is not in this parking lot." Have one person be the parking lot attendant. Then get back to the earlier identified concerns after you have addressed the present concerns. Encourage attendees to summarize what the meeting achieved and what steps should be taken next. One very important role in communication is to be a first person participant and a third person observer so you can realize what you are saying and doing.

Communicating With Superiors

Managers and their superiors can have different opinions on what to expect from each other, particularly how to communicate with each other. Examples of different situations are provided in the following section.

What Kinds of Communication Do You Want From Your Superior?

- Ideal communication is open and candid. You want your superior to be transparent; nothing should be hidden.

- You want predictability. Predictability should be related to the mission of the program; for example, will the superior approve the program's spending plan?

- The superior should know something about your program, how it operates, what is important, and what its needs are. It helps if your superior comes to your office to meet sometimes, especially if you are located elsewhere. If you are trying to implement something that is a top-down mandate, have upper administration meet with faculty to explain the imitative and demonstrate their ability to role-model.

- As a chairperson you can also advocate for faculty to the dean and hope that the dean advocates for your program to administration.

What Kinds of Superior Communication Do Directors Find Most Troublesome?

- Sometimes superiors meet with directors on issues that are predetermined and therefore the superior will not consider alternatives.

- Reneging on requests is another issue. It can become an untenable situation if you say everyone should teach a full load but one faculty goes to the dean and gets a release.

- In an academic setting, a dean may not let a chair share with faculty information such as how many or what percentage of faculty do not meet standards in conducting research.

- If something just feels wrong, you should try to talk about it with the dean/your superior.

What Kinds of Director Communication Do Superiors Find Most Troublesome?

- Complaining or whining, especially when no solutions have been tried. How do you get your opinion out there without complaining or whining? How do you present the concern or frustration in a cerebral versus visceral manner? It is also good to include an understanding of the opposing side of the issue, but even more importantly solutions should be offered, and you should outline the ways you have tried to manage the situation. Essentially, this understanding of all sides of the issue conveys that you want to be a part of the solution, while only complaining or whining about the issue demonstrates that you want to be part of the problem and are not eager to change it.

What Kinds of Communication Do Superiors Want From Directors?

- What is going on in the department, and how can things be improved in the department? Some political deans do not want honest information; he or she wants conniving information.

- Some directors want a lot of advice on people: "What do you suggest we do?"

- Some schools meet weekly or monthly with deans. The frequency of communication allows them to stay informed on a regular basis.

- If you come with a different opinion or complaint, directors want a solution.

- The "no surprise rule" is at the top of the list. Directors do not want to be caught off guard, or informed of an issue that you should have already made them aware of.

What Kind of Solutions Should Directors Employ to Successfully Deal With Superiors?

- Use joint problem solving. Joint problem solving is the mutual ability to work on problems together, as opposed to one party dictating what the solution should be. That helps the micromanager back up a bit. When dealing with micromanagers, ask yourself why are they micromanaging. The answer to that question will help you deal with them.

- If your superior wants untroubled waters, what do you do? Most superiors understand that it is never smooth waters, but nobody really enjoys getting bad news. Therefore you should make every effort to resolve issues in an expeditious manner.

- Superiors want honesty from the directors. Do not get into a we–they approach. A we–they approach means that you are adversarial and are likely focused on a chasm that exists between you and your supervisor rather than confronting the issue that needs to be addressed. If you are adversarial, you are demonstrating that you are not in either group.

- You want some regularity of information flow, but the style and personality of the superior will determine that.

- Decide if it is better to put something in writing or talk in person. Remember an email can be saved and printed.

- Superiors want supervisees to know that they are available, approachable, and need to be able to reach you when they need you.

- What are the consequences of not sharing information with my supervisor?

See Box 3.16 for a case study about department and university missions.

BOX 3.16

COMPETENCY-BASED CASE: DEPARTMENT AND UNIVERSITY MISSIONS

Case study: What are the facts. The mission of the department (research) is different from the mission of the university (teaching). And the budget has been cut every year for several years.

Decide a process for structuring the conversation or the process to deal with this situation.

Revisit the missions of the department and the university. Try to figure out what is important, if the department rewrote its mission. How would you downsize? Look at career possibilities. If a program is not marketable, drop it. What do you need to know and what is nice to know in terms of what classes need to be kept for accreditation?

Look at the budget. Will it continue to go down? If so, act on that. If budget comes back, it may not go back to the department. Politically, once you cut your program you never go back, but also once you start teaching more classes, you will never go back.

Have a plan on what you would do with resource needs relative to others who lost things.

Identify loss to institution of each line that is missing, and loss to society due to fewer practitioners. If you know where your graduates go, and you are the major supplier, should you collect this information and use it?

(continued)

BOX 3.16 *(Continued)*

Other strategies

- Make sure you fill positions if someone retires.
- Mentor new potential candidates.
- Do a strategic plan and a retreat.
- There may be two different camps, so do some politicking prior to any discussion. You do not want one strong voice to sway the group.
- Get some input from the dean. Does the dean have information that would help resolve the issue? You can also have the president speak to the department about the commitment of the university.
- Look into the future. Look at career trends.
- Inventory the department's assets. What does the department want to preserve, what can go away.
- Are the classes underenrolled? Look at the doctoral program.
- Seek mission alignment with the university.
- What can the department look at for future resources?

What if the institution gets some of its money back? Where is the department on the list in terms of getting funding back?

MARKETING AND PUBLIC RELATIONS

Box 3.17 displays the competencies/behaviors in this section.

BOX 3.17

NETWORK FOR SOCIAL WORK MANAGEMENT COMPETENCIES AND PRACTICE BEHAVIORS 17

Marketing and public relations: engages in proactive communication about the agency's products and services (Network for Social Work Management Competencies 17). Practice Behaviors:

- Consistently establishes and maintains positive external relationships with key organizational constituencies such as the media, public governance bodies, actual and potential donors, the business community, professional and service organizations, and the public at large (17.1).
- Builds and conveys to multiple constituencies an organizational brand that reflects competence, integrity, and superior client/customer, and community service (17.2).
- Develops and implements a successful marketing plan that dovetails with the fundraising activities of the organization (17.3).
- Ensures that the work of the agency is featured in various public relations venues to build and maintain visibility, access, and credibility and to ensure maximum usage of program resources (17.4).
- Develops clear guidelines for managing interactions with the press to ensure client confidentiality and accurate representation of agency performance (17.5).

(continued)

BOX 3.17 *(Continued)*

- Maximizes the use of electronic media to communicate the work of the organization and deepens the public's understanding of the mission (17.6).

NPOs have grown significantly in the last few decades. The increase in NPOs has contemporaneously created "competition for the limited funds available to NPOs from individual donors, the government, corporations, and foundations" and thus has also created a greater need for marketing (Pope, Isley, & Asamao-Tutu, 2009). However, marketing NPOs differs from marketing for-profit organizations. For example, the predominant function of traditional marketing is to increase the corporation's bottom line, while the paramount mission of most NPOs is cause driven. In regard to reasons why for-profit marketing strategies are ill fit with NPOs' marketing practices, Pope et al. (2009) explain that

- Perhaps the most obvious reason for this lack of fit is that NPOs have three target markets to which they must appeal: clients or customers, volunteers, and donors or funders (Helmig et al., 2004; Padanyi & Gainer, 2004). Often these three target markets are very distinct and respond to the marketing mix in different ways (Andreasen & Kotler, 2007; Padanyi & Gainer, 2004). Furthermore, the benefits gained by these multiple constituents are often non-monetary in nature, making it more difficult for NPOs to communicate clear benefits to each of these markets (MacMillian, Money, Money, & Downing, 2005; Padanyi & Gainer, 2004). This necessitates the need for NPOs to develop multiple marketing strategies aimed at radically different markets. (p. 186)

NPOs need to rouse emotions. An influential marketing strategy for NPOs is one that tells a compelling, heartfelt story that depicts the impact of the problem and demonstrates how people are affected by the problem. This story is best captured through short videos, showing real people affected by the issue, sharing their lived experiences and concretely explaining how donating time or money to the cause can help. People want to feel good about the charities they select, but they also want to know how their charity will help make a difference.

NPOs usually have a portion of budget allocated to marketing. The size of the budget allocation for marketing will determine how much or how creative the marketing division will need to be. When the budget is limited, NPOs usually make the most of funds by using their public relations and social media to market their mission, fundraising events, and ways to donate. Developing a strategic marketing plan with specific goals is the first step in marketing a program. Also developing and funding a marketing plan (maybe hiring a consultant) is absolutely necessary. Hiring a marketing specialist or assigning someone with marketing expertise is crucial. Producing short statements on the program's distinctiveness or unique features is important and can be used in a variety of communications to the public (Fenton Group, 2007). Furthermore, it is helpful to create and implement marketing plans that dovetail with the fundraising activities of the organization.

The first step to engaging in public relationships is to discover who the key constituents are. Once you identify key constituents, you will want to find out who heads them and be in contact with them, often. Maintaining communication with your constituents helps to establish collaborative relationships, and helps to keep them informed of the work your organization is doing. Finding people who can help to support your cause, spreading the word, and expanding the circle of potential donors or volunteers can be very useful for NPOs. Finally, NPOs are relying more and more on social media networks and other electronic platforms of communication to market their cause. It is important to create clever, compelling, and concise subject lines that capture one's attention. It is equally as important to be sure that the communication is free of jargon and easy to understand (make it short, to the point, and meaningful).

To maximize the use of electronic media to communicate the work of your organization and market your program, there are several questions you should ask. The basic is how do you market? Do you use print materials, website, social media, videos? What are your top marketing goals? Are you marketing for student recruitment, fundraising, staff recruitment, client recruitment? How effective are you at marketing? How would you rate your materials? How would you rate use of social media? Do you use social media to inform you about what your constituents want? What is your biggest challenge (money, time, expertise, or getting started)? What are you most proud of (effective student recruitment, use of Facebook, website, good email list)? If you have great things to offer, you just need to figure out how to promote them. Do you use social media yourself? Do you have a full-time person in charge of marketing? (Fenton Communications, 2010)

More than 80% of Americans use technology. In 2010, more data were generated by individuals than in the entire history of mankind through 2009. With information overload, repetition is the key to marketing. More saturation and repetition is good. Personalization and updating your program information is important. With convergence of everything on one device (such as print, video, interactive media, books), it is much easier to reach your audience. Advertising has gone micro (i.e., Facebook). Transparency is valued—people expect open data from businesses and governments. Authenticity is also valued and requires uniqueness, voice, and sincerity. Websites provide your organization's face to the world. What you put up on your website can make all the difference in providing the world with information on your program. Box 3.18 provides some important information on websites and what is recommended for website format.

BOX 3.18

WEBSITES AND RECOMMENDED FORMATTING

Websites

- Your website is your key communications tool (open 24 hours).
- Your audiences are impatient and critical.
- Audiences do not settle for mediocre design.
- Social networking works (and it is cost-effective).
- Communications (and fundraising) are more personality driven than ever before.
- Your communication must be timely (tweets).
- Third-party testimonials matter.
- Storytelling works.
- Harness the collective creativity of students and clients.

"Must Haves" for your website

- Good design
- Thoughtful and simple interface
- Primary navigation at top
- Lots of white space
- "Content is King" (video)
- Visuals (real people)

(continued)

BOX 3.18 *(Continued)*

- New information
- Social media (shareable)
- Searchability
- Solid "About Us" page
- Details second, stories first
- Easy to find contact info
- Third-party testimonials
- Clear, concise text

Conveying what your organization is accomplishing, how it is positively shaping the community, and how it is contributing to a cause conveys to your constituencies why your organizational products and services matter. There a number of ways to go about conveying your organizational brand, which are in the bulleted list. Note this is not an exhaustive list, but does offer a number of ideas about how to market an organization and engage in community relations:

- Write an annual letter of appeal. This letter should highlight organizational accomplishments; share a client or student success story (remember, compelling and concise); and remind people of why their support matters.

- Use Facebook, blogs, Twitter, and other social media to share success stories and provide information on how to donate (hint: using one-click and mobile devices increases the ease of contributing and therefore the amount of donations). Provide information about how staff are working with clients (i.e., highlight a worker talking about what they love about their work) or a staff event that showcases team spirit.

- Share on the website, Facebook, and other forms of social media the organization's report card—that is, scoring on certain standards or accreditations.

- Showcase on the website what the organization or department is well known for. This display may incorporate information about what former students are currently doing in the field, what populations they are working with, their clinical or administrative roles, their noted publications, and so on.

- Websites should also showcase the competencies that students have learned and student outcomes.

- Develop good relationships with the press. The objective is to publicize when faculty, students, and employees are engaging in community events, working with community agencies, and have been identified as experts in their field to be interviewed on a particular subject matter.

- Create brand and convey it to everyone. The brand should reflect competence, integrity, and superior client/customer and community service.

Developing a strategic marketing plan with specific goals is the first step in marketing a program. Also developing and funding a marketing plan (maybe hiring a consultant) is absolutely necessary. Hiring a marketing specialist or assigning someone with marketing expertise is crucial. Producing short statements on the program's distinctiveness or unique features is important and can be used in a variety of communications to the public (Fenton Group, 2007). Box 3.19 provides a list of a wide variety of methods and strategies.

BOX 3.19

METHODS AND STRATEGIES TO MARKET ACADEMIC AND AGENCY PROGRAMS

There are a number of methods and strategies to market academic and agency programs:

- Newsletter
- Annual report
- E-letter
- Website—include photos of alumnae and success stories
- Photos—can be used in multiple places (online, newsletter, newspaper, etc.)
- Advertise at select events
- Place ad on niche guru websites
- Newspaper story
    - Send out reprints
- Use cosponsors' (conferences, etc.) press/communications department to get word out
- Write press releases
- In-house web/IT person
- Brochure: "What do social workers do?"
    - One-pagers (two-sided) variety of content
    - Standardized format
    - Pictures
- Podcasts
- Radio airtime (timely): topics discussed with call-in opportunities
- Email blasts
- Packets of information that staff and faculty take to conferences, etc.
- Sponsorships of statewide conferences
- Marketing to legislators
    - NASW lobbyist
    - Personal contacts with individual legislators—ask them to speak
    - Written notice of legislators' positions
    - Legislative or lobby day
- Alumni email list
- Celebrations of promotions and retirement (advertise and invite people)
- Lectures around country by endowed chairs
- Thank-you notes on letterhead (handwritten)
- Broadcasting good news
- Special pages/sections of university alumni newsletter

To institute a successful marketing campaign, several questions should be asked and answered. The primary questions are what are your goals, who is your audience, what do you want the audience to do, who can help you reach your audience, what is the best method for reaching the audience, what are the best messages for the audience, how much can you afford to spend, can you do it in-house, how will you measure success, and what is the timeline? All of these questions are addressed in further detail in Box 3.20.

BOX 3.20

QUESTIONS TO PREPARE FOR A MARKETING CAMPAIGN (FROM 2007 FENTON POWERPOINT ON MARKETING 101 SESSION)

1. What are your goals?
   a. Fundraising?
   b. Student recruitment?
   c. Recognition from the administration?
   d. Respect from state agencies?
   e. Other?
2. Who is your audience?
   a. Audience (donors, students, administration, agencies)
   b. Benefit (legacy, job placement, insight, workforce)
   c. Concern (inefficiency, prestige, agenda, skills)
3. What do you want the audience to do?
   a. Give money
   b. Attend
   c. Join
   d. Hire
   e. Collaborate
4. Who can help you reach the audience?
   a. Media
   b. Colleges
   c. Faculty
   d. Alumni
   e. Third-party validators
5. What is the best method for reaching the audience?
   a. Direct mail
   b. Email

(continued)

BOX 3.20 *(Continued)*

    c. Conferences

    d. Publications

    e. Online

    f. Telephone

6. What are the best messages for the audience?

    a. Message platform

        i. Problem—Solution—Action

            a. Messaging

                1. Frames

                2. Values vocabulary

                3. Elevator speech

                4. Audience pitches

7. How much can you afford to spend?

    a. Dollars

    b. Time

    c. Staff

    d. Partnerships

    e. Pro bono

8. Can you do it in-house?

    a. Training

    b. Hiring

    c. Consultants

    d. Creative

    e. Production

9. How will you measure success?

    a. Grants

    b. Attendance

    c. Invitations

    d. Job placements

    e. Media coverage

    f. Retention

    g. Visitors

(continued)

BOX 3.20 (*Continued*)

10. What is the timeline?

    a. Fiscal year

    b. Academic year

    c. 5-Year plan

These tools can be of value when marketing to external agencies. There are also a number of tools that are available for communicating information about your program. Some of these tools are identified in Box 3.21.

BOX 3.21

TOP TOOLS FOR COMMUNICATION

Top tools you can use include the following:

- Netvibes
- Doodle
- Skype
- Tweetdeck
- Zoomerang
- Tagline generator
- Flip camera
- Ning
- Wikispaces
- Social mention

These communication tools can be used to promote the organization as a well-recognized advocate on public policy issues.

Box 3.22 displays the competencies/behaviors in this section.

BOX 3.22

NETWORK FOR SOCIAL WORK MANAGEMENT COMPETENCIES AND PRACTICE BEHAVIOR 8.4

Advocates for public policy change and social justice at national, state, and local levels (Network for Social Work Management Competencies 8). Practice Behaviors:

- When appropriate and in line with organizational mission, promotes their organization as a well-recognized advocate on public policy issues (8.4).

When appropriate, organizations should encourage staff to become involved in advocacy efforts that will advance a cause or improve policies relevant to the population served. Organizations, and staff, can engage and advocate for issues by writing articles on public policy, submitting editorials, sharing information through social media networking, creating a petition, and so on. There are a variety of ways that staff and organizations can get involved in advocacy, but it also is important that they are able to share through their social network and media relations what they have done to advocate on behalf of clients, students, groups, communities, and so on. Here again the marketing director can promote this advocacy by disseminating information about the actions taken.

SUMMARY

Throughout this chapter we explored the various effects of engaging in effective interpersonal communication skills and identified ways to enhance communication, particularly when faced with conflict. Effective communication is needed to motivate staff, to resolve conflict, to manage crisis situations, and successfully navigate press coverage. It is also necessary for being able to successfully market organizational programs and foster public relations. This chapter provides tips for recognizing conflicts, taking action to manage conflicts, establishing rules for productive disagreements, communicating goals and expectations, and establishing healthy work environments.

ACTIVITIES

1. Think of an instance when you engaged in conflict resolution with both an individual and group and use the tips described in this chapter to describe how you might have had a better outcome.

2. Create a marketing plan for your organization. This plan should include information about the purposes and successes of your program. Identify key persons that you will involve and why. Explain how you will market your plan.

REFERENCES

Collis, D., & Rukstad, M. G. (2008). Can you say what your strategy is? *Harvard Business Review*. Retrieved from https://hbr.org/2008/04/can-you-say-what-your-strategy-is

Cullen, A. (2013). 'Leaders in our own lives': Suggested indications for social work leadership from a study of social work practice in a palliative care setting. *The British Journal of Social Work, 43*(8), 1527–1544. doi:10.1093/bjsw/bcs083

Fenton Group. (2007). *Marketing tactics*. CSWE 2007 "Marketing 101" Breakout Session NADD and Social Work Leadership Institute, Naples, FL.

Fenton Marketing. (2010). *How to improve your webpage and marketing*. Presentation at NADD Spring Conference, April 10, Naples, FL.

International City/County Management Association. (2013). *Career compass number 34: Making presentations like a pro*. Retrieved from https://icma.org/articles/article/career-compass-no-34-making-presentations-pro

Lucas, A. F. (2004). *Handling conflict in the department*. Paper presented at 21st Annual Academic Chairpersons Conference, Orlando, FL.

Pope, J., Isely, E.S., & Asamoa-Tutu, F. (2009). Developing a Marketing Strategy for Nonprofit Organizations: An Exploratory Study. *Journal of Nonprofit & Public Sector Marketing, 21*(2), 184–201. doi: 10.1080/10495140802529532

CHAPTER 4

MAKING MEETINGS PRODUCTIVE AND WORKING WITH GROUPS FOR SOCIAL WORKERS

CHAPTER OBJECTIVES

- Modeling and encouraging professional behavior.
- Demonstrating and helping others to achieve balance.
- Seeking input from and listening to all levels of staff.
- Inviting diverse perspectives.
- Encouraging and allowing staff to confer and present issues and problems.
- Managing communication in times of crisis.
- Showing evidence of stakeholder buy-in.
- Working constructively with people and institutions.
- Employing leadership tasks in meetings.
- Preparing for a meeting.
- Organizing a meeting.
- Conducting/participating in a meeting.
- Understanding some traps in planning and conducting a meeting.

INTRODUCTION

Meetings can be incredibly motivating, and conversely, they thwart the momentum of teams. For anyone who has ever heard or expressed frustration about having "another meeting, about another meeting" likely understands the significant impact that meetings have. People want to feel that they are making productive use of their time, and that they are being led in a direction of change and accomplishment. Therefore, leaders and managers need to understand how to effectively plan, organize, direct, and control meetings that are successful. Successful meetings will not only result in positive outcomes but they furthermore can contribute to the perceptions of an organization's, or department's, culture. For instance, when teams feel that they participate in meetings that are relevant, that have purpose and follow-through, they experience greater team cohesion, productivity, and overall satisfaction. On the other hand, when teams experience meetings that are disorganized, lack leadership, are ridden with conflict, or have a sense of redundancy or going through motions without producing results, they will likely experience discordance, discouragement, and diminished commitment and motivation. Throughout this chapter we explore the various ways that leaders and managers can employ skills for making meetings productive when working with teams or groups of staff. Box 4.1 displays the competencies/behaviors in this chapter.

BOX 4.1

COMPETENCIES AND PRACTICE BEHAVIORS ADDRESSED IN THIS CHAPTER

Models appropriate professional behavior and encourages other staff members to act in a professional manner (Network for Social Work Management Competencies 4). Practice Behaviors:

- Demonstrates the ability not to be "consumed" by executive responsibilities and helps others to achieve the balance and maintain a sense of humor and perspective (4.7).

Manages diversity and cross-cultural understanding (Network for Social Work Management Competencies 5). Practice Behaviors:

- Seeks input from all levels of staff, listens attentively, demonstrates fairness and consistency, and conveys information fully and clearly (5.4).
- Invites different perspectives to all client-related and management discussions within the organization (5.5).
- Encourages and allows opportunities for staff to confer and present issues and problems affecting program-related services (5.6).

Demonstrates effective interpersonal and communication skills (Network for Social Work Management Competencies 9). Practice Behaviors:

- Manages communication in conflict and crisis situations in a competent and sensitive manner (9.4).

Encourages active involvement of all staff and stakeholders in decision-making processes (Network for Social Work Management Competencies 10). Practice Behaviors:

- Shows evidence of stakeholder buy-in through such means as meetings or representative groups, and program surveys to the community (10.2).
- Displays the ability to work with people and institutions to achieve creative compromises and "win–win" solutions (10.6).

WORKING WITH GROUPS

As we have drawn upon the similarities between direct practice work and leadership in previous chapters, we would be remiss if we did not briefly examine the similarities found in how social workers facilitate group work and how they lead team meetings. Yalom (2005) provided a rich theoretical background for group work as a platform for us to examine such parallels, particularly in considering group (team) cohesion. Yalom explained that group "membership, acceptance, and approval" is paramount to persons' development throughout all stages of life. Life stages transcend to various arenas of life, or roles one functions in, as well. We spend the vast majority of our time dedicated to work and can therefore experience a sense of belonging and acceptance at work. In addition, people respond to reciprocal appreciation, which can be proportionately vital to individuals' well-being and can be exceptionally influential on professional outlooks and development. For instance, when clients feel they can support and be supported by fellow group members, receive and offer constructive feedback, experience universality, altruism, and catharsis, they are more motivated to attend and be productive members of the group.

Yalom (2005) illustrated that "belonging in the group raises self-esteem and meets members' dependency needs but in ways that also foster responsibility and autonomy, as each member contributes to the group's welfare and internalizes the atmosphere of a cohesive group" (p. 57). Staff can similarly experience a sense of belonging and purpose as they commit themselves to the cause (or the purpose of their work tasks); they can experience altruism as they lend support and creative ideas to teammates, and sense of esteem as they negotiate differences of opinions and ideas; they can experience universality as they endure changes, challenges, and collectively seek solutions; and they contribute their individual talents and autonomously work on the assignments they are responsible for, while appreciating the tasks their fellow teammates are contributing to. The team/group contributes to a cohesion within the workplace when members have good group leadership to facilitate and foster the benefits of group belonging. Affiliative leadership style can be applied to constructs of facilitating meetings, as affiliative leaders can promote loyalty, build a sense of belonging, and foster an atmosphere of trust that supports innovation and risk-taking. Similarly, transformative leadership style can inspire the team to collaboratively engage in the process of goal attainment.

When group members feel that they can give honest feedback to the group leader, the affiliative process will allow the group (i.e., team) to provide support and share ideas about how to solve problems. In order for that process to unfold, the meeting leader has to be transparent and willing to own mistakes. Leaders and managers facilitating groups must also be cognizant that the phenomenon of *strength in numbers* can occur, where the group feels they can confront the leader as a group in a way they may not do alone. Leaders should allow the group to assert themselves in a professional and productive manner and be open to acknowledging what they do not know, or perhaps should have done better. Leaders are encouraged not to personalize this process as an attack, but instead as an opportunity to reflect upon and discuss their mistakes to help the group move forward. Such transparency will allow the leader to make more refined mistakes in the future, rather than repeating the same errors.

Leaders and managers ask staff to take risks and be flexible to change, and must therefore be willing to do the same. Modeling for staff may actually provide rehearsal opportunities (referred to in group processes as "practicing") with group members before performing an act or conversation outside of the group to address other dilemmas at work, such as confronting a client about a difficult issue, revisiting a conversation/confrontation with someone they supervise, or finally having a difficult conversation with a community collaborator. Additionally, when directing a meeting, leaders or managers should keep in mind how they intend to balance structure and freedom. Without structure providing information regarding the purpose, there is no freedom to discuss ideas about how to achieve outcomes and innovate. Thus, one needs to be prepared (planning), thoughtful, and strategic (organized) yet approachable enough to invite and inspire the team to freely express their creative ideas and skills that can contribute to the outcome.

MAKING MEETINGS PRODUCTIVE

Meetings can satisfy four out of the five managerial skills: *information sharing, brainstorming, problem solving and decision making,* and *planning implementation.* Meetings are helpful when collective thinking and consensus is required and synergy is likely. Meetings can produce a collective result that can be better than the sum of its parts. Prior to scheduling a meeting consider identifying the type of meeting or process(es) to be used. There are many types of meetings from small-group, informal, spur-of-the-moment meetings to large-group and regularly scheduled meetings. What will the meeting accomplish? Which of the four managerial methods will you employ in the meeting?

If and when you determine that a meeting is the right tool, how can you most effectively use this tool to process information to achieve quality output? Meetings can make a group of people more productive than they would be as individuals. What is the most critical factor to consider when determining whether a meeting is appropriate? Or is there more than one factor that should be considered? You may need to share information, address problems, plan for events, and so on. There are several questions and tools that help one to tease out the factors that should be considered in determining the appropriate use of meetings.

Questions to Identify a Proper Management Tool

All of the following can be accomplished in meetings by using various management methods (in parentheses below):

- Do I need to find old information? (Managing yourself)
- Do I have to give out new information? (Information sharing)
- Do I want to share/collect information? (Information sharing)
- Do I want to brainstorm? (Brainstorming)
- Do I have to develop a plan? (Planning implementation)
- Do I have to solve a problem? (Problem solving and decision making)
- Do I have to decide something? (Problem solving and decision making)

Factors to Consider in Choosing a Management Method

- Likelihood of questions (Will there be a lot of questions?)
- Importance—nature of information—material—issue (Is this a very important issue that needs to be dealt with quickly? Is there a lot of information and material that requires sorting through?)
- Degree of understanding what is needed (Is this issue complicated? Does it need to be discussed in detail so everyone understands ramifications of any action or decision?)
- Time and deadline (What is the best way to resolve this issue quickly?)
- Number of people involved (How many people need to be involved in discussing the situation or making a decision, and what is the best way to get their feedback?)

Material in the rest of this section has been adapted from Commonwealth of Pennsylvania (1987) and Pennsylvania State University (1987).

In this part of the chapter on making meetings productive, the following topics are covered:

- Leadership tasks in meetings.
- Preparing for a meeting.

- Setting the purpose and objectives of a meeting.
- Organizing meetings.
- Conducting/participating in a meeting.
- Styles of leadership for different settings at meetings.
- Follow-up on meetings.
- Checklists for planning meetings.
- Some traps in planning and conducting meetings.

LEADERSHIP TASKS IN MEETINGS

If your meeting is to be productive—that is, accomplish its goal(s) effectively, before, during, and after the discussion—its members must perform a large number of detailed tasks. In some situations, a *designated leader* performs most of these tasks; in others the *entire membership* shares equally in their performance. In either event, it is important that everyone in the group understands what the tasks are and what is at stake if decisions are not made, action is not taken, and people remain uninformed!

In a lot of ways, managing meetings is no different than managing anything else. Like any tool, no matter what the suitability or quality of the tool itself, if you did not know *how to use* the tool, it would not produce the desired results. *Managing* meetings means applying the four basic management functions to meetings—no more, no less (planning, organizing, directing, and control). Preparation is required to achieve the planning and organizing functions. The directing and controlling functions are controlled by conducting and managing those processes. Planning refers to how one prepares for the meeting to ensure that it is successful and productive. Organizing is marked by systematically gathering and disseminating the materials that are needed to ensure greater participation, understanding, and productivity. Directing relates to how one effectively facilitates the meetings. Finally, controlling denotes an ability to contain topics, side conversations, participants' emotions, and so on, in a manner that does not permit the group to be derailed.

One could hypothesize that about two-thirds of the overall success of a meeting comes from the planning and conducting phases, and, in fact, half may come from planning alone. Table 4.1 displays the percentage of time for each of the three stage of the meeting process.

TABLE 4.1 **Three Stages in the Meeting Process**

PREPARING	CONDUCTING	FOLLOW-UP
50%	15%	35%

Preparing for a Meeting

Preparation involves both *planning* and *organizing*. Key ingredients of an effective meeting are both a common focus on *content* and *process*. Recall from Chapter 2 that content refers to what is actually being discussed, while process refers to how the content is discussed (nonverbal communication, body language, etc.). Shulman (2016) explains that groups can sometime get caught in a false dichotomy; meaning that too much process and not enough focus on the content is ineffective. This dichotomy can occur with passive leadership that creates a dependency on leaders and prevents mutual aid. The equivalent to meetings would be when leaders do not invite participation and feedback from the team members. For instance, a content meeting overly focused on giving information can often create resistance from the team. Therefore, simply delivering the content does not work if you are not also including process work in the meeting. Both content and process need to be integrated and attended.

In all stages of a meeting, including preparation, conduct, and follow-up, both content and process must be addressed. Preparation provides both participants and leaders with a source of power. There are plenty of horror stories about lack of preparation either in the content of a meeting or in the process during a meeting, such as a lack of adequate notification or a lack of understanding as to the purpose of the meeting. Box 4.2 displays the Network for Social Work Management Competencies and Practice Behaviors 10.2 and 10.6.

BOX 4.2

NETWORK FOR SOCIAL WORK MANAGEMENT COMPETENCIES AND PRACTICE BEHAVIORS 10

Encourages active involvement of all staff and stakeholders in decision-making processes (Network for Social Work Management Competencies 10). Practice Behaviors:

- Shows evidence of stakeholder buy-in through such means as meetings or representative groups, and program surveys to the community (10.2).

- Displays the ability to work with people and institutions to achieve creative compromises and "win–win" solutions (10.6).

In advance of meetings there are a number of steps one should take. Box 4.3 lays out several steps that improve meeting outcomes.

BOX 4.3

ADVANCE PREPARATION FOR MEETINGS

- Make careful selection, and/or analysis, of the group members. Try to discover the participants' points of view, their knowledge of the subject, and the probable extent of their participation, and try to foresee possible personality clashes.

- Be sure that all persons who need to study the topic have done so. Make reference materials available or suggest where the participants can find them.

- Arrange for a prediscussion planning meeting, if needed.

- Plan a topic outline, assign areas for study prior to the discussion, and agree on all procedural matters. Be sure that all members are acquainted with one another before the meeting begins.

- Plan for observers, technicians, resource persons, or any other special help needed.

In preparing for a meeting, formulate expected outcomes (what), a statement of purpose or objective of meeting (why), and how you will accomplish meeting objectives (how). See Box 4.4:

BOX 4.4

OUTCOMES, PURPOSE, AND HOW OBJECTIVES WILL BE MET

Expected outcome(s)—WHAT

- What do we expect to accomplish?
- Begins with a noun
    - an understanding of ...
    - a decision regarding ...
    - a solution to ...
    - a list of ...
    - a plan to ...

A statement of purpose (objective)—WHY

- Why are we having this meeting anyway?
- Begins with a verb
    - to decide ...
    - to bring closure to ...
    - to solve ...
    - to plan for ...
    - to update ...
    - to share information about ...
    - to generate ideas concerning ...

Objectives—HOW

- *How* will we accomplish it?
- Stated in terms of *outcomes*
    - clarification of ...
    - awareness of ...
    - understanding of ...
    - agreement on ...
- Things you like to discuss, to examine, to consider are activities not results. They tell you what will happen, but they do not tell you why. Activities are the means of achieving an end; objectives must state the end that is to be achieved.
- Outcomes should be only one sentence; otherwise not well focused
    - should be well-defined
    - should be easily understood
    - should be realistic

Table 4.2 provides examples of meeting expected outcomes, purpose, and how objectives will be accomplished at a meeting.

TABLE 4.2 **Outcome — Purpose — Objectives of Meeting**

OUTCOME/PURPOSE/OBJECTIVE	EXAMPLES
Outcome or what you expect to accomplish	An understanding of the financial status of agency or university so that I can decide "yea" or "nay" on merging with agency or university.
Purpose or why are we having this meeting	Agency or university is in dire financial stress and may not survive without a merger.
Objective or how will we accomplish the purpose	Understanding of pros and cons of merger versus going out of business. Agreement on results to be achieved by decision.

▓ Setting the Purpose or Objectives of a Meeting

People are quick to agree on the importance of having a purpose or objectives for a meeting. Indeed, the very reason for bringing people together at a certain time and place is that someone had a goal or purpose or objective that could best be met by having a meeting. However, it is one thing to acknowledge the importance of having objectives, and quite another to be able to write them out in a way that enables the leader and the group to measure progress, allocate their time appropriately, and evaluate the outcome.

When you write your objectives for your meeting or conferences, check them out to make sure they are *results-oriented, measurable,* and *appropriate.* Let us examine each of these three criteria.

Results-Oriented

Your objectives state the outcome or condition that will occur as a result of the meeting. Often people will state the activities that will occur at a meeting instead of the results to be obtained. For example, take the program that is considering a new curriculum. The department head calls the heads of all affected programs together with this objective: "To explore the feasibility of updating the curriculum to an evidence-based practice curriculum." Unfortunately, "exploring" does not let us know why we are "exploring the feasibility." If our objective is "to reach a group decision on whether to update the curriculum," then this is what we should write about, or, if the decision will be made by the leader or someone else and not by the group, then perhaps we have this objective: "To identify the major advantages and disadvantages that each program head sees in updating the curriculum." Verbs like "to discuss, to examine, to consider," and so on are activities and not results. They tell us what will happen, but they do not tell us why. Activities are the means of achieving an end; objectives must state the end that is to be achieved.

Measurable

Your objectives should describe outcomes that are directly observable and capable of being quantified. That is, you must be able to describe the degree of success you have met in accomplishing an objective. Consider, for example, the head of an academic program who has realized that students are not receiving adequate advisement. A meeting is scheduled with the faculty to discuss advisement issues (the problem could be too many students to advise, the advisement period is too short, faculty are not available, and/or students do not show up for advisement). Let us examine one of the objectives of that meeting: "To provide our students with timely and accurate advisement." This statement is results-oriented (i.e., we want students to take the right courses), but it is not stated in terms that make a behavior measurable. There are two adjectives present: "timely" and "accurate." Unfortunately, we cannot observe or quantify either timely or accurate. Thus, the program head has no way of measuring how successful the meeting is, either during the meeting or thereafter.

How can we make this laudable objective (successful student advisement) measurable? One possibility is to focus on the outcome. For example, consider this objective: "Students take exactly the correct courses and therefore graduate on time." Or, if you want more immediate objectives, consider this: "Students meet with advisors on scheduled meeting times 90% of the time." These objectives enable the head to measure two outcomes: students graduating on time and most students meeting with advisors and coming away with correct advisement.

Appropriate

An objective is appropriate if it moves the organization or individuals attaining it in the direction they want to move. Most objectives are stated because the organization wants to overcome some problem or seize some opportunity. If the objectives do indeed overcome a problem or seize an opportunity, they are appropriate. If they do not, they are not. *Validity* is another word for appropriateness. For example, consider the regional manager who brings his or her district managers (DMs) together in an attempt to tackle the problem that more and more good employees are leaving the company. This objective is placed on the agendum of the meeting: "To identify causes of employee dissatisfaction that are contributing to our rising turnover rate, and to reach agreement on the sequence and methods for improving these causes of turnovers." This objective is certainly results-oriented. It also seems to be measurable (i.e., we can count how many "dissatisfiers" the DMs come up with and see whether they did indeed reach agreement on sequence and methods for improving conditions).

However, this objective is founded on a dangerous assumption. The manager is assuming that, by identifying and correcting the dissatisfiers, turnover will decline. This assumption is not necessarily correct. Employees leave a company for many reasons, of which dissatisfaction is but one. It is possible for a regional manager and the DMs to come up with a fine plan for reducing dissatisfaction that will have little, if any, impact on turnover. Thus, we must question the appropriateness, or validity, of this objective. A better objective would be: "What are the underlying reasons for employee turnover and what are the solutions for reducing turnover based on these reasons?"

Organizing a Meeting

Prior to a meeting there are a number of arrangements that should be made to enhance the likelihood of a successful meeting. Box 4.5 provides a list of premeeting tasks that should be considered.

BOX 4.5

TAKING CARE OF ALL PREMEETING ARRANGEMENTS

- Consider the physical setup—room size, seating, noise level, climate and ventilation, possible interference, audiovisual needs, and lighting.
- Arrange for coffee breaks.

(continued)

BOX 4.5 *(Continued)*

- Publicize and promote meeting. There will be no discussion if people do not show up.
- Identify/gather materials needed by participants—be sure that discussion outlines, handouts, and other materials are ready for distribution and assign someone to this task.
- Determine the time of the meeting.
- Identify the recording method(s).
- Notes to be taken by participants? Or will electronic material be available after the meeting.
- Notes to be taken by recording secretary?
- Minutes to be issued following meeting?
- Use of overhead monitor during meeting?
- Estimate the anticipated length of meeting.
- Determine who should attend (only after establishing focus and formulating purpose, outcome, and objectives).
- Formulate meeting announcement or agenda to contain
  - Subject.
  - Purpose of meeting.
  - Meeting date, time, and duration.
  - Location.
  - Recording method(s).
  - Participants.
  - Background material.
  - Outcome expected.
  - Telephone number that can be used if people have issues getting to meeting.

Send all of the above mentioned out to meeting participants prior to the meeting by at least several days, if not a week!

Agendas are the most necessary item for having successful meetings. A sample meeting agenda is displayed in Table 4.3.

Although a lot of material on planning has been presented, the next stage on conducting a meeting is as difficult, if not more so, for some people.

Conducting/Participating in Meetings

While conducting or participating in meetings, you must continue to be aware of both content and process. Just as the managerial functions of planning and organizing were linked to the preparation stage, the directing and controlling functions link to the conducting of meetings. Let us focus on the content of how to conduct a meeting. You must maintain focus during the meeting on the "what you want to accomplish, why you want to accomplish it, and how you will accomplish it" (the agenda). You have already prepared and sent out the agenda; now briefly review the agenda headings and start the meeting.

Make an effective beginning. Group members will participate more freely and meaningfully if they feel a meeting has been carefully planned in advance and is getting off to a good start.

TABLE 4.3 **Sample Meeting Agenda**

Subject:
Purpose of meeting:
To:
From:
Meeting Date/Time and Duration:
Location:
Meeting Leader(s):
Minute Taker:
Participants:
Background material:
Please bring:

TOPIC	OUTCOME EXPECTED AND DISCUSSION/ DECISIONS	ACTION	PERSON(S)	TIMELINE
ANNOUNCEMENTS				
APPROVAL OF PRIOR MINUTES				
OLD BUSINESS				
COMMITTEE ACTION				
NEW BUSINESS				
ADJOURNMENT				Next meeting scheduled for:

Therefore, do not leave anything to chance. Conversely, know when to not be rigid or respond negatively if the unplanned happens. You need to ensure that everything that was outlined for the meeting was covered and that the group did not deviate from its purpose by getting caught up in ramblings or become hyperfocused on one topic while neglecting the others. When a particular topic seems to require additional time and discussion, then an ad hoc committee or follow-up meeting can be coordinated. Leaders and managers can adopt qualities of pacesetting leadership style, especially when facilitating meetings about project management tasks. Pacesetting can help the meeting facilitator take the meeting topics and stages in stride, while staying committed to outcomes. The suggestions in Box 4.6 will increase the likelihood of a productive meeting.

BOX 4.6

START THE MEETING WITH APPROPRIATE AND EFFECTIVE DISCUSSION

- Always be brief.
- Adapt your opening remarks to the local situation.

(continued)

BOX 4.6 *(Continued)*

- Announce any rules of procedure (ELMO—or Enough Let's Move ON, turn off cell phones, do not talk while someone is speaking, decide on breaks or not, identify bathroom locations).

- Announce the topic(s), point out its timeliness and importance, and suggest possible approaches. Indicate the goal of the discussion.

- Make your opening statement thought-provoking, and give some suggestions for the first step in thinking through the problem.

- Try to develop an atmosphere in which participation is easy and in which the members feel secure, responsible for participation, and that the topic is not over their heads.

- Help the group members to get acquainted.

- Prime someone to lead off the discussion, if necessary.

- Where appropriate, encourage group members to develop procedures such as Robert's Rules of Order.

Box 4.7 discusses competencies/practice behaviors on modeling appropriate behavior at work.

BOX 4.7

NETWORK FOR SOCIAL WORK MANAGEMENT COMPETENCIES AND PRACTICE BEHAVIORS 4.7

Models appropriate professional behavior and encourages other staff members to act in a professional manner (Network for Social Work Management Competencies 4). Practice Behaviors:

- Demonstrates the ability not to be "consumed" by executive responsibilities and helps others to achieve the balance and maintain a sense of humor and perspective (4.7).

The best meetings have maximum participation. Involvement and participation are essentials for good discussion. Try to increase the extent of participation. Box 4.8 provides tips on encouraging relevant discussion at meetings.

BOX 4.8

CONTROLLING DISCUSSION AT MEETINGS

- When stimulating discussion, try to avoid questions that can be answered "yes" or "no."
- Test the information and evidence presented; test the reasoning.
- Do not push the discussion too fast; yet try to keep it orderly.
- Help the members improve the quality of communication, but do not embarrass them in the process.
- Try to keep the discussion from becoming just a series of questions and answers.

(continued)

BOX 4.8 *(Continued)*

- Have group members clarify unclear points.
- Know enough about the subject so that you are in a position to help others.
- Maintain a sense of humor and perspective.

During meetings, encourage democratic progress. Progress is always an aim in discussion, but it should be democratic; leaders and participants, rather than a leader or leaders, should make decisions on content and procedure jointly. Employing a democratic leadership style can promote organizational responsibility and empower teams to share ideas and be active problem solvers.

Box 4.9 displays the Network for Social Work Management Competencies and Practice Behaviors 5.4–5.6.

BOX 4.9

NETWORK FOR SOCIAL WORK MANAGEMENT COMPETENCY AND PRACTICE BEHAVIORS 5.4–5.6

Manages diversity and cross-cultural understanding (Network for Social Work Management Competencies 5). Practice Behaviors:

- Seeks input from all levels of staff, listens attentively, demonstrates fairness and consistency, and conveys information fully and clearly (5.4)
- Invites different perspectives to all client-related and management discussions within the organization (5.5).
- Encourages and allows opportunities for staff to confer and present issues and problems affecting program-related services (5.6).

Box 4.10 discusses different keys to facilitating good discussion at meetings.

BOX 4.10

KEYS TO GOOD DISCUSSION AT MEETINGS

Keep the discussions orderly and logical.

- Point out the significance of the topic early in the discussion.
- Be sure the problem or the goal is clearly defined.
- Suggest and explore all possible solutions.
- Insist on testing the facts, evidence, and reasoning.
- Chart the progress of the discussion.
- Call attention to fallacies in reasoning.

(continued)

BOX 4.10 *(Continued)*

Keep the discussion on the target.

- Permit occasional sidetracks only as a means of relieving tension. Let the group members decide what they wish to do about digressions.
- Provide for frequent summaries to show the progress in discussion. Be sure these are accurate and reflect the thinking of the group.
- Restate the main problem occasionally.
- Use the screen to post ideas.

Keep the discussion moving toward the goal.

- Be sure the goal is understood by all.
- Make clear transitions from one point to another.
- Do not permit points to be considered past the point of interest.
- Use frequent summaries to indicate the progress made.
- Point out areas of agreement and disagreement.
- Do not belabor a point when needed information is missing.
- Obtain early decisions on procedural matters.

Keep the discussion inclusive.

- Be sure all phases of a topic are considered. Point out neglected ones.
- Do not take sides in the discussion. The person or group in the minority loses security whenever the leader is on the other side.
- Try to delay decisions that may be based on incomplete, inaccurate facts.
- Try to get optimum expression from all.

Creating a permissive atmosphere at meetings will encourage maximum participation. The resource potential of any discussion group cannot be utilized unless the members feel that their contributions are wanted and that they are secure in participating. The atmosphere of a discussion group or committee should be conducive to free, cooperative, and critical interaction. Box 4.11 displays how to create a permissive and accepting atmosphere at meetings.

BOX 4.11

PROTECT THE RIGHTS OF INDIVIDUALS AND MAINTAIN INFORMALITY AT MEETINGS

Protect the rights of individuals in the group.

- Protect the right of every individual to express his or her own opinion.
- Keep conflicts focused on issues, not on personalities.
- Do not force a person to talk if he does not want to.

(continued)

BOX 4.11 *(Continued)*

- Even if you think an expressed opinion is wrong, let the group correct it; do not set yourself up as the final arbiter.
- Do not push the group too fast; individual security may be lost and progress slowed.
- Try to be accepting or nonevaluative in reacting to comments by group members.

Maintain informality as keynote of discussion.

- Be sure that the discussants are acquainted with each other, if the group is not too large.
- Be patient, considerate, and friendly.
- Keep the discussion from becoming too "serious."
- Keep the use of status symbols to a minimum.
- Avoid keeping the group under constant pressure for decisions and action.
- Do all you can to create a comfortable and informal physical atmosphere.

Directing

Directing meetings is another important management function that, if done right, will result in productive meetings that are very focused. Who should direct meetings? There will be certain situations where, ideally, the person directing the meeting should not have a vested interest in meeting outcomes, for instance, when there is a sensitive matter that would benefit from outside consultation to lead the meeting. However, in such situations the meeting director must know enough about the purpose and underlying issues to effectively direct the discussion. Coleaders of two to three people can also be effective. Otherwise, it is unrealistic to have persons that do not have vested interests in the subject matter facilitate the meeting. For example, program directors and chairpersons must hold regular meetings with their teams of staff and it is improbable that they do not have a vested interest in the topics concerning the departments they lead. Box 4.12 discusses different tips for directing meetings.

BOX 4.12

TIPS ON DIRECTING MEETINGS

- Maintain focus of meetings by using
    - A purpose statement—what.
    - An expected outcome—why.
    - Objectives—how.
    - A recording method.
    - Anticipated (allotted) time and keep on schedule.
- Reaffirm the role of each participant, if possible.

(continued)

BOX 4.12 *(Continued)*

- Recognize everyone's contributions.
- Test understanding of issues.
- Move to closure on each objective.
- If you concentrate on the objectives of the meeting, you will achieve your outcomes and your purpose.
- At the end of the meeting, summarize the purpose and objectives of the meeting and review assigned responsibilities and timelines.

Controlling

We said earlier that adequate preparation will translate into power at the meeting. To exercise power and to move the meeting toward expectations, content preparation is necessary to direct the flow of the meeting, but process sensitivity is also needed to *control* its flow.

Seating location of all participants is important. The meeting leaders should be centrally located. Circular setups encourage full participation more than a classroom style. Minimizing distractions is also important to stay on schedule and produce positive outcomes. Use of voice (some do this very well without being conscious of it) can vary by volume, cadence, and emphasis. Knowing when to speak can help effectively control meetings. Questioning for understanding, direction, and relevance is also important. Reviewing the process periodically is also a good idea.

Box 4.13 displays the Network for Social Work Management Competencies and Practice Behaviors 9.4.

BOX 4.13

NETWORK FOR SOCIAL WORK MANAGEMENT COMPETENCIES AND PRACTICE BEHAVIORS 9.4

Demonstrates effective interpersonal and communication skills (Network for Social Work Management Competencies 9). Practice Behaviors:

- Manages communication in conflict and crisis situations in a competent and sensitive manner (9.4).

To deal with conflicts from both participants' and leaders' standpoints, you must first determine the characteristics of the person who is causing the conflict. People can exhibit many different types of behaviors, including saboteur, sniper, comedian, silent partner, denier, attention grabber, and side tracker. Some people play more than one of these roles.

To deal with conflict

- Listen, but do not debate.
- Talk privately with members who continually exhibit disruptive behavior.
- Turn negatives into positives.
- Encourage the group to share responsibility.

Maintaining necessary control of meetings is important. Control of discussion does not mean that the moderator or leader determines by him or herself what was said or decided, but rather that the members of the group follow their own rules. Control means that the leader acts accordingly so as to enable the group to achieve its goal(s) quickly and efficiently. Box 4.14 displays different types of psychological and physical controls.

BOX 4.14

UTILIZE THE ELEMENTS OF PSYCHOLOGICAL AND PHYSICAL CONTROL

Utilize the element of psychological control.

- Try to maintain the position of referee. Do not dominate action but instead direct attention. You will "control" the group more easily if members perceive you as a natural referee.

- Do not exercise control over the decisions of the group, but call attention to the ramifications of those decisions.

- Abide by predetermined rules of procedure so that decisions will be made democratically by all.

- Do not avoid conflict, but keep focused on issues. Point out the value of conflict in suggesting possible alternative points of view.

- Take positive and decisive action when action is in the interest of the group. Your decisiveness will develop the group's confidence in you as a leader.

- Try to keep the discussants from idea possessiveness, from feeling that they must defend the points they make.

- Emphasize "we" not "I."

- Employ observers for evaluation and control.

- Maintain the physical appearance of being interested in what is taking place.

Utilize the element of physical control.

- Do not permit aside conversation by a few to disturb the process of discussion.

- Avoid lengthy speeches by a few.

- Be sure that everyone hears all comments. Do not hesitate to ask group members to speak up. Control is easily lost when members do not hear.

- The comfort of the group members is important. Check lighting, room temperature, and seating arrangements.

- Announce rules of procedure before a discussion starts; later it will be easier to enforce these rules. Where appropriate, encourage members to develop procedures.

- Be sure to make all audiovisual arrangements in advance. Few audiences like to wait—nor should they be asked to do so—while someone repairs or locates electronic setups.

- Make constant use of flip charts or projector screens. When members of the audience see an outline of the discussion, or a record of the decisions they have made, they are less likely to lose interest in the discussion.

One final point about meetings is that closing the discussion effectively will impact follow-through. Too frequently the closure of a discussion leaves much to be desired. This step is no less important than the conclusion of a speech. Plan it carefully, do not hurry it, provide a meaningful summary, indicate the next steps to be taken, if any, and give proper credit. Always summarize main points and next steps to be sure everyone is on board with the future actions. Box 4.15 discusses ways to end meetings well.

BOX 4.15

MAKE THE ENDING DEFINITE FROM THE POINT OF VIEW OF CONTENT AND PROCEDURE

Make the ending definite from the point of view of content.

- The final summary should indicate the progress made, differences resolved and unresolved, and possible avenues of future action, and should also review recommendations and decisions made.
- Indicate how reports of the discussion are to be distributed or made available to the discussants.
- Secure a consensus of future dates for meetings and other follow-ups.
- Suggest reading and studying references for future meetings.

Make the ending definite from the point of view of procedure.

- Faithfully observe the time limits. End the discussion before everyone is talked out and leave enough time for a final summary.
- Involve members of the group in making the final summary, if possible.
- Be sure to make assignments for follow-up.
- Give proper credit to the leaders and participants.
- Provide for a method of postmeeting evaluation. Allow time for a quick analysis and report of the evaluation.

We do not intend the above list of leadership tasks to be complete. The suggestions do, however, provide a guide for use in patterning one's own leadership style.

Styles of Leadership for Different Settings

If there is heavy *Content* emphasis, then you should exhibit

- Strong planning in preparation.
- Strong directing in conducting.

If there is heavy *Process* emphasis, then you should exhibit

- Strong organizing in preparation.
- Strong control in conducting.

Another way of looking at styles of leadership is addressed in Table 4.4.

TABLE 4.4 Functions of Leadership for Different Settings

PREPARATION FOCUSES ON	Planning and developing	Content
AND		
CONDUCT FOCUSES ON	Organizing and controlling	Process

Leadership styles that seem to fit this kind of interaction are displayed in Table 4.5.

TABLE 4.5 Leadership Styles for Different Types of Interactions

High Direction : Autocrat High Control	Low Direction : Facilitator (process consultant) High Control
High Direction : Coordinator Low Control	Low Direction : Participant Low Control

Since many of us, even leaders and managers, attend more meetings than we conduct, we can be just as frustrated in this role, so let us look at some things that we might do as participants to make meetings more effective. Box 4.16 displays the participant role in effective meetings.

BOX 4.16

PARTICIPANT ROLE IN EFFECTIVE MEETINGS
Prepare

Ask

- Why am I going to this meeting anyway?
- What is expected of me?
- Who/what am I representing?

Know

- What are the expected outcomes, objectives, issues?
- Who is going to participate?
- Where is the meeting going to be?
- When (and how long) will the meeting be?

(continued)

BOX 4.16 (*Continued*)

- ▩ Why is the meeting being held? (What's the purpose?)
- ▩ Know your position on the issue(s)!

Participate

- ▩ Listen for a statement of purpose.
- ▩ Know your fellow participants.
- ▩ Listen, speak, listen.
- ▩ Look for closure to issues (outcomes).
- ▩ Ask relevant questions to the topic under discussion to meeting objective(s).
- ▩ Ask for clarity when you don't understand.
- ▩ Press for closure on the issues!

Who is responsible for making a meeting work, the leader or the participant? Answer: BOTH! Now that the meeting is over, are we finished? Answer: NO! We need to consider one last thing.

▩ Following Up on Meetings

As we said before, more than a third of the success of a meeting depends on effective follow-up. How many times do you come out of a meeting feeling that you really accomplished something only to discover that a month later nothing was ever implemented? Why?
Answer: Ineffective follow-up.

Meetings are a means to an end! We emphasized *outcomes* of meeting. Follow-up starts in preparation of the meeting. Preparation includes the following:

- ▩ Planning—Outcomes.
- ▩ Organizing—Minutes to be taken? Notes to be taken? Computers or easels to be used?
- ▩ Directing—Who, what, where, and when?
- ▩ Controlling—Make visible and state verbally the above.

Identify follow-up responsibilities as you go along in meetings and make them visible. Types of follow-up include phone calls, emails, instant messages, letters, minutes, another meeting, or any combination depending on the nature of follow-up actions identified. If you are specific on who, when, where, and so on, your chances for success are greatly enhanced.

How can we put this information into practice? Start by implementing some of the many activities listed in the previous boxes. Concentrate on one box per meeting. Then move on to another box at the next meeting until you master the content of all boxes. Obviously you use much of this material in meetings now, but by focusing on one box at a time you will eventually incorporate all of these actions.

The last thing that may be of value in planning meetings is a *checklist(s),* which is probably the most comprehensive meeting preparation list that you will ever see. Even though you may never go down it item for item, you may find it useful and you can add to it also.

A Checklist for Planning Meetings

It is so easy to forget crucial items in the planning of meetings—some materials you wanted to have available, the telephone call to the custodian, the name tags, extra minutes of the last meeting, and many others. Using a checklist as a part of planning and leading meetings can prove to be indispensable. The checklists on the following pages should be a good starter, ones you can add to because all meetings, of course, are different—not every item is relevant for every meeting. But, in our experience, the main headings and most of the items are quite universal.

The checklist is organized under 10 separate headings or checklists:

1. Publicity—Promotion—Notifying
2. Agenda and Resource Materials
3. Responsibilities at the Meeting
4. Meeting Space Checkout
5. Equipment of the Meeting
6. Materials for the Meeting
7. Budget
8. Action Just Before the Meeting
9. Action at the Meeting
10. End of Meeting Action

CHECKLIST 1: **Publicity—Promotion—Notifying**

PUBLICITY—PROMOTION—NOTIFYING	WHO IS RESPONSIBLE	BY WHEN
Notices to whom		
Letters of invitation		
Direction to meeting place		
Phone calls		
News releases		
Contact with media		
Copies of speeches		
Copies of meeting plan		
Pictures/photographs		
Bulletin boards		
Personal contacts		
Other		

CHECKLIST 2: **Agenda and Resource Materials**

RESOURCE MATERIALS	WHO IS RESPONSIBLE	BY WHEN
Copies of agenda		
Contact people on the agenda		
Materials needed (e.g., reprints)		
Previous minutes		
Committee reports		
Previous agreement and time commitments		
Other		

CHECKLIST 3: **Responsibilities at the Meeting**

RESPONSIBILITIES	WHO IS RESPONSIBLE
Leadership assignments	
Documentation or recording assignments	
"Hosting" roles	
Making reports	
Trying out equipment	
Test whether charts, posters are readable	
Preview films for timing and content	
Other	

CHECKLIST 4: **Meeting Space Checkout**

MEETING SPACE CHECKOUT	WHO IS RESPONSIBLE	BY WHEN
Size and shape of space		
Access to meeting room		
Electrical outlets		
Mic outlet		
Names of custodian and tech person and where to be reached		
Acoustics		
Private space for telephone use		
Doors		

(continued)

CHECKLIST 4: Meeting Space Checkout *(Continued)*

MEETING SPACE CHECKOUT	WHO IS RESPONSIBLE	BY WHEN
Wall space for newsprints, etc.		
Bathrooms (where, number.)		
Emotional impact (color, aesthetics)		
Stairs		
Elevators		
Heat/cold regulators		
Ventilation		
Parking facilities (number and access)		
Registration area		
Location		
Room setup arrangements		
Other		

CHECKLIST 5: Equipment for the Meeting

EQUIPMENT	WHO IS RESPONSIBLE	BY WHEN
Tables (number, size, shape)		
Chairs (comfort, number)		
Microphones		
Video or teleconference lines		
Waste baskets		
Extension cords		
Overhead projector and computer linkup		
Coffee, tea dispensers		
Water pitchers		
Cups		
Extension cords		
Duplication equipment		
Other		

CHECKLIST 6: **Materials and Supplies for the Meeting**

MATERIALS AND SUPPLIES	WHO IS RESPONSIBLE
Name tags/tents	
Small- and large-tip felt pens	
Self-adhesive flip chart paper and stand	
Reprints of articles	
Copies of previous minutes	
Copies of reports	
Visual aids	
Directional signs to meeting	
File folders	
Other	

CHECKLIST 7: **Budget for Meeting**

BUDGET COSTS	COST ESTIMATE
Mailing and stamps	
Telephone calls	
Telephone conferences	
Rental equipment	
Rental space	
Paper material (name tags, paper)	
Writing materials (pens, markers)	
Secretarial time	
Transportation	
Meals	
Soda, coffee, tea, juice, water	
Reproduction of materials	
Folders	
Income	**Estimated Income**
Registration fees	
Sale of materials	
Grants	
Sale of meal tickets	

(*continued*)

CHECKLIST 7: **Budget for Meeting** *(Continued)*

BUDGET COSTS	COST ESTIMATE
Donations	
Member fees	
Coffee and tea charges	
Other	

CHECKLIST 8: **Action Just Before the Meeting**

JUST BEFORE THE MEETING	WHO IS RESPONSIBLE
Seating arrangements—general	
Session and subgroupings	
Extra chairs	
Extra tables	
P.A. system checkout	
Equipment (easels, screens, etc.)	
Materials (paper, pens, etc.)	
Tapes	
Operator of projection equipment	
Operator of P.A. equipment	
Speaker fees	
Consultant fees	
Entertainment	
Film reproduction	
Tape reproduction	
Water, glasses	
Thermostat	
Opening and closing windows	
Refreshment setup	
Registration setup	
Check that charts, etc. can be seen everywhere	
Agendas available	
Other materials available for handouts	
Name tags/tents	

(continued)

CHECKLIST 8: **Action Just Before the Meeting** *(Continued)*

JUST BEFORE THE MEETING	WHO IS RESPONSIBLE
Table numbers	
Coffee, tea, etc.	
Evaluation forms ready	
Reproduction equipment	
Audiovisual equipment	
Other	

CHECKLIST 9: **Action at the Meeting**

ACTION AT THE MEETING	WHO IS RESPONSIBLE
Meeting, greeting, seating of participants and guests	
Greeting of latecomers	
Evaluation activity	
Handing out materials	
Operation of equipment	
Announcements	
Other	

CHECKLIST 10: **End of Meeting Action**

END OF MEETING ACTION	PERSON RESPONSIBLE
Collect unused materials	
Return equipment	
Clean up and move back tables and chairs	
Thank helpers	
Read and analyze evaluation/feedback	
Prepare feedback on feedback	
Email follow-up materials	
Remind people of their follow-up	
Commitments—phone/write	
Lay plans for next meeting; dates if there is to be one	
Pay bills	
Other	

A few ideas about the use of these checklists

For your meetings, you may want to create an abbreviated checklist. We suggest you reproduce whatever checklists are appropriate for you, making enough copies so that you and your coworkers can use one for each planning activity. Then you will also have it available to hand to volunteers and other associates to help and support in their planning and leading of meetings. Use the following questions after a meeting to evaluate meeting effectiveness.

- What behaviors helped or hindered the consensus-seeking process?
- What patterns of decision making occurred?
- Who were the influential members and how were they influential?
- How did the group discover and use its information resources?
- Were there resources fully utilized?
- What are the implications of consensus-seeking and synergistic outcomes for intact task groups such as committees and staffs of institutions?
- What consequences might such a process produce in the group's attitudes?

Some Traps in Planning and Conducting Meetings

One of the greatest resources for all of us is the ability to learn from our achievements. Another good resource is the opportunity to learn from our mistakes, and from others who have "tried that before" and have been innovative in finding ways to avoid traps and improve upon their successes.

The planning and conducting of thousands of meetings have preceded the ones you are planning this year. To avoid even a few of these mistakes and to learn from some of the many creative inventions will greatly increase your skills and success.

Here are a few of the most critical traps to planning and leading of successful meetings. No doubt you can add to these right now from your experience, and hopefully will be able to identify, analyze, and share additional traps during the next year. Box 4.17 displays some traps during planning and preparation of meetings and Box 4.18 displays traps during the meeting.

BOX 4.17

TRAPS DURING PLANNING AND PREPARATION

- *Meeting planners often plan with no data about the participants, their hopes, and expectations about the purpose of the meeting.* Often meetings are planned in a vacuum with no idea about who is coming, why they are coming, or really what specifically ought to be accomplished at the meeting. It is critical to plan and prepare fully as discussed earlier and, if one does not have the needed information, discover ways of getting it.

- *Lack of involvement in the planning by those who will be at the meeting.* When potential participants are not involved in some way they will probably not take an active part, or they may not even come. They feel they have been planned for, so their attitude is: let the planners do it; we have no "ownership" of this meeting!

- *Beautiful, but illegible, visual aids.* So often visual aids are produced that are visually very pleasing but have not been tried out in large rooms or have not been tested for the distance from which they can be seen (e.g., font size on a screen). Be sure to check all your visual aids beforehand and all pieces of equipment in the room where they are to be used.

(continued)

BOX 4.17 *(Continued)*

- *Same meeting, same place and plan, same time.* Though sameness gives security to some; it bores others. Why not vary the meeting place and time to suit different people of the group? Or ask group members what, where, when they would like to meet next time. If the meeting extends for a whole day or longer, and participants keep going back to the same seats, suggest they change.

- *Holding meetings only because they are scheduled to be held.* If there is no real reason or agenda for a meeting, why hold it? Yes, even if it is a planned monthly meeting. Can you imagine how motivated members would feel for the next meeting if they could count on it being really meaty and full of content, knowing that if there would be nothing to discuss, you would cancel it?

- *Equipment that does not work.* Check your equipment beforehand, but even when equipment checks out, it sometimes breaks down at the same time you most need it. Have an alternative plan up your sleeve, just in case.

- *Lack of plans if extra people turn up.* Often meetings projected for 50 people have 75–100 people. It is important to have some contingency plans. In case that happens, is there a way to move or walk to a larger room? And/or extra chairs? Or, if the opposite happens, fewer people than were planned for, can the room be made cozy and useful in some way, rather than have people feel as though they are rattling around in an empty room?

- *The unbriefed resource person or speaker who comes in and has no idea about what you really wanted and what the group is like, and gives the usual canned speech that is always given on that particular topic by that particular person.* It is extremely important to brief people beforehand whom you want as resource persons for your meeting. These briefings can be done over the telephone, by email, or in person, depending on the situation. Sometimes the resource person will send an outline of what she or he will cover.

- *No agenda, or the one that omits, among the items, a review of the purposes for this particular meeting.* For some meetings no agenda exists or, if it does, it is only in the head and maybe the hand of the leader. Also it is important to review and communicate the purposes of each meeting.

- *Too many items/activities planned for the time available.* This is a trap that many meetings fall into and a realistic plan is needed in relation to how much time various items or activities will take. If you have more items than the time allows, then cut out some items, or else arrange to put them in as pieces you can work on in small groups after the meeting or substitute these for items of lower priorities.

BOX 4.18

TRAPS DURING THE MEETING

- *No sharing of agenda.* There is only one copy of the agenda available, and the chairperson has it. It is hard for participants/members to feel involved when they cannot see and hear the plans of the meeting. Putting the agenda on a screen will solve this problem.

(continued)

BOX 4.18 (*Continued*)

- *Formal, classroom style seating, or rows of chairs all facing the front.* This setup gives the participants the nonverbal clue that all action and wisdom come from the front of the room. It makes it hard to participate actively. The only reason to have this kind of room setup is when the seats are fastened to the floor. Then participants must be helped to participate in special ways, such as two turning around to the two behind them to talk, or a stand-up break of trios or quintets to discuss a particular question. So long as there are moveable chairs, they can be in a circle or small semicircle or around the tables, or other ways that invite and facilitate communication.

- *Meeting starts with nothing to do for early arrivers.* If you know that your meeting will have a "raggedy start," plan something for early arrivers to do, discuss, or think about. It may be a question you want them to discuss, or it may be the use of the paired interview. There needs to be some programmed ways to utilize the prestarting time constructively.

- *Long introductions of speakers, consultants, helpers, etc.* Such introductions usually produce psychological distance between them and the participants. If you need an extensive introduction/background material on a person in order to acquaint the audience with that person, have those materials photocopied for everyone beforehand or give them out at the beginning of the meeting. Then you can give a short, warm, relevant welcome instead of a long introduction. Often the speakers have ideas on how they would like to be introduced.

- *Long, drawn out speakers, reporters, panels, etc.* Often people go over the time limits they have been given. It is important to go over the ground rules with them at the beginning of the meeting again, after having done so in preparing them to participate. And often it is well to reinforce this publicly by saying to all present "the time of the following presentation is approximately 12 minutes," or "I have discussed with our presenters the amount of time available, so don't worry if I give a warning when the time is almost up."

- *Total reliance on one expert at the meeting, rather than utilizing that person to help uncork the resources of all the participants.* Sometimes it is better to have more than one resource person available so that alternatives can be more openly and fully identified.

- *Too long coffee breaks are often a waste of time and money, and also disrupt the continuity.* Why not have coffee and tea available throughout the meeting and design the meeting in such a way that there will be moving around and stand-up time as part of the way the work of the meeting gets done?

- *Failure to deal with feelings of participants.* Often groups are so task-oriented that they skip even obvious feeling issues that need to be dealt with in order to better proceed with the task. For example, if people are very hostile to one another, it is important to deal with that hostility than overlook it. The task will get done so much better with civility.

- *No record of what has been done or what has been said.* Often, when you most want to go back to what happened at a meeting, there is no record of the proceedings. It is important that for every meeting there is some way to keep its major deliberations and work in documented form. This documentation can then become the history of that meeting and of plans, decisions, commitments made. Put all minutes in an electronic archive.

- *Neglecting to carry the group "into the future" to guarantee that the work of the meeting will pay off.* Be sure that decisions and commitments are made about who will do what and when to follow through.

We hope this list will be helpful in ensuring better meetings for you, your participants, and your programs.

SUMMARY

This chapter provided extensive information on how to make meetings productive. The importance of employing leadership tasks in planning, preparing, and conducting meetings was highlighted, as was using alternative leadership styles in different settings. Setting the purpose and objectives of a meeting was covered, along with how to follow up on a meeting's action outcomes. Important tips on how to effectively participate in a meeting were displayed. A variety of checklists for preparing and running a meeting were provided, as were some tips in planning and conducting a meeting.

ACTIVITIES

1. List at least five leaderships styles and identify how each style can be modified for the purpose of planning, organizing, directing, or controlling meetings (Table 4.3).

2. Using Table 4.3, create a mock agenda for an upcoming meeting (this may be for an internship placement or employment, student group meeting, etc.).

3. Describe the ways leaders and managers can follow up on meeting agenda items that have been approved and assigned for action.

REFERENCES

Commonwealth of Pennsylvania, Department of Public Welfare. (1987). *Effective meetings course.* Harrisburg, PA: Author.

Pennsylvania State University, Department of Speech Communications, Program in Continuing Education. (1987). *Leadership tasks in discussion; and a checklist for planning meetings.* Harrisburg, PA: Author.

Shulman, L. (2016). *The skills of helping individuals, families, groups, and communities.* 8th Ed. Cengage Learning. Boston, MA.

Yalom, I. D. (2005). *The theory and practice of group psychotherapy* (5th ed.). New York, NY: Basic Books.

CHAPTER 5

PROBLEM SOLVING AND DECISION MAKING IN SOCIAL WORK

CHAPTER OBJECTIVES

- Understanding a taxonomy of comprehension for leadership decision making.
- Understanding the various approaches to decision making.
- Knowing when to use individual versus group decision making.
- Understanding and employing the general guidelines and steps in decision making.
- Understanding and employing situation appraisal (SA) to clarify the situation in need of resolution, how to outline concerns and problems, and choose a direction.
- Understanding and employing problem analysis (PA) to determine and define the cause of the problem.
- Understanding and employing PA to resolve people's problems.
- Understanding and employing decision analysis (DA) to identify alternatives and analyze risks.
- Understanding and employing potential problem analysis (PPA) to scrutinize the best alternative against potential problems and negative consequences and actions proposed to minimize risk.
- Employing the PA short-form approach when necessary and appropriate.
- Employing the short-form bits and pieces analysis when necessary and appropriate.
- Understanding how to critique the decision-making process.
- Identifying pitfalls of decision making and employing solutions to overcome them.

INTRODUCTION

This chapter provides extensive detail on several types of problem-solving and decision-making strategies and also offers a wide range of approaches for leaders and managers to employ for resolving problems and considering decisions. This chapter presents various organizational approaches to decision making; it also discusses when to use groups for decision making along with the pros and cons of such decisions. The authors present a 12-step process for decision making and full approaches to the four stages of problem solving and decision making: *situation appraisal (SA), problem analysis (PA), decision analysis (DA),* and *potential problem analysis (PPA).* In addition, a PA methodology is presented for dealing with people problems. Finally, several short-form versions of DA are presented.

In keeping with the notion of parallel process, social work practice principles can align with how leaders and managers approach decision making and problem solving. Just as a savvy clinician knows that the facilitative process with clients requires the use of good, thoughtful questions, sagacious leaders and managers also view questions as the foundation to resolving problems and judiciously and collaboratively reaching decisions. Emerging leaders and managers may initially feel unsure about how to strategically maneuver through complex organizational issues or steer programmatic changes; however, borrowing from practice experiences such as facilitating group work, performing client assessments, and developing treatment plans is a skill that can coextend to the processes related to decision making and problem solving.

All organizations make decisions on a daily basis in response to problems and issues that negatively impact them; some decisions are better informed than others. But *who* should make decisions, *when* should decisions be made, and *how*? It usually falls to the leadership of the organization to start the process. But what is required first? Understanding a taxonomy of comprehension for leadership decision making is a good start. If leaders can master some of the cognitive domains under a taxonomy of comprehension, they will be in a better position to manage the problem-solving and decision-making processes.

Box 5.1 displays the competencies/behaviors in this chapter.

BOX 5.1

COMPETENCIES AND PRACTICE BEHAVIORS ADDRESSED IN THIS CHAPTER

Establishes, promotes, and anchors the vision, philosophy, goals, objectives, and values of the organization (Network for Social Work Management Competencies 1). Practice Behaviors:

- Demonstrates the manner in which the vision, philosophy, and values are applied in making organizational decisions (1.6).

Possesses analytical and critical thinking skills that promote organizational growth (Network for Social Work Management Competencies 3). Practice Behaviors:

- Understands and makes use of historical and current data to inform decision making about the agency (3.4).
- Demonstrates strong critical thinking and problem solving skills (3.6).

Initiates and facilitates innovative change processes (Network for Social Work Management Competencies 7). Practice Behaviors:

- Presents innovations to appropriate decision-makers and stakeholders and makes decisions that are aligned with their feedback (7.2).

(continued)

BOX 5.1 *(Continued)*

Encourages active involvement of all staff and stakeholders in decision-making processes (Network for Social Work Management Competencies 10). Practice Behaviors:

- Provides opportunities for internal and external stakeholders to give feedback before significant program changes are implemented (10.1).

- Shows evidence of stakeholder buy-in through such means as meetings or representative groups, and program surveys to the community (10.2).

- Delegates authority and decision making to appropriate entities and supports their decisions (10.3).

- Uses collaborative teams and other strategies to identify outcomes, design programs, share intervention strategies, conduct assessments, analyze results, and adjust intervention processes (10.4).

- Encourages consumers and underrepresented stakeholders to actively participate in decision-making processes (10.5).

- Displays the ability to work with people and institutions to achieve creative compromises and "win–win" solutions (10.6).

CSWE Competency 1: Demonstrate Ethical and Professional Behavior
Social workers:

- 1.1 Make ethical decisions by applying the standards of the NASW *Code of Ethics*, relevant laws and regulations, models for ethical decision making, ethical conduct of research, and additional codes of ethics as appropriate to context.

CSWE, Council on Social Work Education; NASW, National Association of Social Workers.

Taxonomy of Comprehension

This material on the taxonomy of comprehension for leadership decision making was adapted from a work group session at the Twenty-First Annual Conference: Academic Chairperson (Singleton, 2004), which posed the following question: *What is a taxonomy of comprehension and why does it provide a foundation for leadership development and decision making?* A taxonomy of comprehension for leadership decision making can

- Provide a role for thinking
- Provide a hierarchy for thinking
- Call attention to possible ideas not considered previously
- Encourage sophisticated thinking

Four taxonomies of comprehension by Benjamin Bloom, Thomas Barrett, W. S. Grady, and Lee Shulman (Singleton, 2004) are provided in Table 5.1, which displays a number of cognitive domains with organizational examples by different authors for application. Bloom's (1956) original taxonomy of comprehension concerning key cognitive domains was updated by changing the nouns to verbs by Anderson et al. (2001) and adding "creating and evaluating" to both synthesis and evaluation. All of these cognitive domains can be acquired over time and can be very useful in decision making. The authors of this book (Rofuth and Piepenbring) have added additional examples of verbs for these cognitive domains. An exercise on taxonomy is provided in Box 5.2.

TABLE 5.1 **Taxonomy of Comprehension and Key Cognitive Domains With Examples**

NOUN	VERB	ACTION	EXAMPLES
Bloom and Anderson et. al.	**Bloom and Anderson et. al.**	**Bloom and Anderson et. al.**	**Rofuth and Piepenbring**
Knowledge	Remembering	Ability to recall facts directly stated	Stating facts verbatim in meetings
Comprehension	Understanding	Ability to interpret and infer information	Using facts and information to make decisions that impact organizational functioning
Application	Applying	Ability to transfer information to a different context	Using case examples for different situations
Analysis	Analyzing	Ability to examine and classify information	Making sense out of data such as enrollment or service data and applying to organizational service targets
Synthesis	Creating and evaluating	Ability to organize information into a broader knowledge base	Using organizational management information data to better understand client outcomes
Evaluation	Creating and evaluating	Ability to assess using established criteria	Creating assessment criteria that matches organizational objectives
Barrett	**Rofuth and Piepenbring**	**Barrett**	**Rofuth and Piepenbring**
Literal	Categorize	Ability to recognize details and sequence information	Uncovering specific facts and reorganizing for review
Inference	Infer	Ability to summarize and classify information	Gathering data and packaging into report format
Evaluation	Evaluate	Ability to make a judgment of fact or opinion	Making a decision based on facts such as expanding some program offerings at the expense of others
Appreciation	Empathize	Ability to identify with the characters and/or incidents	Empathizing with situations to provide a better understanding of the impact of decisions
Gray	**Rofuth and Piepenbring**	**Gray**	**Rofuth and Piepenbring**
Recalling	Recall	Ability to recall stated facts	As previously stated under Knowledge domain: stating facts verbatim in meetings
Reading between the lines	Infer	Ability to infer information	Understanding the real meaning of statements on staff and/or program performance
Reading beyond the lines	Extrapolate	Ability to make a personal connection	Extrapolating outcomes from implied information

(continued)

TABLE 5.1 **Taxonomy of Comprehension and Key Cognitive Domains With Examples** *(Continued)*

NOUN	VERB	ACTION	EXAMPLES
Shulman	Rofuth and Piepenbring	Shulman	Rofuth and Piepenbring
Engagement	Engage	Ability to actively engage with information	Beginning the process to interpret and apply information that can impact organizational outcomes such as maintaining and improving programs
Understanding	Interpret	Ability to restate the situation using facts	Simplifying and linking facts to examples of organizational effectiveness
Performance	Action	Ability to take action using the information	Acting on information through a planned process to improve organizational functioning such as effective use of faculty and staff resources
Reflection	Think	Ability to think deeply about the action being taken	Working effectively with individual faculty and/or staff in fair evaluations for performance reviews and in recommendations for promotion decisions
Judgment	Decide	Ability to compare outcomes to criteria	Similar to Evaluation cognitive domain: creating assessment criteria that matches organizational objectives and making decisions related to individual faculty and staff with fairness and objectivity
Commitment	Commit	Ability to use information to make a difference in the world	Expanding program offerings and assuring continuance of service

A new cognitive domain at the forefront today is deciphering alternative facts. Because social workers work with human beings, it is simply "human nature" that perceptions about what is factual or objective, rather than subjective, will inevitably come into play. Even when people believe that they are sticking to the facts, subjectivity can creep in by way of presenting facts in a fashion that exaggerates or prioritizes, presenting only some of the facts based on what the person perceives to be paramount. Thus the true facts are sometimes overlooked because it is human nature that some people will produce alternative facts, which can inadvertently derail teams from analyzing the full, or objective, picture. Modifying or exaggerating facts is a common practice, but *alternative facts* are usually the exact opposite of the true facts. Determining what is true and how to obtain agreement with staff on what is true is the challenge. A good practice is to double-check the facts. Then what is needed is a shared agreement of the facts.

BOX 5.2

TAXONOMY OF COMPREHENSION EXERCISE

Practice using different cognitive domains (Noun/Verb listed in the following box) each week. Complete the last column by reflecting on how you use/apply each domain.

Taxonomy of Comprehension and Key Cognitive Domains Applied

NOUN	VERB	HOW YOU USE/APPLY EACH DOMAIN
Knowledge	Remembering	
Comprehension	Understanding	
Application	Applying	
Analysis	Analyzing	
Synthesis	Creating and evaluating	
Evaluation	Creating and evaluating	
Literal	Categorize	
Inference	Infer	
Evaluation	Evaluate	
Appreciation	Empathize	
Recalling	Recall	
Reading between the lines	Infer	
Reading beyond the lines	Extrapolate	
Engagement	Engage	
Understanding	Interpret	
Performance	Action	
Reflection	Think	
Judgment	Decide	
Commitment	Commit	

Box 5.3 provides examples of general concerns or decisions that typically occur in organizations. These examples can be used to generate ideas for the exercises later in this chapter.

BOX 5.3

CASE AND EXERCISE QUESTIONS THAT WILL HELP GENERATE TOPICS FOR CASES AND EXERCISES

1. What current concerns involve something going wrong (in any area—people, administration, policy, clients, students, day-to-day operations, etc.) for which you do not know the cause?
2. What concerns involve something that's going right, but that you think could be improved?
3. What concerns involve something that may or may not be going wrong now, but that goes wrong on a recurring basis?
4. What current concerns required you to make a final decision on the best of two or more alternatives (you may be choosing people, administration, policy, clients, students, day-to-day operations, etc.)?
5. What current concerns involve a need for you to select the best alternative, which you will recommend to the person who will make the final decision?
6. What recurring decisions do you (or does your group) have to make, regardless of whether you are facing the choice right now (e.g., personnel selection, workload distribution, program design, or policies)?
7. Regardless of whether you participated in the decision making or planning, what current projects/plans are you responsible for implementing?
8. What kinds of recurring situations require you to look toward the future to anticipate and prevent events that could harm your plans?
9. What *changes* that impact your operation are about to occur?
10. In your opinion, what is the greatest threat (internal or external) that faces your operation?
11. In your opinion, what is the greatest opportunity that faces your operation?

SOURCE: Management Supervisory Development Program. (1986). *Problem solving and decision making* Harrisburg, PA Department of Public Welfare, Commonwealth of Pennsylvania.

VARIOUS APPROACHES TO DECISION MAKING

Box 5.4 displays the competencies/behaviors in this section.

BOX 5.4

NETWORK FOR SOCIAL WORK MANAGEMENT COMPETENCIES AND PRACTICE BEHAVIORS 10

Encourages active involvement of all staff and stakeholders in decision-making processes (Network for Social Work Management Competencies 10). Practice Behaviors:

- Delegates authority and decision making to appropriate entities and supports their decisions (10.3).

Prior to the start of the problem-solving and decision-making process, you should decide who will start, lead, and complete the process. However, delegating to the appropriate staff is the first critical action, and, of course, an alternative is to lead the effort yourself. Once started, the process needs to be fully supported, and the decisions publicly reinforced. If using a committee, make sure it is the correct one for the task and that the committee chairperson is capable of leading the effort. As the decision-making process commences, the leader should support both the process and the decisions.

There are multiple approaches to decision making and organizations should consider these options carefully based on the capability of the staff of the organization, timing factors in terms of when a decision must be made and implemented, whether the decision will impact the short- or long-term future of the organization, the importance of the goals and objectives of the organization in relation to the particular issue or problem that requires a decision, whether and how the environment will change in the near future, the adaptability of the decision, and whether the issue is a hot political or personal item.

Golensky (2011) summarized the strengths of various approaches to decision making, including optimizing, satisficing, incrementalism, the garbage can model, mixed scanning, the four-force model, and consensus. Table 5.2 provides variations of these approaches along with assumptions, suggestions, and examples about each.

TABLE 5.2 Approaches to Decision Making

APPROACH	ASSUMPTIONS	SUGGESTIONS AND EXAMPLES
Rational	Any number of rational processes can be applied, taking into account problem identification, option discussions, and best possible solutions with the least adverse consequences.	Few organizations have the time and expertise to engage in this approach. Because it is at the heart of the rational decision-making process model, it is difficult to employ unless someone is trained in the process or an outside consultant is hired. It also takes time and commitment to see it through.
Acceptability	Not necessarily the best overall solution, but this approach is the best within the current situation.	This approach is used frequently by agencies and academic committees because the rational approach won't work.
Slight modification of the status quo	Maintaining the status quo with only minimal modifications is the goal of all decisions.	This approach can happen without much effort or thought. The way of least resistant can prevail. People always resist change so the least amount of change has a better chance of acceptance.
Crisis response decision making	The organization does not have a stable decision-making process or a strategic plan in place. As a result, decisions are made on a daily or short-term basis without spending time on investigating the problems and issues, but instead responding with quick resolutions which may or may not resolve the issue in the long run.	One frequent tactic is to create ad hoc committees to deal with new issues instead of using existing structures.

(continued)

TABLE 5.2 **Approaches to Decision Making** *(Continued)*

APPROACH	ASSUMPTIONS	SUGGESTIONS AND EXAMPLES
Mixed methods	This approach accepts a combination of the rational and the maintaining the status quo approaches, depending on the situation and time and resources available.	The combination adds some rationality to the maintaining the status quo approach. The basic tenets of rational decision making can be used to maintain some aspects of the current situation.
Pressure and influence from above	Preferred decisions are suggested by higher level authorities or for political purposes for which some decisions must be made.	Sometimes choices can be negotiated with higher level authorities. Providing additional information on possible negative impacts of a decision may influence these authorities.
Group agreement or consensus	A shared decision-making process involves everyone that the decision might impact. Members agree on a decision although it might not be the best choice for all.	After long meetings, people more readily compromise to end the process. Sometimes trading solutions resolves differences, which typically occurs with academic committees.

SOURCE: Adapted from Golensky, M. (2011). Strategic leadership and management in nonprofit organizations: Theory and practice. Chicago, CA: Lyceum Books.

At the outset of any decision-making process, participants should agree on which approach or which combinations of approaches should occur. Frequently, organizations will combine the various approaches. For example, in an academic environment, consensus is required but optimizing may be used if there are sufficient time and resources, and satisficing may be required if members of the decision-making team have certain agendas, and finally incrementalism may occur if the process is drawn out over time. An even more simplistic approach proposed by Klein (1993) is the "recognition primed model," which proposes that one does not actually compare any options but instead chooses an option that might work, and, if it does not work, another option is selected and this process continues until the best option that starts to work is accepted. Golensky (2011) has also introduced the term "lateral thinking" or "thinking outside the box" for a process which can result in creative ideas not previously considered. Thinking outside the box can occur at any stage of the decision-making process and the resulting resetting of parameters and options can lead to better outcomes.

INDIVIDUAL VERSUS GROUP DECISION MAKING

Box 5.5 displays the competencies/behaviors in this section.

BOX 5.5

NETWORK FOR SOCIAL WORK MANAGEMENT COMPETENCIES AND PRACTICE BEHAVIORS 7 AND 10

Initiates and facilitates innovative change processes (Network for Social Work Management Competencies 7). Practice Behaviors:

- Presents innovations to appropriate decision makers and stakeholders and makes decisions that are aligned with their feedback (7.2).

(continued)

BOX 5.5 *(Continued)*

Encourages active involvement of all staff and stakeholders in decision-making processes (Network for Social Work Management Competencies 10). Practice Behaviors:

- Provides opportunities for internal and external stakeholders to give feedback before significant program changes are implemented (10.1).

- Uses collaborative teams and other strategies to identify outcomes, design programs, share intervention strategies, conduct assessments, analyze results, and adjust intervention processes (10.4).

- Encourages consumers and underrepresented stakeholders to actively participate in decision-making processes (10.5).

Individuals can make decisions for organizations, and that process is obviously much simpler than group decision making. In most organizations, some decisions need to be made immediately or without delay. In this case, the individual leader or manager should make the decision. However, obtaining buy-in on decisions made from the top can become problematic unless it is a totally autocratic administration. As a result, most nonprofit and academic organizations use group decision making to resolve problems. Who should be on the decision-making team? Obviously, teams should include key staff and, if possible, consumers. Recruiting consumers and underrepresented stakeholders for participation in the process will help determine if all issues impacting various groups are revealed. So, when setting up a decision-making team, encourage the participation of internal and external stakeholders in the process, and, if that cannot happen, give them a chance to provide feedback before decisions are implemented. If their feedback questions the legitimacy or proposed effectiveness of the decision, then provide them with information about the process, including the actual decision-making documents and worksheets; if the feedback identifies new, unknown issues or alternatives that were not considered, then the process should start over again.

For group decision making, employment of the *Delphi method* or technique is a means to produce group consensus. The *Delphi method* involves multiple rounds of responses to specific questions or prompts until the most acceptable solution is found. A simplified version of the process starts with a facilitator collecting anonymous responses that include an explanation for the response to the question or prompt followed by summarizing the responses. The group members then revise their responses based on the feedback, and this process continues until a consensus is reached.

Organizations that use group decision making should be aware of the advantages and disadvantages of group decision making (See Table 5.3).

There is a rational decision model for determining who should make a decision, an individual or the group. The Vroom–Jago decision model (Vroom & Jago, 1988) distinguishes five different situations and outlines an algorithm for determining which one to use. Box 5.6 displays the five possible processes to determine if the leader should make the decision, with or without staff input, or whether the staff should be part of the process or solely responsible for the decision. In addition, 11 questions are provided to help determine which of the five processes should be used.

TABLE 5.3 **Group Decision Making—Advantages and Disadvantages**

Group Decision Making—Advantages
- Acceptance by those affected is increased
- Coordination is easier
- Communication is easier
- Greater number of alternatives can be considered
- More information can be processed (Skidmore, 1995, pp. 72–73 as cited in Bedeian, 1993, pp. 216–217)

Group Decision Making—Disadvantages
- Group decisions take longer to reach than individual decisions
- Groups can be indecisive
- Groups can compromise but the compromise may not be the best decision
- Groups can be dominated
- Groups can play games
- Groups can fall victim to "groupthink" (where the drive to achieve consensus becomes so powerful that it overrides independent, realistic appraisals of alternative actions) (Skidmore, 1995, pp. 72–73 as cited in Bedeian, 1993, pp. 216–217)

BOX 5.6

FIVE PROCESSES DECISION MODEL

1. The leader makes the decision.
2. To help make the decision, the leader requests information from staff. The leader can explain the reason for the request or not.
3. The leader explains to the staff the situation for information sharing purposes, but makes the decision.
4. The leader discusses the situation with the staff and entertains input, but still makes the decision.
5. The leader presents the situation to the staff who discuss alternatives and makes a decision through consensus.

Which process should you use?
Answers to the following 11 questions will assist in determining which of the five decision process would work best:

1. Has the problem been clearly identified?
2. Is there enough information for the leader alone to make the decision?
3. Will the leader's decision be accepted by the majority of the staff?
4. Is the success of the decision dependent on staff implementation?
5. Does the staff believe and trust in the leader's decision-making capabilities?
6. Should the leader make the decision or should the leader continue with the status quo?

(continued)

BOX 5.6 *(Continued)*

7. If the leader does not make a decision, will the leader and the organization be negatively impacted?

8. If the decision has a high probability of failure, should the leader share the responsibility for making the decision?

9. For any number of reasons would it be better for the staff to make the decision?

10. Do the staff and the leader share the same goals?

11. Can the staff make the decision or is there too much disagreement among staff or cliques of staff to be able to make a rational decision?

SOURCE: Adapted from Vroom, V. H., & Jago, A. G. (1988). *The new leadership: Managing participation in organizations.* Englewood Cliffs, NJ. Prentice-Hall, Inc.

GENERAL GUIDELINES AND STEPS IN DECISION MAKING

Box 5.7 displays the competencies/behaviors in this section.

BOX 5.7

NETWORK FOR SOCIAL WORK MANAGEMENT COMPETENCIES AND PRACTICE BEHAVIORS 1

Establishes, promotes, and anchors the vision, philosophy, goals, objectives, and values of the organization (Network for Social Work Management Competencies 1). Practice Behaviors:

- Demonstrates the manner in which the vision, philosophy, and values are applied in making organizational decisions (1.6).

While undertaking problem solving and decision making, the vision, philosophy, and values of the organization should be considered. These questions should be asked:

1. How does the issue or problem impact our vision, philosophy, values, and ethics?

2. How do the choices or alternate solutions impact our vision, philosophy, values, and ethics?

3. When evaluating the implemented strategy, how do we determine if the vision, philosophy, and values have been strengthened?

A simplistic approach first proposed by Fulmer (1988) and highlighted by Skidmore (1995) and this book's authors (Rofuth and Piepenbring) suggests that answers to the following questions can be of genuine help in making sound decisions.

1. What is right?

2. What can go wrong?

3. What could cause this problem to occur?

4. What preventive action can I take?

5. What is my contingency plan?

6. When will my alternative plan go into action? (Skidmore, 1995, p. 73 as cited in Fulmer, 1988, pp. 50–54)

7. How much do you want the best solution?

8. What are the difficulties in achieving the best solution?

Recommended Basic General Guidelines for Decision Making

Typically, general guidelines for decision making are based on rational decision-making models, which follow steps in logical order, weighing alternatives to produce the best result. A rational decision model presupposes that there is one best outcome, and thus it is known as an optimizing decision-making model. The search for perfection is frequently a factor in actually delaying making a decision. Sometimes, because of the complicated nature of the situation, there is a call to consult "experts," which further delays a decision, when in fact there are already many knowledgeable people in the organization who can assist in making a rational decision.

A rational model also presupposes that it is possible to consider every option and know the future consequences of each. Predicting the probabilities of various options is difficult at best. A rational decision-making model requires a great deal of time, energy, imagination, and unfiltered information. Finally, negating the role of emotions in decision making, particularly in group decision making, is difficult.

There are a variety of decision-making models and steps. Skidmore (1995) and Golensky (2011) have produced basic general guidelines for decision making in social work administration, and Kepner-Tregoe (1972) and Welch (2002) also offer some general guidelines. The following model combines aspects of a variety of models—recommended by these authors—and is proposed as a best practice tool for decision making.

1. **Define the situation or problem.**
    Uncover the facts of the current situation or problem, including the specific stated problem and any underlying reasons or motives of people identifying the situation or problem. How does the issue or problem impact your organization's vision, philosophy, and values?

2. **Collect and study the facts pertaining to the issue.**
    Data concerning the problem should be collected from staff, people impacted, records, surveys, and other sources of information. This data should then be carefully analyzed so that the correct priorities can be established to deal with the problem. Allwood and Salo (2014) conducted a study on decision quality and effectiveness and have suggested that a good decision process requires a systematic gathering of decision-relevant information from reliable sources and a systematic and relevant use of this information in the decision processes. However, don't delay moving forward even if you don't have all the data. Information will be uncovered over time as you move through additional steps in the decision process.

3. **Establish and classify objectives.**
    In order to establish and classify objectives, outline the results to be achieved by the decision and list the criteria that any possible alternatives should meet. Classify objectives by determining the relative importance of different results or resources needed for the decision. Also identify what *must* be accomplished versus what is desired but not necessary. Finally, survey the full range of objectives to be fulfilled and the values implicated by the choice.

4. **Formulate the possible choices**.
    Many alternative choices to resolve the problem may be available. Thoroughly canvassing a wide range of alternative courses of action along with intensively

searching for new information relevant to further evaluation of the alternatives is a good idea. Compare alternatives by identifying the choices and the different actions or ways of accomplishing the objectives; compare those choices against the objectives to see which alternative does the best job. Finally, ask how do the choices or alternate solutions impact your organization's vision, philosophy, and values?

5. **Anticipate likely results or outcomes of the choices.**
Each alternative must be considered in regard to what would be likely to happen if a particular direction is chosen. Additional questions that need to be considered concerning a specific alternative are these: When would it happen? Where would it happen? How would it happen? What are the anticipated results in terms of the individual(s) involved, others, and the agency (Skidmore, 1995, p. 69)?

   Also, what values are at stake? Carefully weigh what you know about the costs and risks of negative consequences as well as the positive consequences that could flow from each alternative.

6. **Assess the importance of the decision.**
Will this decision have minor or major consequences? Does this decision need to be made now?

7. **Anticipate adverse consequences or the negative side of an alternative.**
Identify the risk that goes along with an action. Reexamine the positive and negative consequences of all known alternatives, including those originally regarded as unacceptable, before making a final choice.

8. **Consider feelings.**
Feelings and emotions can impact the decision-making process, both positively and negatively. In a group decision-making process, some may have hidden feelings about a particular problem or solution. Open-ended discussion may bring these types of issues to the surface. Also, know yourself and your organization. What are your strengths, weaknesses, skills, values, and interests?

9. **Select the best available solution and choose sound action.**
Making the right decision in a timely manner is important. A short delay in finalizing a decision may be useful, but too long of a delay may impact the decision in a negative way, not to mention that the situation may have changed. One needs to decide how much time and energy to spend on making the decision. More important decisions should be given more time.

   All decisions occur in social contexts. Decision efficiency is also important. Time is always a factor in decision making. Some decisions require quick responses, but if you have time, avoid making quick decisions without all the facts. Making incorrect decisions will either create havoc or lead one to start the decision-making process over again (Allwood & Salo, 2014). Put the benefits and risks of each alternative into perspective and identify several factors that really make a difference in the decision before reaching a conclusion. Decisions should be clearly explicated so as not to waste people's time at a later date interpreting the decision (Allwood & Salo, 2014).

10. **Implement the decision and follow through with action.**
Once the decision has been made and a corresponding implementation plan (ideally using a Gantt chart) completed, obtaining full support is essential for the achievement of the objectives in the plan. There will always be wrinkles in plans, so it is a good idea to develop alternative actions to achieve the objectives.

Accountability is also an important part of decision making (Lerner & Tetlock, 1999). When all key stakeholders participate in the decision process and everyone that the decision impacts are kept informed, the acceptance of the decision will be forthcoming and fewer people will question the decision.

11. **Be flexible to changing the decision.**

    Correctly assimilate and take into account any new information or expert judgment that surfaces, even when the information or judgment does not support the course of action initially chosen. Sometimes the situation and facts change, and another alternative course of action may be necessary. Remain flexible and be able to change direction if necessary and possibly start over again.

12. **Evaluate results.**

    Once action is taken to resolve the situation or problem, evaluate the results within a short period of time to determine immediate impact and again at a later date to assess the long-term impact of the solution. When evaluating the implemented strategy determine if the vision, philosophy, and values have been strengthened. A case example in a university setting is displayed in Box 5.8 and an agency exercise is presented in Box 5.9.

BOX 5.8

OPERATING BUDGET CASE EXAMPLE

The following case example displays guidelines and action steps to deal with an academic department issue: *There has been a 20% reduction in the department's operating budget. How will the reduction be implemented? There are four faculty lines open in a department of 12 faculty and only one will be filled next academic year and the future for filling the other positions is unknown. How will the department cover the course sections and how will the department deal with understaffed committees?*

Guidelines and Action Steps

GUIDELINES	ACTION STEPS
1. Define the situation or problem.	There will be three unfilled faculty lines next year. How will the department cover course sections, understaffed committees, overworked advisors, and a reduction of department faculty on university-wide committees?
2. Collect and study the facts pertaining to the issue.	Are there additional facts? Are there other activities faculty engage in not previously identified?
3. Establish and classify objectives.	What are the objectives for the department for dealing with this problem of understaffing? What are the short-term and long-term objectives? Short-term objectives include covering all courses, assuring committees complete work; long-term objectives include filling all the positions to resume normal staffing levels.

(continued)

BOX 5.8 *(Continued)*

GUIDELINES	ACTION STEPS
4. Formulate the possible choices.	Add more adjunct or part-time teachers; increase class sizes by eliminating some sections of courses, extending time to graduation for students; offer more summer courses; change bylaws to reduce committee size; reduce number of committees by combining purposes of committees.
5. Anticipate likely results or outcomes of the choices.	May be able to add more adjuncts. Can increase class sizes but have never taken steps to push back graduation so not likely to occur now. Can add more summer classes but students have to pay extra. Can change committee size and purposes.
6. Assess the importance of the decision.	Some decisions have to be made as there will not be enough full-time faculty, so it is very important that a decision is made to alleviate the problem.
7. Anticipate adverse consequences.	Hiring more adjuncts should be possible unless the university freezes the adjunct budget. Increase in class size will be more difficult on faculty and will negatively impact student learning experiences. If it takes students longer to graduate, it will cost them more in tuition and enrollments might decline. Summer classes can be offered, but some will have to be cancelled due to low enrollments.
8. Consider feelings.	Some faculty are more amenable to increasing class size, but it also depends on type of course; some courses cannot be expanded. Student consideration should also be taken into account.
9. Select the best available solution and choose sound action.	Depending on student enrollment numbers, some of the proposed solutions may be impacted. Consider the impact of enrollment when selecting best solution.
10. Implement the decision and follow through with action.	Decide on which choice, then let all stakeholders know of decision.
11. Be flexible to changing the decision.	If some of the solutions are not possible, go with the ones that have the greatest likelihood of success.
12. Evaluate results.	Determine if students have dropped out as a result of actions taken. Have teacher evaluations been impacted due to large class sizes? Have more students taken longer to graduate? Are revised committees completing work? Are students advised regularly and correctly? Is the department represented on university-wide committees?

BOX 5.9

AGENCY ISSUES EXERCISE

1. *There has been a 20% reduction in the agency's overall budget. How will the reduction be implemented?*
2. *In anticipation of future funding reductions, can the agency be reorganized to achieve cost efficiencies?*

Using the 12 guidelines list the action steps for each.

Guidelines and Action Steps

GUIDELINES	ACTION STEPS
1. Define the situation or problem.	
2. Collect and study the facts pertaining to the issue.	
3. Establish and classify objectives.	
4. Formulate the possible choices.	
5. Anticipate likely results or outcomes of the choices.	
6. Assess the importance of the decision.	
7. Anticipate adverse consequences.	
8. Consider feelings.	
9. Select the best available solution and choose sound action.	
10. Implement the decision and follow through with action.	
11. Be flexible to changing the decision.	
12. Evaluate results.	

DECISION-MAKING PROCESSES–FULL APPROACH

Box 5.10 displays the competencies/behaviors in this section.

BOX 5.10

NETWORK FOR SOCIAL WORK MANAGEMENT COMPETENCIES AND PRACTICE BEHAVIORS 3

Possesses analytical and critical thinking skills that promote organizational growth (Network for Social Work Management Competencies 3). Practice Behaviors:

- Understands and makes use of historical and current data to inform decision making about the agency (3.4).
- Demonstrates strong critical thinking and problem-solving skills (3.6).

There are four stages of problem solving and decision making: *SA—PA—DA—PPA* (Kepner-Tregoe, Inc., 1973). Although many organizations encounter concerns on a day-to-day basis, some concerns may have greater impact than others. An SA is a method to determine the importance of a concern. If something went wrong in the past, a PA may be required. If something must be done to resolve a problem that is currently occurring, a DA may be required. Finally, if something could go wrong in the future, a PPA may be required. The steps to accomplish a situation analysis are described in Box 5.11. The following material on the four stages has been adapted with permission from Kepner-Tregoe and sourced from the Management Supervisory Development Program (1986) workshop attended by one of the authors (Rofuth). Kepner-Tregoe has continued to evolve these ideas and adapt them for use by businesses and industries worldwide. For more information, go to www.kepner-tregoe.com.

Situation Appraisal

An SA requires four steps: (a) identify concerns; (b) separate concerns; (c) prioritize concerns; and (d) locate and choose an appropriate rational process. These four steps are displayed in Box 5.11.

BOX 5.11

FOUR STEPS OF A SITUATION APPRAISAL

1. *Identify concerns*
    - A concern is something that may require action.
    - The action must lie in your area of responsibility.
    - You should list concerns without discussion.

    To determine what threats and opportunities may be of concern, ask the following questions:
    - What situation bothers me?
    - Who is worrying me?

(continued)

BOX 5.11 *(Continued)*

- Why do I feel a sense of impending doom?
- What changes bother me?
- What issues must I address now?
- What threats am I facing?
- What opportunities are available to me?

2. *Separate concerns*
   Is each of these concerns a single, manageable item? To answer this question, ask:
   - Can you tell me more about it?
   - What evidence do you have?
   - Does it need to be separated?

   Concerns are separated adequately when there is:
   - Deviation from which one must find a cause
   - A choice to make among alternatives
   - A plan that must be implemented and protected

3. *Set priorities*
   To develop a plan to take action you need to consider
   - What is the seriousness of this situation?
     - What is the impact (money, people, or mission)?
     - What are the risks to me?
     - Who says it's serious?
   - How urgent is this situation?
     - What are the deadlines (real ones)?
     - Why must we do it now?
     - Who says it's urgent?
     - What's in it for me to do it now?
   - What is the growth trend?
     - Seriousness over time?
     - What will happen if appropriate action is not taken?

   Set priorities by assigning a value of high, low, and medium.

4. *Locate and choose the appropriate rational process*
   To determine how to proceed the following questions should be answered:
   - Do you have a deviation for which you need to know cause? Or do you have a cause-unknown deviation? Use PA.
   - Do you need to make a choice? Or do you need to select a course of action? Use DA.

(continued)

BOX 5.11 *(Continued)*

▪ Do you need to assure successful implementation? Or do you have a plan to protect? Use PPA.

If you said no to the above lead questions, then a further separation of concerns is required.

5. *Plan for Resolution*

Once the appropriate rational process has been selected you can proceed to resolve the situation using that process.

DA, decision analysis; PA, problem analysis; PPA, potential problem analysis.

SOURCE: Adapted from Kepner-Tregoe, Inc. (1973b). *Problem analysis and decision making.* Princeton, NJ: Princeton Research Press; Management Supervisory Development Program. (1986). *Problem solving and decision making.* Harrisburg, PA: Department of Public Welfare, Commonwealth of Pennsylvania.

One approach to uncover concerns is calling a group meeting and using the Nominal Group Technique (NGT). In NGT, every member of the group identifies what they think the concern is with a short explanation, and then, duplicate concerns are eliminated from a master list and the group proceeds to rank the concerns. Some facilitators encourage the sharing and discussion of the choices made by each group member, thereby identifying common ground and a plurality of ideas and approaches. This diversity often allows for the creation of a hybrid idea (combined parts of two or more ideas), often found to be even better than those ideas initially considered. In the basic method, the numbers each concern receives are totaled, and the concern with the highest total ranking is selected as the final concern to be addressed. Box 5.12 provides an opportunity to rate the concerns, select a rational process, and plan a resolution.

BOX 5.12

SITUATION APPRAISAL EXERCISE

Exercise Example

Complete Situation Appraisal Worksheet using an example from your current or past work.

Situation Appraisal Worksheet

CONCERN	SEPARATE CONCERNS	SERIOUSNESS (HIGH, LOW, OR MEDIUM)	URGENCY (HIGH, LOW, OR MEDIUM)	GROWTH (HIGH, LOW, OR MEDIUM)	RATIONAL PROCESS— SELECT ONE (PA, DA, OR PPA)	PLAN FOR RESOLUTION

DA, decision analysis; PA, problem analysis; PPA, potential problem analysis.

SOURCE: Adapted from Kepner-Tregoe, Inc. (1979b). *Situation appraisal worksheet.* Princeton, NJ: Princeton Research Press.

Problem Analysis

A PA is a process to describe a deviation from some standard in order to isolate the cause of the deviation. There are seven steps in a PA (See Box 5.13).

BOX 5.13

SEVEN STEPS IN A PROBLEM ANALYSIS

1. **A deviation statement (identification of the problem)**
   The deviation statement helps focus the problem by guiding questioning and focusing the data search.
   To better describe the deviation, ask these questions:
   - What is the object with the defect or problem?
   - What is the defect or problem itself?

2. **The specification step identifies the possibilities by**
   - Providing a format for gathering data
   - Limiting the data search
   - Making the information specific
   - Making the problem visible

   To better describe the deviation, ask these questions:
   What, where, when, and to what extent does the problem occur?
   - What may we expect the problem to be, but it is not
     - The object with the defect?
     - The defect itself?
   - Where may we expect the problem to be, but it is not
     - The object of the defect observed (geographical location)?
     - The defect on the object?
   - When may we expect the problem to be, but it is not
     - The object with the defect first observed (clock, calendar, time)?
     - Observed since then (clock, calendar, time)?
     - The defect first observed in the cycle of the object or process?
   - What extent may we expect the problem to be, but it is not
     - How many units of the object have the defect?
     - How much of each unit is affected?
     - How many defects are on each unit?
     - What is the trend?

(continued)

BOX 5.13 *(Continued)*

3. **The third step is to determine distinctions between things (looking for sharp contrasts between people, places, and things)**

   - Information needs to be new (additional—cannot repeat it from specifications) and factual
   - Must be true only of is and not the is not
   - Broadens database
   - Narrows the search for cause—throw out factors that cannot be the cause
   - Ask this question to find cause:
       - What, if anything, is distinctive of the is compared to the is not?

4. **The fourth step is to determine if there are any changes in distinctions**

   - Is the change the cause?
   - What is changed in, around, and about the distinctions?
   - Date all changes to the clock, calendar, time.

5. **The fifth step is to develop hypotheses or possible causes**

   - Take each change and develop a possible cause or hypothesis
   - Use if/then or causal statements (i.e., if there is an X, then Y will change)
   - Note any assumptions

   Ask these questions to find cause:
   - How could each change have caused the deviation?
   - How could a change plus a distinction have caused the deviation?
   - How could a change plus a change have caused the deviation?

6. **In the sixth step, possible causes are tested**

   - An evaluation of probable causes against the evidence of the specification to determine that cause with the fewest or most reasonable set of assumptions
   - Test each hypothesis against all information in specifications
   - Test destructively—try to disprove this hypothesis
   - Look for the most probable cause

   Ask these questions to find cause:
   - For each possible cause ask, if this is a true cause, how does it explain both the is and the is not? What assumptions must you make?
   - What is the most probable cause?

7. **Verification of the problem is the final step. Some options are:**

   - Test reality through observation
   - Monitor results to determine if problem is fixed

A Problem Analysis Worksheet can be used to complete a PA (see Box 5.14).

BOX 5.14

PROBLEM ANALYSIS WORKSHEET CASE EXAMPLE

Problem Analysis Worksheet

Deviation Statement: A number of students are having issues related to social work attributes

SPECIFYING QUESTION	IS	IS NOT	DISTINCTIONS	CHANGES
			WHAT IS DISTINCTIVE ABOUT THE IS?	WHAT HAS CHANGED IN/ON/AROUND THE DISTINCTION? DATE ALL CHANGES.
What: Identity	Students are expelled from field placements for inappropriate attire.	Students are not dressing professionally.	Students expelled are all from the third cohort.	Third cohort advisor left mid second term (Mar 23).
Where: Location	In certain field placement agencies (C and D).	(Could be, but is not) in other agencies (A, B, E, and F), supervisors and students are attired appropriately.	C and D located in poor neighborhoods, so students dress down.	Clients and students dress differently in C and D, even though supervisors do not. Students in poor neighborhoods should still dress appropriately.
When: Timing	During second semester, first year and second semester, second year field placement.	(Could be but is not) during first semester, first year or first semester, second year field placements.	These are high-stress periods during the semester.	Cohort advisor left mid second term.
Extent: Size or magnitude	About 10% of students (10 out of 100).	(Could be, but is not) more or less than 10 students; 10%.	Increased number versus prior years.	No change beyond the distinction is known.

Possible causes from changes and distinctions: Students not receiving sufficient reviews (no advisor) and do not have opportunity to correct behaviors prior to being expelled.	**Test** for probable cause. Which specifying facts make this possible cause improbable? Note any assumptions.
Steps to verify cause: Institute "must have advisor" policy and assess in next year.	Compare remaining students review process/timing and compare to those expelled. What is the correlation between number of advising sessions and termination? What is the correlation between early intervention and not being expelled?

SOURCE: Adapted from Kepner-Tregoe, Inc. (1975). *Problem analysis worksheet.* Princeton, NJ: Princeton Research Press.

(continued)

BOX 5.14 *(Continued)*

Exercise

Complete the Problem Analysis Worksheet using an example from your current or past work.

Problem Analysis Worksheet
Deviation Statement:

SPECIFYING QUESTION	IS	IS NOT	DISTINCTIONS	CHANGES
			WHAT IS DISTINCTIVE ABOUT THE IS?	WHAT HAS CHANGED IN/ON/AROUND THE DISTINCTION? DATE ALL CHANGES.
What: Identity				
Where: Location				
When: Timing				
Extent: Size or magnitude				
Possible causes from changes and distinctions			**Test** for probable cause. Which specifying facts make this possible cause improbable? Note any assumptions.	
Steps to Verify Cause				

SOURCE: Adapted from Kepner-Tregoe, Inc. (1975). *Problem analysis worksheet.* Princeton, NJ: Princeton Research Press.

▨ People Problems and PA

A people problem is a *deviation* where the observed behavior and performance are not normal and for which the *cause* is unknown. Because results and outcomes are the manager's concern, and staff that deviate from normal behavior can negatively impact meeting the bottom line, the manager should focus on understanding the causes of deviation in behavior and performance. People problems are difficult to solve because of intangible factors such as personal problems or working relationship issues and because information available for analysis is often unreliable and distorted.

There are several suggested general guidelines to follow when trying to understand people problems:

- ▨ Separate issues
- ▨ Focus on observed observations
- ▨ Focus on the environment
- ▨ Separate facts from feelings

- ▨ Separate facts from opinions
- ▨ To name is not to blame (i.e., need to identify where the problem is originating because it may not be totally that person's fault)

The following seven-step process is useful in uncovering people problems and producing good outcomes.

1. **Deviation statement**
   - ▨ Who is the person, unit, or group with the problem?
   - ▨ What is the problem?
   - ▨ Do not jump to conclusions or to action. Instead follow a systematic, disciplined approach to analyze information and issues.
   - ▨ Separate ambiguous situations into specific subconcerns.
   - ▨ Focus your attention on behavior. Consider only what you can observe or document about performance deviations. Stay clear of emotional, value-loaded descriptions.

2. **Specification**
   Describe the problem in specific terms before speculating on the causes of the problem. Organize this information into IS and IS NOT columns; write down the SHOULD and the ACTUAL performance. Not only does this categorizing bring your focus to the real problem but it also provides a baseline for developing and testing possible causes. By identifying what is not the current situation, you can better differentiate between the real and not real situation; it also allows you to examine the circumstances in which a situation might not be occurring. Determine if there is a norm for this situation. For example, the lifting of a mandatory retirement age in the United States has had many consequences, both positive and negative. Positive benefits include retaining the knowledge and skills of experienced workers who know the history of the organization. Negative aspects of people not retiring include younger people having fewer opportunities to move up in the organization; people also continue to work with progressive cognitive impairment, impacting client services.

   It is important to focus on facts only. Description questions are listed in Table 5.4. A case example is provided in Box 5.15.

TABLE 5.4 Descriptive Questions by Who, What Where, When, and Extent, and Is and Is Not

	IS	IS NOT
WHO	Who is the person or group with whom you are having difficulty?	Who is the person, persons, or organizational unit with whom you would expect to have this difficulty, but are not?
WHAT	What behavior is occurring that should not be occurring?	What difficulties might you expect to have with this person, persons, or organizational unit that are not occurring? What part of his or her job is going all right, but might be going wrong?
WHERE	Where is the behavior exhibited?	Where might the behavior be expected to occur, but is not happening?

(continued)

TABLE 5.4 **Descriptive Questions by Who, What Where, When, and Extent, and Is and Is Not** *(Continued)*

	IS	IS NOT
WHEN	When do these difficulties occur (time, clock, calendar)? When do these performance difficulties occur on the job?	At what other times might they occur, but do not (time, clock, calendar)? Given that the difficulties occur when they do, when else might you expect trouble, but find performance is acceptable?
EXTENT	To what extent do each of the difficulties occur? How often do they occur? How many occurrences, complaints? Are they increasing, decreasing, or staying the same?	How severe might each of the difficulties be, but are not? How often might they occur, but do not? How many might there be, but are not? What trend might normally be expected, but does not happen this time?

SOURCE: Adapted from Kepner-Tregoe, Inc. (1973a). *Potential problem planning worksheet.* Princeton, NJ: Princeton Research Press.

BOX 5.15

DESCRIPTIVE QUESTIONS CASE EXAMPLE

Complete the following table using one example situation of a people problem.

Descriptive Questions by Who, What Where, When, Extent, and Is and Is Not

	IS	IS NOT
WHO		
WHAT		
WHERE		
WHEN		
EXTENT		

SOURCE: Adapted from Kepner-Tregoe, Inc. (1973a). *Potential problem planning worksheet.* Princeton, NJ: Princeton Research Press.

3. **Possible Causes, Distinctions, and Change**
    To determine the true cause of a problem or distinction from normal, look for something that is new or something that has brought about change. Without change the situation would remain normal. If there is a problem, something caused it, and that something is a change in the environment. Focus on distinctions in the *work environment*, not distinctions within people. Change can occur in a variety of circumstances, including gradual or subtle change (that occurs over time and is not noticed), irrelevant change (change that appears irrelevant may in fact contribute to the problem), change from improvements (may seem good but in fact may be impacting the problem in some way), and unknown changes and speculation (change always occurs, even if no one notices). Remember people can absorb change and may or may not know it.

4. **Determine changes in distinctions**
   Determine if the change is the cause, and what has changed in, around, or about the distinction.

5. **Develop hypotheses or possible cause**
   Take each change and develop a hypothesis. Why is this change occurring?

6. **Testing causes**
   Evaluate each cause against the facts of the situation from the is and is not columns of the PA description worksheet. Ask this question: "If the Possible Cause is the true Cause, why does it affect only the IS facts and not the IS NOT facts?" (Kepner-Tregoe, Inc., 1973, p. 24). Test each possible cause by checking each one against each item in the problem specification.

7. **Verification** is a little tougher to achieve. For example:

   ■ Whom—do you want to talk to?

   ■ What—are you going to say?

   ■ Where—do you want to talk?

   ■ When—is the best time?

   ■ Extent—how deeply do you want to question the person?

   Verify the most likely cause by (a) validating any assumptions that relate to it, and then by (b) judging its true worth though direct observation of job conditions. Look for positive deviations in performance. When dealing with people problems, some of the most valuable insights come from a study of distinctions associated with good, rather than bad, performance. The key to performance improvement often lies in these distinctions associated with positive deviations (Kepner-Tregoe, Inc., 1973, p. 27).

■ DA—When to Use It?

DA is one of the most important functions of management. Making correct decisions can improve an organization's function, while making incorrect decisions can hinder organizational functioning and sometimes its very existence. The following seven steps are a systematic, logical approach to DA.

1. **Create and describe the decision statement**. What is the purpose of this decision? What choice do we have to make? What is the problem? Who does it impact? How long has it existed? Have solutions been attempted? What is the negative impact on the organization? Can the problem be ignored? When should it be resolved? A decision statement requires:

   ■ An action verb and an object—use one of three words: select, pick, or choose

   ■ Results expected—use one or two modifiers to describe in detail

2. **Establish objectives (8–12 maximum).** Review expected results. What are resource limitations in terms of time, staff release, and funding?
   For group processes: Each member should be given the opportunity to state his or her objective(s). This polling of the group could be done in a round-robin fashion (e.g., Delphi technique). Each objective should be written out. After all objectives are written, the group can review them to clarify them or delete any duplicates. Consider the following:

   ■ Results, including effectiveness and output

   ■ Resources, including efficiency and input

- Constraints, including rules, laws, and regulations

There are five key questions to help frame objectives:

- What are the maximum results desired?
- What are the minimum acceptable results?
- What are the maximum allowable resources?
- What are the constraints?

3. **Set priorities or classify objectives**. Which of these objectives are musts and which are wants? What is the weight of each want objective?

- *Identify musts and wants:*
  Separate must and want objectives. A must objective is one in which the objective must be satisfied unconditionally. All other objectives are considered "want" objectives and are prioritized according to the next step.

- *Must objectives*
- Mandatory—required for success of decision statement
- Measurable—now, at the time of decision
- Reasonable/realistic—Can alternatives be expected to be available?
- Hint—only 0 to 3 objectives are necessary to run through the must/want scale
- Can use a "dominate must" vote on very important objectives (a weight of 10). The remaining objectives (the want objectives) are compared with each other and assigned weights from 1 to 10, with 1 being the objective with the lowest importance and 10 with the highest importance.

- *Need to weigh the want objectives on a scale of 10 to 1:*
- Avoid double counting of objectives
- Make sure objective is not rephrased
- Don't include alternatives as objectives
- Avoid use of binary objectives or objectives you really want

4. **List and develop alternatives**. What alternatives are available?

- Identify the potential choices
- Use the set of must and want objectives as a blueprint to guide search
- To get help on suggestions, check with:
  - People with past experience
  - Experts in the area
  - People who have to implement decisions
  - Representatives of the population affected
  - Subordinates
  - People in similar situations

5. **Evaluate alternatives** against each other by scoring them. Which alternatives screen well through the "must" objectives? What is the score for each alternative compared to each want objective? What are the weighted scores for each? What are the total weighted scores? What is your tentative choice?

When evaluating the alternative against a must objective, you need determine only whether you have a go or a no go situation. If the objective can be satisfied with a particular alternative, that alternative is evaluated as a go. If a no go is assigned to an alternative, that alternative is no longer considered as a viable one.

When evaluating against a want objective, the alternatives are assigned a score from 1 to 10. Assigning a 1 means the alternative least satisfies the objective. Conversely, a 10 means that an alternative best satisfies the objective. What you are determining is how well (the degree to which) an alternative satisfies a particular objective. Consequently, it is possible that several alternatives can be assigned the same score.

- Work horizontally on a matrix comparing all alternatives to each objective
- Musts: Score on a go/no go basis
- Wants: Score alternatives on a scale of 10 to 1
  - Assign 10 to that alternative that best meets the criteria of the objective
  - Assign a relative value to the other alternatives as they compare to the 10 alternative
- Multiply the weight of the want objective times the score of the alternative to get the weighted score. Next add all the weighted scores for each alternative. The alternative with the highest score is considered the likely choice.

6. **Identify any adverse consequences**. What are the adverse consequences of the highest scoring alternatives? What is the probability and seriousness of each consequence? For the two highest alternatives, identify any adverse consequences and evaluate each consequence in terms of its probability of occurring and its severity.

- Need to consider potential problems that can go wrong for the tentative choice and runner up
- Ask a set of questions:
  - What could go wrong if I pick the alternative?
  - What did our critics say would go wrong?
  - Check with department critics
  - Assess for threat
  - State concerns in if/then relationships
  - Assess for probability and seriousness
  - Assign value of high, medium, or low

7. **Make the best balanced choice**. What is the most effective balance between benefits and risks?

- If tentative choice has no severe adverse consequences, then pick it
- If the tentative choice has severe adverse consequences, then ask:
  - Will I accept more risk to get a bigger benefit? If yes, choose tentative alternative.
  - Will I accept less benefit to reduce risk? If yes, choose alternative with less severe consequences.

To achieve the maximum benefit of decisions and to assure full and supportive implementation, share decisions with all stakeholders with an explanation of how and why the decisions were made and how you believe these decisions will support the program(s). Key stakeholders include direct consumers, the advisory board, other parts of the organization, funders, and so on. Methods of sharing this information include holding meetings with key, small groups of stakeholders, putting the information on the web page, and adding the information to marketing material. Boxes 5.16, 5.17, and 5.18 provide exercises in table format for establishing and classifying objectives, comparing alternatives, and presenting adverse consequences.

BOX 5.16

DECISION ANALYSIS: ESTABLISH AND CLASSIFY OBJECTIVES EXERCISE

Use an example of a current concern from your place of employment or an example from Box 5.3 to complete this exercise.

Decision Analysis Worksheet
Decision Statement
Establish and Classify Objectives

OBJECTIVES	RELATIVE IMPORTANCE (MUST OR WANT)	WEIGHT FOR WANT OBJECTIVES (10 = MOST INFLUENCE, 1 = LEAST INFLUENCE)

SOURCE: Adapted from Kepner-Tregoe, Inc. (1979a). *Decision analysis worksheet.* Princeton, NJ: Princeton Research Press.

BOX 5.17

DECISION ANALYSIS: COMPARISON OF ALTERNATIVES EXERCISE

Use an example of a current concern from your place of employment or an example from Box 5.3 to complete this exercise.

Decision Analysis Worksheet—Comparison of Alternatives
Decision Statement
Objectives

MUSTS	ALTERNATIVE A	ALTERNATIVE A	ALTERNATIVE B	ALTERNATIVE B
	Information	Go/No Go	Information	Go/No Go

(continued)

BOX 5.17 *(Continued)*

MUSTS	ALTERNATIVE A		ALTERNATIVE A	ALTERNATIVE B		ALTERNATIVE B
WANTS	Weight	Information	Score	Weight Score	Information	Score	Weight Score
Totals							

SOURCE: Adapted from Kepner-Tregoe, Inc. (1979a). *Decision analysis worksheet.* Princeton, NJ: Princeton Research Press.

BOX 5.18

DECISION ANALYSIS: ADVERSE CONSEQUENCES EXERCISE

Use an example of a current concern from your place of employment or use an example from Box 5.3 to complete this exercise.

Decision Analysis Worksheet—Adverse Consequences
Alternatives

ADVERSE CONSEQUENCE	PROBABILITY (LOW, MEDIUM, OR HIGH)	SERIOUSNESS (LOW, MEDIUM, OR HIGH)

SOURCE: Adapted from Kepner-Tregoe, Inc. (1977). *Decision analysis worksheet—Adverse consequences.* Princeton, NJ: Princeton Research Press.

Short-Form and Bit and Piece DA

In most organizations, there is not enough time to invest in a full DA. As meetings are best used for decision making, the meeting participants will want a decision even though the underlying problem was not clarified, or all alternatives were not discussed, and so on. In these situations, a quicker and more expedient version of decision making is available through a short-form DA. Box 5.19 explains when to use the short-form DA and also covers the five basic steps in the process (Kepner-Tregoe, Inc., 1980 as cited in Management Supervisory Development Program, 1986).

BOX 5.19

TECHNIQUE FOR SHORT-FORM DA

Technique
Short-form DA
  The following statements are located in DA, but indicate a need for short-form rather than full DA:

- *Time pressure*—If you need to make a choice quickly, a full DA is probably not possible (e.g., you need to decide which version of a form will be used the next day).

- *Low-priority decisions*—If the impact of choosing a particular course of action is low, the concern is probably not of sufficient priority to warrant a full DA (e.g., you need to decide on the design of business cards).

- *Recurring decisions*—If you are facing a decision that you have made many times in the past, a full DA is probably not needed (e.g., you are selecting an acting director for a brief absence).

- *Simple decisions*—A decision that has a limited number of objectives, alternatives, and adverse consequences probably does not require a full DA (e.g., you need to decide to move a meeting time to another time due to a conflict in scheduling and there is a free day for that new meeting time).

Short-form DA focuses on the five basic steps in the process:

- **Decision statement**—The need for being sure of the exact decision requires that you quickly establish (probably mentally) a decision statement.

- **Objectives**—A run-through of the must objectives follows, along with a listing of key wants, as time allows.

- **Alternatives**—An examination of at least one or two alternatives other than the one that first comes to mind will ensure that you are not blinded by an attractive option.

- **Adverse consequences**—Asking about adverse consequences before choosing a course of action can lead you to change your mind or stimulate a short-form potential problem analysis.

- **Choice**—Your choice, as in full DA, is the alternative that strikes the best balance between benefits and risks.

DA, decision analysis.

SOURCE: Adapted from Kepner-Tregoe, Inc. (1980). *Short form and "bit and piece" (decision analysis)*. Princeton, NJ: Princeton Research Press; Management Supervisory Development Program (1986). *Problem solving and decision making*. Harrisburg, PA: Department of Public Welfare, Commonwealth of Pennsylvania.

Bit and Piece DA

Another expedient decision-making analysis process is the bit and piece DA, which can be employed when only one alternative is discussed and requires a decision whether to go with that alternative or not. The answer to three questions can help make the appropriate decision:

- "What objectives are met by doing it that way?
- What are alternative ways we could go?

▨   What are the adverse consequences of doing it that way?" (Kepner-Tregoe, Inc., 1980, as cited in Management Supervisory Development Program, 1986, p. E/CM94.002)

Bit and piece DA can be used daily for the simplest of decisions. For example, if the boss asks you to attend a meeting, you might use this technique to ascertain if you need to attend or possibly send a subordinate who has the relevant information for the meeting. When you are given a task you might question why the task is necessary, particularly if the information or data are already available. As one issue decisions are required every day, you should consider incorporating the what-type questions into your verbal and/or private analysis of problems that arise. Just remember to ask yourself the three questions when someone wants a quick decision. Boxes 5.20 and 5.21 provide brief analyses for decision making.

BOX 5.20

BIT AND PIECE DA WORKSHEET EXERCISE

For a short-form decision analysis, use the following Bit and Piece Worksheet to indicate objectives, alternatives, adverse consequences, and your choice.

Bit and Piece Worksheet

DA CONCERN	DECISION STATEMENT	OBJECTIVES	ALTERNATIVES (AND CHOICE)	ADVERSE CONSE- QUENCES	CHOICE

DA, *decision analysis.*

SOURCE: Adapted from Kepner-Tregoe, Inc. (1980). *Short form and "bit and piece" (decision analysis).* Princeton, NJ: Princeton Research Press.

BOX 5.21

DECISION ANALYSIS CONCERNS EXERCISE

For bit and piece application, use the Steps to Resolve Concerns/Situation Worksheet to indicate the questions or steps that will be most useful. Consider both current DA concerns and typical daily activities involving decisions.

Steps to Resolve Concerns/Situation

DA CONCERNS/ SITUATION	DAILY ACTIVITIES INVOLVING DECISION	KEY DA STEPS OR QUESTIONS

DA, *decision analysis.*

SOURCE: Adapted from Kepner-Tregoe, Inc. (1980). *Short form and "bit and piece" (decision analysis).* Princeton, NJ: Princeton Research Press.

Potential Problem Analysis

PPA is a methodology for helping managers uncover potential problems by identifying possible problems and planning how to keep those problems from occurring, or at least minimizing the negative impact.

Box 5.22 provides information on how to develop a plan to deal with potential problems.

BOX 5.22

SEVEN STEPS FOR DEVELOPING A PLAN TO DEAL WITH POTENTIAL PROBLEMS

1. **Action Plan Statement**
   - Tells what should take place—the objectives
   - What, where, when, and to what extent?
     - Example: Transfer (what) 50 patients (extent) to unit 15 (where) by January 1 (when).

2. **List Steps in Plan**
   - List in chronological order
     - For each step identify responsible party and the target date for implementation
   - Identify *critical* areas in the plan
     - Where something new, complex, or unfamiliar is tried
     - Where deadlines are tight
     - Where the success or failure of one step determines the outcome of entire plan
     - Where activities have little visibility
     - Where responsibility is difficult to assign
     - Where extensive interaction is required

3. **Identify Potential Problems By**
   - Looking for future deviations
   - Identifying what could go wrong
   - Assessing for threat
   - Using if/then relationships
   - Assessing probability/seriousness

4. **Identify Likely Cause(s)**
   - The reasons deviations will occur (in the first place)
   - Why the potential problem would happen and how would it happen
   - Assess probability for each cause

(continued)

BOX 5.22 (Continued)

5. Preventive Actions

- Design actions to eliminate cause (plan to take action for each cause)

6. Contingent Actions

- Preventive actions: designed to eliminate cause

- Contingent actions: taken against the effects of the problem should they occur

7. Provide for Information

Mileposts tell us where we are and how we are doing in terms of dealing with potential problems and if the threats from these problems have been resolved.

- Responsibility and timing are key (assign someone)

- Choose a date before and after each critical step (assign a person to keep track)

- Watch for triggers that tell the preventive actions have failed and that the contingent actions must be implemented

Box 5.23 applies the seven steps of the PPA to a case example.

BOX 5.23

POTENTIAL PROBLEM ANALYSIS EXERCISE

Apply the seven steps of PPA to the following case:

A nonprofit agency specializes in residential treatment for children and adolescents and has experienced a significant drop in referrals due to policy changes made at the state level. The state funding agency for children and youth has recently had a paradigmatic shift that is focused on drastically reducing and eliminating congregate care facilities throughout the state. The nonprofit agency is considering closing due to the financial hardship these changes have posed. The CEO, executive team, and board of directors examined the possibility of closing and determined that the agency did not have enough cash flow or endowment to close, and therefore have decided to explore options for serving alternative populations to create a desired niche. The agency has a long history of serving children and adolescents with complex childhood trauma and other issues.

Seven Steps for Developing a Plan to Deal with Potential Problems

STEPS	OBJECTIVES	ADD CASE CONTENT
1. Action Plan Statement	• Tells us what should take place—the objectives • What, where, when, and to what extent? • Example: Transfer (what) 50 patients (extent) to unit 15 (where) by January 1 (when).	

(continued)

BOX 5.23 *(Continued)*

STEPS	OBJECTIVES	ADD CASE CONTENT

2. List Steps in Plan	• List in chronological order
	  • For each step identify responsible party and the target date for implementation
	
	• Identify *critical* areas in the plan
	  • Where something new, complex, or unfamiliar is tried
	  • Where deadlines are tight
	  • Where the success or failure of one step determines the outcome of entire plan
	  • Where activities have little visibility
	  • Where responsibility is difficult to assign
	  • Where there is extensive interaction required	

3. Identify Potential Problems By	• Looking for future deviations • Identifying what could go wrong • Assessing for threat • Using if/then relationships • Assessing probability/seriousness	
4. Identify Likely Cause(s)	• The reasons deviations will occur (in the first place) • Why the potential problem would happen and how would it happen • Assess probability for each cause	
5. Preventive Actions	• Design actions to eliminate cause (plan to take action for each cause)	
6. Contingent Actions	• Preventive actions: designed to eliminate cause • Contingent actions: taken against the effects of the problem should they occur	
7. Provide for Information	Mileposts tell us where we are and how we are doing in terms of dealing with potential problems and if the threats from these problems have been resolved. • Responsibility and timing are key (assign someone) • Choose a date before and after each critical step (assign a person to keep track) • Watch for triggers that tell the preventive actions have failed and that the contingent actions must be implemented	

PPA, potential problem analysis.

Once the plan has been completed, there are several questions that you should ask to make sure the implementation plan correctly addresses the PPA (see Table 5.5). Chances of success are improved if you can answer these questions with a reliable degree of certainty.

TABLE 5.5 **Questions to Ask Prior to Implementation of Plan to Address the Potential Problem Analysis**

By asking the following questions, you will more likely ensure that the implementation plan addresses the potential problem analysis:

1. Things always go wrong; if these actions are taken what could possibly go wrong?

2. Both internal and external threats to successful implementation can occur, can you identify possible threats?

3. What are the causes of possible impediments?

4. What type of action will reduce the likelihood of negative outcomes?

5. Are there alternative actions that will enhance the likelihood of success?

6. What is the methodology that will be used to measure program achievement?

SOURCE: Adapted from Kepner-Tregoe, Inc. (1973b). *Problem analysis and decision making.* Princeton, NJ: Princeton Research Press.

Box 5.24 provides an opportunity to develop an action plan to solve a problem.

BOX 5.24

POTENTIAL PROBLEM ANALYSIS WORKSHEET

Use an example of a current concern from your place of employment or an example from Box 5.3 to complete the exercise.

Potential Problem Analysis Worksheet

Action Plan Statement

SPECIFIC POTENTIAL PROBLEMS	LIKELY CAUSES	PREVENTION (TAKE PREVENTIVE ACTION OR ACCEPT RISK)	PROTECTION (SET CONTINGENT ACTION OR ACCEPT RISK)	PROVIDE FOR INFORMATION (PROGRESS, TRIGGER)

SOURCE: Adapted from Kepner-Tregoe, Inc. (1973a). *Potential problem planning worksheet.* Princeton, NJ: Princeton Research Press.

Short Form PA

The primary purpose of PA is to help you think about problems in a systematic fashion. When confronted with a problem, the tendency is to immediately assume what is causing the problem without reflecting on the problem. A short-form PA with four logical steps helps avoid this tendency (see Box 5.25).

BOX 5.25

PROBLEM ANALYSIS SHORT FORM LOGICAL STEPS

Problem Analysis Short Form Logical Steps

1. Collect information.
   - *What* is the problem?
   - *Where* is the problem occurring?
   - *When* is the problem occurring?
   - To what *extent* is the problem occurring?
2. Once you have the information, analyze it with particular attention to any changes that have occurred relating to the problem.
   Changes_____
3. Ask yourself, how could this change(s) cause the problem?
4. Test your conclusions to see if your suspected cause is the real cause.

In addition, a short-form PPA may also be useful (See Box 5.26).

BOX 5.26

SHORT FORM—POTENTIAL PROBLEM ANALYSIS

Use an example of a current concern from your place of employment or an example from Box 5.3 to complete this exercise.

Short Form—Potential Problem Analysis

STEPS IN PLAN	PERSON RESPON-SIBLE	TARGET DATES	POTENTIAL PROBLEMS IN THE STEPS INCLUDING LIKELY CAUSE OF PROBLEM	ACTIONS TO PREVENT POTENTIAL PROBLEMS	ACTIONS THAT SHOULD CORRECT PROBLEM IF IT DOES OCCUR	HOW TO OBTAIN INFORMA-TION ON PLAN'S PROGRESS

HOW TO CRITIQUE VARIOUS DECISION-MAKING PROCESSES

Box 5.27 displays the competencies/behaviors in this section.

BOX 5.27

NETWORK FOR SOCIAL WORK MANAGEMENT COMPETENCIES AND PRACTICE BEHAVIORS 10

Encourages active involvement of all staff and stakeholders in decision-making processes (Network for Social Work Management Competencies 10). Practice Behaviors:

- Displays the ability to work with people and institutions to achieve creative compromises and "win–win" solutions (10.6).

Understanding and following the decision-making process is itself the most important aspect of selecting which approach to employ. Discussions that occur during meetings may or may not be relevant to the issue or problem at hand. Agreement to use a decision-making process should be discussed and agreed upon, hopefully with group consensus.

The Management Supervisory Development Program (1986) has proposed several guidelines for focusing on process rather than content:

1. Listen for the logical purpose underlying each question or comment. Is the suggestion a possible objective or outcome that could be accomplished, or is it an adverse consequence that will occur if no action is taken or is it an alternative solution?

2. Document all aspects of the decision-making process that occurred during the meeting. Was the issue or problem properly identified? Were solutions discussed that would lead to positive outcomes? Were adverse consequences discussed for each possible action and solution? Were all possible alternatives discussed and compared?

Many pitfalls occur during the decision-making process. Can you identify them? The next section identifies 16 pitfalls that can occur during the decision-making process.

PITFALLS OF THE DECISION-MAKING PROCESS

Box 5.28 displays the competencies/behaviors in this section.

BOX 5.28

NETWORK FOR SOCIAL WORK MANAGEMENT COMPETENCIES AND PRACTICE BEHAVIORS 10

Encourages active involvement of all staff and stakeholders in decision-making processes (Network for Social Work Management Competencies 10). Practice Behaviors:

- Shows evidence of stakeholder buy-in through such means as meetings or representative groups, and program surveys to the community (10.2).

There are many pitfalls in the decision-making process; however, there are possible solutions to resolving them. Carlisle (1987), Skidmore (1995), and the Management Supervisory Development Program (1986) have identified a number of them. Solutions for each pitfall are provided:

1. Most people do not always think rationally in most situations, particularly if crucial information about the situation is not known. *Solution: For rational decision-making gathering, in-depth information and knowledge of the situation is the first step in making a rational decision, along with believing that rational decisions may make for better resolutions.*

2. As they arise, issues and problems are resolved by making quick decisions. Decision-makers do not always take the time to collect the necessary information to resolve the issue or problem. *Solution: Make sure all information is gathered, and schedule more time for meetings if necessary.*

3. Solutions to the issue or problem do not necessarily adhere to the organization's goals and objectives. *Solution: Incorporate the goals and objectives of the organization at the beginning of whichever decision-making process you employ.*

4. When issues and problems arise, the person(s) who identified them may have an agenda or simply are bringing forward a situation without the correct information. *Solution: Stick to the facts and do not allow individual emotions to cloud judgement.*

5. One management practice is to delay making a decision when there is insufficient time to gather information and to discuss and resolve the situation. And sometimes, the problem resolves itself or no longer is an issue. However, the issue or problem could actually get worse if it does not resolve, and then the solutions can be more complicated. *Solution: Use delays judiciously.*

6. Issues and problems can be complicated; so if all the factors impacting the issue or problem are not identified, the solution might be oversimplified. *Solution: Make sure all underlying factors that impact the problem are identified.*

7. People frequently behave irrationally for a number of reasons, such as self-interest, biased opinions, and so on. If irrational acts are allowed to influence decisions instead of facts, the underlying issue or problem will not be resolved. *Solution: Always stick to the facts.*

8. Mistakes are always made and as a result people can get discouraged. *Solution: Mistakes will always occur, but alternative solutions can be proposed, and moving forward again is the best way to minimize discouragement in the process.*

9. There are always alternative options to an issue or problem; however, these may not correlate with the program's objectives. As a result, alternative solutions may move the organization in an unintended direction. *Solution: Do not select alternatives until the complete decision-making process is finalized. If one alternative sounds good, resist accepting it as the solution and ending the process. And make sure the program's goals and objectives are considered when proposing a solution.*

10. When considering alternative solutions, some alternatives may have more pro features and fewer con features, and as a result, not all alternatives are fully evaluated, or the favorable features may only be short-term benefits. Quantifying the possible results of each alternative may not be possible either. *Solution: Consider all alternatives and make sure each is tested to determine if it is the best solution.*

11. Almost all alternative solutions will have adverse consequences, although some have more than others. *Solution: Examine alternatives that were not considered because they appeared to have adverse consequences and therefore could not be the likely solution.*

12. Alternatives are selected that are too general, broad-based, or all-encompassing because they offer hope for a solution, even though they do not provide specific information on achieving a positive outcome. *Solution: Always gather facts that can provide specific information about the alternatives and consider all information no matter how dated the information might be.*

13. In considering solutions, objectives that are absolutely necessary (musts) should be considered over solutions that one wants to use that might solve the problem. Identifying the strengths and weaknesses of the must and want objectives is not conducted. *Solution: Some objectives are absolutely necessary, whereas others may be necessary but, considering the situation, are not absolutely necessary. Differentiate between musts and wants and identify the relative importance of wants.*

14. All alternatives, whether or not they satisfy all musts or wants, are reviewed and compared. Devoting too much time to considering alternatives that will not meet must objectives is time-consuming and can result in a selection that might not solve the issue or problem. *Solution: Make sure that only must objectives are fully vetted.*

15. The outcome of decision choices that are selected cannot necessarily be correctly predicted. *Solution: Attempt to estimate different probabilities of success by projecting multiple scenarios of possible outcomes.*

16. When employing a decision statement as part of the decision-making process, make sure to keep focused on it and do not start the process over again by reviewing different options. *Solution: Stick with the problem identified through the SA process. If other problems surface, deal with them separately.*

SUMMARY

This chapter introduces a variety of effective decision-making strategies. The chapter begins with introducing a taxonomy of comprehension.

There are multiple approaches to decision making and organizations should consider these options carefully based on a number of factors. Organizations typically use a combination of the several approaches, including optimizing, satisficing, incrementalism, the garbage can model, mixed methods, and four-force model and consensus. Organizations may not use any approach at all except intuition or spur of the moment selection of limited options that may or may not be related to the underlying question or issue.

There are advantages and disadvantages in decision-making depending on whether an individual or group is making the decision. The question of who should make decisions is usually left up to the leader; mechanisms are available to help decide on whether an individual or group should make a decision. There are many advantages and disadvantages to group decision making and these should be taken into consideration when deciding on who should be involved in the decision-making process. The Vroom–Jago decision model distinguishes five different situations and outlines an algorithm for determining which one to use.

There are a variety of guidelines, steps, and questions that can be asked to guide the decision-making process. A 12-step general model is proposed as a comprehensive rational decision-making process.

There are four stages of problem solving and decision making: SA, PA, DA, and PPA (Kepner-Tregoe, Inc., 1973). Many organizations encounter concerns on a day-to-day basis. Some concerns may have greater impact than others. To determine the importance of a concern may require an SA. If something went wrong in the past, a PA may be required. If something must be done to resolve a problem that is currently occurring, a DA may be required. Finally, if something could go wrong in the future, a PPA may be required. The steps to accomplish all these forms of analysis are provided in this chapter along with tables that display actions to accomplish each form of analysis.

To provide a critique of the decision-making process focus not on the content of any given meeting but on the process itself. The basic process or approach to decision making is critical to the success of managers. Content information is important in only that one situation. If managers are aware of the decision-making process, they can tackle new situations and new jobs with more assurance. Three guidelines for putting the spotlight on process rather than content are provided in this chapter.

Sixteen pitfalls and concomitant solutions are provided to assist in avoiding mistakes in decision making.

Competency-based questions are provided in Box 5.29.

BOX 5.29

COMPETENCY-BASED DISCUSSION QUESTIONS

1. Which cognitive domains do you already use and which ones do you need to develop?

2. Which decision-making approach(es) does your organization commonly use and why do you think that approach, or combined approaches, is used? Could your organization use a different approach(es)?

3. Are there types of decisions you typically make that would be better served by using a group decision-making process? Are there instances when group decision making has not worked out, and what are the reasons?

EXERCISES

1. Decide which approach or combination of approaches you plan to use the next time a major decision needs to be made and, if using a group, explain why.

2. When your organization needs to use a group process for its next big decision, apply the 12-step approach and keep a record of what occurred during each step. After reviewing the record, make a list of what worked well and what did not. Also note if there were steps that were not used or could be skipped next time. Finally, did you circle back on any of the steps?

3. Complete all of the worksheets in this chapter for each of the four problem-solving and decision-making processes, and also complete the short-form and bit and piece decision analysis and the problem analysis short form.

4. Track the decision-making process of a meeting. Use a graph to do this, noting every minute on each of the following phases: establishing objectives, classifying objectives, and comparing alternative, adverse consequences and choices (and miscellaneous, if necessary).

5. Listen for some of the common pitfalls that happen to people when making decisions.

6. Review the solutions to pitfalls, and, when engaging in decision making, apply two of the solutions to each full decision-making process.

REFERENCES

Allwood, C. M., & Salo, I. (2014). Conceptions of decision quality and effectiveness in decision processes according to administrative officers and investigators making decisions for others in three Swedish public authorities. *Human Service Organizations: Management, Leadership & Governance, 38*(3), 271–282. doi:10.1080/23303131.2014.893277

Anderson, L. W., Krathwohl, D. R., Airasian, P. W., Cruikshank, K. A., Mayer, R. E., Pintrich, P. R., . . . Wittrock, M. C. (2001). *A taxonomy for learning, teaching, and assessing: A revision of bloom's taxonomy of educational objectives.* New York, NY: Pearson, Allyn & Bacon.

Bedeian, A. G. (1993). *Management* (3rd ed.) Fort Worth, TX: Dryden Press.

Bloom, B. S., Engelhart, M. D., Furst, E.J., Hill, W. H., & Krathwohl, D. R. (1956). *Taxonomy of educational objectives, Handbook I: The cognitive domain.* New York, NY: David McKay Co., Inc.

Carlisle, H. M. (1987). *Management essentials: Concepts for productivity and innovation* (2nd ed.) Chicago, CA: Science Research Associates.

Fulmer, R. M. (1988). *The new management* (4th ed.) New York, NY: Macmillan.

Golensky, M. (2011). *Strategic leadership and management in nonprofit organizations: Theory and practice.* Chicago, CA: Lyceum Books.

Kepner-Tregoe, Inc. (1972). *General guidelines for decision making.* Princeton, NJ: Princeton Research Press.

Kepner-Tregoe, Inc. (1973a). *Potential problem planning worksheet.* Princeton, NJ: Princeton Research Press.

Kepner-Tregoe, Inc. (1973b). *Problem analysis and decision making.* Princeton, NJ: Princeton Research Press.

Kepner-Tregoe, Inc. (1975). *Problem analysis worksheet.* Princeton, NJ: Princeton Research Press.

Kepner-Tregoe, Inc. (1977). *Decision analysis worksheet—Adverse consequences.* Princeton, NJ: Princeton Research Press.

Kepner-Tregoe, Inc. (1979a). *Decision analysis worksheet.* Princeton, NJ: Princeton Research Press.

Kepner-Tregoe, Inc. (1979b). *Situation appraisal worksheet.* Princeton, NJ: Princeton Research Press.

Kepner-Tregoe, Inc. (1980). *Short form and "bit and piece" (decision analysis).* Princeton, NJ: Princeton Research Press.

Klein, G. A. (1993). *A Recognition-Primed Decision (RPD) model of rapid decision making.* New York, NY: Ablex Publishing Corporation.

Lerner, J. S., & Tetlock, P. E. (1999). Accounting for the effects of accountability. *Psychological Bulletin, 125*(2), 255–275. doi:10.1037/0033-2909.125.2.255

Management Supervisory Development Program. (1986). *Problem solving and decision making.* Harrisburg, PA: Department of Public Welfare, Commonwealth of Pennsylvania.

Singleton, A. Union University. (2004). *Using a taxonomy of comprehension for leadership decision making.* Twenty-First Annual Academic Chairpersons Conference. Adams Mark Hotel. Orlando, FL.

Skidmore, R. A. (1995). *Social work administration: Dynamic management and human relationships* (3rd ed.) Needham Heights, MA: Allyn & Bacon.

Vroom, V. H., & Jago, A. G. (1988). *The new leadership: Managing participation in organizations.* Englewood Cliffs, NJ. Prentice-Hall, Inc.

Welch, D. A. (2002). *Decisions, decisions: The art of effective decision making.* Prometheus Books Amherst, NY.

CHAPTER 6

DEVELOPING AND MOTIVATING STAFF IN SOCIAL WORK

CHAPTER OBJECTIVES

- Understanding employee motivation.
- Designing effective reward systems.
- Implementing of staff orientation, training, and development.
- Being sensitive to inequities.
- Promoting and ensuring diversity.
- Dealing with faculty performance.
- Learning how to lead by example.
- Learning how to give directions.
- Understanding generational differences.
- Understanding the importance of effective communication.
- Learning how to use empathic language.

INTRODUCTION

Throughout this chapter we canvas a variety of constructs pertaining to staff motivation and development. Because leaders and managers are persistently required to monitor and facilitate improved performance, productivity, and quality of outcomes to service recipients, the impact on advancement must focus on how to motivate and develop staff to be able to consistently adapt to new demands, and this usually requires implementation of new or adaptive approaches. Innovative approaches in performance and productivity can be immensely beneficial in the long run, and social workers as a profession, of course, value the idea of change; but acclimatizing practice and learning behaviors to meet new demands can take time and consume additional energy and focus that may already be stretched thin. Box 6.1 displays the competencies/behaviors in this chapter.

BOX 6.1

COMPETENCIES AND PRACTICE BEHAVIORS ADDRESSED IN THIS CHAPTER

Possesses interpersonal skills that support viability and positive functioning of the organization (Network for Social Work Management Competencies 2). Practice Behaviors:

- Develops the value of optimizing the human potential of staff and ensures that the organization develops healthy and productive practices that develop staff in all ways (2.9).
- Demonstrates the ability to assemble a leadership team of individuals whose skills and abilities supplement one's own and to be a "team player" (2.10).

Models appropriate professional behavior and encourages other staff members to act in a professional manner (Network for Social Work Management Competencies 4). Practice Behaviors:

- Encourages staff to become involved in the identification and planning of their own professional development (4.4).
- Encourages staff to engage in a variety of activities including inquiry research, workshops, institutes, and observation/feedback (e.g., peer coaching and mentoring) (4.6).

Manages diversity and cross-cultural understanding (Network for Social Work Management Competencies 5). Practice Behaviors:

- Provides opportunities for staff to learn about different groups to enhance their practice, and encourages open discussion about issues to promote sensitivity (5.2).
- Seeks to employ a diverse workforce to align with clients served by the organization (5.3).

Plans, promotes, and models lifelong learning practices (Network for Social Work Management Competencies 11). Practice Behaviors:

- Positions the organization as a "learning organization," providing ongoing opportunities for all staff to receive professional development to assure quality service delivery (11.1).
- Ensures that the organization offers competent and regular supervision to staff at all levels of the organization (11.2).
- Whenever possible, offers staff an opportunity to learn from experts, as well as make presentations themselves, at outside conferences and meetings (11.6).

(continued)

BOX 6.1 *(Continued)*

■ Whenever possible, allows staff to take classes or work on advanced degrees with support of the agency. If agency funds are not available, flexibility in scheduling or other nonmonetary support should be offered to support learning (11.7).

CSWE Competency 6—Engage With Individuals, Families, Groups, Organizations, and Communities

■ 6.2 Use empathy, reflection, and interpersonal skills to effectively engage diverse clients and constituencies.

CSWE, Council on Social Work Education.

The exigencies of social work practice and educational innovations toward greater productivity and performance outcomes in the context of a global ethos of expediency, combined with the crisis-ridden work of direct practice and push for faster education accomplishments, can particularly heighten emotional exhaustion, stress, and burnout for social work employees, which, in turn, may compromise motivation. As employees reorient to new electronic systems, benchmarks, protocols, and so on, they may feel frustrated that their attention and energy have shifted away from how things "used to be" and is now being spent on novel approaches that may not yet feel productive or impactful. Leaders and managers who provide feedback, resources, and motivation to staff, especially during times of change and project implementation, can help ward off feelings of frustration, stress, and uncertainty. Attending to how the climate of the workplace is shaped through monitoring and managing the stress for the masses will result in improved employee performance. Remaining astute and sensitive to any real or perceived inequalities and barriers to staff development must be at the forefront of leaders' and managers' minds, and regular practice behaviors, in order to help motivate teams.

BOX 6.2

NETWORK FOR SOCIAL WORK MANAGEMENT COMPETENCIES AND PRACTICE BEHAVIORS 2

Possesses interpersonal skills that support viability and positive functioning of the organization (Network for Social Work Management Competencies 2). Practice Behaviors:

■ Develops the value of optimizing the human potential of staff and ensures that the organization develops healthy and productive practices that develop staff in all ways (2.9).

■ Demonstrates the ability to assemble a leadership team of individuals whose skills and abilities supplement one's own and to be a "team player" (2.10).

The competencies listed in Boxes 6.1 and 6.2 imply that one of the primary aims of leadership and management is to build a collective unit, a united front, *a team*. Teams are the essence of productivity and effectiveness, and it is the team's collaborative efforts that prove the repute of an organization. The essence of team membership is to work together to continuously improve individual talents that collectively contribute to the desired outcome. We begin our discussion about ways to apply practice behaviors 2.9 and 2.10 by providing some examples of ways "coaches," that is, leaders and managers motivate teams and instill values of collaboration and commitment to succeed. It is an essential task of leaders and managers to either shape or further reinforce individuals' drive to act as "team players." By creating teams that can work together and complement the talents of fellow teammates, the collective group can be highly impactful. Additionally, being among supportive coworkers, bonded by purpose, can help buffer times of stress. As the Chinese proverb states: "If you want to go fast, go alone. If you want to go far, go together."

Teams can be gratifyingly full of comradery, support, enthusiasm, and drive or, conversely and discouragingly, be tainted with torpor and infectious querulousness. Gratton and Erickson (2013) explained that when team membership is large, complex, and dispersed (either through virtual worksites or distinct department locations), the tendency to collaborate diminishes—*unless* the organization's leadership has taken active measures to create and maintain a culture of collaboration. They further explain that disparate skills and viewpoints are necessary for any contemporary organization to thrive. Consider if the manager of a professional baseball team spent his entire annual recruitment and hiring budget only on closing pitchers but had an outfielder that was injured and another who might be traded. How do you think the team's season will go? Teams need diverse skill sets, knowledge bases, and viewpoints, but diversity is sometimes challenged by human beings' penchants for similarity.

Gratton and Erickson (2013) noted that "the differences that inhibit collaboration include not only nationality but also age, educational level, and even tenure" (p. 56). It may seem peculiar to think that teams of social workers would have their collaborative spirits stifled by differences and diversity, but sadly our profession is not immune to this occurrence. However, examining the trends of 55 large teams revealed several common patterns that fostered high levels of collaboration, which suggest that leaders can promote an attitude of acceptance that embraces differences and influences cohesion (Gratton & Erickson, 2013). Gratton and Erickson's (2013) findings synthesize how leaders and managers can adopt various approaches for enhancing team collaboration, which include (a) investing in building and maintaining social relationships throughout the organization; (b) modeling collaborative behavior; (c) using coaching to reinforce a collaborative culture; (d) ensuring that new team members know other team members (i.e., beyond introductions); (e) modifying leadership styles as the team develops through stages of project implementation; and (f) assigning distinct roles to individual team members to work autonomously, but that are simultaneously geared toward the team's goal attainment as well. Furthermore, it is suggested that human resources departments can (a) provide training about specific skills of collaboration to employees, such as engaging in meaningful conversations, acknowledging others' work, and respectfully and productively resolving conflicts; and (b) support a sense of a work community through events such as sponsoring activities within the community (Habitat for Humanity, Special Olympics, sponsored walks to support a community/national/global cause).

A study by Petland (2013) examined the chemistry of high-performing groups and concluded that a critical "it factor" of successful teams was in how they communicated in informal settings. Observing communication patterns among teams in the workplace gave impetus to the idea of scheduling coffee breaks for all workers in a large call center of a banking firm at the same time to encourage socializing with their teammates. One manager, who was initially reluctant and worried about the potential loss of productivity this would cause, was pleasantly surprised to find that the experiment resulted in the average handling time of calls being reduced by more than 20% among lowest performing teams and by 8% across all groups. Moreover, employee satisfaction rates increased by more than 10%. The estimated savings to the company following this change were a forecasted $15 million (Petland, 2013).

If taken at face value, the correlations between coffee breaks, greater productivity, and job satisfaction may initially sound rather simplistic, one might even say misguided, advice. Petland (2013) in fact cautioned that many corporations attempt to create social opportunities and fail to get a return on their investment; specifically, she referred to one company that arranged "beer nights" for employees to meet outside of work, which was ineffective at increasing team productivity. She underscores that the critical factor of team performance improvement is the quality of communication among teammates. The quality of social communication among the teammates included elements of energy, engagement, and exploration (Petland, 2013). Thus, it was the way they interacted and showed interest and concern in informal settings that influenced how they worked together in their formal roles that contributed to greater productivity. Furthermore, Petland was surprised to find that an individual's reasoning and talent did not contribute as much to team success as one might imagine and instead suggests that "the best way to build a great team is not to select individuals for their smarts or accomplishments but to learn how they communicate and to shape and guide the team so that it follows successful communication patterns" (p. 7). So, what are those patterns? According to Petland, successful teams demonstrate the characteristics in Box 6.3.

BOX 6.3

CHARACTERISTICS OF SUCCESSFUL TEAMS

1. Everyone on the team talks and listens in roughly equal measure, keeping contributions short and sweet.
2. Members face one another, and their conversations and gestures are energetic.
3. Members connect directly with one another—not just with the team leader.
4. Members carry on back channel or side conversations within the team.
5. Members periodically break, go exploring outside the team, and bring information back (Petland, 2013, p. 7).

In many ways, social work leaders and managers can rely on their knowledge of group work theories and skills to develop cohesive teams (groups). What Petland describes as successful communication patterns within teams is akin to the process of mutual aid in group work. It is up to leaders and managers to facilitate meetings that allow processes to emerge. Shulman (2011) imparts that mutual aid is the process of helping others to help others, and is an inherent experience of group work. We propose that it is also an essential process to teamwork. The mutual aid process in group work is more than just lending support to fellow group members: it involves a group of people with similar problems, or what Shulman refers to as the all in the same boat phenomenon—joining together to help one another. Oftentimes group members will chat during breaks or after the group ends; they will share resources that have helped them outside of the group; and they communicate directly with one another, not the leader, when exuding empathy or sharing advice. Essentially, the group begins to run itself (Shulman, 2011).

An inexperienced or ostentatious group facilitator may erroneously overlook the fact that it is the group members who own the group, rather than the group leader. The leader of the group is predominantly responsible for getting the group to work together and adopts the stance that clients are the experts of their own lives, and in a like manner the team members are viewed as the experts of their realms of responsibilities. Allowing the team to run the meeting does not imply that the leader sits back and does nothing, particularly during an unstructured group meeting. It simply means that the leader is able to pose questions that elicit participation and idea sharing from all members, manage any mic stealers (those individuals who tend to take up an unfair share of airtime and monopolize the conversation), guide staff to connect with everyone (e.g., eye contact and body position are not aimed toward the leader the entire meeting, but with all members), and provide direction for members to work together outside of the meeting (sometimes this entails a project, or merely following up on a conversation outside of the meeting). Above all, the leader who is able to provoke mutual aid never delusively positions her or himself as the "expert" of the group, but instead welcomes and even solicits feedback and ideas from team members, and furthermore, proves that they authentically value this input by making adjustments as needed. The leader who is comfortable enough to facilitate this type of process will likely observe his or her team sharing information, purpose (all in the same boat), skills that promote innovation and goal attainment, and ultimately enhanced **team commitment**. Team commitment is defined as "the extent to which people are proud to belong to a team or organization and believe that everyone is working toward the same objectives" (Spreier, Fontaine, & Malloy, 2006, p. 53). The more a team experiences shared values, the greater performance commitment they share, and the higher team pride they hold. When teams are infused with mutual aid, mutual aid can optimize individuals' potential, improve performance, and promote productivity and collective problem solving.

Box 6.4 describes an example of why teamwork is important.

BOX 6.4

EXCERPT FROM PRESIDENT JOE INTERVIEW

Giving the team the freedom to share and interact is very important. If one sits in a leadership team here, I say X and let the team engage conversation. Team is important.

Challenge one another, support one another. (President Joe Bertalino, Interview on Leadership Style from March 5, 2018, SCSU, New Haven, Connecticut)

SCSU, Southern Connecticut State University.

BOX 6.5

NETWORK FOR SOCIAL WORK MANAGEMENT COMPETENCIES AND PRACTICE BEHAVIORS 4

Models appropriate professional behavior and encourages other staff members to act in a professional manner (Network for Social Work Management Competencies 4). Practice Behaviors:

- Encourages staff to become involved in the identification and planning of their own professional development (4.4).
- Encourages staff to engage in a variety of activities including inquiry research, workshops, institutes, and observation/feedback (e.g., peer coaching and mentoring) (4.6).

UNDERSTANDING EMPLOYEE MOTIVATION

In this section, we discuss ways to motivate staff through increased involvement, review considerations for providing desired rewards, and examine ways to nurture lifelong learning through supervision approaches and training opportunities (see Box 6.5 which displays the competencies/behaviors in this section). There are several factors of motivation that leaders and managers must be cognizant of, which include *leading by example, effective communication, empowerment, talent development,* and *incentivizing.*

We begin our discussion about motivation with the idea of threat. You may be thinking: "Threat?!" Yes, threat. Leaders and managers not only need to be conscientious of what motivates staff but also what demotivates them, as the latter is often directly the result of a perceived threat to one's sense of security in their social/professional realm. Rock (2008) suggests that perceived threats to one's social world can have physical, emotional, and behavioral reactions that are similar to response threats toward one's primal needs. Hallowell (2015) congruently asserts that when staff chronically perceive their work environment as a threat (e.g., they are overwhelmed by the task beyond their ability to cope with it), this "disables the brain and makes performance worse" (p. 14). The intersection of social neuroscience and leadership and management illustrates how individuals' behaviors are motivated to maximize rewards and minimize threats. The SCARF model, first introduced in 2008 by David Rock, suggests that individuals are motivated by *status, certainty, autonomy, relatedness,* and *fairness.* **Status** refers to the person's degree of importance to others. **Certainty** is concerned with the person's ability to predict outcomes, and since our brains are predicting "mapping machines" (Rock, 2006), this motivation is fairly common and is also the reason people prematurely jump to conclusions since the brain is trying to map outcomes. **Autonomy** is about a person's perceived sense of control in his or her environment and life events. **Relatedness** pertains to a person's sense of security and trust within her or his social/professional orbit. Finally, **fairness** is about a person's perception of fair exchanges between people in his or her social/professional group (Rock, 2008). As Rock (2006, 2008) explains, we are wired to maximize rewards and minimize threats, but this construct is not telescoped to our most basic, or primitive, needs. Rather it has evolved to include our social needs that drive our behavior and emotional responses. Hence, if a person perceives a threat to one of the five SCARF domains, she or he will respond to the threat stimuli. For instance, if a person who highly values autonomy perceives that he or she is being micromanaged, the situation will activate a social behavior and emotional response, which ultimately impacts performance and productivity. Interestingly enough, 20% of a person's productivity is based on the perception of fairness. So, if an employee does not sense that there is parity in their work environment, the organization is operating at a significant deficiency. Add another one or two employees that feel similarly and, well, you get the point. But just to belabor it a bit more, consider what Kim and Mauborgne (2017) had to say about this:

> 50% of employees merely put in their time, while the remaining 20% act out their discontent in counterproductive ways, negatively influencing their coworkers, missing days on the job, and driving customers away through poor service. Gallup estimates that the 20% costs the US economy around half a trillion dollars each year. (p. 1–2)

Understanding what individual staff value helps leaders understand what may cause staff to feel threatened, and consequently stimulate a fight, flight, or freeze reaction. Leaders and managers may unknowingly, and we certainly hope unintentionally, activate threat stimuli. Without pausing to reflect on how the staff may have become demotivated (i.e., threatened), they run the risk of exacerbating the staff's response to the perceived threat. Engaging in open and empathic dialogues is one of many antidotes to this, but proactively attending to ways that outright avoid posing threat stimuli is always preferable and helps to ensure staff are able to perform at their peak. Hallowell (2015) imparts that perpetual or excessive fear neurologically impairs *peak performance*. Peak performance is defined by Hallowell as "consistent excellence, with improvement over time at a specific task or set of tasks" (2015, p. 14). He summarizes the factors that contribute to peak performance in five steps:

1. Select. Leaders and managers need to figure out what employees should do. To achieve peak performance, leaders can help them select tasks that they (a) are good at, (b) like to do, and (c) will add value to the organization or project at hand.

2. Connect. When people feel connected to people, to their work, and the organization, they are more inclined to be committed, loyal, and "make sacrifices to preserve that sense of attachment" (p. 17). Leaders and managers can model this by:

   a. Noticing and acknowledging your employees

   b. Allowing for idiosyncrasies and peccadilloes

   c. Encouraging conversation

   d. Encouraging breaks

e. Offering food and drink (nurturing gesture)

f. Fostering impromptu get-togethers

3. Play. Defined here to mean *"any activity that involves the imagination"* (p. 20). Ways to encourage staff to engage in creative problem solving include:

   a. Asking open-ended questions (use the Socratic method)

   b. Modeling a questioning attitude

   c. Decorating and arranging your workplace with an eye toward facilitating play (color themes, team tables in break rooms, appropriately humorous pictures or quotes)

   d. "Retrograde synthesis" (start with the goal and work backward, step by step)

4. Grapple and grow. This step involves mastering difficult tasks that "matter," which enhances feelings of well-being and accomplishment. Hallowell (2015) cautions that prior to asking people to do more, leaders and managers must first ask if they are operating in the junction of what they like, are good at, and offer value to the organization.

5. Shine. Provide affirmations for what and how staff have accomplished work.

Leading by example. It seems commonsensible to state that leaders and managers must be able to *lead by example*, but unfortunately not everyone follows this principle. If a leader/manager is not exhibiting passion for the work, avoids certain tasks or people in the work environment, is apathetic or easily discouraged or frustrated, how will they possibly motivate others to work with passion and purpose? Do not get us wrong: we are not suggesting that leading by example means that one ceases to perform the daily tasks they are responsible for and actually do the tasks of their subordinates. Instead, we mean that a leader/manager's ability to find her or his own style of exemplifying what she or he wants to see more of in the work environment and attitudes of staff. For instance, a CEO of a children's clinical school made a habit of taking all students who earned honors out to breakfast every marking period, along with his staff. As he sat with the staff and students, the staff were able to see him engage firsthand with the students and see his compassion and concern for them. A secondary gain was that he also got to know the frontline staff better, and they got to learn that he was genuinely interested in hearing about the minutia of quotidian operations they deal with, and he made it a point to make organizational changes based on the input he received during those breakfast chats. Another example is of an executive at a 24-hour care facility who knew that the frontline staff was having difficulty with a resident who recently became floridly psychotic. One evening she stopped in to see how the resident and staff were doing and found the resident's one-to-one staff sitting in the resident's room looking emotionally exhausted and hurriedly eating his dinner in a hard chair. She offered to sit with the resident so the staff was able to take a break to finish, and enjoy, his dinner and take a short respite from the client. One last example is the executive director who is not above picking up garbage during a walk on campus because she believes that the clients and staff deserve to serve and be served in an aesthetically welcoming, and clean, environment. As you can see from these examples, it is not about doing anything just for the sake of doing it, it is also about what drives the leader/manager. In the examples depicted, the leaders believed that they were doing what is right, and not for the sake of a show. This is true leadership by example—and people will always sniff out the difference. Leaders and managers must demonstrate their commitment to the clients, the cause, and the staff authentically, and cultivate their own genuine style of leading by example.

Second, leaders and managers need to be able to *effectively communicate*. Leaders and managers must be clear in their message, aware of their tone and body language. Above all, leaders and managers need to communicate by showing up, and not just communicate through technology.

When staff members are able to connect with leaders, face-to-face communication can significantly improve. Why? We are wired to pick up on social nuances to help make sense of the message being delivered. Our mirror neurons (connected with theory of mind) are activated by the behavior of others, which not only helps us to understand others' actions and intentions but helps us learn new skills by mimicking the observed actions. Additionally, who is going to feel motivated by a phantom leader or manager who is never physically around to see the work results anyway? In-person communication may have its time constraints, but it shows an unrivaled level of interest in and commitment to the staff.

Third, staff who are *empowered* are more likely to feel motivated than staff who feel they do not have a say in matters. For instance, the manager of a group home sensed the grumblings of staff who were recently mandated to work additional shifts due to an increased census and position vacancies. She met with the team of staff to better understand their dissatisfaction, and they explained that they do not feel they can manage work–life balance when they are mandated to stay for another shift. The manager, who had also worked additional shifts to help provide coverage, empathized with the team and asked if they would like to work together to create a schedule that builds in overtime shift coverage in a way that seemed predictable and fair for everyone. The manager explained that the team would have to work with each other to determine which days they would stay on for an additional shift. So if staff A knew that staff B had to leave on time for childcare reasons on Wednesdays, and staff C had class in the evening on Wednesdays, then staff A would work the double on that day, and staff B would cover Thursdays, while C would cover Fridays. If any staff needed to switch days they would work with teammates to have the shift covered in advance, so they could all avoid the unanticipated, and undesirable, mandates to stay. The manager noticed after using this approach that the staff was no longer calling out for their shifts; she presumed it was primarily because they did want to let their teammates down, but also because they were empowered to take ownership of the schedule.

Fourth, staff need to have *opportunities for growth*. Providing opportunities for professional development and advancement helps staff to feel that they are a valued asset worth investing in. Offering opportunities for professional growth can include providing continuing education and conference attending, in-service training, or projects that are designed to help staff meet stretch goals. Many staff have untapped talents. Good leaders and managers take the time to understand what an individual's professional goals are (hint: what will motivate them) and connect work tasks with staff's long-term goals. Some organizations are concerned about the time and fiscal demands talent development will consume; however, research indicates that the cost of recruiting new talent is an estimated 150% of an employee's salary (Gostick & Elton, 2018). Thus, it is mutually beneficial to the organization and the individual to retain and develop staff.

Finally, leaders and managers need to *provide incentives to staff*. We mentioned in Chapter 2 that external rewards need to be enticing to the employee, and there is no one-size-fits-all model for this. Leaders and managers need to know what drives their staff, individually and as a team, and tailor the incentives accordingly (more about this later).

▧ UNDERSTANDING GENERATIONAL DIFFERENCES AND SIMILARITIES OF MOTIVATION

There is an anthology of literature dedicated to managing millennials, particularly alongside baby boomers, which elucidates the chasms that exist between age cohorts in terms of what they value, and hence, what motivates them when it comes to work. Millennials are the fastest growing population entering the labor force, an estimated 56 million, closely followed by Gen Xers at 53 million, with baby boomers averaging 41 million in the workforce (Fry, 2018). Additionally, there will soon be a burgeoning of postmillennials working alongside baby boomers, who are trending toward later life retirement in comparison to the generations that preceded them. The relevance of the topic on generational differences found in the literature suggests universal workplace tensions that exist between generations, particularly about the way things "ought to be" versus how things have "always been." For instance, millennials' top three complaints about older employees are that they are (a) resistant to change, (b) lack recognition of (millennials') efforts, and (c) micromanage. On the other hand, older employees typically complain that millennials have (a) a poor work ethic, (b) informal behavior and language, and (c) inappropriate dress (Gostick & Elton, 2018, p. 30). While value clashes can create some divisiveness in the workplace, it can also offer opportunities to integrate values, work ethics, and ideas that capitalize on the best of the distinct cohorts. We posit that the examination into generational differences is important for understanding motivation and can correspondingly aid leaders and managers in creating inclusive work environments that promote creativity, diversity, learning, and ultimately performance and productivity.

Espinoza and Ukleja (2016) explained that the generational clashes are normative because, "as each age cohort's self-identity is strengthened, it makes comparisons of itself to other generations. Social comparison exaggerates the differences between groups (Baby Boomer/Millennial) but strengthens in-group similarity and cohesion" (p. 24). The key for managers and leaders is to first help all members embrace the differences among them and "suspend the bias of your own experience and not compare yourself to them" (p. 58). Second, leaders and managers have to evoke the greatest assets across the age groups to complement, rather than clash, with one another. The differences in generational values are imperative to understand not only for the purpose of unifying teams but also for retaining staff, especially those from younger generations. Whereas baby boomers are more likely to enter into "psychological contracts," or an informal and unwritten contract of job security and trust with employers (ultimately influencing employee loyalty), millennials are less likely to agree to this elusive contract (Espinoza & Ukleja, 2016). Furthermore, millennials are more likely to leave their jobs if their needs (i.e., what motivates them) are unmet. The adage "employees don't leave jobs, they leave managers" holds water especially for millennials, and we believe it will for postmillennials, too.

In order to extract the best from different age cohorts, we must first seek to understand the characteristics, values, and motivating forces within the distinct populations. Fitch and Van Brunt (2016) provide an outline of the generational characteristics of leaders and managers, as excerpted in Table 6.1.

TABLE 6.1 Generational Characteristics: Leaders and Managers

Millennials leaders: Tend to be passionate but may lack experience leading and inspiring others to follow or implement their creative ideas. It is important to focus on their passion as this is a primary strength that can be used to create goals for growth opportunities related to leading others.

Millennials managers: May not be as focused on the minutia of details involved in daily tasks, especially when compared to previous generations such as baby boomers. In the role of manager, they tend to thrive and achieve better outcomes when they are somehow invested in the end results. It is helpful to offer information that helps them see their sense of purpose and belonging, while also mentoring them on how to focus on the details of tasks and projects, and to illustrate the connections for increased awareness of why the details matter to management.

Generation X leaders: May be a combination of practical thinkers and idealizers who are capable of thinking big. They often have passion and big hearts that help them collaborate well with others and also inspire those they lead. One of their greatest assets may be motivating others, which is a strength that can be capitalized on to help inspire those who are not as passionate or motivated.

Generation X managers: May be a combination of practical thinkers and idealizers who are capable of thinking big. They often have passion and big hearts that help them collaborate well with others and also inspire those they lead. One of their greatest assets may be motivating others, which is a strength that can be capitalized on to help inspire those who are not as passionate or motivated.

Baby boomers as leaders: May be quite likeable and charismatic leaders who have a robust base of knowledge and experience, which may be an asset for mentoring others.

Baby boomers managers: May hold a wealth of knowledge about an organization as they may be more likely to have longer tenure with the organization. The historical knowledge and propensity for expansive networks can be shared and taught to others.

As you can see, there are clear differences in the strengths and weaknesses outlined for each generation. Leaders and managers who are aware of these differences can facilitate discussions that help to further develop staff across generations, tapping into their unique skills and characteristics, while also rounding out weaknesses by leveraging the strengths of different generations.

Because Gen Xers and baby boomers have been working together for a number of years, and thus both cohorts have greater experience negotiating perceived differences, Espinoza and Ukleja (2016) focused on the perceived orientation and rapport-building competencies of millennials, in comparison with boomers. According to Espinoza and Ukleja (2016), the *Perceived Orientations of Millennials by Baby Boomers* include the following:

- *Autonomous*: Unlikely to conform to office processes, so long as their work is completed.
- *Entitled*: Want to move up quickly and guarantees for performance, not just the chance to perform.
- *Imaginative:* Can offer fresh perspectives, unique ideas, but also distract from participating in processes.
- *Self-absorbed:* Predominantly concerned with how they are treated versus how they treat others. Focused on their own needs for trust, encouragement, and praise.
- *Defensive:* Want to receive only positive feedback and not constructive feedback, and can be guarded and resentful when they are told what they are not doing well.
- *Abrasive:* This behavior is likely due to growing up in an era of technological communication, and social courtesies and pleasantries are overlooked, which appears disrespectful.
- *Myopic:* Difficulty making causal connections and, due to their internal interests, they struggle to understand how others are impacted.
- *Unfocused:* While recognized for their intellectual abilities, they lack attention to detail, are easily bored, and are unable to focus on tasks that are uninteresting to them.
- *Indifferent:* Perceived as lacking commitment and care (p. 41–42).

It is important to recognize that these perceptions outlined earlier are taken from a sample of individuals and may not be representative of all individuals due to the subjective bias in self-reporting. Additionally, it is critical to underscore that assuming all of these perceptions to be true and applicable to all millennials may inherently bias one's view. Therefore, we underscore that this list of perceptions is merely one view of many, and primarily serves to highlight that all working groups are diverse, have diverse values, and have different perceptions of others. The relevancy to this material is understanding how differences in values, traits, and beliefs can be discussed and mediated with others in order to form a diverse, productive, and supportive work environment. The *Generational Rapport Competencies* suggested by Espinoza and Ukleja (2016) to enhance working relationships and motivate millennials based on the perceived orientations described include the following:

- *Flexing (be flexible):* Modify workplace expectations and behaviors. Call for empathically listening and adapting to new ways of doing and viewing things.
- *Incenting (create the right rewards):* Know the reward expectations and design a path that matches with performance expectations. Requires the ability to identify the values and pair recognition and reward with those values. This approach also entails providing information to millennials about advancement opportunities and regular performance feedback.

- *Cultivating (put their imagination to work):* The art of seeing and supporting the creativity in others. This action requires that leaders/managers create a work atmosphere where staff can feel free to release their imagination and have fun in the process.

- *Engaging (build a relationship):* Relationally connect and take interest in the millennial as an individual to discover the points of connections.

- *Disarming (be positive when correcting):* Proactively respond to conflict. This includes de-escalating intense interactions, working with any resistance, and active listening and fairness.

- *Self-differentiating (do not take things personally):* This action is simply about your ability to self-regulate your emotions and "trigger" events in a manner that allows you to respond, rather than react, and compartmentalize emotions to prevens you from personalizing things.

- *Broadening (show them the big picture):* The ability to help millennials make causal connections to better understand the link between daily tasks and the bigger picture. It involves teaching organizational awareness and the ability to assess potential ramifications of daily actions and decisions.

- *Directing (include the details):* The capacity to clearly communicate what is expected. This action requires that communication is not ambiguous and does not assume that the listener decoded the message that was intended, and requires some questioning and listening to be sure that message was fully understood. This process of questioning and listening helps to determine the millennial's readiness for the task.

- *Motivating (make it matter to them):* The ability to inspire millennials to discover the meaning, or purpose, of everyday work to better understand how their contribution matters. (p. 41–42)

Here again, we use these examples to underscore that leaders can benefit from understanding the individual differences in communication, recognition, motivation, and values to address the diverse needs of staff from all generations and backgrounds.

Gostick and Elton (2018) also provided an overview for understanding what motivates different generations, further reinforcing the point that understanding differences in motivational forces can help connect teams across generations. They culled 23 of the top motivators from research in the behavioral science field and, contrary to Espinoza and Ukleja's (2016) findings of perceived millennial characteristics, concluded that older generations actually preferred to work more autonomously (listed as the eighth out of 23 motivators), while millennials ranked this among the bottom of their motivators (21st out of 23 motivators). This finding suggests that the perceived orientation of millennials as autonomous may not be such a cogent motivator for millennials after all, and moreover indicates that leaders must be able to distinguish the degrees of autonomy given to and expected from their individual employees. Interestingly, millennial workers are seeking "more direction, coaching, and inclusion" (Gostick & Elton, 2018, p. 31). Older generations were more inclined to feel frustrated by this perceived need for "handholding" the millennials, who felt the lack of mentoring and collaboration was frustrating (Gostick & Elton, 2018, p. 33).

The top three motivators found across millennials, Gen Xers, and boomers were impact, learning, and family (Gostick & Elton, 2018). Impact refers to the desire to know that one's work is important and making a positive difference. Learning is the desire to continue to expand knowledge and develop skills. Finally, family refers to the desire to have work–life balance and make family members proud. Another common finding across generations that Gostick and Elton (2018) reveal is that money was listed in the bottom three of motivating factors. Millennials also listed prestige and autonomy, while Gen Xers and boomers listed fun and prestige as the bottom motivators.

Millennials' desire for more collaboration and mentoring directly ties to the second significant difference between the generations, which is that they also desire and are strongly motivated by recognition for their work. Gostick and Elton (2018) explained, "In fact, overall, the data indicates that Millennials as a group are almost *twice* as likely to be motivated by recognition as Gen X and *three-and-a-half times* more likely to be motivated by recognition than Boomers" (p. 35). Perhaps the best finding for leaders and managers to be aware of is that millennials are drawn to a sense of community and purpose. They want to feel that they are contributing to a cause and that their work is filled with purpose. This desire is, of course, excellent news for social work leaders and managers. But as previously mentioned, leaders and managers need to employ competencies such as broadening, directing, and clearly explaining how their work is contributing to the overall purpose (mission, vision, values, and goals) of the organization.

Box 6.6 provides a list of questions to unlock answers about what motives staff and what they value the most.

BOX 6.6

DISCOVERING STAFF VALUES

Questions to unlock answers about what motivates staff and what they value the most

- What do you feel you are best at doing?
- What skills do you have that you value the most?
- Can you give me some examples of how you can, or already do, apply what you are best at in your current role?
- What do you enjoy doing the most? How can we build more of that into your work routine (caveat here: presumes that the answer to the first part of the question is appropriately aligned with a professional goal and mutually beneficial to the individual and organization)?
- What would you like to be better at?
- What type of situations and teams do you work best in?
- What do you want to be doing, which you are not currently doing?
- What would help you do that?
- What are the three most important things to your career life?
- What do you least like about your work?
- What would you like to improve?
- What is something you have improved that you feel really proud of? How did you do it? What helped you?
- What would you like to be doing a year from now?
- What do you hope to contribute to the team?
- What would you like the team to know about your talents? How can they get to know that? How can they demonstrate to you that they know that? What is the best way for me to show you that I recognize that?
- What is the best way to offer you feedback? How will you know if it did not sit well? What do you need from me?

Effective communication requires that we use emotional intelligence to engage, explain, and pick up on the nuanced and unspoken information conveyed during an interaction. Communicating effectively with millennial staff compels leaders and managers to confirm that the message conveyed was accurately understood, most notably when discussing recognition and reward (Espinoza & Ukeleja, 2016). For instance, when a professor states "If you do the readings, have good class attendance and participation, and avail yourself of office hours and the writing lab," what students likely hear is "If I turn in all my work and show up for class, I'll get an A." Another example is when a manager suggests "Taking a student intern will be good experience for you to gain skills that can be applied to clinical supervision," and the worker hears "If I take an intern, I will be promoted to the supervisor position." The interpreted message about the potential outcomes, or incentives, can be misconstrued as guarantees because of selective perception, a process that unintentionally screens out parts of the intended message because it contradicts with one's hopes about the possible outcome (Espinoza & Ukeleja, 2016). In layman's terms, this ineffective communication can be thought of as "hearing what one wants to hear," which can sometimes provoke frustration in both the communicator and the listener, but it is important to note that this is an unintentional process. It is therefore critical for the communicator to clarify what the listener has understood from the message delivered. Finally, effective communication can prevent emotional exhaustion, stress, and burnout of staff. The risk of job burnout, emotional exhaustion, and decreased well-being is high among human service workers; ambiguity in work responsibilities and conflicting work roles can heighten this. Leaders and managers can help prevent emotional depletion and promote staff well-being through clear explanations of role expectations and responsibilities.

Leaders and managers often need to communicate to teams to provide direction and motivation. Some leaders/managers are more comfortable with and adept at delivering motivational talks to their teams than others. Many borrow from prior experiences of listening to former coaches, managers, or other inspirational figures, but few have relied on the science behind pep talks according to McGinn (2018). McGinn (2018) outlines the three-part formula that has been studied to energize teams, which includes *direction giving, expressions of empathy*, and *meaning making*. Note that these three key ingredients are in concert with Espinoza and Ukeleja's (2016) rapport-building competencies for working with millennials. The field of research on this matter has been coined as the motivating language theory (MLT), and McGinn suggests that leaders who understand the three key elements embedded in MLT can skillfully, and we would add artfully, apply them.

Direction giving entails the use of "uncertainty-reducing language" (McGinn, 2018, p. 110). This requires the leader to explain exactly how to do the task staff are being asked to do, provide clear and complete instructions (i.e., easily understood), give clear definitions of the work, and provide ample information on how the work will be evaluated. For instance, you may hear a sports coach explain in a pregame speech:

"We are going to need to keep moving the puck. They have fast skaters, and they will be looking to put the puck on their leading scorer's stick. So, Smith, Gold, and Johnson, I want you to mark him every shift you're out there. If you get beat, you guys have to get back to help out in the defensive zone."

Similarly, an executive preparing a team for a meeting might explain:

"The state is looking to cut money wherever they can. We need to show them how we can help to reduce the cost of congregate care by providing intensive wraparound services. Megan, we need you to prepare data from this year and the last two that shows the reduction in emergency room presentations and emergency placements since we implemented this program. Steve, we need you present on the quantitative and qualitative measures of the program's success, and Bonnie, we need you to drive it home with the cost savings data that you've compiled over the three years. I will conclude with some of the new visions we have for using technology to have more frequent check-ins with clients to continue to support them in their communities."

Empathic language demonstrates concern for the individuals performing the task. This language can include "praise, encouragement, gratitude, and acknowledgement of the task's difficulty" (McGinn, 2018, p. 110). Checking in with staff by asking how everyone is doing, verbalizing your understanding that the task is challenging but that you believe in the team's ability to rise to the challenge, and expressing that their well-being is important are examples of empathic language. For instance, a leader might say

I know this work is difficult. You come here every day, and regardless of what you are dealing with in your own lives—sleepless nights of a new baby, taking care of your ill parent, worrying about your kid who just left for college—you bring your best self here to do really hard work. It takes very committed, compassionate, and smart individuals to what you do. I know our clients appreciate you, even if they have funny ways of showing it sometimes. And I appreciate you all, too. I know that the budget cuts have meant that you have each needed to take on additional cases, and I want to check in and see how everyone is handling the recent changes, and how we can support each other through these changes.

Meaning-making language provides an explanation for why the task is important. McGinn notes that this entails making a connection between the organization's purpose and mission to the individual team member's goals. Additionally, meaning making often incorporates the use of stories "about people who've worked hard or succeeded in the company, or about how the work has made a real difference in the lives of customers or the community" (McGinn, 2018, p. 110). For example, a leader might share with their team:

"I know that you are all here because you believe that change, and recovery is possible. You're here to help make a difference in the lives of our clients and their support networks." Or: "I know that you all believe in educating and inspiring the minds of our future clinicians, policy advocates, and leaders in our field."

An effective pep talk includes all three factors of direction giving, empathic language, and meaning making, but as with many things in life, balance is key. Balancing the three-part formula means that the leader/manager understands who his or her audience is and emphasizes one of the three factors to a greater or lesser degree as the social context calls for. For example, staff who are skillful at the task being asked of them will require less direction giving (and their audience may be put off if the talk is overly focused on this). A tight-knit team may not need as much empathic language and overemphasizing this factor may cause the team to believe that you do not know them well (or be put off by the overuse of your social work ways!). McGinn suggests that meaning making is typically useful, but to a lesser degree when the goals are obvious to everyone. We would add that because the field of social work can be stressful, and staff are exposed to complex and discouraging conditions, providing reminders about the meaning of their work is always helpful when they are expressed thoughtfully and artfully (i.e., never out of habit or in a mechanical fashion).

In academia, the tenure and promotion processes play a significant role in motivating faculty. If they do not produce, they lose their jobs. To obtain a promotion, one must also produce and meet certain standards. All universities have unique promotion and tenure procedures in terms of what qualifies one for tenure or a promotion. However, once a faculty achieves tenure, what can motivate them? Promotion from assistant to associate professor (although in most instances faculty seek and obtain tenure and promotion to associate simultaneously)? Then promotion to the next level of full professor can have some motivating value. However, what can motivate full professors who have tenure? Most universities have a post-tenure review process every 6 years. That said, the post-tenure review process usually has minimal ramifications. So we are left with believing faculty will be motivated by the intrinsic value of their work!

DESIGNING AND ALLOCATING REWARDS

Rewards are defined as "a reflection of whether people feel they are given regular, objective feedback and are rewarded accordingly. While compensation and formal recognition are important, the main component is feedback that is immediate, specific, and directly linked to performance" (Spreier et al., 2006, p. 53). An inherent challenge in leadership and management is designing and allocating rewards for staff that will provide the desired affirmation about their performance. The social work profession is significantly different from business professions that are more profit driven and therefore more endowed to fiscally incentivize staff with commission and bonus rewards. However, as the emerging research on rewards illustrates, staff across diverse professions are looking for more than financial recognition (Fitch & Van Brunt, 2016; Kohn, 2018). Furthermore, the social service sector is composed of individuals who are not primarily driven by salary, and thus organizations are at significant advantage to create job satisfaction through nonmonetary contingencies, including positive work environments, fulfilling supervisory relationships, and providing opportunities for ongoing professional development through a variety of work assignments (Smith & Shields, 2012).

Incentivizing staff through external rewards, such as stipends for additional work, a floating holiday for successful outcomes, increased pay or fringe benefits, and so on, continue to be embraced with some enthusiasm, but Kohn (2018) elucidates that the enthusiasm can be short-lived. The mistake that many leaders make is failing to ask staff directly what they value. Reward programs can fail to have the impact executives hope if they overlook the participation of staff in the design process. Ignoring the values of staff is referred to as *need-based programs*, or reward programs that strictly rely on management's assumptions about what staff value; as a result the reward program is based only on this assumption (Espinoza & Ukkleja, 2016). Leaders and managers need to be cognizant of how staff participate in designing the type of rewards employees seek, and the employees will thus be grateful and incentivized by the rewards. Additionally, leaders and managers need to "create an environment in which a person becomes self-motivated or intrinsically motivated" (Espinoza & Ukleja, 2016, p. 57). For instance, knowing that autonomy is intrinsically valued by some means that providing opportunities for autonomous work assignments becomes the intrinsic motivation. Therefore, a manager that can create some flexibility in the work environment will successfully fuel the staff's intrinsic motivation. We strongly encourage a direct conversation that helps staff understand that you are invested in them and tailoring tasks to their individual talents and career aspirations:

> *Carrie, I know we've talked about some of goals, and as we have gotten to know each other, I've grown to understand that you enjoy and value tasks where you can work independently on some community engagement activities that can really help our outreach department. The reason I am asking you to work on the community networking project is because you successfully engaged the parent group and helped increase their participation and buy-in, and also because I want to give you an opportunity to use your outreach and engagement skills on a similar project. Again, this is part of a larger organizational initiative and you will need to provide us with a monthly summary of your progress. Let's start by you telling me a little about what ideas you might have for this project, and how you see them connecting with the organization's goals.*

In the example, Carrie was provided with an opportunity to work on a stretch goal, provided with positive feedback about a specific performance, and informed about what she is receiving (reward) and will be expected to provide back to the team. As the conversation ensues, the manager might ask questions about what Carrie's professional goals are and they might discuss how this task can help her professional development. Carrie is likely to feel that she is valued, understood, and encouraged to work on her professional goals and become invested in the project. In sum, Carrie is more likely to be internally rather than externally motivated.

Incentive programs do not always work. Kohn (2018) presents data on the use and impact of reward systems that challenges conventional thinking about incentivizing staff. He offers several compelling reasons for why incentive plans are ineffective, including

1. Pay does not motivate. While money is a concern, it is not of principle concern. Anyone who has worked alongside Mental Health Technicians or Direct Care Counselors or Certified Nursing Assistants may be more apt to believe this reason outlined by Kohn. They have tough jobs that are physically and emotionally taxing, they are often the first to be assaulted by clients, and among the lowest financially compensated. They could just as easily secure a job at a local retail store, restaurant, and so on, for roughly the same hourly wage and less physical and emotional strain. So, it is fairly safe to assume that it is not the money they care about, but the purpose of why they work in a caretaking industry.

2. Rewards punish. Just as coercive leadership styles demotivate staff, rewards may have a similar effect. Kohn suggests that establishing a contingency based on performance means that the manager is manipulating the staff, "and that experience of being controlled is likely to assume a punitive quality over time." (p. 118)

3. Rewards rupture relationships. Forcing people to compete for rewards can erode team cohesion, collaboration, and performance.

4. Rewards ignore reasons. A common error managers make is to develop reward plans to get their teams back on track before understanding the true issues that led them off-track and ignoring the core problem(s). Kohn warns that rewards are sometimes used as a substitute for providing staff with the resources needed to perform a task well. For example, an agency aimed to reduce restraints tried to incentivize departments with the lowest percentages with an additional floating holiday. The problem is, how will staff learn other ways of de-escalating clients to accomplish this goal? Similarly, instructing a staff to develop an evidence-based group curriculum and suggesting they will be promoted to lead clinician if they do a good job places a lot of pressure on that staff (threat response = poor performance). How will the staff develop the group if they do not have access to scholarly journals or is unable to attend relevant training? Thus, we cannot dangle rewards in lieu of resources and comprehensive understanding of the core issues or needs.

5. Rewards discourage risk-taking. Because the focus is on the reward, this motivator can diminish one's creativity and outside-the-box thinking.

6. Rewards undermine interest. Extrinsic motivators cannot match intrinsic motivators. As Kohn states, "People who do exceptional work may be glad to get paid and even more glad to be paid well, but they do not work to collect a paycheck. They work because they love what they do." (2018, p. 117–120)

Kohn concludes that behaviorist theory is implicitly responsible for the construction of incentive programs and suggests the psychological assumption of "bribes to accomplish" underpinning reward plans is ineffective. Kohn also shares a critical observation of the research, which has essentially ascribed to a behaviorist doctrine of evaluating quantitative outcomes of productivity versus qualitative measures of performance. Consider the following excerpt:

Do rewards work? The answer depends on what we mean by "work." Research suggests that, by and large, rewards succeed as securing one thing only: temporary compliance. When it comes to producing lasting change in attitudes and behavior, however, rewards, like punishment, are strikingly ineffective. Once the rewards run out, people revert to their old behaviors. Studies show that offering incentives for losing weight, quitting smoking, using seatbelts, or (in the case of children) acting generously is not only less effective than other strategies but often proves worse than doing nothing at all. Incentives, a version of psychologists call extrinsic motivators, do not alter the attitudes that underlie our behaviors. They do not create an enduring commitment to any value or action. Rather, incentives merely—and temporarily—change what we do. (Kohn, 2018, p. 116)

BOX 6.7

NETWORK FOR SOCIAL WORK MANAGEMENT COMPETENCIES AND PRACTICE BEHAVIORS 11

Plans, promotes, and models lifelong learning practices (Network for Social Work Management Competencies 11). Practice Behaviors:

- Positions the organization as a "learning organization," providing ongoing opportunities for all staff to receive professional development to assure quality service delivery (11.1).
- Ensures that the organization offers competent and regular supervision to staff at all levels of the organization (11.2).
- Whenever possible, offers staff an opportunity to learn from experts, as well as make presentations themselves, at outside conferences and meetings (11.6).
- Whenever possible, allows staff to take classes or work on advanced degrees with support of the agency. If agency funds are not available, flexibility in scheduling or other nonmonetary support should be offered to support learning (11.7).

As we have discussed in this chapter thus far, leaders need to recognize the various ways staff are motivated and subsequently what they will regard as rewards that continue to drive them. It is important to note that we are not implying that you hastily extinguish the use of external rewards, but that instead you reflect on an omnipotent paradigm shift about the design of reward systems that includes input from staff. We encourage leaders and managers to work to create an atmosphere that promotes intrinsic motivation. Some final points on recognition:

Give recognition. Respond in a timely manner to offer recognition for staff's work. Include fellow teammates and superiors as situationally appropriate.

Create a positive work environment. A workplace that is imbued with positive energy can directly influence staff's dedication to the organization. Allow for informal gatherings and celebrations to increase social connectedness among teammates. Share success stories that focus on what is going well, rather than everything that is wrong. Attitudes are infectious.

Help build and develop skills. Providing opportunities for professional development and growth is a significant motivating factor. When staff are provided with continuing learning and professional development, they perceive their organization more positively, which can directly increase their motivation to enhance their performance.

Empower team members to participate in decisions. When F.D.R. was facing the banking crisis during the Great Depression, he implored the American people to understand that the crisis was not just his problem, it was everyone's problem and therefore everyone needed to be a part of the solution. Empowering others to be active decision makers, whether with conflict resolution, new innovations, or projects, increases motivation. Why? Well, if you helped think of it, you are more likely to be passionate about it, and you will have an increased commitment to its successful outcome. There are certainly times when a leader or manager cannot implement the ideas of staff, and may need to present teams with the limited choices due to constraining factors. In such situations it behooves the leader to clearly explain why these are the only options and facilitate a collaborative discussion about the pros and cons of the potential directions and what is needed to reach the best possible outcome.

Be fair. Fairness is not a cookie-cutter action. It should be tailored to individuals, but in a fashion that is fair to all. It requires thought and intentionality to be objective toward all staff and provide respect, feedback, and opportunities for advancement. The activities for advancement are designed with the individual in mind, but are available to all members.

A prominent reward for staff is the recognition of their potential and working with them to identify ways to advance their skills, while enhancing innovation and performance within the organization or academic institution. Leaders and managers should dedicate time to engage in meaningful discussions with staff about their career aspirations and conjointly think of opportunities for staff to develop the skills needed for their professional development. Leaders and managers can promote peer-led in-services, faculty presentations that showcase current works in progress, sharing by staff who recently attended a conference of the salient themes and resources, and so on. There is a plethora of ways to help staff develop skills that are aligned with their career plans and aspirations. A commonly held assumption is that after investing in talent development, the staff will take their new talent someplace else; however, staff who are continuously provided with learning and skills development are less likely to get bored and more likely to stay. Why? Because they are both internally and externally motivated and appropriately rewarded.

STAFF TRAINING AND DEVELOPMENT

Goleman (2011) asserts that the one trait all leaders possess is motivation, which has been described as an intrinsically driven desire to achieve. According to Goleman (2011), motivated individuals "seek out creative challenges, love to learn, and take great pride in a job well done" (p. 41). One explanation for the internal motivation Goleman (2011) describes is that leaders are consummate learners, passionate about what they do, are driven to expand their knowledge bases, skills, and, above all, are open to learning from others—including those they lead. According to Espinoza and Ukleja (2016), intrinsic motivation contains three fundamentals: (a) autonomy, (b) mastery, and (c) purpose. It is the responsibility of leaders/managers to create an environment that permits autonomy that is balanced with interdependence, opportunities for talent development, and mastery. See Boxes 6.8, 6.9, and 6.10 for examples of staff training and development.

BOX 6.8

COMPETENCY-BASED EXAMPLE OF TRAINING SERIES FOR NEW AND EMERGING MANAGERS

A growing agency discovered they had a lot of potential talent within their pool of workers. As many of the senior-level managers had climbed the ladder, they valued being a part of an agency that developed talent and gave them chances. The team decided to offer a series of in-service trainings to new (within the last year) managers as well as emerging team leaders who demonstrated qualities and skills that could be further developed. They wanted to ensure that they were providing staff with the appropriate resources and designed a training that included coaching sessions on

- Session 1: Labor laws and employee relations
- Session 2: How to facilitate and document performance reviews and provide professional coaching

(continued)

BOX 6.8 (Continued)

- Session 3: How to facilitate productive meetings
- Session 4: How to create program and performance goals and design and evaluate measures that can be linked with the organization's strategic plans
- Session 5: How to manage stress and model professional communication and emotion regulation skills
- Session 6: How to practice self-care and promote it in others

BOX 6.9

COMPETENCY-BASED EXAMPLE: CLINICAL LUNCH AND LEARN SERIES

A bustling inpatient unit established a Clinical Lunch and Learn series facilitated by clinicians on a rotating basis.

When the *DSM-5* came out, three out of eight clinicians attended an outside training and developed a series of trainings on various disorders over the course of 6 months. All eight members would read a particular section (e.g., anxiety disorder) prior to the Lunch and Learn, and bring a potluck lunch. Three that attended the formal training took turns presenting on different disorders, and then the group engaged in discussions about the topic. Interestingly, the conversations sometimes led to thoughts about clients and new insights about differential diagnoses. They would then raise these new ideas in rounds with the attending psychiatrist and modify treatment plans as clinically indicated. This practice helped to empower the staff who presented and participated, and enhanced the cohesion and collaboration of team members. Additionally, within 18 months all three of the presenters were promoted to clinical leadership positions.

BOX 6.10

COMPETENCY-BASED EXAMPLE: SHARING AND SHOWCASING SCHOLARLY WORK

All faculty in a university department were encouraged to "share and showcase" their scholarly endeavors among peers. The small forum allowed presenters to not only receive affirmations and findings from their peers but also to solicit ideas from colleagues about method designs, questionnaires, and so on. This forum also allowed faculty to share resources. The monthly share and showcase times were scheduled just before lunch. As peers became interested in sharing and gaining creative ideas from one another about their projects, this led them to continue conversations over lunch. The team was genuinely interested and engaged with each other and began checking in with their peers and sharing articles and resources that could be of interest to others' scholarly pursuits.

The paradigm of managing others, which has historically instilled ideologies of teaching, has shifted toward a coaching methodology. Frankovelgia (2015) compares the differences embedded in both teaching and coaching approaches, highlighting that teaching—a directive approach—instructs and provides answers, while coaching—a supportive approach—encourages independence and serves as a resource. She further underscores that teaching is restricted to what one knows, while coaching facilitates an interactive exchange that sparks discovery and creativity.

In order for staff to commit to a team, they must feel that the their "coach" (leader/manager) is committed to them. Every player has a hope, and it is up to the coach to help them him or her that hope into an achievable goal by providing them with practice drills, encouragement, and feedback to keep him or her motivated. Leaders and managers should inculcate staff with motivation and nurture their growth through strategic training and development opportunities. Talent development requires pluralistic methods that infuse a variety of learning experiences for the staff to internalize and subsequently integrate with their skills and knowledge repertoires. Staff training is a fluid process that can, and should, shift based on the needs of the organization and the individual members comprising the organization.

The manner in which newly hired staff are oriented to the organization sets critical attitudinal pathways, which usually lead to enthusiasm, doubt, or pessimism. Informal orientation to an organization can include the provision of mentorship, a period of shadowing, one-on-one supervision, and regular check-ins, and also inclusion in the established social circles (conversations during breaks and seats made available at lunch tables, invitations to outside work gatherings, etc.). A staff who enters a new organization and is paired with one to three teammates for shadowing and mentoring will be more likely to be introduced to fellow teammates, be shown where and how to access resources they will need on a regular basis, and be provided explanations for protocols, as well as more likely to feel included and valued from the start. Compare that approach to an employee who finished the new employee orientation session and then is left alone, even if unintentionally, to meet others, find out where the copier is, or which building the monthly staff meeting is held, essentially left to "sink or swim." How will this staff feel about her or his new employment? We suspect rather unwelcomed, isolated, confused, and very likely overwhelmed.

Orienting new staff occurs formally and informally. Formal orientation typically provides new employees with information (yes, this is oftentimes very dry material) on agency policies and procedures, documentation and IT training, restraint procedures, and any agency-specific models used, such as trauma-informed care, motivational interviewing, and so on. This is not an exhaustive list, but you get the idea here. However, some agencies are now including more formal orientation trainings about distress tolerance to help manage stress and burnout and teach effective professional communication skills. The concepts of distress tolerance, emotional regulation, or mindfulness skills are provided in formal training sessions, and the application of skills is then followed up in one-on-one coaching sessions. When an agency has the opportunity to provide staff with one-on-one coaching from an outside consultant, the neutral party can help enhance a sense of security for employees. When this is not possible, an agency can assign a coach from a different department to increase the employee's comfort level.

Investing in staff through ongoing training and mentoring can set a course for ongoing commitment and continuous organizational advancement. Ongoing training can also occur through a number of lexicons including opportunities to attend external trainings/conferences, supervision meetings, and in-services. Staff training and development can also include staff-directed learning that provides resource materials (slide presentations from trainings the supervisor attended, relevant research articles, and videos on how to use particular interventions, etc.) as well as crafted opportunities for the staff to expand their comfort zones and skills. For instance, a staff with career aspirations for leadership but who lacks confidence in presenting to large groups might start by providing a brief presentation on a topic she or he feels well versed in to a small group of peers. Another example is a clinician who has aspirations to return to school to earn a PhD or DSW degree but is not very comfortable with research. The supervisor acknowledges the creative work he or she has done with a difficult population and shares a local mental health news article with him or her, encouraging him or her to draft a single case study and submit for publication. The supervisor offers to be a soundboard and help with edits and ideas as needed. The possibilities of staff development are endless. What is important to note is that leaders and managers facilitate discussions with their supervisees in order to design work tasks that can be a catalyst for their growth. Attending to staff's development helps to increase the likelihood that leaders/managers will retain staff; decrease the potential that staff will become bored, restless, and demotivated; and prevent stress as staff feel invested in and are not habituating to any one particular task.

BOX 6.11

NETWORK FOR SOCIAL MANAGEMENT COMPETENCIES AND PRACTICE BEHAVIORS 5

Manages diversity and cross-cultural understanding (Network for Social Work Management Competencies 5). Practice Behaviors:

- Provides opportunities for staff to learn about different groups to enhance their practice, and encourages open discussion about issues to promote sensitivity (5.2).
- Seeks to employ a diverse workforce to align with clients served by the organization (5.3).

CSWE Competency 6—Engage With Individuals, Families, Groups, Organizations, and Communities

- 6.2 Use empathy, reflection, and interpersonal skills to effectively engage diverse clients and constituencies.

CSWE, Council on Social Work Education.

Box 6.11 displays the competencies/behaviors in this section. A common misperception about developing talent is that leaders and managers think there is simply not enough time in their already packed schedules. However, coaching is not an aggrandized task. Yes, it requires forethought and planning, but the reality is that coaching can occur in the moment, and knowing the right questions to ask allows great coaching to happen in less time than one might think. Jen Su (2015) outlines three types of coaching sessions: *long-term development, debriefing,* and *short-term problem solving. Long-term development* focuses on a particular professional development goal that typically requires practice and takes anywhere from 6 months to 1 year to attain. Once the long-term goal is made and practice objectives are set, hold monthly meetings or "coaching session" to review progress and scaffold learning from prior sessions. **Debriefing** meetings on an event or project focus on reviewing what occurred in order to learn what can be done differently in the future (some refer to this as "root cause analysis"). The important thing to keep in mind when facilitating a debriefing meeting is that staff are likely to feel guarded and threatened by the very idea of this type of meeting, and it is crucial to create a safe environment where staff do not feel blamed but heard. Asking questions such as "What did learn from this? What did we do well? What do you think we need to work on? How are you all feeling about what happened?" can help to empower staff to think of creative solutions while exuding a stance of openness and empathy rather than blame and shame. **Short-term problem solving** focuses on a specific problem in need of a quick resolution. Due to the sense of urgency associated with short-term problem solving, managers can easily fall into the trap of directing/advising/teaching before taking a few moments to ask questions. When a staff presents you with a problem, they usually have a good deal of information about the problem and tend to already have some good insight to possible resolutions: hear them out. They may not have the best answer for the situation, or they may have only partially thought the resolution through and need some coaching to connect the dots to the larger picture and possible outcomes, but actively listening to their ideas will provide you with information that can (a) reveal a long-term development need, (b) provide an opportunity to model critical thinking, and (c) coach through questioning.

One approach to asking good coaching questions pertaining to staff development is the *GROW model.* The GROW model stands for goal, current reality, options, and will (or way forward). This model empowers staff to come up with new ideas and insights to their professional development, as well as performance, problem-solving, and decision-making skills (McCarthy, 2018).

Goal setting should incorporate the S.M.A.R.T. rule of being specific, measurable, attainable, realistic, and timely. Ask questions such as

- What would you like to accomplish?
- Why are you hoping to achieve this goal?
- What are the benefits of achieving this goal?
- What is the ideal outcome of achieving this goal?
- What is a realistic timeframe for achieving this goal?
- What will you need to achieve this goal?

Current *Reality* appraisals are helpful to understand the framework and scale of the goal. Ask questions such as

- What steps have you already taken toward the goal/what have you already tried?
- Where are you now with your goal?
- What has helped you toward reaching your goal?
- What has hindered you?
- Where do you see any adjustments that need to be made to help you reach your goal?

Exploring *Options* helps to create solutions and advances the individual toward goal attainment. Ask questions such as

- What are the options you are working with?
- What do you think needs to happen first?
- What do you think would happen if you did A, B, or C? What are the pros and cons of each option?
- What do you believe would happen if you did nothing at all?
- Who else might be of value to help you with this?
- What is the biggest challenge in this for you?
- Is there anything you have considered doing differently? What has prevented you from taking that approach?

Will, or way forward, provides an opportunity for the coach to gauge the individual's commitment. Ask questions such as

- What are your plans for going about that?
- What will you need to do that?
- What is getting in the way of doing that?
- How will you know when you have reached that point?
- How would others know when you reached it?
- What will you need from me, and other members of the team, to help you get there?
- What is the cost of not getting there? (self and others)
- How will you know if you are detracting from your goals?
- How will I know? What do you need from me to help you if you do detract?

Pace the GROW questions to ensure that person has time to reflect and actively listen to avoid diving in to provide answers. Leaders and managers should practice self-reflection and also seek feedback from the staff about what was helpful and what was not helpful. It is also helpful to create a working document (you can think of this document as a contract) outlining the salient points discussed and use it to refer back to and evaluate progress. A note of caution: do not dub this "performance improvement goals" or etch it into a performance evaluation from the start. Sure, you can use this as a tool for appraising performance down the line, but some staff may feel overwhelmed and intimidated if the "coaching contract" is linked to such a formal document being shared with HR. Additionally, it can inadvertently diminish the value you are trying to exude, which is that professional development matters to you because staff matter to you (not because you are required by agency policy to conduct coaching).

Developing your own coaching style takes time, practice, and the confidence to admit and address mistakes that you will inevitably make. There are a few common mistakes that neophyte managers make including what Wilkins (2015) calls coaching the "mini-me." Just as we say in clinical practice "it is not about *you*, it is about the client," the same principle applies in coaching. Embrace and nurture the fact that members of your team are unique individuals that can share their own strengths and weaknesses, and do not aim to develop a replica of yourself. Additionally, patience really is a virtue. Coaching your team members requires a good deal of patience and the willingness to let them let stumble just enough to ultimately find their way. You can, and should, establish timeframes for stumbling and also set clear benchmarks for appraising progress and providing feedback. Finally, you need to be aware of your frustration triggers and monitor your tone and approach when things are not going as expected (Wilkins, 2015). Box 6.12 displays an interview with Alicia Davis on leadership.

BOX 6.12

EXCERPT OF INTERVIEW WITH ALICIA DAVIS ON LEADERSHIP

Alicia Davis is an Executive, Leadership and Wellbeing Coach for Speaker Sisterhood, LLC and Institution for Professional Excellence in Coaching (iPEC) in Hartford, Connecticut. The following excerpt is taken from an interview with Alicia about leadership. In this conversation she shares some of the findings from her research on women in leadership.

Basically, most of the women don't feel that they have a community to go to, or don't feel like they have that mentoring on how to get ahead, or even feel supported by their team.

I think that drilling down into that, I honestly think that in a corporate environment that this is probably more prevalent than in a social services environment, because there's more competition and there's a whole edge to the corporate approach [not] there is in social services. I actually think that part of—and this is just my interpretation—what I see is that women in general, or caregivers in general, are always about giving to others; they put themselves on the bottom of the list, if they're on the list at all. It's really hard for women, I think, in social services and behavioral health organizations, to ultimately allow others to support them.

I think that part of it is there might not be as many women in the upper leadership roles that are showing younger leaders or leaders that are middle managers who want to continue on, there just aren't a lot of role models because there aren't a lot of women in those higher positions. (Interview on Leadership with Alicia David, March, 15, 2018).

Thomas and Ely (2016) explain that companies have historically embraced diversity because they asserted that discrimination was legally and morally wrong, but today organizations embrace diverse work teams because they can increase organizational effectiveness. Many social work students are taught through class lectures and readings about diversity and the influence of culture on rapport building and applied interventions. Similarly, seasoned social workers are required to obtain continuing education credits that satisfy cultural competence credits. We understand at a cognitive level that diversity plays a vital role in the work we do: But how do we actually experience this value and integrate it in our work as teams? To start with, we must cultivate our own cultural intelligence by identifying our strengths and weaknesses. Earley and Masakowski (2016) suggest that cultural intelligence requires the ability to "think before acting," a reasoning that is similar to emotional intelligence (p. 2). Earley and Masakowski (2016) avow that

> *A person with high emotional intelligence grasps what makes us human and at the same time what makes each of us different from one another. A person with high cultural intelligence can somehow tease out of a person's or group's behavior those features that would be true of all people and all groups, those peculiar to this person or this group, and those that are neither universal nor idiosyncratic. The vast realm that lies between these two poles is culture. (p. 2)*

Green, Lopez, Wysocki, and Kepner (2012) define diversity as the celebrated, valued, accepted, acknowledged, and understood differences among individuals with regard to race, age, class, ethnicity, gender, sexual orientation, spiritual practice, and physical and mental abilities. Workplace diversity is defined by the extent of heterogeneity related to personal and functional attributes (Stevens, Plaut, & Sanchez-Burks, 2008). The literature on diversity in the workplace has significantly expanded as the demographic composition of organizations and institutions has grown increasingly diverse (Stevens et al., 2008). The flourishing of underrepresented individuals in organizations, combined with the drive to develop cohesive and successful work teams, has captured the attention of leaders and managers in varied professions (Earley & Masakowski, 2016; Green et al., 2012; Stevens et al., 2008). Interestingly, the literature illustrates thematic perceptions of the pros and cons of diverse workplaces. For instance, workforce diversity can positively influence production, creativity, high-quality social relationships, and positive organizational change. Contrariwise, negative influences reported include heightened social conflict, diminished social inclusion, and obstruction in decision making and change processes (Stevens et al., 2008).

As previously stated, heterogeneous teams are more likely to demonstrate creativity, innovation, quality performance, and greater productivity. However, this characteristic of heterogeneity holds true when teams are cohesive and able to collaborate in a manner that leverages each individual's talents, skills, and knowledge. Viewing diversity as an opportunity, rather than a problem or threat, expands the potential for increased understanding, acceptance, and value. Many organizations have committed to enhancing diversity and promoting inclusion in the workplace. These are well-known values and beliefs within the social work profession, but how are organizations working to achieve diversity?

Stevens et al. (2008) examined three approaches—*colorblindness, multiculturalism,* and *all-inclusive multiculturalism*—to dislodging the benefits of diversity and creating positive organizational change. The colorblind approach to organizational diversity is rooted in American ideals of individualism, equality, and assimilation. As the name suggests, it turns a blind eye to cultural group identities to realign them with the superordinate identity (in this case the broader organization) to increase the person's organizational identity, which concurrently decreases the significance of individual differences. This approach is evident when organizations promote minority–nonminority collaboration, and as Stevens et al. (2008) summarized, "The irony of this practice is that diverse employees are discouraged from acting and thinking in the unique ways associated with their social categories, which does not allow them to utilize fully the viewpoints of their distinctive social group membership" (p. 120). The colorblind approach fundamentally believes in treating all people the same; however, this is commonly perceived by minorities/underrepresented individuals to be exclusionary. Organizations that adopt this approach evoke feelings of devaluation of cultural differences, frustration, discontentment, and are likely fraught with conflict that derives from such sentiments.

A multicultural approach to diversity underscores the advantage of workplace diversity and seeks to overtly recognize differences as a strength. Underrepresented groups find organizations that take a multicultural approach more appealing than organizations taking the colorblind approach as they appreciate the recognition of the differences in backgrounds and group identities (Stevens et al., 2008). Organizations apply a multicultural approach in numerous ways, including mentoring and networking programs that offer additional resources for underrepresented groups, diversity luncheons where food from different cultures is brought in, and diversity awareness days where different backgrounds and traditions are celebrated, as well as seminars and workshops on cultural awareness. Unfortunately, these initiatives fade all too quickly when they are met with opposition, especially when the nonminority members are nonparticipators and seemingly resistant. Coincidently, Stevens et al. (2008) explained that nonminority members frequently complain of feeling excluded when multicultural approaches are implemented, which can create feelings of resentment in the workplace. Instead, Stevens et al. (2008) suggested that organizations consider an all-inclusive multicultural (AIM) approach.

An AIM approach gains both minority and nonminority support through the acknowledgment and recognition of the importance of differences of both groups. Thus, neither group is excluded or disadvantaged from a predominant focus on either group, but rather a collective focus on inclusivity. Stevens et al. (2008) explained:

> Essentially, the AIM approach addresses deficiencies in the standard multicultural ideology without reverting to colorblindness. Whereas AIM acknowledges that the demographic groups which people belong to have important consequences for individuals, it also explicitly endorses this vision equally across members of all groups, including minorities. Given the pervasiveness of American values of equality and egalitarianism, which drive individualistic ideology, this equal emphasis on groups is less of a mismatch for nonminorities. Moreover, AIM lifts perceived threats to unity that may form in reaction to multicultural policies. (p. 123)

The implementation of an AIM approach firstly and primarily requires a shift in language. For instance, rather than asking staff to bring a favorite "ethnic" dish and recipe, ask them to bring a favorite "family" dish and recipe. Stevens et al. (2008) advise that using AIM-based communication entails avoiding language that seems to be exclusive.

Social worker leaders and managers can promote awareness and acceptance of individual and cultural differences that exist within the teams they lead, which can extend to how the organization as a whole cultivates a shared culture that values diversity. Cultivating a work environment allows all members to share ideas, expertise, creativity, and strategic approaches that are necessary; but these efforts can be futile if diversity is not actively nurtured, embraced, and discussed in an open and trusting atmosphere.

SUMMARY

This chapter examined the multifarious ways to enhance staff motivation and foster employees' professional growth and development. Leaders and managers must be mindful of how they frame reward systems and include input from employees to effectively develop positive contingencies—but above all leaders and managers need to recognize and nurture the talent of their staff. By attending to the growth of individual staff and cohesion among teammates, leaders and managers can facilitate innovative changes and motivate staff performance and productivity. Leading and managing others also requires one to be cognizant of any inequalities and create a work atmosphere that embraces diversity.

ACTIVITIES

Complete the SCARF self-assessment online at https://neuroleadership.com/nli-scarf-assessment/.

1. What surprised you about the results? How do express these values? How do you express yourself when a primary SCARF domain feels threatened? What can you do to become more aware of your threat responses? What can you do to become more aware of others' threat responses?

2. Your supervisor has asked you to steer a project that will help other staff learn about different groups and encourage transparent discussions about issues that will enhance sensitivity and workforce diversity. How would you go about this? Which approach—or elements of the colorblind, multicultural, and integrated multicultural approaches—would you adopt for your framework, and why? Discuss any potential barriers and how you would seek to mitigate them.

REFERENCES

Earley, C., & Masakowski, E. (2016). Cultural intelligence. In *On managing across cultures*. Boston, MA: Harvard Business School.

Espinoza, C., & Ukleja, M. (2016). *Managing the millennials: Discover the core competencies for managing toady's workforce*. New Jersey, NJ: John Wiley & Sons.

Fitch, P., & Van Brunt, B. (2016). *A guide to leadership and management in higher education*. New York, NY: Routledge.

Frankovelgia, C. (2015). Shift your thinking to coach effectively: You're learning right along with your employees. In *HBR guide to coaching employees: Give effective feedback. Foster steady growth. Motivate start performers*. Boston, MA Harvard Business Review Press . Boston, MA: Harvard Business Review Press.

Fry, R. (2018, April). Millennials are the largest generation in the U.S. labor force. *Pew Research Center*. Retrieved from http://www.pewresearch.org/fact-tank/2018/04/11/millennials-largest-generation-us-labor-force/

Goleman, D. (2011). What makes a leader? In *On leadership: HBR's 10 must reads*. Boston, MA: Harvard Business Review Press.

Gostick, A., & Elton, C. (2018). *The best team wins*. New York, NY: Simon & Schuster.

Gratton, L., & Erickson, T. J. (2013). Eight ways to build collaborative teams. In *On teams*. Boston, MA: Harvard Business Review Press.

Green, K. A., Lopez, M., Wysocki, A., & Kepner, K. (2012, February). *Diversity in the workplace: Benefits, challenges, and the required managerial tools*. University of Florida, IFAS Extension.

Hallowell, E. M. (2015). Set the stage to stimulate growth: A practical, concrete plan for achieving peak performance. In *HBR guide to coaching employees: Give effective feedback. Foster steady growth. Motivate start performers*. Boston, MA: Harvard Business Review Press.

Jen Su, A. (2015). Holding a coaching session: Ask questions, articulate goals, reframe challenges. In *HBR guide to coaching employees: Give effective feedback. Foster steady growth. Motivate start performers*. Boston, MA: Harvard Business Review Press.

Kim, W., & Mauborgne, R. (2017). *Blue ocean leadership*. Boston, MA: Harvard Business School.

Kohn, A. (2018, August). Why incentive plans cannot work. *The Harvard Business Review*, 114–121.

McCarthy, D. (2018, May 2). Coaching questions for managers using the GROW model. *The Balance Careers*. Retrieved from https://www.thebalancecareers.com/coaching-questions-for-managers-2275913

McGinn, D. (2018, August). The science of pep talks. *The Harvard Business Review*, 108–113.

Petland, S. (2013). The new science of building great teams. In *On teams*. Boston, MA: Harvard Business Review Press.

Rock, D. (2006). *Quiet leadership: Six steps to transforming performance at work*. New York, NY: Harper Collins.

Rock, D. (2008). SCARF: A brain-based model for collaborating with and influencing others. *NeuroLeadership Journal,* Retrieved from http://web.archive.org/web/20100705024057/http://www.your-brain-at-work.com: 80/files/NLJ_SCARFUS.pdf

Shulman, L. (Speaker) (2011, August 22). Leading mutual aid support groups: Exactly how can people with the same problems help each other? [Audio Podcast]. Retrieved from http://www.insocialwork.org/episode.asp?ep=78

Smith, D. B., & Shields, J. (2012). Factors related to social service workers' job satisfaction: Revisiting Herzberg's motivation to work. *Administration in Social Work, 37,* 189–198. doi:10.1080/03643107.2012.673217

Spreier, S., Fontaine, M. H., & Malloy, R. (2006, June). Leadership run amok: The destructive potential of overachievers. *The Harvard Business Review.* Retrieved from the World Wide Web: https://hbr.org/2006/06/leadership-run-amok-the-destructive-potential-of-overachievers

Stevens, F. G., Plaut, V. C., & Sanchez-Burks, J. (2008). Unlocking the benefits of diversity. All-Inclusive multiculturalism and positive organizational change. *Journal of Applied Behavioral Science, 44*(1), 116–133. doi:10.1177/0021886308314460

Thomas, D. A., & Ely, R. J. (2016). Making a deference matters: A new paradigm for managing diversity. In *On managing across cultures.* Boston, MA: Harvard Business School.

Wilkins, M. M. (2015). Avoid common coaching mistakes: Pitfalls to watch out for-and how to remedy them. In *HBR guide to coaching employees: Give effective feedback. Foster steady growth. Motivate start performers.* Boston, MA: Harvard Business Review Press.

## CHAPTER 7

PROFESSIONAL DEVELOPMENT IN LEADERSHIP AND MANAGEMENT IN SOCIAL WORK

CHAPTER OBJECTIVES

- Understanding how to foster your own continued learning.
- Demonstrating self-confidence in your leadership skills.
- Capitalizing your strengths and compensating for your limitations.
- Understanding personal and professional development.
- Understanding how to move up in leadership.
- Learning how to take care of oneself (psychologically and physically).
- Developing and mentoring future leaders.
- Learning managerial skills to increase productivity.
- Organizing an effective workspace.
- Planning to achieve goals.
- Avoiding time wasters.

INTRODUCTION

Throughout this chapter, we explore the process of transitioning into positions of leadership and management. Rising to these positions means that a social worker will undergo multiple transitions as he or she assumes new leadership tasks, establishes and manages new expectations, develops new relationships, and creates new professional goals. The transition to leadership can also result in shifting power dynamics, especially in relationships with former coworkers who may now be supervisees. Because a number of transitions occur quickly, the novice manager can benefit greatly from mentorship as well as ongoing self-care. An organization that creates an atmosphere committed to nurturing the professional development of emerging leaders and managers will reap benefits by way of decreased turnover and financial loss associated with said turnover; their employees will exhibit increased performance, productivity, and job satisfaction.

In discussing the benefits of mentorship, we highlight the ways mentors profit from the experience, which can regenerate the practice of lifelong learning. Inherent to mentorship is a mutual commitment to the processes of learning, discovery, self-reflection and self-awareness, and an appreciation of mistakes that can result in lessons that contribute to better future outcomes. Finally, we explore ways to inspire confidence and establish trust, and explore managerial methods for enhancing productivity. Box 7.1 displays the competencies/behaviors in this chapter.

BOX 7.1

COMPETENCIES AND PRACTICE BEHAVIORS ADDRESSED IN THIS CHAPTER

Plans, promotes, and models lifelong learning practices (Network for Social Work Management Competencies 11). Practice Behaviors:

- Assumes a mentorship role for less experienced managers (11.3).

- Keeps up-to-date with research on instructional practices, management, and leaderships, as well as on effective practices in professional development, and shares those practices with staff (11.4).

- Engages in a variety of activities to foster the manager's own learning, such as participating in collegial networking and subscribing to journals and listservs (11.5).

- Demonstrates self-confidence in leading the organization, capitalizing on his or her own strengths, and compensating for his or her own limitations (11.8).

Developing Leaders

We all have an idea of what leadership is and is not. Take a moment to consider someone in your life—a coach, teacher, supervisor, colleague—that you consider to be a leader. What characteristics come to mind when you think of that person? How do/did they lead? What are/were you drawn to about their leadership style? And now how about yourself? Maybe you have been in a leadership role historically, or presently hold a position of leadership. How do people view you as a leader? How would you like them to view you as a leader?

Chances are that in doing a brief self-appraisal you perhaps overlooked some of your strengths as well as your blind spots. Perhaps you even had difficulty articulating what defines a leader, whether you were considering someone else or yourself. If you find yourself in this position, this can be a signal that it is time to pause and take inventory. Taking time to reflect, to be purposeful in seeing yourself as a leader and others as future leaders with greater clarity, can be a formidable task when you consider the quotidian crisis-oriented nature of the social work field, especially against the backdrop of diminished funding streams and resources, but it is incumbent upon you as a leader to create the time and space needed to crystalize your thinking on this matter.

Before reading further, take a moment to list 10 leadership qualities that immediately come to mind for you. See Box 7.2.

BOX 7.2

TEN LEADERSHIP QUALITIES ACTIVITY

1. _____
2. _____
3. _____
4. _____
5. _____
6. _____
7. _____
8. _____
9. _____
10. _____

- What are the top three qualities that you value most in leaders? Are they on your list?
- What are your top three strengths as a leader? Are they on this list?
- What are three qualities that you would like to improve to become a better leader?

Moving Up in Leadership

"I never had any training!" This omnipresent sentiment has been expressed by and to many leaders holding positions that range from mid-level to executive-level management in the field of social work. It is sometimes countered with the notion that on-the-job-training (OJT) is the training—a point worthy of consideration as it can offer cogent experiential learning. But as with any pedagogy, leadership and management training must be ripe with multimodal opportunities for learning and evaluating one's competencies across various dimensions, or practice behaviors. However, the construct of leadership, and specifically leadership development, is often overlooked not only in social work curricula but, moreover, in organizations. The tacit expectation under these conditions is that social workers moving through the ranks in the field will somehow instinctively develop a successful style of leadership. In the absence of leadership development trainings, novice social work managers and leaders may be challenged with a Darwinian task of survival of the fittest.

Moving up in leadership presents many opportunities to apply previously untapped skill sets to present and future challenges. Moving up can also result in shifts in relationships with coworkers, as transitioning from colleagues to supervisor–supervisee can be marked by uncertainty for both parties. A coworker may initially express excitement and sincere happiness for the new appointment, but this feeling can also be imbued with uneasiness about what changes this new hierarchy may evoke in the working relationship. In some cases, individuals may even end up supervising former supervisors, and sometimes individuals move into a position of higher ranking than their former supervisor. This inversed relationship can initially be an awkward and delicate transition; it must be handled with humility, open communication, and mutual understanding and respect so both parties move forward productively and collaboratively. It is important to recognize that newly appointed managers may experience a loss of reference group that previously supported the novice manager's identity. This loss can be validated, normalized, and balanced through the mentorship process.

Novice—and even seasoned—managers and leaders can sometimes suffer from "imposter syndrome," or the self-perception that they are not truly qualified for the position. This self-doubt can be quelled through good mentoring so that the novice manager can embrace the experience, as opposed to repressing it or trying to overcompensate for it. Imposter syndrome can evoke both hesitation and disbelief, convincing managers that they do not have the skills or experience to effectively lead others. Instead of attempting to veil a lack of knowledge, managers can use it to their advantage by embracing their blind spots and asking the team for solutions, clarification of the problem, or input to better understand how the problem arose in the first place. When managers are able to embrace vulnerability—that is, acknowledge that they may not be the expert in a given situation—they are able to conjure confidence and increase collaboration and trust; managers who project their vulnerability by giving ill-informed directives will more likely induce sentiments of doubt and distrust in their leadership style and abilities. The bottom line is, it can be healthy, inspirational, and respectable for managers to show they are comfortable learning alongside those they lead (see Box 7.3).

BOX 7.3

COMPETENCY-BASED STRATEGIES FOR MANAGING FORMER RELATIONSHIPS AS YOU MOVE UP IN LEADERSHIP

When you become the boss, your relationships with colleagues may change.

A staff person may say or feel, "I know you as a colleague but not as my boss. You are now in a position of power," and he or she may be wondering how you will use that position of power.

Will your leadership role change your relationship with your friends? Not necessarily, if you treat them the same at work as you treat everyone else.

Moving up means that you will need to exhibit a willingness to be vulnerable and take the arrows, but stick to your values and core.

You will also need to determine how you will measure the adaptations of your relationships. How can you objectively tell how the relationship has changed? From whom will you seek feedback about your relationships, and what makes them the best people from whom to solicit feedback?

The Mentorship Impact

Box 7.4 displays the competencies/behaviors in this section.

BOX 7.4

NETWORK FOR SOCIAL WORK MANAGEMENT COMPETENCIES AND PRACTICE BEHAVIORS 11

Plans, promotes, and models lifelong learning practices (Network for Social Work Management Competencies 11). Practice Behaviors:

- Assumes a mentorship role for less experienced managers (11.3).

As discussed throughout Chapter 6, leaders and managers not only inspire people and manage projects but also assume the role of mentor or coach to help develop aspiring, emerging, and, in some cases, stagnated managers. Many social work clinicians find themselves advancing to leadership and management positions because they performed well as clinicians or caseworkers. They have very likely demonstrated good social work skills, maintained unyielding productivity levels, juggled heavy caseloads, successfully navigated complex clinical situations, and perhaps contributed sound input during team meetings. They may be the informal leader on the team to which other clinicians gravitate for practice wisdom or expertise on a particular subject matter. Likewise, those in academia may find themselves advancing to chairperson or director or dean positions because they have excelled in their faculty role, garnered the respect of colleagues, and are fairly knowledgeable about some, but not all, of the inner workings of an academic institution.

Similar to the business world where the highest earners and greatest producers become the obvious choices for promotions, social workers may rise through the ranks when they stand out among their peers. However, all too often, social workers transition to managerial roles that require leadership skills in which they have never been formally trained. Given the fast-pace nature of the social work field, training can be a careless afterthought, haphazardly choreographed, or altogether overlooked. A dangerous assumption is that new managers will step into their newly appointed role with inherent skills to swim upstream through the administrative challenges—but more likely they will sink. This philosophy places the responsibility solely on the individual and attributes characterological blame rather than evaluating the environmental factors that contribute to a novice manager's demise.

Shanks, Lundström, and Bergmark (2014) highlighted that when social workers are promoted to leadership positions as a result of their achievements as practitioners, it is often assumed that they will continue to apply their clinical skills in their managerial role. While we have underscored the parallels between social work practice that can be transferred to leadership style and skill, we concur with Shanks et al.'s point that applying practice skills alone will not maximize leadership advancement opportunities. Thus, managers need leadership training programs to capitalize on social workers' tacit strengths of innovation, collaboration, planning, mediation, and empowerment.

But nobody really has the time to commit to training, right? Wrong. In fact, according to Gallup (2015), only one in 10 people enter management positions with the talent to manage others. Furthermore, when leaders and managers adopt the notion that OJT is the only training necessary for new managers, there is a 60% chance that the novice manager will fail. Recall from Chapter 6 that coaching takes less time than one typically believes it will. Hence, it is unrealistic for organizations and academic institutions to presume that new or underperforming managers will learn only by experience and become socialized to administration simply by being in their role and transferring their social worker skills.

Benefits of Mentoring

It is mutually propitious to offer mentorship to novice and potential managers for a few reasons. First, and as previously mentioned, it increases the likelihood of success for the individual, for the teams the individual manages, and for the organization as a whole. When managers flounder in their new roles, it costs the organization not only money but also morale. The new manager will likely feel discouraged, embarrassed, and frustrated; their coworkers, who may have been looking to take a leap and apply for a management position, may become disenchanted about the idea of advancement (at least in this organization); human resources will likely feel dispirited by the turnover and redundancy of recruitment; the business office will likely feel outraged by the cost of turnover; and the supervisor will likely feel overwhelmed that they need to absorb the tasks of the vacant position.

Second, the prevalence of change results in rapid shifts in the organizational structure, meaning that as an agency expands, merges, affiliates, or reorganizes in any way, it can create a swift need to fill managerial positions that are either new, newly structured, or newly vacant. Additionally, shifts seen by way of retirement announcements and resignations can also create a void within the organization. Organizations can deepen their players' bench by proactively preparing, aspiring, and developing managers through proper training and mentorship to quickly suit up for a new position.

Finally, when mentorship is successful, it not only improves the mentee but also improves the mentor. Assisting the mentee provides the mentor an opportunity to reflect on his or her own experiences and identify his or her own areas of strength and weakness. The mentor may make adjustments in the way he or she is currently leading, analyzing problems, or practicing self-care. Thus, there is an inherent learning process for the mentor, and this process can provide new opportunities and ideas about leadership philosophies, behaviors, and skills.

Approaches to Mentoring

As mentioned in brief, OJT is often seen as an approach for unseasoned managers to learn how to perform their new roles. This traditional approach relies heavily on self-directed learning, usually through online courses, checklists, and various reading materials. While this approach affords the autonomous learner fundamental tools, the limitations of such an approach are the lack of interpersonal skills trainings. This approach also assumes that the individual does not have any learning challenges that would deter him or her from completing or fully benefiting from the training materials. Even if one does not have a learning difficultly, providing unidimensional training overlooks the fact that individuals have varied learning styles. When applying the traditional approach, it is critical to follow up during mentoring sessions to gauge the mentee's level of understanding of the material and how he or she would apply said knowledge to various situations.

A blended approach to training appends classroom training to the traditional approach of self-directed learning. Training classes can afford individuals new skills, new abstract concepts and ways to modify existing abstract concepts, and, overall, can provide rich information. However, this approach is limited by a lack of opportunities to practice what Kolb and Kolb (2011) referred to as reflective observation and active experimentation. Reflective observation allows the learner to reflect on inconsistencies between experience and understanding. Active experimentation permits the learner to enter a new experience and apply reflective observations and new or modified abstract conceptualizations to test the results.

An integrated approach is a fusion of self-directed learning, blended learning, and learning that is customized to the individual. Customized learning entails that the mentor first inquires what the mentee would like to learn, or learn more about; designs tasks to match the learning goals; and facilitates ongoing reflective discourse about the process and experience of applying the new skills and related concepts. Mentoring commences by developing a relationship with the mentee, which requires that trust is built and that goals are both established and attended to over the course of working together. Stanier (2016) suggested using the TERA quotient as a foundation for growth and coaching. The TERA quotient stands for *tribe, expectation, rank*, and *autonomy*.

Tribe represents the question pervading the minds of both mentee and mentor: Are you with me or against me? Both parties need to establish trust and feel that they can depend on one another.

Questions about expectations underscore the importance of contracting and clarifying how the mentorship process will proceed and what both parties expect from one another. Knowing and understanding expectations can promote a sense of safety and predictability, which enhances trust and willingness to fully engage in the process.

Rank refers to the issues of power or hierarchy that may manifest. If a person feels that their rank, or status in the relationship, is reduced, they will guard themselves by becoming disengaged; risk-taking will be inhibited in their ongoing performance activities.

Autonomy signifies omnipotence, or the importance of having a say in the relationship. When people have higher levels of input, they are more likely to be engaged and take ownership. When there are practical reasons for constrained input, or autonomy, these should be discussed openly;

the mentor and mentee should identify ways to employ degrees of autonomy wherever and whenever possible.

Once the mentorship establishes this framework, the ongoing coaching ensues and the mentor continues to encourage the mentee to reflect on what has been useful to his or her learning journey, and seeks to know what will help the mentee in the next phase of learning.

As a mentor, being human can deepen the rapport between mentor and mentee and may abate any angst or pressure the mentee may feel about needing to know and master everything at once. Sharing your prior experiences, mistakes, and lessons learned can open the mentee up to sharing what he or she may be finding difficult. Additionally, when mentors share their growth experiences, they are modeling the importance of reflective thinking skills and self-awareness. It is also a good opportunity to share concrete learning that is acquired through formal training or continuing education credits.

A mentor has typically experienced a multitude of challenges and should ask their mentee what challenges they are facing. Difficulty in organizing meetings? Difficulty in managing an employee or a task? Then, the mentor can follow up with specific, focused questions that enable the mentor and mentee to reach a solution together. Essentially, the mentor coaches the mentee on how to apply critical thinking skills to a new task as the mentee evaluates the myriad ways to resolve the matter at hand. This process helps the mentee obtain clarity of thought and articulate the rationale for the selected solution while also preparing for other potential outcomes that may arise in the process. Listen for clues about the mentee's communication and negotiation skills, as well as mind-set about the issue. When you hone in on any potential blind spots, you proactively coach your mentee using an effective communication process.

One cannot be a leader without knowing the art and impact of communication; strong communication is a cognate of both emotional intelligence and emotional maturity. Bunker, Kram, and Ting (2015) highlighted that one's talent, ambition, and productivity held less weight than one's emotional maturity, or the ability to influence and persuade others and effectively regulate one's own emotions, especially in times of crisis and stress. Emotional maturity is marked by one's capacity to forge strong interpersonal skills, actively listen to and empathize with others, and offer patience and understanding. Emotional maturity may come with time and experience, but these alone do not always account for one's emotional maturation. Mentees may not have a wealth of experience dealing with high levels of stress or crises and therefore may not be attuned to how they interpersonally relate during times of stress. Mentorship can help the mentee self-assess their emotional maturity and emotional intelligence, and ongoing reflective discourse around this topic can help the mentee improve her or his capacity for influencing and persuading teams toward desired changes.

What Good Mentors Do

Tjan (2017) assessed an estimated 100 venerated leaders in various business, culture, arts, and government industries and distilled the characterizations that make exceptional mentors. He noted that the best mentors help mentees to become the best versions of one's professional self that they can be. Hence, the best leaders are not focused on creating a following, rather they are focused on developing other leaders. Tjan outlined four patterns of behavior that the best mentors demonstrated: *relationship building, character building, optimism*, and *loyalty*.

First, the best mentors hold the relationship above the mentorship. Tjan (2017) noted that one study out of the University of Wisconsin–Milwaukee showed that mentees who lacked a fundamental rapport with their mentor were not discernably different from those who did not have a mentor at all. Mentoring relationships need to be genuine and synergistic in order to motivate people and move them beyond the bounds of boss/employee roles to find a commonality for working together that transcends crossing items off a list.

Second, the best mentors are concerned with one's character before competency. While helping employees master skills is essential, the best mentors at times overlook competency building and instead help mentees develop and articulate their leadership style, values, and emotional intelligence. Mentors who facilitate character building are more likely to have committed workers who are eager to achieve goals. Of course some managers have a pervasive worry that they will invest their energy and time in developing people who will take their skills and find another position. On the other hand, some managers think mentees will be strong contributors during their tenure and will be more likely to give ample notice if they do leave, as a professional gesture of gratitude for the mentor's commitment to their professional development.

Third, the best managers amplify optimism and restrict cynicism. Mentees may bring fresh ideas that are simply unrealistic or heedless in nature, and while you might feel compelled to immediately point out mentees' flawed reasoning, doing so will very likely kill the buzz of their energy. Instead, the best mentors are able to address the positive facts: it is great to have mentees take initiative; you admire their ability to think outside the box; you respect their unwavering commitment to trying to solve a difficult problem; and there are positive aspects to their plan. To address the underdeveloped areas, it is best to take a curious stance. Ask questions about the part of the plan that the mentee needs to consider from various angles and help her or him to identify the blind spots in her or his plan. Additionally, be sure to check yourself: Do you believe it is a poor plan because it is never been done before? Has it been tried and failed? Will it require additional time and energy from you? If so, these may not be valid reasons to dismiss the mentee's ideas and might require you to think of the issues differently before rejecting the mentee's input altogether.

Fourth, the best mentors demonstrate a loyalty to their mentee that is unrivaled to the organization. Do not get this last point wrong—we are not suggesting that a mentor act disloyal toward the organization or engage in any unprofessional dialogues with a mentee that demean the agency in any way. What Tjan (2017) insinuates is that mentoring and developing the professional skills of others is a self-effacing commitment to others' professional development. Mentors do not telescope their focus to identify the mentee's strengths that can be further developed but instead help them to discover their passions as well. The best mentors may help a mentee discover that they are better suited for another role within the organization, or sometimes elsewhere, but the integral principle is that the mentor helps the mentee to move forward and achieve. Tjan concluded from all four best practices of mentorship have to do with being "good people" and surrounding oneself with "good people" who are dedicated to helping others become the best professional versions of themselves (p. 4).

BOX 7.5

NETWORK FOR SOCIAL WORK MANAGEMENT COMPETENCIES AND PRACTICE BEHAVIORS 11

Plans, promotes, and models lifelong learning practices (Network for Social Work Management Competencies 11). Practice Behaviors:

- Keeps up-to-date with research on instructional practices, management, and leaderships, as well as on effective practices in professional development, and shares those practices with staff (11.4).

- Engages in a variety of activities to foster the manager's own learning, such as participating in collegial networking and subscribing to journals and listservs (11.5).

Box 7.5 displays the competencies/behaviors in this section. The history of the social work profession is richly laced with leadership. The many pioneers who advanced social work's reputation and legitimacy did so through leadership, which underpins the field's code of ethics. However, there has been increasing concern over the past two decades about the lack of attention paid to the preparation of social work leaders (Bliss, Pecukonis, & Snyder-Vogal, 2014; King Keenan et al., 2018). Bliss et al. (2014) highlighted that the lack of focus on social work leadership in education curriculum resulted in the development of strategic plans and core competencies, all specific to social work leadership, by the professional organization national Network for Social Work Management (NSWM). Furthermore, the 2008 Educational Policy and Accreditation Standards (EPAS) directly noted the critical role that education has on leadership among the professional community (Bliss et al.).

The diminished focus on leadership training for social work students is partly due to an increase in MSW students entering clinical concentrations and significantly fewer students declaring macropractice, including administrative, community organization, and/or policy specializations (Bliss et al., 2014). As previously discussed, many clinicians are promoted to leadership and management positions without any administrative or leadership training opportunities, which may prevent them from further advancing in the future. The dearth of formal education and continuing education trainings in social work leadership has likely contributed to the sharp rise in other professionals—from the fields of law, medicine, public administration, and business administration—assuming the highest leadership positions in social service agencies. Social work leaders and managers, both within academia and organizations, must take active and varied measures to ensure effective practices in both their own development and the development of others.

There are a variety of leadership development programs, but access to them varies by geographic location. Although some leadership development training programs are designed for generic leadership development, there are others geared toward nonprofit leadership and, to a lesser extent, social work leadership specifically, although the National Association of Deans and Directors (NADD) provides some sessions on leadership development at its semiannual meetings. Training programs can include in-person classes, online classes, or a hybrid of both. Leaders and managers can enhance their mentees' development by integrating course learning with experiential learning through specific leadership assignments that take place in the work environment. The Network for Social Work Management has encouraged and supported social work programs in developing certificate programs in social work management; currently more than a dozen schools have adopted these programs.

There are several other ways that leaders and managers stay current on effective practices and leadership trends, including journal subscriptions, registering for email lists, engaging in forums and discussion boards, listening to podcasts and audiobooks, reading new texts, keeping current with news coverage relevant to the field, and exploring the websites of other agencies and academic institutions to see if they have cornered the market on an educational, treatment, advocacy, or policy trends. Leaders and managers must remain informed and committed to their own lifelong learning and share their knowledge and resources with colleagues and mentees.

Professional networking offers opportunities to increase footholds, influence others, and obtain useful information. It can occur both within and outside of the institution or organization, although most consider networking to be external. External networking connects leaders and managers with other professionals and affords leaders with new insights, ideas, and information about what is trending and how others are responding to trends. External networks should include diverse professions and not be narrowed to the field of social work. That is not to say that you should not network with fellow social workers, but leading and managing both present multifarious tasks and problems and therefore networking with other professions can offer varying schools of thought about how to tackle diverse issues. Internal networking requires leaders and managers to not only know staff but know them well enough to understand how they will be inspired, what their strengths are, and what they are passionate about—and this will come in handy when you need to lead a major change effort and positively persuade people to embark on a growth mind-set. Furthermore, knowing and being known by internal constituents can influence their confidence in leaders (see Box 7.6).

BOX 7.6

NETWORK FOR SOCIAL WORK MANAGEMENT COMPETENCIES AND PRACTICE BEHAVIORS 11

Plans, promotes, and models lifelong learning practices (Network for Social Work Management Competencies 11). Practice Behaviors:

- Demonstrates self-confidence in leading the organization, capitalizing on his or her own strengths and compensating for his or her own limitations (11.8).

Personal and Professional Development

Is it possible to evolve in one sphere of your life and leave another sphere uninfluenced? Chances are, as you reflect back on a significant personal development, it also somehow shaped your professional development as well. A new routine for home organization, for instance, may have had a contagious effect on staying organized in the office. Breaking down a task with your team at work may trigger an idea to break down personal weight loss goals that initially seemed overwhelming and unattainable—the point being that self-efficacy builds momentum from prior experiences. An aspiring leader or manager is more inclined to gain confidence when she or he can relate new challenges to previous ones that resulted in successful outcomes or positive lessons learned.

Bandura's (1977) model of social cognitive learning is expressed in the dynamic, reciprocal interplays between the individual, her or his environment, and her or his behavior. Bandura delineated several interlocking concepts including behavioral capacities, observational learning, reinforcement, and environmental influences, later adding self-efficacy as it related to one's learning. While Bandura described how social learning occurs within one's environment, he also focused on the intrinsic motivation required for learning and fostering desired changes. Concepts of self-efficacy contained in Bandura' theory suggest that individuals hold capacities for building upon prior experiences that evinced mastery of tasks and skills. Bandura advises that self-efficacy is also a critical factor in self-regulating emotional states. He further suggests that, in order to learn new behaviors, individuals must possess self-reflection capabilities and evaluate their progress toward a desired outcome; these skills must then be combined with evaluation responses from key members in the person's environment.

Since the inception of social cognitive learning theory, the phenomenon of self-efficacy has been evaluated in a variety of studies concerning topics that range from public health campaigns, characteristics of leadership, athletics, academic performance, life satisfaction, and well-being. Self-efficacy is described as one's perceived ability to perform a particular task with mastery and success. Contrastingly, self-inefficacy is marked by an absence of persistence, frequently caused by self-doubt, even when individuals are equipped with knowledge about the situation at hand. Self-efficacy is thereby viewed as the perceived confidence in one's ability to exercise control over one's life by mobilizing efforts to persevere as well as by utilizing cognitive resources and completing action steps toward goal attainment (Bandura, 1977).

BOX 7.7

EXCERPT OF INTERVIEW WITH ALICIA DAVIS

Alicia Davis an Executive, Leadership and Wellbeing Coach for Speaker Sisterhood, LLC and Institution for Professional Excellence in Coaching (iPEC) in Hartford, Connecticut. The following excerpt is taken from an interview with Alicia about leadership. In this conversation, she shares some of the findings from her research on women in leadership.

The perception of self-confidence was the number one area that women said they needed support in. That was really surprising to us because we thought it would probably be more along the lines of work–life balance. Confidence was 33%, then balance, then recognition and equality. So, again, that also ties in with that perception as well as the business practices or the ways that we discriminate even if we don't know that we're discriminating sometimes. (Interview on Leadership with Alicia David, March, 15, 2018)

As seen in Box 7.7, **confidence** is the pillar of leadership because of the instinctive tendency to trust people who exude confidence. That said, let us clarify what confidence is *not*. It is not aggressive, it is not boastful, it is not excessive in any way—these are behaviors that more closely resemble narcissism and bullying. Having confidence simply means that one is comfortable with oneself; that is, one is at ease with one's ability to make decisions, create good working relationships, accept one's shortcomings with a self-assurance that allows one to utilize intrinsic and extrinsic resources to succeed, welcome others to contribute and offset one's own deficits, and acknowledge mistakes and shortcomings with poise and resilience. How do people first recognize a leader's confidence? By the way the leader treats *everyone* she or he interacts with. It may seem obvious that a good leader needs to demonstrate that he or she is confident in leading meetings with purpose, presenting information, or having a keen ability to solve problems, but people must realize that a leader is trustworthy, and a first step to establishing trust is through respectful and genuine interactions. A leader who concentrates on people first will gain the trust that scaffolds confidence.

Establishing trust does take time, but fortunately the assiduous nature of work presents numerous opportunities for trust to rapidly develop as numerous and complex challenges are tackled on a regular basis. Trust begins with how every member of the team is approached, engaged, and made to feel valuable; in sum, it is how the team is shown respect. The argument can be made that "respect needs to be earned," and we are not dismissing the value of this age-old saying, but the reality is that the leader who is first to show respect and genuine concern to others is the first to lower the resistance of others; this interaction will lay the foundation of trust. A leader who needs to remind subordinates of their importance or position, or similarly demonstrates a desire to impress his or her superiors, is not acting with confidence. On the other hand, a leader who recognizes the value of others regardless of their roles, treats everyone with human decency, and genuinely listens to their concerns and ideas is likely a confident leader, and this demeanor is more apt to garner the trust of others. The establishment of trust and confidence in a leader propels teams forward.

Leaders also show trust in how they oversee projects. For example, if a leader delays giving information, or gives partial information such as a new fiscal year's budget and then expects a team member to complete their budget report on short notice, the supervisee may not trust that her or his supervisor has her or his best interest at heart. Similarly, when a leader provides short notice for an assignment that requires detailed information (i.e., time to complete), it can appear as if the supervisor is disorganized or forgetful, which can also be perceived as the supervisor being emotionally reactive to pressure from her or his superiors. Hence, the supervisee will experience diminished trust and confidence in their supervisor, which can erode the supervisee's passion for the work. On the other hand, teams that trust their leader and are confident in his or her ability to lead will make great sacrifices for that leader; they will work harder, dedicate themselves to the mission, and step outside their comfort zones to accomplish the desired outcomes.

One final thought on trust: it has been said that people do not trust words but actions; however, what they *mostly* trust are patterns of actions. It is not enough to let your actions speak louder than words on a few occasions, it needs to be a pattern—many actions over many situations that are consistent with your words. Be mindful of and reflect on the patterns you choose to reflect your leadership (see Box 7.8).

BOX 7.8

PATTERN OF ACTIONS EXERCISE

We encourage leaders to evaluate not only their actions but their established patterns. Take a moment to list five different situations that required you to use leadership skills. What was consistent throughout all five scenarios? What contradicted? Describe the actions you took, and then describe what pattern the actions represent.

Confidence in one's leadership is paramount when implementing changes or seeing teams through uncertain times. A team that has trust in a leader will have the confidence in the leader's ability to steer them through the contours of the unknown. The confident leader will navigate change by remaining open to ideas and feedback from staff, and also by providing information that is necessary to help the team think of the best possible ideas to match a given situation. Confident leaders are not threatened by this process; rather they encourage it and realize that promoting different ways of thinking and doing things are in the best interest of the team, organization, and constituents. This also means that the confident leader is not interested in tooting his or her own horn, but instead focuses on acknowledging and nurturing the efforts and talents of everyone, or the team as a whole.

Confident leaders tend to want their actions to speak for themselves, and do not feel the need to verbalize their own importance or their accomplishments, because they mainly intend on inspiring and motivating their teams and not on acquiring the prestige and power of their roles. They enjoy seeing positive outcomes and teams working in a collaborative manner, and that can be reward enough for them. Having humility does not mean that they are unable to accept compliments with comfort and grace; however, and in fact, the manner in which one accepts a compliment can also be very telling about their confidence (see Box 7.9).

BOX 7.9

ACCEPTING A COMPLIMENT

Review the following examples and reflect on how you might react to such response.

1. Thanks, I was just doing my job, though.
2. You are very generous. I do not think I am quite that deserving of such a compliment, though.
3. Thank you. I appreciate you sharing that. We all worked hard together on this project and learned a lot along the way, too, and it is nice that others see the results of that.

Confidence in Times of Stress

Confident leaders are able to regulate their emotions when faced with highly stressful situations. Their ability to "keep calm and lead on" evokes confidence from their teams. Leading teams through stress requires that the leader remind her or his team what they have control over and how each individual's strengths will help pull the team through the storm, thus reminding members that they are valuable, empowered, and in it together.

Aside from navigating through turbulent times, confident leaders are also good at providing staff with the resources that they need to continue to learn and grow. As mentioned previously, leaders and managers who take a coaching/mentorship stance are able to help their staff reach professional goals that enhance organizational well-being and individual drive. Good leaders facilitate productive dialogues in mentoring sessions (i.e., supervision meetings) that tap into the individual's professional goals, and they are able to connect the individual with the necessary resources that will help him or her attain those goals. Finally, as we have reminded the reader throughout the chapters leading up to this one, confident leaders always *lead by example*.

Confident Leaders

- Build solid working relationships.

- Take an interest in others.

- Actively listen to the ideas and values of others.

- Make others feel they are important and have a significant role to play in the big picture.

- Explain situations to help others understand the bigger picture.

- Are transparent when they cannot divulge all of the details, but remain committed to sharing as much information as they can, when they can.

- Own their mistakes, not just by saying "I made a mistake" but by taking a further step to explain why they made a particular decision and what they now realize they would have done differently.

- Engage people who seem disengaged and listen to understand where their disengagement is coming from, and do not try to convince them to think differently; instead, they ask the right questions, permitting the employee to think for him or herself.

- Smile. Maintain a positive attitude and model positive interactions.

- Give respect first to earn respect.

- Keep commitments and promises. When something beyond their control interferes with their ability to stay true to their word, confident leaders advocate as needed and appropriate to help increase the chances that they can keep their promises, and, if advocating proves futile, they candidly discuss the situation with their teams. They share their disappointment and hopes; they act human.

MANAGERIAL SKILLS TO INCREASE PRODUCTIVITY

People across all industries are now required to do more with fewer resources while simultaneously achieving high performance and productivity levels. While this "do more with less" trend may result in positive fiscal outcomes, it has spawned a neurological phenomenon that Hallowell (2014) referred to as *attention deficit trait* (ADT). ADT is not a psychiatric diagnosis like attention deficit disorder, but a side effect of taxing working conditions, including taking in excessive amounts of information that overwhelms the brain's ability to effectively process, prioritize, and respond effectively. Hallowell explained it as follows: "Marked by distractibility, inner frenzy, and impatience, ADT prevents managers from clarifying priorities, making smart decisions, and managing their time" (p. 27). Hence, managers who are perfectly capable of performing well can become overstimulated by environmental demands, which essentially short-circuits their ability to effectively process the information required for them to perform at their optimal capability.

Recall from Chapter 6 that perceived threats to one of the SCARF domains can have noxious effects, which result in underperformance. Hallowell (2014) concurs with this idea; when our frontal lobes near capacity, they ignite a fear that one cannot "keep up" and the higher brain, the executive functioning, yields to the lower brain, the amygdala, and limbic system, transferring to survival mode. As Hallowell (2014) explained

> In survival mode, the deep areas of the brain assume control and begin to direct the higher regions. As a result, the whole brain gets caught in a neurological catch-22. The deep regions interpret the message of overload they receive from the frontal lobes in the same way they interpret everything: primitively. They furiously fire signals of fear, anxiety, impatience, irritability, anger, or panic. These alarm signals shanghai the attention of the frontal lobes, forcing them to forfeit much of their power. Because survival signals are irresistible, the frontal lobes get stuck sending messages back to the deep centers saying, "Message received. Trying to work on it but without success." These messages further perturb the deep centers, which send even more powerful messages of distress back up to the frontal lobes. (p. 37)

Although Hallowell's examination of ADT focused mainly on corporate industries, we propose that social workers (both in direct practice and academia) are perhaps at an even greater risk of experiencing ADT given our intense exposure to devastating human conditions, perpetual crisis management of complex human experiences, and keen awareness of the suffering and oppression that exists in tandem with numerous administrative demands. The conjecture that social workers may be more prone to ADT leads us to further dismantle the ways that leaders and managers can use their awareness of ADT when managing themselves, managing others, and influencing organizational culture. Hallowell (2014) offered several ways to manage ADT, including the following:

1. Promote positive emotions. Interact with a colleague you enjoy every 4 to 6 hours (a cautionary note: this should not be someone you enjoy complaining with, as that will only serve to further entrench negativity and fear; the purpose is to simply enjoy the company of others). It is not surprising that being connected with colleagues actually improves executive functioning.

2. Take physical care of your brain. Ensure adequate sleep, a nutritious diet, and exercise. Stand up and walk around throughout the day, as sitting for prolonged periods of time reduces blood flow and decreases mental acuity.

3. Organize for ADT. Prevent disorganization by ordering your workstation in manner that fits you. Organize your time by carving out specific times to attend to specific tasks.

Newell and Nelson-Gardell (2014) illustrated that professional burnout, vicarious trauma, and compassion fatigue are occupational hazards for social workers and require a better understanding of how social work students can learn self-care. For those moving into leadership positions, practicing self-care is equally vital and comparable to students because of the multiple realms of adaptation and exposure to new learning one must undergo. For instance, changes in schedules, longer days impacting family life, and the increased volume of emails and on-call expectations can make work seem ineludible. Layers of vicarious strain include added demands to developing leaders in the field of social work. The secondary stress no longer stems directly from the clients' turmoil, but can expand to envelop clinicians' reactions to clients' turmoil and, thus, begin to include the vicarious stress of those directly serving clients (distant secondary trauma). The overall pressure of balancing the kaleidoscopic demands of leadership positions, in combination with empathically leading others who may be at their own threshold for stress, can contribute to burnout (see Box 7.10).

BOX 7.10

COMPETENCY-BASED CASE STUDY

Allison, a seasoned LCSW working in a residential treatment facility, has always loved being a clinician and is an exemplary role model for other clinicians within her organization. She has a warm, approachable demeanor, and many staff gravitate to her for informal support and advice on how to approach complex cases. She is always supportive, straightforward, conscientious, and thorough.

When the organization restructured, Allison was approached by her supervisor to fill the position of clinical supervisor. This position allowed her to apply her innate interpersonal skills, clinical knowledge, and expertise to supervise others. The position also required her to cut her caseload back to a handful of residents.

Allison was eager to embrace the new challenges of her supervisory role and had a balanced sense of her strengths and areas of improvement. She was a quick learner who seemed to intuitively have a firm handle on her new responsibilities. However, in the initial months, Allison found herself staying at the office late several nights a week and rationalized that it was just while she adjusted to the new demands of the position, but she did miss being at her children's evening activities and having family dinners. Even on the evenings that she did make it home in time for dinner, she was frequently interrupted by phone calls from staff in need of clinical directives. Her husband was supportive and helped out by preparing dinners, but this too was something that Allison missed as she had always enjoyed cooking and found it to be relaxing after work.

Her supervisor had started to observe that her upbeat, calm, and focused manner was gradually eroding and decided to share these concerns with her. Allison explained that she felt that the days were packed with tasks, and she always felt like she needed to "be on." She was struggling to escape from the job even during her off times. Her supervisor encouraged her to consider what she needed for her own self-care practices, and Allison developed a self-care plan. The supervisor would periodically check in with Allison about her implementation of self-care, to continue to encourage her to attend to her well-being.

LCSW, Licensed Clinical Social Worker.

There are a number of reasons that allocating time for self-care can seem challenging for leaders, particularly for those who are just beginning to find their way in their new roles. The escalation of responsibilities entails augmented assignments, greater oversight of people and projects, accelerated learning of new skills and new acronyms, and collaborating with unfamiliar subsystems that can appear intensely fast-paced and foreign. When combined with the ancillary objective of gaining a deeper understanding of who one is as a leader, this escalation can all be quite stressful. There is more to do and less time to do it in; more people to attend to and less focus on oneself. However, returning to the axiom of emotional intelligence, both the emerging and the seasoned leader can apply the skills of self-awareness and regulation, empathy, and motivation to anchor themselves in the present and practice self-care with intentionality.

New leaders may feel overwhelmed by the plethora of role changes and the potential resistance they meet from others about organizational changes. They may begin to question their ability to gain consensus. They may even begin to displace their office stress at home and project their tenuous professional relationships onto loved ones, creating personal stress in addition to professional. While there are a number of activities to engage in, self-care—like self-awareness—is also about being realistic with expectations. Self-care does not need to be extravagant, such as going for a massage or weekend getaways to clear the mind, but can include simple daily exercises to stay present, focused, and energized.

Taking time to nurture one's own well-being does not need to be luxurious or far-reaching, just practical enough to practice with consistency. Telling oneself there is not enough time and too much to do, of course, impedes the practice of self-care and permits stress to metastasize. However, by raising awareness of the present, one can increase clarity, focus, and energy to stay the course—and also stay healthy. One can do many activities in the name of self-care, but unless one has fully committed to being present in the moment, allowing the static noise of countless to-dos and looming pressures of the day to fade into the background, it will be a desultory exercise and frustrating attempt—and one truly does not have any time for that. Simply put, it is about paying attention to what we are doing, when we are doing it. It is not thinking about the next thing, which will inevitably be there waiting anyway. In essence, it is about being mindful.

Mindful leaders can practice self-care throughout the day. Set the day, or make a list the night before, with purpose and intention by asking: *What do I want to bring to this day? What are the three things that I want to accomplish today?* The answers do not need to be lofty; instead they should be purposeful and practical, which can feel attainable and rewarding. There are times throughout the day that mindfulness can be employed by using some of the following self-care activities:

- **Refresh.** Give yourself brief breaks in between emails, calls, meetings, and so on to go for a short walk. The idea is to take your surroundings in along that walk. Notice your breathing, feel the chill of the air or the warmth of the sun on you, notice the swing of your arms and the pace of your steps.

- **Listen to music**. Stand up and stretch; take a couple of minutes to meditate.

- **Recharge.** A lunch break may not always be possible, but taking some time to enjoy your meal and not read emails, listen to messages, or take calls is a healthy compromise. Pushing the pause button while chewing on your lunch can result in feeling recharged and refocused. Taking a midday or lunch break by getting out of the work environment will do wonders for your performance, and if you cannot exercise during that time, perhaps do it after work. Exercising either before work or at lunch will serve a beneficial function.

- **Breathe**. Do a short deep breathing activity at various intervals throughout the day.

- **Reconnect.** Connections are both intrapersonal and interpersonal. Connect with a loved one during the day. A brief phone call or text message with a loved one can be anchoring, and slowing down for just a moment to connect with support networks can be energizing.

- **Connect** back to yourself and check in on your set intention for the day, reflect on the intention, and modify it as needed.

- **Refocus.** One can use instrumental exercises to help refocus. Strategies like using a calendar and setting agendas and time limits for tasks can also help bring what is essential into clear focus.

Self-care can include taking the time to create, relax, and have fun. By creating the space for these activities, you organically build in time to self-reflect, to be among those you love, to spend time on yourself, and to simply be in the moment.

Time to create

- Try new things: a new recipe, a new exercise routine, jewelry making, or a new gadget.
- Write about whatever you want; journaling can be a way of articulating ideas and discovering ways for how to create changes.
- Color.
- Try a painting class.
- Create a comfortable space: both at home and at work.

Time to learn and engage in new skilled activities

- Mental activities: learning a new language, musical instrument, cerebral games such as bridge and chess.
- Physical activities: learning a new sport, painting, pottery, sewing.

Time to relax through

- Yoga.
- Deep breathing.
- Meditation.
- Hypnosis.
- Taking in nature.
- Reading.

Time to have fun

- Attend enjoyable events.
- Spend time with friends.
- Spend time with family.
- Exercise.
- Walk.
- Hike.
- See a play/movie.
- Tap into your inner kid and let go. Go for a bike ride, enjoy an ice cream cone, be silly, have fun!

Whatever activities you choose, stay *in the moment* and focus your attention on what is happening and when it is happening; redirect any thoughts that drift back to your to-do lists. That is how you set the intention to care for yourself, by allowing yourself to recuperate so that you can attend to your "to-dos" later at your optimal performance.

The University of Buffalo offers a number of self-care resources, including self-assessments and a variety of self-care activities (see Boxes 7.11 and 7.12).

BOX 7.11

ADDITIONAL RESOURCE

For more information, go to: https://socialwork.buffalo.edu/resources/self-care-starter-kit.html.

BOX 7.12

COMPETENCY-BASED SELF-CARE PLAN

List the self-care things that you like to do, then think about the best time to engage in these activities. Once you have done that, add them to your monthly calendar.

Enhancing Productivity

The managerial methods that can be used to enhance productivity include *managing yourself effectively* (in this chapter), *information sharing* (Chapter 3), *brainstorming* (Chapter 14), *problem solving and decision making* (Chapter 5), and *planning implementation* (Chapter 14). The communication tools to best achieve success can include using the telephone, emails, social media, memos, informal contact, and meetings (small or large). The question is, which method should you use? Three strategies for more effective personal results are organizing an effective workspace, planning to achieve goals, and avoiding time wasters.

Organizing an Effective Workspace

The organization of a workplace will either enhance or detract from effective management practice. Too much clutter makes it difficult to find material and can be psychologically challenging. By eliminating clutter, you can be more effective. A Chinese proverb offers a solution: "The person who removes a mountain begins by carrying away small stones." Answer the question posed in Box 7.13.

BOX 7.13

QUESTION FOR READERS

Question: An office with piles of clutter is a sign of

  a. A disorganized person

  b. A genius

  c. Laziness

  d. Being overworked

  e. A poor manager

  f. A good manager

What do you think is the correct answer? You decide which combination of answers from a to f are correct. Piles of clutter are clearly a sign of a disorganized person. You could be a genius or maybe not! With clutter others may quickly jump to the conclusion that you are disorganized, as it will be difficult to find material when you need it and you seem lost as you rifle through materials to find what you need, or what you may have buried and forgotten about.

Some of the following tables and boxes on managing yourself were adapted from Crandell (2004).

There are three steps one can take to start organizing an effective workplace: setting up a filing system, gathering essential tools, and managing workflow. The three steps to start organizing an effective workplace are displayed in Box 7.14.

BOX 7.14

THREE STEPS TO START ORGANIZING AN EFFECTIVE WORKPLACE

- **Setting up a filing system—either hard copies or electronic folders**

  - Working files—kept close at hand, easy to reach them, go to them often. Working files and other file systems listed below can also be done electronically with folders and subfolders.

  - Reference file—not used on a regular basis, further removed from the desk.

  - Archival files—things to keep for legal reasons; kept farther away.

  - Tickler files—a complete system would contain separate file folders for months of the year and days of the month. Drop things into tickler file in advance. Consult it on a daily basis. However, electronic calendars are what most managers use today (e.g., Microsoft Office and calendars on smart phones).

  - When setting up filing systems, use words you will remember; people's names are better than topics.

- **Gathering essential tools**

  - Trays (4)—incoming material to place things temporarily in the first tray, then sort to the middle tray things that are pending, then day-to-day material, then in the last tray place things to be distributed, such as outgoing documents.

  - Computer—create folders in a way that you will remember them, e.g., in a hierarchical order. For example, if you attend a conference every year, create subfolders by year.

  - Telephone—office and/or cell phone. Make sure you can remotely access your office messages. Have your phone and email messages transferred to your smart phone.

  - Standard office supplies including a labeler for files (portable).

  - Finally, a folder for whatever you are working on right now, either a hard copy or electronic folder.

- **Managing workflow**

  - Collecting—pull together all things you have to do in the next week or month, using in-baskets (paper and/or electronic).

  - Processing—if it takes less than two minutes, do it now. Otherwise trash it or file it; or delegate it; or defer it.

  - Organizing—use calendars and lists. Use calendars for meetings and appointments; a tickler file for placing major responsibilities into categories through an annual calendar. For example, in February, schedule or assign courses; in March, submit budget. Scheduling can be done using an Area of Responsibility Calendar (see Table 7.4). Use lists to keep track of projects, next actions, waiting for something, sometimes/maybe items, and lists of unscheduled tasks:

    - Lists

      - Projects: anything that requires more than one step to complete. Examples in academia include online education, curriculum changes, and revisions of the policy manual. Examples in agencies include planning and budgeting reorganizing (see Table 7.5).

(continued)

BOX 7.14 *(Continued)*

- Next actions: one step to carry a specific project forward. Do as soon as you can (see Table 7.6).

- Waiting-for list: if good at delegating responsibility, need to know when things will come back. Develop a spreadsheet: name, topic, requested date, expected date (see Table 7.8).

- Sometime/maybe list: something you want to do eventually. Also in a spreadsheet: name, topic, requested date, expected date (see Table 7.9).

- List of unscheduled tasks (see Table 7.10).

How do you transition to this system?

To get started, take two days and process all of the information in your office and files. If you cannot finish in this time, take another day or two the following week. Do one piece of paper/document, or one thing at a time, such as saving or deleting a folder's contents. Attack a particular area or pile of work until everything is sorted. Whenever a new piece of information comes in, identify it according to the four Ds, of daily planning (urgent and important, important and not urgent, urgent and not important, and not important and not urgent) and deal with it accordingly. This system may seem silly at first, but consider how many pieces of information are addressed to you every day. Now layer the everyday interruptions on top of that, and add another layer of the unforeseen interruptions, and another layer of the projects that you should be working on. It's a lot, isn't it? And while you may have a decent, or even good, handle on managing all of the items you need to follow up on now, the chances are that the more you advance, the more information will be thrown at you. Hence, now may be an ideal time to create a system that can handle the bounteous information that you receive.

Planning to Achieve Goals

Many leaders and managers have ideas about what goals they want and need to accomplish. However, there are many times during the day that one's focus is interrupted. For academic deans, directors, or chairperson, these interruptions may include time redirected toward search hires, the spontaneous student review meeting, consultation sought on event planning, and so on. Someone working in an organization that provides services may be derailed by acute crises (at the client or employee level), unforeseen compliance issues, or short notice on a grant or request for proposal opportunity that must quickly be addressed.

In other words, leaders can fall into the habit of getting sidetracked. One way to monitor your schedule is to complete a time study for how you are relegating your time. For instance, what percentage of your day demands email response, returned phone calls or accepting calls, talking to staff, meetings, documentation reviews, and so on? What percentage of time do you allocate each week to working on projects that are aimed at meeting your goals? You may be surprised to find how little time is actually devoted to the activities that move you toward achieving your goals. Based on your findings, you can visualize where more or less of your time would best be allocated. Part of allocating your time involves being able to plan and prioritize tasks. Below are some suggestions to help guide your short- and long-term planning.

Short-term planning should be done weekly by reviewing and updating calendars on Monday morning and reviewing and updating all lists. For daily planning, identify what is important and urgent. Table 7.1 provides examples on when to deal with issues that are urgent and important, urgent and not important, important and not urgent, and not important and not urgent.

Many leaders and managers frequently get overwhelmed. When leaders or managers do get overwhelmed, what can they do about it? One suggestion is to concentrate on finishing what one absolutely has to get done that day. All less important tasks can be put off to a later time. Put off to later less important tasks. The most important tasks are usually ones demanded by your boss. Do them first. Other tasks of importance might pertain to urgent client or student needs and require immediate action. Essentially, leaders and managers need to understand how to prioritize tasks, which by extension can help them to manage stress.

TABLE 7.1 **Daily Planning by Urgency and Importance**

WHAT IS	WHEN TO DEAL WITH IT	EXAMPLES
Urgent and important	Deal with right away	Sexual harassment incidents, budget requests, significant client incident
Urgent and not important	Deal with it when you have the time	Reassign office space
Important and not urgent	Make sure it is dealt with but not right away. Build time in to schedule to ensure it is attended to	Plan meetings, share information, scheduling, revamp performance improvement committee
Not important and not urgent	File at least once a week and take action once a month	Review of phone records

How do you spend most of your time? Do you only deal with urgent and important or important and not urgent issues and ignore the others? Table 7.2 provides a list that requires rating by the four Ds.

Long-term planning should also be done regularly but at longer intervals, such as once a month. To make long-term planning operational, develop action plans for projects. Table 7.3 provides examples of projects and how to identify outcomes for these projects, the steps to achieve these outcomes, and completion dates.

See also Box 7.15 which gives advice to new leaders.

BOX 7.15

EXCERPT OF INTERVIEW WITH PRESIDENT JOE

Question: *What advice would you give someone going into a leadership position for the first time?*

Good leadership requires having a passion. Know what your purpose is. Need to plan. Three p's. When I think about career, had a passion and knew what I was doing, had a purpose, and I was a planner.

Two other things: need to understand and make every effort to live your values. If these values don't match with the institution, then you need to gracefully exit. As part of core value system, you need to acknowledge when you are wrong and when you faltered. Authenticity matters. (President Joe Bertalino, Interview on Leadership Style from March 5, 2018, SCSU, New Haven, Connecticut)

SCSU, Southern Connecticut State University.

TABLE 7.2 **Activities Over the Last Month by Four Ds**

ACTIVITY	WHAT IS	COMPLETED? YES OR NO	TOTAL PERCENT OF WHAT ACTIVITIES COMPLETED
1.	Urgent and important		
2.	Urgent and important		
3.	Urgent and important		
Total			
1.	Urgent and not important		
2.	Urgent and not important		
3.	Urgent and not important		
Total			
1.	Important and not urgent		
2.	Important and not urgent		
3.	Important and not urgent		
Total			
1.	Not important and not urgent		
2.	Not important and not urgent		
3.	Not important and not urgent		
Total			

List activities over the last 30-day period and then identify what percent of them were completed after designating them urgent and important, urgent and not important, important and not urgent, and not important and not urgent.

TABLE 7.3 **Develop Action Plans for Long-Term Planning**

PROJECT	IDENTIFY OUTCOMES	STEPS TO ACHIEVE OUTCOMES	COMPLETION DATES
Renovate office	Find funding	Seek funds from current and new sources	6 months
Reaccreditation	Timeline created	Develop timeline	3 months
Reaccreditation	Tasks assigned	Email tasks to staff	4 months
Reaccreditation	All sections edited	Drafts of sections completed by staff	12 months
Reaccreditation	Report finalized	Edit final report	15 months
Reaccreditation	Sign-off from head	Submit to head	7 months
Reaccreditation	Report accepted	Email and hard copy submitted to accrediting agency	17 months

Avoid Time Wasters

Both short- and long-term planning can help you stay on task, but there are a number of things that can happen on a daily basis that waste precious time, including not being able to find things (lost sheep), telephone interruptions, drop-in visitors, and the constant bombardment of email. Tips on avoiding these time wasters are listed in Box 7.16.

BOX 7.16

AVOID TIME WASTERS

- Lost sheep—for example, a piece of paper you cannot find. To avoid not being able to find things:
  - Process information as it comes in, or on a regular basis.
  - File materials at the end of the day.
  - Eliminate clutter on a weekly basis so it does not pile up.
- Telephone Interruptions
  - Screen calls when working on projects or tasks to avoid interrupting the flow (make sure your number is not in a general call location unless you want it there).
  - Return calls in batches; do not return them as they come in.
  - If you have an open door policy, limit each call to 5 minutes or less. If it is a call that you anticipate will take longer, schedule the phone meeting so you have a start and stop time, which you can coordinate with the other party in advance.
- Drop-in Visitors
  - Screen visitors.
  - Prepare responses in advance.
  - Limit time of intrusion. You can still be approachable without being overly accessible. Remember setting limits for others allows them to see and learn how to do the same for themselves. If the reason they sought you out is important enough to schedule a follow-up meeting, do so. If the matter is acutely urgent, prioritize the steps for addressing it quickly and check back in about the follow-up needed.

Email overload can also cause one to lose valuable time. Box 7.17 provides some valuable tips on expeditiously handling email and other forms of instant messaging (IM). Today, people can switch back-and-forth between using email and IM apps. Common IM apps include WhatsApp, Facebook Messenger, Slack, Skype, and messenger apps that come with your smart phone. A new generation of workplace apps (Shellenbarger, 2018) is becoming available for use and include Microsoft Teams, Stride by Atlassian, and Google Hangouts, all of which bundle IMs with team collaboration, web conferencing, and social networking tools.

BOX 7.17

HOW TO HANDLE EMAIL AND INSTANT MESSAGING

- Emails, texts, and other forms of instant messaging (IM) communication: Process several times a day or in batches. For example, emails are best handled in the morning, and then again at midday, the end of the day, and in the evening. Texts and other short messaging apps sometimes require immediate responses. Delete, delegate, respond, or defer (adding to another list). Do not scan list of messages for important things; do it all in batches.

  - Process email like paperwork

    - We have become so reliant on email that people can become saturated, and thus what is vital may get overlooked because people are on "information overload." Keep your messages brief, use bullet points, remind staff when they do not need to "reply all" and flood others' mailboxes, and make sure your subject lines capture the essence of your message and the attention of the reader. Finally, the shorter the message, the greater likelihood that someone will actually read the email. If the message is too long, break it down and send multiple messages. Always read your responses before sending back to ensure clarity.

    - People scan emails, so if you have multiple points to make, either send multiple short emails or bullet important points (but not more than three bullets).

    - Texts are usually shorter so it is easier to respond quickly. One problem with texts is that people tend to respond to every one, back-and-forth in a never-ending cycle, which is not necessary. However, if you urgently need to get a message, you will have more success than email.

  - How to manage email

    - Create folders for email by person.
    - Create an action folder or other folders by topic area.
    - Create a waiting-for folder.
    - If an email is really important, print it out and put into tickler file or an action folder.

  - How often do you clean out email?

    - Clean out incoming email on a daily basis.
    - Go to action folder regularly.
    - To clear out items in action folder, do at least one item each week.

Procrastination can be a problem for anyone, particularly perfectionists. To reduce the likelihood of procrastination, break large tasks into smaller ones, set deadlines for yourself, and identify the next action.

WHERE TO BEGIN WITH VARIOUS LISTS?

One place to start is to create a table called an "Area of Responsibility Calendar by Month" and update it regularly. Table 7.4 provides examples of responsibilities and activities to achieve by month.

TABLE 7.4 **Area of Responsibility Calendar by Month**

FEBRUARY	
Responsibility/topic	**Activities**
Schedule	Assign undergraduate and graduate courses
	Agency meetings
Budget	Check ledger statement for February
	Estimate budget by category
Personnel	Annual review due
	Modify evaluation instruments

The next step is to create a "Projects List." All organizations have projects that need to be completed. One way to stay on top of projects is to create a projects list that contains all major and minor projects by activities, due dates, person or group in charge, resources needed, and a description of the final product (see Table 7.5).

TABLE 7.5 **Projects List**

MAJOR PROJECTS	ACTIVITIES	DUE DATE	PERSON OR GROUP IN LEAD	RESOURCES NEEDED	DESCRIPTION OF FINAL PRODUCT
Online education	Identify which courses are suitable	End of academic year	Curriculum committee	Monthly meetings	List of online courses
Curriculum changes	Review curriculum and identify best practices	End of semester	Curriculum committee	Monthly meetings	Revised curriculum
Revision of policy manuals	Edit and update manuals	Before start of new year	Program coordinators	Time	New year manuals
MINOR PROJECTS					
Office renovations	Determine which offices need updating	First of the year	Office manager	Develop and send survey to staff	List of which offices need renovation
Office renovations	Find funding sources	February 1	Office manager	Identified amount per office	Allocation of funds to start renovation

Another tool is to create a "Next Actions List." See Table 7.6 to identify actions that need to be undertaken soon and ways to achieve them.

TABLE 7.6 **Next Actions List**

NEXT ACTION	ACTIVITIES	DUE DATE	PERSON RESPONSIBLE	FINAL PRODUCT
Course schedule	Update schedule from previous year	December 1 for the following fall semester	Department chairperson	New fall course schedule
	Add new courses and times	"	"	"
	Assign faculty	"	"	"
Hire secretary	Create job description	March 1	Personnel committee	Job description completed
	Advertise	March 15	Personnel committee chair	Ad appears
	Screen candidates	April 15	Personnel committee	Screening complete and candidates for interviews selected
	Interview	May 1–10	Personnel committee	Interviews completed
	Make tentative offer	May 12	HR department	Offer made
	Conduct background check	May 12–17	HR department	Check complete
	Hire secretary	May 18	HR department	Start date set

TABLE 7.7 **To-Do List**

CATEGORY	DATE DUE
Send emails	
Return phone calls	
Meetings	
Complete work on computer and forward	
Forward hardcopy material	
Personal items	
Errands	

Most managers can benefit from a personal to-do list. There are a number of ways to create such a list. One way is to create a table that contains everything listed by categories (you could have separate tables by categories, but if you have too many categories, you may find it difficult to add things to the correct categories). Table 7.7 is an example of a simple, one-table "To-Do List" by categories and due dates.

Sometimes actions and projects cannot be completed until someone else completes certain actions or, perhaps, the material is not due until a certain date. This dilemma may require creating a "Waiting-for List." See Table 7.8, which includes the name of the person responsible, the topic, the requested date, and the expected date.

TABLE 7.8 **Waiting-for List**

NAME OF PERSON RESPONSIBLE	TOPIC	REQUESTED DATE	EXPECTED DATE
Dr. Jack	Assessment form	12/11/18	1/6/19
Jackie	Travel form	12/17/18	1/24/19
Bill	Release form	2/15/18	2/17/19

Sometimes, there are projects or actions in which you are not sure of their importance. In these cases, it is best to create a "Sometime/Maybe List." See Table 7.9, which contains the topic, who should be responsible, and the due date.

TABLE 7.9 **Sometime/Maybe List**

TOPIC	WHO SHOULD BE RESPONSIBLE	DUE DATE
Revise curriculum	Curriculum committee	March 2019
Update strategic plan	Director	January 2019
Read this book	Myself	Next month

When you have back-to-back meetings and do not have time to handle input or information, create a "List of Unscheduled Tasks." See Table 7.10, which contains the name of the meeting, unscheduled tasks, what will get done by the end of the week, and how much time is required to get the task done. Aim to get things done by the end of the week. The week is the planning period.

TABLE 7.10 **List of Unscheduled Tasks**

NAME OF MEETINGS	UNSCHEDULED TASKS	WHAT WILL GET DONE BY END OF WEEK	HOW MUCH TIME REQUIRED TO GET DONE

SUMMARY

This chapter identified the process of transitioning to leadership and management roles. There are multiple benefits to mentoring emerging managers, and mentorship offers additional gains for both the mentor and the mentee. Offering mentorship to new managers and aspiring leaders also promotes an organizational culture that values professional development and can enhance performance and productivity. When best practices are employed by mentors, it highlights their commitment to relationship building, character building, optimism, and loyalty. Mentors can apply the TERA quotient at the commencement of mentorship to establish trust and expectations. Characteristics of confident leaders include the importance of proactively engaging staff in a respectful manner and demonstrating authenticity, transparency, and interest in learning from coworkers at all levels of the organization. The neurological phenomenon of ADT may leave social work managers and leaders susceptible to information overload, which consequently highlights the importance of creating strategies for attending to one's self-care. Finally, this chapter outlined the managerial skills needed to increase productivity, offering tools for time management, workspace organization, managing time flow, developing project lists, and managing multiple sources of information.

ACTIVITIES

1. Consider a project that is currently assigned to you and a group of people with whom you either work or attend classes. This project may be a work or school assignment. Write a brief confidence-building memo to two or more of your peers. What do you see as their strengths and abilities to perform the task successfully? What do you know about their characteristics and previous accomplishments that will help them succeed in the task?

2. Now complete the same memo for yourself. Reflect on your comfort level in completing both memos. Compare and contrast what it was like writing to others and then to yourself.

3. Complete a time study. Keep track over a 3- to 5-day period of how you spend your time and energy. What tasks consume the most amount of time? What tasks do you need to dedicate more time to, and how can you do that?

4. Create a bulleted outline to describe your action plan for leading with confidence. Detail what you will do to establish trust with others and how you will know when you have gained the trust and confidence of others (i.e., what behaviors will they demonstrate, what will the relationships be like?).

REFERENCES

Bandura, A. (1977). Self-efficacy: Toward a unifying theory of behavioral change. *Psychological Review, 84*, 191–121. doi:10.1037/0033-295X.84.2.191

Bliss, D. L., Pecukonis, E., & Snyder-Vogal, M. (2014). Principled leadership development model for aspiring social work managers and administrators: Development and application. *Human Service Organizations: Management, Leadership & Governance, 38*(1), 5–15. doi:10.1080/03643107.2013.853008

Bunker, K. A., Kram, K. E., & Ting, S. (2015). Coaching rising managers to emotional maturity. Give effective feedback. Foster steady growth. Motivate star performers. In *HBR guide to coaching employees*. Boston, MA: Harvard Business Review Press.

Crandell, G. (2004)., *It's about time: Managing yourself for more effective results*. 21st Annual Academic Chairperson Conference, Adams Mark Hotel, Orlando, FL.

Gallup   (2015).   Manager   and   team   leader   development.   Retrieved   from
https://www.gallup.com/workplace/215384/gallup-manager-team-leader-development.aspx

Hallowell, E. M. (2014). Overloaded circuits: Why smart people underperform. Renew your energy.
Lighten the load. Strike a better balance. In *HBR guide to managing stress at work*. Boston,
MA: Harvard Business Review Press.

King Keenan, E., Sandoval, S., & Limone, C. (2018). Realizing the potential for leadership in social work.
Journal of Social Work, 0(0), 1–19. doi:10.1177/1468017318766821

Kolb, D., & Kolb, A. (2013). The kolb learning style inventory 4.0: Guide to theory,
psychometrics, research & applications. Retrieved from https://www.researchgate.net/
publication/303446688_The_Kolb_Learning_Style_Inventory_40_Guide_to_Theory_Psychometrics
_Research_Applications

Newell, L. M., & Nelson-Gardell, D. (2014). A competency-based approach to teaching professional
self-care: An ethical consideration for social work educators. *Journal of Social Work Education, 50*(3),
427–439. doi:10.1080/10437797.2014.917928

Shanks, E., & Lundström, T., Bergmark, Å. (2014). Embedded in practice? Swedish social work managers
on sources of managerial knowledge. *Human Service Organizations Management, 38*(5), 435–447.
doi:10.1080/03643107.2013.866605

Shellenbarger, S. (2018, April 18). The instant message generation gap. *The Wall Street Journal*, A9.

Stanier, M. B. (2016). *The coaching habit: Say less, ask more & change the way you lead forever [audiobook]*.
Toronto, ON, Canada: Box of Crayons Press.

Tjan, A. K. (2017). What the best mentors do. *Harvard Business Review*. Retrieved from
https://hbr.org/2017/02/what-the-best-mentors-do

CHAPTER 8

MANAGING THE ORGANIZATIONAL FUNCTIONS FOR SOCIAL WORKERS

CHAPTER OBJECTIVES

- Learning effective communication with both internal and external constituencies.
- Understanding ways of creating and maintaining a positive organizational culture.
- Identifying ways to create a favorable organizational climate and culture through teamwork, mutual respect, and confidence.
- Recognizing organizational dysfunction and ways to overcome it.
- Understanding ways of addressing cynicism and complacency.
- Valuing professionalism and role modeling.
- Promoting diversity and culturally competent practice.
- Modeling professional and ethical behavior.
- Establishing and maintaining a professional and productive organizational culture.
- Inspiring your workforce to produce in a superior manner.
- Understanding how to turn around a dysfunctional organization.
- Encouraging diversity and different perspectives.
- Ensuring all services are culturally competent.
- Motivating members of the organization at all levels.
- Advocating for an organizational culture that benefits all employees and clients.

INTRODUCTION

Leaders and managers are responsible for managing and overseeing key organizational functions. These functions include diverse tasks such as managing staff, budgets, and information technology; creating and implementing strategic plans; and cultivating an atmosphere where staff are motivated and encouraged to achieve the organizational goals and mission.

Managers need to ensure that staff are provided with the skills, knowledge, and access to resources to successfully perform their jobs to help the organization meet its goals and objectives. Change is constantly occurring within organizations, and leaders need to be able to model for staff how to effectively adapt to and capitalize on change. Oftentimes, dealing with change requires that leaders develop an entrepreneurial mind-set, which is typified by proposing change and innovation. It is highly unlikely that the vast majority of working teams will celebrate and embrace change; the reality is that most people will resist it. Leaders and managers need to prepare for this reluctance and help teams transcend cynicism and complacency to enhance performance, productivity, and morale. Advancing teams beyond cynicism may command that leaders and managers model appropriate professional behaviors that demonstrate ethical conduct and shield the integrity and reputation of the organization.

In order to effectively model for teams, leaders must be knowledgeable about the diverse aspects that contribute to the daily operations and functions of the organization, such as budgeting, human resources, external relations, and having a pulse on the work occurring within different programs that make up the organization. Leaders and managers need to model that they are attentive to staff, evinced by attentively listening and seeking input from various levels of staff by providing them with opportunities to meet and discuss programmatic concerns or ideas. Furthermore, leaders and managers need to demonstrate their commitment to acknowledging diversity and take steps toward providing services that are culturally competent. This chapter addresses the competencies/behaviors in Box 8.1.

BOX 8.1

COMPETENCIES AND PRACTICE BEHAVIORS ADDRESSED IN THIS CHAPTER

Possesses interpersonal skills that support viability and positive functioning of the organization (Network for Social Work Management Competencies 2). Practice Behaviors:

- Establishes and maintains an organizational culture that recognizes and rewards professionalism, quality customer service, employee engagement and empowerment, and programs and services that further social justice (2.1).
- Inspires the workforce to move beyond cynicism and complacency, and perform and produce in a superior manner (2.2).

Possesses analytical and critical thinking skills that promote organizational growth (Network for Social Work Management Competencies 3). Practice Behaviors:

- Demonstrates a working knowledge of budget and finance, human resources, communication and marketing, applications of information technology, fundraising, and external relations; and an understanding or "feel" for the core work of the organization (3.1).
- Demonstrates an entrepreneurial spirit and attitude (3.2).
- Demonstrates strong skills in turning around dysfunctional organizations (3.5).

(continued)

BOX 8.1 *(Continued)*

Models appropriate professional behavior and encourages other staff members to act in a professional manner (Network for Social Work Management Competencies 4).

- Engages in and promotes ethical conduct (4.1).
- Protects the integrity and reputation of the organization (4.2).
- Creates and supports an organizational culture that values professionalism, service, and ethical conduct (4.3).

Manages diversity and cross-cultural understanding (Network for Social Work Management Competencies 5). Practice Behaviors:

- Publicly acknowledges the diversity of the staff and clients and creates a climate that celebrates the differences (5.1).
- Seeks input from all levels of staff, listens attentively, demonstrates fairness and consistency, and conveys information fully and clearly (5.4)
- Invites different perspectives to all client-related and management discussions within the organization (5.5)
- Encourages and allows opportunities for staff to confer and present issues and problems affecting program-related services (5.6).
- Takes steps necessary to assure that all services provided by the organization are culturally competent (5.7).

Develops and manages both internal and external stakeholder relationships (Network for Social Work Management Competencies 6). Practice Behaviors:

- Consistently and effectively motivates governance body members, employees, volunteers, clients, and other key constituencies to work toward achieving the organizational mission (6.1).

Organizational culture is the perceived and expected behaviors within an organization that are often a manifestation of the expectations, values, and philosophy of the organization. Culture is often based on the beliefs, attitudes, and practices that can be either written or unwritten, which have developed over time. Is organizational culture a stable state? Or is it constantly evolving? Most people describe it as a stable state; however, cultures evolve on a regular basis. For example, every time a new staff begins to work at an organization she or he may bring something that can slightly modify the organizational culture. For instance, a new faculty member is very tech savvy. He or she collaborates with other faculty and, as a result, the new status quo is a high-tech environment where all workers are expected to participate at a high level of technological efficacy. Professionalism is a part of most organizational cultures, but exactly how that is defined varies from organization to organization. However professionalism is defined by an organization, leaders typically seek to reinforce the organization's interpretation of professionalism among their staff.

Rewarding Professionalism

Professionalism is the way people appear, dress, present, and represent the organization's values, mission, purpose, and communicate in a respectful manner. Professional behavior does not engage in or encourage gossip, bullying behaviors, excluding behaviors, bad-mouthing people, or complaining about fellow coworkers, the organization as a whole, or clients they serve.

The ideal behaviors are rewarded by promoting the people who have a pattern of demonstrating professionalism. Professionalism is sometimes recognized in public mentions among teams, or referred to in coaching, or mentoring, stories during supervision. Professional behaviors are expected by the leaders, stakeholders, and fellow colleagues, and when people diverge from professionalism, it is apparent to others and can have a noxious effect on the organization. Finally, professionalism ensures that workers are providing the best care to clients/students.

Ensuring Quality Customer Service

Leaders and managers must model through their actions that the customers (clients or students) are the very reason everyone shows up for work . . . and gets paid! Thus, leaders and managers need to set a precedent in the organization that the customer comes first, and they can model this behavior by how they treat their staff. For instance, leaders and managers should

- Respond to people in a timely manner.
- Treat people with respect and dignity.
- Not put people off.
- Show up for their team on time.
- Be prepared for meetings.
- Listen to staff.

Engaging and Empowering Employees

Engaging staff begins with understanding what they value, how they are motivated, and what their aspirations are. Once a leader or manager gains this insight, he or she can develop tasks and projects that are tailored to the staff's strengths, talents, and stretch goals. To empower staff, the leader or manager has to provide the appropriate access to information, assistance, and linkage with other staff to work on projects together. Ideally, members of the team—with diverse skill sets—should be assigned individual projects that are contributing to the team's success while also showcasing individuals' skills. Holding regular team meetings where staff provide updates on their projects is one way to promote information sharing that helps others know what all individuals are working on that is contributing to the overall goals.

People also want to know that they are valued; so you, as a leader or manager, need to communicate how they are valued members of the team. If they are actively engaged, they will want to be involved, and if you give them the opportunities to be creative, they will be empowered.

Developing Programs and Services That Promote Social Justice

Academia

Leaders and managers should create programs that have a direct impact on social justice. In an academic setting, for example, a department might promote lobby day experience, poverty simulation, or sponsor events that fundraise for social justice institutions. Additionally, departments should incorporate social justice topics into the curriculum (as either a course or through course assignments). Students are involved in social justice activities as part of their field practicum assignments. Faculty can engage in social justice activities through service on boards of community agencies.

Community Agency

Community agencies want to create services that have an impact and incorporate social justice in the service provisions, for instance, holiday food and gift donations, advocating for families of color who are viewed differently than families of the majority group, and so on. Programs within a community agency should incorporate social justice ideals, which may require acknowledging internally that people are engaged in social justice activities.

CYNICISM AND COMPLACENCY

Box 8.2 displays the competencies/behaviors in this section.

BOX 8.2

NETWORK FOR SOCIAL WORK MANAGEMENT COMPETENCIES AND PRACTICE BEHAVIORS 2, 6, AND 3

Possesses interpersonal skills that support viability and positive functioning of the organization (Network for Social Work Management Competencies 2). Practice Behaviors:

- Establishes and maintains an organizational culture that recognizes and rewards professionalism, quality customer service, employee engagement and empowerment, and programs and services that further social justice (2.1).
- Inspires the workforce to move beyond cynicism and complacency, and perform and produce in a superior manner (2.2).

Develops and manages both internal and external stakeholder relationships (Network for Social Work Management Competencies 6). Practice Behaviors:

- Consistently and effectively motivates governance body members, employees, volunteers, clients, and other key constituencies to work toward achieving the organizational mission (6.1).

Possesses analytical and critical thinking skills that promote organizational growth (Network for Social Work Management Competencies 3). Practice Behaviors:

- Demonstrates strong skills in turning around dysfunctional organizations (3.5).

Cynicism and complacency can set in for manifold reasons. Sometimes employees are impacted by difficulties in their personal lives that can impact their overall well-being and negatively affect their workplace performance as well as their career outlook. There are also times when workers can become disengaged due to the workplace atmosphere, as well as the macrolevel socioeconomic and political climate, which may have cascading effects on their professional mind-set.

Organizational transitions and implementation of complex changes can also influence people's professional demeanor. Transition periods are ripe with opportunities for employees to become easily frustrated and discouraged, and can consequently result in complacency, complaining, or both. Changes in the macroenvironment, such as funding cuts, new regulations, inauguration of a new administration with viewpoints sharply opposed to those akin to the mission and values of an organization (as well as the profession), and discontinuation of services to clients, can cause workers to feel pessimistic, angry, and disempowered in their roles as helping professionals. Regardless of the cause of the change, the consequences of withered spirits in the workplace can have grave implications. As we mentioned in Chapter 6, workers who are disengaged, dispassionate, and dissatisfied with their work are extremely costly to employers. Additionally, the likelihood of performance errors dramatically increases. Leaders and managers need to be aware of the signs of employee complacency and cynicism to put it to an immediate halt. However, beyond identifying and stopping it, leaders and managers can be more influential in preventing cynicism and complacency from creeping in to begin with by looking out for the following situations:

- Workers may not feel challenged.
- Workers may feel they have too many tasks and not enough resources.

- Workers may feel they are not provided with enough feedback (coaching/mentorship).
- Workers may believe they are undervalued (i.e., "my boss has no idea all that I do around here").
- Workers may not see their supervisor getting involved enough and thus feel they need to figure things out and fend for themselves.
- Workers may not feel they are supported or understood by their supervisor.
- Workers may feel they are never able to contribute to the decision making but are always responsible for implementing the changes that are made at the "top."
- Workers may be experiencing compassion fatigue, burnout, or high stress.
- Workers may feel the overarching system they work in causes burnout or stress that may be unrivaled with compassion fatigue or burnout associated with client care.

Any one of the previous reasons can contribute to workplace cynicism, but the most common has to do with leadership. When staff do not trust the motives of leaders, cynicism is usually the direct result of such distrust.

Results of cynicism can include:

- Decreased commitment
- Politicking
- Divisiveness
- Pessimism
- Negativity
- Sarcasm

And these results only continue as the employee's tenure continues.

How to Deal With Cynicism

Prevent it! Do not be cynical yourself, and do not permit people to engage in cynical chatter. Lead with passion for what you do, and model an upbeat attitude. If you lack energy and enthusiasm, why should others be any different? Recognize that people may be dealing with things outside of work and their stamina and heart for the work may just need a little care. Understand what motivates people—can more opportunities be provided for employees to learn, grow, and contribute? How are they recognized for their contributions?

One common pitfall is leaders overcompensating for cynicism that results from dire situations by strictly focusing on the bright side. While optimism could seem to be a positive approach, followers may feel that they are not understood, that the leader is either hiding or blind to issues— which strips away confidence in leadership. Leaders sometimes default to this approach because they do not have the answers, or they want to fix the wrong things. Therefore, leaders need to get to the heart of why people are cynical and then attempt to deal with the cause. While listening to staff, it is important to try to hear from them what solutions they would offer to remedy the situation. It is equally important that, while you validate staff, you also explain the limitations you face in ameliorating the situation. Sometimes staff report that cynicism exists because of past actions that have impacted them negatively; however, situations change and staff need to be aware that changes have occurred that have improved the conditions that caused the cynicism.

For example, the dean and administration have, over the years, asked the department to increase enrollments to supplement the overall decrease in university enrollments. The department has responded in the past by increasing enrollments; these increases were supposed to be supported with increases in resources such as new faculty lines. However, the new resources were never provided. So now, when the administration is asking again for enrollment increases, the faculty are very cynical and respond that they will not fall into that trap again. However, the department recently implemented a new Doctor of Social Work (DSW) program and the university has fully funded the program, that is, provided increased and new resources to the department. So now, the chair has suggested to the faculty that the university is actually willing to provide the resources necessary to expand enrollments because of the recent precedent with the DSW program. By educating the faculty on this development, faculty cynicism should decrease.

▧ Turning Around Dysfunction

Because organizations are made up of groups of people, group dynamics inherently create conflict. It is important to note that conflict does not equal dysfunction, rather how the group handles the conflict can be functional or dysfunctional. Dysfunction can set in when teams are performing well below their potential. Underperforming teams can result from leaders lacking a clear vision about what should be done and what is needed to achieve the task. Under these circumstances, staff may carry on believing that they are progressing toward the goal, only to later discover that their efforts were in vain, causing them to feel confused, frustrated, and discouraged. If a leader is unable to provide feedback along the way, because of a lack of vision, interest, or are too consumed with other tasks, then the staff will quickly band together to resist the project. Conversely, when leaders can articulate what is needed for the project, and how the project fits in with the organization's mission and goals, staff feel well informed and as a result will complete tasks well and the project in a timely manner.

Other causes of dysfunction are connected to a lack of group consensus about what the actual problems are and how they should be solved. Typically, groups that cannot reach consensus have less group cohesion. When groups are able to trust one another, feel understood and supported by their teammates, and engage in conflict productively rather than destructively, they are more cohesive, collaborative, and productive. Finally, organizational leaders must attend to how the resources match with the staff's needs and abilities. Having a lack of resources to function in one's role can create tension, frustration, and wilted morale. See Box 8.3 for examples of organizational dysfunction.

BOX 8.3

EXAMPLES OF ORGANIZATIONAL DYSFUNCTION

1. **The culture of complacency.** In academic organizations, faculty can easily become complacent due to the tenure system. Once a person gets tenure, she or he has a secure job for life, provided she or he does not do something extremely egregious to compromise her or his position. As a result, tenured faculty may become more complacent and not participate in committees or community work, conduct research and publish, or update their courses.
   How to overcome the culture of complacency: Most universities have a posttenure review process; however, sometimes these reviews are perfunctory and therefore the challenge is to make the reviews have meaning. Providing faculty with detailed verbal and if possible written performance assessments on an annual basis will strengthen the posttenure review process.

(continued)

BOX 8.3 *(Continued)*

2. **Organizational camps.** Organizations and staff frequently gather in silos because they may pursue similar interests that place them in that silo, but silos do not collaborate, cooperate, or share information or work with each other to achieve the program's goals and objectives.
   How to overcome organizational camps: Strategically assign different silo members to work together on a team comprised of members from another silo to get people to work together, essentially breaking down the silos.

3. **The stale state.** The stale state occurs when the organization does not need to worry about competition and therefore is no longer willing to innovate. When an academic program that receives more applications than it can accommodate, and therefore does not need to compete with other programs or market the program, it can become stale.
   How to overcome stale states: The leader and/or manager should always be encouraging and modeling innovation and creativity, and that should apply to all programs within the larger group. Additionally, leaders need to always entertain the belief that the organization can do better.

4. **Chasing the tail.** Chasing the tail can happen when there are multiple responsibilities with competing levels of importance and too many people are involved to truly know who should do what. Staff members feel, report, and look like they are constantly running in circles, and the demonstrable outputs of their efforts are minimal due to the overlap of tasks without one clear direction.
   How to overcome chasing the tail: Help to limit staff involvement in too many committees.

5. **Not instituting decisions.** When leaders do not act and implement the changes resulting from the agreed upon decisions, the staff will continue to revisit the issue and waste time discussing the issue rather than implementing the change. An example is when faculty has voted to approve something and at the next meeting staff brings up the issue again for discussion, and the change resulting from the decision voted upon should have already been implemented but was not.
   How to overcome noninstituted decisions: Leaders and managers need to be sure that everyone is aware of the decision and how it will be implemented, as well as the timeline for implementation.

6. **The favorites.** Staff can become annoyed, angry, and jealous of other staff who may appear to have a close working relationship with the leader or manager.
   How to overcome the perception of favorites: The leader can offer to share assignments with other staff, particularly those who are complaining, thus giving them the opportunity to establish a working relationship with the leader.

7. **Where have all the good ones gone?** In large bureaucracies with multiple levels of decision making and the resulting time that it takes for a decision to be made, staff can become frustrated. As a result, staff may leave the organization. There are times when "the good ones" move on to more challenging and action-oriented positions, leaving the organization with people who are merely showing up for work.
   How to overcome losing the good ones: Promote them! Try to develop ways to fast-track decisions within the organization, and if this is not possible, provide good staff with challenging assignments to prevent boredom.

(continued)

BOX 8.3 *(Continued)*

8. **Lack of clear direction.** A lack of focus, clear instruction, and direction results in people being uncertain about the organization's goals. Without direction, people will focus on either crisis issues or whatever they want to work on, and as a result their work may not move the organization towards goal achievement.
   How to overcome lack of clear direction: Be concise with direction and use the strategic plan as a roadmap for people to follow.

9. **Operating in crisis mode.** When the strategic plan is pushed aside so that you can deal with an immediate crisis, another crisis typically follows; therefore, the organization is perpetually focused on managing crises and cannot attend to the strategic plan and its corresponding mission, goals, and objectives.
   How to overcome operating in crisis mode: Designate core members of the team to manage ongoing crises. This task can be their primary function while others work to implement the strategic plan.

Motivating Others

Leaders motivate the masses, including their teams, volunteers, clients, governance body members, and constituencies. Leaders inspire people to believe in a cause, push their performance, and work together as a united team. Motivating others is not strictly about being able to give a persuasive speech to teams and groups; it actually takes a leader's behaviors to motivate others. Leaders who are able to set goals for themselves and for others are able to motivate others. Why? Because it demonstrates that they are passionate, driven, and logical in their ability to prioritize tasks, flexible in their ability to adjust along the way as needed, focused enough to see the tasks through, and humble enough to evaluate their progress and correct the course if necessary. See Box 8.4 on communicating expectations.

BOX 8.4

COMMUNICATING EXPECTATIONS

When creating goals, it is important to convey the following expectations to teams:

- What (what results are to be; what is to be accomplished)
- Why important (contributions of goals to unit)
- Specificity (finer definitions of what)
- Developmental opportunity (trust employees to use developmental/learning opportunity)

Leaders motivate others by strengthening relationships and communicating effectively with people. Leaders who invest in their teams by getting to know them through face-to-face conversations, offer opportunities for learning more about what motivates them. Getting to know people helps to identify the ways to utilize their strengths, passions, and skills, and creating opportunities for staff to put their talents to good use will likely motivate them. Creating unique work tasks for individuals also demonstrates that the leader trusts their ability to complete or lead a task, which can be an inspiration for them to complete it successfully. Finally, leaders need to provide good doses of positive, and specific, feedback to continuously motive others. See Box 8.5 on effective communication and Box 8.6 on motivation through planning.

BOX 8.5

STRENGTHENING RELATIONS AND EFFECTIVELY COMMUNICATING

Clarify Authority and Resources

- Clarify the authority or the latitude to act on a continuum from "do not bother me" to "do not do anything without me."
- Clarify resources: Aim to try to develop autonomy. Ask employee: What do you need? How long will it take you? Are other players involved?

Agreed Upon Method of Control or Follow-up

- Provide opportunities for collaboration
- Provide a wider variety of types of feedback
- Let employees know schedule of times to meet and location
- Let employees know your level of availability (this will lower anxiety over a new assignment, the person can come to you if unclear on how to proceed)
- Provide mindfulness opportunities

Test for Understanding

- Ask employee: Are we on the same wavelength?
- Reinforce process (allows for clarification)
- Foster development, which helps motivate employees. Do not just dump a project on an employee, provide coaching, resources, and proper controls.

BOX 8.6

MOTIVATING BY PLANNING

What Is Planning?

- Acting to influence future events
- Planning and coordinating an organization's activities helps it remain focused on goal attainment
- Planning is future oriented
- Selecting among alternative future courses of action
- A rationale approach to preselected objectives
- Deciding in advance what needs to be done; best ways and times to do it; and who is the best choice to do it

(continued)

BOX 8.6 *(Continued)*

- A continuous process requiring ongoing monitoring and revision
- Should generate a surplus (contribute more to improved client services than it takes away from them)

Good planning makes a positive contribution to organizational climate

- Fosters teamwork, confidence, certainty, and trust, all of which positively affect staff morale
- Can also produce negative results such as inefficiencies
- Overplanning can be destructive to teamwork, confidence, and so on

Goals

- More specific than a mission
- Organizational outcomes toward which staff aim
- Management decisions evaluated with reference to organizational goals
- As conditions/needs change, goals should change; goal succession or abandonment can occur
- Goals are often only theoretically attainable

Objectives

- Make it possible to determine if goals have been achieved
- Have time deadlines
- Management by objectives—written objectives for all staff
- Targets are negotiated and measurable
- Ongoing assessment of progress
- Builds objectivity into employee evaluation

SOURCE: Adapted from Weinbach, R. W. (1998). *The social worker as manager: A practical guide to success* (3rd ed.). Needham Heights, MA: Allyn and Bacon.

Role Modeling

Box 8.7 displays the competencies/behaviors in this section.

BOX 8.7

NETWORK FOR SOCIAL WORK MANAGEMENT COMPETENCIES AND PRACTICE BEHAVIORS 4

Models appropriate professional behavior and encourages other staff members to act in a professional manner (Network for Social Work Management Competencies 4). Practice Behaviors:

- Engages in and promotes ethical conduct (4.1).
- Protects the integrity and reputation of the organization (4.2).
- Creates and supports an organizational culture that values professionalism, service, and ethical conduct (4.3).

As we have mentioned throughout the previous chapters, leaders and managers need to be consummate role models. Internal and external figures have their eyes fixed on leaders to obtain a sense of what the organizational culture is. How the leader performs, responds to others, leads meetings, addresses difficult issues, and so on reveals what the organizational culture is—that is, what the values, expectations, behaviors, and so on that are considered acceptable professional behaviors. For instance, if an external agency (that also happens to fund the program) is meeting with a director to discuss a concern about frontline staff not seeming to engage a client, that is, acting indifferent toward the client, and the director is not paying attention during the meeting, the behavior would reinforce the hunch that the organizational culture is that of indifference and lack of concern (i.e., from the top down). In this particular situation, it would be easy to see how the director has not only overlooked the behavior of the staff but has reinforced it by modeling the same behavior.

Modeling for staff also relates to ethical standards of practice. Staff must see the leaders and managers promoting ethical behaviors, first through role modeling, and then through addressing any unethical matters to immediately put a halt to them. Leaders and managers may also be required to report certain unethical behaviors and should always follow the organizational procedures, professional code of ethics, and laws. By modeling behaviors that are ethical and professional, leaders and managers are able to create and support an organizational culture that values professionalism, service, and ethical conduct.

MANAGING DIVERSITY

Box 8.8 displays the competencies/behaviors in this section.

BOX 8.8

NETWORK FOR SOCIAL WORK MANAGEMENT COMPETENCIES AND PRACTICE BEHAVIORS 5

Manages diversity and cross-cultural understanding (Network for Social Work Management Competencies 5). Practice Behaviors:

- Publicly acknowledges the diversity of the staff and clients and creates a climate that celebrates the differences (5.1).
- Takes steps necessary to assure that all services provided by the organization are culturally competent (5.7).

Organizations that employ diverse staff are better positioned to provide culturally competent services. When organizations are comprised of diverse staff adopt an organizational culture of inclusivity and respect for differences and embrace collaboration among diverse teams, this culture can result in better service to clients. Additionally, when clients or students feel that employees or faculty are representative of the client/student population served, this balance enhances their trust in the organization that their needs will be met.

How does an organization publicly acknowledge diversity of staff and clients? Organizations can publicly acknowledge the diversity of staff by providing statistics and information on the diverse backgrounds of staff and educational and service experience. Likewise, publicly acknowledging the clients to a large audience will provide all stakeholders and funders with a better understanding of who the agency serves.

Celebrating differences among staff can happen in a variety of ways, but it is first important to identify which approach your organization is willing to take—for example, a colorblind approach, multicultural approach, or an all-inclusive multicultural (AIM) approach (for more information, refer to Chapter 6).

To ensure that you are providing culturally competent services, there are a number of steps that you can take including

- Sending staff to multicultural training.

- Completing continuing education units (CEUs) in culturally competent domains.

- Hosting open discussions about the impact of diversity in using particular interventions.

- Talking openly in supervision about how clients or students are affected by issues of diversity.

Finally, organizations should evaluate their culturally competent service provision. There are several ways to evaluate this, such as

- Client surveys

- Staff surveys

- Data collected from employee relations claims

- Data collected from grievances

Box 8.9 displays the competencies/behaviors in this section.

BOX 8.9

NETWORK FOR SOCIAL WORK MANAGEMENT COMPETENCIES AND PRACTICE BEHAVIORS 5

Manages diversity and cross-cultural understanding (Network for Social Work Management Competencies 5). Practice Behaviors:

- Seeks input from all levels of staff, listens attentively, demonstrates fairness and consistency, and conveys information fully and clearly (5.4)

- Invites different perspectives to all client-related and management discussions within the organization (5.5)

- Encourages and allows opportunities for staff to confer and present issues and problems affecting program-related services (5.6).

Leaders manage diversity and cross-cultural understanding within organizations by being attuned to staff, creating opportunities to listen to staff concerns, asking directly about the perception of fairness, and providing information on a consistent basis that is clear and reflects the importance of understanding cross-cultural issues. Input solicited by the leader from staff members can occur during supervision, staff meetings, and online surveys. During decision-making meetings, leaders can ask (a) how can we be more culturally competent, and more specifically, (b) how does the decision impact different cultural populations? If you ask the latter question and the answer is that there will be a strong negative impact on a population group, then rethink the decision.

MULTIPLE SKILLS FOR LEADERS AND MANAGERS

Box 8.10 displays the competencies/behaviors in this section.

BOX 8.10

NETWORK FOR SOCIAL WORK MANAGEMENT COMPETENCIES AND PRACTICE BEHAVIORS 3

Possesses analytical and critical thinking skills that promote organizational growth (Network for Social Work Management Competencies 3). Practice Behaviors:

- Demonstrates a working knowledge of budget and finance, human resources, communication and marketing, applications of information technology, fundraising, and external relations; and an understanding or "feel" for the core work of the organization (3.1).
- Demonstrates an entrepreneurial spirit and attitude (3.2).

Leaders need to demonstrate analytical and critical thinking skills that can be applied to all areas of organizational functioning. Leaders can specifically demonstrate a working knowledge of all core functions by learning how each core function works and actually demonstrating expertise in each area by modifying and creating new functional processes.

Budget and Finance

Leaders need to be able to understand how to use Excel and Excel-type spreadsheets used by their organizations. The best way to learn is to create spreadsheets that provide the information needed to manage programs and make decisions.

Human Resources

Leaders need to be informed and up to date on labor laws and other human resource issues. Leaders who oversee programs typically arrange to meet with the human resources director on a regular basis to review procedures for hiring staff, evaluating staff, managing staff benefits, managing the reputation of the organization (e.g., monitoring how the organization is rated online by employees and former employees and how it is described), managing staff conflict, and reviewing the processes for promotions, terminations, and other forms of progressive discipline.

Communication and Marketing

Even if the organization has a designated marketing director, leaders need to be involved in marketing the organization and communicating with external resources. Leaders need to be in touch with other community collaborators to know what, where, and how they are marketing their organizations in order to effectively position your organization to maximize marketing strategies.

Applications of MIS

Organizations can develop teams to vet management information system (MIS) programs. The identification and implementation of MIS programs will require teamwork, and sufficient training.

For additional information on MIS refer to Chapter 12 (Management Information Systems and Managing Technology for Social Work Environments).

Fundraising

Leaders, particularly leaders in nonprofit organizations, need to discover and employ the most cost-effective methods to raise funds. One method might include focusing on major donors. Organizations also need to determine if they can create staff positions that focus exclusively on fundraising. As the adage "You need to spend money to make money" goes, to be successful at fundraising requires a large amount of time to work with potential donors and a large amount of time to keep track of the databases and communication with donors and potential donors. For additional information on fundraising see Chapter 16 (Strategic Resource Development in a Social Work Environment).

External Relations

There are a variety of external organizations that agencies interact with on a regular basis. Determining who should be in contact and liaise with them will likely be based on the position one holds, the charisma one exudes, and the feasibility of maintaining positive relations. Leaders need to develop a list of contact information on all of their external relations so they can contact them on a moment's notice. Some examples of external relations include funders, fellow providers, licensing departments, accreditation organizations, donors, and board members.

Understanding the Core of the Organization

Leaders need to articulate to internal and external constituencies the most important aspects of the organization, as well as what aspects may be missing or neglected.

SUMMARY

In this chapter, we explored how leaders manage organizational functions. Inherent to managing organizational functions is the ability to lead, inspire, and motivate staff to move beyond cynicism and complacency in order to perform in an optimal manner. This chapter identified examples of organizational dysfunction and ways to overcome various organizational dysfunction. Leaders and managers are encouraged to model exemplary behaviors to inspire staff and to engage in ethical behaviors. Finally, we reviewed the importance of acknowledging diversity and taking steps to ensure that the organization provides culturally competent services to clients or students.

ACTIVITIES

1. Identify what dysfunctions exist in your organization or academic institution. Discuss ways that you would seek to overcome the organizational dysfunction.
2. Describe your organizational culture. Describe the diversity of your staff and clients. If staff diversity does not represent the clients served, how might that impact the provision of services, as well as clients' perceptions of service provision?

3. Identify five external constituencies that interface with your organization. Explain who typically maintains communication with external constituencies and how often, and discuss why that is.

4. What type of behavior have you modeled in your organization? What type of modeling behaviors do you recognize as a strength, and what modeling behaviors do you plan to work on?

5. What are the factors that you believe go into professionalism? How would you describe the practice of professionalism in your organization?

REFERENCE

Weinbach, R. W. (1998). *The social worker as manager: A practical guide to success* (3rd ed.). Needham Heights, MA: Allyn and Bacon.

PART 2

RESOURCE MANAGEMENT PRACTICES IN SOCIAL WORK

CHAPTER 9

ACCOUNTABILITY IN SOCIAL WORK

"Your accountability partner keeps you on track and moving forward in all aspects of your development."

Mike Stazer

"Creating a culture of integrity and accountability generates a respectful, enjoyable and life giving setting in which to work."

Tom Hanson, Birgit Zacher Hanson

CHAPTER OBJECTIVES

- Establishing a system of internal controls.
- Establishing a system of accountability for revenue.
- Maintaining financial records.
- Protecting against liability.
- Maximizing the use of funds.
- Maintaining safety of people, facilities, and equipment.
- Establishing a succession plan.

INTRODUCTION

Social workers are held accountable for organizational and professional compliance. Pollack (2009) elucidated that "recently, and more frequently, a new venue of accountability has emerged—the courtroom" (p. 837). He further explained that the social work profession has worked tirelessly to alter its original image of friendly visitors to respected professionals and "either despite or because of this effort, and coincident with political and socioeconomic transitions, dissatisfaction and litigation against social workers and social work organizations have increased considerably" (p. 839). Pollack highlighted that, since social work has garnered professional status, the public has acknowledged the vast needs social workers are called upon to meet, and the newfound respect for the social work profession from the public has produced greater expectations of and scrutiny over social workers' performance. For these reasons, and others, it is crucial that social work organizations understand the benefits of accountability and transparency, as well as the dangers of a lack thereof.

Any organization will function better with transparency and accountability. These are critical concepts because they win the trust of employees and constituents and cultivate a positive work environment in which staff have a better understanding of how the work they do meets the organization's mission and goals. Thus, when there is transparency and accountability within an organization, workers tend to feel more appreciated and know that they are contributing to both short- and long-term accomplishments and goals. Conversely, when an organization lacks transparency and accountability, it can create a culture of suspicion and a lack of ownership, which ultimately diminishes the likelihood of teamwork. When staff feel they are not valued or respected enough to be informed, they are less likely to believe that their work is valued and more likely to blame others, particularly the administration that has failed to inform them, for any subpar outcomes.

It should be noted that leaders will inevitably face situations in which transparency can actually be detrimental to the staff, as it may evoke anxiety and fears of the unknown; or because strategic information disclosed too soon could adversely impact the organization (such as leaking information to competitors); or because the strategy that will eventually be executed is in the nascent stages of development and revealing change processes to all levels of staff too soon will create ambiguity, confusion, and frustration. Thus, there will be times when leaders need to be selectively transparent and pace the release of disclosures in order to act in the best interest of the majority of staff or the cause the organization is seeking to advance. One such example is when leaders are negotiating new budgets or are uncertain about the budget cuts that might impact employment by retaining, replacing, or restricting organizational positions. Disclosing the possibility of cuts and changes too hastily, or before all of the facts are gathered and options are analyzed, can have a negative impact on workers. If the situation is unstable and multiple outcomes are not yet known, the leader would be wise to wait until more information can be gathered to avoid causing a fight, flight, or freeze reaction among staff. In such an instance, staff anxiety can result in workers' abrupt departures (flight) or reduced productivity and enthusiasm for the work (freeze), or increased office grumblings that can have an infectious impact among coworkers and create a negative work environment (fight).

Most organizations have established governance policies for processing information and decision making. These policies are typically made clear in the bylaws and the organizational table, which provides an overview of the system's hierarchy. Organizational tables need to be developed to define the lines of authority by positions within the agency so that everyone will know who is accountable for particular aspects of organizational functioning. There are also committee structures within the organizational hierarchy, which are prominent in academic institutions in particular, designed to develop structure for committee decision making and then a process for providing formal recommendations to the larger group. Decisions should be accepted through a standardized workflow that allows the organization to move forward in meeting its mission and goals. The participants need to understand the regulatory processes and be active contributors in these processes in order to establish and maintain a system of internal controls that protect against liability.

This chapter focuses on how leaders and managers promote a culture of accountability and transparency, as well as engage in the numerous financial responsibilities that ensure an organization's optimal functioning and survival (see Box 9.1 for the competencies and practice behaviors covered in this chapter).

BOX 9.1

COMPETENCIES AND PRACTICE BEHAVIORS ADDRESSED IN THIS CHAPTER

*Establishes and maintains a system of internal controls to ensure transparency, protection, and accountability for the use of organizational resour*ces (Network for Social Work Management Competencies 14). Practice Behaviors:

- Prepares and manages organizational budgets in a manner that maximizes utilization of available funds for client service and complies with requirements of funders (14.1).
- Develops and implements a system of internal controls that adequately safeguards the resources of the organization (14.2).
- Demonstrates effective actions to protect the organization and its employees from liability by both managing and ensuring risks incurred within the scope of discharging established responsibilities (14.3).
- Assures the maintenance of financial records that comply with generally accepted accounting standards (14.4).
- Assures the appropriate safety, maintenance, protection, and utilization of other organizational resources, such as facilities and equipment (14.5).
- Helps design and manage a process of succession planning to assure the organizational continuity of executive, professional, and service leadership (14.6).
- Establishes strong systems of accountability for revenues received from various sources (14.7).

Advocates for public policy change and social justice at national, state, and local levels (Network for Social Work Management Competencies 8). Practice Behaviors:

- Challenges broad regulatory expectations and advocates for efficient and well-tailored polices with potential to impact client's welfare (8.5).

Manages risk and legal affairs (Network for Social Work Management Competencies 19). Practice Behaviors:

- Protects the agency from undue risk by ensuring that appropriate policies and procedures exist in all areas of operation (19.1).
- Establishes systems of monitoring in all areas of the organization where there may be potential risk (e.g., client services, recordkeeping, accounting, purchasing) (19.2).
- Ensures adherence to all laws, regulations, contracts, and legal agreements (19.3).

CSWE Competency 5—Engage in Policy Practice
Social workers

- 5.2 Assess how social welfare and economic policies impact the delivery of and access to social services.
- 5.3 Apply critical thinking to analyze, formulate, and advocate for policies that advance human rights and social, economic, and environmental justice.

CSWE Competency 8—Intervene With Individuals, Families, Groups, Organizations, and Communities
Social workers

- 8.5 Facilitate effective transitions and endings that advance mutually agreed-on goals.

CSWE, Council on Social Work Education.

TRANSPARENCY

Box 9.2 displays the competencies/behaviors in this section.

BOX 9.2

NETWORK FOR SOCIAL WORK MANAGEMENT COMPETENCIES AND PRACTICE BEHAVIORS 14

Establishes and maintains a system of internal controls to ensure transparency, protection, and account-ability for the use of organizational resources (Network for Social Work Management Competencies 14). Practice Behaviors:

- Prepares and manages organizational budgets in a manner that maximizes utilization of available funds for client service and complies with requirements of funders (14.1).
- Establishes strong systems of accountability for revenues received from various sources (14.7).

Transparency drives the operations and activities of the organization in a manner that is scrupulous, fastidious, and judicious enough to withstand public scrutiny. The public, in this sense, may refer to the actual public, a licensing board, accreditation boards, professional association, and judicial as well as civil or class action lawsuits.

Organizations, especially nonprofit organizations (NPOs), have legal and ethical obligations, to their funders and the general public, to manage the financial activities with transparency and accountability. Under most circumstances this responsibility requires the organization to provide information about its finances to the public, generally by filing the 990 form. The 990 form is an annual federal document for tax-exempt organizations with gross receipts of $200,000 and gross assets of $50,000; NPOs with gross receipts and assets less than that typically complete the 990-EZ or 990-N tax documents. The 990 report is a crucial statement of transparency that conveys the organization's mission and programs and provides financial information that is available to the public and the Internal Revenue Service (IRS). This public document can help organizations obtain donations because it offers information about the organization's mission and programs and can demonstrate that it is conducting its financial matters ethically, legally, and responsibly. Transparency is essential for potential donors, assessing information about the results and impact of the organization's programs, which, along the financial record, will better inform donors about the organization and cause to which they want to contribute.

In addition to providing financial transparency to constituents and the public, there are several other ways for organizations to promote transparency and accountability. These include, but are not limited to, the completion of annual assessments of the chief executive officer (CEO) or president, as well as regular assessments of the board of directors' performance, when applicable. Assessing the CEO and board demonstrates that those who hold the most power and authority over organizational decision making are held accountable. Establishing a whistleblower policy in writing, and ensuring that all staff are aware of the procedures for enacting the policy, is essential. Note that a good whistleblower policy protects the employee's anonymity and also protects employees from retaliation. Organizations should also establish performance improvement committees, a committee that evaluates the outcomes of programs including client satisfaction, and, wherever possible, involve clients or family members to serve as advisors. The findings that are generated from performance improvement committees, as well as the corrective action plans, should be disseminated and explained to all staff who have a shared responsibility in the organization's performance.

Preparing and Managing Organizational Budgets

Organizations cannot operate without well-managed budgets. Social work leaders and managers are typically well versed in the mission of the organization and are focused on delivering services that promote the organization's mission and goals. However, very few social workers are comfortable working with financial data since they do not typically have training or experience in this area. As such, many attempt to translate their experiences with their personal finances (such as household expenses, savings goals, investments, paying down debts) to the skills necessary for preparing and managing budgets within an organization. In transferring one's skills and knowledge of managing one's personal finances, the manager is likely cognizant of the general principle that you cannot spend more than you take in. The reality is that, depending on one's position and role expectations, managing a departmental budget may be as basic as insuring that the line item expenses are covered in the budget and do not exceed the budgeted amount. However, managing all aspects of an organization's finances is very complex—far too complex, in fact, to be covered in this text—particularly considering the size of the organization, the number of programs within the organization, and the amount of funders and regulations that must be incorporated in the analysis. As one's scope of responsibilities expands, overseeing the budget will more than likely require one to work closely with members of the business department. A business department may be composed of a CFO, assistant CFO, accounts receivable, accounts payable, and other key accounting positions that oversee the organization's fiduciary health. It is important to identify the key players within an organization and establish working relationships with them to collaboratively prepare, manage, and make the best use of budgets.

Preparing and managing budgets requires an understanding of how to read budgets to better be able to analyze them and make well-informed programmatic decisions according to the financial realities and projections. Some organizations passively permit a culture where managers do not take an active role in managing the budget. For instance, a manager may receive monthly or quarterly budget reports from their business office but may only give the reports a quick glance because they do not understand them, are more focused on service-related tasks, or assume that it is the responsibility of the business office to monitor budgets and inform them when changes are needed. These are all precarious assumptions for leaders and managers to make, and, in the worst case scenarios, can even be considered nefarious. Yes, nefarious—if one has access to critical financial information and one's job description includes responsibility for budgetary outcomes, than either carelessly reviewing or avoiding the budget reports altogether is a sign of total irresponsibility. Likewise, if managers are expected to have budgetary oversight and are not getting the information needed to manage or prepare budgets, then the manager also has a responsibility to seek out the information and address these concerns with a supervisor and other key positions as needed.

The budget can be used to monitor financial information (think compliance and financial auditing) and objectively and strategically guides decisions based on what is actually in the budget and therefore managing it is imperative. Most NPOs have to comply with sundry regulations that dictate how dollars can be spent, within what timeframes, and how the organization will provide accurate records of income and expenses. The first step to managing budgets is to know and understand the financial parameters that can impinge the budget. This step also includes acknowledging each budget category and what line items are included in the budget, such as office supplies, staff positions, training costs, travel funds, and rent. Another requirement is to understand the rules and regulations that are set in the budget, such as when funds must be spent by, how unspent funds can be allocated or returned to the funder, and what constitutes *operating costs* versus *capital investments*.

For instance, some grant-funded programs may disallow capital investments and only approve funding for operating costs. Operating costs are essentially the expenses associated with conducting day-to-day business and are recorded on budget reports, sometimes referred to as income statements, as expenses to the agency. Operating expenses can include line items such as office supplies, training, travel funds, licensing fees, and general maintenance and repairs made to equipment or buildings *as long as* the repairs do not increase the useful life of an asset. Because operating expenses cover short-term expenses within a given time period, anything that enhances assets may be considered a capital investment. Capital investments are considered long-term expenditures that either add a new asset or enhance the value of an existing asset. See Box 9.3 for further explanation and an exercise.

BOX 9.3

COMPLYING WITH GRANT REGULATIONS

A nonprofit agency is awarded a $1 million grant to implement an electronic health record system. The grant requires that the agency match 50% of the awarded amount ($500K) before the agency can submit an invoice to the grantor for reimbursement. The grant funds must be fully spent within one year and the project must be operational within 18 months of signing the grant. All invoices must include receipts and dates of the expenses along with documentation providing explanation for the expenses. The grant will cover the operating expenses for a total of three years, which includes software licensing fees, an information technology position, and a consulting project manager during the implementation phase only. However, the grant does not include the installation of new hardware to existing computers or the purchase of new computers as either is considered to be a capital investment (i.e., the agency would increase their useful assets by installing new hardware and increase overall assets by purchasing new computers). The $500K match amount can include *in-kind funds*. In-kind funds are goods or services donated but not cash. The agency sought computer donations from a for-profit business looking to get rid of some computers; that business could in turn receive a tax benefit for the donation made. The in-kind donation was an estimated $250K in computer equipment. Because of the size of the organization, additional computers, laptops, and tablets are still needed. Updates to hardware and the organization's Wi-Fi systems at several locations are also still required.

Exercise

1. Create a list of the benefits, both short- and long-term, for the organization to implement the electronic health record system.

2. Create three options for how the organization will meet the remaining $250K match funding.

3. Consider how the agency will continue to pay for ongoing licensing fees that total $100K beyond the three-year grant period. For example, take the working knowledge you have in a particular organization and apply it to this scenario—what areas of an organization would you first examine to either increase revenue or decrease costs?

There may be times when the budget does not yet reflect income or expenses that will be calculated at a later time. This budget issue is sometimes caused by delays in payments received by insurance companies, federal grants, or tuition payments. Usually the accounting department will note the amount earmarked in accounts receivable and accounts payable as a way to flag that the budget will adjust once funds are either received or cleared to then accurately reflect the income over or under expenses. Additionally, there are times when a quarterly budget may present exceptionally well, or exceptionally poorly, but the key to managing budgets is to understand the story behind the numbers. For instance, if, over the last quarter, the agency was required to pay a large sum of money for an investment, the numbers may present in the red for that quarter. However, considering that the large one-time payment will fold into the annual budget and can also be depreciated, the ultimate bottom line (year-end) may not be as grave as it originally appeared in the quarterly report. The numbers also tell a story about service-related trends and can provide valuable information that guides decisions about whether or not to expand or consolidate programs.

Preparing Budgets

Managing the budget is essential to maintaining financial balance and reporting to funders on how dollars are spent; preparing the budget demonstrates how you plan to allocate and balance funds in the upcoming fiscal year. A *fiscal year* is the period of time an organization or government uses for accounting purposes, which can sometimes run from July 1st of a given year through June 30th of the following year. Preparing a budget prior to the commencement of a fiscal year is a projected plan that connects the service delivery and financial goals of an organization. By setting the trajectory of a program, managers can identify clear benchmarks for when additional resources or positions may be financially justified to further contribute to the expansion of a department. Additionally, preparing a budget provides a realistic picture of the status of the program and organization as a whole, financially speaking, and helps to identify trends in funding shortages and projected losses to help proactively determine what adjustments are required. Examining the financial trends and projections equips the manager with knowledge to make accurate decisions, have realistic conversations about what is and is not feasible, and presents opportunities for creative and proactive problem solving.

When preparing budgets, the social work manager must consider the organization's mission and evaluate not only the programs but also the activities within those programs given the known and projected income and expenses. Evaluating programs requires an understanding of their costs, such as those in staffing, rent, supplies, utilities, equipment, as well as any fees associated with staffing such as health benefits, short- and long-term disability benefits, unemployment costs, and so on. Typically, members of the business office can provide an overall cost, or formula, for calculating the costs associated with full-time, part-time, and per diem staff. Preparing budgets for upcoming fiscal years also requires knowledge of the fiscal trends of the current year and years prior to help project and plan for the future. For instance, if the organization generated $1 million in revenue by serving 600 clients, and there is currently a waitlist for services, then one can prepare a budget that reflects the projected income if the census increased to 700 clients (the programmatic goal) and can calculate the estimated costs of additional staff, training, and supplies that would be needed to serve an additional 100 clients.

When preparing budgets that are bound to requirements set by a funder, it is important to remember that the projected budget should comply with said requirements. For instance, if the funder requires that a particular position is filled by a licensed clinical social worker (LCSW), you must, of course, adhere to that requirement while also ensuring that your proposed budget accurately reflects the salary of a LCSW and not a master-level social worker. Hence, the budget must incorporate any restrictions set by the funder. When estimating expenses and income, it is important to be as realistic as possible, but it is also prudent to prepare *conservative estimates*. Conservative estimates tend to project expenses high and income low. Preparing conservative estimates allows some room for unforeseen expenses and also increases the likelihood that programs will stay within budget because they are created with cautious estimations from the onset.

Box 9.4 provides an example of how to prepare a program budget. The program has designated the growth goal and also identifies the resources that are needed once certain benchmarks are attained. This plan was outlined by the program director—who later worked with the chief financial officer (CFO) to confirm the financial calculations—and submitted the proposal using accounting software. This is an example of how managers and finance staff collaborate to prepare budgets. Box 9.4 provides details on preparing a program budget.

BOX 9.4

PREPARING A PROGRAM BUDGET

Target population: Youths aged four through 21 diagnosed with ASD.

Our target geographic locations for the FY18 year will focus on X, Y, and Z counties.

Objective: IN-HOME will establish a census of 25 clients by year-end.

The following analysis was completed based on the outlined assumption(s): We estimate that during the course of FY18, we will have 250 IHSS hours per week and 25 behaviorist hours per week.

For **FY 18,** we estimate that we will establish a census of 25 clients per week. We estimate that each client served will be authorized 10 hours per week of in-home support (in-home support staff). Based on Medicaid requirements that 10 authorized hours of direct services requires one hour of supervision provided weekly to the IH support staff, we assume that there will be 25 hours of behaviorist services per week.

SERVICE PROVIDER	REIMBURSEMENT RATE	PAY RATE
IHSS	$45	$19.50–$20
Behaviorist Contractor [a]Assumption 1: BCBA, LCSW, or LMFT	$75	$35

Conservatively, the billable hours were based on a 48-week year to account for vacations, holidays, inclement weather, etc. Assuming that all billable hours are fully reimbursed by Medicaid and other private insurance companies, by establishing a client census of 25 hours IN-HOME program could generate a total of $576,000 of billable services. Note: This number is also conservative based on the fact that initial evaluations, or FBAs, are not accounted for in this forecast. The calculation assumes total utilization.

WEEKLY BILLABLE	IHSS	BEHAVIORIST
Total Medicaid based on 48-week year	$540,000	$90,000
Total DDS based on 48-week year	**IHSS**	**Behaviorist**
	$115,600	$39,208
Annual total	$655,600	$129,208
		$784, 808

Current staff in IN-HOME

- One FT BCBA to cover 25 hours of behavior services
- One FT IHSS staff to provide direct service
- Program coordinator: 40 hours per week
- Ten per diem IHSS staff to provide direct service
- Contractors: LCSW working approximately 13 hours per week
- BCBA 20 hours per month

(continued)

BOX 9.4 *(Continued)*

We estimate the following annual costs for FY 18:

POSITION	ANNUAL COST
FT BCBC	$70,000
FT IHSS	$40,560
Program coordinator	$37,744
Contracted LCSW	$21,840
Consultant[a]	$15,000
Per diem IHSS staff	$262,378
20 hours IN-HOME director	$40,000
Total staff cost[b]	$492,448
Total staff cost with benefits	$600,602
Total overhead and other[c]	$134,614
Total operating expenses	**$735,216**

[a]Cost of the consultant will absolve in FY18 after a period of overlap with the new IN-HOME BCBA director, estimated to occur by December 31, 2017.

[b]Additional costs to include fringe benefits is $108,154.

[c]Additional $134,614 including $79,000 for G&A, with remaining amount covering overhead, training and related fees.

Goal for FY18

Establish census of 25 clients in IN-HOME and provide a total of 250 direct service ABA hours per week, and 25 behavioral service hours per week, for 48 weeks of the year.

In order to meet this goal IN-HOME will need

1. Increased per diem pool of IHSS per diem staff to a total of 31. This assumes that one per diem staff average 9–10 hours per case, per week. As more clients are added throughout the year, we will need to continue to hire and train per diem staff.

2. The FT BCBA will be required to complete 19.5 billable hours per week for 48 weeks of the year.

3. The newly appointed IN-HOME director will assume marketing responsibilities and work with the program coordinator to recruit per diem staff and will provide technical oversight.

ABA, applied behavioral analysis; ASD, autism spectrum disorder; BCBA, board certified behavior analyst; DDS, Department of Developmental Disability; FBA, functional behavioral assessment; FY, fiscal year; IHSS, In-Home Supportive Service; LCSW, licensed clinical social worker; LMFT, licensed marriage and family therapist.

While many social workers do not come into the field as experienced financial administrators, as they rise through the ranks and have increased oversight of the organizational budgeting, they begin to require more skills, experience, and confidence. What is helpful for learning this process will vary by individual. Some have found it helpful to mirror their understanding of how to manage household finances, some may have exposure from previous jobs to build upon, some independently read and research this topic, and some may quickly find that spending ample time with members of the accounting team (CFO or other business and accounting administrators) helps to mentor them through unfamiliar territory. It is important that social work managers connect and collaborate with various members of the business or accounting division and remain curious.

Internal Controls

Box 9.5 displays the competencies/behaviors in this section.

BOX 9.5

NETWORK FOR SOCIAL WORK MANAGEMENT COMPETENCIES AND PRACTICE BEHAVIORS 14 AND CSWE PRACTICE BEHAVIOR 8.5

Establishes and maintains a system of internal controls to ensure transparency, protection, and accountability for the use of organizational resources (Network for Social Work Management Competencies 14). Practice Behaviors:

- Develops and implements a system of internal controls that adequately safeguards the resources of the organization (14.2).
- Demonstrates effective actions to protect the organization and its employees from liability by both managing and ensuring risks incurred within the scope of discharging established responsibilities (14.3).
- Assures the maintenance of financial records that comply with generally accepted accounting standards (14.4).
- Assures the appropriate safety, maintenance, protection, and utilization of other organizational resources, such as facilities and equipment (14.5).
- Helps design and manage a process of succession planning to assure the organizational continuity of executive, professional, and service leadership (14.6).

CSWE Competency 8—Intervene With Individuals, Families, Groups, Organizations, and Communities
   Social workers
8.5 Facilitate effective transitions and endings that advance mutually agreed-on goals.
CSWE, Council on Social Work Education.

Internal controls are management practices that are systematically employed to obviate the misuse or misappropriation of funds and shield the organization from potential risks and liabilities. Related competencies can be found in Box 9.5. Internal controls try to ensure achievement of the organization's goals, mission, and objectives using operational effectiveness and efficiency. Pollack (2009) offers a framework for distinguishing between organizational goals and expectations and advises that "goals precede expectations, and expectations should be set before someone can be held accountable for meeting them" (p. 839). In order to adequately safeguard organizational resources, systems of control are typically established through written policies that outline the procedures that will be followed to protect the financial information of an organization as well as its employees. Internal controls are designed to promote practices that are legal, ethical, and effectual, and to help safeguard the organization from lawsuits, financial ruin, and a sullied reputation.

Organizations have a mixture of both internal and external controls over its finances, as well as its compliance with service-delivery standards. Compliance standards are addressed in detail later in this chapter, but for now we focus on internal and external controls. Within an organization, there are key positions charged with examining the operating budget and maintaining records that are compliant with governing bodies. Business departments that are carefully knitted into the organizational structure are responsible for balancing the financial records and providing detailed analytics on how dollars were generated and spent. The minutia of details required for maintaining financial records is beyond the scope of this book, but the crucial point here is that leaders are encouraged to have multiple reviewers of the budget and financial record keeping. For instance, some organizations' bylaws prescribe that a finance committee must review financial information on a regular basis. A *finance committee* is typically comprised of a few board members—who ideally have knowledge of accounting principles—and the CFO, assistant financial officer, or other bookkeepers in accounting, and is typically chaired by the board treasurer. The ideal composition should include individuals with some knowledge of financial recordkeeping, which may include an attorney, a certified public accountant, bookkeeper, bank investor, and so on, and, most importantly, the individuals should not have a financial stake in the organization.

The finance committee helps to ensure that the organization's board is satisfying its fiduciary responsibilities, keeping with the mission, and shielding the organization from potential risk and liability. Creating a finance committee that does not have a financial stake in the organization allows members to objectively oversee the organization's financial dealings. Generally, financial committees' primary tasks are to identify possible problems and offer consultation to correct fiscal issues. The committee members are familiar with the organization's budget because they review the budget reports on a regular basis and monitor cash flow and debts. Consistent budgetary reviews also provide opportunities for the committee to ensure that funds are spent legally and ethically, in accordance with the funding requirements. If a finance committee does identify illegal activity, it is ethically obligated to report the finding to the CEO, president, or board president. Reporting illegal activity can mitigate any further risks to the organization, whereas delays in reporting malfeasance can subject the board to lawsuits and the organization to additional penalties and fines.

In addition to finance committee reviews, organizations should conduct annual financial audits. An *annual financial audit* is a review of the organization's financial records and statements, as well as minutes from finance committee meetings, all of which provides a summation of the accuracy of financial reporting and compliance with regulations. Financial audits may be conducted by an employed accountant in addition to a consulting accounting firm external to the organization. The board treasurer or chairperson of the finance committee may interact with the auditing firm, as well as the CFO. The findings of the audit should be reported to the CEO or president, board treasurer, and chair of the finance committee, as well other chief executive positions such as CFO, executive vice president, and chief operating officer. If an audit ever reveals that a key executive member is responsible for wrongdoing, the executive should be omitted from participating in the meeting and not be privy to the summarized audit findings until appropriate actions are taken. Completing annual financial audits can help to assure that the financial records comply with the generally accepted accounting standards.

As mentioned earlier, safeguarding the organization occurs at various levels. It is found in bylaws and policies and demonstrated in the protocols in which the organization engages. Departments within the organization can contribute to protecting the agency from fraud, financial exploitation, or accounting errors by creating systems of checks and balances and auditing program-specific financial records. For instance, managers of group homes may be tasked with completing audits, collecting receipts, and recording expenses allocated within the budget for an individual program. The program director who oversees the house manager can assure that monthly spending is on target and the program manager should meet regularly with the business office to review the budget. Additionally, when an agency requires that staff have access to purchasing household goods, there must be systems in place to monitor that the funds are not being used improperly—or worse, illegally, as in cases where staff use agency funds to purchase personal items. In such cases, the staff is exploiting not only the agency but moreover the clients, who are the rightful recipients of the funds. In this type of situation, the staff in question may be legally charged and also reported to the state protection agency for financial abuse of the client, in addition to being terminated from his or her position. It is therefore vital for the organization to have safeguards in place to monitor purchases.

Organizations, ideally, have many built-in layers that collectively establish internal controls. There should be controls at every level within the organization where multiple positions are accountable for assuring the success of the organization by remaining in compliance with governances. Organizations can also use external resources and software in the system of controls. For instance, there is a variety of accounting softwares that track and electronically monitor records. Additionally, many nonprofit agencies have external auditors who review both financial and clinical records and submit their findings about the organization's record keeping and status of compliance in accordance with regulations. Box 9.6 shows a case study on budgeting.

BOX 9.6

COMPETENCY-BASED CASE STUDY: A HOUSE MANAGER UNDER BUDGET

The manager of a therapeutic group home is responsible for reconciling the monthly expenses. The manager reports that they remained $200 under budget this month. "How wonderful!" the supervisor thinks, until he or she takes a look at the breakdown of expenses firsthand and notices that there were multiple charges to the local office supplies store. The agency has a contract with a wholesale vendor, and requests for office supplies are supposed to go through central office. Additionally, the supervisor notices multiple charges to a local gas station on the same day, which is curious because the residents did not have that many planned community outings that week. The supervisor is growing more curious about the appropriation of funds and worries that this quick audit of expenses may be suspicious.

Questions

1. What is the first thing that the supervisor should do?
2. How should the supervisor approach the manager about what was discovered in this audit?
3. What are some possible human errors that might have occurred?
4. Should the supervisor report this finding to anyone else in the agency? If so, who and at what point?
5. Why should there be multiple layers, or multiple persons, to review budgets within an organization?

Protecting the Organization and Employees From Liability

There are many things that place an organization at risk, including financial malfeasance, professional malpractice and ethical misconduct, workplace harassment, general welfare and safety of employees and clients/students, and many more. Clinicians who have worked in direct practice are familiar with methods of shielding oneself from liability, such as maintaining proper documentation, adhering to the profession's code of ethics, and submitting accurate billing information.

Organizations are expected to adhere to the policies and standards outlined by a number of regulating entities. It is unusual for any organization to have a single regulation system, as there are various mandates established at the federal, state, and local levels in addition to professional licensing and accreditation boards specific to the mission of agencies, institutions, and specific departments. For instance, a nonprofit agency may be accredited by the Council on Accreditation (COA) or Joint Commission on Accreditation of Healthcare Organizations (JCAHO). A social work department at a university is accredited by the Council on Social Work

Education (CSWE). In addition to accreditation, many organizations are also licensed by any number of administrations, such as the Department of Public Health (DPH), Department of Developmental Disabilities, Department of Children and Families, Department of Mental Health and Addiction, and Substance Abuse and Mental Health Services Administration (SAMHSA). Beyond accrediting and licensing standards that regulate compliance outcome measures, an organization is also accountable to standards outlined by various funders such as Medicaid, Medicare, private insurance, or federal financial student aid.

As you are probably beginning to realize, there can be a lot of regulations with which an organization must stay in compliance, and, on top of that, organizations must also keep up-to-date with any changes made by their regulation systems. Pollack (2009) explained that the "multiplicity of accountability relationships may lead to accountability overload and an overall fragmented and fuzzy accountability in an environment ripe for litigation" (p. 839). Organizational leaders must understand the standards and devise policies and practices that incorporate all of the regulations from each entity that accredits, licenses, and funds its operations. Developing systems of accountability can include procedure, process, or effort (Pollack, 2009). Procedural accountability implies that the worker is adhering to the prescribed guidelines. Consequential accountability, the responsibility for an outcome or the outcome of actions taken or not taken, whether or not intentional, is often encountered in social work and healthcare-related professions. The organization is responsible for making the accountability policy clear and available to workers (Pollack, 2009). How are all of these regulations kept track of, and who is responsible for evaluating how the organization is doing with its compliance metrics?

Protecting the organization and employees from liability must happen on multiple fronts, but tracking can be consolidated to one committee that is responsible for overseeing the organization's compliance. Such a committee is often referred to as a corporate compliance committee; however, we refer to it throughout this section simply as a compliance committee. Organizations may be required to have a *compliance committee* based on the funding it receives, particularly those that receive financial reimbursement from Medicare or Medicaid. Even if the compliance committee is not mandated, it is best practice. These committees are desirable within organizations because (a) they protect the organization and can provide documentation in the event that the organization must prove that it made reasonable efforts to proactively identify risks and addressed them accordingly, and (b) they can serve a dual purpose of conducting program evaluations while also assessing overall organizational compliance.

A compliance committee is usually chaired by the compliance officer, whose primary role is to oversee the organization's compliance. The primary purpose of a compliance committee is to gather and assess information from all divisions to ensure that all aspects of the organization are in compliance with all regulations and, when necessary, develop corrective action plans to bring about improvements. Effective compliance committees develop procedures for assuring that the organization is acting in accordance with applicable laws and regulations; promoting an atmosphere of transparency and accountability; adhering to all professional and ethical standards; preventing noncompliance issues such as the misuse or misappropriation of funds or any type of financial fraud; identifying noncompliance issues early and developing corrective courses of action that are swiftly taken; and enhancing the trust and confidence of employees and constituents.

The composition of compliance committees should be multidisciplinary in order to represent all departments and functions of the organization, including human resources, finance, service delivery (when there are multiple service programs all should be represented), information technology (electronic record keeping and the Health Insurance Portability and Accountability Act [HIPAA]), and general operations (including maintenance and safety). Creating a committee comprised of diverse professionals and multidisciplinary roles capitalizes on the expert knowledge within the group. For instance, having an IT representative, who assumedly has greater knowledge than a social worker or finance representative about the security of the agency's database, can offer expert recommendations about software updates that will protect the electronic system from being hacked. Similarly, a representative from human resources will be able to inform the group about the most recent changes in labor laws to which the organization needs to adhere. Note that a compliance committee is only as good as the data points selected to evaluate outcomes and compliance metrics, and only as impactful as the corrective actions taken in response to identified problems. Data points should be informed by the regulations outlined from accrediting, licensing, and funding entities, which can be compartmentalized to divisions within the organization that can monitor and correct.

Larger, more complex organizations with multiple service divisions and greater infrastructure may develop several subcommittees to collect and evaluate compliance data and then report back to the compliance committee. For example, members of a human resource department can collect data about how many workers' compensation cases were filed in the last quarter. A clinical representative can provide information from an audit of client records that assesses the outcome of a treatment goal and the accuracy of clinical documentation. A financial representative can confirm and report back that the finance committee is reviewing the quarterly audit. Thus, compliance committees can divide the organization's departments into subcommittees to monitor key functions and outcomes of each program in the organization. Each subcommittee might be designated the responsibility of evaluating the risks inherent to that particular division as well as their outcomes, which serve as benchmarks to demonstrate the actions that the organization took to promote the safety and well-being of staff and clients/students, and thus actions that are mitigating risks. The subcommittees will gather and assess the compliance standards applicable to the operations within their particular division, and then the representatives serving on both a subcommittee and compliance committee will report back to the compliance committee. The compliance committee must then review the findings shared by the subcommittees and make inquiries to ensure that no risks have been overlooked.

For smaller organizations, member representation might be assumed by the directors, managers, or leaders of a particular division. It is, however, wise to promote staff membership from all levels of the organization whenever possible, as it encourages inclusion and can offer rich insights and information from frontline staff about operations and any barriers that exist. Organizations can structure their compliance committee review process into an open or closed system. For instance, some organizations have employees on the compliance committee (closed), while others open their committees to external members that may also include external multidisciplinary professionals, clients, or family members of clients. The purpose of both closed and open compliance committees is to review the process and progress of compliancy, identify risk, and develop strategies for mitigating risks. Again, risks can range from client satisfaction, staff satisfaction, and fiduciary appropriations to environmental risks and much more.

Compliance committees typically generate and submit reports to designated members of the organization, including the CEO/president and board. Additionally, minutes should be recorded and detail the findings and follow-up actions that will be reviewed at the next meeting. An annual report of the compliance committee's activities and outcomes should also be generated and submitted to the CEO/president and board.

Assuring the Appropriate Safety

Organizations are responsible for providing a work environment that is safe and protects workers from emotional and physical harm. Organizations are also legally bound to comply with Occupational Safety and Health Administration (OSHA) regulations. Employees' rights to a safe and healthy work environment should be posted in areas visible to all staff. There are a number of OSHA standards that may overlap with the compliance committee measures and should be incorporated into the organization's written policies and procedures, such as protecting whistleblowers from retaliation. Frequent OSHA citations include risk of falling and the necessity of providing employees protection from exposure to bodily fluids or hazardous waste.

Similar to devising systems for evaluating the financial and operational compliance matters, organizations must also establish systems for monitoring and ensuring the safety of the work environment. The metrics for safety committees should infuse OSHA standards, along with other regulations applicable to the organization such as physical management training (PMT) and crisis de-escalation techniques. There are a variety of factors that should be considered for assuring the safety of staff and protection of organizational resources. For that reason, it is wise for organizations to establish safety committees dedicated to gathering and assessing information relevant to overall safety. For universities, the most appropriate person to chair the safety committee may be a member or director of the campus security, while for organizations this person may vary based on the availability of a relevant position and organizational infrastructure. In organizations, the director of human resources, maintenance, compliance, or other key positions may be charged the task of chairing a safety committee.

Academic institutions must provide Title IV training to staff to inform them of mandated reporting of criminal activity, sexual assault, harassment, stalking, domestic violence, and acute mental health (suicide or homicide) risks. For agencies, staff are similarly trained in mandated reporting. Safety also includes how staff and those served by the staff (students or clients) are trained or informed of safety prevention, such as potential evacuation protocols, fire drills, active shooter drills, or how to manage physically aggressive clients. Additionally, the safety committee should gather and evaluate information about workers' comp claims, the physical safety of the environment including managing risks to safety imposed by those served, and how vital equipment such as agency vehicles, phone, and alert systems are maintained.

A safety committee should include members from various divisions of the organization who can contribute to the overall assessment and monitoring of safety. For instance, a supervisor within each program may be required to submit a daily vehicle inspection report noting things such as low tire pressure, an upcoming oil change, or a need to restock items in the first aid kit kept in the vehicle. A human resource manager may submit a monthly report summarizing the type of injuries recorded in worker compensation claims. A compliance officer may submit a report documenting allegations of client abuse or neglect. For organizations that have video surveillance, a report should outline any significant findings from the surveillance. The facilities' maintenance director should submit a report documenting all of the maintenance completed on equipment or the physical plant.

Box 9.7 provides a case example of one such complaint regarding client aggression toward staff.

BOX 9.7

COMPETENCY-BASED CASE STUDY: OSHA COMPLAINT

Staff working on an inpatient psychiatric unit filed a complaint with OSHA alleging a hostile work environment. The reporter claimed that the unit is unsafe for staff because the following incident occurred:

While working on the second shift, a staff was struck in the face by a patient. The patient was admitted to the psychiatric unit for a psychotic disorder and was noted to be floridly psychotic at the time of admission, experiencing auditory and visual hallucinations as well as delusions of persecution. The patient was admitted on a physician's emergency certificate due to being gravely disabled and unable to provide consent for treatment. On the evening the patient was admitted, the staff was attempting to direct the patient to his room from the common area. The patient became agitated and struck the staff in the face with an open palm. Other staff nearby quickly intervened and placed the patient in a PMT-approved hold until the patient could safely be released and escorted to his room. The reporter is filing a claim stating that the environment poses significant risk to the physical safety and well-being of staff.

(continued)

BOX 9.7 *(Continued)*

Questions

1. In the scenario, is there any evidence that the inpatient psychiatric unit of the general hospital violated an OSHA standard(s)? Explain how you reached your answer.

2. If an OSHA investigation were to be opened, what supporting documentation would need to be provided to demonstrate that the hospital and unit took precautionary efforts to minimize the risk to employees and patients? Explain why each piece of supporting documentation would be needed, and what should be included.

OSHA, Occupational Safety and Health Administration; PMT, physical management training.

In the example provided, neither the inpatient unit nor hospital is found to be at fault, and the claim is dismissed for the following reasons: the job description clearly noted that staff are, at times, required to use physical management techniques to protect against aggressive patients; and staff must be physically able to perform certain work duties, such as restrain patients and lift objects up to a certain weight. There is adequate documentation that the staff received training in the proper use of PMT, which included how to verbally de-escalate patients, how to block and protect against aggressive patients, and how to physically restrain patients. There was adequate documentation reporting on each prior incident of physical restraint and the subsequent debriefings held to analyze the root cause and develop corrective action steps; and the corrective action steps had adequate follow-through and an assessment of the action steps taken in response to findings. There was adequate information that the compliance committee regularly reviewed information pertaining to these procedures. There was also adequate information that the hospital makes information available to staff about employee assistance programs, recurring trainings, and grievance policies.

Undergoing investigations of this sort can be time-consuming and frustrating, as many feel that it takes away from time that should be dedicated to serving clients and managing programs; however, investigations are part of managing programs. The better prepared an organization is in its system of internal controls and monitoring ongoing compliance, safety, and so on, the less time-consuming and overwhelming it can seem when undergoing an investigation of any kind. This brings us back to the omnipotence of transparency and accountability. The more transparent and accountable the system of controls are, the lower the risk of successful litigation, citations, or fines.

Succession Planning

Succession planning can, and should, occur at all levels and positions of an organization. In Chapter 7, we discussed the benefits of developing mentorships for emerging and aspiring leaders and identified that one of the benefits is reduced turnover. Developing future leaders demonstrates a commitment to employees' career paths and conveys that they are valuable. Establishing plans for developing staff should also consider the impact of the unpredictable exiting of staff in management or other key positions. Building an internal pool of candidates who can quickly step into the role of manager is challenging in organizations that recently restructured and eliminated middle management positions, as these positions are often stepping stones to senior management roles. Restructuring can often result in people being assigned greater responsibility and duties within their existing roles, compressing the time that may be needed to enhance skills and knowledge required for senior-level positions. However, opportunities for development may be embedded in some of the newly assigned tasks and responsibilities, and these should be articulated and explained in a manner that promotes and inspires a growth mind-set to reduce the potential of employees feeling overwhelmed, overstretched, or undercompensated.

The services and programs that are inherent to the mission and values of the organization need to be sustained beyond individual talent and tenure. Cross-training staff and managers is one strategy for preparing for planned and unplanned vacancies across the organization. Although there are many hurdles that social service and academic organizations face in terms of developing future leaders, the reality is that planning is essential to the organization's stability and sustainability. How an organization goes about preparing for this process may vary, but creating succession plans is paramount.

Change in executive leadership can occur for a multitude of reasons, most commonly retirement or advancement to another organization. Under these circumstances the CEO, the board of directors, and executive leadership members usually have a reasonable amount of time to plan the exiting of the CEO and recruitment of his or her successor. However, there are times when a CEO leaves the position unexpectedly, perhaps due to sudden illness, disability, or death; there are also times when a board might abruptly terminate or request the immediate resignation of a CEO. When the departure of the CEO is sudden and unexpected, it can evoke an array of emotions from staff such as shock, disappointment, betrayal, worry, fear, or relief, but perhaps the most ubiquitous of all is a prevailing feeling of uncertainty about what will happen next, how things will change, and how they will be affected by the changes yet to unfold. Even when the exit is planned well in advance, it is evitable that the CEO and board will experience what Gothard and Austin (2013) referred to as "psychological and task-oriented adjustment," which is marked by considerable self-reflection and evaluation (p. 272). The task-oriented adjustments pertain to how the exiting CEO and board might identify the competencies of the succeeding CEO and discuss the vision for the future of the agency. The CEO can aid in succession planning by offering opportunities for the board of directors to better acquaint themselves with "high-level talent inside the agency" (p. 274). There are times when the board and CEO might have radically different views about the future direction of the organization and what steps should be taken. Under these circumstances, the differences in perspectives can lead the board and CEO to evaluate the future by taking all parties' ideas into consideration and reaching consensus, or the differences can create an irrevocable rift between the CEO and board, which will invariably impact the recruitment, onboarding, and transition processes.

Gothard and Austin (2013) noted that it is ultimately the board of directors' responsibility to establish a succession plan, albeit boards often rely on the CEO to begin the planning process. Boards may rely on the CEO to initiate the process out of respect to the autonomy of the CEO; but as Gothard and Austin (2013) cautioned, this reliance on the CEO can sometimes result in an absence of conversations about the planning process altogether. Emotions can run high during any transition, and a transition of such magnitude—no matter how well planned or how ideal the circumstances are—will inevitably be tinged with emotion. Many effective leaders and CEOs apply the concept of *self-leadership*, an internal system of rewards and notions about performance effectiveness and outcomes, which contribute to their professional advancement. Thus, it can become difficult to untangle the personal from the professional. Sometimes the emotion is due to the stage of life adjustment the CEO is making, which can stir up questions such as, "Am I really ready for retirement? What will I do with my time? How did I leave my mark here? How will my successor evaluate me? How do other people feel about my exit?" Finally, Gothard and Austin (2013) asserted that "boards need to examine their own composition in the succession planning process, as board diversity can affect both the selection and success of the new ED" (p. 274).

There are several key elements to consider in succession planning, which include (a) beginning the formalized process of succession planning, (b) pacing the announcement of the exit with the process of identifying viable candidates, and (c) structuring the onboarding and overlapping of CEOs.

Formalizing the process of succession planning begins with identifying and developing the competencies, skills, and knowledge of a potential successor. The board should be informed by the executive about a potential candidate prior to initiating any formal conversation with the candidate about grooming her or him for succession. Once the board has approved the candidate as a potential successor, part of the grooming should include increasing the candidate's exposure to and interaction with the board members.

Pacing the announcement of the exit is crucial to maintaining organizational equilibrium; it is essential to maintain order and prevent intense positive or negative emotions over the change. The process of recruitment should be timed so that fellow executives are informed and invited to contribute to the process of identifying the skills, competencies, values, knowledge, and experience of the ideal future leader. However, if the process is prolonged—that is, if the announcement has been made that the executive is stepping down and there is significant lag time in the recruitment process—this can incite unsettling emotions and great uncertainty among staff about what will be, as they wait with anticipation to discover who the next "boss" will be. Will he or she be able to work with them? Will he or she want to come in and change how we do everything? Will he or she bring his or her "own people" in to replace us? Recall from Chapter 6 that our minds are wired to predict, and a lack of predictability can lead us to draw conclusions, which may be so far off that it only enhances fear and ambiguity, and, ultimately, affects performance and commitment.

Once the successor has been selected, and assuming that the succession is planned rather than abrupt for any reason, the executive and succeeding executive, along with the board of directors, should devise a plan for onboarding. The amount of time where the two executives overlap should be given careful consideration. While the exiting executive can help to orient the new executive in many areas and functions of the position, too much overlapping can have negative ramifications. An extended overlap can confuse the staff on whom to report to. For instance, out of habit or comfort, staff might find themselves still going to the exiting executive rather than establishing a working relationship and reporting to the new executive. It can also be difficult for the new executive to establish him- or herself in his or her role with the former executive lingering in the shadows. An extended overlap can cause the incoming executive to be overreliant on the exiting executive; this reliance may be out of respect to the exiting executive or simply an uncertainty about how to proceed in a manner that might live up to the exiting executive's standards. Conversely, if the new executive introduces new ideas about how things can be done or handled differently, it can stir up harsh feelings in the exiting executive who may feel that his or her accomplishments will soon vaporize. A sapient approach to overlapping the incoming and exiting executives is to establish well-articulated objectives that will be met within a short span of time. Once that period has been met, the exiting executive might remain on-call as a consultant to both the board and the new executive.

The following points can be considered in developing a succession plan:

- Hire from within, or look for an external candidate? What are the potential pros and cons of either?

- How will this change impact the organization? How will the organization sustain relationships with donors, state representatives, funding agencies, clients, and other key constituents?

- Develop a vision for the future. What do the programs, services, revenue streams, and so on, need to look like? And what are the competencies needed in potential candidates to meet those needs?

- What are the needs of the staff? What are the personal qualities that the potential candidate should have to effectively lead the staff, motive and inspire teams?

- How will the future candidate promote and support a diverse work team?

- What are the requisites needed for this position? Education level, experience, accomplishments, and references.

- What needs to remain intact? What needs to change? What are the skills that will be needed to ensure both?

ACCOUNTABILITY

Box 9.8 displays the competencies/behaviors in this section.

BOX 9.8

NETWORK FOR SOCIAL WORK MANAGEMENT COMPETENCIES AND PRACTICE BEHAVIORS 8 AND COUNCIL ON SOCIAL WORK EDUCATION PRACTICE BEHAVIORS 5

Advocates for public policy change and social justice at national, state, and local levels (Network for Social Work Management Competencies 8). Practice Behaviors:

- Challenges broad regulatory expectations and advocates for efficient and well-tailored polices with potential to impact client's welfare (8.5).

CSWE Competency 5—Engage in Policy Practice
Social workers

- 5.2 Assess how social welfare and economic policies impact the delivery of and access to social services.
- 5.3 Apply critical thinking to analyze, formulate, and advocate for policies that advance human rights and social, economic, and environmental justice.

CSWE, Council on Social Work Education.

Social work leaders and managers need to understand how regional, state, and federal policies and regulations impact their work with clients. This understanding requires leaders and managers to keep informed of new laws and regulations that are sometimes inserted in massive federal bills which ultimately influence and impact local service providers. However, the crucial point here is that social workers need to be aware of these changes as they are being proposed and voted on. Why? Not only can these changes have negative effects on service delivery to clients and how clients can access or be considered eligible for social services but also because social workers have opportunities to advocate on behalf of clients prior to new regulations being passed.

Federal and state regulations can be modified by engaging in advocacy work in the public comment process. For example, a federal or state agency will issue regulations that are required by law to solicit public comment; advocates can then engage in defined regulatory processes to change policy. Advocates have an opportunity to impact the regulations during the review process, hopefully in ways that will improve client welfare. When new policies are instituted, one initial approach is to meet with legal aid, which can assist you in understanding the policy and regulatory changes and can become part of the process to push the government to consider modifying the new policies and regulations. Organizations should also intervene after policies and regulations are promulgated to make sure that these regulations are properly enforced in a manner that benefits clients.

Leaders and managers at agencies need to be able to prepare testimony and provide stories about the clients they serve. One strategy that has a great impact on legislators is to bring clients in to testify on how the proposed regulations will impact their lives, either in a positive or negative way. One can advocate at both the legislative and executive branches. When the executive branch holds public hearings, advocates can provide adjustments to soften a harsh regulation or strengthen a positive regulation to improve lives of clients. Box 9.9 is an example of a private agency impacted by state agency regulations.

BOX 9.9

COMPETENCY-BASED CASE STUDY: ADVOCACY

A state department serving persons with developmental disabilities historically served persons with intellectual disabilities and adults with developmental disabilities. However, given the sharp increase in the prevalence of children diagnosed with ASD, the department began to serve youths (children and teens) diagnosed with ASD. The public sector outsourced treatment services to the private sector, which received funding directly from the state agency. The private sector was therefore overseen by the state agency for compliance with treatment service outcome measures, processes of working with families, and funding regulations. One funding regulation outlined strict guidelines for reimbursing services rendered when a youth did not have school. The regulation stated that youths must be out of school for 10 consecutive days before the servicing agency is eligible for reimbursement. For youths being served in residential treatment, private agencies were gravely impacted by this regulation, since most school vacation days were either one-day holidays or five-day breaks, and inclement weather days were scattered days, as were delayed openings or early dismissals. Staffing, of course, was needed for the youths during these weeks and dispersed days throughout the academic calendar year. For an agency that primarily served youths and provided a number of residential placement options, the financial loss of this policy would be too high. The CFO calculated the amount of money it would take to staff all nonschool days, with the exception of weekends, and it totaled nearly $1 million. The executive team believed in the mission of the organization that served youths, and also knew firsthand that families, as well as the youths, needed the support of residential treatment services.

Questions

1. How should the executive team handle this matter? What are the first steps they should take in addressing this matter, and why?

2. What does the leadership team need to consider and how should it proceed?

3. What should the executive advocate for? Who should the executive advocate to? Explain your reasoning.

ASD, autism spectrum disorder; CFO, chief financial officer.

▦ Organizational Procedures

Box 9.10 displays the competencies/behaviors in this section.

BOX 9.10

NETWORK FOR SOCIAL WORK MANAGEMENT COMPETENCIES AND PRACTICE BEHAVIORS 19

Manages risk and legal affairs (Network for Social Work Management Competencies 19). Practice Behaviors:

- ▦ Protects the agency from undue risk by ensuring that appropriate policies and procedures exist in all areas of operation (19.1).

(continued)

BOX 9.10 *(Continued)*

■ Establishes systems of monitoring in all areas of the organization where there may be potential risk (e.g., client services, record keeping, accounting, purchasing) (19.2.).

■ Ensures adherence to all laws, regulations, contracts, and legal agreements (19.3).

So far in this chapter we have reviewed a number of ways to mitigate organizational risks and protect organizational resources, including employees. Within each section, we suggest providing written policies to all staff to describe the procedures for enacting a given policy. Organizational policies and procedures should be reviewed frequently, at least annually. There are times that an organization will have to make changes throughout the course of a year, so there should be a process for reviewing and approving policies. This process can be in the form of a committee dedicated to reviewing the policy draft, offering critical feedback, and approving the establishment or change of a given policy. Once the committee has approved the policy, the CEO or compliance officer may request that the agency's attorney review the policy. Finally, the policy should be shared with the board of directors for final review and approval before it is published and made available to all staff.

Policies and procedures need to be clear to the reader, thus they should not include a lot of jargon but should be written in a comprehensible manner. Additionally, simply having written policies and procedures is not sufficient to protect the organization against risk. The burden of proof falls on the organization to demonstrate how the information was originally distributed to staff and how the information was made accessible and comprehensible for staff to review. Many organizations require staff to sign a document stating that they received a copy of or access to the policies and procedures (P&P) manual. With the use of technology, many organizations can now streamline their data tracking through emails that provide links to electronic P&P manuals and updates to any policies and procedures. Other organizations have links to P&P manuals and training updates that are accessible through electronic paystub portals. However the information is made available, a system of tracking its use should be audited regularly. Auditing can help to identify and address any gaps that are preventing employees from obtaining information and/or training on policies and procedures. Findings from this internal audit should be shared with the compliance officer.

BOX 9.11

NETWORK FOR SOCIAL WORK MANAGEMENT COMPETENCIES AND PRACTICE BEHAVIORS 19

Manages risk and legal affairs (Network for Social Work Management Competencies 19). Practice Behaviors:

■ Establishes systems of monitoring all areas of the organization where there may be potential risk (e.g., client services, record keeping, accounting, purchasing) (19.2).

■ Ensures adherence to all laws, regulations, contracts, and legal agreements (19.3).

Box 9.11 details the importance of monitoring organizational risks and adhering to company policies. Understanding the potential risks to clients, staff, and the organization—from errors in accounting, student outcomes, and clinical record keeping—is an essential task for compliance committees, but must involve multiple arenas of the organization that could be impacted. While every organization's needs for monitoring and minimizing risks will differ, there are several accountability tools drawn from the work of Pollack (2009), as outlined below.

- Contracts: These are legal documents that describe the legal expectations regarding who is responsible for what. They provide a timeframe, a reporting mechanism, a review procedure, and a payment schedule.

- Program or financial audits: These are procedures to verify after-the-fact operational aspects of the workers and organization.

- Periodic reports: These are documents that summarize activities or accomplishments which elaborate on an entire program or specific aspect of a program.

- Periodic interviews: These are face-to-face contacts or site visits used as opportunities to view and review service in action.

- Client satisfaction surveys: These are documents that focus on client satisfaction which are vital to meeting legal expectations. (Pollack, 2009, p. 840)

We suggest adding staff satisfaction surveys to Pollack's list. Staff surveys focused on employee satisfaction are imperative to meeting department of labor expectations as well as offering internal information about employee morale. These periodic reports should include information about the safety of employees, such as worker compensation claims, staff and client injuries, and the demographic composition of clients served and staff positions. Providing data about the staff composition can help organizations identity possible inequities and call attention to a potential need for greater inclusion. Periodic reviews might also include information about sponsored research activities to ensure staff are acting in accordance with regulations, and to report on the accomplishments of such activities. Any legal consultation or actions that have occurred within a designated time should also be included in periodic reports, which are primarily submitted to the board of directors. Periodic interviews may include meeting with clients or clients' family members to assess the quality of care and services delivered. Face-to-face interviews can also be conducted with staff to assess knowledge and skills, and gather information about future trainings that can help to improve performance, or identify potential risks to employees, clients, and the organization.

SUMMARY

Throughout this chapter we discussed the need for organizational transparency and accountability. Social work leaders and managers have a responsibility to clients, as well as various regulatory systems, to ensure that programs are operating ethically and legally. The multiplicity of regulations to which organizations must adhere requires ongoing planning and evaluation, which should be accomplished through the strategic efforts of multidisciplinary teams. It is imperative that social work leaders and managers have a comprehensive understanding of the various regulations that guide daily functions and develop judicious habits that safeguard clients, employees, and the organization from manifold risks. Various committees can be developed to oversee compliance with a number of regulations, including financial regulations, safety, and overall risk prevention aims, along with policies and procedures outlined as organizational expectations. Organizational expectations offer the foundation for organizational and programmatic goals to be established. Finally, we briefly revisited the concept of mentoring or grooming staff for the purpose of succession planning and dismantled some of the processes inherent to succession planning.

ACTIVITIES

1. Consider a program within an organization, academic, or social service. Develop a program goal and outline the budgetary goals and needs that will either help to balance a program budget or increase income over expenses (profit). Be sure to include time frames for completing the goal, and identify the people you will need to collaborate with to develop the plan and continuously monitor the plan.

2. Review an organizational policy (for students this may also include field manuals) and critique it. Your critique should include (a) identifying the purpose and importance of the policy; (b) discussing the clarity of how the policy is written; and (c) discussing how the policy meets a compliance issue.

REFERENCES

Gothard, S., & Austin, M. J. (2013). Leadership succession planning: Implications for nonprofit human service organizations. *Administration in Social Work*, *37*, 272–285. doi:10.1080/03643107.2012.684741

Pollack, D. (2009). Legal risk, accountability and transparency in social work. *International Social Work*, *52*(6), 837–842. doi:10.1177/0020872809342663

CHAPTER 10

HUMAN RESOURCE FUNCTIONS IN A SOCIAL WORK ENVIRONMENT

CHAPTER OBJECTIVES

- Recognizing how to create a diverse workforce to align with clients served by the organization.
- Creating a positive and supportive culture and climate for the workplace and those served.
- Understanding employee relations policies and practices that are fair, adhere to law, and are implemented in a consistent manner.
- Learning how to recruit, hire, train, and conduct performance assessment and promotion/termination based on established criteria.
- Understanding the importance of a discrimination- and harassment-free work environment.
- Learning how to recruit and retain a diversity of employees to reflect the communities and constituencies served by the organization.
- Employing civil service and union rules to ensure that the most qualified employees are selected to carry out agency responsibilities.
- Learning the essentials of creating job descriptions.
- Understanding the best recruitment practices.
- Understanding affirmative action and equal employment opportunities rules.
- Learning how to create an employment evaluation rubric.

INTRODUCTION

This chapter reviews and discusses best human resource practices aligned with the Network for Social Work Management (NSWM) and Council on Social Work Education (CSWE) practice behaviors. Emerging and seasoned leaders and managers will inevitably find themselves in situations that they are not prepared for; in terms of human resource issues, the saying goes, "truth is stranger than fiction." In other words, you will be exposed to complex employee relations situations that are unexpected, disappointing, and downright shocking at times. When dealing with human resource matters there are three key rules of thumb: (a) always have your documentation in order; (b) always use emotional regulation and professional communication to handle the situation, and in some situations, it is wise to ask a third party to be present; and (c) address the situation early on to develop corrective action plans and prevent perpetuation of the issue. Managing human resource issues requires that you have proactively provided the best possible working environment for all staff and that you have led with a philosophy of equity. Box 10.1 displays the competencies/behaviors in this chapter.

BOX 10.1

NETWORK FOR SOCIAL WORK MANAGEMENT COMPETENCIES AND PRACTICE BEHAVIORS

Manages diversity and cross-cultural understanding (Network for Social Work Management Competencies 5). Practice Behaviors:

- Seeks to employ a diverse workforce to align with clients served by the organization (5.3).

Effectively manages human resources (Network for Social Work Management Competencies 12). Practice Behaviors:

- Designs and manages the workplace to ensure a positive and supportive culture and climate for staff and clients (12.1).
- Designs and manages employee relations policies and practices that are fair, adhere to law, and are implemented in a consistent manner (12.2).
- Supervises recruitment, hiring, training, performance assessment, and promotion/termination based on established criteria (12.3).
- Creates, maintains, and fosters a discrimination- and harassment-free work environment for employees, clients, and general public (12.4).
- Successfully recruits and retains a diversity of employees to reflect the communities and constituencies served by the organization (12.5).
- In settings with Civil Service and Unions, works within existing systems to ensure that the most qualified employees are selected to carry out agency responsibilities (12.6).

MANAGING THE WORKPLACE TO ENSURE A POSITIVE AND SUPPORTIVE CULTURE

BOX 10.2

NETWORK FOR SOCIAL WORK MANAGEMENT COMPETENCIES AND PRACTICE BEHAVIORS 12

Effectively manages human resources (Network for Social Work Management Competencies 12). Practice Behaviors:

Designs and manages the workplace to ensure a positive and supportive culture and climate for staff and clients (12.1).

Box 10.2 displays the competencies/behaviors in this section. A workplace that offers a positive and supportive culture and climate is an environment that fosters cohesion among different individuals and teams and encourages employees to provide input and use their creativity. The focus of a growth-oriented environment should be on both the provision of client/student services and the provision of staff training and opportunities for growth. Leaders need to consider how staff are recognized for their work, dedication, and creativity. This recognition can vary depending on the collection of individuals (refer to Chapter 6 for more information on rewards). The best way to determine how the staff want to be acknowledged is to survey the staff directly and solicit ideas about what appeals to them. Finally, a positive workplace environment is focused on inclusivity: staff at all levels, from diverse backgrounds (racial, gender, sexual orientation and expression, etc.), are valued for their work, are recognized and paid equitably, and have the same opportunities for input, which are heard and applied by the administration.

Understanding the pulse of the organization is critical if leaders are to maintain a positive and supportive culture and climate. Implementing an open systems environment that creates a positive workplace atmosphere where staff are driven to help clients/students, and also feel supported by managers, will encourage the continuance of a positive workplace environment. To establish and maintain a positive workplace environment, staff need to feel that the higher-ups are supportive of their growth, development, and well-being (i.e., work–life balance, burnout, etc.).

Box 10.3 provides an example of ethnocentrism behavior and prompts a question.

BOX 10.3

COMPETENCY-BASED QUESTION: CULTURAL DIFFERENCES

When managers hear complaints from staff who view cultural differences (dress, speech, etc.) as "unprofessional," those staff are exhibiting ethnocentrism behavior (judging others' behaviors and tastes in the context of one's own culture, values, etc.).

Question:

1. In what ways do cultural differences impact the effectiveness of professionals?

BOX 10.4

NETWORK FOR SOCIAL WORK MANAGEMENT COMPETENCIES AND PRACTICE BEHAVIORS 12

Effectively manages human resources (Network for Social Work Management Competencies 12). Practice Behaviors:

   Designs and manages employee relations policies and practices that are fair, adhere to law, and are implemented in a consistent manner (12.2).

EQUITY

Box 10.4 displays the competencies/behaviors in this section. Equity can be defined as an environment that deals with people based on performance rather than biases and prejudices. Equity applies to all types of employment including merit employment. Think about managing results, not personalities. Applying the rules of Equal Employment Opportunity (EEO) and Affirmative Action (AA) legislation helps assure equity in the workplace. Applying EEO and AA practices can be of great value to managers because they

- Prohibit managers from establishing irrelevant, non-job-related standards that interfere with employee performance.
- Create a more diverse workforce.
- Develop a workforce more representative of the community and more responsive to clients' or students' needs.
- Give direction.
- FOLLOW THE LAW.

Managers can be held personally liable if they do not follow the law. In the case of *Faraca v. Clements*, the superintendent of a mental health facility in Georgia refused to hire a mixed race couple to serve as house parents. He stated that "the community was not 'ready' for this situation." He was fined $7,000 (in 1980). The State Legislature wanted to let the accused superintendent off the hook, but the court ruled that he was personally liable for his actions.

   EEO and AA provide certain strategies that can assist managers in performing their jobs in an equitable way:

- EEO eliminates adverse impact and applies only to job-related criteria.
- AA aims to address past discrimination practices and prevent the future occurrences.
- AA is a set of guidelines, case law, and legislative law aimed at gaining a workforce representative of society.
- EEO guides employers in eliminating future discrimination.

The EEO Act of 1972 states

- Because of race, color, religion, sex, and so on, it is unlawful to discriminate with respect to compensation, terms of employment, conditions of employment, privileges, or to deprive or adversely affect employment opportunities, or to refuse to refer for employment, or to discriminate with respect to training, retraining, and apprenticeship.

If a case goes to court, the court is likely to ask

- Does the decision adversely impact any particular section of society?
  - If yes, is that rule, qualification, screening process job related?
  - If yes, there is no discrimination (i.e., must be physically able to perform the job).
- If a situation adversely impacts a group and it is not job related, it's discriminatory.

Why are so many people hostile to these concepts? Perhaps because most people do not understand them. And if they do understand them, they may not believe that these rules should be the law and therefore may not believe that their own actions are discriminatory. Although we as a society have made legal advances, institutional racism, discrimination, and oppression practices, as well as microaggressions, sadly still exist, and such behaviors should never be tolerated. It is the responsibility of leaders, managers, and organizations to be aware of the laws, legal ramifications, and impacts resulting from inequalities, racism, discrimination, oppression, and microaggressions in the workplace.

RECRUITMENT

BOX 10.5

NETWORK FOR SOCIAL WORK MANAGEMENT COMPETENCIES AND PRACTICE BEHAVIORS 12

Effectively manages human resources (Network for Social Work Management Competencies 12). Practice Behaviors:
   Supervises recruitment, hiring, training, performance assessment, and promotion/termination based on established criteria (12.3).

Box 10.5 displays the competencies/behaviors in this section. The following section addresses recruitment, hiring, training, performance assessment, and promotion and termination with the primary focus on how these actions pertain to faculty at a university, although most of these same methods can be used by public service agencies.

Recruitment requires a number of steps, including establishing a personnel committee, creating the job description, and advertising academic positions through marketing.

Establishing a Personnel Committee

The first step in the hiring process, after obtaining approval from the administration that a position can be filled, is to create a personnel committee. Some university programs use existing personnel committees, and others create a new committee to manage the job search. To assure that diversity in hiring is considered, it is wise to have a diverse committee and, ideally, people on the committee who have had prior experience on personnel hiring committees, as they will know some of the dos and don'ts. The personnel committee may commence with tasks that include drafting the position and identifying sites for posting the position. The focus of the academic institution, that is, research focuesd (commonly referred to as R1 and R2 schools) or teaching focused (R3 schools), will influence how the position should read and where it is posted for recruitment. For instance, posting the academic position in a chronicle that is centered on research social work would be better suited for an R1 or R2 school, rather than an R3 school. The human resources (HR) department plays a vital role in helping to ensure that the committee is able to select from a diverse pool of candidates. For instance, many institutions will ask candidates to complete a demographic form in order to ensure that the candidate pool is sufficiently diverse. The makeup of the personnel committee is also vital to the process of ensuring that diversity remains a key component of the search process. In addition, how the personnel team proceeds with every candidate should be a uniform process, whereby all communication, questions, and time allotted for each candidate's interview is consistent with all candidates. It also is prudent to have HR staff train the personnel committee about the protocols and laws that need to be consistently followed.

In some organizations, the team of people responsible for creating the job description and facilitating the interview process may be less formal than a committee, but should nonetheless follow the basic principles of how search committees are structured, using consistency in questions for each candidate and creating an objective means of rating candidates.

Creating the Job Description

Start the process of creating a job description by obtaining information from the faculty on the needs of the program in terms of teaching areas; for organizations, identify what programmatic service areas need coverage. Sometimes you will be replacing newly retired faculty who covered specific curricula areas. Other times you will be hiring faculty for newly created positions that may be aligned with specific content areas. The university provost and human resources office usually have specific language and formatting for job ads. Similarly, within organizations the HR department typically has specific language that needs to be incorporated in the job ad. Professor-level (i.e., assistant, associate, professor) appointments are usually decided by the provost's office, depending on several factors such as funding for the position, whether a more experienced faculty is needed, and so on. Likewise, for organizations, positions typically will require certain requirements in education level, experience, licensing, and so on, and the salary range will be determined by the budget. Program heads may have to lobby for approval for open-level positions and support their case for why additional staff are needed. As approval for positions is typically linked with the budget, deans, directors, and chairpersons will need to demonstrate the need for the position (i.e., accreditation requires that there are a certain number of full-time faculty or a contract with the funding source specifies the number of clinicians the program will employ).

The job description itself should contain information about the university/organization and the program along with specific job responsibilities. Required and preferred qualifications should be identified along with the application process and submission information. To obtain a more diverse application pool, the job description should contain language that identifies diversity as important, such as seeking candidates with research and scholarship on diversity, experiences with diverse populations both on campus and in communities, strategies for teaching multiculture practice and working with cultures other than their own (Springer, 2006).

Advertising Academic Positions Through Marketing

Prior to advertising the job, identify your program's strengths and create a message based on those strengths, and find images to convey those strengths. Create language that sells the community, university, and program strengths. Be strategic on how to communicate the message, such as where you place print ads (*The Chronicle of Higher Education, Black Issues in Higher Education, The Hispanic Outlook in Higher Education, Council on Social Work Education, Society for Social Work Research,* and the *National Association of Social Workers Newsletter*). To disseminate the ads, use email lists from the academic organizations in social work, such as the National Association of

Deans and Directors of Social Work Graduate Programs, the Association of Baccalaureate Social Work Program Directors, and the Group for the Advancement of Doctoral Education in Social Work. If your program is in a moderate to big city, it may be more likely that you will draw from a qualified pool of people who do not have to move, and thus, you may get more applications. If you live in a small city or rural area, you will probably have to look outside of your area.

Communicating with applicants is very important. Decide early in the process who will be responding to applicants. Explore with the applicants the possibility of a preliminary information meeting at the CSWE annual program meeting or the Society for Social Work Research annual meeting. Interviews can be conducted off-site and used as a preliminary screening. You can allow faculty who are not on the personnel committee to meet with potential applicants. These sessions can be less than 45 minutes: 15 minutes marketing the school and 30 minutes interviewing the applicant. Even if you would not consider a candidate, you want the applicant to want to be considered. Use any initial conversation as an opportunity to market your organization's strengths. Inform candidates of possible timelines. Remember–each contact is a chance to market your school. If your interviewing process is on a fast track, you also might consider formal interviewing at these conferences; however, most of the personnel committee should attend these interviews.

THINNING THE POOL OF CANDIDATES

To reduce the applicant pool to a manageable number, all the personnel committee members should evaluate all the application materials, usually a letter of interest, curriculum vitae, and three letters of recommendation. Instead of letters of recommendation, you can ask for reference contact information, but then the committee members will have to contact the references by telephone interview. Requiring the submission of reference letters will expedite the process, plus you can always call the references if you have any questions about the candidate. If you have any questions or concerns about the applicant, contact the references. The typical goal is to invite three to five candidates for telephone or airport interviews (preliminary interviews that are completed expediently to avoid the additional costs of hotel stays and meals) per position (if you have multiple positons in which candidates may apply for more than one, you can reduce the number invited per position).

To select these interviewees, each member of the personnel committee should complete a rating rubric for each applicant and the average score of all ratings can be combined into a master sheet in order to rank the applicants' aggregate scores. Appendix 10A displays an example of a rating rubric, which can be modified for service organizations as well. All of the criteria in the rubric must come directly from the job description. The rubric can be created in Excel, which can self-calculate total scores for each applicant. However, first the committee must decide on the weight for each of the criteria. To make use of this rubric as an exercise, create a table in Excel, take your current or past job descriptions, take out the key words and add to the rubric, then put in the computing formulas. Read applications closely for candidate history; however, do not let the history too negatively influence your decision (i.e., nontraditional hires). Once the applicants are ranked, the committee should review the list and discuss applicants who some committee members believe should be considered even though their ranking was lower than others. Consider whether you selected the best overall candidate or the person who most meets your immediate needs. Also consider interviewing applicants who are ABD (if you do not have otherwise highly qualified candidates or want to promote more diversity of some kind), maybe local people or your adjuncts. For this preliminary interview, create a short list of interview questions (see Box 10.6). The whole personnel committee should conduct the interviews and each person assigned different questions in advance to ask candidates during the interview.

BOX 10.6

TELEPHONE OR SKYPE INTERVIEW QUESTIONS

Interview Questions

First, briefly introduce personnel committee members.

The personnel committee chair will state that the committee members will ask a series of questions and will be taking notes. The committee chair also will let the applicant know that there will be an opportunity for the candidate to ask additional questions.

1. There is often a disconnect between what students learn in their classes and what they experience in the field. How do you help them bridge that gap?
2. Would you give some examples of the types of assignments that you use and your thoughts about the relationship between assignments and students' learning styles?
3. What do you hope students will learn in their social work education both on the BSW and MSW levels? (and DSW)?
4. In what ways have you worked with and supported diverse communities and students? What particular strategies have you used?
5. What has been a significant, formative experience in your development as a social worker?
6. What prompted you to pursue a career as an (social work) academic?
7. In what university and departmental committee work or other forms of university service would you hope to participate?
8. At this university (add name), professors are often called upon to perform administrative tasks. Describe a challenging administrative task you have performed in a work setting.
9. What are the unique qualities that you will bring to this university (add name)?
10. What questions do you have for us?

One final point on asking questions: what you ask can hurt you, so you should know what you can ask and what you cannot ask.

What CAN you talk about?

- Work histories, references
- Ability to perform essential functions of the job
- Educational experience
- Interpersonal skills
- Potential starting date of employment
- Relationship with current or last employer
- Criminal convictions
- Career goals, objectives
- Hypothetical situations to gauge skills
- Salary, benefits, hours, working conditions

What CANNOT you talk about?

- Marital status

- Childcare arrangements

- Health concerns (except to inquire if applicant can perform "essential functions" of the job)

- Arrest record (except in some states for security-sensitive positions)

- Religious affiliation (except for some church-affiliated institutions, certain positions)

- Childbearing or other family concerns (Wilson, 2004)

INVITING THE CANDIDATES TO CAMPUS OR AGENCY

The personnel committee chairperson should invite the candidates for an in-person interview. Working out the dates when the faculty and possibly students will be available for interviewing is a first step. Then provide the candidates with several possible dates. Once a date has been set, send them a detailed schedule (make sure to build in some downtime). Arrange hotel accommodations and have a faculty member transport them. Take candidates out to a restaurant (and no, alcohol is never covered) that is quiet and somewhat private and invite personnel committee members to join the meal. The Personnel Committee Chairperson should collect all receipts to submit to the university/agency for reimbursement; note that these expenses should receive prior approval from the business department (typically this comes out of a recruitment line item in the budget). Inform the candidates in advance who will be interviewing them, where they will be staying, and provide them with information about the community that they may want to independently explore during their stay. Also tell candidates to keep all their receipts and how they will process them for payment (Rofuth, 2009).

For campus interviews, make sure that the candidates get a welcome package including materials from a real estate agent about housing and community strengths. Schedule breaks and let people eat–use meal time discussions and connections made over breaking bread to sell the department or school/university. Make sure that the schedule includes exposure to "selling points" such as students, libraries, sports facilities, technology labs, and so on.

Finally, it is important that the academic institution is a welcoming environment to all individuals and demonstrates an atmosphere that embraces diversity and a culture of inclusion. Promoting an environment that is welcoming and inclusive will assure that candidates find the institution appealing and increase the odds that new hires stay at the academic institution for the long haul. To increase the likelihood of candidates accepting the position, sometimes institutions have to provide added incentives such as relocation packages and offering free tuition for immediate family members.

Candidates' Presentations

Provide information to candidates on the purpose of their presentations, as decided by the committee (Rofuth, 2009). Does the committee want the candidates to

- Prove the subject has good communication skills?

- Demonstrate knowledge of a particular subject area that person might teach?

- Demonstrate that person is a scholar by presenting on a research topic?

Once these parameters are decided, tell the candidates the purpose of the presentation, the amount of time for their presentations, and the audience. Also tell them what type of computer will be available and if can they bring a jump drive; whether they should talk about their research (one study or multiple); and if the presentation will be a "mini" teaching class with students or just faculty who will evaluate their presentation and communication skills? Will there be people from other programs and from different fields? Will there be any higher-ups from the administration in attendance, such as the provost who makes the final hiring decision? For the candidate's job talk, recruit faculty, students, and staff to come to the candidate's presentation during a convenient time, such as during regularly scheduled class time for students. After the session is over, obtain input from faculty, students, and staff through the use of an evaluation form.

CANDIDATE INTERVIEWS

Candidates typically are interviewed by the search or personnel committee, the head of the program and/or dean if the program is located within a larger school or college, and the provost. The committee should prepare a detailed in-person interview questionnaire for the candidate (see Appendix 10B).

Wooing On-Site or at Work Location

Once the candidate is on-site, it is important to sell the program and how the person would fit in for teaching, research, committee work, and administration. Explain the teaching load credits. Describe the working culture and the office hours requirement and field agency visit requirements if teaching a practicum (teaching the field practicum can sometimes be worth more than one course credit). If in a unionized environment, discuss its pros and cons: how the union protects faculty job security and promotes annual wage increases; if nonunion, the pros and cons should also be discussed (Rofuth, 2009).

Show Off the Physical Environment

The physical work environment is very important to people in all fields. Show the candidate the typical office space or the actual office space that the person might inhabit. Do a tour of teaching rooms, the library, workout facility, and faculty dining. If parking is very convenient and free, talk about that (Rofuth, 2009).

Status of Technology in Classroom and in Curriculum and Expectations About Teaching Delivery Methods

Discuss the curriculum delivery options, such as percentage of on-ground, hybrid, and online courses and type of platforms used by the university. Also, if there are off-site teaching locations, describe them to new faculty and inform them if they will be expected to teach off site (Rofuth, 2009).

Tell Candidates What They Need to Know About the Program

Provide information on the basic program design and the strengths and weaknesses of the program (Rofuth, 2009). Note the next reaccreditation date and the strengths and weaknesses identified by the site team from the previous self-study report. Tell candidates about the background and specialties of the faculty and staff. Provide a general description of student demographics and student successes, such as retention, publications, and participation in governance.

Develop a list of the university's strengths along with vision and mission statements and package this material to give to candidates, both hard copy and electronic, and then verbally tell them about the strengths that your campus offer such as the following:

- Location (part of the town and suburbs and what is nearby)
- Educational opportunities (for family members and available scholarships)

- Pool of students at university (regional, national, international students)
- Libraries (especially social sciences)
- Resources (technology, space, labs, start-up funding, collaboration across departments)
- Cultural and sports events (Rittner, 2009)

Describe the uniqueness of the town and what makes it a great place to live:

- What are the strengths of the area, including the character of community and community programs and activities?
- What does the town offer, including assets of the community and how the university fits into the community?
- What are key links that can be provided that highlight specific details about the town? (Rittner, 2009)

Provide examples of town strengths such as the following:

- A great place to live
- Affordable housing
- A good biking town
- A good transportation system
- Accessible and affordable cost of living
- Arts and culture including multiple theater companies, many museums
- Great outdoors with access to the ocean and mountains nearby
- Many multicultural restaurants in town and nearby
- Great public and private schools
- Large city(ies) are nearby

HIRING

Box 10.7 displays the competencies/behaviors in this section.

BOX 10.7

NETWORK FOR SOCIAL WORK MANAGEMENT COMPETENCIES AND PRACTICE BEHAVIORS 12

Effectively manages human resources (Network for Social Work Management Competencies 12). Practice Behaviors:

In settings with Civil Service and Unions, works within existing systems to ensure that the most qualified employees are selected to carry out agency responsibilities (12.6).

There are a variety of issues that can affect the hiring process. The first issue is who should actually approve the hiring of candidates. Is the person who will directly supervise the new hire the best person to make the decision? In larger organizations and in universities, the direct supervisor usually does not make the hiring decision. This practice has its pros and cons. The biggest con is the concern whether and to what extent the person given the authority to hire the candidate really understands what the program needs in terms of the best hire.

The compensation that is offered can also have an impact on the candidate accepting or rejecting the job offer. One dilemma in civil service and union environments is that the salaries of current workers are locked in to certain yearly increases or no increases at all for several years. So when a potential hire seeks a competitive wage, it may not be available as this person might be paid more for the same job as current employees in that same job function. There is also the issue of deciding what the person should be paid based on the candidate's work history. In academia that calculation can be difficult, especially in social work when the extensive, long-term nonacademic work experiences of a candidate are sometimes not as valued as years of teaching experience (a person with this type of background might be considered a nontraditional hire in academia).

Accreditation requirements for staffing levels can have an impact on the number of faculty hired, as the CSWE requires a ratio of 25:1 for undergraduate students to faculty and 12:1 for graduate students per faculty. However, the formula for how to count part-time faculty is left up to the university. Hiring the right number of staff can also be an issue, particularly the percentage of time the program heads and coordinators devote to administrative duties. Secretarial support is also important. Hiring of secretaries should go through some of the same procedures as faculty hiring, except the presentation or job talk is not required. A rating scale for a secretary search can be found in Appendix 10C.

Affirmative Action requirements can be made available by the human resources departments in large state agencies and public universities. Information on which populations are underrepresented are available and should be considered when making hiring decisions. When making hiring decisions, the Americans with Disabilities Act (ADA) and special accommodations should also be reviewed and made available.

In making the hiring decision, a lot depends on the performance of the candidate during the interview. Some candidates perform well during an interview, but that does not mean they are the best fit for the job. Other candidates may not perform well during an interview because of nervousness, but they may be the best candidates. How good are you at making hiring decisions? Box 10.8 gives questions to ask yourself prior to conducting an interview.

BOX 10.8

COMPETENCY-BASED QUESTIONS–EXPERIENCES AS AN INTERVIEWER

How did you perform in the interview for the job you currently have?
What was the best job interview you ever had and why?
What was the worst job interview you ever had and why?
What has been your experiences when you interviewed over the phone or video? Did it go well or not? Explain.
When was the last time you interviewed someone on the phone, via video, or in person? What did you learn about the interview process from those interviews?
What would you change?
SOURCE: Modified from Wenger, L. (2014). *Hiring high performers. Workforce Performance Group.* Retrieved from https://socialworkmanager.org/wp-content/uploads/2016/05/Hiring-ppt_kbf_LW.pdf

Making the wrong hiring decisions can come back to haunt you. Fortunately, research shows that 70% of new hires are consistently satisfactory performers, 15% are superstars, but 15% are hiring mistakes (Wenger, 2014). Bad things happen when you hire the wrong people:

- Turnover is expensive and can defeat quality and quantity of work.
- Clients are dissatisfied and as a result the reputation of the organization can be ruined.

- Staff become "burned out" after taking on the new hire's responsibilities because the new hire may not complete work in a timely manner or is incompetent.

- Operational mistakes can occur, which can impact total organizational functioning.

- Investment in orientation and training is wasted on the person.

- The reputation of the organization in the community may be damaged from these actions and future funding can be negatively impacted.

Box 10.9 provides strategies to strengthen your interviewing skills.

BOX 10.9

SIXTEEN TIPS TO BECOME A BETTER INTERVIEWER

1. Remember your goal: Get as much info as possible about applicant; get behind the mask. Seek out additional information if possible, such by as talking to one of the references. Applicant's goal: Hide weak areas; get job offer.

2. An interview is not a relaxed, social conversation, and is not about developing a good relationship, at least at first. Treat the interview in a totally professional manner.

3. Be prepared for the interview; have the applicant's material in front of you along with the interview questions, which you will have perused beforehand.

4. Make sure you have a clear understanding of what the open job is about, including the specific duties the applicant will perform on the job.

5. Reduce the effect of a first impression, particularly the halo–horn effect. The influence of physical appearance can be overwhelming, but do not let it cloud your judgement, unless of course the person is dressed in a totally inappropriate manner.

6. Watch out for positive "chemistry" and discussion of similar interests, and if your gut tells you this is the right person.

7. Stay away from canned questions and be creative in following up on questions.

8. Compare the applicant's qualifications and experience to the job skills requirements, not to the rest of the applicant pool.

9. Do not ask what would you do? Ask what have you done? Ask for a specific situation, include an obstacle, and smile and nod.

10. Do not let urgency to fill this position influence your decision.

11. The applicant should talk about 80% of the time. You should be willing to wait for an answer (is the applicant uncomfortable with silence?).

12. Do not give the applicant a job description or even an agency brochure before the interview.

13. Watch for red flags such as too many jobs in too little time; poor personal hygiene; inappropriate dress; arriving late or failing to appear for appointment; vague reasons for leaving last job.

14. Listen and do not be distracted; have the interview in a quiet place where there aren't distractions.

(continued)

BOX 10.9 *(Continued)*

15. You should dress appropriately and be alert and attentive.

16. Avoid prejudgment about the applicant. And if you did have prejudgments, note how the interview has overcome them.

SOURCE: Modified from Wenger, L. (2014). *Hiring high performers. Workforce Performance Group.* Retrieved from https://socialworkmanager.org/wp-content/uploads/2016/05/Hiring-ppt_kbf_LW.pdf

There are several things you should look for in an applicant during the interview:

- Does the applicant exhibit a can-do attitude, which he or she can support by providing examples on how he or she overcame some problems in a previous job?
- Does the applicant have a passion for the work?
- Does the applicant put in the time and get things done, and like what she or he does?
- Does the applicant have the necessary skills to do the job successfully?
- Is the applicant totally overqualified, and if so, does he or she have a good explanation as to why he or she wants the job.

At the conclusion of the hiring process, all those involved should meet to discuss how the process worked and the level of satisfaction with the hire(s). If changes in the process have been identified that will improve the process, these changes should be implemented in the future. At reasonable intervals, such as 6 months and 1 year, a review of the applicant's performance should be conducted. If the new employee is not working out, steps can be taken to improve performance, and if that does not work, then termination will be required.

In conclusion, there are no perfect candidates out there; everyone will have flaws needing to be coached/mentored and areas in need of strengthening. And if you fired everyone who is flawed, there would be no employees left.

Regardless of how good a job you do making hiring decisions, employee training and development should always be available.

Selecting the Final Candidate

After all the interviews are completed, committee members should rank the candidates again using the postinterview rubric (see Appendix 10D). The committee then should discuss how to rank the candidates from first to third.

Negotiations

At universities, usually the dean or provost negotiates with the candidates. However, you can steer the candidate in the right direction in terms of salary, rank, years of service, and so on. For example, if a person is qualified, suggest they seek a higher rank or pay grade, describe who they need to impress, what points would strengthen their case, and inform them about who makes the ultimate decision. If the situation is right, you can sometimes bring a person in at a higher rank than was originally offered, assuming the advertisement stated open rank or associate or full professor (i.e., associate professor based on years and degree of experience vs. assistant professor). Ultimately, you need to prepare the candidate for the dean and provost negotiations.

Assessing the Search Process and Outcome

All searches have the potential for errors in process and decision making. It is crucial that the members of the personnel committee take an active role in evaluating and assessing the entire search process once it is completed and identify any issues that impeded the search. Examining what went well and what steps and actions could be better in the future is a first step. Identifying key processes that can be improved on and incorporated in future searches is the goal of this assessment process. In addition, written minutes of the meetings, with particular attention given to issues that arose during the search, should be passed on to the next personnel committee.

TRAINING

Training should be available to all staff and faculty. You as a manager should ask yourself, what does this individual actually need to succeed and be a better employee? Is it something that can be provided in-house, or does the employee need the time and potentially financial resources to attend a specialized training or workshop? Organizations need to also consider offering opportunities to assist staff with educational advancement (tuition reimbursement, loan forgiveness assistance, money toward continuing education units (CEUs), etc.).

PERFORMANCE ASSESSMENT

Ongoing assessment of performance is required in all organizations, both private and nonprofit agencies and universities. Information on performance assessment in universities is described later in this chapter under the Tenure and Promotion Process section. However, unless your organization forbids it, there are some basic performance assessment tenets that apply to all organizations.

Performance assessment entails staff performance evaluations, progressive discipline if necessary, promotion if eligible and earned, and terminations when necessary. Positive performance management (PPM) is a term used to describe how to improve the performance of employees through forward-looking proactive employee-centered actions and to consider negative sanctions in a positive manner. Each step in PPM looks at improving performance, except termination.

Objectives of a performance counseling interview are to

- Collect data on performance.
- Let employee be heard.
- Clarify performance rules.
- Clarify actual performance.
- Identify with employee and take corrective actions.
- Identify support and provide resources.
- Impose consequences.
- Identify follow-up consequences of continued inadequate performance.
- Notify employee of his or her right to be heard.

Staff value performance evaluations because the person being evaluated can learn about her or his superior's perceptions of the staff member's strengths and weaknesses. Evaluations are of value to the evaluator because the superior now has a documented record of the staff's performance along with suggestions on how to improve performance. The organization will benefit from the staff's improved performance as will the receivers of services. Additional values of the evaluations to the evaluator include

- Providing a periodic vehicle to call staff attention to individual and organizational mission, goals, and objectives.
- Determining how well each worker's daily activities contribute to the organization's mission, goals, and objectives.

- Providing a way to reinforce desirable behavior.
- Laying the legal groundwork for reassignment, denial of merit pay, demotion, and termination.
- Suggesting specific areas where improvement will be required (Weinbach, 1998).

Criteria for performance assessments should be predetermined by the manager, with input from the employee. It is unfair to change the rules between evaluations. The instruments and criteria should be presented and explained to the staff at the start of the meeting. Two common management errors can occur: (a) evaluating the worker using the manager as a reference point, and then (b) evaluating all aspects of the worker's performance consistent with that rating.

When conducting a performance assessment, several realistic expectations should be considered concerning the person under review, including (a) the worker's stage of career development, professional background, stated career objectives, and previous work experience, and (b) whether or not there is consensus on what is the desirable outcome of an employee's work activities and whether this outcome has been clearly stated. Other questions to be considered for a staff evaluation:

- Was the worker given good and consistent supervision and timely training?
- Was adequate clerical support provided?
- Was the worker forced to carry an unreasonably heavy load?
- Were coworkers supportive and helpful?
- Were environmental conditions impeding?
- Were there extenuating circumstances? (Weinbach, 1998).

Both hard and soft criteria can be considered when undertaking a performance assessment.

- Hard criteria: absenteeism, tardiness, initiative, conduct, job knowledge and quality, and timeliness of work
- Soft criteria: attitude, cooperativeness, adaptability, use of supervision, ability to work with peers, and value to the organization (Weinbach, 1998)

There are several rules that managers should follow to achieve good performance assessment interviews.

- Put the employee at ease.
- State the purpose of interview.
- Let the employee speak.
- Listen for content and feeling.
- Give information clearly.
- Summarize the interview.

However, there are also several barriers to good communication that managers should be aware of including

- Nonverbal ques such as space, body language, and voice.
- Verbal/semantic language such as jargon, talking up or down, using acronyms and trigger words.
- Poor listening skills.

To overcome poor listening skills, managers can engage and practice active listening that requires one to

- Not make hasty judgements.
- Resist distractions.
- Wait to respond.
- Rephrase for content.
- Reflect feelings.
- Use "lag time" and work at listening.

When employees are underperforming, progressive discipline should commence. Several steps of progressive discipline can be taken.

- Verbal reprimands should be direct, one-on-one, private, and confidential, and documented (never do group reprimands).
- Written reprimands provide a specific warning spelling out in detail what is inadequate, what is expected, and by what date.
- Transfers should be used sparingly, do not pass the problem along to someone else (Weinbach, 1998).

Discipline can be used for punishment or chastisement and result in a penalty due to negative past behavior. Rules and regulations are used for what one should or should not do. Discipline can also be used to control and enforce behavior. Use discipline in guiding and strengthening people not only toward positive, future-oriented performance but also to ensure that they have the adequate tools to move on to a more positive track. The benchmarks of corrective action plans should also be reviewed regularly to evaluate and provide feedback about the observable and measurable changes in the staff's performance.

Immediate terminations can occur in several instances, such as when gross misconduct occurs and thus termination requires no prior warning and is immediate, and when unsatisfactory work performance continues over time with several poor performance evaluations over one or more probationary periods. It is wise to schedule the termination interview at the end of the workday or week. During the interview, be direct, discuss benefits, and then finally place a confidential memo in the person's file (Weinbach, 1998). Additionally, when facilitating termination meetings, it is advisable to have a member of the human resources department participate in the meeting as well.

When creating performance rating documents, whether to evaluate staff or for staff to evaluate a manager, first identify all key aspects of the pertinent employee job description and then create a rating scale so each aspect can be rated. An example of such a scale is in Appendix 10E.

PROMOTIONS AND TERMINATIONS

Organizations may have rules and procedures for promotions and advancement that include policies on when a person can apply for a position. When there are prescribed rules for the process, there are likely committees that review promotion applications and provide the recommendation for promotion. There are sometimes, especially in academia, multiple levels for the approval process, and you must learn to be well versed in how that process works. For example, at a university the levels of review for tenure, promotion, and posttenure professional reviews can include the department evaluation committee; the department head such as dean, director, or chairperson; the dean of the school or college; the university promotion and tenure committee, the provost; and finally the president. The final decision is made by the provost and president based on all the other recommendations. State agencies sometimes operate similarly to academia, in that there is a highly formalized process for applying for promotion and standardized reviews for approving the promotion. In nonunionized agencies, there may be fewer layers to promoting individuals. There are pros and cons to all of the processes.

In considering promotions, most managers should use information on whether outside constraints such as labor unions rules, seniority, and AA play a role; whether promoting from within would be of value to the organization or not; whether past performance is any indicator of future performance and the likelihood that the staff person can take on a more advanced role; whether personal characteristics such as initiative, intelligence, conceptual abilities, problem-solving skills, integrity, communication skills, and commitment to the organization's goals will make a difference; and finally will this promotion benefit the organization (Weinbach, 1998).

Similarly, the rules of termination will slightly vary depending on a few factors, including whether or not the organization is unionized and, to some extent, the workplace culture. The rules, of course, can and should only vary as much as the laws set forth by the Department of Labor. Whenever an employment agency is considering termination, there are multiple factors that will likely invade the decision-making process. Some of these include (a) Will the position be refilled? (b) How will this termination impact staff morale? (c) Would the termination be upheld in a labor law dispute case? There is a loss of investment whenever there is staff turnover, and it is therefore best to always try to work with the employee and provide her or him with the tools needed to improve performance. However, sometimes it is unrealistic or impossible for the employee to improve performance and you may be faced with no other alternative than to terminate the employee. When this is the case, you need to ensure that you have robust documentation, have reviewed the labor laws, and have attempted to professionally counsel the employee and can demonstrate a clear lack of improvement. Try to separate with the employee in a way that is neutral/emotion-free.

TIPS ON RETAINING AND PROMOTING FACULTY AT UNIVERSITIES

Supporting new faculty during their early years will make a big difference in the long run if they are to succeed in obtaining tenure and promotion. Some recommendations include

- Providing less of a teaching load if possible (possibly reduce the load by one to two courses in the first semester).
- Offering multiple sections of the same course.
- Scheduling them to teach field courses, which can provide a way to integrate theory and practice and to better understand the curriculum and are sometimes the equivalent of two courses.
- Not putting them in a course they have never taught before (at least without a mentor and a lot of support) (Rofuth, 2009).

When assigning mentors, provide faculty mentors who can relate to new faculty members as persons. Furthermore, the academic head should

- Share with the new faculty course syllabi and teaching methodologies.
- Send them to hi-tech training so they are familiar with all the computer programs their university uses for teaching and administration.
- Make sure they get a computer right away and all of their account information.
- Not overburden them with committee assignments.
- Suggest that the faculty member joins one university-wide committee (so that the faculty member will become known throughout the university, which will help during future promotion and tenure) (Rofuth, 2009).

Help new faculty members with their creativity and research by

- Suggesting they publish an article on their dissertation or some piece of it.
- Setting up a meeting with the university's sponsored research office.
- Letting the faculty know about all internal grants and opportunities, such as small summer grants, curriculum development grants, and so on.
- Including the new faculty on a grant you personally are working on.
- Offering to work on a grant with them in an area of their interests and tell them who in the university might have a similar research interest.
- Providing contacts from local organizations that need research assistance (Rofuth, 2009).

Finally, make sure new faculty are aware of any new faculty programs at the university and opportunities for community involvement.

- Provide the names of local organizations seeking board members.
- Have new faculty orientations for all faculty members hired across the campus (Rofuth, 2009).

SUPPORTING ESTABLISHED FACULTY

Some of the same steps taken to support new employees should be used to support established faculty as well. However, a few more steps are applicable to faculty who have been at the university for some time, particularly those still pursuing tenure and promotion.

Tenure and Promotion Process

Tips for working with faculty on the tenure and promotion process:

- Make sure faculty understand the tenure and promotion process and direct them to the website of the university that explains the process.
- Explain how the process works and what is required.
- Strongly suggest they go to presentations that are sponsored by the university's promotion and tenure committee.
- Share with faculty members extra departmental requirements or standards.
- Tell faculty going through the process what type of language and expectations you typically put in your letter of support.
- Negotiate with the dean or other higher level administrator on what the faculty member will need to be successful.
- Make sure everyone understands the expected outcomes each year (Rofuth, 2009).

Provide technical support to faculty on building a personal file by describing

- How to begin to develop a good file.
- What are the attributes of a good file.
- How to build a first-year file, second-year file, and files thereafter.

- What format is required by the university.
- What content should go in what area of the file.
- How to save and add all the student teaching evaluations to the file.
- How to save and add letters of support.
- How to document all work, including committee work, research, publications, classes taught, conferences attended, community work, and so on (Rofuth, 2009).

Different types of schools have different expectations for promotion and tenure.

- Large research universities with doctoral programs can require yearly publications, obtaining grants but teaching less.
- Programs that have both MSW and BSW programs may require publishing consistently and showing a progression and excellent teaching reviews.
- Single MSW or BSW programs may have expectations similar to combined programs.
- However, universities may have differing expectations at all levels (Rofuth, 2009).

PROMOTION PROCESS FOR AGENCIES

The promotion process within human and social service agencies will vary depending on whether or not there is a union, and whether there is an established organizational culture that influences the promotion process. For unionized agencies, the process of promotion is analogous to academic processes in that there may be a highly structured application and review process. Some agencies treat promotion applications as they would new hires, where the position is formally posted and employees must submit an application, updated resume, and complete online materials (i.e., course completion and test results in some instances). The employee is then interviewed for the position, and the interviewing team (i.e., personnel committee) asks the same questions of each applicant and scores the answers, using promotion application materials to guide their decision. There may be multiple rounds of interviewing, and previous performance evaluations are taken into consideration.

Some agencies adopt a culture where the employee is selected to step into a promotional position. This type of appointment typically only occurs in nonunionized agencies. Selecting the employee to step into a promotional position may occur because of organizational restructuring, that is, the creation of a new position or the transfer of an employee which then leaves another higher ranking position vacant, or when new programs are being developed and a person who has been working on the implementation is the best fit to step into the role of leading or managing the program. Adopting a less formal process to promoting employees can have many pros, including expediting the process; however, quick appointments can also create some disadvantages to the agency culture if staff perceive that the opportunities for advancement have benefited a select few, rather than providing equal opportunities for all to apply for promotional positions. Some nonunionized agencies only adopt this practice when they know that the internal pool of candidates qualified for the position is extremely limited and may have other growth opportunities in mind for the few employees that might be in that pool of qualified professionals. Thus, they do not use this selective approach to fill other, entry or mid-level, positions within the agency. It is important that leaders recognize when using this approach that there may be negative feelings evoked in staff as a result of this practice, and leaders need to be willing to adjust the promotion process in order to preserve staff morale.

DISCRIMINATION

BOX 10.10

NETWORK FOR SOCIAL WORK MANAGEMENT COMPETENCIES AND PRACTICE BEHAVIOR 12

Effectively manages human resources (Network for Social Work Management Competencies 12). Practice Behaviors:

Creates, maintains, and fosters a discrimination- and harassment-free work environment for employees, clients, and general public (12.4).

Box 10.10 displays the competencies/behaviors in this section. Discrimination and harassment can occur in the workplace because of the diversity of the people who work there. Primary forms of diversity cannot be changed (i.e., age, ethnicity, disabilities, sexual orientation, and gender) and secondary types of diversity reflect choices people make (i.e., marital status, parental status, religious affiliation, and work experience; Weinbach, 1998). Diversity or lack of diversity in the workplace can play a role both in increased conflict and incidents of discrimination and harassment. Universities are required to follow Title IX regulations and must train responsible employees regarding reporting mandates.

Box 10.11 is an example of a student reporting to a faculty member that another faculty member is sexually harassing female students.

BOX 10.11

COMPETENCY-BASED EXAMPLE: A CASE OF HARASSMENT

You are a faculty member and a student asks to speak with you after class. She has seemed withdrawn and preoccupied of late, which is uncharacteristic. The student begins to tell you that she feels very uncomfortable in one of her other classes because the professor has made sexually inappropriate comments to several female students on a number of occasions. She reports that during the last class, the professor asked her where she likes to go out, and if she ever goes out to have after-class drinks with friends. The student explains that she is unsure of what the professor intended, but that she is certain that she feels very uncomfortable in that particular class.

If you were the faculty this is being reported to

1. How would you respond to the student?
2. What information would you want to provide the student with?
3. What will you do with this information now?

Box 10.12 lists questions about diversity and harassment.

BOX 10.12

COMPETENCY-BASED DIVERSITY AND HARASSMENT QUESTIONS

Will situations in which the organizational climate for diversity is unfavorable foster conflict?
How can increased diversity influence the workplace?
What types of harassment have you witnessed in the workplace?

Discrimination can impact managers in many ways. Managers' ability to recognize discrimination is essential for good management practice. Discrimination can take many forms, including a lack of informal social contacts within the organization, withholding of critical information to function in the job, lack of promotion opportunities, wage disparities, and stereotyping people.

Informal social contacts with managers/peers exist in many organizations and some staff do not have access to these informal contacts due to not belonging to any particular group or clique. Managers should attempt to get groups together informally instead of just letting them form on their own.

Managers should also make sure that everyone has the same information about current events and issues, and if a staff person is working on a project, the person should be given access to all the necessary information.

Access to promotion may be limited to certain groups or stereotypes of people. Managers should make sure that all staff know about promotion opportunities and are encouraged to apply.

In many organizations, males are still offered higher starting salaries than females and higher pay raises and/or bonuses. All new employees should be given the same consideration in terms of starting salary, especially when multiple people are starting in the same job. Furthermore, new hires should be paid the appropriate starting wage regardless of what other currently employed staff are paid. Erroneous stereotypes can exist in all organizations and managers should not let these stereotypes impact any decision on job assignments, wages, and promotions.

Clients and the general public should also be treated in the same way in terms of information sharing and protection against stereotypical behaviors of the staff.

Workplace harassment and bullying can take place at any time and in any setting. Requiring staff to complete mandatory training on harassment will at least educate people on the negative impacts of it and how to recognize it when it occurs. Reporting of incidents should be made to superiors, whether the person reporting is positive or not harassment actually occurred.

BOX 10.13

NETWORK FOR SOCIAL WORK MANAGEMENT COMPETENCIES AND PRACTICE BEHAVIORS 5 AND 12

Manages diversity and cross-cultural understanding (Network for Social Work Management Competencies 5). Practice Behaviors
    Seeks to employ a diverse workforce to align with clients served by the organization (5.3).
Effectively manages human resources (Network for Social Work Management Competencies 12). Practice Behaviors:
    Successfully recruits and retains a diversity of employees to reflect the communities and constituencies served by the organization (12.5).

Box 10.13 displays the competencies/behaviors in this section. It is helpful if leaders understand their clients and staff in terms of demographics and have a well-informed understanding of client and staff needs. Understanding of clients and staff is critical because it provides insight into what they desire, what they can relate to, and what type of culture they will gravitate to or seek out. As we discuss in other chapters, diversity in the workforce is a catalyst for enhanced productivity, creativity, and can significantly improve performance measures. Diversity in the workforce also brings unique perspectives and awareness of the needs and barriers to working with diverse client populations. For instance, in a social service agency having multilingual staff may result in the capacity to serve more clients. In academia, diversity can help to represent the student population and result in more students feeling drawn to a program that represents diversity. Asking how do the vision/mission/values reflect cultural understanding that appeals to clients and to potential employee candidates can reveal important information about how your organizational culture embraces and promotes a diverse workforce.

REEXAMINING AND CHANGING HIRING BIASES

When making final hiring decisions, the committee should look at the candidate's holistic achievements and avoid biased decision making that is narrowly focused only on where the candidate obtained educational degrees and recent employment (Mickelson & Oliver, 1991). The candidate should be evaluated based on what she or he has produced and achieved, how successful her or his job talk was, and how well-suited she or he is for the position. Try to avoid the common mistake of hiring faculty who look just like others in the department (Light, 1994).

After faculty are hired, the level of support they receive will determine if they will stay. And you do not want to get a reputation that newly hired faculty leave after a short period of time.

Bailey, Pearlmutter, and Sable (2015) created a long list of strategies to recruit and retain faculty of color (see Appendix 10F).

In order to be effective, Latino recruitment and retention within social work education requires an intentional integrative, comprehensive strategy sustained over time. Considerations of such a strategy need to include a number of factors (Ortiz & Hernández, 2012):

- The culture and nuance of academia is socially constructed and often foreign to Latino/a students and faculty.
- Beyond teaching, research, and scholarship, doctoral programs need to socialize students to the culture of academia.
- Create a safe environment at the college/university that respects Latino culture and sufficient role models to serve as mentors.
- Determine if there are factors in the admission process, or at other points, that seem to trip up Latino/a students.
- Find ways to integrate student services with academics that are more holistic and organic and consistent with Latino culture.
- Assess curriculum for relevancy to culturally and contextually appropriate practice behaviors for working with Latino/as.
- Evaluate the learning environment–implicit curriculum–for its welcoming of Latino/a students.
- Develop a multifaceted mentoring program that includes alumni practitioners, field instructors, and faculty (even if outside the department/school).

■ Mentoring should focus on the individual's strengths and contributions rather than on deficiencies. Latino/as are often reluctant to participate in mentoring if it is perceived that they are somehow deficient or less capable.

■ Avoid having Latino/a faculty become "projects" (Ortiz & Hernández, 2012).

BOX 10.14

NETWORK FOR SOCIAL WORK MANAGEMENT COMPETENCIES AND PRACTICE BEHAVIORS 12

Effectively manages human resources (Network for Social Work Management Competencies 12). Practice Behaviors:

In settings with Civil Service and Unions, works within existing systems to ensure that the most qualified employees are selected to carry out agency responsibilities (12.6).

Box 10.14 displays the competencies/behaviors in this section. Civil service and union environments have specific rules and procedures for conducting job searches. Universities will frequently advertise all job openings in the university in combined ads. Creating the job descriptions in conjunction with and with approval of the human resources office is usually required. HR requirements will typically not rule out the most qualified candidates for jobs, but they may restrict the size of the pool. Creating rating rubrics with the approval of the human resources office will also assure that the most qualified candidates are hired (see Appendices 10A, 10C, and 10D; Rofuth, 2009).

There are advantages for people hired in civil service and union environments, such as more job security, wage increases in most years, and health insurance coverage for the employee and family. These benefits can serve as good recruiting pitches to the most qualified candidates and candidates from diverse backgrounds.

SUMMARY

Throughout this chapter, we discussed human resource functions, including job designs and processes of recruitment, hiring, and promoting staff. Examples of rubrics that can be modified to fit academic and service agencies are provided to create an objective scoring card for candidates based on the job description and requirements. This chapter also examined critical employment relation policies and delineated the laws that organizations must adhere to. Organizations that understand, respect, and live by nondiscriminatory practices can create a workplace environment that is free of harassment, racism, and microaggressions. It is vital that leaders and managers understand the labor laws, AA rules, and EEO rules and promote an atmosphere that values inclusion of diverse people.

ACTIVITIES

1. Describe the diversity that exists within your organization or student community. Are the agency's managers and staff representative of the client population? Or is the college/university's faculty representative of the student population?

   a. How could this agency or academic institution create greater diversity among managers/faculty?

2. Practice creating a job description.

   a. Use a current, previous, or ideal role that you have held, or would like to someday hold, and outline what the requirements and preferred qualifications are for the position.

   b. Describe the tasks that are essential functions of the job.

   c. Note any additional tasks that may be asked of the employee, which should be included in the job description.

   d. Describe the reporting structure for the position.

   e. Provide an overview of the organization and program. Hint: What would make this an appealing place to work? What are some of the benefits? What type of organization does this seem to be?

REFERENCES

Bailey, D., Pearlmutter, S., & Sable, M. (2015). *Strategies for recruiting and retaining faculty of color.* Paper presented at the NADD Spring Conference, San Diego, CA.

Licata, C., Rudnicki, W., Logan, S., & Gross, A. (2004). *Feedback for administrators: Adding value to the evaluation/development process.* Twenty-First Annual Academic Chairpersons Conference. Adams Mark Hotel. Orlando, FL.

Light, P. (1994). Diversity in the faculty "not like us": Moving barriers to minority recruitment. *Journal of Policy Analysis and Management, 13*(1), 163–186.

Mickelson, R. A., & Oliver, M. L. (1991). Making the short list: Black candidates and the faculty recruitment process. In P. G. Altbach & K. Lomotey (Eds.), *The racial crisis in America higher education* (pp. 149–166). Albany, NY: SUNY Press.

Ortiz, L., & Hernández, S. H. (2012, April). *Recruiting and sustaining Latino faculty and students.* Paper presented at the National Association of Deans and Directors Spring Conference, Marriott Hotel, Fort Lauderdale.

Rittner, B. (2009, March 18). *Branding & marketing to potential faculty.* The Association of Baccalaureate Social Work Program Directors (BPD) Annual Meeting. Power point presentation, Scottsdale, AZ.

Rofuth, T. (2009, March 18). *Human resources in BSW programs.* The Association of Baccalaureate Social Work Program Directors (BPD) Annual Meeting. Power point presentation, Scottsdale, AZ.

Springer, A. (2006). *How to diversify the faculty.* American Association of University Professors. Washington, DC.

Weinbach, R. W. (1998). *The social worker as manager: A practical guide to success* (3rd ed.). Needham Heights, MA: Allyn and Bacon.

Wenger, L. (2014). *Hiring high performers. Workforce Performance Group.* Retrieved from https://socialworkmanager.org/wp-content/uploads/2016/05/Hiring-ppt_kbf_LW.pdf

Wilson, L. V. (2004). *Avoiding lawsuits in higher education: Risk management strategies for academic administrators.* Paper presented at the 21st Annual Academic Chairperson Conference, Adams Mark Hotel, Orlando, FL.

APPENDIX 10A: PREINTERVIEW RUBRIC

Preinterview Clinical Position

Rating Scale:
The following six-point scale is used to rate the candidate on each criterion. The rating score is multiplied by the weight for that criterion for the total points.
(0) No Pass: Applicant's experience and training are below that which would be considered qualifying for this factor. Candidate's background clearly falls below minimum acceptable standards for the job. Applicant's description reveals serious deficiencies in experience and/or training in important areas of the factor, or across the breadth of the factor. A rating of zero (0) in a key factor may disqualify a candidate from further consideration.
(1) Low Pass: Applicant's experience and training indicate that she or he possesses the factor at a level that is minimally acceptable for the job. Candidate's description shows experience and/or training which adequately covers the most important aspect of the factor.
(2) Between Low Pass and Pass: Applicant's experience and training indicate that she or he possesses the factor at a level that is between minimally acceptable to satisfactory for the job. Candidate's description shows experience and/or training which is more than adequate but less than full coverage of the most important aspect of the factor.
(3) Pass: Applicant's experience and training indicate that she or he possesses the factor at a level that is satisfactory for the job. Candidate's description shows experience and/or training covering the important areas of the factor.
(4) Between Pass and High: Applicant's experience and training indicate that she or he possesses the factor between satisfactory and at or above the level for the job. Candidate's description shows experience and/or training between covering the important areas of the factor to a deep or broad experience and/or training across all areas of the factor.
(5) High Pass: Applicant's experience and training indicate that she or he clearly possesses the factor at or above the level required for top performance on the job. Candidate's description indicates deep or broad experience and/or training across all areas of the factor.

PREINTERVIEW CLINICAL POSITION RUBRIC

STEP ONE: Initial Screening—Candidate must get a YES for all three of these categories in order to undergo further consideration.

Criteria	As measured by	Weight	NAME:	
			Score	Total (Score × Weight)
Must possess MSW (accredited program)	Yes or No	No weights		
		(Required)		
Doctoral degree by (date)	Yes or No	No weights		
		(Required)		
Minimum 2 years post-MSW practice experience	Yes or No	No weights		
		(Required)		

(continued)

Preinterview Clinical Position *(Continued)*

PREINTERVIEW CLINICAL POSITION RUBRIC				
STEP TWO: *Committee–If candidate passes initial screening, then full committee will review and rank application using the following criteria.*				
Criteria	As measured by	Weight	NAME:	
			Score	Total (Score × Weight)
SCHOLARSHIP AND CREATIVE ACTIVITY				
Capacity to produce peer-reviewed scholarship	Range of peer-reviewed scholarship, works in progress, scholarly agenda, other	10 (Required)		0
Record of empirical research and scholarship/creative activity	Number and types of peer-reviewed scholarship, works in progress, scholarly agenda, other	8 (Preferred)		0
TEACHING				
Demonstrated potential for excellence in teaching	As expressed in letter of interest, interviews, or presentation (i.e., teaching philosophy, teaching strategies, examples of effectiveness), student or faculty evaluations, letters of support, other	10 (Required)		0
Two or more years teaching social work at undergraduate and/or graduate levels	Number of years teaching	5 (Preferred)		0
CLINCIAL PRACTICE				
Effectiveness in working with diverse populations	Range or types of experiences (such as teaching, research, practice, community involvement), areas of expertise, examples of effectiveness, other	8 (Preferred)		0
Clinical practice experience in one or more of C&F, MHSA, SSWK, OA, or related fields	Range or types of clinical practice experiences, areas of expertise, future agenda, other	8 (Preferred)		0
LCSW or equivalent social work license	Yes or No	8 (Preferred)		0

(continued)

Preinterview Clinical Position *(Continued)*

OTHER APPLICATION ITEMS				
Quality of letter of interest	Demonstrates knowledge and interest in position, qualifications, and strong written communication skills	10 (Required)		0
Strength of letter 1	High recommendation from supervisor or colleague	4 (Required)		0
Strength of letter 2	High recommendation from supervisor or colleague	4 (Required)		0
Strength of letter 3	High recommendation from supervisor or colleague	4 (Required)		0
TOTALS			0	0

C&F, Children and Family; MHSA, Mental Health and Substance Abuse; OA, older adults/elders; SSWK, School Social Work.

Preinterview Policy Position

Rating Scale:
The following six-point scale is used to rate the candidate on each criterion. The rating score is multiplied by the weight for that criterion for the total points.
(0) No Pass: Applicant's experience and training are below that which would be considered qualifying for this factor. Candidate's background clearly falls below minimum acceptable standards for the job. Applicant's description reveals serious deficiencies in experience and/or training in important areas of the factor, or across the breadth of the factor. A rating of zero (0) in a key factor may disqualify a candidate from further consideration.
(1) Low Pass: Applicant's experience and training indicate that she or he possesses the factor at a level that is minimally acceptable for the job. Candidate's description shows experience and/or training which adequately covers the most important aspect of the factor.
(2) Between Low Pass and Pass: Applicant's experience and training indicate that she or he possesses the factor at a level that is between minimally acceptable to satisfactory for the job. Candidate's description shows experience and/or training which is more than adequate but less than full coverage of the most important aspect of the factor.
(3) Pass: Applicant's experience and training indicate that she or he possesses the factor at a level that is satisfactory for the job. Candidate's description shows experience and/or training covering the important areas of the factor.
(4) Between Pass and High: Applicant's experience and training indicate that she or he possesses the factor between satisfactory and at or above the level for the job. Candidate's description shows experience and/or training between covering the important areas of the factor to a deep or broad experience and/or training across all areas of the factor.
(5) High Pass: Applicant's experience and training indicate that she or he clearly possesses the factor at or above the level required for top performance on the job. Candidate's description indicates deep or broad experience and/or training across all areas of the factor.

(continued)

Preinterview Policy Position *(Continued)*

PREINTERVIEW POLICY POSITION RUBRIC				
STEP ONE: Initial Screening–Candidate must get a YES for all three of these categories in order to undergo further consideration.				
Criteria	As measured by	Weight	NAME:	
			Score	Total (Score × Weight)
Must possess MSW (accredited program)	Yes or No	No weights		
		(Required)		
Doctoral degree by (date)	Yes or No	No weights		
		(Required)		
Minimum 2 years post MSW practice experience	Yes or No	No weights		
		(Required)		

PREINTERVIEW POLICY POSITION RUBRIC				
STEP TWO: Committee–If candidate passes initial screening, then full committee will review and rank application using the following criteria.				
Criteria	As measured by	Weight	NAME:	
			Score	Total (Score × Weight)
SCHOLARSHIP AND CREATIVE ACTIVITY				
Capacity to produce peer-reviewed scholarship	Range of peer-reviewed scholarship, works in progress, scholarly agenda, other	10 (Required)		0
Record of scholarship/creative activity	Range of peer-reviewed scholarship, policy proposal or evaluations, works in progress, scholarly agenda, other	8 (Preferred)		0
TEACHING				
Demonstrated potential for excellence in teaching	As expressed in letter of interest, interviews, or presentation (i.e., teaching philosophy, teaching strategies, examples of effectiveness), student or faculty evaluations, letters of support, other	10 (Required)		0

(continued)

Preinterview Policy Position (Continued)

Two or more years teaching social work at undergraduate and/or graduate levels	Number of years teaching	5 (Preferred)		0
POLICY PRACTICE				
Effectiveness in working with diverse populations	Range or types of experiences (such as teaching, research, practice, community involvement), areas of expertise, examples of effectiveness, other	8 (Preferred)		0
Community and/or policy practice experience	Range or types of practice experiences, areas of expertise, examples of effectiveness, other	8 (Preferred)		0
OTHER APPLICATION ITEMS				
Quality of letter of interest	Demonstrates knowledge and interest in position, qualifications, and strong written communication skills	10 (Required)		0
Strength of letter 1	High recommendation from supervisor or colleague	4 (Required)		0
Strength of letter 2	High recommendation from supervisor or colleague	4 (Required)		0
Strength of letter 3	High recommendation from supervisor or colleague	4 (Required)		0
TOTALS			0	0

Preinterview DSW Position

Rating Scale:
The following six-point scale is used to rate the candidate on each criterion. The criterion rating score is multiplied by the weight for that criterion\a for the total points.
(0) No Pass: Applicant's experience and training are below that which would be considered qualifying for this factor. Candidate's background clearly falls below minimum acceptable standards for the job. Applicant's description reveals serious deficiencies in experience and/or training in important areas of the factor, or across the breadth of the factor. A rating of zero (0) in a key factor may disqualify a candidate from further consideration.
(1) Low Pass: Applicant's experience and training indicate that she or he possesses the factor at a level that is minimally acceptable for the job. Candidate's description shows experience and/or training which adequately covers the most important aspect of the factor.
(2) Between Low Pass and Pass: Applicant's experience and training indicate that she or he possesses the factor at a level that is between minimally acceptable to satisfactory for the job. Candidate's description shows experience and/or training which is more than adequate but less than full coverage of the most important aspect of the factor.

(continued)

Preinterview DSW Position *(Continued)*

(3) Pass: Applicant's experience and training indicate that she or he possesses the factor at a level that is satisfactory for the job. Candidate's description shows experience and/or training fully covering the important areas of the factor.
(4) Between Pass and High: Applicant's experience and training indicate that she or he possesses the factor between satisfactory and at or above the level for the job. Candidate's description shows experience and/or training between covering the important areas of the factor to a deep or broad experience and/or training across all areas of the factor.
(5) High Pass: Applicant's experience and training indicate that she or he clearly possesses the factor at or above the level required for top performance on the job. Candidate's description indicates deep or broad experience and/or training across all areas of the factor.

PREINTERVIEW DSW POSITION RUBRIC

STEP ONE: Initial Screening–Candidate must get a YES for all three of these categories in order to undergo further consideration.

Criteria	As measured by	Weight	NAME:	
			Score	Total (Score × Weight)
Must possess MSW (accredited program)	Yes or No	No weights		
		(Required)		
Doctoral degree by (date)	Yes or No	No weights		
		(Required)		
Minimum 2 years post-MSW practice experience	Yes or No	No weights		
		(Required)		

PREINTERVIEW DSW POSITION RUBRIC

STEP TWO: Committee–If candidate passes initial screening, then full committee will review and rank application using the following criteria.

Criteria	As measured by	Weight	NAME:	
			Score	Total (Score × Weight)
SCHOLARSHIP AND CREATIVE ACTIVITY				
Record of peer-reviewed scholarship	Number and types of peer-reviewed scholarship, works in progress, scholarly agenda, other	10 (Required)		0
Record of empirical research and scholarship/creative activity	Number and types of peer-reviewed scholarship, works in progress, scholarly agenda, other	8 (Preferred)		0

(continued)

Preinterview DSW Position *(Continued)*

TEACHING				
Demonstrated excellence in teaching	As expressed in letter of interest, interviews, or presentation (i.e., teaching philosophy, teaching strategies, examples of effectiveness), student or faculty evaluations, letters of support, other	10 (Required)		0
Two or more years teaching social work at graduate level	Number of years teaching	5 (Preferred)		0
Online teaching experience	Range and types of online teaching and delivery methods, online curricular development, advanced training in online teaching (e.g., quality matters), other	8 (Preferred)		0
CLINCIAL/LEADERSHIP/MANAGEMENT PRACTICE				
Effectiveness in working with diverse populations	Range or types of experiences, areas of expertise, examples of effectiveness, other	8 (Preferred)		0
Clinical practice experience	Range or types of clinical practice experiences, areas of expertise, future agenda, other	8 (Preferred)		0
Leadership/ management experience	Range or types of leadership experiences, areas of expertise in leadership, future agenda, other	8 (Preferred)		0
OTHER APPLICATION ITEMS				
Quality of letter of interest	Demonstrates knowledge and interest in position, qualifications, and strong written communication skills	10 (Required)		0
Strength of letter 1	High recommendation from supervisor or colleague	4 (Required)		0
Strength of letter 2	High recommendation from supervisor or colleague	4 (Required)		0
Strength of letter 3	High recommendation from supervisor or colleague	4 (Required)		0
TOTALS			0	0

APPENDIX 10B: IN-PERSON FACULTY INTERVIEW QUESTIONS

INTERVIEW QUESTIONS

First, briefly introduce the personnel committee.

The personnel committee chair will state that the committee members will ask a series of questions and will be taking notes. Committee chair also will let the applicant know that there will be an opportunity for the candidate to ask additional questions. (The bolded questions are the same as from the preliminary interview questions.)

1. **There is often a disconnect between what students learn in their classes and what they experience in the field. How do you help them bridge that gap?**
2. How would you characterize your relationships with students?
3. How have you dealt with difficult students? Or students who are struggling?
4. **Would you give some examples of the types of assignments that you use and your thoughts about the relationship between assignments and students' learning styles?**
5. What type of clinical, policy, or management/leadership experiences and skills do you bring to teaching?
6. What type of courses would you ideally like to teach?
7. What have been your online teaching experiences? (Doctoral position)
8. What program do you prefer to teach in and what courses? (Clinical and Policy)
9. What is your philosophy on how to improve student writing?
10. **What do you hope students will learn in their social work education both on the BSW and MSW levels? (and Doctoral)?**
11. **In what ways have you worked with and supported diverse communities and students? What particular strategies have you used?**
12. How would you incorporate cultural competencies and sensitivity into your courses?
13. How would you be involved in the community here?
14. **What has been a significant, formative experience in your development as a social worker?**
15. What are you passionate about? What interests you?
16. We have all had a lot of successes in our lives, but we have had some things that we have learned from as well, so what are some of those?
17. If I were to talk to a group of people who have worked with you in different roles, what would they say that is good about you, and then, what are the two things they would change about you?
18. Tell me who your favorite boss was and why.
19. In your previous jobs, what successes are you really proud of?
20. How would one of your peers describe you?
21. **What prompted you to pursue a career as an (social work) academic?**
22. Please describe your scholarly interests and research agenda.
23. What type of grants would you like to work on?

24. Why are you interested in this position?

25. Why do you want to come to this department or organization?

26. What do you like about our mission?

27. **In what university and departmental committee work or other forms of university service would you hope to participate?**

28. What type of collaborative work have you been involved in?

29. **Professors are often called upon to perform administrative tasks. Describe a challenging administrative task you have performed in a work setting.**

30. **What are the unique qualities that you will bring to this job?**

31. What type of new ideas would you bring to our faculty?

32. What do you do when you fail? Tell me an example of something you thought was a great idea and why it did not work. What did you learn about why it failed?

33. What was the best leadership experience you have had?

34. Do you see yourself as a leader?

35. **What questions do you have for us?**

APPENDIX 10C: SECRETARY POSTINTERVIEW RUBRIC

Rating Scale:
The following six-point scale is used to rate the candidate on each criterion. The rating score is multiplied by the weight for that criterion for the total points.
(0) No Pass: Applicant's experience and training are below that which would be considered qualifying for this factor. Candidate's background clearly falls below minimum acceptable standards for the job. Applicant's description reveals serious deficiencies in experience and/or training in important areas of the factor, or across the breadth of the factor. A rating of zero (0) in a key factor may disqualify a candidate from further consideration.
(1) Low Pass: Applicant's experience and training indicate that she or he possesses the factor at a level that is minimally acceptable for the job. Candidate's description shows experience and/or training which adequately covers the most important aspect of the factor.
(2) Between Low Pass and Pass: Applicant's experience and training indicate that she or he possesses the factor at a level that is between minimally acceptable to satisfactory for the job. Candidate's description shows experience and/or training which is more than adequate but less than full coverage of the most important aspect of the factor.
(3) Pass: Applicant's experience and training indicate that she or he possesses the factor at a level that is satisfactory for the job. Candidate's description shows experience and/or training covering the important areas of the factor.
(4) Between Pass and High: Applicant's experience and training indicate that she or he possesses the factor between satisfactory and at or above the level for the job. Candidate's description shows experience and/or training between covering the important areas of the factor to a deep or broad experience and/or training across all areas of the factor.
(5) High Pass: Applicant's experience and training indicate that she or he clearly possesses the factor at or above the level required for top performance on the job. Candidate's description indicates deep or broad experience and/or training across all areas of the factor.
POSTINTERVIEW SECRETARIAL POSITION RUBRIC
STEP ONE: Initial Screening–Candidate must get a YES for all three of these categories in order to undergo further consideration.

Criteria	As measured by	Weight	NAME:	
			Score	Total (Score × Weight)
Three years' experience beyond routine clerk level in office support or secretary experience	Yes or No	No weights		
		(Required)		
One year of the general experience must have been at secretary 1 or equivalent	Yes or No	No weights		
		(Required)		

(continued)

Secretary Postinterview Rubric (Continued)

College training in the secretarial sciences may be substituted for the general experiences on the basis of 15 semester hours equaling 1/2 year of experience to a maximum of 2 years				

POSTINTERVIEW SECRETARIAL POSITION RUBRIC				

STEP TWO: Committee–If candidate passes initial screening, then full committee will review and rank application using the following criteria.

Criteria	As measured by	Weight	NAME:	
			Score	Total (Score × Weight)
PREFERRED QUALIFICATIONS				
Designs and creates fillable PDF forms	Example of PDF forms created	10 (Preferred)		0
Documents policies and procedures	Reports, flow charts, and spreadsheets produced	10 (Preferred)		0
Handles web page management via content management	Examples provided	10 (Preferred)		0
KNOWLEDGE, SKILL, AND ABILITY				
Considerable knowledge of office systems and procedures		10		0
Considerable knowledge of proper grammar, punctuation, and spelling		8		0
Knowledge of business communications		5		0
Knowledge of department's/unit's policies and procedures		5		0

(continued)

Secretary Postinterview Rubric *(Continued)*

Some knowledge of business math		6		0
Interpersonal skills		7		0
Ability to schedule and prioritize office workflow		7		0
Ability to operate office equipment, including computers and other electronic equipment		8		0
Ability to operate OfficeSuite software		8		0
Ability to take notes (shorthand, speedwriting, or other acceptable method)		7		0
OTHER				
Effectiveness in working with diverse populations	Range or types of experiences, areas of expertise, examples of effectiveness, other	5		0
Effectiveness in working in a union environment	Range or types of experiences, areas of expertise, examples of effectiveness, other	5		0
Familiarity with program expressed interest in	Interview	5		0
Management and organizational skills	Interview	5		0
Ability to work independently	Interview	5		0
Ability to be proactive	Interview	5		0
Ability to handle difficult situations	Interview	6		0
Oral/verbal communication skills	Interview	7		0
Written communication skills	Interview	7		0
Professionalism	Interview	7		0
TOTALS			0	0

APPENDIX 10D: POSTINTERVIEW RUBRICS

Postinterview DSW Position

Rating Scale:
The following six-point scale is used to rate the candidate on each criterion. The rating score is multiplied by the weight for that criteria for the total points.
(0) No Pass: Applicant's experience and training are below that which would be considered qualifying for this factor. Candidate's background clearly falls below minimum acceptable standards for the job. Applicant's description reveals serious deficiencies in experience and/or training in important areas of the factor, or across the breadth of the factor. A rating of zero (0) in a key factor may disqualify a candidate from further consideration.
(1) Low Pass: Applicant's experience and training indicate that she or he possesses the factor at a level that is minimally acceptable for the job. Candidate's description shows experience and/or training which adequately covers the most important aspect of the factor.
(2) Between Low Pass and Pass: Applicant's experience and training indicate that she or he possesses the factor at a level that is between minimally acceptable to satisfactory for the job. Candidate's description shows experience and/or training which is more than adequate but less than full coverage of the most important aspect of the factor.
(3) Pass: Applicant's experience and training indicate that she or he possesses the factor at a level that is satisfactory for the job. Candidate's description shows experience and/or training covering the important areas of the factor.
(4) Between Pass and High: Applicant's experience and training indicate that she or he possesses the factor between satisfactory and at or above the level for the job. Candidate's description shows experience and/or training between covering the important areas of the factor to a deep or broad experience and/or training across all areas of the factor.
(5) High Pass: Applicant's experience and training indicate that she or he clearly possesses the factor at or above the level required for top performance on the job. Candidate's description indicates deep or broad experience and/or training across all areas of the factor.

POSTINTERVIEW DSW POSITION RUBRIC
STEP ONE: Initial Screening–Candidate must get a YES for all three of these categories in order to undergo further consideration.

Criteria	As measured by	Weight	NAME:	
			Score	Total (Score × Weight)
Must possess MSW (accredited program)	Yes or No	No weights		
		(Required)		
Doctoral degree by (date)	Yes or No	No weights		
		(Required)		
Minimum 2 years post-MSW practice experience	Yes or No	No weights		
		(Required)		

(continued)

Postinterview DSW Position *(Continued)*

POSTINTERVIEW DSW POSITION RUBRIC				
STEP TWO: *Committee–If candidate passes initial screening, then full committee will review and rank application using the following criteria.*				
Criteria	**As measured by**	**Weight**	**NAME:**	
			Score	**Total (Score × Weight)**
SCHOLARSHIP AND CREATIVE ACTIVITY				
Record of peer-reviewed scholarship	Number and types of peer-reviewed scholarship, works in progress, scholarly agenda, other	10 (Required)		0
Record of empirical research and scholarship/creative activity	Number and types of peer-reviewed scholarship, works in progress, scholarly agenda, other	8 (Preferred)		0
TEACHING				
Demonstrated excellence in teaching	As expressed in letter of interest, interviews, or presentation (i.e., teaching philosophy, teaching strategies, examples of effectiveness), student or faculty evaluations, letters of support, other	10 (Required)		0
Two or more years teaching social work at graduate level	Number of years teaching	5 (Preferred)		0
Online teaching experience	Range and types of online teaching and delivery methods, online curricular development, advanced training in online teaching (e.g., quality matters), other	8 (Preferred)		0
Able and willing to teach in multiple areas across programs	Range and types of teaching experience such as level (BSW, MSW, DSW), formats (evening, weekend, hybrid), student populations (traditional, adult), and topic areas (sequences, courses)	7		0
CLINCIAL/LEADERSHIP/MANAGEMENT PRACTICE				
Effectiveness in working with diverse populations	Range or types of experiences, areas of expertise, examples of effectiveness, other	8 (Preferred)		0

(continued)

Postinterview DSW Position *(Continued)*

Clinical practice experience	Range or types of clinical practice experiences, areas of expertise, future agenda, other	8 (Preferred)		0
Leadership/ management experience	Range or types of leadership experiences, areas of expertise in leadership, future agenda, other	8 (Preferred)		0
Community involvement	Range or types of involvement, areas of expertise, evidence of effectiveness, future agenda, other	4		0
OTHER APPLICATION ITEMS				
Quality of letter of interest	Demonstrates knowledge and interest in position, qualifications, and strong written communication skills	10 (Required)		0
Strength of letter 1	High recommendation from supervisor or colleague	4 (Required)		0
Strength of letter 2	High recommendation from supervisor or colleague	4 (Required)		0
Strength of letter 3	High recommendation from supervisor or colleague	4 (Required)		0
Familiarity with program content for this position	As expressed in letter of interest, interview, and/or presentation	5		0
Committment to department mission	As expressed in letter of interest, interview, and/or presentation	6		0
Oral/verbal communication skills	As demonstrated in interviews, presentation, etc.	7		0
Written communication skills	As demonstrated in letter of interest, presentation, correspondence, other	7		0
Professionalism	Performance at interviews, presentation, timeliness, comportment	6		0
Other strengths, abilities, experiences that would contribute to department mission and goals		5		0
TOTALS			0	0

Postinterview Clinical Position

Rating Scale:
The following six-point scale is used to rate the candidate on each criterion. The rating score is multiplied by the weight for that criterion for the total points.
(0) No Pass: Applicant's experience and training are below that which would be considered qualifying for this factor. Candidate's background clearly falls below minimum acceptable standards for the job. Applicant's description reveals serious deficiencies in experience and/or training in important areas of the factor, or across the breadth of the factor. A rating of zero (0) in a key factor may disqualify a candidate from further consideration.
(1) Low Pass: Applicant's experience and training indicate that she or he possesses the factor at a level that is minimally acceptable for the job. Candidate's description shows experience and/or training which adequately covers the most important aspect of the factor.
(2) Between Low Pass and Pass: Applicant's experience and training indicate that she or he possesses the factor at a level that is between minimally acceptable to satisfactory for the job. Candidate's description shows experience and/or training which is more than adequate but less than full coverage of the most important aspect of the factor.
(3) Pass: Applicant's experience and training indicate that she or he possesses the factor at a level that is satisfactory for the job. Candidate's description shows experience and/or training covering the important areas of the factor.
(4) Between Pass and High: Applicant's experience and training indicate that she or he possesses the factor between satisfactory and at or above the level for the job. Candidate's description shows experience and/or training between covering the important areas of the factor to a deep or broad experience and/or training across all areas of the factor.
(5) High Pass: Applicant's experience and training indicate that she or he clearly possesses the factor at or above the level required for top performance on the job. Candidate's description indicates deep or broad experience and/or training across all areas of the factor.
POSTINTERVIEW CLINICAL POSITION RUBRIC
STEP ONE: Initial Screening–Candidate must get a YES for all three of these categories in order to undergo further consideration.

Criteria	As measured by	Weight	NAME:	
			Score	Total (Score × Weight)
Must possess MSW (accredited program)	Yes or No	No weights		
		(Required)		
Doctoral degree by (date)	Yes or No	No weights		
		(Required)		
Minimum 2 years post-MSW practice experience	Yes or No	No weights		
		(Required)		

(continued)

Postinterview Clinical Position *(Continued)*

POSTINTERVIEW CLINICAL POSITION RUBRIC				
STEP TWO: Committee–If candidate passes initial screening, then full committee will review and rank application using the following criteria.				
Criteria	As measured by	Weight	NAME:	
			Score	Total (Score × Weight)
SCHOLARSHIP AND CREATIVE ACTIVITY				
Capacity to produce peer-reviewed scholarship	Range of peer-reviewed scholarship, works in progress, scholarly agenda, other	10 (Required)		0
Record of empirical research and scholarship/creative activity	Number and types of peer-reviewed scholarship, works in progress, scholarly agenda, other	8 (Preferred)		0
TEACHING				
Demonstrated potential for excellence in teaching	As expressed in letter of interest, interviews, or presentation (i.e., teaching philosophy, teaching strategies, examples of effectiveness), student or faculty evaluations, letters of support, other	10 (Required)		0
Two or more years teaching social work at undergraduate and/or graduate levels	Number of years teaching	5 (Preferred)		0
Interest and ability in teaching in multiple areas across programs	Range and types of teaching experience such as level (BSW, MSW), formats (evening, weekend, hybrid), student populations (traditional, adult), and topic areas (sequences, courses)	7		0
CLINCIAL PRACTICE				
Effectiveness in working with diverse populations	Range or types of experiences (such as teaching, research, practice, community involvement), areas of expertise, examples of effectiveness, other	8 (Preferred)		0
Clinical practice experience in one or more of C&F, MHSA, SSWK, OA, or related fields	Range or types of clinical practice experiences, areas of expertise, future agenda, other	8 (Preferred)		0

(continued)

Postinterview Clinical Position *(Continued)*

LCSW or equivalent social work license	Yes or No	8 (Preferred)		0
Community involvement	Range or types of involvement, evidence of effectiveness, future agenda, other	4		0
OTHER APPLICATION ITEMS				
Quality of letter of interest	Demonstrates knowledge and interest in position, qualifications, and strong written communication skills	10 (Required)		0
Strength of letter 1	High recommendation from supervisor or colleague	4 (Required)		0
Strength of letter 2	High recommendation from supervisor or colleague	4 (Required)		0
Strength of letter 3	High recommendation from supervisor or colleague	4 (Required)		0
Familiarity with program content for this position	As expressed in letter of interest, interview, and/or presentation	5		0
Committment to department mission	As expressed in letter of interest, interview, and/or presentation	6		0
Oral/verbal communication skills	As demonstrated in interviews, presentation, other	7		0
Written communication skills	As demonstrated in letter of interest, presentation, correspondence, other	7		0
Professionalism	Performance at interviews, presentation, timeliness, comportment	6		0
Other? Professional activities, student advisement?		5		0
TOTALS			0	0

C&F, Children and Family; MHSA, Mental Health and Substance Abuse; OA, older adults/elders; SSWK, School Social Work.

Postinterview Policy Position

Rating Scale:
The following six-point scale is used to rate the candidate on each criterion. The rating score is multiplied by the weight for that criterion for the total points.
(0) No Pass: Applicant's experience and training are below that which would be considered qualifying for this factor. Candidate's background clearly falls below minimum acceptable standards for the job. Applicant's description reveals serious deficiencies in experience and/or training in important areas of the factor, or across the breadth of the factor. A rating of zero (0) in a key factor may disqualify a candidate from further consideration.
(1) Low Pass: Applicant's experience and training indicate that she or he possesses the factor at a level that is minimally acceptable for the job. Candidate's description shows experience and/or training which adequately covers the most important aspect of the factor.
(2) Between Low Pass and Pass: Applicant's experience and training indicate that she or he possesses the factor at a level that is between minimally acceptable to satisfactory for the job. Candidate's description shows experience and/or training which is more than adequate but less than full coverage of the most important aspect of the factor.
(3) Pass: Applicant's experience and training indicate that she or he possesses the factor at a level that is satisfactory for the job. Candidate's description shows experience and/or training covering the important areas of the factor.
(4) Between Pass and High: Applicant's experience and training indicate that she or he possesses the factor between satisfactory and at or above the level for the job. Candidate's description shows experience and/or training between covering the important areas of the factor to a deep or broad experience and/or training across all areas of the factor.
(5) High Pass: Applicant's experience and training indicate that she or he clearly possesses the factor at or above the level required for top performance on the job. Candidate's description indicates deep or broad experience and/or training across all areas of the factor.
POSTINTERVIEW POLICY POSITION RUBRIC
STEP ONE: Initial Screening–Candidate must get a YES for all three of these categories in order to undergo further consideration.

Criteria	As measured by	Weight	NAME:	
			Score	Total (Score × Weight)
Must possess MSW (accredited program)	Yes or No	No weights		
		(Required)		
Doctoral degree by (date)	Yes or No	No weights		
		(Required)		
Minimum two years post-MSW practice experience	Yes or No	No weights		
		(Required)		

(continued)

Postinterview Policy Position *(Continued)*

POSTINTERVIEW POLICY POSITION RUBRIC				
STEP TWO: Committee—If candidate passes initial screening, then full committee will review and rank application using the following criteria.				
Criteria	As measured by	Weight	NAME:	
			Score	Total (Score × Weight)
SCHOLARSHIP AND CREATIVE ACTIVITY				
Capacity to produce peer-reviewed scholarship	Range of peer-reviewed scholarship, works in progress, scholarly agenda, other	10 (Required)		0
Record of scholarship/creative activity	Range of peer-reviewed scholarship, policy proposal or evaluations, works in progress, scholarly agenda, other	8 (Preferred)		0
TEACHING				
Demonstrated potential for excellence in teaching	As expressed in letter of interest, interviews, or presentation (i.e., teaching philosophy, teaching strategies, examples of effectiveness), student or faculty evaluations, letters of support, other	10 (Required)		0
Two or more years teaching social work at undergraduate and/or graduate levels.	Number of years teaching	5 (Preferred)		0
Interest and ability in teaching in multiple areas across programs	Range and types of teaching experience such as level (BSW, MSW, DSW), formats (evening, weekend, hybrid), student populations (traditional, adult), and topic areas (sequences, courses)	7		0
POLICY PRACTICE				
Effectiveness in working with diverse populations	Range or types of experiences (such as teaching, research, practice, community involvement), areas of expertise, examples of effectiveness, other	8 (Preferred)		0
Community and/or policy practice experience	Range or types of practice experiences, areas of expertise, examples of effectiveness, other	8 (Preferred)		0
Community involvement	As expressed in letter of interest, interview, and/or presentation	4		0

(continued)

Postinterview Policy Position *(Continued)*

OTHER APPLICATION ITEMS				
Quality of letter of interest	Demonstrates knowledge and interest in position, qualifications, and strong written communication skills	10 (Required)		0
Strength of letter 1	High recommendation from supervisor or colleague	4 (Required)		0
Strength of letter 2	High recommendation from supervisor or colleague	4 (Required)		0
Strength of letter 3	High recommendation from supervisor or colleague	4 (Required)		0
Familiarity with program content for this position	As expressed in letter of interest, interview, and/or presentation	5		0
Committment to department mission	As expressed in letter of interest, interview, and/or presentation	6		0
Oral/verbal communication skills	As demonstrated in interviews, presentation, other	7		0
Written communication skills	As demonstrated in letter of interest, presentation, correspondence, other	7		0
Professionalism	Performance at interviews, presentation, timeliness, comportment	6		0
Other? Professional activities, student advisement?		5		0
TOTALS			0	0

APPENDIX 10E: FACULTY EVALUATION SURVEY OF DEPARTMENT HEAD

Social Work Program

Check your rank

_____Professor

_____Associate Professor

_____Assistant Professor

_____Temporary Full Time

_____Adjunct

_____Other

Rate the effective performance of the program head on each function using the following scale: 0 = Cannot Rate, 1 = Very Poor, 2 = Poor, 3 = Average, 4 = Above Average, 5 = Exceptionally Well

TABLE 10E.1 **Rating of Program Head General Performance**

#	PERFORMANCE	0	1	2	3	4	5
1	Recognizes faculty in accordance with their contributions to the program						
2	Guides development of a sound organizational plan to accomplish the program's vision, mission, and goals						
3	Arranges the equitable allocation of faculty responsibilities such as committee assignments, teaching loads, etc.						
4	Facilitates the recruitment of promising faculty and staff						
5	Provides the necessary supports for good teaching in the program						
6	Guides curriculum development						
7	Encourages an appropriate balance among academic fields of practices within the program						
8	Stimulates and supports research and scholarly activity in the program						
9	Maintains faculty morale						
10	Resolves conflicts						
11	Fosters development of each faculty member's special talents or interests						
12	Communicates expectations of the campus administration to the faculty						

(continued)

TABLE 10E.1 **Rating of Program Head General Performance** *(Continued)*

#	PERFORMANCE	0	1	2	3	4	5
13	Communicates the program's needs (personnel, space, budget) to the administration						
14	Facilitates obtaining grants and contracts from extramural sources						
15	Improves the program's reputation in the total campus community						
16	Chairs program meetings						
17	Orients new faculty						
18	Represents the program externally						
19	Serves as a channel of communication between the program and external entities						
20	Keeps faculty informed of program activities						
21	Conducts annual evaluations fairly						
22	Fosters professional development						
23	Encourages senior faculty to take special responsibility to assist junior faculty in professional development						
24	Ensures advisement of students is shared equally between all faculty in the program						
25	Encourages appropriately high academic standards						
26	Encourages teaching effectiveness						
27	Leads the program in periodic review of program vision, mission, goals, objectives, and curricula						
28	Assures that the program's vision, mission, goals, and objectives are consistent with the university's strategic plan						
29	Plans and completes the program's self-study for reaccreditation						
30	Deals fairly with students' academic concerns						
31	Deals fairly with the faculty's academic concerns						
32	Consults with the faculty when developing the program's annual budget						
33	Monitors budgetary allocations within the program						
34	Assigns teaching duties fairly						
35	Develops a schedule of classes for the program						

(continued)

TABLE 10E.1   **Rating of Program Head General Performance** *(Continued)*

#	PERFORMANCE	0	1	2	3	4	5
36	Exercises leadership in all aspects of program functioning						
37	Encourages development toward academic excellence for the program						
38	Encourages development toward professional excellence for program						
39	Develops sound procedures for assessing faculty and staff						
40	Oversees critical administrative matters (i.e., support staff, space allocation, physical facilities, equipment)						
	Total Points for each column						
	Total points for all columns						
	Average score						

Indicate how frequently each of the following statements is descriptive of the program head's action and/or performance using the following scale:

0 = Cannot Rate, 1 = Never, 2 = Occasionally, 3 = Frequently, 4 = Always

SOURCE: Licata, C., Rudnicki, W., Logan, S., and Gross, A. (2004). *Feedback for administrators: Adding value to the evaluation/development process.* Twenty-First Annual Academic Chairpersons Conference. Adams Mark Hotel. Orlando, FL.

TABLE 10E.2   **Rating of Program Head Action and/or Performance**

#	PERFORMANCE	0	1	2	3	4
1	Makes own attitude clear to the faculty					
2	Tries out new ideas with the faculty					
3	Works without a plan					
4	Maintains definite standards of performance					
5	Makes sure his or her part in the program is understood by all members					
6	Lets faculty members know what is expected of them					
7	Encourages faculty members to work to their maximum potential					
8	Makes sure that the work of faculty members is coordinated					
9	Does little things that make it pleasant to be a member of the faculty					
10	Presents information that is understandable					
11	Keeps to himself or herself					
12	Looks out for the personal welfare of individual faculty members					

(continued)

TABLE 10E.2 Rating of Program Head Action and/or Performance *(Continued)*

#	PERFORMANCE	0	1	2	3	4
13	Refuses to explain actions					
14	Acts without consulting the faculty					
15	Is slow to accept new ideas					
16	Treats all faculty members as his or her equal					
17	Is willing to make changes					
18	Makes faculty members feel at ease when talking to them					
19	Puts faculty suggestions into action					
20	Gets faculty approval on important matters before going ahead					
21	Postpones decisions unnecessarily					
22	Is more a reactor than an initiator					
23	Makes it clear that faculty suggestions for improving the program are welcome					
24	Is responsive to one "clique" in the faculty but largely ignores those who are not a member of the clique					
25	In expectations of faculty members, makes allowance for their personal or situational problems					
26	Lets faculty members know when they've done a good job					
27	Explains the basis for his or her decisions					
28	Gains input from the faculty on important matters					
29	Acts as though visible program accomplishments are vital to him or her					
30	Acts as though high faculty morale is vital to him or her					
31	Encourages faculty participation					
32	Recognizes and values diversity among faculty					
33	Creates an atmosphere of confidence and trust					
34	Exhibits supportive behavior					
35	Creates an atmosphere where open communication is encouraged (about job, conflicts, goals, ideas, etc.)					
36	Values ideas and opinions of others and makes constructive use of these ideas and opinions when appropriate					
37	Provides clear direction for the future of the program					
37	Provides clear direction for the future of the program					
38	Recognizes personnel for contributions or achievements made to program, school, university, or community					

(continued)

TABLE 10E.2   **Rating of Program Head Action and/or Performance** *(Continued)*

#	PERFORMANCE	0	1	2	3	4
39	Stimulates research and scholarly activities					
40	Is a role model					
	Total points for each column					
	Total points for all columns					
	Average score					

Use the following scale to answer questions about yourself or the program in general:

0 = Cannot Rate, 1 = Strongly Disagree, 2 = Disagree, 3 = Neither Disagree or Agree, 4 = Agree, 5 = Strongly Agree

SOURCE: Modified from Licata, C., Rudnicki, W., Logan, S., and Gross, A. (2004). *Feedback for administrators: Adding value to the evaluation/development process.* Twenty-First Annual Academic Chairpersons Conference. Adams Mark Hotel. Orlando, FL.

TABLE 10E.3   **Rating of Yourself or Program in General**

#	PERFORMANCE	1	2	3	4	5	6
1	I enjoy my committee work in this program						
2	I enjoy teaching in this program						
3	I enjoy my scholarly work in this program						
4	I enjoy working with the community for this program						
5	My teaching schedule works for me						
6	I am able to attend the conferences I need to attend each year						
7	I have a positive relationship with my colleagues						
8	I have a positive relationship with the program head						
9	I agree with the priorities that have guided recent developments in the program						
10	The program has been getting stronger in recent years in terms of the curriculum						
11	The program has been getting stronger in recent years in terms of status in the university						
12	The program is managed well by the program head						
13	The program head is a good leader						

(continued)

TABLE 10E.3 **Rating of Yourself or Program in General** *(Continued)*

#	PERFORMANCE	1	2	3	4	5	6
	Total points for each column						
	Total points for all columns						
	Average score						

Use the following scale to rate how the program head's effectiveness has been seriously impaired by the following items:

0 = Cannot Rate, 1 = Strongly Disagree, 2 = Disagree, 3 = Neither Disagree or Agree, 4 = Agree, 5 = Strongly Agree

SOURCE: Modified from Licata, C., Rudnicki, W., Logan, S., and Gross, A. (2004). *Feedback for administrators: Adding value to the evaluation/development process.* Twenty-First Annual Academic Chairpersons Conference. Adams Mark Hotel. Orlando, FL.

TABLE 10E.4 **Rating of Items that Impair the Program Head's Effectiveness**

#	PERFORMANCE	1	2	3	4	5	6
1	Enrollment problems in the program						
2	Inadequate facilities for the program						
3	Bureaucratic requirements and regulations						
4	Inadequate financial resources to support the program						
5	Relatively low priority given to the program by the head's immediate superior						
6	Obstructionism/negativism from one or more members of the faculty						
7	Inadequate support from human resources						
8	Inadequate support staff						
9	Inadequate technological support						
	Total points for each column						
	Total points for all columns						
	Average score						

SOURCE: Modified from Licata, C., Rudnicki, W., Logan, S., and Gross, A. (2004). *Feedback for administrators: Adding value to the evaluation/development process.* Twenty-First Annual Academic Chairpersons Conference. Adams Mark Hotel. Orlando, FL.

Responses to the following questions will be compiled and presented in a narrative format. Which matters need priority attention in the department during the next year or two? Identify any departmental policies or procedures that you feel need immediate improvement. What is the most important observation you can make about the department chairperson.

a. Administrative effectiveness?

b. Administrative style?

c. What area of performance should be changed and how?

Other comments:

Please return the completed form to program evaluation committee.

APPENDIX 10F: STRATEGIES FOR RECRUITING AND RETAINING FACULTY OF COLOR

1. Start the pipeline early—by cultivating students in the BSW program.

2. Cultivate/support programs to mentor/support doctoral candidates of color.

3. Hear and validate the experiences of faculty of color; cultivate an environment of respect.

4. Establish a campus-level diversity committee that helps to match people from the campus to visiting applicants.

5. Advocate for a provost that provides support on a competitive basis for recruitment of outstanding underrepresented scholars.

6. Explore creating an incentive program to hire diverse faculty.

7. Identify supports in the university and larger community.

   a. Association of Latino and Latina Social Work Educators (ALLSWE) has built a national community of scholars.

   b. Explore establishing a campus Latino faculty and staff association.

8. Have direct one-on-one conversations with candidates.

   a. Show people that they matter.

   b. Do not make assumptions.

   c. Help to ensure that each new faculty member can achieve success.

   d. Make sure people are writing and able to earn tenure and demonstrate productivity.

9. Pay competitively.

10. Be explicit about wanting diversity in job announcements and recruitment literature.

11. Use already existing faculty networks.

12. Support and build networks with faculty of color on campus.

13. Make sure to facilitate interactions with faculty and students of color when candidates are on campus.

14. Look for shared positions with gender, race, and identity-type departments.

15. Emphasize mentoring in scholarship and work climate.

16. More on mentoring: it is not just one-to-one; there are network options and functionally-based mentoring.

17. Develop a mentoring fund to purchase research consultation.

18. Use a three-person mentoring committee for the promotion and tenure process within the program and tailored to faculty of color.

19. Identify mentoring that goes beyond promotion and tenure to groom folks for leadership.

20. Assure that mentors or other established faculty provide a culture interpreter.

21. Carefully assign mentors who are available and committed to the success of the new faculty member.

22. Provide external mentoring contracts for specialized needs to build collegial relationships beyond the institution or to broaden opportunities for scholarship.

23. Develop mentoring networks—in-unit, university, and national—and provide financial resources and a development team that assists with research and activities, and prepares a draft of the person's annual review.

24. Have mentors at multiple levels to capture the complexity of being a faculty of color, and at least one of them needs to be a faculty of color.

25. Build mentoring relationships with multiple mentors within and outside of the school.

26. Create promotion and tenure avenues and products that would assist faculty of color.

27. Forge relationships with university diversity offices for additional supports and resources.

28. Foster interdisciplinary collaboration.

29. Engage in minority Council on Social Work Education (CSWE) fellow's community and network.

30. Provide diversity training to search committees and have at least one external member on the committee.

31. Address bias within the existing faculty.

32. Assist with introducing candidates' partners or significant others (within legal constraints) to communities of color and leaders of color in the community.

33. Bring partners/spouses for a site visit, recognizing that a family system is moving to the community.

34. Employ policies that support the family and special circumstances (e.g., citizenship).

35. Make explicit links to the broader community for faculty and their families.

    a. Consider supports and possible affinity groups.

36. Seek out a local consortium that provides an inventory of available positions for spouses'/partners' job searches.

37. Pay attention and help people locate/integrate into communities and resources that match their needs.

38. Proactively provide continuing professional education opportunities; assure there are financial resources for participating in special projects.

39. Directly address any failures in support from faculty colleagues.

40. Orientation does not stop after the first month; have continuing supports in place.

41. Pay attention to the "psychological contract" and interpret it so it is spoken, rather than silent.

42. Assure understanding of the department's/school's cultural norms.

43. Let faculty of color know that you are their advocate.

44. The psychological contract has to be made explicit, that is, concerned with shared values and reality of the experience.

45. Encourage growth and development over time to support self-efficacy—belief in competence.

46. Make sure the university has a terrific retirement plan.

47. Find creative ways to advertise positions (beyond the chronicle).

48. Assure racial and ethnic diversity on the search committee—without overburdening existing faculty/staff of color.

    a. Ensure members have explicit training about diversity, race, ethnicity, and other differences and include a member of the college's/university's diversity committee in training events.

49. Include community partners in the search process to allow information exchange.

50. Ensure university commitment (including higher administration) to development of faculty of color.

51. Creatively try to minimize and manage faculty workload.

52. Protect faculty from overcommitment to service in the university and community.

53. New faculty should not shoulder education and service on race or ethnicity.

54. Need a fierce commitment to developing and retaining faculty of color among programs and faculty.

55. Create and sustain a supportive culture; be able to recognize what that is and what it means.

56. Rules of engagement—share the culture of the school and larger college/university.

57. Be honest about the culture in the environment of the program, school, college, and university.

58. Provide protection with integrity and standards, with flexibility and sensitivity.

59. Promote faculty development on issues in academia of power and privilege.

60. Provide clear information about what it takes to be successful, a system of ongoing feedback.

61. Share resources and ideas between institutions.

62. Develop a partner support program.

63. Increase ability to make counter offers, and provide financial support through the partner support program.

64. Develop institution-wide linkages with faculty and staff of color.

65. Assure a nurturing environment in widening circles in the institution.

66. Build connections across institutions.

67. Challenge institutional traditions regarding support for faculty.

68. Encourage institutional leadership to explore approaches elsewhere.

69. Select a real estate professional familiar with many different communities to assist with relocation of faculty.

70. Ask about pressures the individual may feel, acknowledge them, and help to strategize a response.

71. Ensure that saying no is okay.

    a. Create a committee to help support/guide faculty about use of time in service.

72. Support participation in training opportunities.

73. Explicitly acknowledge the value added by faculty of color and appreciate their work.

74. Ask leading questions to increase understanding of the needs, pressures experienced, and perceptions/experiences of faculty of color to the program's culture and climate.

75. Focus on student/faculty engagement in the organizational/school climate.

76. Recognize that faculty of color contribute to intellectual pluralism and there are multiple roads to success.

77. Encourage faculty of color to brag about their accomplishments, even if this behavior is against their cultural/ethnic/gender norm.

78. Encourage faculty of color to be true to themselves in finding a research passion.

79. Make sure that curriculum has strong content regarding people of color.

80. Develop multiyear strategic hiring priorities to hire faculty of color in order to support and build a diverse school environment.

81. Champion having diverse faculty, strengths, and accomplishments to college/university administration.

82. Monitor wider university/community culture.

83. Recognize that even with a diverse faculty the white majority can still exist (hold power); be sure to listen and value all voices, create safety, and encourage people to use their voices.

84. Make research connections for interdisciplinary collaboration.

    a. Get involved in grants, grant writing.

    b. Continue investing in people's growth through leadership development (Harvard Leadership, Leadership in Aging, Child Welfare).

85. Recognize when to help someone move on.

86. Fix structural problems in which the systems are rigged against so many.

    a. Build a structure in which faculty can thrive within the school and university communities.

87. Bring people to campus to meet them even if their application is not an obvious pick.

SOURCE: Modified from Bailey, D., Pearlmutter, S., & Sable, M. (2015). *Strategies for recruiting and retaining faculty of color.* Paper presented at the NADD Spring Conference, San Diego, CA.

CHAPTER 11

SUPERVISING STAFF IN A SOCIAL WORK ENVIRONMENT

CHAPTER OBJECTIVES

- Ensuring that your organization offers competent and regular supervision to all staff.
- Designing and managing a positive, supportive, and fair workplace.
- Creating and establishing criteria with which to recruit, hire, train, and so on.
- Communicating well in crisis.
- Guiding professional judgment and behavior using supervision or consultation.
- Understanding multiple roles of the supervisor and methods of supervision.
- Identifying elements of good supervision.
- Describing key aspects of delegating assignments
- Discussing dilemmas and key concepts about keeping good people.
- Understanding formal and informal feedback and performance evaluations.
- Discussing creating systems and documents for performance evaluations.
- Specifying how to take corrective action steps to change behavior.
- Identifying action steps of progressive discipline.
- Identifying ways of handling incompetent and destructive employees.
- Identifying how to diagnose employment problems.
- Describing aspects of dealing with legally protected employees.
- Managing staff diversity.

INTRODUCTION

Supervisors respond to diverse needs within organizations and are credible leaders that help to foster an atmosphere of trust and positivity within the workplace, while also attending to the individual needs of supervisees to help grow their professional identity and skills. To achieve optimal performance within the organization, supervisors must exemplify their own practices of lifelong learning and demonstrate exceptional interpersonal communication and conflict-resolution skills. Supervisors must also be well informed about employment laws and adhere to consistent and ethical methods whether they are assessing performance and providing feedback or in the process of recruitment, promotion, and addressing performance issues. Being able to manage employee relations and supervise in a manner that is predictable and fair for all supervisees is critical to effectively lead and supervise others. This chapter discusses the broad spectrum of tasks that supervisors engage in and identifies the ways that competencies and practice behaviors can be further developed.

Box 11.1 displays the competencies/behaviors in this chapter.

BOX 11.1

COMPETENCIES AND PRACTICE BEHAVIORS ADDRESSED IN THIS CHAPTER

Plans, promotes, and models lifelong learning practices (Network for Social Work Management Competencies 11). Practice Behaviors:

■ Ensures that the organization offers competent and regular supervision to staff at all levels of the organization (11.2).

Effectively manages human resources (Network for Social Work Management Competencies 12). Practice Behaviors:

■ Designs and manages the workplace to ensure a positive and supportive culture and climate for staff and clients (12.1).

■ Designs and manages employee relations policies and practices that are fair, adhere to law, and are implemented in a consistent manner (12.2).

■ Supervises recruitment, hiring, training, performance assessment, and promotion/termination based on established criteria (12.3).

Demonstrates effective interpersonal and communication skills (Network for Social Work Management Competencies 9). Practice Behaviors:

■ Manages communication in conflict and crisis situations in a competent and sensitive manner (9.4).

CSWE Competency 1—Demonstrate Ethical and Professional Behavior

■ 1.5 Use supervision and consultation to guide professional judgment and behavior.

CSWE, Council on Social Work Education.

MULTIPLE ROLES OF THE SUPERVISOR

Supervisors wear many hats. They are leaders, coaches, experienced clinicians, advocates, community organizers, budget analysts, ethics specialists, program developers, program evaluators, teammates, mentors, teachers, learners, superiors, subordinates, and much more. In light of the multiple roles they balance, it is no wonder that the act of supervising can be a pendulum between exhausting challenges and invigorating rewards. Supervision is a long-standing hallmark of social work practice and was originally used as a forum for practitioners, researchers, and teachers to formulate social work practices and frame theories (Hughes, 2010). Supervision in social work has since expanded to include a collection of approaches for supervising staff. Thus, the roles of supervisors have increased to serve more diverse purposes. The responsibilities of supervisors have grown increasingly complex and can span from one-on-one supervision in order to maintain and enhance quality of care to the management of resources that encompass the breadth of service delivery processes and systems (Hyrkas et al., 2005).

The expansion in the scope of supervisory requirements has predominantly been influenced by the socioeconomic climate, which has resulted in more social service agencies progressively adopting business models of practice and oversight. According to Hair (2013), adopting a business-oriented approach to human services has meant that supervisors' tasks have sharply refocused from the supervision relationship to administrative assignments. This shift in focus has caused concern over the ability to attend to the practice needs of social workers. Additionally, unabated cuts in government funding have caused organizations to drastically reduce the number of social workers, who are therefore assigned higher caseloads and may find themselves selecting treatment modalities for clients based on availability of resources rather than the individual needs of clients. Hence, more human service organizations are applying the business model of "doing more with less."

Today's supervisors must be highly adaptable, visionary thinkers, who are credible and fair, and, moreover, must also be able to demonstrate balanced attention to the supervisory relationship and administrative demands. In the wake of swelling administrative oversight, supervisors may be susceptible to drifting away from the social work traditions of the supervisory relationship. Pack (2015) described supervision as "the guided process of reflection on practice in an established ongoing relationship" (pp. 1821–1822). She further asserted that this reflective practice allows the supervisee's professional self to emerge and informs future practice and ethical actions. Facilitating reflective discourse is an essential process of supervision that must be maintained in order to cultivate clinical excellence, provide high standards of ethical care, and retain quality staff. The dilemma facing supervisors today is how to allot the time that is needed for reflective discourse and practice.

There are several types of supervision that range from individual, group, and peer supervision. Each modality of supervision has a distinct structure and offers varying benefits to the supervisee. The commonly known one-to-one supervision is required for social workers prior to sitting for clinical licensure exams, but is also frequently used on an ongoing basis within organizations to review clinical cases. Group supervision incorporates a collective approach for sharing knowledge and experiences and can produce an "all in the same boat" benefit of normalizing shared experiences, stressors, and practice ideas. Peer supervision involves seeking professional supervision from counterparts and is often used by clinicians in private practice for case consultation. The primary function of supervision, regardless of the form it takes, is to ensure the protection of clients through competent and ethical provision of services by the social worker (National Association of Social Workers Association of Social Work Boards [NASW], 2013). The task of the supervisor is to establish an environment of trust, empathy, support, and confidentiality to help advance the supervisee's knowledge, technical skills, and capacities for self-reflection and self-awareness.

Supervision can involve administrative, educational, and supportive methods to establish the goals of improved quality care for clients. Administrative, or management, supervision seeks to align organizational policy and work demands with the supervisee's focused work assignments. Educational supervision pertains to case-related processes that are geared toward expanding the supervisee's knowledge and use of skills related to assessment, treatment, and the use of self in practice. Finally, supportive supervision guides the supervisee in managing the stressful demands of the job and facilitates a process of professional efficacy and the development of professional identity (NASW, 2013). Williams (1997) discussed three process-oriented methods of supervision: patient-centered, therapist-centered, and process-centered supervision. Patient-centered supervision is a dyadic process whereby the supervisee presents the client's presenting problems and is offered clinical advisement by the supervisor. Therapist-centered supervision helps to elucidate issues of countertransference impacting the supervisee's work with the client. Finally, process-centered supervision detects parallel processes in supervision and explores the triadic interactions between client, supervisee, and supervisor. The supervisor who is adept at interweaving varying methods of supervision, and intuitively knowing when the supervisee is in need of more or less of one of the three, can create a rich supervisory experience that generates sustainable gains for the supervisee, the organization and clients, and the supervisor.

IDENTIFYING ELEMENTS OF GOOD SUPERVISION

The five E's associated with good supervision are *empathy, exemplary modeling, ethical behaviors, empowering,* and *educating*. Supervisors are responsible for providing regular supervision to supervisees and promoting a spirit of lifelong learning while also demonstrating such practices, in accordance with the Network for Social Work Management Competency 11, as shown in Box 11.2.

BOX 11.2

NETWORK FOR SOCIAL WORK MANAGEMENT COMPETENCY AND PRACTICE BEHAVIOR 11

Plans, promotes, and models lifelong learning practices (Network for Social Work Management Competencies 11). Practice Behaviors:

- Ensures that the organization offers competent and regular supervision to staff at all levels of the organization (11.2).

Empathic Supervision

Empathetic supervisors are emotionally attuned to their supervisees and can have a strong pulse on when the supervisee is feeling overworked, unsure of her or his skills, out of kilter in her or his work–life balance and self-care, and over- or underemotionally invested in clients. Exuding empathy does not mean that the supervisor is a "push-over," nor does it mean that the supervisor is overly aware of the supervisee's personal life or heavily involved in helping her or him manage her or his assignments. Showing empathy to supervisees simply means that the supervisor demonstrates awareness and understanding of the supervisee's experience of work and associated feelings. These experiences are validated by the supervisor (always keeping in mind not to validate the invalid), who brings a supportive awareness to mutually engage in problem solving.

Empathic supervisors are cognizant of both the client-specific and organizational stressors that can impact supervisees and potentially cause diminished work performance. Westerlund et al. (2010) unpacked the psychosocial work environment factors and reinforced the theory that work overload, lack of involvement in decision making, and conflicting demands are negatively correlated with psychological health and well-being. They further noted that supervisors who embrace relationship-oriented or transformational leadership styles that show consideration for the worker were associated with lower rates of work-related stress. This belief underscores that supervisors have the ability to influence perceptions of work-related stress independent of the perplexing macrolevel demands that commonly have a trickling impact on supervisees. Supervisors can provide a buffer to environmental stressors within an organization through their empathic responses and also provide supervisees with tools for managing the identified stressors. Conversely, when supervisors lack empathy, they run the risk of their supervisees becoming guarded and void of the emotional elements that are experienced in social work practice.

Ingram (2013) identified the importance of emotions in relation to practice and supervision, and highlighted that "separation of feelings from professionalism can be seen as an anathema in an interpersonal profession" (p. 5). If supervision is not emotionally inclusive, the clinician will attempt to remove emotions from the clinical case discussion with the supervisor, which subsequently prevents them from making sense of and using their emotional responses in their practice with clients. Ingram (2013) offered that the conceptualization of emotional integration in supervision has been debated in the literature on the basis that knowledge should undergird professional practice; however, this argument is futile when one considers the concept and value of emotional intelligence in practice. Emotional intelligence is attributed to self-awareness and the ability to identify emotional responses in oneself and others, which are qualities that are highly revered within the social work profession.

The caveat to embracing an emotionally inclusive supervisory process is that the supervisor must establish professional boundaries for the emotional content that is explored and processed in supervision, as the focus should be aimed at improving practice and not for the purposes of therapy for the supervisee. Williams (1997) explained that the difference between supervisory work and therapy work is that in therapist-centered supervision, the supervisor facilitates technical changes that may also result in personal growth for the supervisee, but the focus remains judiciously aimed at professional skills development.

Exemplary Practice

Supervisors employ skills of leading and teaching by example for supervisees. They are constantly being observed by supervisees who turn to them for a professional learning experience, whether it is leading a meeting, managing workplace conflicts, or addressing the needs of clients. Thus, supervisors have numerous opportunities to be exemplary models of professional practice that can range from effective communication, professional boundaries, critical thinking skills, uniting teams, and applying ethical behaviors. Supervisors may demonstrate ways to address a difficult client situation and model how the supervisee can handle these difficulties in practice. For instance, a clinician, who is struggling to articulate feeling "stuck" and uncertain about how to use motivational interviewing skills when working with a substance abusing client, can have the approach modeled by the supervisor to catalyze the clinician's awareness about the application of techniques with the client. Similarly, to cultivate the supervisee's cultural competence in engaging diverse clients, supervisors should model how to discuss the diversity that exists in their working relationship. Modeling awareness of diversity and displaying how to facilitate open and respectful conversations in supervision about differences in cultural backgrounds, age, language, sexual orientation or expression, physical abilities, gender, and so on, can help supervisees become more aware of the aspects of diversity in their work with clients; their own values, beliefs, and biases; and contribute to their development of culturally competence practices. Through the supervisor's modeling, clinicians may be able to safely process their own readiness to change their approach to practice work with clients, begin to experience how the approach can be helpful in lowering clients' resistance to engage in the difficult topic, and enhance their empathy for what the client may be experiencing in session. This approach is referred to as process-centered supervision.

Process-centered supervision is concerned with understanding the transactional nature of communication between the client, supervisee, and supervisor. The potent affective responses of clients can be reenacted by supervisees, as they unknowingly identify with the client's affect during impasses and times of difficulty in therapy (Williams 1997). The supervisee may unconsciously portray the difficulties in supervision, which in turn leads the supervisor to address them. The supervisee is then able to watch and learn from the supervisor, and as the supervisee works through this parallel process, she or he steps into the role of the client to better understand the utility of techniques that can be used in practice. Similar to therapist-centered supervision, process-centered supervision can be prone to erring into a therapeutic focus on the supervisee, and supervisors are exhorted to maintain the boundaries of the supervision relationship.

Ethical Supervision

BOX 11.3

COUNCIL ON SOCIAL WORK EDUCATION COMPETENCY 1

CSWE Competency 1—Demonstrate Ethical and Professional Behavior

■ 1.5 Use supervision and consultation to guide professional judgment and behavior.

CSWE, Council on Social Work Education.

Box 11.3 displays the competencies/behaviors in this section. Supervisors increasingly manage resources, which requires them to make judgment calls that prioritize the use and allocation of such resources; these decisions may unavoidably result in the restructuring, reduction, or elimination of services and/or staff (Hyrkas et al., 2005). These are difficult decisions that will impact supervisors, supervisees, and clients. But, as previously mentioned, the supervisor can cushion the reactions of supervisees and prepare supervisees to manage and mitigate the rippling effects on the clients they serve as well. It is critical to note that judgment calls should always keep the clients' best interests in mind. It is the ethical responsibility of supervisors to advocate for supervisees and clients when the threat or reality of reduced resources may cause deleterious outcomes for clients due to changes in the service delivery.

Furthermore, encouraging ethical behaviors and decision making is essential for supervisors to model and teach. The NASW (2013) affirms that ethical decision making is both a cognitive and emotional process. Ethical decisions can encompass issues of dual relationships, such as assignment to supervise or treat someone known to the worker outside of the agency; dilemmas about how to best advocate for a client to remain in treatment even though the funder will no longer authorize payment; how to document in a manner that protects the client, organization, and the social worker; and even how to engage clients in topics that go against one's personal values. Ethical behaviors are guided by professional standards, but individual values can creep into decisions and behaviors as well. The supervisor's role is to illuminate value clashes, help weigh possible consequences and benefits of a given action taken by the supervisee, and consider how to promote social justice and respect for individuals.

BOX 11.4

NETWORK FOR SOCIAL WORK MANAGEMENT COMPETENCY AND PRACTICE BEHAVIOR 9

Demonstrates effective interpersonal and communication skills (Network for Social Work Management Competencies 9). Practice Behaviors:

- Manages communication in conflict and crisis situations in a competent and sensitive manner (9.4).

Box 11.4 displays the competencies/behaviors in this section. It is important to be aware that once trust is firmly established, the supervisee may grow more comfortable unveiling their professional vulnerabilities, and a good—and ethical—supervisor will seize these opportunities to help the supervisee crystalize their professional identity. Supervisors should treat these disclosures respectfully and protect their supervisee's confidentiality. Confidentiality in supervision, in the sense described previously, pertains to maintaining the professional dignity of the supervisee and not using the information revealed to exploit or hold against him or her (Dewane, 2007). When a supervisee is courageous enough to be self-reflective and is seeking guidance on how to process as a professional—which inevitably ties to who the supervisee is as a person—the supervisor must maintain this information in confidence and compassionately engage the supervisee in safe and meaningful discussions. Likewise, the supervisee who lowers his or her guard to request help in refining skills should not have to later regret asking for help from the supervisor who consequently thinks less of them. Supervisees who either directly or indirectly hear supervisors talk about another supervisee's inept skills, personal life, or failed efforts will quickly lose confidence and trust that they are safe to be vulnerable and authentic in supervision, which will undoubtedly foil opportunities for their growth.

Confidentiality is a numinous custom in social work practice and, just as a clinician has legal and ethical limitations to safeguarding information, there are times that the supervisor must report certain information that is disclosed or observed. These ethical dilemmas of confidentiality should flow from the social work professional code of ethics, but there are additional constraints to supervisor–supervisee confidentiality that must include agency policy. Administrative supervision provides information and guidance about the policies and procedures that employees are expected to adhere to within an organization, and the parameters of these should not come as a surprise to supervisees. Nonetheless, there are times when supervisees step completely outside these parameters or touch gray zones, and the supervisor must bring these cases to her or his superior(s) and possibly the human resources department as well. If such situations do arise, the supervisor can preserve the supervisory relationship by respectfully informing the supervisee of the steps the supervisor is required to take and, as applicable to the circumstances, keep the supervisee informed of the next steps and potential disciplinary actions that will ensue. See the case study in Box 11.5.

BOX 11.5

COMPETENCY-BASED CASE STUDY—TED GIVES A PROMOTION

Ted is a clinician on an inpatient psychiatric unit that serves adults and adolescents. He has been employed at the hospital for 2 years and has proven to be a fine clinician. One year ago, he was promoted to the

(continued)

BOX 11.5 *(Continued)*

charge clinician, which expanded his duties to supervise the MHTs on unit. During a scheduled supervision meeting, he disclosed to his supervisor that he had eloped over the weekend and was now married. The supervisor offered her congratulations to Ted, who quickly interjected to explain that he was sharing this information because he was concerned that there was a possible conflict of interest. Encouraged by the supervisor to elaborate, he went on to explain that the person that he married was his subordinate, whom Ted had recently promoted to the position of lead MHT. Ted stated that he was aware of the nepotism policy, but that he was not quite sure how this would impact him and his partner now. The supervisor appreciated that Ted made her aware of this, and transparently shared her ethical concern over the fact that Ted, in his position of authority, had promoted someone he was in a relationship with.

Questions

1. Did Ted do the right thing by informing his supervisor? How do you think the supervisor should respond?
2. Should Ted have promoted his partner? What could he have done differently?
3. If you were the supervisor, what would you do next? How would you address this situation with Ted?

MHT, mental health technician.

▨ Empowerment

Empowering supervisees embodies the principle that individuals need to be intellectually stimulated and fare better when work tasks are not monotonous and their skills are not at risk of growing stale (Westerlund et al., 2010). Empowering supervisees is a methodical process that needs to be carefully scaffolded in order to maximize its benefits. The supervisor who delegates tasks to a supervisee who has no prior experience and limited understanding of the task will, counterproductively, disempower (and very likely frustrate) the supervisee. Empowering staff often requires that the supervisor has equipped them with the essential tools; empowerment includes building their professional efficacy to incrementally augment their ability to master tasks. Supervisors should have well-defined guidelines for the decision-making capabilities and scope of autonomy that the supervisee holds and build upon the supervisee's strengths by creating "stretch goals" to further develop his or her skills. Empowering staff can occur in subtle—yet significant—ways, such as asking for their ideas about how to resolve a team or task problem, assigning ongoing oversight of data input, or creating a new protocol. Hence, delegating tasks and creating new work assignments can serve to empower supervisees.

KEY ASPECTS OF DELEGATING ASSIGNMENTS

Delegation of tasks is a thoughtful approach to determining the best person to be assigned specific tasks. The general rule of 80/20 can be applied when delegating assignments: 80% of the time it should be based off of what you know the supervisee can do successfully, and 20% off of what she or he has the potential to do. This rule protects supervisees from feeling overwhelmed, and potentially defeated, by the tasks delegated to them. Factors that go into this decision can include questions about who should be assigned the task given expenses and the level of sophistication the task requires, who can complete the task in a timely manner and with the most efficiency, and who would benefit the most—and for what reason—from completing the task (Certo (2006)). The act of delegating demonstrates to employees that their expertise and insights are valued and can produce a greater overall impact on the organization than if supervisors or managers alone completed the task(s). When delegating assignments to supervisees, it is helpful to inform them why they were selected for the task at hand. By conveying their unique talents that you see befitting for the assignment, you are employing positive psychology to remind them of their strengths and skill sets that can contribute to their successful completion of the assignment and also reinforcing their professional identity. It is equally important to supportively acknowledge their underdeveloped skills that may be exposed during the course of the assignment and discuss ways for managing this proactively. The supervisor and supervisees can craft a plan for checking in and determine in advance what the supervisees may need from the supervisor to reach their stretch goals and learn new skills. See the cast studies in Boxes 11.6 and 11.7.

BOX 11.6

COMPETENCY-BASED CASE STUDY—EMILY'S INTERN

Emily has worked as a clinician in an outpatient setting for 5 years. She enjoys her work with clients, but whenever her supervisor engaged her in conversations about professional growth opportunities, she would shy away and quickly dismiss the ideas. Having a solid supervisory relationship with Emily, her supervisor was eventually able to peel back her qualms about advancement, which included concerns about work–life balance, since Emily is a single mother and also lacks confidence in supervising other clinicians; she particularly did not want to have to lead meetings as many other supervisors did. Emily and her supervisor processed this dilemma in supervision and eventually the supervisor posed the idea of having her supervise an intern. The supervisor knew that Emily could offer a student a wonderful learning experience, and thought it also might help to empower Emily and gradually increase her confidence in supervising other clinicians in the future.

Questions

1. Was this approach appropriate? Why?
2. Due to Emily's personal situation should one not encourage her to take on a supervisory role?
3. Is there another approach?

BOX 11.7

COMPETENCY-BASED CASE STUDY—CLINICAL GROUP

During a group supervision meeting, several clinicians of a residential treatment facility expressed their concerns about direct care staff, saying that they are being manipulated by the residents. The clinicians are worried that they may be frustrated due to the limited understanding of the residents' needs and symptoms of their mental health diagnoses. After obtaining more information from the group, the supervisor suggests that the team offer a series of in-services to the direct care staff on a variety of topics that could help increase their understanding and provide them with some tools for managing difficult behaviors. The supervisor acknowledges each clinician's areas of strengths and expertise that could be shared with the staff, and together they develop a plan for offering several brief in-service trainings.

Questions

1. Is this the right approach for this situation? Why or why not?
2. Does it address the real problem?
3. What would be another approach?

Educational Supervision

Educational supervision includes teaching and developing knowledge, skills, and self-awareness. Supervision often involves socializing the supervisee, especially those new to the field, to the profession, organization, and their affiliated teams/departments. Socialization may involve teaching the supervisee how to manage anxiety and develop ways for coping with the high stress and demands of the work (Hughes, 2010). Helping supervisees develop skills for managing work demands by encouraging self-reflection also contributes to the process of supervisees' development of professional identification. Educating supervisees, however, also involves learning processes that may be applied indirectly, interactively, experientially, and directly. Indirect learning can include reading case assessments and notes and engaging in reflective discussions and problem solving, while direct learning involves supervisor-led discussions that are more didactic in nature. Interactive learning includes role-playing, use of two-way mirrors, and video recordings. Experiential learning can also include role-playing and case simulations as well as hands-on experiences.

Educating and training supervisees can have excellent returns on investment, and good supervision is marked by continuously raising the bar, or incrementally increasing the rigor, expectations, and exposure to tasks that will help supervisees grow. How supervisors increase expectations and enhance learning opportunities should be strategic and align with the supervisee's position and potential for growth. For instance, you would not try to raise the bar for an entry-level clinician by expanding his or her purview from directly intervening with clients to budget analyses. Supervisors must stay current, share resources, connect supervisees with training opportunities outside the agency, and contribute to the development of training opportunities within the agency. The purpose of educating supervisees is to develop knowledge and utility of skills that promote optimal practice.

As mentioned earlier in this chapter, **patient-centered supervision** involves the supervisor teaching and honing fundamental skills that the supervisee applies in practice. Within the supervisory relationship, the concept of learning can induce transference reactions from the supervisee due to the supervisor's superior role. Williams (1997) suggested that supervisees may develop feelings of admiration, as well as fear and opposition, in the context of the learning relationship. Dweck's (2007) conceptualization of mind-sets explains that individuals can have either a *fixed* or *growth* mind-set toward learning new concepts and skills. A fixed mind-set prefers easy tasks, avoids seeking help, and is quick to lose motivation in response to mistakes, whereas a growth mind-set prefers tasks that may be hard, welcomes help, and does not lose motivation after a mistake, which leads to higher learning outcomes. Understanding the mind-sets of supervisees can allow supervisors to modify their teaching approaches to lower the resistance of those with fixed mind-sets and capitalize learning opportunities with those who have growth mind-sets. See the case study in Box 11.8.

BOX 11.8

COMPETENCY-BASED CASE STUDY—KIM AND BETTY

Kim has been supervising Betty, a clinician for an in-home therapy program, for 6 months now. Kim's patience is wearing and she is growing frustrated by what seems to be a problem for every solution she offers to Betty about her cases. One day in supervision Kim could not muster the energy to engage in what felt like a pointless attempt to try and coach Betty about the family dynamics at play with her most challenging case. She instead decided that she would downplay her own knowledge and ask Betty to explain the techniques she was using and their theoretical underpinnings. Betty initially answered in

(continued)

BOX 11.8 *(Continued)*

vagaries, but Kim innocuously asked for clarifications and greater details. Kim quickly discovered that the root of her resistance was a fixed mind-set, which suddenly explained why she was dismissive of the help Kim offered and seemed to lose motivation. Kim decided that discussing the techniques in supervision was perhaps too threatening for Betty at this time, and instead offered her some readings and an external training opportunity.

Questions

1. How can Kim help Betty modify her fixed mind-set?
2. What type of learning approach might be most successful for Kim to use with Betty?
3. As the supervisor, how would you address Betty's resistance?

DILEMMAS OF KEEPING GOOD PEOPLE

Undesired attrition of staff poses significant fiscal strain on organizations and academic institutions. In fact, the average cost of turnover is estimated at one-fifth of a worker's salary (Turnover and Retention, 2016). There is anecdotal endorsement that social service agencies in particular are susceptible to higher rates of turnover resulting from greater risks of burnout; high stress and low wages are thought to be the common factors that contribute to attrition. However, the anecdotes typically expressed within organizations can eclipse a comprehensive approach to better understanding the dilemma of retaining good people.

Retention has become a global issue, and many companies across diverse industries are turning their attention to examining the reasons why employees leave in order to guide retention efforts (Turnover and Retention, 2016; Hagel, Wong, Benko, & Erickson, 2014; Schwartz, 2015). Traditional philosophies around keeping good staff have taken resolute actions to engage employees in aligning their personal professional goals and experiences with the organizational purpose. However, Schwartz (2015) warns against maintaining an outdated assumption that those who are extremely engaged and committed to their jobs put in longer work days, exceed expectations, and are constantly accessible or connected to their work. These attributes were prevailingly robust indicators of loyalty to organizations that signified employees would be in it for the long run. Contemporary trends, however, suggest that these work habits are actually more predictive of burnout and can consequently lead to attrition. Similarly, Hagel et al. (2014) illuminated that concentrating on retention alone is a misguided effort for organizations, as the modern workforce is seeking more dynamic rewards. The dilemma, in part, becomes deciding how, when, and why to invest in employees' holistic work experience.

It is projected that by the year 2025, 89% of workers aged 55 to 64 and 34% of millennials will make up the global workforce (Hagel et al., 2014). Millennials are driven more by the purpose of the work and less attracted to traditional work habits of putting in long office hours as described earlier. Their purpose-driven outlooks are drawn to opportunities for tackling societal issues such as income inequality and social justice (Hagel et al., 2014), which can offer opulent benefits for social service organizations and academies. They also hail work–life balance as paramount, and they are not alone. From baby boomers to millennials, work–life balance is increasingly valued, and sought after, by employees.

Providing opportunities for greater flexibility is very appealing across generations and sexes. Both men and women report that flexibility is a vital condition for maintaining a work–life balance, with women reporting greater preference of increased time over money and men also reporting strong desires to work fewer hours (Hagel et al., 2014). The challenge for social service organizations is figuring out how to meet the au courant desires of employees while balancing the needs of the organization, especially given the fact that our work mainly requires direct client care and contact. Some ways organizations can help promote the work–life balance are through scheduling, allowing employees to work 40 hours in 4 days to build in an additional day off, permitting workers to remotely log into electronic health records to securely enter documentation away from the office; and flexing schedules to allow employees to attend to caretaking tasks, whether for children, pets, or elderly parents. Organizations that demonstrate regard for their employees' work–life balance can help prevent attrition; however, it is not enough for employees to feel that they benefit from flexibility—they are also looking to feel that organizations and leaders are willing to invest in their professional growth and development.

The dilemma of whether or not to invest time, human, and financial resources in employees involves potential investment risks for agencies, and many agencies fear they will lose staff once the investment has been made. Investing in employees' skill sets can seem like a gamble, but, then again, so is not investing—the question in the cost–benefit analysis is what outweighs this risk? Will the investment in training help staff complete their tasks with greater precision, efficiency, and knowledge? Will providing the training, regardless of how many staff the organization can potentially lose, provide good corporate compliance strategies (i.e., decrease liability)? What will an investment in staff mean to stakeholders—clients, staff, funders, the community? Chances are that when all of the abovementioned are taken into consideration, the benefits far outweigh the risks.

Deciding exactly how much and where to invest is crucial, and often requires strategic decision-making methods. Examining how to instill an organizational culture that values staff development and learning opportunities is advantageous not only for individual employees but the agency as a whole. One needs clarity of the purpose of the investment, and knowing the reasons for the investment must come into focus. When considering investments in staff training and development, the following questions can help guide decisions:

- What is the purpose of the investment?
- Who will benefit from the investment (clients, staff, stakeholders)?
- How far-reaching will the investment be (maximizing gains)?
- What are the short-term gains?
- What are the long-term gains?
- What sacrifices need to be made to make this investment?
- How is the organization compensating for the lack of investment? What is the cost of not investing?
- How will the organization sustain the gains of this investment? And what resources are needed in order to do so?

Human Resources

The following section explores ways for supervisors to effectively manage human resources and engage in practice behaviors that can positively impact organization culture. Managing conflicts and employee relations are some of the ways that supervisors lead by example to promote positive workplace culture, but these should always be well-informed by agency procedures and employment laws to ensure parity within the organization. Aspects of effective management of human resources are discussed and case examples are offered to reflect on practice behaviors. Box 11.9 displays the competencies/behaviors in this section.

BOX 11.9

NETWORK FOR SOCIAL WORK MANAGEMENT COMPETENCIES AND PRACTICE BEHAVIORS 12

Effectively manages human resources (Network for Social Work Management Competencies 12). Practice Behaviors:

- Designs and manages the workplace to ensure a positive and supportive culture and climate for staff and clients (12.1).

- Designs and manages employee relations policies and practices that are fair, adhere to law, and are implemented in a consistent manner (12.2).

- Supervises recruitment, hiring, training, performance assessment, and promotion/termination based on established criteria (12.3).

UNDERSTANDING FORMAL AND INFORMAL FEEDBACK

Performance Evaluations

Performance evaluations are traditionally associated with anniversaries: another year spent with the organization and time to capture feedback on how one is doing. But unlike the "let's pop some champagne" celebratory rush that comes from recognizing life's other milestones, performance evaluations can evoke feelings of dread and anxiety over what criticisms and areas of improvement might pop up. This, of course, is not the sole intention of performance evaluations, as they should highlight the employee's areas of strengths and acknowledge successful outcomes as well. However, supervisors need to consider how they systematically provide feedback throughout the year, both formally and informally. It would seem odd for one to express love to his or her significant other only on anniversaries; the absence of such during the year would likely not get the couple to the next anniversary. So why should it be common practice to wait a year to give formal performance appraisals? Lack of consistent performance feedback causes people to question "where is the love?"—they need reassurance on how they are doing and to be taught ways to improve before reaching that milestone. Performance evaluations and feedback are not static; rather, they are fluid. To further examine how performance is evaluated, let us consider the two types of performance feedback. Feedback can use both formal and informal strategies.

Systems and Documents for Performance Evaluations

Formal: Formal performance evaluations (PE) use standardized measures developed or adopted by the agency to appraise essential functions of the employee's position. They are administered at set intervals, usually annually but can be quarterly, as determined by the organization. They are also administered during working test periods, usually for new employees, but can also be included in progressive discipline plans. The implementation process is subject to influence by the organizational culture. (How does the organization value the PE process? Is it arbitrary, i.e., "we do them because we have to"? Or are they highly regarded as being constructive? Is there an organizational push to complete them by a deadline—a race to get them done? Or is it an ongoing practice that promotes a quality experience between supervisor and supervisee?) Skills and skill deficits are articulated. Goals and objectives, along with benchmarks for examining future progress, are mutually agreed upon.

Informal: With informal PE, the provision of feedback occurs organically and can be individual or team- or department-oriented. Expressions of jobs well done and appreciation of efforts are thoughtfully conveyed beyond a "thanks!" and "great job." Coaching is embedded in the process of informal feedback to enhance skills and skills deficits. There is communication fluency between the supervisor and supervisee; both are speaking the same language and hearing the same message. Informal PE can be influenced by organizational culture. (Are we attending to the feedback needs of staff? Are we proactive or reactive in providing feedback?)

Formal Feedback

Formal performance evaluations are not created in a vacuum. In most organizations, the standard forms used to complete evaluations have likely evolved through time and conscientious efforts aimed at capturing the multiple dimensions the position entails. Performance evaluations also include nuanced measures for assessing how well the employee's values align with the agency's mission and values. For instance, an organization well-known for providing trauma-informed care will likely have measures related to how well the employee adopts this paradigm in everyday practice. The evaluation forms are often created within teams of interrelated departments overlapped with human resources to avoid taking a myopic view and insure that the organizational goals are imbued in metrics.

Performance evaluations tend to use an integrated approach of quantifying and qualifying performance by using a combination of Linkert scales with room to provide examples of performance related to a measured domain. Ideally, the measure will cover domains related to the supervisee's knowledge, application of skills, ethics, cultural competence, interpersonal skills, and ability to gather data to inform practice. For leadership positions, evaluations should include the employee's ability to manage fiscal and programmatic outputs, interface with and influence community stakeholders, and execute strategic plans.

Supervisors are fraught with the task of amassing a year's worth of performance into the annual review. When that time of year comes, it can seem like a daunting assignment, especially if multiple supervisees are due their evaluations at the same time. This crunch can result in providing supervisees with limited examples to support their ratings and leave employees feeling uninspired and unmotivated, and unsure of their future direction. See the case study in Box 11.10.

BOX 11.10

COMPETENCY-BASED CASE STUDY—ELLEN'S DISMISSAL

Ellen was recently dismissed from her position and decided to appeal her dismissal to the executive director. In her appeal she stated that she did not have a performance evaluation in more than a year. The executive director was confounded by this not only because human resources had reported that all evaluations were current but also because the agency completes quarterly evaluations and not just annual performance appraisals. Upon consulting with HR it turned out that Ellen did in fact have her annual and quarterly evaluations, which caused the executive director to wonder—why was the employee's evaluation experience so forgettable? As he took a closer look, he observed that the form contained

(continued)

BOX 11.10 *(Continued)*

quantitative feedback and scantly included examples of the employee's performance. He realized that the evaluation was completed just for the sake of being completed.

Question

1. How could this situation be improved so the employee better understands the outcome of the PE?

PE, performance evaluation.

Whether completing annual or quarterly performance evaluations, supervisors can obviate diminishing the effectiveness and purpose of evaluations by regularly preparing for it. For example, supervisors can keep notes and gather emails related to performance. Supervisors can also share their reflections by email, or log in supervision notes, and ask that supervisees maintain their own self-evaluation file as well, which can be reviewed by the supervisors and supervisees together prior to and at the time of evaluation.

Informal Feedback

Fluid feedback can lend copious benefits to the employee and to the supervisor–supervisee relationship. Unfortunately, even with the best intentions and beliefs they are conveying their points clearly, supervisors' feedback can at times be misconstrued. There are many reasons for misunderstandings in communication—certain words can have different connotations to different people; individuals unintentionally skew the information they are receiving; and the substance of what is said can get lost in the style of how it is said. Therefore, feedback conversations must allow for a "check-in" to clarify and confirm the understanding of messages being sent and received. In the typical busy day at work, it is easy to take for granted that communication sometimes requires additional efforts (and time) aimed at mutually decoding meaning to ensure that conversations are as productive and beneficial as hoped. The skills of reflective listening and clarification are often applied when working with clients. The clinician asks them to share what they heard the clinician say, and the clinician summarizes what she or he heard the client say to be sure that they are mutually understanding what is actually being communicated. But this practice is sometimes overlooked in the supervisory relationship—perhaps supervisors take for granted the value of this practice behavior applied to many aspects of their work; perhaps they assume that since they know the art of communication it will translate to their work with supervisees; or maybe they just have a big agenda to get through and do not feel there is time to pause and check in. Regardless of the reasons it stems from, it behooves supervisors to be more consistent in their approach with supervisees.

Make your feedback count. All too often supervisors and leaders believe that they are attending to the needs of employees by giving praise. There are two potential pitfalls with this: (a) it is too vague and (b) it stops at praise. Telling someone that you appreciated their work and that they did a "great job" can assuredly give the warm fuzzies, but the reality is this feeling will likely be fleeting and does not leave the individual with a lasting impression that you see their worth, because it does not give attention to the details. Consider the differences between the following two compliments:

- *Vague:* You are a good leader.
- *Specific:* Your confidence in leading this project had a positive impact. You took initiative without being overbearing on the group and encouraged them to get involved, which helped successfully see this project through, and I can tell the team respects you for that.

When giving feedback to supervisees, supervisors need to be specific with their compliments and constructive comments (Stone & Heen, 2014). It is not enough to say "you did a great job with that case." Rather the supervisee must hear what it was that they did that was so great, for example: "I was really impressed by how you phrased your questions in an open-ended way to supportively push the client to talk about that. Asking good questions like that is a measure of how attuned you were with him."

Vague feedback may feel good in the moment but leaves supervisees with a vapid appraisal of their performance. Specific feedback is meaningful and enduring, and it has the power to become etched in the recipient's mind and can fuel ongoing growth. The attuned supervisor understands that supervisees need appraisals composed of reflections about both their impact and style for continued development.

But do not let feedback stop at complimentary comments about the supervisee's abilities. Feedback should also be used as an inducement to delve further into mentoring. Mentoring involves developing the supervisee's professional self. The idea is to help the supervisee build upon her or his capacities based on her or his strengths and to become more aware of blind spots by providing candid, supportive, and descriptive feedback about how the supervisee can continue to grow.

PROGRESSIVE DISCIPLINE AND TAKING ACTION TO CHANGE BEHAVIOR

Box 11.11 displays the competencies/behaviors in this section.

BOX 11.11

NETWORK FOR SOCIAL WORK MANAGEMENT COMPETENCY AND PRACTICE BEHAVIOR 12

Effectively manages human resources (Network for Social Work Management Competencies 12). Practice Behaviors:

- Supervises recruitment, hiring, training, performance assessment, and promotion/termination based on established criteria (12.3).

Providing thorough verbal and written communication is critical when addressing progressive discipline with supervisees. Some supervisors see progressive discipline as a means of protecting themselves and the agency from legal ramifications, in that providing adequate documentation for a "three strikes" philosophy or similar policy shields them legally. In many ways it becomes a compilation of incidents that substantiate the employee's subpar performance, insubordination, or lack of adherence to agency policies. Documentation is omnipotent when handling disciplinary matters, but supervisors are warned not to get so mired in documenting that they neglect the process of progressive discipline.

Progressive discipline typically follows a lockstep approach that may eventuate in the employee's termination. Usually progressive discipline begins with documenting a warning to the supervisee, followed by a suspension, a demotion, and finally dismissal (Certo (2006)). A warning compiles information pertaining to the problem behavior the employee has demonstrated and must illustrate how the behavior negatively impacts the organization, or those served by the organization. Warnings detail what action steps will be taken to improve the behavior and potential actions that will be taken by the organization if the behavior is not corrected by the employee. Suspensions outline a number of days that the employee shall not report to work and are typically unpaid. The intended purpose of suspensions without pay is to elevate the progressive process of disciplining the employee, and sometimes suspension is applicable due to the severity of the problem behavior.

Demotion of an employee transfers him or her to another position, of lower status, within the organization. There are opposing views on the effectiveness of demotions. Some supervisors may see it as merely transplanting the problem to another department in the organization, and others may see it as an opportunity for the employee to better apply his or her skills in a position that is more fitting for him or her. In the latter case, the employee may feel a sense of relief because he or she felt ill-equipped and overwhelmed in his or her previous position; but despite this feeling the employee may be also embarrassed and ashamed that he or she could not meet the performance expectations at the higher position. In such instances, supervisors should support the supervisee in navigating this change and handling his or her affective responses. An unproductive and hazardous rationale for demotion, which is detrimental to the organization and the person, is relocating the person with the problem behaviors from one position to another without addressing the problem behaviors.

Dismissal of an employee is the permanent separation between the organization and employee. When an employee is dismissed from their employment, there should be ample documentation to support the decision, which includes comprehensive understanding of labor laws. Dismissals may result from an employee's failure to change problem behaviors and comply with corrective action plans, or may be due to an egregious act committed by the employee. Thus, dismissals can be insidious or abrupt; neither one is ever easy for an organization since destructive behaviors of employees can have deleterious systemic effects and drain resources.

When addressing problem behaviors, progressive discipline must be clear and must take action to resolve the identified problem. Disciplining supervisees should not be punitive in nature; a supervisor who takes a condescending or authoritative stance will likely exacerbate the problem because the employee is more likely to be resistant to this approach (Certo, 2006). However, when a supervisor utilizes positive discipline, an approach that seeks to prevent the problem, the supervisee is more apt to comply. In order to effectively execute progressive discipline, the supervisor must clearly articulate, both in writing and in verbal communication with the supervisee, the problem, the impact of the problem, and the steps, or rules that need to be followed. Using positive discipline incorporates the use of empathy, as the supervisor also seeks to understand the circumstances that caused the behavior or poor performance in the first place and seeks to modify the behavior by providing sufficient conditions for optimal performance. It is incumbent on the supervisor to reflect about the supervisee's past performance and determine whether the supervisee has been properly trained, had adequate feedback on her or his performance (formal and informal), and has been recognized and compensated fairly (i.e., do they have a reason to be disgruntled?) (Certo, 2006).

When supervisors become aware of problem behaviors in supervisees, they need to take immediate action. Avoiding the issue will not only perpetuate the problem behavior of the identified employee, but can have cascading effects on the morale of their counterparts. There is a strong likelihood that the supervisee's fellow employees have already noticed or heard about his or her behaviors, and if they go unaddressed for too long the consequences of the continued behavior can erode morale and instill a perception of organizational injustice. When addressing the matter with the supervisee, the supervisor must keep the focus to solving the problem behavior, and keep emotions out of it (i.e., self-regulate). These meetings should maintain the dignity of the employee and be held confidential, which means ensuring that the place of meeting provides privacy. It is sometimes a good idea, depending on the circumstances, to have a third party, such as a human resources representative, attend the meeting.

Progressive Discipline and Corrective Action Steps

Step One

Supervision meetings should

- Document supervision meetings by:
  - Topics covered, areas of concern(s).
  - Follow-up steps to be taken.
  - Person(s) responsible for follow-up steps.
  - Time frame/completion dates for action steps (note, when a series of steps needs to be taken these can effectively be broken down into a timeline that delineates the dates for portions of action steps that will be taken).
  - Method(s) for reporting back and evaluating outcome(s).
- Provide written description of patterns that are cause for concern in an objective fashion.
- Document assistance that was or will be provided to help the supervisee improve.

Step Two

Written warnings should

- Objectively state issue(s) of concern.
- Reference any previous conversation(s) or professional counseling that occurred in prior supervision meetings to address the issue(s) of concern.
- Document the following:
  - Topics covered, areas of concern(s).
  - Follow-up steps to be taken.
  - Person(s) responsible for follow-up steps.
  - Time frame/completion dates for action steps (note, when a series of steps needs to be taken these can effectively be broken down to a timeline that delineates the dates for portions of action steps that will be taken).
  - Method(s) for reporting back and evaluating outcome(s).
  - Potential outcome(s) that will result if performance improvement plan is not adhered to.

Step Three

Personnel conferences should

- Include written documentation of meeting held to address critical areas of performance concerns.
- Document the following:
  - Topics covered, areas of concern(s).
  - Follow-up steps to be taken.

- Person(s) responsible for follow-up steps.

- Time frame/completion dates for action steps (note, when a series of steps needs to be taken these can effectively be broken down into a timeline that delineates the dates for portions of action steps that will be taken).

- Method(s) for reporting back and evaluating outcome(s).

- Potential outcome(s) that will result if performance improvement plan is not adhered to.

- Statement supervisee was offered the opportunity to respond in writing to the personnel conference and provide a written rationale for any items addressed verbally or in writing that he or she does not concur with regarding his or her performance, or the performance improvement plan.

- Summary document signed by all parties (supervisor, supervisee, and HR representative) with copies to personnel file, supervisor, and supervisee.

Step Four

Suspension without pay

Note: There are times that call for immediate suspension without pay where the supervisor is not able to hold a personnel conference prior to the supervisee being placed on leave. In such instances, the performance issue is typically egregious and the act of suspension may be following policies and procedures of the organization based on the nature of the performance issue. For instance, a report of child abuse or neglect perpetrated by the employee should require the employee be placed on administrative leave—or suspension without pay—until an investigation is complete. Report of an employee stealing from clients' funds may, similarly, require the employee to be placed on administrative leave until a full investigation is completed.

When an employee is placed on administrative leave pending an investigation, a representative from the organization is advised to maintain contact with the employee to provide information regarding the process and timelines for completion of the investigation. Employees are at times wrongly accused of harming clients, which can be a very demoralizing experience. This possibility requires the supervisor and agency to take an unassuming approach until the investigation can conclusively determine whether or not the employee can return to work. In the event that an employee is wrongly accused and there is sufficient evidence to determine that they did not harm anyone, the supervisor should discuss ways to support the employee in her or his return to work. This process should include discussing the experience with the employee to drain off possible feelings of demoralization and informing her or him of her or his rights (i.e., back pay for time missed).

- Documentation should include the following:

  - Topics covered, areas of concern(s).

  - Follow-up steps to be taken.

  - Person(s) responsible for follow-up steps.

  - Time frame/completion dates for action steps (note, when a series of steps needs to be taken these can effectively be broken down to a timeline that delineates the dates for portions of action steps that will be taken).

  - Method(s) for reporting back and evaluating outcome(s).

  - Potential outcome(s) that will result if performance improvement plan is not adhered to.

■ Statement supervisee was offered the opportunity to respond in writing to the personnel conference and provide a written rationale for any items addressed verbally or in writing that she or he does not concur with regarding her or his performance, or the performance improvement plan.

■ Summary document signed by all parties (supervisor, supervisee, and HR representative) with copies to personnel file, supervisor, and supervises.

Step Five

Termination

Note: At times employees may be offered the opportunity to resign from the position, but this is typically offered when the reason for termination is not egregious.

■ Employee is

    ■ Informed about procedures for filing an appeal.

    ■ Provided information about final paycheck and, if applicable, insurance coverage and other fringe benefits.

■ Documentation should include the following:

    ■ Topics covered, areas of concern(s).

    ■ Follow-up steps to be taken.

    ■ Person(s) responsible for follow-up steps.

    ■ Time frame/completion dates for action steps (note, when a series of steps needs to be taken these can effectively be broken down to a timeline that delineates the dates for portions of action steps that will be taken).

    ■ Method(s) for reporting back and evaluating outcome(s).

    ■ Potential outcome(s) that will result if performance improvement plan is not adhered to.

    ■ Summary document signed by all parties (supervisor, supervisee, and HR representative) with copies to personnel file, supervisor, and supervises.

■ When indicated, the agency may seek consultation from an employment attorney.

See the case study in Box 11.12.

BOX 11.12

COMPETENCY-BASED CASE STUDY—TROUBLE AT THE UNIVERSITY

In a university department, a faculty member is demonstrating performance issues such as not being present for office hours and sporadic attendance at department meetings and classes. Because the university faculty is unionized, the use of formal, progressive discipline is not possible. For example, the department chairperson (who is in the same union as the faculty) cannot put in writing any statements about performance except when the faculty member is up for renewal, tenure, promotion or post-tenure assessment.

Questions

1. What can the department chair do to improve the faculty member's performance?
2. How can the chairperson prevent a fall in department morale?

HANDLING INCOMPETENT AND DESTRUCTIVE EMPLOYEES

Handling incompetency and destruction in the workplace can be very time-consuming and, in spite of the supervisor's best efforts to ameliorate the issue, the supervisor may not get the result expected. Incompetency can grossly impact the ways clients receive treatment and care, and can be challenging for supervisors for a number of reasons. Supervisors expect that supervisees come into the field and into their positions with a certain caliber of knowledge and skills; so when a supervisee demonstrates that she or he does not possess certain rudimentary assets, the supervisor needs to allocate much more time and resources to bring the supervisee to a level of adequate performance. Additionally, the situation can cause the supervisor anxiety and concern that she or he is not providing quality care to clients, and may perhaps even weigh down the rest of the team.

There are many examples of incompetence, including insufficient assessment skills, inability to engage clients, limited use and knowledge of interventions, poorly written and poorly conceptualized treatment plans, disorganized oral presentation of cases, and so on. In an academic setting, incompetence can include poor andragogy, poor student advisement, and not completing student assessment rubrics correctly, or at all. At the core of incompetence appears to be a dearth, or at times simply an avoidance, of the application of critical thinking skills. Incompetencies can often be addressed through supervision, but the supervisor should maintain good documentation of her or his concerns and corrective actions taken to address the incompetencies.

Critical thinking involves clarity of mind and rationality of thought that is informed by evidence. In its simplest form critical thinking is knowing the "why." Why is it this differential diagnosis? Why is this happening now? Why is it important to start the case presentation with the client's demographic information and brief history of illness? Why has the client not shown up for treatment? Why select this intervention over that one? To effectively challenge incidents of incompetence, the supervisor can supply the supervisee with proper resources to expand his or her repertoire of evidence-based knowledge and apply an inquisitive and Socratic approach to help him or her refine his or her cognitive process and approach to servicing clients and contributing to designated treatment teams. The supervisee may need prompting from the supervisor to consider multiple possible outcomes and be supportively challenged to review the situation through a holistic lens, rather than narrowed focus. A lack of critical thinking can sometimes signal that the supervisee also needs help to raise self-awareness. For instance, the supervisee may be rigidly focused on only one aspect of the situation that appears to evoke a visceral response, but unaware of his or her own drives, he or she is consequently missing the bigger picture. Sometimes a supervisee will even require a little reality testing. For example, the supervisee may see him- or herself as compassionate and engaged, while the supervisor notices different patterns of interaction during supervision where the supervisee seems to present as indifferent or even judgmental when discussing client cases.

The destructive employee can take many forms. Destructive employees can be thieves (stealing large or small amounts from organizations), can act hostilely toward others or bully them, can passive-aggressively infuse a spirit of adversity, fraught with personal problems that get dragged into the workplace environment, or have inappropriate boundaries with clients, staff, or students.

Any of the aforementioned can manifest in insubordination and uncooperativeness (Certo, 2006). Addressing problem behaviors of incompetent and destructive staff should follow the progressive disciplinary actions, and may also include connecting the supervisee to an employee assistance program (EAP). Maintaining documentation of behaviors, meetings that addressed the behaviors, and clearly written action steps is essential. Finally, supervisors must be sure that they act consistently and fairly. Fair does not equate to a cookie-cutter approach or assume that one size fits all. Consider the following parable:

Lucy has a cut on her finger and goes to the nurse, who gives her a Band-Aid to cover the cut. Jack has an earache and goes to the nurse, who gives him a Band-Aid to cover his ear. Kathleen has a sore throat and goes to the nurse, who gives her a Band-Aid to place on her throat.

Hence, being fair does not mean doing the same thing for everyone, because everyone's situation is different and therefore requires a different solution. But it does mean that the solution offered is equitable and is offered justly to all. See the case study in Box 11.13.

BOX 11.13

COMPETENCY-BASED CASE STUDY—OVERTIME HOURS

Linda, a program director at a skilled nursing facility, could not understand why overtime hours had crept up so much over the last three pay periods. She combed through the vacation and sick time, as well as workers' compensation/light duty, for answers, but to no avail. Determined to figure out the cause of this increase, she decided to get to the office early one morning so she could have a jump-start. As she looked out her office window, she watched several third shift staff walk to their cars and drive away. She looked at her clock, took another sip of coffee, and got back to her work. Later that day it occurred to her to check the timecards and noticed that the staff she had watched leave earlier that morning had punched out an hour and a half after she watched them drive away. After consulting with HR, Linda scheduled individual meetings with all of the employees whom she watched leave early and punch out late. During the meetings all but one of the staff confessed that they had been punched in earlier and out later than they had actually worked over the last 6 weeks, and also revealed the names of others who had helped them punch in/out when they were not actually present at work.

Questions

1. Did this group of employees steal from the organization? Explain.
2. What are the next steps that Linda should take to handle this matter?

DEALING WITH LEGALLY PROTECTED EMPLOYEES

Box 11.14 displays the competencies/behaviors in this section.

BOX 11.14

NETWORK FOR SOCIAL WORK MANAGEMENT COMPETENCY AND PRACTICE BEHAVIOR 12

Effectively manages human resources (Network for Social Work Management Competencies 12). Practice Behaviors:

- Designs and manages employee relations policies and practices that are fair, adhere to law, and are implemented in a consistent manner (12.2).

Supervisors should not shy away from taking necessary actions to address problematic behaviors out fear of legality (Certo, 2006), but must seek out knowledge of labor laws and consult their human resources representatives when handling problem behaviors of supervisees. Employment laws are beyond the scope of this chapter, but supervisors are obliged to consider how legislation impacts the work environment. Equal Employment Opportunity laws prohibit discrimination of persons based on race, religion, sex, and national origin. The Equal Pay Act requires equal pay for equal work among men and women, and the Pregnancy Act protects women from discrimination due to pregnancy and childbirth. The Americans with Disabilities Act prohibits employers from discriminating against disabled individuals, and the Age Discrimination Act interdicts discrimination against persons 40 years old and older due to age. There are a number of laws in place to protect employees, and ultimately the burden of proof rests on employers when discrimination cases are filed. The employer is potentially liable for punitive damages and compensation, and it is therefore in an organization's best interest to develop training programs, corporate compliance committees, and provide regular consultation to supervisors to mitigate discrimination risks to employees, supervisors, and the organization. See the case study in Box 11.15.

BOX 11.15

COMPETENCY-BASED CASE STUDY—BOB THE CLAIMS MANAGER

Bob is a claims manager at an insurance company with a background in social work. He is responsible for reviewing the authorization claims of his supervisees within 48 business hours. When there is a higher volume of cases to review, Bob is permitted overtime and paid time and a half for those hours. Recently, he has not been performing his assigned tasks, so his supervisor requests a meeting to discuss ways to improve his performance. Bob became hostile toward his supervisor as evidenced by raising his voice and standing up at times while shouting his defense that he was doing his job. The supervisor explained that he was acting in an insubordinate manner and that she would now have to consider this meeting a written warning. Bob angrily told her that she cannot do that because of his disability. The supervisor was confused by this since there was never any documentation provided that requested any employment modifications. Bob went on to state that he would obtain a doctor's note. A few days later Bob submitted a letter from his doctor that indicated he had received treatment for a condition, but the doctor specifically noted that Bob's condition did not require modifications at work. Over the next 2 weeks, Bob's insubordination continued as he was tardy, absent several days, did not attend to his duties, and demonstrated an uncooperative demeanor toward his supervisor, who at this point requested a meeting with Bob and a representative from HR. Following this second meeting, Bob continued to be absent from work and, upon his return, it was determined that he would be demoted. Bob, appalled at this idea, submitted his letter of resignation. One month later HR received notification that Bob was bringing a claim against the organization, alleging that he was discriminated against for his disability and subjected to a hostile work environment. The compilation of documentation from the supervisor, along with the documentation that was submitted by Bob's physician, was in favor of the organization.

Questions

1. Is Bob a legally protected employee?
2. Was Bob discriminated against?
3. Given that the burden of proof is on the employer, what documentation should be compiled and submitted by the organization if a discrimination case is filed?

Managing Staff Diversity

Diversity in the United States has historical roots, as the nation's rich history of immigration propelled economic and cultural growth. Thus, the United States has thrived on diversity and the implications of diversity can be advantageous within the workplace when cultural competency exists at organizational and individual levels. According to the NASW standards, social workers are required to obtain continuing education credits (CEC) in cultural competence every year. This core competency and the CEC requirement signifies the importance of addressing diversity and understanding the impact that diversity has on clients, service delivery, and broader social environments—including the workplace. Supervision and leadership enjoins the supervisor to attend to aspects of diversity between the supervisee and client, the supervisor and supervisee, and the organizational culture as a whole.

Diversity can include, but is not limited to, race, ethnicity, class, religion, age, sexual orientation, gender and gender identification and expression, marital status, and physical and cognitive abilities. The organizational culture, or values, norms, and beliefs that govern organizational behavior, influence the hiring, training, and interactive styles and behaviors within an agency (Certo, 2006) sets the tone for how individual employees are treated. Discrimination is the act of treating others unfairly secondary to prejudicial thoughts, or judgments about individuals or groups; stereotypes are generalized ideas of others. Supervisors must be aware of the subtle, and sometimes overt, ways that prejudicial thoughts, discriminatory actions, and stereotypes can impact employees and contribute to a biased—and perhaps even an oppressive—organizational culture.

There are many aspects of diversity to consider. Sexism, for example, is the discrimination of persons based on gender stereotypes. While an organization may combat this by educating employees about sexual harassment, sexist discourse, and discrimination of members of the lesbian, gay, bisexual, trans, queer, intersex, asexual (LGBTQIA) community, there are times when a supervisor is faced with more nuanced forms of sexism. For instance, an organization that allows for flextime due to childcare must evaluate whether this treatment is equal—are mothers and fathers provided equal flextime? And what are the ramifications of providing flextime for childcare to parents, but not for nonparents? Is the man who leaves early to pick up his children viewed the same way as the woman who also leaves early for her children? Is the woman without children who leaves promptly after her 8-hour day frowned upon for not staying later, while the woman with children who leaves promptly after an 8-hour day considered more socially acceptable within the culture of the organization?

Ageism, another discriminatory action which can creep into the workplace, treats employees differently based on their age, stereotyping older generations as less tech-savvy and less effective performers who are out of touch with modern approaches. However, as Certo (2006) noted, older workers have much to offer organizations, including work ethic, loyalty to an organization, a wealth of experience, and the ability to mentor younger coworkers.

Supervisors must be aware of the many possibilities of diversity and seek to understand and promote understanding and acceptable behaviors of others in accordance with social work values and employment laws. Supervisors must also be cognizant of the ways that both verbal and nonverbal communication is provided and received. For instance, considering how eye contact is culturally symbolized, how smiles are construed, and understanding the various salutations across cultures are all critical. It is also important to pay attention to spoken language, and what messages are being implicitly and explicitly conveyed through discourse.

Within the supervisor–supervisee dyad, discussions about how the complexities of diversity impact particular clients, or client groups and families, are essential to facilitate change work. However, supervisors must also be conscientious about the diversity that exists in the supervisor-supervisee dynamic. Schmidt (1972) noted that the act of supervising entails oversight, advisement, and direct and critical evaluation of the supervisee. Given the tasks required of a supervisor, the supervisee will naturally view the supervisor as an authority figure and potentially perceive the supervisor similarly to authority figures she or he has previously known throughout her or his life. Depending on the supervisee's prior experiences with authority figures, responses to issues of diversity, combined with the supervisee's values and cultural ethos, can be stirred up in the supervisory relationship. It is essential that supervisors mind this potential gap and are comfortable discussing the diversity that exists between them. This understanding not only helps to ensure that effective communication can occur but also models for the supervisee the importance of acknowledging and discussing diversity issues which are applicable to direct practice learning as well. See the case study in Box 11.16.

BOX 11.16

COMPETENCY-BASED CASE STUDY—MOLLY AND FRANK

Molly is a 31-year-old African American female who is being supervised by Frank, a 61-year-old Caucasian male. Molly finds it difficult to meet with Frank for supervision, as she often feels nervous about asking him to clarify his directives. She describes their meetings as one-sided and perceives that Frank is often talking at her, rather than with her, and as such she is reluctant to share her ideas and points of views about her cases. She worries that her supervisor will not hear her ideas and perhaps even become frustrated and upset if she is not always so agreeable to his supervision. Molly was raised in a family and in a community that valued respecting one's elders—by never "talking back"—and acquiescing to people in authority, particularly Caucasians. Overall she enjoys her job and the clientele she works with, but has considered leaving her job on multiple occasions. She feels intrinsically stuck by her own ambiguity of whether or not to remain at her job, and is not quite sure what she should do.

Questions

1. What elements of diversity have impacted Molly?

2. As a supervisor, how could Frank enhance his awareness and understanding of Molly's experience?

3. How can Molly be empowered?

4. How does this supervisory dyad reflect on the agency as a whole? What are some areas of potential risks, negative perceptions, and areas of improvement for the organization?

SUMMARY

Supervisors have increasingly diverse roles, but the long-standing tradition of supervision is still venerated for providing supervisees with administrative, educational, and supportive methods to ensure quality care is provided to clients. Effective supervision can be attributed to the five E's: empathy, exemplary modeling, ethical behaviors, empowering, and educating supervisees. Delegating assignments is a thoughtful approach for empowering supervisees and fostering advancement of their skills, critical thinking, and leadership potential. Supervisors must provide clear directives and support to contribute to the successful outcomes of the tasks they delegate.

Providing feedback is a critical aspect of supervision and supervisors must be mindful of the ways they are providing feedback and creating opportunities to receive feedback as well. Feedback can be formal and informal, and supervisors are charged with the task of ensuring that feedback is mutually understood (i.e., are we both hearing the same message?). Specific, rather than vague, feedback is helpful to promote professional growth of supervisees. Supervising staff may necessitate that progressive discipline steps are taken to address performance concerns. Performance concerns can be a wide range of issues that may include dealing with incompetent and destructive employees or addressing subpar performance. Supervisors should consult with human resources and provide documentation of meetings that address performance concerns. There are always shades of gray when considering how to approach personnel concerns, but following progressive discipline steps can provide opportunities for the supervisee to improve her or his performance and request assistance needed to reach better outcomes. Following a progressive discipline course can protect both the employee and organization.

Supervisors should anticipate that they will manage diverse staff and must be aware of the social work values and employment laws. It is incumbent upon supervisors, being in positions of authority, to understand how diversity impacts the supervisees, clients, and organizational culture. As leaders, supervisors must promote culturally competent practices within an organization and facilitate conversations about diversity in a respectful manner to ensure that the workplace is free of prejudice, discrimination, and stereotypes.

ACTIVITIES

1. Identify the benefits of supervisors providing therapist-centered, patient-centered, and process-centered supervision.

2. Reflect on your own supervisory attributes and provide examples for how to employ the five E's in your supervision style and practice.

3. What tasks can you delegate to supervisees that can promote their skills development? What are the areas that they will require support in? How will you monitor their tasks and balance a supportive and autonomous approach?

4. Track the feedback that you provide to supervisees over a 1-week period. Take note of the ways that you offer specific feedback and create opportunities for confirming that feedback given and received is mutually understood.

5. Describe how staff performance evaluations could be improved at your agency. (a) Describe specific criteria that could be used in an evaluation of personnel in one position. (b) Describe the agency's procedures for progressive discipline (if the agency does not have procedures, how would you create them?). (c) Describe the agency's termination policies and procedures.

6. Consider those you supervise, and who you report directly to as your supervisor. (a) What aspects of diversity exists among you? (b) How comfortable are you in discussing the diversity that you notice? (c) What are the potential benefits of dialoguing about the diversity you observe?

REFERENCES

Certo, S. C. (2006). *Supervision: Concept and skill-building*. New York, NY: McGraw-Hill Irwin.

Dewane, C. (2007). Supervisor, beware: Ethical dangers in supervision. *Social Work Today, 7*(4), 34.

Dweck, D. (2007). *Mindset: The new psychology of success*. New York, NY: Penguin Random House.

Hagel, J., Wong, J., Benko, C., & Erickson, R. (2014, March 7). *Beyond retention: Build passion and purpose*. Deloitte University Press. Retrieved from https://dupress.deloitte.com/dup-us-en/focus/human-capital-trends/2014/hc-trends-2014-beyond-retention.html

Hair, H. J. (2013). The purpose and duration of supervision, and the training and discipline of supervisors: What social workers say they need to provide effective services. *British Journal of Social Work, 45*, 1562–1568. doi:10.1093/bjsw/bcs071

Hughes, J. M. (2010). The role of supervision in social work: A critical analysis. *Critical Social Thinking: Policy and Practice, 2*, 59–77.

Hyrkas, K., Appleqvist-Schmidlechner, K., & Kivivmaki, K. (2005). First-line managers' views of the long-term effects of clinical supervision: How does clinical supervision support and develop leadership in health care? *Journal of Nursing Management, 13*, 209–220. doi:10.1111/j.1365-2834.2004.00522.x

Ingram, R. (2013). Emotions, social work practice and supervision: An uneasy alliance? *Journal of Social Work Practice, 27*(1), 5–19. doi:10.1080/02650533.2012.745842

National Association of Social Workers Association of Social Work Boards. (2013). *Best practice standards in social work supervision*. Retrieved from https://www.socialworkers.org/LinkClick.aspx?fileticket=GBrLbl4BuwI%3D&portalid=0

Pack, M. (2015). "Unsticking the stuckness": A qualitative study of the clinical supervisory needs of early-career health social workers. *British Journal of Social Work, 45*, 1821–1836. doi:10.1093/bjsw/bcu069

Schmidt, D. M., *Supervision: A sharing process*. Paper presented at the CWLA Southwest Regional Conference, Albuquerque, NM.

Schwartz, T. (2015, March 13). When employee engagement turns into employee burnout. *The New York Times*. Retrieved from https://www.nytimes.com/2015/03/14/business/dealbook/when-employee-engagement-turns-into-employee-burnout.html

Stone, D., & Heen, S. (2014). *Thanks for the feedback: The science and art of receiving feedback well*. New York, NY: Penguin Books.

Turnover and Retention. (2016, August 12). *Catalyst: Knowledge center*. Retrieved from https://www.catalyst.org/knowledge/turnover-and-retention

Westerlund, H., Nyberg, A., Bernin, P., Hyde, M., Oxenstierna, G., Jappinen, P., & Theorell, T. (2010). Managerial leadership is associated with employee stress, health, and sickness absence independently of the demand-control-support model. *Work, 37*, 71–79.

Williams, A. B. (1997). On parallel process in social work supervision. *Clinical Social Work Journal, 25*(4), 425–435. doi:10.1023/A:1025748600665

APPENDIX : TEN STEPS FOR SUPERVISION

1. To Examine Rules for Reasonableness, Ask Yourself
   - Is this rule necessary?
   - Do other organizations have this rule? (Is this rule a common or accepted practice in similar types of operations?)
   - Can it be enforced?
   - Can I apply it to myself?

2. To Examine Standards for Reasonableness, Ask Yourself
   - Has the standard ever been reached?
   - What have good, but not exceptional, workers been able to do?
   - Do other organizations have this rule?
   - Can I apply it to myself?

3. Tips for Clarifying Rules and Standards
   - Provide written copies of rules/policies and discuss with staff for understanding
   - At least an annual review of rules, even if rules are already in place
   - At least a semiannual review of standards
   - Provide clarification before enforcing a lapsed rule

4. Identify a Range of Consequences: Both Positive and Negative
   - Positive consequences for exceeding standards (letter of commendation, more responsibility, attend conferences)
   - Penalties for not meeting rules and standards (letter of reprimand, low performance evaluation)

5. Keep Performance Records
   - Have one for each employee
   - Update every 2 weeks (this will help you latter when evaluating performance)
   - Make available to employee
   - Add positive and negative performances

6. Gather Information
   - Stick to the facts
   - Talk to employee first (it is bad for the employee to find out you have been talking to others first)
   - Gather data objectively
   - Do not go into the interview with a negative attitude

7. Provide Assistance
   - Orientation
   - Training
   - Time (availability of yourself)
   - Tools, job aids, materials, other resources
   - Allow working with peers
   - Feedback and other information
   - Open communication

8. Ensure Consistency
   - Applying consequences should focus on performance only
   - You lose credibility if you reward someone more positively than another
   - If you punish inconsistently you also lose credibility and arbitration
   - Rules must be applied to all employees in a similar work situation
   - Review your prior actions and check with personnel

9. Identify Appropriate Consequences
   - Positive consequences: verbal praise, letter of commendation, bonus, promotion
   - Negative consequences
   - Evaluative penalties: oral and written warnings (generally imposed for minor reasons, but check with personnel first)
   - Adverse actions: suspension, demotion, termination (must check with personnel)

10. Steps in Progressive Discipline
    - Oral warnings
    - Written warnings
    - Suspensions without pay
    - Demotion
    - Termination

- Oral warnings
    - Identify as such and is the first step in process (use to correct future behavior)
    - Describe behavior
    - Describe corrective action
    - Explain consequences of continued substandard performance
    - Put it in performance record
- Written warnings
    - Identify as such
    - State when oral warning was given (date)
    - Statement of rule or standard violated
    - Description of unacceptable behavior (including review of standards)
    - Identify consequences of continued substandard performance
    - Notification of right to grievance
    - Notification that warning or letter will be put in personnel file—it will be made part of the record
    - Notification of right for employee to provide his or her own version
- Suspension without pay
    - Use same procedure as written warning
    - Better be sure everything was done up to this point
    - Intent is to correct behavior
- Demotion
    - Two conditions must be present to consider demotion:
        - The person must have inadequate skills
        - Organization must have an available position for which the person is qualified
    - Termination
    - Only point where the supervisor is not interested in improving supervisee's performance
    - Everything up to this point, supervisor was interested in improving performance
    - In many instances, personnel departments have standard suspension, demotion, and termination letters; use them
- Consider mitigating circumstances
    - No two circumstances are identical
    - There are two rules to keep in mind:
    - Cannot increase penalty due to overall performance (X is late in getting in reports and late to work; need two lines of progressive discipline)
    - Can reduce penalty due to overall exceptional performance—ONCE

- Benefits of following the 10-step process
    - Allows for the greatest chance of correction behavior. May take time in short run, but in the long run, it is good for the organization
    - Supervisor can create a positive environment where performance can occur
    - Process is sustainable—will help the organization avoid the grievance process (no surprises)
    - Improved management. control of workplace
    - Improved communication among workers and management

CHAPTER 12

MANAGEMENT INFORMATION SYSTEMS AND MANAGING TECHNOLOGY FOR SOCIAL WORK ENVIRONMENTS

CHAPTER OBJECTIVES

- Understanding benefits and use of management information systems (MIS).
- Linking organizational mission, goals, and objectives to MIS outcomes.
- Assessing the quality of information.
- Identifying the types of data and information needed in various departments of the organization.
- Selecting or creating programs to collect and analyze data.
- Developing integrated information systems.
- Defining organizational impact.
- Developing, modifying, and using outcome measures.
- Assessing program effectiveness and using data and information to achieve excellence and ensure organizational consistency and integrity.
- Producing reports and creating a feedback loop to improve data collection and organizational programs.
- Managing technology, computer systems, malware, and data storage.
- Using technology to improve organizational effectiveness such as jointly working on documents.

INTRODUCTION

The use of technology has significantly influenced how we live and work. Just consider how technology has made its way into our lives over the past quarter of a century: connecting people through Facebook, Twitter, Snapchat, online dating, GoToMeeting, Survey Monkey, LinkedIn, Instagram, Facetime, and so on. The technological boom has created greater access to information and greater connectedness. The advent and rapid evolution of technology offers more options than ever, which naturally leads to more decisions about which technological platforms to use and how to get the most from them. Coincidently, technology has also contributed to how decisions are reached because it can rapidly provide intel to analyze data that are then used to objectively guide decision-making processes.

The social work profession has also been progressively shaped by advances in technology. Consider the fairly recent spike in fully online and hybrid MSW programs, telemedicine, and, more recently, the introduction of a talk therapy app that provides therapy anywhere, anytime by using texting applications. There are also a variety of apps that social workers can use that provide assessment and diagnostic tools, information about psychiatric medications, social skills apps, relaxation apps, and a wide assortment of many others. These tools have quickly become integrated in work with clients and can offer adjunctive benefits and support to clients, especially in between therapy sessions. Furthermore, organizations use technology for widespread dissemination of information, such as emergency alerts or changes to policy or protocol, as well as for ongoing tasks, including the provision of trainings, which can be offered and tracked by the organization with greater efficiency.

The use of technology in social work has, of course, been a topic of some debate within the professional community, particularly about whether or not such advances will lead to the corrosion of social work practice and education. On one side of the debate, there is concern about the lack of engagement and face-to-face contact, while on the other hand some recognize that electronic means of communication has rapidly become the mainstream, often preferable, form of interpersonal engagement in contemporary society. In fact, it is rare for people to talk on the phone anymore; they more often opt to text, email, or use some form of social media to communicate with others, perhaps because it is thought to be less time-consuming or perhaps it is simply the evolution of human interactions. So how does the social work profession adapt to these trends and modify ways of communicating, gathering, and conveying information?

Throughout this chapter that is the very question we intend to explore. This chapter examines the use of management information systems (MIS) and considers the ways organizations and academic institutions can make the most of organizing and managing MIS programs to maximize efficiency and productivity. There are a host of considerations that must be factored into how organizations go about selecting, implementing, and making the most of the organization's MIS, while also staying true to the core values, ethics, and practice competencies etched in the profession. Box 12.1 displays the competencies/practice behaviors addressed in this chapter:

BOX 12.1

COMPETENCIES AND PRACTICE BEHAVIORS ADDRESSED IN THIS CHAPTER

Manages all aspects of information technology (Network for Social Work Management Competencies 15). Practice Behaviors:

- Identifies and utilizes technology resources to enhance the organization's process (15.1).
- Uses resources to promote the effective use of technology for clients and staff (15.2).

(continued)

BOX 12.1 *(Continued)*

- Remains current with developments in technology and upgrades the organization accordingly (15.3).
- Encourages adaptation of technology for service tracking and for other purposes that enhance efficiency and quality (15.4).

CSWE Competency 1—Demonstrate Ethical and Professional Behavior

- 1.4 Use technology ethically and appropriately to facilitate practice outcomes.

CSWE Competency 4—Engage in Practice-informed Research and Research-informed Practice
  Social workers

- 4.1 Use practice experience and theory to inform scientific inquiry and research.

CSWE Competency 7—Assess Individuals, Families, Groups, Organizations, and Communities
  Social workers

- 7.1 Collect and organize data, and apply critical thinking to interpret information from clients and constituencies.

CSWE Competency 8—Intervene With Individuals, Families, Groups, Organizations, and Communities
  Social workers

- 8.1 Critically choose and implement interventions to achieve practice goals and enhance capacities of clients and constituencies.

CSWE, Council on Social Work Education.

USING TECHNOLOGY TO ENHANCE ORGANIZATIONAL PROCESSES

Box 12.2 displays the competencies/behaviors in this section.

BOX 12.2

NETWORK FOR SOCIAL WORK MANAGEMENT COMPETENCIES AND PRACTICE BEHAVIORS 15

Manages all aspects of information technology (Network for Social Work Management Competencies 15). Practice Behaviors:

- Identifies and utilizes technology resources to enhance the organization's process (15.1).

There has been a burgeoning use of information technology (IT) in healthcare and social service industries and universities. IT offers more efficient means of gathering information and refining systems of internal controls, which allows organizations to not only track performance but also guide administrative decision making. MIS can support evidence-based and evidence-informed practices and teaching methods. MIS programs can be designed to help track the use of evidence-based treatment (EBT) techniques through an integrated means for collecting data on client or student outcomes, essentially establishing metrics for analyzing fidelity to treatment interventions or teaching methodologies. Thus, there is a significant connection between direct practice outcomes and administrative decision making, as administrative decision making often requires analyses of client or student outcomes as they correlate with treatment or course plans. Various data collected from direct practice or teaching in higher education settings, and their associated outcomes, can be integrated into the evaluation of the services delivered, which is used to guide administrative decisions.

Identifying Technology Resources

The organization's informational objectives, combined with the cost-effectiveness of the MIS, will factor into the decision about what type, or types, of MIS an organization will benefit from the most. Gillingham (2016) observed:

> It has been suggested that a minimum data set, defined in relation to good agency functioning rather than the affordances of an IS, may be a good starting point to guide such designs—further that a critical approach be taken in the evaluation of new designs, with an emphasis on the extent to which the investment required matches any increases in the ability of both managers and practitioners to achieve relevant goals. (p. 59)

A central MIS decision is whether to buy an existing program or to have an electronic system designed and custom-built for the organization. Again, the best choice obviously comes down to both cost-effectiveness and taking into account the needs of the organization as a whole, which, of course, should consider the needs of the majority of departments that will be operating the system. All departments that will be using the system, ideally, should contribute to this decision-making process. Regardless of whether an MIS program is custom-built or purchased, the organization or academic institution will need to begin the process of making this decision by first outlining the priorities and needs of the various programs. To that end, the organization will need to consider what the overarching goals and purpose of the MIS are, and concomitantly identify the specific needs of each department that are process-driven, compliance-driven, and outcome-driven.

There are certainly benefits of building a system that is tailored to the organization's and departments' needs, including the fact that the design, workflow, and interface of process and outcomes data can be tailored to the unique needs of the organization. The downside of building an MIS is that the process can be arduous and require a great deal of human and financial resources. Purchasing an established MIS can be helpful when there is limited expertise to design and build a system, and time and funds are limited. However, it is important to note that buying licenses for an MIS product will still require plenteous amount of human and financial capital to proceed through the various phases of data collection, vetting, planning, and implementation. Furthermore, it is very rare that an out-of-the-box MIS program will have everything that an organization is looking for to meet *all* of its needs. Therefore, intrinsic to the process of vetting MIS programs is the internal negotiations made among departments about what can be sacrificed and what possible "work-around" protocols can either be devised within the system to address needs or via procedural trainings if the system cannot be modified. The organization will need to determine the level of modifications that can be made to the base product, the additional costs incurred from such changes, and whether or not members from within the organization can be trained on how to make modifications well after the implementation phase is completed. In other words, how self-sustaining will the organization be once they launch the MIS program?

Implementation of the MIS program will need a project manager to oversee the teams, monitor tasks, and, most importantly, motivate the masses. Any change, especially a change of such magnitude as launching or altering an MIS program, can potentially evoke anxiety and resistance from a portion of staff. Change that involves key members enthusiastically mobilizing others to take action will stand a much better chance of creating staff buy-in, and, in the end, successful implementation and ongoing use of the MIS.

Prior to making a decision about whether or not to buy or build, a strategic process needs to carefully examine the workflow, regulations specific to the departments, and critical client/student outcome metrics. The vanguard of this process should have IT expertise, which may mean that the organization needs to hire a consultant or consulting firm. Additionally, the team should include lead members who have sufficient knowledge of the programs or service areas and can provide information about the type of services, expected outcomes, protocols, regulations, and funding mechanisms. Once the MIS team has delineated the organizational needs, it can begin to flesh out what the organization needs in an MIS program. The organizational needs can be turned into benchmarks that are used to create a rubric to score and compare MIS programs. In addition to the needs of all programs, the rubric should also include factors such as upfront and ongoing costs, access to ongoing service support, and automatic updates. It is often beneficial to vet at least a handful of companies before narrowing the decision to the top three. If the team determines that none of the MIS companies will meet the multifarious needs of the departments and organization as a whole, then the next step might be to explore how an MIS program can be custom-built. If the team decides to custom-build the MIS program, several companies should again be vetted and ranked before reaching a decision.

Box 12.3 offers some examples of the possible axioms that can be included in designing a rubric for scoring different MIS software during the vetting process.

BOX 12.3

DESIGNING AN MIS SOFTWARE RUBRIC

- *Ease of use:* How user-friendly, or intuitive, is the system? Consider that varied levels of staff within the organization will need to use the program. Based on the needs of all departments, how usable is the program? What features does it offer that will minimize the information overload of work, such as autopopulated fields and dropdown menus? Consider also the optics of the program. Is it aesthetically pleasing to the eyes, or is the amount of information appearing on each screen busy and overstimulating?

- *Security:* How will the database remain secure to protect client or student information and operate in accordance with HIPAA standards and other essential compliance regulations? Depending on one's position, a worker may need only partial, rather than complete, access to clients' or students' records. Aside from protecting client or student data, granting permission only to what is essential can safeguard erroneous data entry.

- *Functionality:* Evaluating the functionality of an MIS program will entirely depend on the needs identified in the initial project phase (i.e., identifying the needs of all departments). The functionality should be able to extract data points that can be filtered in various ways and analyzed and used to generate reports. The functionality of the program should also include the ease of access to and usefulness of information. What features/options will enhance the monitoring of compliance? What features will improve client services? For instance, can students download an app and keep track of assignments with their mobile device? Similarly, are clients able to log in to a patient portal and access information about upcoming appointments or resources they obtained at their last appointment? Will the program be able to integrate with other software systems? For instance, billing, marketing, and other electronic medical record systems? As the needs of the organization grow, or contract, how easily can requirements be modified? What additional costs or penalties are involved in making scalability changes?

- *Ongoing customer service*: Once the system is fully implemented, will there be ongoing support services to address any software issues? If so, what are the time frames in which they will be available (consider business hours in different time zones)? Will the software be available for the duration of the license, or a closed window of time? What software updates will the organization be eligible for, and will there be additional costs?

HIPAA, Health Insurance Portability and Accountability Act; MIS, management information system.

Selecting the MIS program that best fits organizational needs is a multilayered and multi stepped process that involves thoroughly vetting the MIS program and company through a strategic process that involves key staff positions from all departments. Since each department has its own set of needs, and thus its own set of questions about how the MIS will meet these needs, it is best to involve all groups from the start. This involvement does not mean that everyone from each department should be asked to participate; rather key members can serve as representatives and advisors to the process. Mildon and Shlonsky (2011) suggested that people should be integrally involved in training, testing, and designing processes related to the outcomes and outputs that will be needed. Much goes into selecting the MIS system that will be the most useful for the organization. Through an extended vetting process, each department can get a sense of functionality of the electronic system and begin to understand how the system can integrate with other data points that are needed for reporting requirements.

Having representation from each department not only increases the likelihood that the system selected will meet the multitude of needs but also ensures that each department will have a stake in the success of the program. When vetting the MIS, it is critical that the functionality does not operate in silos, but instead can interact with other data points that inform decisions about how to grow, maintain, or correctively adjust to the identified trends. Assuring functionality requires that members of the vetting process have knowledge of the programs, including how treatment fidelity and client outcomes are measured, as well as how compliance goals and objectives are measured.

It is, however, important to note that involving staff is not a guarantee of success. Some staff members may be eager to assist in the processes, and some may simply go through the motions, too overwhelmed with their other tasks and responsibilities and not fully able to commit to the time this process actually takes. One way to help mitigate the latter is for leadership to assess what tasks can be reassigned to others during this project development period. Additionally, it is crucial that the staff involved understand that they are being asked to think about the long-term picture and day-to-day functioning. The project manager may need to help them make causal connections about the significance of the project and how they can contribute to the successful outcomes. Although involving staff is critical, leaders need to be cognizant of the fact that the representatives may not have a sophisticated understanding of how the product will shape the future of their work. They may not know what questions to ask, and may be overwhelmed by technical jargon. It can be helpful to have IT support or external consultants available to the team throughout the vetting, planning, and implementation process. Having IT support or an external consulting firm can help to ensure that the right questions are being asked and that information is explained in a manner that is easily understood, which will in turn enable the staff to provide relevant information about the workflow and data points that will be most useful to integrate into the system. Along the way, team members will require inspiration, coaching, positive reinforcement, and transparency to maintain energy levels and stay engaged and motivated.

Utilizing Technology Resources

There are a number of benefits to utilizing technology resources for enhancing the organization's processes. Prior to deciding what type of MIS program the organization will pursue, the organization must identify the purpose and potential benefits of the MIS. Johnson (2018) provides rich insights about the role of MIS in social work management and identifies several crucial ways that MIS benefits social workers and organizations.

> *Throughout my research, it became apparent there are five information system domains: executive information, decision support, management information, office support and transaction processing. MISs incorporate basic data, information and explicit knowledge. MIS documents best practices, program and client information that can be utilized for planning, initiating, organizing, and improving a social service*

organization. MIS is a strategic data tool that can be used to move the mission of social service organizations forward.

MIS has the capacity to provide Social Workers with outcome data, service analysis, program outcome indicators, individual/family community trends and information about stewardship of funds. This information also supports opportunities for engagement, project management, and build upon Social Work competencies. Further, these efforts support the ability to adapt to internal and external shifts in human service organizations, as well as the information required to evaluate a program's effectiveness and create a corrective action plan to meet the needs of the community (Johnson, 2018, n.p.)

As Johnson (2018) illustrated, there are numerous advantages to MIS for social service organizations. Some of the benefits include, but are certainly not limited to, improved financial management, improvements in program operations, monitoring client and student outcomes, planning and decision making, and improvements to policy and practice. Jonson-Reid, Kontak, and Mueller (2001) explained that "when such systems are designed collaboratively by line social workers and researchers, the information collected is more responsive to immediate practice and policy needs, as well as more valuable to ongoing evaluation research" (p. 210).

In order for an organization to maximize the potential advantages, as outlined by Johnson (2018), a core team developed for the purpose of leading the MIS project must identify the critical ways the data will be collected, and for what purpose (i.e., potential gain). The core focus of this foundational process is to articulate how the MIS will be used to steward funds and advance the mission of the organization.

▨ Planning and Implementation Phases

Whether the organization is introducing the MIS for the first time or transitioning from another MIS program, there are several phases of decision making and strategic planning that should occur leading up to the implementation process. When organizations transition from one MIS product to another, the MIS team may have the advantage of knowing what worked well and what did not. Knowing this information not only helps to critically evaluate the utility and functionality of the MIS program but also lends insight about the process of training staff and launching the program successfully. Hence, the organization may have a fairly good idea about what capacity and functionality the new system should have, how data collection and reporting might be integrated with newfound intention, and how to lead staff through a large-scale change.

The decision making, strategic planning, and implementation of the MIS can be conceptualized in four phases, as described in the following sections. Variations to these phases depend on organizational culture and needs. The team must consider the baseline capabilities of the organizational culture to know how to implement the changes in a way that promotes buy-in and the use of the technology. It should be acknowledged that technology is still designed and operated by humans—creating user-defined options requires multiple rounds of consideration about the potential outcomes. There may be times when the core team needs to revisit a previous phase in order to successfully complete the phase they are currently operating in and before diving into the next phase.

Phase I

The first phase focuses on laying the foundation for decision making that will help determine if the organization will select or create an MIS. Before determining whether to buy or build the MIS, the team will need to define the organizational impact being sought. Once the desired impact is clearly defined and agreed upon, the team will need to begin to conceptualize how to link the organizational mission, goals, and objectives to policy and compliance outcomes.

Conceptualizing how the mission, goals, objectives, policy, performance, and compliance aims should be carefully sewn in to the electronic system will guide the team in identifying the types of data and information need to be gathered, reported on, and analyzed by various departments within the organization. Thus, in this initial phase, the team begins to conceive the data points that will need to be gathered and defines exactly why these data will be important.

Phase II

The second phase crystalizes the conceptualization of data points and purposes. The primary aims of this phase are to evaluate the quality of information that is both currently and conceivably necessary to effectively meet goals, objectives, and regulations, and to offer meaningful analytics. The process of conceptualizing data points is marked by a process of weeding out informational overload and developing or refining a universal means for data collection, analysis, and reporting. Organizations, especially those that do not yet have an MIS or perhaps have an archaic MIS, may be susceptible to informational overload due to the multiple datasets that might also have different meanings depending on the users. Informational overload can suffuse an organization as new regulations or protocols are introduced and each department develops its own way of managing the data. Data gathered in silos, rather than through uniformed methodologies, can result in the creation of multiple forms that amass duplicative information, resulting in the diminishment of data cogency and limitations to the reliability of data. If information from one department is collected differently, or not at all by another department, it will result in the skewing of aggregate data. Therefore, teams can and should view this phase as an opportunity for weeding out or rethinking, reorganizing, and redesigning how information is gathered, why it is needed, and how it can integrate with other systems and departments. To that end, the team is able to develop and modify the outcome measures. Workflow processes can provide road maps for the team to begin to identify and understand how to prevent the perpetuation of data silos and information overload.

Phase III

The third phase primarily focuses on beginning to implement the system. System implementation involves product testing, usually by creating mock examples entered into the system to test for bugs, and troubleshooting any errors before going live. This phase also involves training teams of staff. Ideally, organizations can use "train the trainer" models in which a number of staff are trained to become proficient in using the system and can provide training to other teams of staff. The trainers can be available to staff for questions as they begin to learn and independently use the system. Implementation can be completed in stages: a small department or percentage of records is transferred to the electronic system, while others incrementally follow. Conversely, organizations may opt to launch a full implementation where all programs go live simultaneously. The potential pros and cons of both options should be weighed by the team as choice will be driven by the organization's culture and resources.

Phase IV

The fourth phase is about managing and maintaining the system, including assessing how programs are using and making the most of the MIS. During this phase, reports offer informational feedback about how the data are collected and organized by the programs, in a way that informs decisions and evaluates service outcomes. This phase is an ongoing process of managing technology, computer systems, malware, and the storing and use of data.

Having implementation targets, detailed project lists, meeting minutes, and action lists are critical for the project manager to monitor and disseminate to the team to continuously evaluate how the project is progressing. Teams should, however, anticipate Murphy's Law in the process of implementing an MIS program no matter how well-prepared, well-paced, and thorough they have been throughout the various phases. The team cannot think of everything from the outset and will discover some things even if only accidentally after the product has gone live. However, the more methodical teams are in their planning, the better off they will be in managing the hiccups that will undoubtedly occur along the way.

MIS Use for Planning and Decision Making

In an academic setting MIS can assist with planning and scheduling courses, assessing and assigning the workload of staff, and determining the course times and days that are most appealing for students (i.e., increased student enrollment). The ideal MIS would have the student course plan information included in the MIS, since students take different combinations of courses over multiple years. A university would want to use this information for academic planning and projecting into the future estimated program growth. The MIS can also provide information about student enrollment as it pertains to student-to-faculty ratios, which can offer information about the number of faculty positions that are needed both now and in the future. Additionally, an MIS system is helpful for tracking the workload of staff by determining their credit-load assignments. MIS programs can be designed to track and measure student outcomes, such as the Council on Social Work Education (CSWE) competencies. Reporting on student outcomes based on CSWE competencies is useful for conducting self-studies and preparing for accreditation or reaccreditation.

Organizations that provide direct care services to clients can also benefit greatly from MIS systems. These benefits can be experienced throughout the organization, including in the business office, human resources, and clinical and medical services, as well as any ancillary services. As we discussed in Chapter 9, organizations are responsible for adhering to multiple regulations that impact various programs within the organization. MIS programs can offer features such as flagging key persons when critical data points are missing, such as signatures from a supervisor, or having a supervisor receive notice that a treatment plan is near or past due, and helping the billing department track and calculate client contact hours and meaningful use when submitting billing claims. Box 12.4 displays the competencies/behaviors in this section.

BOX 12.4

NETWORK FOR SOCIAL WORK MANAGEMENT COMPETENCIES AND PRACTICE BEHAVIORS 15 AND COUNCIL ON SOCIAL WORK EDUCATION PRACTICE BEHAVIORS 4, 7, AND 8

Manages all aspects of information technology (Network for Social Work Management Competencies 15). Practice Behaviors:

- Uses resources to promote the effective use of technology for clients and staff (15.2).

CSWE Competency 4—Engage in Practice-informed Research and Research-informed Practice Social workers

- 4.1 Use practice experience and theory to inform scientific inquiry and research.

CSWE Competency 7—Assess Individuals, Families, Groups, Organizations, and Communities Social workers

- 7.1 Collect and organize data, and apply critical thinking to interpret information from clients and constituencies.

(continued)

BOX 12.4 *(Continued)*

CSWE Competency 8—Intervene With Individuals, Families, Groups, Organizations, and Communities
   Social workers

▦   8.1 Critically choose and implement interventions to achieve practice goals and enhance capacities of clients and constituencies.

CSWE, Council on Social Work Education.

Evaluating client outcomes is an essential competency. However, given large caseloads, it can be quite challenging for social workers to evaluate the results of their work without a technology system that can quickly and accurately generate outcome reports. MIS can assist social workers in providing a timely snapshot of treatment progress, which is essential for the care of the client but equally as imperative for performance-based reporting. Programs may be mandated by funding regulations—grants or managed care—to produce information about the client outcomes. Performance-based reporting essentially requires organizations to report on metrics of progress to demonstrate the effectiveness of care, which has steadfastly been linked with reimbursement measures. For instance, some funders have created a scaled system for reimbursement that requires providers to demonstrate the evidence-based practice employed and the measurable treatment outcomes, which are then converted into a tiered system of reimbursement. Organizations, thus, need to efficiently generate reports that support their billing claims.

▦ Technology to Maximize Resources

In this section, we discuss the various ways technology can be used to maximize organizational resources and promote the effective use of technology for clients and staff.

Cost Savings

While the costs associated with purchasing and maintaining an MIS may initially seem high, the long-term cost savings can be significant. Materials such as paper, printing costs, copy machines, ink cartridges, and fax machines often consume a great deal of programs' budgetary expenses. Voluminous paper files and records need to be stored, which ultimately translates to a need for greater space; and overhead costs can be significantly reduced through digitizing the records. Staffing costs can also be reduced by implementing a well-designed and integrated MIS, as the time needed for staff to manage, record, compile, and analyze information can be done with greater efficiency. The process of obtaining and releasing records can be done much faster and more economically. By reducing the amount of time that is allocated to administrative paperwork, staff can instead allocate more time to services and ways to advance the organizational mission.

Funding

MIS programs can help organizations and academic institutions obtain more funding from outside sources or from primary funders by documenting achieved outcomes. Thus, an organization can demonstrate that clients have achieved treatment goals, and follow-up measures may indicate sustained treatment gains. For an academic institution, an MIS can help to record student learning outcomes needed for reaccreditation. Information can also be generated from process and outcome data that are described in annual letters of appeal to showcase to potential donors how and what has been achieved.

Compliance

As discussed in Chapter 9, there are numerous elements of compliance that need to be tracked and monitored. Having an MIS program that can quickly analyze how many treatment plans were completed on time, the percentage of goals that were attained and how many critical instances or reports of abuse or neglect were filed, all at the click of a button, allows organizations to efficiently analyze and report data. The CSWE requires that all schools advertise on their websites the results of student learning outcomes to ascertain whether or not students are meeting learning benchmarks. Additionally, because information recorded in an MIS is timestamped and can be linked to the staff entering the data, there is an inherent level of compliance protection built into the system. Granting user rights further protects sensitive information by limiting the amount of information staff can access, depending on the staffs's roles. Thus, there is a greater ability to ensure the organization is adhering to Health Insurance Portability and Accountability Act (HIPAA) regulations. MIS programs that are designed to collect the specific data that measure such benchmarks can generate analytics that capture this information. Finally, paper records are at risk of becoming lost or damaged due to flooding, mold, fires, or other natural disasters. Having an MIS that is backed up by a server, or multiple servers, helps to ensure the security of records.

Billing

Errors in billing can be reduced through the use of MIS programs as well. Because the billing department will have access to the information in a timelier manner, reimbursement claims can be submitted faster and with fewer errors. Additionally, MIS programs can help track the trends of reimbursement, such as the reasons claims were denied, and also help track claims that need to be resubmitted and followed up on.

Compiling Data

As can be seen from the previous examples, the overarching theme is how quickly the MIS can compile the data encased in the program, which would otherwise require hours of human labor to complete. Additionally, the time historically spent on entering data into another system, such as Excel, to calculate and graph findings for analytic reports can be done much faster thanks to sophisticated algorithms and integrated data systems. The amount of time saved on these laborious tasks can now be expediently completed with a few simple clicks. Furthermore, multiple departments are able to simultaneously access the electronic files, eliminating the need for copying information. Some MIS programs are even designed for collaborative use, where concurrent changes can be made to the record while preventing conflicting edits, which can reduce the number of errors caused by redundancy or information overload.

An integrated MIS has the ability to connect information that evaluates administrative and service delivery outcomes. As mentioned earlier in this chapter, service delivery outcomes can improve how programs monitor and report on client outcomes. Service delivery outcomes can be used by administrators to make decisions and report on critical data points, such as client contact hours, that are factored in the analysis of program costs, as well as identify client outcomes for analyzing treatment efficacy. The ability to evaluate treatment efficacy can directly connect to the use of evidence-based practices employed and can guide clinical administrative decisions about treatment interventions and modalities that prove to be most effective for a particular client population. Monitoring client contact hours can aid the administrative task of analyzing budget outcomes, as well as staff performance outcomes that can be objectively measured and evaluated. Therefore, an integrated MIS aids in the ability to evaluate programmatic factors that may correlate with client outcomes, as well as performance outcomes of staff that then inform both administrative decisions and practice decisions.

In addition to using the information to monitor variables that contribute to client outcomes, data can also highlight information that leads to administrative decision making about what adjustment may be needed to enhance or correct service delivery issues. For instance, if the data indicate that clients presenting for anger management treatment who received both individual and group therapies demonstrated significant and sustained treatment gains when compared to those who received only group therapy, the administrative decision may be whether or not to combine the treatment modalities. The additional data that will need to be explored are whether or not clients were offered individual treatment, and reasons they may have declined or discontinued services. For instance, are individual therapy appointments offered at various times of the day, making it possible for those working to attend individual therapy appointments? Hence, the client outcome data help to raise questions about how to best serve clients since they provide information about what is working and flags ideas about how to continue to improve client outcomes.

Client/Patient Portal

The social work profession adheres to the value of clients' rights to self-determine and be collaborators in their treatment. One way that MIS can help to further promote this value is through the use of a client portal, more commonly referred to as a patient portal. Patient portals are part of many MIS programs, although sometimes they are an additional cost to the base product.

A patient portal provides clients with access to information including their upcoming appointments, their demographic and insurance information prior to arriving for an appointment, the type of service they received, educational information about medication side effects, and ancillary information such as domestic violence resources or suicide prevention hotlines. Providing clients with electronic access to additional resources, or education about their diagnosis or medication, helps to promote clients' rights to treatment. Organizations can also use electronic means to check in with clients between appointments, particularly those clients at risk of relapse or suicide. A related best practice and compliance standard is strengthening and promoting clients' natural support systems. Patient portals can be used to promote supportive members' involvement in care. For instance, children of aging parents living with dementia can access information about their parents' medical and psychosocial appointments by accessing the patient portal (provided there is a release of information permitting this, of course). This remote access is especially helpful for adult children who are geographically distant from their parent(s) but want to remain involved in their caretaking and know that their parent will not be able to convey information about their treatment.

A patient portal is also a way for organizations to track best practice procedures and compliance with regulations. Ultimately, patient portals can track data that demonstrate that the client was provided information regarding their treatment and educational resources related to their presenting concerns. Electronic communication has helped many agencies send and receive client satisfaction surveys, which are a rich data source that can be used for marketing and programmatic improvement.

Technology Is Changing

Box 12.5 displays the competencies/behaviors in this section. The field of technology is constantly improving: software and hardware updates occur often, and new programs are continuously developed and enhanced. Prudent organizations commit themselves to staying informed about the advances technology offers. With the constant upgrading of mobile technologies, staff can now access most programs for data entry using their smartphones. Mobile devices can also interact with MIS programs. Gillingham (2014b) noted that information systems (IS) accessed through smartphones and tablets can be a useful and empowering tool for social workers to enter and obtain information in timely fashions.

BOX 12.5

NETWORK FOR SOCIAL WORK MANAGEMENT COMPETENCIES AND PRACTICE BEHAVIORS 15 AND COUNCIL ON SOCIAL WORK EDUCATION PRACTICE BEHAVIOR 1

Manages all aspects of information technology (Network for Social Work Management Competencies 15). Practice Behaviors:

- Remains current with developments in technology and upgrades the organization accordingly (15.3).

CSWE Competency 1—Demonstrate Ethical and Professional Behavior

- 1.4 Use technology ethically and appropriately to facilitate practice outcomes.

CSWE, Council on Social Work Education.

> *The use of mobile devices such as smartphones and tablets may improve the way that frontline practitioners access IS to enter and retrieve data. The increasingly customizable reporting functions of IS can also facilitate the collection of specific data for the evaluation of interventions (see O'Connor et al., 2011). The increased accessibility to IS provided by mobile devices may also be used to empower service users by allowing them to access and enter data in agency records. (Parrot & Madoc-Jones, 2008, p. 134)*

Remaining current with ongoing developments in technology is typically a task dedicated to the IT department within an organization. Just as social workers receive continuous education in their field of expertise, IT staff are also expected to keep up to date with evolving technology knowledge, skills, and programs that allow them to best inform and advise organizations about how to maximize the benefits and utility of technology.

Leaders and managers can also remain informed about advances in technology by registering with various professional email lists that publish information about new or improved programs. Networking is another way that leaders and managers can stay informed about the various MIS programs available; they can ask members within their networking circle about the programs they use, the issues they might have with the programs, and the ways they have resolved any issues. The organizational culture must always be considered when exploring MIS options to help guide how future changes can be implemented and to best understand how to promote staff buy-in and understanding of the impact of technology to capitalize on its use.

When organizations upgrade to new computer programs for management, interacting, and tracking, the faculty and/or staff need to be trained in how to access and use the programs. Training on the use of new programs should be made available to all and could be considered a mandatory requirement. When updating or changing systems, consider which data will be migrated from the old system to the new. For every choice made about a piece of data that should be collected, consider that some data may not be available either because they do not exist in the IS or it is technically impossible to capture them, or perhaps staff are not able to enter the data. The process of upgrading will invariably result in additional decision making.

Validity of Data

Box 12.6 displays the competencies/behaviors in this section. Although MIS programs are designed to enhance efficiency, organizations and academic institutions need to realize that, in order for the MIS to do so, time and human capital must be dedicated to managing the entering of data, assessing the value of data, and monitoring that the data are valid and reliable.

BOX 12.6

NETWORK FOR SOCIAL WORK MANAGEMENT COMPETENCIES AND PRACTICE BEHAVIORS 15

Manages all aspects of information technology (Network for Social Work Management Competencies 15). Practice Behaviors:

- Encourages adaptation of technology for service tracking and for other purposes that enhance efficiency and quality (15.4).

Organizations and project management teams need to understand that technology is still designed and operated by humans, and, as such, is not immune to human error. A common challenge of MIS programs—whether launching a system for the first time or changing systems—is the validity of data. The data may not be as valid or reliable as it needs to be because of gaps in the design of data fields that may not exactly correlate with process or outcomes measures, or basic or advanced information points that are needed to complete comprehensive analytics. Validity is all about obtaining data on what you are trying to measure. Oftentimes, design gaps are due to the differences between the experts designing and training on the MIS, and the program people who are experts about the type of data that need to be recorded, submitted, analyzed, and communicated within and outside the system. It is therefore helpful to have program people explain the intricate information and workflow processes to the IT experts or MIS consultants. When there is a lack of collaboration and understanding of the workflow processes and why certain data collection is vital, the system will be developed with information gaps that will most likely be completed inconsistently or in worse cases jeopardize compliance with regulations. Gillingham (2014a) explained that a primary area of concern for human service organizations is that "they may struggle to complete tasks, data that is entered by occasional users may be inaccurate or incomplete, which undermines claims that the IS can be the single source of truth for an organization" (p. 173).

Box 12.7 provides an example of data validity pertaining to a service organization.

BOX 12.7

COMPETENCY-BASED CASE EXAMPLE: DATA VALIDITY

One example of risks to compliance is the type of treatment modality that may be listed as data fields in a base product MIS. A clinic needs to document the type of session as either individual, group, family, or medication management, and is also required to record the session duration. The MIS program only encased individual and group therapies for treatment modality choices and suggested that the session duration be noted within the body of the therapy note. This limitation created significant concern as the agency had worked tirelessly to maintain high marks on the audits completed by the state licensing department. Additionally, the clinicians were required to submit monthly reports to the state department that calculated the number, type, and total duration of therapy minutes provided in the last 30 days. Although the MIS program was intended to improve efficiency, its supplier was unable to modify this feature needed by the organization.

(continued)

BOX 12.7 *(Continued)*

Questions

1. Not initially knowing that the MIS program did not offer the data fields needed, the organization signed a contract with the MIS company. How should the team now proceed?

2. What type of adaptations will the team need to create and/or advocate for?

Classifying faculty workload in a university setting (e.g., courses taught, research release time, and administrative assignments for credit) must be defined accurately each semester and year as this information is needed for documentation purposes for both administrators and faculty. For example, a faculty member up for tenure, promotion, or assessment needs to have access to the MIS files on her or his history of workload. This type of file can easily be created in Excel with automatic computing for overload credits and these data will be of great value to the director when assigning work.

Box 12.8 provides a description of how performance-based budgeting and the shift to better use of data improved organizational functioning.

BOX 12.8

COMPETENCY-BASED CASE EXAMPLE: PERFORMANCE-BASED BUDGETING IN A DEPARTMENT OF CHILDREN AND FAMILIES

This excerpt is taken from a study.

In New Jersey, the state Department of Children and Families was uniquely positioned to be able to respond to the call for performance-based budgeting and the more prominent shift toward the use of data in overall agency management. Both the children's behavioral health system and the child welfare system had undergone significant reforms that included the development of robust data management systems. As a result, the department's leadership recognized the need to develop the skills of middle managers to help them utilize data in their daily decision making . . .

An important aspect of this program is that the department's leadership team has utilized the findings of the fellows each year as the basis for policy and practice change and for new service development.

This initiative quickly became an essential part of our organizational culture and succession planning. Five years into this very successful program as leaders we have come to realize that we have done a very good job of educating our staff to ask questions about their work and to expect to see results through observable changes in data. We have also educated our staff to expect our interventions with families to be successful and/or to expect that the services we refer our families to will result in positive differences in their lives and in the lives of their children (Blake, 2016, pp. 89–90).

Reliability of Data

How information is entered can also pose threats to the reliability of data. Once an organization has determined the type of data points needed, the team needs to judiciously plan, provide ongoing training, and manage the data that are entered. Gillingham (2014b) noted that a primary issue is ensuring that the data being entered means what it was intended to mean, otherwise the validity is diminished. Additionally, how data are entered by numerous people can threaten the reliability of data. Box 12.9 illustrates how data entry can be inconsistent and thus threaten the reliability of data and overall compliance with a particular regulation.

BOX 12.9

COMPETENCY-BASED CASE EXAMPLE: DCFID

According to regulations, an organization must include youths' Department of Children and Families identification number, known as the DCFID, as part of its demographic information. The organization will be
cited when officially audited if the DCFID is not listed in the record. The MIS program does not have a field
specifically designated to record the DCFID, but does have fields for medical record numbers and social
security numbers. None of these fields can be modified within the MIS program, so staff troubleshoot by
recording the DCFID either in the medical record or SSN fields as the default way to ensure that they have
input the data. The problem with this solution is that when the audit occurs, auditors cannot consistently
determine if the DCFID has been recorded because the data have been input by several staff in different
ways, and some staff stopped entering it altogether because they were no longer visually prompted to
complete a field that was specifically labeled DCFID.

   In the previous case example, the agency was faced with a dilemma about a missing data point
which could not be entered because the MIS program's base product did not include a field specific
to the agency's need. Since the agency and MIS consultants could not add or modify fields, the best
approach to dealing with this situation would be to have ongoing training and oversight of data
entry. Prior to training, the project manager of the MIS implementation might inquire with several
key members who have the primary responsibility for inputting these data what other field may
make sense to set as the default for recording the DCFID. Once consensus is reached, the training
should include multiple mock entries to ensure that the data are entered correctly. The training
should include instruction manuals that can be provided to the current staff and used as a training
document for future staff. After going live with the MIS program, the data should be monitored
and cross-referenced to confirm that DCFID numbers are consistently recorded in the designated
field. Finally, the agency may want to create a table of contents for the auditor that describes where
certain information can be found in the electronic chart, which is now labeled as "x."

SUMMARY

Throughout this chapter, we discussed the various benefits of using MIS to enhance organizational
processes, resources, and outcomes. We outlined four phases related to implementing an MIS
that can aid organizations in identifying technology resources and launching an MIS program.
Additionally, we explored the utility of technology resources and discussed how technology aids
administrative and clinical decisions. Finally, we examined the ways that MIS improves efficiency
in planning, billing, and compliance monitoring.

ACTIVITIES

1. Create a workflow list to describe the process within your department about how information is gathered, evaluated, and reported.

2. Create a rubric for evaluating an MIS program that meets your organization's needs. Include
   benchmarks about the type of data points that need to be collected, ease of use, and how
   information can be analyzed to guide clinical and administrative decisions.

3. Identify at least three ways that using an MIS could guide your clinical and/or administrative
   decision making.

REFERENCES

Blake, A. (2016). The impact of our changing environment on the management practices in Public Human Service Organizations. *Human Service Organizations: Management, Leadership & Governance, 40*(2), 89–91. doi:10.1080/23303131.2016.1165039

Gillingham, P. (2014a). Information systems and human service organizations: Managing and designing for the "occasional user". *Human Service Organizations: Management, Leadership & Governance, 38*(2), 169–177. doi:10.1080/03643107.2013.859198

Gillingham, P. (2014b). Repositioning electronic information systems in human service organizations. *Human Service Organizations: Management, Leadership & Governance, 38*(2), 125–134. doi:10.1080/03643107.2013.853011

Gillingham, P. (2016). Electronic information systems and human service organizations: The needs of managers. *Human Service Organizations: Management, Leadership & Governance, 40*(1), 51–61. doi:10.1080/23303131.2015.1069232

Johnson, K. (2018). Role of management information systems (MIS) in social work management. *Network for Social Management*. Retrieved from https://socialworkmanager.org/press-blogs/community-voice/role-management-information-systems-mis-social-work-management-kimson-johnson/

Jonson-Reid, M., Kontak, D., & Mueller, S. (2001). Developing a management information system for school social workers: A field-university partnership. *Children & Schools, 23*(4), 198–211. doi:10.1093/cs/23.4.198

Mildon, R., & Shlonsky, A. (2011). Bridge over troubled water: Using implementation science to facilitate effective services in child welfare. *Child Abuse & Neglect, 35*(9), 753–756. doi:10.1016/j.chiabu.2011.07.001

CHAPTER 13

FINANCIAL MANAGEMENT IN SOCIAL WORK

CHAPTER OBJECTIVES

- Understanding budgeting and the budgeting process in the organization.
- Understanding types of income and expenses.
- Managing finances to meet program goals.
- Maximizing financial resources.
- Developing investment strategies.
- Developing contracts.
- Using the budget as a management tool.
- Understanding financial statements, analysis, and planning.
- Dealing with limited resources, cutbacks, reductions, and environmental challenges.
- Developing downsizing strategies.

INTRODUCTION

Social work leaders and managers are responsible for understanding the organization's budget processes. The organization's budget can be considered a blueprint for knowing how to programmatically proceed. For instance, there will be times when the budget can help to identify costs that need to be reduced and resources that may need to be reallocated. Budgets are also used as management tools in and of themselves since they provide a picture of how the program is operating. When there is a budget deficit, the root cause must be fully understood in order to effectively produce solutions to the problems resulting in fiscal losses. Conversely, when programs are operating at profit, or at income over expense, it is equally as important to understand the cause(s) of the program's success.

There are a number of environmental influences that challenge an organization's budget. The socioeconomic climate can have significant power over the funding for social services and public universities. Even programs that are not funded by the government, such as private colleges and universities, can be impacted by environmental influences that manifest in enrollment trends, which ultimately affect the budget process. Social workers are very well acquainted with how austerity can affect clients, families, groups, communities, as well as the organizations that service them and academic institutions that teach about them.

Social work leaders and managers need to be comfortable reviewing, analyzing, and preparing budgets to understand how to maximize financial resources and make decisions about the future direction of programs and financial sustainability of departments. However, because the span of financial management tasks is beyond the scope of this chapter, the Appendix offers key financial terms for social work managers to become familiar with.

In this chapter, we explore how social work leaders and managers perform financial management responsibilities. Box 13.1 displays the competencies/practice behaviors addressed in this chapter.

BOX 13.1

COMPETENCIES AND PRACTICE BEHAVIORS COVERED IN THIS CHAPTER

Possesses analytical and critical thinking skills that promote organizational growth (Network for Social Work Management Competencies 3). Practice Behaviors:

- Makes creative use of agency resources to serve the needs of diverse clients (3.3).

Effectively manages and oversees the budget and other financial resources to support the organization's mission and goals and to foster continuous program improvement and accountability (Network for Social Work Management Competencies 13). Practice Behaviors:

- Manages utilization of resources to ensure that they are in line with the organization's mission and goals (13.1).
- Ensures that expenditures are allowed and appropriate and that allocated funds are available throughout the fiscal year (13.2).
- Monitors revenue and expenditures at regular intervals to ensure that budget assumptions are consistent with anticipated income and expenses (13.3).
- Ensures that financial activities are consistent with organizational policies and are sufficiently documented for audit (13.4).
- Oversees equitable allocation of funds based on such indicators as visits, outcomes, and historical precedent (13.5).
- Monitors expenditures to ensure that operating units have sufficient resources to offer quality services, using dashboards and other visual tools to link expenditures to outcomes (13.6).

BUDGETING

Box 13.2 displays the competencies/behaviors in this section.

BOX 13.2

NETWORK FOR SOCIAL WORK MANAGEMENT COMPETENCIES AND PRACTICE BEHAVIORS 3 AND 13

Possesses analytical and critical thinking skills that promote organizational growth (Network for Social Work Management Competencies 3). Practice Behaviors:

- Makes creative use of agency resources to serve the needs of diverse clients (3.3).

Effectively manages and oversees the budget and other financial resources to support the organization's/program's mission and goals and to foster continuous program improvement and accountability (Network for Social Work Management Competencies 13). Practice Behaviors:

- Manages utilization of resources to ensure that they are in line with the organization's mission and goals (13.1).

- Oversees equitable allocation of funds based on such indicators as visits, outcomes, and historical precedent (13.5).

Many social work leaders and managers professionally advance without formal training and education on how to manage and oversee budgets. However, managing the resources within an organization, or department within an organization, is critical to ensuring that resources are aligned with the mission and goals. The organization's budget provides an operating plan for a given fiscal year. Thus, the budget conveys, in financial language, how the organization will fulfill its mission. Social work leaders and managers may initially be unfamiliar with the financial jargon that is expressed in the budget or throughout the process of preparing the budget with members of the business office; however, with increased exposure, experience, and curiosity, many can quickly learn the fiscal lexicons.

The budget is usually approved by the board of directors and executive leadership who will decide which programs will be ventured, based on a program's budgetary forecast and collective budgetary forecasts of all programs within the organization. Preparing a conservative budget for the upcoming fiscal year allows the board of directors or other key decision makers to review how resources have been allocated for service delivery and about fiscal barriers or problems that could potentially unravel the budget over the fiscal year. Understanding the potential fiscal problems that might arise within a program is yet another reason why managers and leaders should monitor the budget at regular intervals to assess the financial strengths and weaknesses of the program and to identify modifications that need to be made. Modifications can materialize through a process of reallocation of resources, cost reduction strategies, downsizing strategies, or investment strategies, such as considering ways to increase or diversify revenue streams.

A primary task for leaders and managers is to determine which resources are allocated to which goals, and then analyze whether or not the allocation is sufficient to reach the desired goals. When it is decided that the allocation of funds is insufficient to attain the stated goals, leaders and managers must consider if reallocation is possible, and if so, determine how to reallocate the funds. Reallocation is sometimes accomplished by restructuring cost centers.

▨ Cost Centers

A cost center is defined as a distinct unit or department within an organization that has an identified manager who is responsible for the oversight of the income and expenses associated with the unit and ensures the adherence to the unit's budget. Managers may sometimes oversee more than one cost center, depending on the scope of their responsibilities. Resource reallocation to a different cost center within the agency may be necessary, not only to effectively manage resources but to balance budgets. For instance, there may be a program within the organization that is deemed essential for the mission of the agency, albeit it does not breakeven. In this case, the costs associated with operating this particular department/unit (cost center) could potentially be reallocated to another department. Box 13.3 provides an example of reallocating resources between cost centers.

BOX 13.3

COMPETENCY-BASED EXAMPLE: REALLOCATING RESOURCES BETWEEN COST CENTERS

A mental health agency provides a continuum of services to adults living with HIV and AIDS. Some of the services they provide include outpatient mental health counseling, substance abuse treatment, residential treatment and housing support, medical case management, advocacy services, medication management, and syringe exchange program. The mission of the agency is to meet the complex and nuanced needs of persons living with HIV and AIDS. As part of the case management services, the agency offers primary support with food, utilities, medical expenses, and transportation. The costs and income for these services have traditionally been recorded in the case management services cost center. However, with the inflating costs associated with providing transportation assistance as well as much needed medical supplies, combined with the shrinking funds available for case management services, this cost center is operating at a 20% loss. The organization and board of directors believe that these services are essential to the mission of the organization and do not believe they should be cut, but know that if the program continues to operate at a loss for another year, then they will have to make some tough decisions. The director worked with the chief financial officer to examine how costs or services could be potentially reallocated among various cost centers. They began by looking at the cost centers that are operating at income over expenses or break-even levels. Three cost centers, the outpatient, residential, and medication management programs, were operating slightly above income over expenses (enough to collectively absorb the 20% deficit). Because all three of these programs frequently utilize case management services, it was determined that each of the programs will pay a proportionate fee toward the case management cost center for services rendered. By reallocating how the funds are distributed between these programs, the case management center was projected to be able to operate at breakeven for the duration of the upcoming fiscal year.

Leaders and managers can use the budget as a management tool which provides information about programmatic performance. The management of resources is predominantly focused on balancing budgets and deciding where and how to make adjustments so that the allocation of resources is being used in the best possible way as to maximize the outcomes for clients or students. Social work leaders and managers must also ascertain what services and related resources are crucial to the organization's mission and goals. The budget, which captures the financial state of operations, alerts management to necessitous changes. This alert can sometimes mean that difficult decisions need to be made about how to restructure positions within the organization to trim a top-heavy assembly of management positions, and/or to evaluate other resources that are consuming a significant percentage of the budget.

An essential task of monitoring resources is to maximize the outcomes for clients/students as they conjoin with the organization's mission and values. The management of resources covers an array of line items that need to be understood in context; meaning the utility of the resources must be measured in context with the programmatic aims and budgetary abilities. For instance, the following shortlist of items may need to be adjusted to improve the viability for a balanced budget: (a) agency vehicle: Associated costs include insurance, lease/car payments, maintenance and gas; (b) licensing fees for various software programs: Are there more licenses being paid for than necessary?; (c) travel authorizations: Associated costs include parking fees, air/rail/car travel expense, lodging, meal costs, and related conference fees; and (d) office space: How large is the space, how much of the space is actually being utilized and how much space is actually needed? Is there a way to decrease costs associated with this resources?

Managing the utilization of resources should occur at multiple levels within an organization. To determine whether resources expended are not relevant to the mission, and to monitor for budgetary compliance, there should be regular budget reviews. The budget reviews should analyze the financial statements and operational performance as they are tethered to the organizational mission. As mentioned in Chapter 9, organizations can become vulnerable to financial exploitation and malfeasance; however, by establishing procedures whereby the budgets are reviewed regularly, and by several key persons, the organization may prevent—or at least provide early identification of—financial fraud.

Performance-Based Budgeting

Setting up a performance-based budgeting (PBB) system, which is tied to defined program outcomes, is a first step in determining the best allocation of resources. Demonstrating how dollars fund day-to-day activities and the specific amounts per category, and tying these expenditures to expected program outcomes, will allow the organization to later determine whether resources need to be reallocated to increase the likelihood that program outcomes will be met. PBB is interchangeable with the concept of accounts-based reporting discussed in Chapter 12. Funders want to confirm that dollars are being spent to produce maximum outcomes. As Blake (2016) notes in the excerpt below, today's budgetary climate demands confirmation of results:

> In essence, [you] need to show the outcomes you intend to achieve and how the funding is supportive of those outcomes. In practice it can be very difficult. There are still serious capacity issues for many public and nonprofit organizations when it comes to management information systems and the overall collection of data. Human service and child welfare organizations in some parts of the country are still struggling to develop management information systems that can track relevant data indicators and help them answer questions from their funders such as whether the individuals and families they are working with are achieving the outcomes they have identified as goals. Sophistication of systems runs the full gamut from Excel spreadsheets to reliance on multiple discreet systems that do not interact with each other to robust data warehouses that allow for integration and assessment of multiple data sets to facilitate an understanding of outcomes. Many organizations do not have the data that would enable them to answer questions about the value of the funding being allocated.

Box 13.4 provides basic information on the value of PBB.

BOX 13.4

DESCRIPTION OF PERFORMANCE-BASED BUDGETING

The purpose of performance-based budgeting is to document progress toward achieving measurable goals. Performance-based budgeting uses evidence-based information to maximize the allocation of funds toward successful programs and reduce funds to programs that are not working as prescribed. Performance-based budgeting can also be described using other names such as outcomes-based budgeting, results-based budgeting, or priority-based budgeting. PBB uses evidence-based data to reallocate funds to achieve organizational goals and objectives.

During periods of fiscal constraint, performance-based budgeting allows organizations to fund programs that advance progress on the organization's mission, goals, and objectives.
Following are the five methods for implementing performance-based budgeting:

1. Align the performance-based budgeting process with the budget cycle and start the decision-making process early in the year.

2. Use the strategic plan to tie tasks and action items to the budget.

3. Create a team that represents all key programs or units and allow that team to make recommendations and options in terms of budget requests.

4. Establish a management team as the final arbitrator for budget requests.

5. Use a management information system to monitor spending and reallocation when necessary.

Performance-based budgeting permits organizations to be transparent in making budget decisions and allows organizations to

- Allocate funds to programs or units based on their ability to fulfill the overall organizational mission, goals, and objectives.

- Establish accountability for those managing programs.

- Shift the budget focus away from specific program or unit goals and toward overall organizational goals.

- Provide opportunities for all key stakeholders to become engaged in the budgeting process.

SOURCE: GovEx (2018, September 9). *Performance-based budgeting & steps for implementation*. Retrieved from https://govex.jhu.edu/wiki/performance-based-budgeting-2/

Box 13.5 provides additional characteristics of PBB along with advantages and challenges.

BOX 13.5

PERFORMANCE-BASED BUDGETING: FACT SHEET FROM THE NATIONAL CONFERENCE OF STATE LEGISLATURES (2008) (MODIFIED)

"The traditional approach to budgeting focuses on incremental changes in detailed categories of expenditures. PBB differs by focusing on results rather than money spent. The basic principle of PBB is accountability, not merely on compliance with law and previous funding decisions." PBB allows budget authorities to reconsider priorities and provides the flexibility to make decisions that are not easily permissible under traditional budgeting systems.

(continued)

BOX 13.5 *(Continued)*

A performance-based budget has the following characteristics:

- "It presents the major purpose for which funds are allocated and sets measurable objectives.
- It tends to focus on changes in funding rather than on the base (the amount appropriated for the previous budget cycle) ...
- It offers agencies flexibility to reallocate money when conditions merit, rewarding achievement and possibly imposing sanctions for poor performance."

PBB

- Assists budget authorities with helpful background information on the purposes of funded programs and the results they achieve.
- Helps explain previous funding decisions.
- Aids in estimating and justifying the potential consequences of new funding decisions.
- Allows deeper understanding of agency activities.
- "Instead of focusing on the preservation of existing programs and associated spending levels, both agency personnel and policymakers may gain understanding of program effectiveness."

Challenges: While there are many advantages with PBB, there are a number of concerns about the process, including

- Agency personnel and funding authorities having different ideas regarding what is important about an agency's work.
- Programs with a large number of performance indicators, and performance indicators set forth by various regulation bodies, can distract and overwhelm managers when making crucial funding decisions.
- Confidence that performance information is reliable and valid.
- The proper use of incentives and disincentives improving agency performance.

National Conference of State Legislatures (NCSL) Resources

- Legislative Performance Budgeting
- Legislating for Results: How Using Performance Information can Help You
- Asking Key Questions: How to Review Program Results
- Five Actions to Improve State Legislative Use of Performance Information

Other Resources

- Performance-Based Program Budgeting in Context: History and Comparison, Florida Office of Program Policy Analysis and Government Accountability.
- Making Results Based State Government Work, The Urban Institute

PBB, performance-based budgeting.

There are many issues with PBB, however. Too many performance measures can make the system burdensome and costly. PBB can create competition between competing entities. If, for example, PBB is used in a university system, the same measures will apply to all campuses in the system but each campus may be uniquely different. For small organizations, though, it may be an effective way to control and allocate scarce funding.

PBB can be a time-intensive process for review, matching performance against expectations, then allocating dollars against those outcomes.

Whatever budgeting system is used by your organization, the staff need to be able to understand the reasons why this particular system is used, how it works, and how it can help the organization achieve its mission, goals, objectives, and outcomes.

Budgetary Oversight

Box 13.6 displays the competencies/behaviors in this section.

BOX 13.6

NETWORK FOR SOCIAL WORK MANAGEMENT COMPETENCIES AND PRACTICE BEHAVIORS 13

Effectively manages and oversees the budget and other financial resources to support the organization's/program's mission and goals and to foster continuous program improvement and accountability (Network for Social Work Management Competencies 13). Practice Behaviors:

- Ensures that expenditures are allowed and appropriate and that allocated funds are available throughout the fiscal year (13.2).

- Monitors revenue and expenditures at regular intervals to ensure that budget assumptions are consistent with anticipated income and expenses (13.3).

- Ensures that financial activities are consistent with organizational policies and are sufficiently documented for audit (13.4).

A primary purpose of creating procedures for budgetary oversight is to ensure that funds are being spent ethically, legally, and responsibly. Ensuring that funds are spent legally means that the organization is not committing financial fraud, bribery, theft, or any other type of financial malfeasance. Ensuring that funds are ethically spent means that members of the organization are not taking advantage of financial resources. For example, if a staff were to submit a travel receipt for four days of lodging when the conference lasted only three days, this reimbursement would be unethical and possibly fraudulent. Similarly, if a staff traveled 50 miles to meet a client and after meeting with the client decided to travel another 25 miles to visit a friend in the area, submitting mileage reimbursement for 75 miles, rather than 50 miles, it would be unethical and fraudulent. Identifying illegal and unethical spending within the organization can sometimes be difficult because the person(s) committing the act is typically adept at concealing malfeasance, either through limiting the actions as to avoid calling too much attention, or knowing when to halt or distract because she or he senses she or he is close to being caught.

Ensure that funds are spent responsibly and aren't wasted on lavish items such as fancy office furniture, expensive retreats, unnecessary positions with inflated salaries, or even purchasing bottled water when water fountains are available.

Social work leaders and managers charged with budgetary oversight of programs need to ensure that financial decisions are made in responsible ways. Leading programs by being financially responsible means that there is not excessive spending. Evaluating how to reduce costs on a regular basis and acting on these recommendations is also a good practice. Every organization has varying intervals for reviewing budgets: some are monthly, some are quarterly, and others are every six months. If the financial state of a program is in flux, budgets should be reviewed monthly. When reviewing budgets, it is important to determine what the contributing factors are for the financial state, whether the balance is in the red or in the black. As discussed in Chapter 9, it is vital to understand the story behind the numbers, to understand what is helping or hurting the financial status. By understanding the story that underpins the financial data, leaders and managers are better equipped to make decisions about what can alter the financial trajectory.

Social work leaders and managers must know and understand the organization's financial policies, and be responsible for ensuring that everyone is aware of the financial policies. This practice is part of holding others accountable. Leaders and managers must also consider how they will implement a system of accountability in terms of reviewing budgets on a regular basis. For instance, will staff be required to report on the budget at meetings, demonstrating their knowledge of the financial state, and will staff make recommendations as applicable? Or will staff be required to sign off on the budgets as a way of acknowledging they have received and reviewed the budget? However the system of understanding the budget is designed, it must be executed with consistency to truly be effective.

The availability of funds can vary for a variety of reasons, including economic downturns and delay of payments or accounts receivable. The availability of funds tends to have a snowball effect when it comes to delayed payments. For instance, the state government may be delayed in sending funds to the regional public sector, and the regional sector may then be delayed in paying the private sector. Because the private sector tends to be nonprofit organizations that cannot operate as corporations do, they may not be permitted to charge financial penalties for delayed payments; however, they are still expected to pay their bills—and they certainly want to be sure to make payroll. In situations like these, an organization may need to draw on a line of credit to make the payments, and then pay off the credit loan immediately upon receiving payments that are expected, per the accounts receivable records. It is important to distinguish that a lack of available funds refers to the *liquid assets* available, such as cash that can be used for immediate funds; it does not refer to *fixed assets*, which cannot be readily converted to cash and immediately used for an urgent requirement.

Not having funds available creates a number of hardships for organizations, including how to make difficult decisions about (a) taking a line of credit for certain items, and how much; (b) what absolutely needs to be funded now, and what can perhaps wait (i.e., payroll and insurance vs. membership dues); and (c) what line items will need to be immediately cut due to the lack of available funds.

Audits

When organizations complete independent audits, whether required by law or not, they are demonstrating their commitment to financial transparency. As discussed in Chapter 9, an organization may publish their financial report on their website so that potential donors and the general public who review it can be assured that the organization's financial conduct is ethical, legal, and responsible. Some board of directors may want an audit completed as it offers assurance that the financial statements that have been submitted for review are in fact accurate and correct. Completing an annual independent audit is a prudent practice. However, small nonprofits may not be able to fund the cost of an independent audit, and therefore cost–benefit analysis should be considered. For smaller nonprofit organizations, typically those with operating budgets less than $1 million, there are a number of other ways to demonstrate financial transparency. Smaller nonprofits can share their policies on conflict of interest, financial management, and internal control procedures; post their 990 form; and adopt an executive compensation policy that requires the board of directors to approve the executive director/CEO's salary. Box 13.7 displays the competencies/behaviors in this section.

BOX 13.7

NETWORK FOR SOCIAL WORK MANAGEMENT COMPETENCIES AND PRACTICE BEHAVIOR 13

Effectively manages and oversees the budget and other financial resources to support the organization's/ program's mission and goals and to foster continuous program improvement and accountability (Network for Social Work Management Competencies 13). Practice Behaviors:

- Monitors expenditures to ensure that operating units have sufficient resources to offer quality services, using dashboards and other visual tools to link expenditures to outcomes (13.6).

Retrenchment Planning

Retrenchment planning has become more and more endemic to organizations today due to anticipated or mandated budget cuts. Retrenchment planning is a process of reevaluating the organization's budget based on the internal and external changes in the environment that can negatively impact goals and objectives. Retrenchment planning is important because changes frequently occur in both the internal and external environments, and it would be detrimental to wait until the next budget cycle to evaluate. Thus, retrenchment planning must take place under short time deadlines, yet may significantly reshape the operations of the program.

Table 13.1 provides examples of two different resource planning scenarios.

TABLE 13.1 **Planning With Increasing Resources Versus Planning With Stable/Decreasing Resources (Higher Education Examples)**

PLANNING WITH INCREASING RESOURCES	PLANNING WITH STABLE/DECREASING RESOURCES
The future is predictable. With a new governor of the same party, past funding practices will continue or there may be more funding to higher education.	*The future cannot be predictable and is therefore unknown.* With a new governor of a different party, higher education funding will be drastically reduced due to less state funding support as a result of the elimination of the state income tax.
Funding is a given from the same sources. A state university receives funding allocation of one quarter of its funding from the legislature.	*Funding is not a given and can vary from year to year and the sources may dry up.* The legislature used to fund the university at 60%, and now funds only 15%, and therefore the challenge is how to raise money to maintain the budget. Two options are to raise tuition and fundaising; however, the institution needs to obtain approval from the legislature to raise tuition (which may or may happen) and fundraising targets are not usually achieved immediately.
A university can be creative in programing and spending. A university has more flexibility in spending on innovative activities.	*A university must maintain the status quo, adding no new programs and maintaining programs.* A university has to closely watch its budget expenditures and cannot approve any new or extravagant initiatives.

(continued)

TABLE 13.1 **Planning With Increasing Resources Versus Planning With Stable/Decreasing Resources (Higher Education Examples)** *(Continued)*

PLANNING WITH INCREASING RESOURCES	PLANNING WITH STABLE/DECREASING RESOURCES
Funding can be spread around to different units in the system. In a state university system, the governing body is freer to provide funding for the requests from the other state universities.	*Conflict may occur and some units may see a reduction in funding.* Each state university will be competing for funding—some will win and some will lose.
Goals and objectives can be maintained or expanded with incremental or major change. The university can consider making improvements in programs and possibly expanding them.	*Retrenchment may require hard choices; do you cut all components or just some?* With reduced funding, the university may have to modify its goals and objectives, and as a result the mission may be unattainable.
With stable or expanding funding, separate units have potential for growth and are encouraged to be creative. The system office will focus on the university in the system that can better serve graduate students.	*Multiple components may need to be reviewed for efficiencies.* The system office might want to encourage universities to combine programs.
Moderate- to long-term time frame. With stable state funding, a university's programs are secure for the entire fiscal year.	*Short-term time frame,* With unstable state funding, a university program should plan on reducing funding for programs and concomitant services.

When cutbacks occur, there are several steps that can be taken: (a) Assess the historic strengths of the program as strengths should be maintained at all costs (if you make across-the-board cuts, the stronger components of programs will be negatively impacted along with the weaker components of programs); (b) evaluate the adaptability of the staff (can staff take on different and expanded assignments or be transferred to program components that will continue if the components they work in are eliminated); (c) restructure programs to be more cost-effective and efficient and still achieve goals and objectives; or (d) create smaller programs that will achieve the same purposes.

Alternatively, when program funding is increased, several initial steps should be considered, such as (a) upgrading the historic core of the program, particularly the stronger components, thus positioning the organization to even better obtain its mission, goals, and objectives and increase the likelihood of future enhanced funding and (b) developing new program initiatives that might better help the organization meet its mission, goals, and objectives.

There are two dimensions of a core program: (a) Maintaining representativeness or concern for the past and the historical continuity of all aspects of the program and (b) adapting to a changing environment to maintain the current and future version of the program. When retrenchment is necessary, there are several possible core programming sequences that can be considered (Management and Behavior Science Center, 1983): (a) Reduce the program to its historic core, (b) make the core more efficient through either consolidation or increased productivity, (c) upgrade the core, and (d) develop new core roles that better adapt to reduced funding. One example of how to implement a funding reduction in a core Master of Social Work Graduate program might be to (a) reduce enrollments to the target during the years before expansion occurred; (b) offer more joint courses with other departments such as Women's Studies, Public Health, and so on; (c) make improvements in the core aspects of the program so the program is more efficient; and (d) redesign aspects of the program that are more cost effective.

When an organization is considering cuts in funding, several approaches should be seriously considered. One assumes most leaders of organizations understand that across-the-board cuts punish the efficient and reward the inefficient, yet most organizations resort to across-the-board cuts. When programs that are meeting or exceeding their goals are cut, the staff can become unmotivated and discouraged mainly because they have to now reduce funding support for all of their key programs, unless they decide to eliminate a program and keep other programs intact. Thus, the efficient are punished, and their passion and performance are undermined. Programs that are inefficient will be less impacted because the assumption is that the staff are not motivated or passionate, or the programs are poorly designed. Across-the-board cuts are easy to implement and can be conducted quickly. A message goes out that all programs or units within programs or cost centers will be cut 5% during a certain funding period. Across-the-board cuts are simple and quick and do not require a review of selected cuts to programs, even underperforming programs. Making significant cuts requires a hard evaluation of goals and objectives, and as a result, a redesign of programs may be the most adaptive strategy.

When considering cuts, the first place to start is a review of the organizational structure and staffing. Some organizations can be considered inflated and overstaffed with too many managers, too short a span of control, and too many layers between decision makers. Lean organizations would reduce staff and managerial functions, eliminate some manager positions and reduce the layers of organizational decision making, and increase the spans of control. The consequences of these actions might be fewer vertical career opportunities for employees, significant job enlargement, and downward delegation. Finally, organizations cannot afford "crash diets" consisting of laying off direct line staff and then rehiring them when the organization's situation improves. In some institutions, such as universities, replacing staff can take an extended period of time.

To begin the process of deciding what to cut, an examination of the organization's mission and marginal investments is a good first step. Box 13.8 provides a list of organizational mandates and functions along with an in-depth list of questions about which services or programs are marginal investments.

BOX 13.8

LIST OF QUESTIONS FOR EXAMINING THE ORGANIZATION'S MISSION AND MARGINAL INVESTMENTS

Examine the Organization's Mission

  A. What are the organizational core values and are they incorporated into daily operations?

  B. What are the organization's required mandates?

  C. What are the activities the organization engages in that are nonmandated functions?

  D. What are the functions that the organization delivers exceedingly well?

  E. What are the functions that the organization does not deliver well?

  F. What recent trends are impacting the organization and its attainment of its mission, goals, and objectives?

  G. What aspects of the organization have not been reviewed?

(continued)

BOX 13.8 (Continued)

Examine Marginal Investments

A. Does the program have a high cost per student or client?

B. Does the program serve a small population and is this population declining?

C. Is the program competing with other entities?

D. Is the program meeting its mission, goals, and objectives?

E. If the program was cut back or be eliminated, would there be adverse consequences?

F. If the program is cut back or eliminated, will the result be greater costs in the future?

There are several approaches to cutting back on programs. Box 13.9 provides three recommended approaches for how to reduce funding yet improve productivity, cut services, and shift costs.

BOX 13.9

APPROACHES TO SURVIVE CUTBACKS

1. Maintain services through improved productivity
   - Reorganize tasks and assignments to be more efficient
   - Reorganize the organizational structure and responsibility chart
   - Adapt and use current and future technologies and communication systems
   - Offer education and training to managers and staff
2. Reduce services
   - By the number of offerings
   - By the depth of the service
   - By reductions in service availability through fewer offerings
   - Through staff reorganizations, retirements, and terminations
   - By offering services only in high-demand locations
3. Transfer costs
   - To students or clients
   - By requiring direct payments
   - To other programs
   - By temporarily stopping service delivery

There are a variety of responses that are available in times of funding reductions. Considering these will help a manager in reviewing alternative approaches and developing an overall strategy. Levine, Rubin, and Wolohojian (1981) identified nine types of responses to cutbacks, as shown in the first column of Table 13.2.

TABLE 13.2 **Nine Types of Responses to Cutbacks in Academic and Agency Settings**

TYPES OF RESPONSES	ACADEMIC SETTING	AGENCY SETTING
Service or program termination	Arrange for students to transfer to another institution	Close a service division of an outpatient clinic
Transfer of activities, services, or programs	Shift technological support from a central office to departments	Shift the responsibility of benefits coordination for clients from the public to the private sector
Defer activities, services, or programs to the future	Put hold on maintenance and building repairs	Put on hold all upgrades to new computers, phone systems, or maintenance and building repairs
Improve efficiencies	Provide laptops instead of desktops so faculty can work more productively at home and at meetings	Implement concurrent charting using laptops or mobile devices
Use cheap labor	Hire more graduate assistants and part-time workers	Develop internship programs and obtain volunteers
Replace working hours with better technology	Allow faculty to use up-to-date computer systems to complete work instead of using secretary	Use MIS to complete billing faster, using fewer staff hours to complete and resulting in more efficient claims management
Employ better decision making through better data analysis	Maintain budget spreadsheets at the department level and use to adjust spending	Use MIS to inform program outcomes, performance outcomes, and compliance outcomes
Cut services	Reduce the number of adjunct instructors and the number of courses offered	Reduce the number of services offered within a particular program, and therefore reduce number of staff needed
Increase capacity for resource development	Obtain more grants and other funding	Obtain more grants and other funding and diversify revenue streams

As you can see from the examples outlined above, there are a number of ways to deal with retrenchment planning. Levine et al. (1981) found that common practices occur across varied types of organizations

1. To avoid termination of services and programs, engage in practices that produce greater efficiencies, delay funding support, ration services, and move services to another entity.

2. Most organizations are not able to reduce or replace labor with capital such as technology.

3. Across-the-board cuts in services are still the most predominate way of dealing with cuts.

4. The process of cutting back on services can create inefficiencies and changes in goals and strategies to attain goals. Cutbacks can negatively impact personal planning and can really impact units that already are understaffed. As a result, some units can become so understaffed that the overall existence of the organization will be called into question.

5. Drastic action will not be taken in time to resolve the situation.

Once a course of action has been determined to deal with the cutbacks, leaders and managers need to identify which resources can be matched to the necessary action. Types of resources may include facilities, equipment, computers, and parking spaces; materials needed to operate the organization, such as supplies, phones, and other equipment; and staff. The questions to ask are to what extent does planning dealing with cutbacks involve each of these types of resources that are required (for a typical planning period) and how much of each type is expected to be available? What is the shortfall between what resources are required and what are available? How can this gap in resources be filled? If the gap cannot be filled, then the goals and objectives of the organization should be modified accordingly.

There are a variety of ways to deal with resource shortages or gaps between what is required and what is available. Table 13.3 provides a template for dealing with resource shortages or gaps in funding in both academic and agency settings.

TABLE 13.3 Competency-Based Exercise: Ways to Deal With Resource Shortages in Academic and Agency Settings

WAYS OF DEALING	ACADEMIC SETTING	AGENCY SETTING
How can you provide substitute services? Identify which services can be substituted for others. How will you implement these changes?		
Can these services be provided in-house or by current staff? Who will provide the service(s) that is being cut and how will it impact other aspects of organizational staffing?		
Can services be replaced or redesigned, and if so, will service recipients still receive sufficient and acceptable service?		

There are a variety of implications for leadership in organizations that result from retrenchment planning actions. Table 13.4 provides eight implications that can impact leaders of organizations as they attempt to deal with retrenchment planning.

TABLE 13.4 Implications of Retrenchment Planning on Leadership

1.	For years if not decades now, organizations have been experiencing reductions in funding. This trend does not appear to be likely to change. So managers should assume that fiscal austerity is here to stay and plan accordingly.
2.	Managing resources requires a large amount of the manager's time, so managers should plan their workload accordingly.
3.	Budget decisions are usually made by staff responsible for accounting or budget functions, and these staff may have little knowledge of the programs that they may be cutting. So program managers need to take an active role in fiscal planning and implementation.
4.	Resource management is a year-round job that needs to be monitored on a constant basis. Funding decisions can occur outside of the normal fiscal planning process, so managers should be prepared to deal with budget issues on an ongoing basis.

(continued)

TABLE 13.4 **Implications of Retrenchment Planning on Leadership** *(Continued)*

5.   When considering budget cuts, take into consideration all possible ramifications in service provision. Never make across-the-board cuts. If necessary, eliminate some programs so that well-functioning programs that are well connected with the organization's mission and goals will survive.

6.   Consider ways of combining services and organizational units.

7.   Reimbursement systems can have differential impact on the organization's staff. Investigate how reimbursement systems are impacting organizational function and causing the organization to move away from its mission, goals, and objectives. An organization will shift its focus to obtain funding, sometimes with negative results.

8.   Crises can create opportunities to change operations that might be of long-term value to the organization and its mission.

Leadership in today's environment of constant cutbacks is like sailing a boat instead of steering a powerboat. Careful attention should be paid to the contextual conditions, a sense of destination, and a willingness to take many different tacks to get to the goal of keeping the boat afloat and reaching your destination safe and sound.

SUMMARY

Throughout this chapter we examined the budgeting process within organizations. Budgets will invariably be influenced by environmental challenges. In response to various challenges, organizations will need to understand ways to reallocate funds, manage limited resources and cutbacks, and at times develop strategies for downsizing. Additionally, this chapter addresses concepts of retrenchment planning and resource planning. Understanding the processes for approving budgets and analyzing the types of income and expenses is an important task of leaders and managers.

ACTIVITIES

1.   Are you using resources correctly to meet your organization's vision, mission, and goals? How can you determine you are?

2.   Review the mission/goals alongside the budget statements. Determine whether the program is budgeting and spending funds on items that are relevant to the mission and goals. Explain your answer.

3.   Identify and explain whether or not the budget has allocated investment funds, that is, is the program investing in the future (trainings, technology/capital expenses). Based on your findings, do the resources seem to be used in a manner that supports services? Or is there a better way to use the resources currently available that might provide better services?

4.   If budget problems are identified, how will you reallocate funds?

REFERENCES

Blake, A. (2016). The impact of our changing environment on the management practices in public human service organizations. *Human Service Organizations: Management, Leadership & Governance, 40*(2), 89–91. doi:10.1080/23303131.2016.1165039

GovEx. (2018, September 9). Performance-based budgeting & steps for implementation. Retrieved from https://govex.jhu.edu/wiki/performance-based-budgeting-2/

Levine, C., Rubin, I., & Wolohojian, G. G. (1981). *The politics of retrenchment: How local governments.* Beverly Hills, CA: Sage Publications.

Management and Behavior Science Center. (1983). *Planning module #5: Resource assessment.* Philadelphia, PA: The Wharton School, University of Pennsylvania.

National Conference of State Legislatures. (2008). *Performance based budgeting: Fact sheet.* Retrieved from http://www.ncsl.org/research/fiscal-policy/performance-based-budgeting-fact-sheet.aspx

APPENDIX: KEY FINANCIAL TERMS

Accounts Payable: the amount owed to others for the services or merchandise received.

Accounts Receivable: the amount owed to the organization for services or merchandise provided to others (i.e., clients, students).

Accrual Basis Accounting: system of financial recordkeeping that records transactions as expenses when they are incurred and as income when earned, versus when cash is paid or received. Accrual basis accounting is more precise than the alternative cash basis accounting, but is a more complex system of recordkeeping.

Accrued Expenses: the costs of services that have been used, but are not yet due or payable.

Accrued Interest: the accumulated interest cost that is not yet due or payable.

Annual Report: a report that is published by the organization which describes its activities. This report is often used as an effective means of informing the community about the organization's activities, outcomes, and grant funds used.

Area of Interest Fund: a designated fund held by a community foundation or donor that is used for a specific charitable purpose.

Articles of Incorporation: a document filed with the secretary of state or other appropriate state office for the purpose of establishing a corporation. This filing is the first legal step in forming a nonprofit corporation.

Allocation: a method of dividing expenses to different program, administrative, and fundraising categories.

Assets: refers to what the organization owns.

Financial Audit: an examination conducted by a certified public accountant(s) which the organization's board of directors uses to provide assurance to both internal and external constituencies that the organization's financial statements are in accordance with generally accepted accounting principles.

Balance Sheet: a snapshot of the financial condition of the organization at a particular moment in time. Balance sheets may also be referred to as statements of financial position.

Board-Designated Funds: funds that the organization's board of directors earmark for a specific purpose, such as operating reserves. Board-designated funds are still considered unrestricted funds for accounting purposes because the condition was not specified by a donor.

Capitalizing an Asset: a recording of the cost of land, building, or other necessary equipment as fixed assets included on the balance sheet, rather than as an expense, which would be recorded on the income statement.

Cash and Cash Equivalents: funds that can be quickly and easily converted to cash.

Cash Basis Accounting: a financial recordkeeping method that records transactions when cash is received or spent.

Cash Flow Statement: a report presenting cash inflows and outflows during a specific period of time.

Chart of Accounts: a list of all accounts used in an accounting system, which includes assets, liabilities, equity, income, and expenses.

Conditional Promise to Give: a pledge by a donor to make a contribution to the organization if a specific requirement is met.

Contribution: can be a donation, gift, or transfer of cash or other assets.

Current Assets: the cash, investments, accounts receivables, and other assets that are estimated to be available as cash within the next 12 months.

Deferred Revenue/Deferred Income: income for which payment has been received before a service of merchandise has been delivered. It is reflected as a liability on the balance sheet until it is actually delivered and thus can be recognized as income.

Deficit: when expenses exceed income there is a deficit. Deficits may also be referred to as net losses or a negative changes in net assets.

Depreciation: the decrease in value of a fixed asset over the course of its expected physical or economic life. Depreciation is recorded as an expense each year.

Discretionary Fund: a grant or donation fund that may be distributed at the discretion of a designee (typically the executive director) and does not usually require prior approval by the full board of directors.

Endowment: refers to the principal amount of gifts and bequests that are received subject to a requirement that the principal be maintained intact and invested to generate a source of income for the organization. Donors may require that the principal continuously remain intact or may define a set period of time or until sufficient assets have been accumulated to achieve a designated purpose.

Fixed Assets: assets that have a useful life of several years or more, such as property, buildings, vehicles, furniture, computers, and other equipment.

Fiscal Year: a 12-month period that is used by the organization to plan the use of its funds. This period may be a calendar year but can also be any other 12-month period.

Form 990: an annual tax return document used by public charities to report information about their finances.

Functional Expenses: expense categories outlined by the type of expense, such as program services, general administrative, and fundraising. Functional expenses are required reporting categories for the IRS Form 990 and audited financial statements.

Fundraising Expense: the total costs incurred in soliciting contributions, gifts, grants, and other funding sources.

Generally Accepted Accounting Principles (GAAP): a customary framework of guidelines for financial accounting established by the Financial Accounting Standards Board (FASB) to help ensure the accuracy and reliability of financial records and reports.

Income Statement: a report that summarizes the organization's financial activities (income and expenses) during a specific period of time. Income statements may also be referred to as statements of activities, statement of changes in net assets and profit and loss (P&L).

In-kind Contribution: contribution made of goods or services as opposed to a cash donation.

Liabilities: what the organization owes.

Management and General Expense: the expenses related to the general operations of the organization, but not related to fundraising or programs.

Net Assets: the difference between the organization's total assets and total liabilities recorded on the balance sheet to reflect the net financial worth for the organization.

Permanently Restricted Funds: contributions such as endowment gifts that are invested to generate income.

Prepaid Expense: an expense that is paid prior to use of the good or service purchased.

Reserves: the amount of funds set aside by the organization to be used in case of losses or unexpected expenses.

Restricted Funds: contributions that are restricted by the donor for a specific use, and can be temporary or permanent in nature.

Unrestricted Funds: contributions given to an organization without the donor placing any restrictions or limitations as to their use.

PART 3

STRATEGIC
MANAGEMENT AND
ADMINISTRATIVE
SKILLS FOR
ORGANIZATIONAL
GROWTH AND SUCCESS
IN A SOCIAL WORK
ENVIRONMENT

STRATEGIC PLANNING IN A SOCIAL WORK ENVIRONMENT

- Understanding and applying the planning process as an inherent management activity.
- Understanding where and when to use the three categories of planning: ends planning, means planning, and action planning.
- Understanding a variety of planning terms.
- Using specific planning and techniques on the job, such as scanning the environment.
- Creating a vision and mission statement and keeping the mission current.
- Writing clear, specific, and measurable goals and objectives.
- Translating an idealized design into goals and objectives.
- Developing a strategic plan.
- Developing a business plan.
- Creating an alternative scenario analysis.
- Implementing planning and project management to support mission, goals, and objectives.
- Assessing whether the plan has been achieved.

INTRODUCTION

Throughout this chapter, we discuss the importance of organizational vision, goals, objectives, and strategic plans. When creating strategic plans, it is important to obtain initial agreement about the process, have a clear understanding of the benefits of the strategic planning process, evaluate the internal and external environments that may influence future plans, and develop alternative plans. As part of the strategic planning process, organizations need to develop a vision, core values, a mission statement, goals, objectives, outcomes, and benchmarks. This chapter provides examples for completing both a full and abbreviated strategic planning process. Several steps in the strategic planning process can be understood through the lens of clinical practice. For example, defining the situation parallels identifying the presenting problem or reason for referral; collecting the facts parallels the clinical assessment process; establishing and classifying objectives parallels the process of creating a treatment plan and establishing mutually agreed upon goals and objectives; formulating the possible choices mirrors the process of engagement and right to self-determination; anticipating the outcomes, assessing the importance of the decision, and understanding possible adverse outcomes parallels the process of discussing the risks and benefits of treatments; and finally selecting the best available solutions parallels the process of engaging in an evidence-based practice. Strategic plans should be reviewed regularly to ensure that the organization and programs are meeting the prescribed benchmarks, and should also be reviewed to assess the overall outcomes of the plan in its entirety. Box 14.1 displays the competencies/practice behaviors covered in this chapter.

BOX 14.1

COMPETENCIES AND PRACTICE BEHAVIORS ADDRESSED IN THIS CHAPTER

Ensures strategic planning (Network for Social Work Management Competencies 20). Practice Behaviors:

- Understands the organization's relationship to its environment, the emerging internal and external forces affecting the organization, and the ability to position the organization within that environment for future and current success (20.1).
- Directs staff effectively in identifying areas of future growth and development in all areas of agency operations to be used in a strategic planning process (20.2).
- Demonstrates competence in the ability to orchestrate and support an inclusive and organization-wide strategic planning process designed to position the organization for success in achieving its mission in the mid- and long-term future (20.3).
- Constructs or directs the construction of an adequate business plan that details the pathway, timelines, and accountability for the accomplishment of identified strategic objectives (20.4).

Establishes, promotes, and anchors the vision, philosophy, goals, objectives, and values of the organization (Network for Social Work Management Competencies 1). Practice Behaviors:

- Creates, communicates, and anchors a vision for the organization (1.1).
- Works to ensure that all programs align with the overall organizational mission (1.2).
- Reviews the mission periodically to determine its relevance to client and the community needs (1.3).
- Works closely with management staff to establish benchmarks to show alignment with vision, mission, philosophy, and goals (1.4).
- Identifies potential organizational drift from vision, mission, philosophy, and goals (1.5).

(continued)

BOX 14.1 *(Continued)*

Possesses analytical and critical thinking skills that promote organizational growth (Network for Social Work Management Competencies 3). Practice Behaviors:

- Monitors economic and political trends, shifts in trends, values, and mores (3.8).
- Displays keen skills in strategic thinking (3.9).

Develops and manages both internal and external stakeholder relationships (Network for Social Work Management Competencies 6). Practice Behaviors:

- Plans, thinks, and acts strategically in concert with key stakeholders to position, evolve, and change the organization to assure success in the current and future environments (6.3).

CSWE Competency 5—Engage in Policy Practice
Social workers:

- 5.2 Assess how social welfare and economic policies impact the delivery of and access to social services.

CSWE Competency 6—Engage With Individuals, Families, Groups, Organizations, and Communities
Social workers:

- 6.1 Apply knowledge of human behavior and the social environment, person-in-environment, and other multidisciplinary theoretical frameworks to engage with clients and constituencies.

CSWE Competency 7—Assess Individuals, Families, Groups, Organizations, and Communities
Social workers:

- 7.4 Select appropriate intervention strategies based on the assessment, research knowledge, and values and preferences of clients and constituencies.

CSWE Competency 8—Intervene With Individuals, Families, Groups, Organizations, and Communities
Social workers:

- 8.1 Critically choose and implement interventions to achieve practice goals and enhance capacities of clients and constituencies.
- 8.5 Facilitate effective transitions and endings that advance mutually agreed-on goals.

CSWE Competency 9—Evaluate Practice With Individuals, Families, Groups, Organizations, and Communities
Social workers:

- 9.1 Select and use appropriate methods for evaluation of outcomes.
- 9.3 Critically analyze, monitor, and evaluate intervention and program processes and outcomes.

CSWE, Council on Social Work Education.

PLANNING IN GENERAL

All organizations need planning. Planning is needed when there is a deviation between what one would like the future to be (one's desired future) and what one believes is likely to occur if nothing changes (the projected future). The discrepancy between one's desired future and the projected or likely future is a planning gap that needs to be acted upon if one's desired future is to be attained. The likely future is predicated on the condition that not much will change with present conditions and, therefore, the future will follow the same projection. The program will continue as expected. A desired future is a hypothetical projection of what the future program could be if one can make changes in the system that will increase the likelihood of attaining that future state. Selecting future ideals or goals for a program and then instituting a planning process to achieve those ideal goals is the hallmark of good management practice, or possibly also good leadership. One premise of good leadership is to set almost impossible goals and then get people to work toward achieving them (e.g., human mission to Mars, curing cancer). Achievement of planning goals depends largely on the amount of control that managers have to influence the process. If managers have a high level of control and are not happy with the current situation, they will be able to institute a planning process to create a more desirable future.

Managers can take several approaches to planning based on what they "like" or "do not like" about the present situation and possible future scenarios, and what they believe can take place in the present and the future. They can employ the "inactive approach" (do nothing) in the present because they like the current situation, and by not taking action nothing will change, and/or they can do nothing to create a desired future and therefore it will not occur. They can employ the "reactive approach" (conserve the status quo) in the present situation because they like the current conditions and/or apply the same reactive approach if they do not like future options. They can employ the "preactive approach" (predict and prepare) in the present if they do not like the current situation and/or also employ this approach if they like the future options. Finally, managers can employ a "proactive approach" (create a desired future), if they do not like the present situation and also do not like what the likely future will be.

Most management texts suggest that the managerial role consists of four functions: organizing, planning, controlling, and coordinating. Planning is just one part of the manager's overall role, and planning is the focus of this chapter.

Within the planning aspect of the managerial role, there are three types of planning: ends planning, means planning, and action planning. How much time managers devote to these three types of planning depends on the manager's management style and her or his level of control. A manager with a high level of control can engage more readily in "ends planning" in which the manager can design a desired future and propose ways to bring about that future state. A manager with a mid level of control can engage in "means planning" in which the manager develops the means for attaining acceptable goals. A manager with a low level of control is usually called upon to engage in "action planning" in which the manager simply implements the project in accordance with the established ends and means.

Managers are in a position to influence the work environments in most organizations, both in positive and negative ways. Work environments can have a positive or negative impact on employees. All work environments can experience episodes of high demand, high levels of stress, and sometimes even total chaos! How does one go about spending time on "planning" when deadlines are approaching? A good manager will build in time for planning and help employees realize the value of their working on something that they want to work on. The first step is to get everyone involved in a planning process. Schedule planning meetings and make them as important as meeting deadlines. If planning is done right, high-demand deadlines will not occur as often.

The ability to engage in planning activities can also be influenced by uncertainty emanating from higher level managers and uncertainty from within the manager's staff. Managers can deal with uncertainty by explaining how planning can overcome it when the right steps are taken. Conversely, managers can discuss how uncertainty is impacting the organization and that uncertainty is hindering the organization's progress in attaining its mission, goals, and objectives.

As previously stated, planning consists of three interrelated activities (ends, means, and action). To engage in "ends" planning, the manager works with the staff to uncover the problems that are negatively impacting the organization and propose opportunities that might help alleviate these problems. By comparing the present situation with a desired future, a manager with staff agreement can clarify or propose a new mission, core values, and goals for the organization. To engage in "means" planning, the manager and staff generate all possible alternative solutions to the problems impacting the organization. Each alternative should be assessed in terms of organizational and resource impacts. Select the alternative with the highest likelihood of success that also correlates with the organization's mission and goals. Finally, to engage in "action" planning, the manager, with the support of the staff if possible, should assign responsibility for carrying out activities and tasks that will achieve the identified goals and objectives, assess the plan's implementation, and if necessary, identify corrections to the plan. According to Ackoff (1978), to implement these three types of planning activities, a manager should employ the three principles of proactive planning: participative, continuous learning and adaption, and holistic. Participative planning requires the belief that the principle benefit of planning is engaging in the process and that everyone's opinion is valid and necessary to achieve synthesis in designing ideal programs or outcomes. The process of continuous learning and adaptation necessitates that a plan becomes an ongoing, changing experiment, not a directive. Finally, a holistic process requires the integration of the organization along vertical lines and coordination across horizontal lines. Furthermore, solutions seldom exist where the problem appears, and the larger the system, the larger the ramifications of any action.

ESTABLISHING A STRATEGIC PLAN

I skate to where the puck is going to be, not where it has been.

Wayne Gretzky

Most organizations have strategic plans, although not all have gone through a complete strategic planning process. Strategic plans should be relatively short-term (two to three years) and dynamic, although some organizations, particularly academic institutions, create strategic plans with five-year or longer timelines. A lot can change in five years, and those plans can and should be updated. Whenever new leadership takes over, strategic plans should be either modified or scratched and started anew. It is difficult to administer an organization without a plan for the future. Planning is all about the future; taking action to influence future events can be very advantageous to organizations. Planning is future oriented, and selecting among alternative future courses of action is a recommended course of action that will be discussed in this chapter.

Box 14.2 presents several examples of university strategic planning processes.

BOX 14.2

SEVERAL DIFFERENT MODELS OF UNIVERSITY STRATEGIC PLANNING PROCESSES

Nichols College (Murphy, Wilson, & Schneider, 2007) uses SWOT analysis as the main component of its planning process. A SWOT will provide information, but it is only one of several steps for developing a successful strategic plan. Most national accrediting organizations in higher education call for a bottom-up strategic planning process. However, some universities use their board of directors to create a top-down process for the mission, goals, and objectives, and then the university for a bottom-up approach for implementing the plan. Nichols College uses a four-year model that is updated each year. The board is driven by the Higher Education Act, Patriot Act, State Legislature, the Sarbanes/Oxley Act. So boards are now becoming more actively involved. Some universities use a top-down approach throughout the process and other universities use a bottom-up approach, even allowing the faculty to direct the process from start to finish (Southern Connecticut State University, 2001).

(continued)

BOX 14.2 *(Continued)*

At Norwich University in Vermont (Murphy, et al., 2007), 65 people were interviewed, particularly newer faculty members. The interviews led to a 20-page plan. The plan contained facilities and development plans. Funds were needed to implement the plan, therefore the plan outlined the vision expected to come to fruitition if the university obtained financial support. Norwich's long-range planning process has 10-year and three-year goals and operates on a five-year cycle. There is an academic unit plan and an administrative plan that focus on the human resources plan, enrollment management, marketing plan, leadership development plan, and technology plan. Underlying all of these plans is the vision, mission, guiding values of the institution, and essential goals.

At Mount Holyoke College, a prior strategy was to set up meetings and public forums to discuss the mission and goals of the school (Creighton, 2007). Constituents were invited to share in the discussion. The intent was to make planning operational. Establishing a positive agenda was crucial; managers did not want to start the process with "we are in trouble." They started with what was unique and special, what the core mission was, and what constituents can do to enhance the mission. There were no sacred cows such as financial deficits, applicant pool, or escalating costs of need blind admission. The next step was to draft a mission statement and identify challenges. Draft documents helped the development of the iterative process, and kept people informed and involved. A second draft was sent to all 30,000 alumni with the invitation to respond by email or web. Three draft plans were ultimately developed. In the second plan, innovative processes were used to spin out new ideas and plans. The final result was a six-year plan, which included new initiatives, increased giving, and surpassing the fundraising goal of $250 million. As a result of this planning process, the college regained excellence and leadership.

SWOT, strengths, weaknesses, opportunities, and threats.

FULL STRATEGIC PLANNING MODEL

Box 14.3 displays the competencies/behaviors in this section. Producing a strategic plan requires the commitment of the organization and staff. As part of the strategic planning process, organizations need to develop a vision, core values, a mission statement, goals, objectives, outcomes, and benchmarks. An in-depth strategic planning model is provided next.

BOX 14.3

NETWORK FOR SOCIAL WORK MANAGEMENT COMPETENCIES AND PRACTICE BEHAVIORS 6 AND 20 AND COUNCIL ON SOCIAL WORK EDUCATION PRACTICE BEHAVIOR 8

Develops and manages both internal and external stakeholder relationships (Network for Social Work Management Competencies 6). Practice Behaviors:

- Plans, thinks, and acts strategically in concert with key stakeholders to position, evolve, and change the organization to assure success in the current and future environments (6.3).

Ensures strategic planning (Network for Social Work Management Competencies 20). Practice Behaviors:

- Demonstrates competence in the ability to orchestrate and support an inclusive and organization-wide strategic planning process designed to position the organization for success in achieving its mission in the mid- and long-term future (20.3).

(continued)

BOX 14.3 *(Continued)*

CSWE Competency 8–Intervene With Individuals, Families, Groups, Organizations, and Communities
Social workers:

■ 8.5 Facilitate effective transitions and endings that advance mutually agreed-on goals.

CSWE, Council on Social Work Education.

A full strategic planning model consists of ten steps:

I. Identifying the Present Perceived Situation
II. Developing Projections of the Present Perceived Situation
III. Projecting the Logical Future of the System
IV. Developing Alternative Futures (Scenarios)
V. Identifying Strategic Issues
VI. Using Alternative Objectives to Create a Composite Scenario
VII. Describing the Organization of the Future
VIII. Developing Strategic Goals and Strategies
IX. Creating an Action Framework
X. Realizing Change

I. **Identifying the Present Perceived Situation**

A. *Initial Agreement on a Strategic Planning Process*
If developing a strategic plan for an agency, obtain an initial agreement on the process or a "Plan for Planning" (Bryson, 1988). The organization and staff must commit to create the plan; obtain the commitment of multiple staff to work on the process and production of the document so that everyone participates in creating the organization's future.
Reaching an initial agreement typically proceeds through the following stages:

1. "Introducing the concept of strategic planning.
2. Developing an understanding of what it can mean in practice.
3. Thinking through some of its more important implications.
4. Developing a commitment to strategic planning.
5. Reaching an actual agreement" (Bryson, 1988, p. 74), usually through vote or collaboration among key people who can influence the process and act as instrumental sources of expertise and information.

The greater the number of decision makers and the less they know about strategic planning, the more time-consuming the process will be and the more indirect the route to agreement. The support and commitment of key decision makers are vital; they supply information crucial to the planning effort, including identifying who should be involved, deciding when key decision points will occur, and providing critical resources such as staff assignments, budget, and meeting space.
A well-articulated initial agreement benefits the organization because it includes

1. A clear definition of the group(s) to be involved and the process by which it is to be maintained so everyone knows who is working on the plan.

2. An outline of the general sequence of steps in the strategic planning effort.

3. Mechanisms, such as a strategic planning coordinating committee for buffering consultation, negotiation, or problem solving.

4. Guarantees from key decision makers of their time commitment.

B. *Mandates*

Before starting the planning process, the organization needs to identify and clarify the nature and meaning of the externally imposed mandates, formal and informal, affecting the organization. For example, the organization may be mandated to serve a certain population. Identifying the mandates will assist the organization in achieving the following outcomes:

1. "Compilation of the formal and informal mandates faced by the organization.

2. Interpretation of what is required as a result of the mandates.

3. Clarification of what is not ruled out by the mandates–the rough boundaries of the unconstrained field of action" (Bryson, 1988, p. 94)–what is not explicitly forbidden. What you might do can lead to valuable discussions about what the organization's mission should be.

Additional benefits of reviewing mandates include

1. "Clarity about what is mandated increases the likelihood that mandates will be met" (Bryson, 1988, p. 95).

2. When areas that the mandates do not rule out are reviewed, there is a greater possibility of developing a mission not limited to mandates.

II. **Developing Projections of the Present Perceived Situation**
Box 14.4 displays the practice behaviors covered in this section.

BOX 14.4

NETWORK FOR SOCIAL WORK MANAGEMENT COMPETENCIES AND PRACTICE BEHAVIORS 3 AND 20 AND COUNCIL ON SOCIAL WORK EDUCATION PRACTICE BEHAVIORS 5 AND 6

Possesses analytical and critical thinking skills that promote organizational growth (Network for Social Work Management Competencies 3). Practice Behaviors:

- Monitors economic and political trends, shifts in trends, values, and mores (3.8).
- Displays keen skills in strategic thinking (3.9).

Ensures strategic planning (Network for Social Work Management Competencies 20). Practice Behaviors:

- Understands the organization's relationship to its environment, the emerging internal and external forces affecting the organization, and the ability to position the organization within that environment for future and current success (20.1).
- Directs staff effectively in identifying areas of future growth and development in all areas of agency operations to be used in a strategic planning process (20.2).

(continued)

BOX 14.4 *(Continued)*

CSWE Competency 5–Engage in Policy Practice
  Social workers:

■ 5.2 Assess how social welfare and economic policies impact the delivery of and access to social services.

CSWE Competency 6–Engage With Individuals, Families, Groups, Organizations, and Communities
  Social workers:

■ 6.1 Apply knowledge of human behavior and the social environment, person-in-environment, and other multidisciplinary theoretical frameworks to engage with clients and constituencies.

CSWE, Council on Social Work Education.

Developing projections of the present perceived situation without new interventions that could alter the system is the second step. However, uncovering the current problem based on perceptions of the present situation is the initial task. But first, discover key elements, in both the *external environment* and the *internal environment*, that have an impact on the present perceived situation and will have an impact on projections of the present situation into the future.

A. *External and Internal Environments*
   The purpose of this step is to provide information on the internal strengths and weaknesses and the external threats and opportunities. This information sets the stage for providing valuable information for understanding strategic issues.

   Outcomes that can be expected:

   1. Creation of a strengths, weaknesses, opportunities, and threats (SWOT) analysis that is a list of internal strengths and weaknesses and external opportunities and threats.

   2. Identification of specific steps to deal with threats and weaknesses.

   3. Creation of an environmental scanning team to produce detailed analyses of the external environment and to keep other participants informed of the findings.

   4. Development of an effective management information system that includes input, process, and output categories so that the organization can assess its strengths and weaknesses efficiently and effectively.

   Benefits that can be expected:

   1. Information vital to the survival and prosperity of the organization is uncovered, thus allowing the planning team to view the organization as a whole in relation to its environment.

   2. Creation of a future rather than worrying about it!

   3. Clarification of the tension fields within which the organization exists. These actions juxtapose the positive (strengths and opportunities) with the negative (weaknesses and threats), the present (strengths and weaknesses) with the future (opportunities and threats).

   4. Timely action may be taken to deal with strengths and weaknesses.

Components of a SWOT analysis include
External Environment

- ▨ Forces/trends: political, economic, social, and technological
- ▨ Clients/customers/payers
- ▨ Competitors: competitive forces
- ▨ Collaborators: collaborative forces

Internal Environment

- ▨ Resources: people, economic situation, information, and competencies
- ▨ Present strategy: overall, functional or departmental
- ▨ Performance: results and history

Table 14.1 provides examples for each of the four categories in SWOT: strengths and weaknesses in the internal environment and opportunities and threats from the external environment.

TABLE 14.1 **Strengths, Weaknesses, Opportunities, and Threats**

INTERNAL ENVIRONMENT	
Strengths	**Weaknesses**
• Staff • New staff • Management/leadership • Values and ethics displayed	• Union environment • Funding not stable • Some staff need to retire • Unreliable management information system
EXTERNAL ENVIRONMENT	
Opportunities	**Threats**
• New programs are unique • Geographic locations • Programs are evidenced based	• Changing state funding environment • Lack of legislative support • More competitors

III. **Projecting the Logical Future of the System**

The logical future of the system is an "image of an extended present system." Planners put together all of the information gathered in the preceding steps and develop *reference projections* of three different images of the extended present system: *a realistic image, an optimistic image, and a pessimistic image* (see Box 14.5).

BOX 14.5

EXAMPLES OF REFERENCE PROJECTIONS FOR REALISTIC, OPTIMISTIC, AND PESSIMISTIC IMAGES

Realistic image: State funding will continue to be restrictive with 5% reductions each year.

Optimistic image: State funding will actually increase each year with a new administration that believes supporting programs will reduce long-term expenditures.

Pessimistic image: State funding will decline 5%–15% a year for the foreseeable future.

IV. **Developing Alternative Futures (Scenarios)**

The purpose of developing alternative futures scenarios is fourfold:

1. To serve as a vehicle for penetrating the problematique (the problematique is the underlying issue that impacts everything).

2. To serve as idea generators (i.e., novel hypotheses, values, strategies), not detailed descriptions of future states.

3. To serve as devices used to suggest new alternative objectives toward which the current system should be redirected. The scenarios should develop freely; you should ignore system constraints. These scenarios are not written to describe feasibility.

4. They begin to reveal, most importantly, the objectives toward which planning will be directed.

These scenarios are imposed upon the reference projections. Identification of strategic issues is the next step.

V. **Identifying Strategic Issues**

To identify strategic issues, use reference projections to uncover the fundamental policy choices facing the organization. This step outlines the basic direction along which the construction of a new social reality might take place.

Outcomes to be expected:

1. Creation of a list of the strategic issues faced by the organization.

2. Arrangement of the issues on the list in some order that is logical and prioritized.

To obtain these outcomes, you need to be able to describe the issue, discuss the factors that make the issue strategic (mandates, mission, external and internal environmental features), and discuss the consequences of failure to address the issue.

As a result, you may find that immediate action needs to be taken, no action needs to be taken but a close monitoring of it is necessary, and/or that the issue can be handled as part of the regular strategic planning cycle.

Benefits to be expected:

- Attention is focused on what is truly important.

- Attention is focused on issues, not answers. Often conflicts arise when discussing solutions to problems when the underlying problem is in fact not known.

- Useful clues are identified as to how to resolve the issues—*because* one has to discuss the mandates, mission, external and internal environments that make them strategic.

    ▪ The creation of useful tension is often necessary to prompt organizational change.

    ▪ If key decision makers decide to move forward and not terminate the planning efforts, the organization's character will be strengthened.

VI. **Using Alternative Objectives to Create a Composite Scenario**
The integration of the scenarios that proved most consonant with the envisioned ends or an idealized design (see Appendix 14A) becomes a composite scenario of what the "system ought to be." To create a composite scenario, follow these steps:

1. A synoptic version of the reference projection is introduced at the beginning (so you can compare it with what follows).

2. Different environmental frames describing the most generally expected evolution of the overall situation are then introduced (e.g., the cybernetics age is evolving into the artificial intelligence age; a new governor is elected with obvious state policy implications, etc.).

3. The scenarios that were produced in Step IV are composed together, manipulated, and transformed into the above environmental frames.

4. This operation yields an image of the system's future that is most desirable. Lines of interim evolution are defined and detailed, until they represent the outcome toward which you want the system to evolve.

VII. **Describing the Organization of the Future**
A description of the organization of the future should include a clear and succinct description of the organization as it implements its strategies and strives to achieve its full potential, including how the organization will function when it is working well.
Outcomes to be expected:

1. A written statement that includes

    ▪ a vision statement

    ▪ mission statement

    ▪ basic philosophy and core values

    ▪ goals and objectives

    ▪ basic strategies

    ▪ performance criteria

    ▪ important decision rules and

    ▪ ethical standards expected of all employees.

2. This descriptive statement should be widely circulated among organizational members and other key stakeholders after the appropriate sign-offs have been obtained.

3. It should be used to inform major and minor organizational decisions and actions.

Benefits to be expected:

1. Employees will have specific, reasonable, and supportive guidance about what is expected of them and why.

2. The more specific the vision of success, the more likely members will pursue and achieve it.

3. Leadership will have more time to focus on moving forward instead of debating what to do, how to do it, and why.

4. Organizational members and stakeholders will become more aware of the barriers to realization of the vision.

5. A reduction of incidences of conflicts will occur.

The mission statement provides the purpose for the organization, so clarifying the mission statement is necessary. You should ask what is the purpose of the organization or why should it be doing, what it does, and what are the philosophy and values that guide it.

Several outcomes result from clarifying the mission/values:

1. Creation of a mission statement if one does not exist.

2. Completion of a stakeholder analysis including

   - Identification of stakeholders, both internal and external.

   - Defining the criteria stakeholders use to judge the organization.

   - Determining how the organization is performing against those criteria.

3. Satisfying stakeholders is the key to success!

Stakeholder Mapping

Stakeholder mapping is a method to assess the possible impact of all stakeholders, given a set of objectives or a specified plan of action. It broadens the view of the organization and increases the opportunities for dealing with the total constellation of stakeholders. Understanding stakeholders will aid in preventing the familiar phenomenon of putting out unexpected fires as they develop from various dissatisfied groups. It is a method for the management of change. The process is a set of steps designed to facilitate a full and systematic consideration of stakeholders and their potential impact on the organization.

Step 1: State the organizational objectives.

Step 2: Brainstorm with stakeholders.

Step 3: Characterize stakeholders' attitudes toward organizational objectives or planned change.

Step 4: Identify stakeholders' power with respect to the adoption and/or implementation of the issue.

Step 5: Identify conditions—who do stakeholders influence and who influences stakeholders.

Step 6: Rethink solutions to increase implementation chances.

Step 7: Strategies (role-playing of discussion with stakeholders and simulation of possible strategies are powerful ways to explore all the possible implications of various strategies).

Benefits of clarifying the mission/values

- Focuses discussion on what is truly important.

- Clarifies organizational purpose.

- Gives explicit attention to the organization's philosophy and values and reduces the likelihood of error in the strategy formulation step.

- Questions to ask in developing a mission statement:

  - "Who are we?

  - In general, what are the basic social and political needs we exist to fill or the social and political problems we exist to address?

▨   In general, what do we want to do to recognize or anticipate and respond to these needs or problems?

▨   How should we respond to our key stakeholders?

▨   What is our philosophy and what are our core values?

▨   What makes us distinctive or unique?" (Bryson, 1988, p. 105)

VIII.   **Developing Strategic Goals and Strategies**
Developing strategic goals and strategies is the how-to step. Start by developing specific strategic goals, and then develop alternative strategies that will assist in attaining each goal. Formulation of strategies requires an extension of the mission to form a bridge between an organization and its environment. Strategic goals outline the organization's response to policy choices and define the essence of the organization, what it does, and why it does it.
Outcomes to be expected:

1. The organization may or may not wish to have a formal strategic plan.

    a. The plan would include

        i. Organization's mission statement.

        ii. Mandates to be met.

        iii. SWOT analysis.

        iv. Strategic goals, issues, or a vision of success.

        v. Strategies, including guides for implementation.

2. Formal agreement to move ahead.

3. Actions to be taken when they are identified and become useful or necessary.

Benefits to be expected:

1. A clear picture emerges of the strategies to achieve an ideal future derived from broad concepts to a detailed implementation plan.

2. Enhanced organizational creativity in solutions to problems.

3. The emergence of a new reality, provided actions are taken as identified.

4. Heightened morale among team members in the resolution of important issues.

IX.   **Creating an Action Framework**
Creating an action framework involves the development and implementation of "tactics" or activities that are needed to implement the strategies. Once organizational planning activities are implemented, a system of monitoring and control should be implemented to track progress. A monitoring and control system should contain four functional components: (a) an acceptable description of the expected outcomes, (b) ability to monitor actions, (c) ability to understand discrepancies in actions, and (d) ability to make changes in the plan to get it back on track if necessary. Several strategies are available to establish an implementation plan and then monitor it. A "back-step analysis" can be used to identify the reverse hierarchical order of action steps by working backward from the final objective or outcome. To order all of the action steps in a format for monitoring and control, a Gantt chart is recommended because it can exhibit project schedules by identifying tasks to be undertaken, the level of effort, persons responsible, and target completion dates. A wide variety of Gantt

charts are available, including those in the *Ultimate Guide to Gantt Charts* at
www.projectmanager.com/gantt-chart. Appendix 14B provides an example of a Gantt
chart designed for a strategic plan.

X. **Realizing Change (The System Responds)**
    When a description of the "organization of the future" is produced and
    implementation of the framework occurs, controlled interventions begin to make
    impacts upon the system and the system alters its behavior. This pattern of change has
    been "planned" and the change that occurs is willed and planned.

AN ABBREVIATED STRATEGIC PLANNING PROCESS

Not all organizations have the time, resources, and knowledge to conduct a full strategic planning
process. However, the full process can be adapted to an organization's resources. For example, an
abbreviated strategic planning process can be conducted in a relatively short period of time, such
as over several months. One example of an abbreviated strategic planning process is described
below.

Steps in an Abbreviated Strategic Planning Process

1. Obtain an initial agreement on a strategic planning process.

2. Identify and clarify the nature and meaning of the externally imposed mandates,
    formal and informal, affecting the organization.

3. Discover key elements in the *external environment* that have an impact on the "present
    perceived situation" and will have an impact on *internal environment* projections of the
    present situation into the future.

4. Develop a clear and succinct description of what the organization of the future should
    look like as it implements its strategies and achieves its full potential.

5. Create statements of vision, mission, core values and why the organization exists, goals,
    objectives, basic strategies, performance criteria, and ethical standards expected of all
    employees.

6. Create an action framework that involves the development and implementation of
    "tactics" or activities that are needed to implement the strategies. Implement
    organizational planning activities.

7. Change has occurred that is willed and controlled. Controlled interventions begin to
    make impacts upon the system and the system alters its behavior. The pattern of change
    has been planned.

VISION STATEMENTS, CORE VALUES, MISSION STATEMENTS, GOALS, AND OBJECTIVES

Box 14.6 displays Network for Social Work Management Practice Behavior 1.1, which is covered
in this section.

BOX 14.6

NETWORK FOR SOCIAL WORK MANAGEMENT COMPETENCIES AND PRACTICE BEHAVIORS 1

Establishes, promotes, and anchors the vision, philosophy, goals, objectives, and values of the organization (Network for Social Work Management Competencies 1). Practice Behaviors:

- Creates, communicates, and anchors a vision for the organization (1.1).

All organizations should have a vision, core values, mission, goals, objectives, outcomes, and benchmarks to meet the objectives. Understanding the meaning of these terms and their differences is an important first step.

Vision Statements

Differentiating between an organization's vision and mission can be challenging. Vision statements should be short and all about the future. That future is a desired end state that might not actually be achievable, but which the organization should consistently strive to achieve. The vision is what the organization wants to attain.

There are several characteristics of an effective vision. Vision statements should

- Imagine the future.
- Appeal to stakeholders.
- Be realistic.
- Be resilient.
- Be communicated with ease.

A description and four examples of vision statements are provided in Table 14.2.

TABLE 14.2 **Vision Statement Description and Examples**

DESCRIPTION	EXAMPLES
Vision statements should be short and all about the future. That future is a desired end state that might not actually be achievable, but which the organization should consistently strive to achieve. The best visions are inspirational, clear, memorable, and concise, not more than 15 words.	Human Rights Campaign: A world where lesbian, gay, bisexual, transgender and queer people are ensured equality and embraced as full members of society at home, at work and in every community. Feeding America: A hunger- free America. Alzheimer's Association: A world without Alzheimer's disease. Oxfarm: A just world without poverty. The Nature Conservancy: A world where the diversity of life thrives, and people act to conserve nature for its own sake and its ability to fulfill our needs and enrich our lives.

Establishing a vision is challenging and involves risk taking, but it will lead an organization in a direction that it should move toward. New leaders of an organization may want to review the organization's vision and values. And if a new vision is to be created and accepted, everyone in the organization should be involved in creating the vision. Vision statements should be true to the organization's actual situation. A vision statement that is disconnected from reality will only lead to trouble. For example, how can a university be a "preeminent graduate institution" if the faculty teach a four-course load?

Core Values

How do you encourage visionary thinking? One place to start is by creating or reviewing the organization's core values. All organizations are driven by a core set of values, whether these values are known or not. Effective organizations identify their core underlying values and use them in developing and implementing mission, goals, objectives, and the strategic plan. Every organization has core values that are vital to its survival and enhance the possibility of flourishing. If the organization has core values that are vital to flourishing, it can make decisions faster, which are also easier to support and can get support from the community. Core values do not have to be fixed values, and as a result, they can then be shared by generations of staff. Box 14.7 provides examples of core values questions to help the organization achieve its vision, mission, goals, and objectives.

BOX 14.7

CORE VALUES QUESTIONS

Core values—Does one's department function using its identified core values? Are core values producing positive behaviors on a daily basis? A review of the structure and culture of the organization could suggest an avenue for change if core values are being ignored.

What if there are conflicting core values (the university values access yet it raises tuition every year by 5%)?

What is the organization's mission, where is it going, and what are its core values? Can you state your organization's mission and core values in one minute?

What are the core values in your department which are vital to its survival and flourishing?

Core values do not have to be fixed values; they can evolve over time as the organization's vision, mission, and goals evolve. They can then be shared by generations of staff. If not all groups in the organization embrace the core values, how do you work with them so they become part of the culture?

(Ritt, Lewis University, 2004).

A description and examples of academic program core values are provided in Table 14.3.

TABLE 14.3 **Core Values Description and Examples**

DESCRIPTION	EXAMPLES
All organizations should be driven by a core set of values. Effective organizations identify their core underlying values and use them in developing and implementing mission, goals, and objectives.	Examples of academic core values: collegiality / autonomy / academic freedom / specializations/expertise / reason and the scientific method / experiential education / integrity / excellence / community service / ethics / lifelong learning / what is in the best interests of the students.

Box 14.8 provides an opportunity to examine one's own organization's core values.

BOX 14.8

COMPETENCY-BASED EXERCISE: VALUES CLARIFICATION EXERCISE

At your place of current or past employment:

- What core values are at work in shaping how people in the organization think and act?
- Do espoused values differ from those actually acted upon? If integrity is the primary value but some people are engaging in activities that have questionable integrity, what should you do about it? One way to stop conflicting value behavior is to model good behavior and show that negative behavior is not acceptable.
- Does everyone know the core values and do they understand how they can influence behavior? If not, how can you better define the core values and point out how they impact the organization?
- What change is necessary to fully realize the core values?
- Are there core values that may conflict, and if so, is there common ground among these conflicting values?

Box 14.9 provides examples of core academic setting values and why these core values are important.

BOX 14.9

EXAMPLES OF CORE ACADEMIC VALUES

Examples of university core values from its strategic plan (Norton, 2007)

- Excellence: The university values exemplary and distinguished performance in all aspects of university life by all members of the university community, especially in the areas of teaching, learning, scholarship, and service.
- Student Success: The university values all students, believes in their potential to achieve, and commits to challenging, supporting, and empowering them to transform their lives.
- Access: The university values its responsibility to provide opportunities for individuals with potential and motivation to become productive members of the university community and demonstrates that value by eliminating barriers that hinder full participation.
- Diversity: The university values an educational and work environment in which individuals and cultures are celebrated and respected for the unique talents, insights, and perspectives that they contribute.
- Lifelong Learning: The university values the pursuit of knowledge and provides an environment for all individuals to learn and develop throughout the various phases of their lives.
- Community Involvement: The university values community service, civic engagement, and social responsibility by all university members; encourages the integration of these principles in the learning experiences of students; invites community participation in university affairs; and promotes local, regional, national, and international collaborations.

Mission Statements

Mission statements should consist of the broadest and most general plan. Mission statements tend to be idealistic and altruistic. Although vagueness is palatable to everyone, mission statements do not provide specific guidance for influencing staff behavior. It is best to distill all elements of a mission into a single sentence or just a few sentences (e.g., how would you write a mission statement in a single sentence that include the following: women, diversity, liberal arts, purposeful engagement?).

Key issues today that preoccupy boards and trustees are related to missions. For example, how can the mission be adapted to market demands and how can the mission evolve to respond to demand? If you adapt, do you erode the old mission and market positions?

Purpose and content of mission statements:

- A mission statement is a statement by an organization or program (or project or service) that contains detailed information about the overall direction and purpose of the organization or program.

- It is an administrative statement, which guides planning and decision making, and is not restricted by any time element.

- It should contain the philosophy of the organization or program, specify the level and type of services provided, set forth the major functions of the organization/program, and identify the service area or population and special formal and informal relationships with other organizations/programs.

- It is an enduring vision of future direction and values.

- It sets forth the basic purpose of the program or project.

- Goals and objectives fulfill the mission statement (Family Planning Initiative and HIV Planning Council, 1992).

What is your organization's mission, what are its goals, and what are its core values? You should be able to answer in one minute! Box 14.10 provides several examples of agency mission statements and an example of a university mission statement.

BOX 14.10

MISSION STATEMENT EXAMPLES

Agency Mission Statement Examples

- "The AIDS/HIV Service Group is a non-profit, volunteer, and community-based organization serving the City of Charlottesville and Albemarle, Greene, Louisa, Nelson and Fluvanna Countries (other areas are served as resources allow and as needed). The purpose of this agency is

    - To help people infected with HIV, their loved ones, family, and friends cope by providing emotional, practical, and educational support.

    - To prevent the spread of HIV by educating people about the risks of acquiring HIV.

    - To promote in the public an informed and compassionate response to the epidemic and all the people if affects."

(continued)

BOX 14.10 *(Continued)*

- "The mission of the HIV Planning Council is to develop and coordinate an effective and comprehensive community-wide response to HIV/AIDS, to reduce the incidence of HIV infection, and to maintain the highest possible quality of life for all persons infected with or affected by HIV disease, including those traditionally not served or underserved."

- "The mission of the Centre for AIDS Services of Montreal (Women) is to provide support, education and referrals for women living with HIV/AIDS and STDs based on the needs of women. We offer these services to empower women to determine the quality of their own lives" (Family Campus Initiative and HIV Planning Council, 1992).

- "Southern Connecticut State University (SCSU) provides exemplary graduate and undergraduate education in the liberal arts and professional disciplines. As an intentionally diverse and comprehensive university, Southern is committed to academic excellence, access, social justice, and service for the public good" (Papazian, 2015).

For academic programs, the first step is to review the institutional mission, how it is distinct, and how it aligns with the program's mission. If rewriting the program mission, identify key themes from the institutional mission and make sure these themes are added to the program mission. The University of Phoenix scans the market for business opportunities, the ones traditional academic institutions are not picking up, and then delivers in those areas. When those opportunities shift, the University of Phoenix shifts quickly to seize those opportunities, but traditional institutions do not. So when doing a SWOT analysis, look at what the for-profits are doing in your area, how they are working in your markets. They are more resilient and quicker to seize opportunities. If you are going to explain your mission to a parent, could you do that? Most are too long. Mission statements should be a couple of sentences, up to five at the most. Box 14.11 provides two distinct examples of a mission statement at two different points over a decade at the same university (mission statements can and should change).

BOX 14.11

EXAMPLE OF A SOCIAL WORK DEPARTMENT MISSION STATEMENT

This university is one of four universities in the university-wide system and the Department of Social Work is the only program in this system and state that offers both undergraduate and graduate programs in social work. The program curriculum emphasizes a perspective that views people as having the capacity to change and adapt while in continuous and reciprocal interchange with all elements of their environment. The academic and field practicum components are designed to teach professional social work knowledge and to impart tools for scholarship, critical thinking, and evidence-based practice. We are committed to ethical practice and the integration of social work values in all educational activities and practice. The purpose of undergraduate education is to prepare students to work in entry-level agency-based social work positions. The focus of graduate education is professional education for students, who will provide clinical or management services.

Another example: The mission of the Department of Social Work is to provide quality social work education to undergraduate and graduate students and to advance knowledge through study, practice, and research. Further, the Department is also committed to preparing social workers to promote system change to achieve economic and social justice in the life of communities impacted by rapid economic

(continued)

BOX 14.11 *(Continued)*

and social shifts. We are committed to students in the program being able to engage in practice with diverse populations in metropolitan settings. In addition, the Department is committed to educating social workers to be effective practitioners and leaders in the public and private sectors. The Department is also committed to developing partnerships with the community to further both the Department's and the University's commitment to scholarship and professional preparation.

Would a new faculty member at your institution describe the mission differently than someone who has been there 15 years? How does the university mission get conveyed, and is the program in alignment with it? Box 14.12 provides several questions that could help in redefining a mission statement.

BOX 14.12

COMPETENCY-BASED MISSION STATEMENT EXERCISE

- Why does your academic department exist? Some departments are underfunded. To act on this issue, define how your department fits into the university mission and why this department is important. From a financial and mission orientation, explain why the department exists. As a department head, you have to advocate for resources, so explain why the department exists, point by point. Identify what revenue streams are coming into the university because of the department (graduate enrollments may be higher than other graduate programs).

- What are the department's major activities (curricular products and student services)?

- What are the target markets the department serves?

- Who are the students? (Most are 18–22 years old, some nontraditional, some commuters, some not.) Graduate students and doctoral students represent a large percentage of all graduate enrollments in the university.

- What are future directions for your department? What new markets can be captured?

A description and examples of a variety of mission statements are provided in Table 14.4.

TABLE 14.4 Mission Statements Description and Examples

DESCRIPTION	EXAMPLES
Mission statements should consist of the broadest and most general plan. Mission statements tend to be idealistic and altruistic.	LinkedIn: To connect the world's professionals to make them more productive and successful. BBC: To enrich people's lives with programs and services that inform, educate, and entertain. SCSU: Provides exemplary graduate and undergraduate education in the liberal arts and professional disciplines. As an intentionally diverse and comprehensive university, Southern is committed to academic excellence, access, social justice, and service for the public good.

BBC, British Broadcasting Corporation; SCSU, Southern Connecticut State University.

Box 14.13 is a group exercise for defining a mission statement.

BOX 14.13

COMPETENCY-BASED EXERCISE: DEFINING A MISSION STATEMENT

Group exercise

- Select a partner.
- Define the mission of your organization in 60 seconds.
- Give one example.
- Give one example of the mission in action, such as (a) train students to be lifelong learners, (b) educate citizens to meet demand in the state workforce, and (c) serve the metropolitan community.
- Identify three major projects and their alignment with the mission.
- How is your organization's mission different from similar programs at other institutions?
- State your institutional mission. How is it distinct?

Goals

Goals are more specific than a mission. Goals serve as the organizational outcomes toward which staff aim. Management decisions should be evaluated with reference to organizational goals. As conditions/needs change, goals should change. Goal succession or abandonment can also occur. Goals are often only theoretically attainable.

Goals include two basic components: (a) who will be affected and (b) what will change because of the program (Family Planning Initiative and HIV Planning Council, 1992).

Examples of a program goal

- To help staff manage their own stress.
- To reduce the incidence of HIV infections in the community.
- To help clients and their families deal with lifestyle changes after a diagnosis of AIDS (Family Planning Initiative and HIV Planning Council, 1992).

To be successful in developing, maintaining, or expanding programs, both the mission statement and the goals need to be accepted, understood, and supported by everyone in an organization and all external stakeholders.

Box 14.14 provides an example of goals that are derived from a mission statement.

BOX 14.14

CASE STUDY EXAMPLE: MISSION STATEMENT AND GOALS

Sample Mission Statement: Lotus Community Wellness Center

The Lotus Community Wellness Center, a dynamic partnership with Pacific HealthCare and the surrounding community, is committed to empowering men, women, and children of all backgrounds to enhance and maintain their health through the concept of holistic care. Therefore, the spiritual, intellectual, emotional, physical, and social dimensions of this larger community will be addressed through an active integration of the talents and resources of the partnership. Ongoing services and other educational programs, activities and support, all of which are affordable and accessible.

Goals

The Wellness Center will

1. Use approaches that intergrade the spiritual, intellectual, emotional, physical, environmental, and social dimensions of life.
2. Provide health educational and support groups to encourage health life choice for all ages.
3. Be a personal, caring service, assisted by volunteers trained in methods consistent with the mission of the Center.
4. Listen to the needs of all voices in the community in planning the current and future directions of the Center.
5. Provide a visible, regularly staffed, and accessible resource facility.
6. Target audiences through maintaining an ongoing communication/public relations strategy.
7. Be a nonprofit, self-sustaining endeavor (Family Planning Initiative and HIV Planning Council, 1992).

An example of a university's goals is offered through the Board of Trustees' goals for Nichols College, which include these basic statements. Goals should:

- Be mission driven and specific.
- Encourage students to actively engage in lifelong learning educational experiences.
- Strengthen the university financially (Murphy, et al., 2007).

Box 14.15 provides information on building support for goals and steps to assess a strategic plan.

BOX 14.15

BUILDING FACULTY INVESTMENT IN ASSESSMENT AND INSTITUTIONAL EFFECTIVENESS

How do you build support for the goals of the strategic plan?

- Need provost and dean's leading effort.

(continued)

BOX 14.15 *(Continued)*

- Create faculty advisory group.
- Create faculty learning communities.
- Sponsor and attend internal and external conferences.
- Create a context for change.

Assess implementation of the plan to determine if changes in it need to be made:

- Ask employers to assess and give feedback on student competence.
- Administer a general survey.
- Encourage ongoing department assessments.
- Survey students.

Summary:

- Articulate a persuasive vision, convince faculty about the value of the vision.
- Encourage academic leadership to be involved.
- Provide support such as funding, creating learning communities and advisory groups.
- Create an environment for change.
- Sustain, recognize, and reward the effort put into developing the strategic plan.
- Remember that this is a work in progress (Freeland, 2007).

A description and examples of goals are provided in Table 14.5.

Much of the literature on goals and objectives focuses on what constitutes a "good" objective and how it should be formulated (e.g., quantifiable, specific, and measurable). Much less attention has been focused on the factors that influence the perception of what are desired goals. External influences certainly can impact goal development. The extent that an organization needs to follow external mandates, in some cases, can influence goal development.

TABLE 14.5 **Goals Description and Examples**

DESCRIPTION	EXAMPLES
Goals should • Have a specific function (e.g., program goals, educational goals). • Have a different definition from that of a mission statement and from that of an objective. • Be a statement of a desired future state or condition. • Express long-term hopes and aspirations. • Not be directly measurable but are attainable. • Be accomplished by activities. • Lack deadlines, be relatively broad in scope, and provide guidance for the establishment of objectives.	• To help staff manage their stress. • To reduce the incidence of HIV infections in the community. • To help clients and their families deal with lifestyle changes after a diagnosis of AIDS. • To encourage students to actively engage in lifelong learning educational experiences. • To strengthen the university financially. • To create and strengthen community partnerships to further the department and university's shared commitments to scholarship, professional preparation, and advocacy.

Additional factors, such as other types of external and internal influences (emanating from key outside stakeholders or the chief operating officer), can impact the perception and formulation of desired goals. These external and internal influences are displayed in Box 14.16.

BOX 14.16

EXTERNAL AND INTERNAL INFLUENCES IMPACTING GOALS

External Influences

- Policies and decisions that the organization must follow
- Legislative mandates from all levels
- Court orders such as decrees
- Lobbying by interest groups and advocates
- Higher level administrative support or lack of support
- Funding

Internal Influences

- Past and present levels of performance by staff
- Staff support for goals
- Predictions of what the future will be
- Continuity of staff and management
- Staffing levels

Because the larger environment can influence goal development, goals should not be created unilaterally, but through a negotiated process (formal or informal) involving stakeholders at three different levels (Management and Behavior Science Center, 1983):

1. The level of the unit itself or the unit that is creating the goal.
2. The larger system in which the planning unit resides.
3. The parts that make up the planning unit (the component programs that are part of the planning unit).

In different situations, these three levels can have different degrees of influence over the formulation of desired outcomes. For example, if the desired outcome is "planning for new ways to increase funding," then the unit level would have the highest degree of influence over attaining this outcome because staff at this level would be actively engaged in planning and participating in fundraising activities. The larger system would have a low level of involvement and the component parts of the unit would have a low to medium level of involvement. In another example with an outcome of "planning for determining participant eligibility," the larger system would have the highest degree of involvement and the unit and component parts of the unit would play a lesser role. Finally, with the example of a national meeting and advocacy organization, the component parts of the unit would have the most influence as the organization consists of many component parts and this organization makes decisions that impact all of the desired outcomes that the organization establishes.

Objectives

Objectives make it possible to determine if goals have been achieved; they also have time deadlines. Objectives outline the specific tasks essential to accomplish already determined goals. Each separate objective should be the partial accomplishment of a goal. Objectives have baselines that use valid and reliable data derived from currently established data systems. The baseline date provides the point from which a target can be set (e.g., increase enrollment by 10% a year and to no more than 300 students after five years). Only when objectives have been spelled out in measurable activities should resources be allocated to accomplish the goals and mission.

Objectives can serve a number of purposes, such as providing written objectives for all staff (management by objectives), creating targets that can be negotiated and are measurable, assessing ongoing programs, and building objectivity into employee evaluations.

A description and examples of objectives are provided in Table 14.6.

TABLE 14.6 **Objectives Description and Examples**

DESCRIPTION	EXAMPLES
<ul><li>Objectives must be measurable by specifying who, to what extent, under what conditions, by what standards, and within what time period certain activities are to be performed and completed.</li><li>Objectives provide direction for action.</li><li>Objectives may be short-term or long-term. As programs become more complex, more objectives are needed. (Family Planning Initiative and HIV Planning Council, 1992).</li></ul>	<ul><li>Students will demonstrate the abilities and attributes of the profession as evidenced by participation rubric scores in field seminar courses.</li><li>Achieve 90% admission rate for all BSW students who apply to graduate school.</li><li>Achieve LMSW passing rates and LCSW passing rates that are above the national average for that year.</li><li>Create a case statement for fundraising plan during spring 2019 semester.</li></ul>

Objectives can also be used to specify what programs hope to accomplish and can measure different levels of programming, such as awareness, knowledge, attitudes, skill development, access, behavior, risk reduction, and health status. Behavioral terms can determine who will do how much of what, to whom, when, where, and for what purpose. Another way to define objectives is to consider the condition or magnitude of change in the target group on an outcome measure, or consider the content or type and direction of change on the target population and the magnitude or degree of change, including the way change will be measured, all within a certain timeframe. So another example is: "By graduation, 80% of the class will have mastered the adaptation of practice skills in using CBT with culturally diverse populations" (Family Planning Initiative and HIV Planning Council, 1992).

A structured approach can be used by plugging in words into a formula as long as all the descriptive content is provided. The content of the formula includes a verb/action word, a noun/outcome, the date/time, and the cost or level or condition. One example is:

The program will provide placements (verb/action) for five clients (noun/outcome) by May 1 (date/time) in a sober living house (cost or level or condition).

Another example using the same content but in a different order is:

By May 1 (date/time), the program will provide placements (verb/action) for five clients (noun/outcome) in a sober living house (cost or level or condition),

Verbs to describe objectives should show action, and be specific, detailed, and not vague.

Precise verbs that are open to few interpretations include the following:

- Discuss / evaluate /identify / list /diagram / compare / translate / recall and state / integrate /illustrate / select / interpret / differentiate / summarize / classify /predict / apply / write / recite / solve /construct / complete /prepare /make / run / draft / draw / contract / develop / open / define / describe / tabulate / answer / report / state / / feeling level / challenge / defend / dispute / join / judge / offer/ praise / question / share / attempt / visit / accept / support (Family Planning Initiative and HIV Planning Council, 1992).

Verbs that are less precise can be open to many interpretations and therefore should be avoided. Examples of less precise verbs and verb phrases that should not be used include the following:

- Know / realize / fully realize / enjoy / believe / understand / understand / feel responsible for / appreciate / value / comprehend / be aware of / tolerate / be familiar with / desire / feel / have faith in / desire / feel / have faith in / grasp the significance of / acknowledge / know / be motivated / experience / be informed of / be involved in (Family Planning Initiative and HIV Planning Council, 1992).

Each objective should always be assessed to ensure it is clear, measurable, and specifies some level of results. However, most organizations usually start with process objectives, which delineate action. Once process objectives are created, which typically denote type of service provided, by whom, and by a set date, then outcome objectives can be created that denote what results will be achieved. For example, see Table 14.7, which relates various process objectives to corresponding outcome objectives.

TABLE 14.7 Process Rather Than Outcome Objectives

PROCESS OBJECTIVE		RESULTS OBJECTIVES
Staff are able to submit record keeping data in a timely manner	rather than	Updated data is used to obtain additional funding as program has capacity to serve and assess
Planning activities took place	rather than	Plan resulted in changes in program operations, which improved client outcomes by 10% in all components of the program
Spend total budget by the end of the year	rather than	Budget provided a 10% increase in services
Staff processed all applications in a timely manner	rather than	Program enrollment increased by 10%
Provide temporary shelter for more clients	rather than	Moved 20% of clients into permanent housing after assistance provided

Objectives can also be classified under three categories related to what type of outcome is desired. If the desired outcome is to continue the existing programs as currently structured, then the objectives can be classified as "maintenance objectives." If the desired outcome is to improve existing programs, then the objectives can be classified as "performance objectives." If the desired outcome is to create new programs that will help the organization better meet its mission, goals, and objectives, then the objectives can be classified as "innovation objectives." When creating the plan, these three categories of maintenance, performance, and innovation should be used in association with corresponding objectives that match each type of outcome.

According to Management and Behavior Science Center (1983b), formatting of objectives by addressing the what, how much, when, why, and how questions helps in objective creation and definition. Several examples below show how these questions can be applied:

- What condition needs to be changed and does this change require a new direction?—We are serving too many students/clients and we need to change admissions requirements.

- How much change needs to occur to make the condition manageable?—Reduce admissions by 20%.

- When will this change take place?—At the start of the next enrollment cycle.

- Why is this change recommended?—The organization's mission statement states that quality service will be provided, and as the program has expanded too rapidly, service has deteriorated.

- How will this change be implemented?—A revision to the strategic plan will be required that addresses this issue and creates new objectives.

Objectives should also be prioritized, as not all are equally critical and urgent. According to the Management and Behavior Science Center (1983b), criteria for prioritizing objectives include the importance of the objective to the organization, its urgency, its cost/benefit, the location or source of the objective, and the degree of organizational change that will occur if this objective is implemented.

Importance and urgency can be assessed by asking the following questions:

- Is the objective critical or important and urgent? If so, it should be given the highest priority.

- Is the objective critical or important and should be done soon, or is urgent? If so, it is desirable and should be acted on sooner rather than later.

- Is the objective critical or important or useful but unnecessary or unimportant yet with long-range consequences? If so, it is a desirable objective that can be acted on at some point.

- Is the objective useful but unnecessary or unimportant yet has long-range consequences, orhould be done soon? If so, it is a desirable objective that can be acted on at some point.

- Is the objective critical or important or useful but unnecessary or unimportant and time is not a factor? If so, do not consider action any time soon.

To determine the cost/benefit of implementing an objective, ask the following key questions:

- For this objective, will a small increase in cost result in a disproportionate increase in benefit?

- For this objective, will a large increase in cost result in an even greater disproportionate increase in benefit?

- Conversely, for this objective, will a small reduction in cost result in a disproportionate increase or decrease in benefit?

- And will a large reduction in cost result in an even greater disproportional increase or decrease in benefit?

The location or source of the objective is an important consideration mainly concerning what level of control one might have over acting on the objective. If the objective is located outside of the manager's span of control, it may be difficult to oversee the successful implementation of the objective.

Finally, implementing objectives can create organizational change in many ways and some may be beneficial and some not so beneficial. Considering the impact that the objective will have on organizational behavior, each one should always be weighed prior to implementation.

Evaluating Objectives

Before finalizing objectives, a good practice is to review each objective to determine whether objectives meet the requirements for being a true objective. Is the objective stated as a declarative sentence? Does the objective contain the what, how much, and when information? Does the objective describe a future outcome that can actually be attained? If any of these are missing, make sure to add content to satisfy the requirement for defining a good objective.

Establishing Benchmarks

Box 14.17 displays the Network for Social Work Management (NSWM) Practice Behavior 1.4 and Council on Social Work Education (CSWE) Practice Behavior 9.1 that cover benchmarks.

BOX 14.17

NETWORK FOR SOCIAL WORK MANAGEMENT COMPETENCIES AND PRACTICE BEHAVIORS 1 AND COUNCIL ON SOCIAL WORK EDUCATION PRACTICE BEHAVIOR 9

Establishes, promotes, and anchors the vision, philosophy, goals, objectives, and values of the organization (Network for Social Work Management Competencies 1). Practice Behaviors:

- Works closely with management staff to establish benchmarks to show alignment with vision, mission, philosophy, and goals (1.4).

CSWE Competency 9–Evaluate Practice With Individuals, Families, Groups, Organizations, and Communities
   Social workers:

- 9.1 Select and use appropriate methods for evaluation of outcomes.

CSWE, Council on Social Work Education.

As part of the strategic planning process, establishing benchmarks to show alignment with mission, goals, and objectives should be undertaken as part of the implementation process. What is the best way to establish benchmarks? Retreats with key staff can sometimes be useful. Benchmarks can be used in two ways: either as numeric targets for objectives or as outcome indicators that document what percentage was obtained for each objective (if the objective had a percentage target). There are formal and informal ways to determine if benchmarks have been met and if the organization's objectives are still aligned with the mission and goals, as organizational drift can occur over time. Formal methods include monthly, biannual, or annual reviews of the status of the strategic plan. Informally, one can usually notice when things are not aligned because activities seem to have no bearing or relationship to the mission and goals.

IMPLEMENTION OF STRATEGIC PLANS

Box 14.18 presents NSWM Practice Behaviors 1.1, 1.2, and 1.4 and CSWE Practice Behaviors 7.4 and 9.1, all of which are focused on implementing strategic plans.

BOX 14.18

NETWORK FOR SOCIAL WORK MANAGEMENT COMPETENCIES AND PRACTICE BEHAVIORS 1 AND COUNCIL ON SOCIAL WORK EDUCATION PRACTICE BEHAVIORS 7 AND 9

Establishes, promotes, and anchors the vision, philosophy, goals, objectives, and values of the organization (Network for Social Work Management Competencies 1). Practice Behaviors:

- Creates, communicates, and anchors a vision for the organization (1.1).
- Works to ensure that all programs align with the overall organizational mission (1.2).
- Works closely with management staff to establish benchmarks to show alignment with vision, mission, philosophy, and goals (1.4).

CSWE Competency 7–Assess Individuals, Families, Groups, Organizations, and Communities
Social workers:

- 7.4 Select appropriate intervention strategies based on the assessment, research knowledge, and values and preferences of clients and constituencies.

CSWE Competency 9–Evaluate Practice With Individuals, Families, Groups, Organizations, and Communities
Social workers:

- 9.1 Select and use appropriate methods for evaluation of outcomes.

CSWE, Council on Social Work Education.

Leaders and managers need to develop programs that align and then assess them regularly. Are the programs doing what the organization says it believes in? Program evaluations can be telling, as can client satisfaction surveys. Any strategic plan should have operationally defined goals and objectives that can measure the success of the mission. In addition, employing tacit ways to gauge success can be helpful, such as interpreting communications from clients, community and staff to detect any hidden or implied meaning.

Once a strategic plan is completed, implementing the plan is a process that frequently falls short. A strategic plan should coordinate an organization's activities and help it remain focused on goal attainment. Implementation should be a continuous process involving ongoing monitoring and revision. Deciding in advance what needs to be done, the best ways and times to do it, and who is the best choice to do it requires an implementation plan. Appendix 14B displays an implementation plan in an action framework with a simple example.

A tip for ensuring that implementation will take place: Post a one-page summary during meetings. At the top of the agenda and minutes of the department meeting, include the mission and vision and identify several key strategic initiatives. Boards and trustees in higher education look for several things that can make strategic plans a success. Building a governance team that can accomplish goals is a primary objective. Using the strategic plan as the glue to hold together a collaborative and cohesive governance team will help everyone know the institution is driving toward goals and objectives. The strategic plan must be a continuous process which ties the president (who is willing to bet his or her career on obtaining the objectives) and the board. The president needs to communicate the process for planning and implementation. If the board believes in the plan, it will raise funds for the program and the next capital campaign. If the board believes in the changes being made, it will help. Leaders must have ownership in the plan from the board, administration, faculty, alumni, donors, and so on (Murphy, et al., 2007).

Table 14.8 is a simplified version of an action plan.

TABLE 14.8 **Strategic Planning Process Action Plan**

STRATEGY/ACTION STEPS	PERFORMANCE MEASURES	TIMELINE	RESPONSIBILITY	RESOURCES

Updating and Keeping Current Strategic Plan

Box 14.19 is covered in this section.

BOX 14.19

NETWORK FOR SOCIAL WORK MANAGEMENT COMPETENCIES AND PRACTICE BEHAVIORS 1 AND COUNCIL ON SOCIAL WORK EDUCATION PRACTICE BEHAVIORS 8 AND 9

Establishes, promotes, and anchors the vision, philosophy, goals, objectives, and values of the organization (Network for Social Work Management Competencies 1). Practice Behaviors:

- Reviews the mission periodically to determine its relevance to client and the community needs (1.3).
- Identifies potential organizational drift from vision, mission, philosophy, and goals (1.5).

CSWE Competency 8—Intervene With Individuals, Families, Groups, Organizations, and Communities
  Social workers:

- 8.1 Critically choose and implement interventions to achieve practice goals and enhance capacities of clients and constituencies.

CSWE Competency 9—Evaluate Practice With Individuals, Families, Groups, Organizations, and Communities
  Social workers:

- 9.3 Critically analyze, monitor, and evaluate intervention and program processes and outcomes.

CSWE, Council on Social Work Education.

Once strategic plans are accepted and implementation has occurred, it will only be a matter of time before some goals and objectives become either achieved or obsolete. Therefore, on some regular (e.g., yearly) basis, the plan should be assessed. To begin with, ask the following questions:

- How and when do you ensure that mission reviews are up-to-date with stakeholders?
- How do you determine if organizational drift is occurring and, if it is, what you should do about it?
- When should you assess the program? When creating and implementing mission, goals, and objectives, how do you establish ways of knowing there will be red flags? A review every six months to determine if you are adhering to your mission, goals, and objectives is recommended.

As most strategic plans extend three to 10 years, it is important to review the implementation status and also the relevancy of the plan's vision, mission, goals, and objectives. Organizational drift can occur with changes in external and internal environments. Updating the SWOT analysis every several years will provide information on the current environment. An analysis of implementation status at a minimum every year will determine what has been achieved, what still needs work, and what should be eliminated from the plan. If some goals are achieved, new goals may be instituted.

Business Plan

Box 14.20 displays Network for Social Work Management Practice Behavior 20.4, which deals with the construction of a business plan.

BOX 14.20

NETWORK FOR SOCIAL WORK MANAGEMENT COMPETENCIES AND PRACTICE BEHAVIORS 20

Ensures strategic planning (Network for Social Work Management Competencies 20). Practice Behaviors:

- Constructs or directs the construction of an adequate business plan that details the pathway, timelines, and accountability for the accomplishment of identified strategic objectives (20.4).

Business plans differ from strategic plans in that they are used to describe and plan for a new business or program development (or a new program within a larger, preexisting organization) or to obtain funding, whereas strategic plans are predominantly used to implement or manage a strategic direction in an existing organization or program. While business plans are typically short-term (one year) and are created to evaluate the feasibility of starting a new service or program, strategic plans are longer term (three to five, even 10 years) plans that assume that programs can be implemented within the timeframes, without questioning the economic feasibility.

When creating your business plan, an important first step is to draft your executive summary. The executive summary provides an overview of the program or service you are seeking to deliver. Included in the executive summary is the description of the service(s) that will be provided, to what target audience, and solutions to alleviate the problem. The goals and objectives of the service delivery plan can be derived from the organization's strategic plan, and should cover the organizational mission, vision, and values. The executive summary must provide some information about the competition and underscore what will make this program unique and marketable. Subsequently, develop marketing strategies for ideal clients or students. Part of the business development plan must include a plan for building a team of qualified people to carry out the business plan. Finally, the executive summary should provide information about the budget plans and delineate how funds will be used and what will be needed in order for the program to be profitable, or generate income over expense.

Following the executive summary in the business plan comes a description of the organization that includes the vision, mission statement, goals, target market, service field, and legal structure.

Vision includes the statement of the organization's values, direction, and what the organization ideally seeks to accomplish.

Mission statement provides some direction on how to accomplish the vision statement and explains the reason the organization exists.

Goals include more specific information on how the organization will achieve the mission and includes both the long- and short-term strategies.

Target market is a brief description of the clients or students that the organization intends to serve, including demographics of the target population and their needs.

Marketing plan should be informed by research on the estimated start-up costs (consider the availability of existing staff and resources), the cost of providing services, cost of marketing and advertising the program, and need for specialized technical support.

Service field refers to the professional practice arena (i.e., a subspecialty in healthcare, specific populations), and thus the plan should emphasize how the service field can develop a niche to serve a target population. Also describe what will set proposed program apart from others.

Legal structure simply refers to whether the organization is a corporation, limited liability, or sole proprietor entity, and also whether it is a public for-profit or public nonprofit, or private for-profit or private nonprofit, or finally a university organization.

There are a number of business plan templates available online that can be modified and used as a framework for creating a business plan.

SUMMARY

This chapter provided an overview of planning in general. It provided examples of strategic plans, and also delineated a full, creative, and futurist strategic planning process as well as a short abbreviated version. This chapter displayed descriptions and examples of vision statements, core values, mission statements, goals, and objectives. Finally, it also discussed the implementation, keeping current, and updating of strategic plans.

ACTIVITIES

1. Review the strategic plan for your organization and edit it using the information on correct use of vision, mission, goals, and objectives.

2. Design an implementation plan for your organization's strategic plan, and if one already exists, add additional columns that might be missing and add relevant material.

REFERENCES

Ackoff, R. (1970). *A concept of corporate planning*. New York, NY: Wiley.

Ackoff, R. (1974). *Redesigning the future*. New York, NY: Wiley.

Ackoff, R. (1978). *Planning (Lecture Notes)*. Philadelphia, PA: The Wharton School, University of Pennsylvania.

Bryson, J. M. (1988). *Strategic planning for public and nonprofit organizations*. San Francisco, CA: Jossey-Bass.

Creighton, J. (2007). *Vision, planning and assessment*. New England Association of Schools and Colleges (NEASC) Conference, Boston, MA.

Family Planning Initiative and HIV Planning Council. (1992). *Developing goals, objectives, and outcomes*. New Haven, CT: Yale University.

Freeland, R. (2007). *Building faculty investment in assessment and institutional effectiveness*. New England Association of Schools and Colleges (NEASC) Conference, Boston, MA.

Management and Behavior Science Center. (1983). *Planning: Overview of planning course (Module #1)*. Philadelphia, PA: The Wharton School, University of Pennsylvania.

Management and Behavior Science Center. (1983a). *Idealized design*. Philadelphia, PA: The Wharton School, University of Pennsylvania.

Management and Behavior Science Center. (1983b). *Developing goals and objectives*. Philadelphia, PA: The Wharton School, University of Pennsylvania.

Murphy, D., Wilson, E. B., & Schneider, R. (2007). *Vision without resources is hallucination*. NewEngland Association of Schools and Colleges (NEASC) Conference, Boston, MA.

Norton, C. J. (2007). *Pursuing excellence, fostering leadership, empowering communities. A strategic plan for Southern Connecticut State University*. New Haven, CT.

Papazian, M. (2015). *Discover Southern: A university for the 21st century. A strategic plan for Southern Connecticut State University, 2015–2025*. New Haven, CT.

Ritt, E., Lewis University. (2004). *Crafting strategy that sticks–aligning with institutional mission*. Twenty-First Annual Academic Chairpersons Conference. Adams Mark Hotel. Orlando, FL.

APPENDIX 14A: IDEALIZED DESIGN

The idealized planning process was developed by Ackoff (1970, 1974); the following material has been modified from the Management and Behavioral Science Center (1983a).

Idealized design is based on the premise that the longer-term future depends more on what we do between now and the future than on what has happened up until now or what happened in the past. In creating an idealized redesign, one clarifies and specifies an ideal system if the current system constraints are removed. By creating an idealized redesign (a future state for a system) and then making the minimum number of compromises to make it feasible, one often makes significantly more progress than if one accepts the present constraints as given and tries to improve the system.

A helpful starting point for idealization is to assume that the system one wishes to redesign (the scope can vary from a unit within an institution to an entire function or department) has been completely destroyed and must be reinvented. The criterion that it be operationally viable means that if the system could be magically implemented, it would be able to work in the environment that contains it. Idealization does not mean one can wish problems away by assuming a different environment.

Specifying Desired Properties of the Unit

A good way to get started in creating an idealized redesign is to generate a list of desired properties by asking a series of questions concerning clients/customers, services, organization and management, and the environment:

1. *For Clients and Consumers*
    - Who should be the primary clients?
    - Who else could benefit from services provided?
    - How should the services be marketed or made available?

2. *For Services*
    - What services should be offered?
    - What should differentiate the services from those of other providers?
    - What role should the organization play with respect to other service providers?
    - How should internal development of new services be organized and carried out?

3. *Organization and Management*
    - How should the unit be structured and managed?
    - Which of the functions or activities should be carried out by the unit itself and which should be obtained by contracting or other means?

4. *The Environment*
    - To whom should the unit be accountable?
    - How should the unit relate to its stakeholders?
    - How can the unit engage in effective scanning of the environment?

Process of Idealization

◼ The process of idealization consists of eight steps:

1. Introduce the concept of idealization and the intended project.
2. Agree on the unit of analysis, the scope, and the assumptions.
3. Individuals create idealized designs.
4. The staff should draft the document and identify contradictions and circulate the initial report.
5. Group discussion should take place with healthy debate, followed by further development of the idealized design.
6. Steps 3, 4, and 5 can be repeated if necessary.
7. Idealized redesign is completed and it may contain explicit experiments to test alternatives around which there was disagreement.
8. A minimum number of modifications can be made to enhance the feasibility of the design.

Fine-Tuning the Idealized Redesign

1. Some action items appear immediately.
2. Some areas for new research and inquiry are identified.
3. There is a sharpened awareness of a desired direction.

After a consensus version of the idealized design has been obtained, the process of specifying ends is as following:

1. Compare the design to a reference scenario (what the present system would look like in the future if nothing changes).
2. Identify the differences that constitute gaps between what is desired and what will happen if nothing changes and the known future evolves.
3. Organize the gaps into three categories:
   ◼ Objectives that can be fulfilled within the planning period.
   ◼ Goals that can almost be attained within the planning period but will eventually be achieved.
   ◼ Ideals that will never be attained but can be held as ends that should focus the future direction of the organization.

An idealized design differs from utopia because what is conceived as ideal may change over time (ideals are not static), a less-than-perfect knowledge of the system makes certain parts difficult to design (a learning capacity should be built into design), and the system and its environment will change in ways that cannot be anticipated (flexibility and adaptability should be built into the system).

There are six reasons why an idealized design is an important part of the planning process:

1. The process converts planning from a retrospective to a prospective orientation.
2. The process invites and facilitates the participation of stakeholders who are affected by the design. Broad participation generates different points of view, which leads to an

enriched concept of the new system, and as a result all participants have learned something new.

3. The process tends to generate consensus among the participants because people tend to agree on the things they ultimately want (people disagree most on the means of achieving what they want and what they immediately want).

4. The process encourages participants to look at the whole system and not just isolated parts of it because it stimulates synthetic rather than analytic thinking.

5. The process stimulates creativity among participants because it values imaginative and far-fetched solutions, rather than conformity, because it allows the participants to downplay constraints on their thinking.

6. The process enlarges the participants' concepts of what is feasible (planning should be the art of converting the impossible to the possible).

Conclusion

The process of creating an "idealized design" gets organizations to think about a future that would be better than the projected status quo. Once an ideal future is described, staff will be motivated to attain it because they know it will improve the organization's outcomes and they will be a part of that success. Moving forward in a new direction does require innovation and change, and people typically resist change, but with change occurring almost on a daily basis in most organizations, change is becoming an acceptable norm. Leaders and managers need to stay ahead of the curve in terms of future opportunities, as when larger system changes start to occur, there are usually opportunities that should be considered, especially if by changing direction the organization will become more effective and productive.

APPENDIX 14B: ACTION FRAMEWORK (GANTT CHART) FOR A STRATEGIC PLAN

To put the plan in context, one should insert a vision and mission statement and a strengths, weaknesses, opportunities, and threats (SWOT) analysis to be followed by the Gantt chart on how to implement the strategic plan (Table 14B.1).

TABLE 14B.1 Action Framework for a Strategic Plan

GOALS	PERFORMANCE TARGET	MEASURABLE PERFORMANCE OBJECTIVES	ACTION/TASKS	RESPONSIBLE PARTIES	KEY PARTNERSHIPS	RESOURCES AND BUDGET	TIMELINE/ ACTION DATE
(1) To enhance and develop leadership capacity of members	(a) Provide knowledge, values, and skills training—subgroups based on new, intermediate, and senior administrators— grounded in developmental stage, university culture and context	(i) At least one professional development session should be offered at each meeting	Schedule at a minimum one session at both fall and spring meeting	Program chair	Organization staff and board	Hotel space and AV	September for fall meeting; March for spring meeting

CHAPTER 15

DESIGNING AND ASSESSING PROGRAMS FOR SOCIAL WORK

CHAPTER OBJECTIVES

- Understanding, interpreting, and using best evidence-based practices to improve organizational effectiveness.
- Creating needs assessments.
- Designing a logic planning model.
- Identifying elements of good design.
- Understanding how to implement the program.
- Evaluating the program.
- Providing feedback mechanisms: program redesign and organizational survival.

INTRODUCTION

This chapter examines the process of program design, focusing on how agency and university leaders can initiate this process by assessing need, and then using the information gathered to effectively plan programmatic interventions to address these needs. It describes the use of logic models as a program planning tool and identifies the elements of good program design. The chapter also examines effective approaches for implementing programs and discusses how evaluation can be used to provide valuable feedback to those seeking to further adjust these programs to make them more effective. Box 15.1 displays the competencies/behaviors in this chapter.

BOX 15.1

COMPETENCIES AND PRACTICE BEHAVIORS ADDRESSED IN THIS CHAPTER

Designs and develops effective programs (Network for Social Work Management Competencies 18). Practice Behaviors:

- Guides program staff in designing and implementing interventions consistent with the mission of the organization that respect all types of clients from diverse circumstances (18.1).

- Supports and assists staff in planning evidence-based programs, based on performance standards, assessments, client data, research on effective practice, community, and user needs, demographics, resources, and economic and technological trends (18.2).

- Develops and enforces procedures for collecting, reporting, and analyzing data to measure program quality and achievement of defined outcomes (18.3).

CSWE Competency 4—Engage in Practice-informed Research and Research-informed Practice
Social workers

- 4.2 Apply critical thinking to engage in analysis of quantitative and qualitative research methods and research findings.

- 4.3 Use and translate research evidence to inform and improve practice, policy, and service delivery.

CSWE Competency 7—Assess Individuals, Families, Groups, Organizations, and Communities
Social workers

- 7.2 Apply knowledge of human behavior and the social environment, person-in-environment, and other multidisciplinary theoretical frameworks in the analysis of assessment data from clients and constituencies.

- 7.3 Develop mutually agreed-on intervention goals and objectives based on the critical assessment of strengths, needs, and challenges within clients and constituencies.

- 7.4 Select appropriate intervention strategies based on the assessment, research knowledge, and values and preferences of clients and constituencies.

CSWE Competency 8—Intervene With Individuals, Families, Groups, Organizations, and Communities
Social workers

- 8.2 Apply knowledge of human behavior and the social environment, person-in-environment, and other multidisciplinary theoretical frameworks in interventions with clients and constituencies.

CSWE Competency 9—Evaluate Practice With Individuals, Families, Groups, Organizations, and Communities
Social workers

- 9.2 Apply knowledge of human behavior and the social environment, person-in-environment, and other multidisciplinary theoretical frameworks in the evaluation of outcomes.

CSWE, Council on Social Work Education.

PROGRAM DESIGN PROCESS

Box 15.2 displays the competencies/behaviors in this section. Program design is a process, one that begins with the identification of a problem to be addressed and then proceeds through evaluation. It has been suggested that this process constitutes "an intermediate level of policymaking situated between broad policy goals on the one hand, and specific setting of policy instrument combinations on the other" (Howlett, Mukerjee, & Raynor, 2014, p. 2). The program design process is initiated by the identification and specification of a clearly defined social problem. Social problems are conditions that are seen as undesirable by society as a whole, or segments of it. Whether particular conditions are seen as problematic depends upon values. In social work, values of social and economic justice are central to identifying problematic conditions. What does—or does not—constitute a social problem depends greatly on the values of those doing the identification. Consequently, social work values, as exemplified in the National Association of Social Workers (NASW, 2008) code and related documents, are foundational to the field's approach to social problems, and, therefore, to program design. Critical to determining the manner in which problems are addressed, then, is the manner in which they are defined, and in how their etiology is understood.

Etiology refers to the examination of causation. Social work's values of social and economic justice emphasize a broad, systemic understanding of the causes of social problems. As Gil (2013) asserted, "Social problems . . . are usually rooted in prevailing societal institutions, policies and values rather than in any inherent attributes and shortcomings of people" (p. 110). Such a value-based understanding of the causation of social problems leads to programmatic designs addressed toward the root causes of these problems, rather than their symptoms.

BOX 15.2

NETWORK FOR SOCIAL WORK MANAGEMENT COMPETENCIES AND PRACTICE BEHAVIORS 18 AND COUNCIL ON SOCIAL WORK EDUCATION PRACTICE BEHAVIORS 7 AND 9

Designs and develops effective programs (Network for Social Work Management Competencies 18). Practice Behaviors:

- Supports and assists staff in planning evidence-based programs, based on performance standards, assessments, client data, research on effective practice, community, and user needs, demographics, resources, and economic and technological trends (18.2).

CSWE Competency 7—Assess Individuals, Families, Groups, Organizations, and Communities
  Social workers

- 7.3 Develop mutually agreed-on intervention goals and objectives based on the critical assessment of strengths, needs, and challenges within clients and constituencies.

- 7.4 Select appropriate intervention strategies based on the assessment, research knowledge, and values and preferences of clients and constituencies.

CSWE Competency 9—Evaluate Practice With Individuals, Families, Groups, Organizations, and Communities
  Social workers

- 9.2 Apply knowledge of human behavior and the social environment, person-in-environment, and other multidisciplinary theoretical frameworks in the evaluation of outcomes.

CSWE, Council on Social Work Education.

The program design process, then, should begin with a clear understanding of the causation of the identified problem, informed by social work values of social and economic justice. It is only then that the process can shift into the gathering of data to determine the extent to which particular populations, or subsets of these populations, are impacted.

Needs/Resources Assessments

Once a problem has been identified, its extent needs to be understood and identified. Problem identification requires the collection of data on the degree the problem or need affects certain populations. Such data collection efforts, commonly referred to as needs assessments, are undertaken to determine the extent of services needed to address the identified problem. As with the understanding and specification of the social problems that underlie them, needs also should be clearly defined.

Definitions of Need

One useful framework for understanding needs was developed by the British social scientist Jonathan Bradshaw (1972, 2013). Bradshaw identified four distinct ways in which need was defined by social program administrators. Each of these four types of need—normative, felt, expressed, and comparative—focuses on a different aspect of how need can be understood.

Normative Need

In this understanding of need, "a 'desirable' standard is laid down and is compared with the standard that actually exists—if an individual or group falls short of the desirable standard then they are identified as being in need" (Bradshaw, 2013, p. 2). The determination of need is based on the values and perceptions of experts.

Felt Need

In this type of need, those experiencing the need are those who define need. This approach adds another dimension to the understanding of need, one not captured by normative standards. Felt need is "limited by the perceptions of the individual—whether they know there is a service available, as well as a reluctance in many situations to confess a loss of independence" (Bradshaw, 1972, p. 641).

Expressed Need

Expressed need is defined in terms of a demand for service. It is, as Bradshaw (2013) noted, "felt need turned into action" (p. 3). A common mechanism for measuring this form of need is waiting lists for various social programs. Although expressed need is an imperfect measure of need, it can supplement other dimensions of need.

Comparative Need

Comparative need is determined by comparing the characteristics of those receiving services with those with similar characteristics who are not receiving a service (Bradshaw, 1972, 2013). It is well known, for example, that not all those who meet eligibility criteria for many social programs are receiving aid. This intentional lack of provision of services may differ by geographic area, or within subgroups of a larger population.

Ideally, a good needs assessment looks at all four of these aspects of need. Such assessments should gather client data, and also examine the perceptions of community residents and social service personnel, community leaders and other key informants, and then use this information to determine community and service user needs. Such assessments should combine "interviews or surveys with key informants and analysis of existing data, available from the U.S. Census or agency databases" (Hardina, 2002, p. 112).

Detailed demographic data on populations in need should be obtained. Additionally, community resources, and economic and technological trends, should be examined. Good needs assessments, in short, should be as comprehensive as possible. They should also include the assessment of community resources, as noted previously. Over the last several decades, the field of social work has increasingly recognized that a focus solely on needs, or deficits, is limiting, and that it is important to look at the strengths and resources of communities and individuals (Kretzmann & McKnight, 1993; Saleeby, 1997; Sherraden, 1991).

Designing a Logic Planning Model

As the program design process moves from assessing needs to developing interventions, a useful tool to conceptualize this process is the logic model, sometimes also called a logic planning model or program logic model (Kettner et al., 2017; Sousa, 2010). Logic models are used to examine the links between program components. The logic model consists of "constructs of carefully worded statements that together provide a comprehensive cognitive structure of a change process," such as the design of new programmatic intervention (Alter & Egan, 1997, p. 87). While logic models may differ in some of the specific elements which are included, they are typically characterized by four components (Sousa, 2010):

1. Resources

2. Activities

3. Outputs

4. Outcomes

The logic model connects these elements. In a more detailed formulation that breaks down these elements a bit more precisely, Alter & Egan, 1997 identified seven basic elements of a logic model which are represented in Figure 15.1, proceeding from the identification of the problem or need, to the development of goals and objectives, and then moving to the marshaling of inputs and methods that will achieve these goals and objectives, which then will lead to short-term results and long-term outcomes. Underlying this model is a program hypothesis which assumes that if the specified activities—that is, the inputs and methods—are implemented then the identified outcomes, both short-term and long-term, will be achieved.

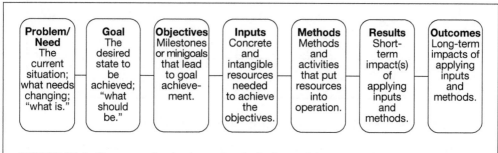

FIGURE 15.1 The seven basic elements of a logic model.

SOURCE: Alter, C., & Egan, M. (1997). Logic modeling: A tool for teaching critical thinking in social work practice. *Journal of Social Work Education, 33*(1), 85–102. doi:10.1080/10437797.1997.10778855

These seven basic elements lay out the essential aspects of the logic modeling process. However, real-world applications of this model require more complex structures, with multiple interventions. Alter and Egan (1997) present a useful tool that takes this shortcoming into account, which is reproduced in Figure 15.2. Essentially what the tool does is break down the goal into incremental steps, each of which requires different inputs and methods and will produce different results. This diagram presents a three-objective framework, which can be extended to include whatever number of program objectives may be needed to achieve the short-term results which will then lead to the desired program outcomes.

Logic models, then, are useful tools which can inform program design. In order to more thoroughly examine this process, however, we must conduct an additional review of the elements of program design.

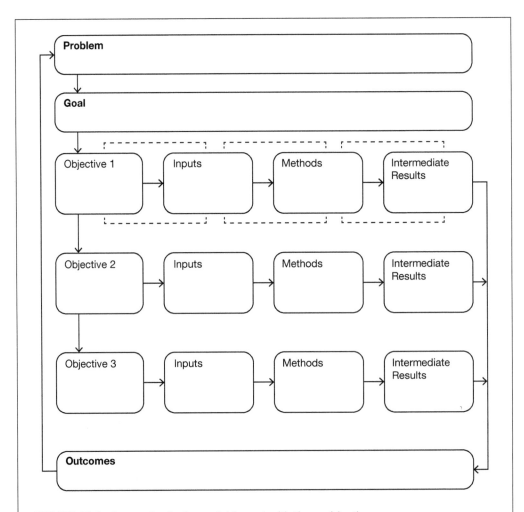

FIGURE 15.2 A complex logic model format with three objectives.

SOURCE: Alter, C., & Egan, M. (1997). Logic modeling: A tool for teaching critical thinking in social work practice. *Journal of Social Work Education, 33*(1), 85–102. doi:10.1080/10437797.1997.10778855
Note: Dashed lines represent how building a logic model requires working back and forth between elements as alternative statements are considered. This process usually must occur between all horizontally linked elements, and sometimes between vertically linked elements.

Elements of Good Design

Box 15.3 displays the competencies/behaviors in this section. Organizational leaders guide program staff in designing interventions consistent with the mission of the organization. Missions, ideally, are consistent with social work values and describe the aspirations of the organization. The mission, as an overarching statement of a human service organization's mission, also guides the program design processes conducted by the organization. The elements of program design, then, operate within an organizational context established by the mission statement. These elements are, essentially, the same elements that comprise the logic model. What is presented in the following section is a framework for assessing elements of good program design.

BOX 15.3

NETWORK FOR SOCIAL WORK MANAGEMENT COMPETENCIES AND PRACTICE BEHAVIORS 18 AND COUNCIL ON SOCIAL WORK EDUCATION PRACTICE BEHAVIORS 4.2, 7, AND 8

Designs and develops effective programs (Network for Social Work Management Competencies 18). Practice Behaviors:

- Guides program staff in designing and implementing interventions consistent with the mission of the organization that respect all types of clients from diverse circumstances (18.1).

CSWE Competency 4—Engage in Practice-informed Research and Research-informed Practice
Social workers

- 4.2 Apply critical thinking to engage in analysis of quantitative and qualitative research methods and research findings.
- 4.3 Use and translate research evidence to inform and improve practice, policy, and service delivery.

CSWE Competency 7— Assess Individuals, Families, Groups, Organizations, and Communities
Social workers

- 7.2 Apply knowledge of human behavior and the social environment, person-in-environment, and other multidisciplinary theoretical frameworks in the analysis of assessment data from clients and constituencies.

CSWE Competency 8— Intervene With Individuals, Families, Groups, Organizations, and Communities
Social workers

- 8.2 Apply knowledge of human behavior and the social environment, person-in-environment, and other multidisciplinary theoretical frameworks in interventions with clients and constituencies.

CSWE, Council on Social Work Education.

Needs/Resource Assessment

As discussed previously, the program design process begins with a comprehensive analysis of the needs and resources of the target population. This analysis involves extensive data gathering and analysis and the use of research skills and techniques that are beyond the scope of this book. Generally, this process involves the gathering of both primary and secondary data, depending on the resources available. Gathering primary data, whether qualitative or quantitative, involves more costs for the organization, for whatever methodology employed, from more qualitative focus groups to major community surveys, this involves an investment of resources. The collection of secondary data, from governmental sources like the U.S. Census Bureau or state and local agency databases, is typically less costly; however, the data will not always exactly correspond with the specific needs/resources information desired, so some approximation will likely be needed. On the other hand, if information is needed quickly or cost is an issue, using secondary data will be a highly desirable approach to get a sense of the needs and resources of the target population.

Goals and Objectives

Once information on needs and resources has been gathered, program designers are in a good position to identify needs and goals. As discussed earlier in the chapter, this process is informed by the agency's overall mission statement and values, as well as by the specific problems or issues that are the target of intervention.

In developing goals, it is useful to consider these as guiding statements for the program, similar in purpose as the mission is to the organization. They "serve as a transition between mission and objectives" (Kettner et al., 2017, p. 112) and are the frameworks that help to achieve the mission. Kettner and his colleagues contend that programs typically have "only one goal, and from this will flow a set of objectives and activities designed to move toward the achievement of the goal" (p. 112). However, in some instances programs may have multiple goals, but usually still in the single digits. Additionally, while "goals are abstract[,] . . . objectives should be as concrete as possible" (Alter & Egan, 1997, p. 93). For example, the goal of a program to serve people experiencing homelessness might be "to reduce homelessness in this community." As seen in this example goals are typically general, aspirational statements.

Objectives, in contrast, are more specific statements that, as the logic model framework presented earlier shows, are derived from the goal and typically indicate both the concrete action or result to be achieved and the timeframe within which they will be accomplished. Generally, program objectives are of two types, process and outcome. Process objectives detail what actions will be taken to achieve the desired results, that is, the means to be used. Outcome objectives refer to the concrete results of these interventions, that is, the change in the target population related to the identified problem. In other words, they specify the desired ends of the program interventions (Kettner et al., 2017).

Activities/Resources

In order to accomplish the desired program objectives and achieve the identified goal, specific actions must be taken to achieve them. These are typically described as activities, and they require that organizational resources be marshaled to implement them. The logic model shown earlier divides these elements into inputs and methods. Methods refer to the activities, whereas inputs refer to the resources needed to put methods into practice (Alter & Egan, 1997). Together, these constitute the means, or processes, by which the program outcomes will be achieved.

Inputs can be defined as "the raw materials required by the change process" and include elements such as "clients or participants, personnel with specific knowledge or training, financial resources, physical facilities and equipment, time and commitment from personnel in leadership roles, legitimacy and community sanction, and the willingness of similar organizations to collaborate or coordinate efforts" (Alter & Egan, 1997, p. 94).

Methods (sometimes called "throughputs") consist of "the procedures that will be implemented to carry out the program" (Kettner et al., 2017, p. 135). These are the specific actions taken by program personnel using the inputs available to achieve the desired change. Actions include various forms of therapeutic or material intervention that may address the identified problem and may be divided into service definition, service tasks, and method of intervention.

Service definition refers to the specific statement, usually a sentence or two, of what the service entails. Service tasks identify the activities that will be performed as part of the service, and the method of intervention concerns the specific technology for service delivery, that is, the manner in which it is delivered (Kettner et al., 2017).

Outputs

Outputs refer to the actual products of a program, sometimes referred to as units of service. They can be defined and measured in three different ways, as episodes or contact units, material units, or time units (Martin & Kettner, 2010). Examples of units of service include the number of counseling sessions, the amount of food provided, course contact hours, and the like. Kettner et al., 2017 distinguished between *intermediate outputs,* such as units of service, and *final outputs,* which refer to service completion. In an academic setting, for example, course contact hours would constitute the intermediate output, whereas course completion would constitute the final output.

Outcomes

Outcomes refer to the results of an intervention and consist of a measurable change with respect to the identified problem or issue that is achieved by a recipient of the services that constitute the program intervention (Kettner et al., 2017). Alter and Egan (1997) distinguished "between the short term results of an intervention or action, and the longer-term outcomes" (p. 95). The latter are often harder to track as, over time, there is typically a loss of contact between the service recipient and program officials. Nonetheless, in thinking about program outcomes, agency administrators should consider both manifestations of this phenomenon.

Short-Term Results

Short-term results are the immediate outcomes of participation in the services provided as part of a program intervention. These are also sometimes termed intermediate outcomes, and can be defined as "changes in the quality of life . . . that can be measured at the point of completion of the services provided" (Kettner et al., 2017, p. 153). They consist of some sort of reduction in the identified problem. To the extent that short-term results are assessed, they are measured by the difference in status with respect to the target problem preceding service and then shortly afterward. In the case of substance abuse treatment, for example, short-term results may be measured by the extent to which the client remains drug-free after treatment. With regard to the immediate outcomes of university courses, results may be determined by graded assignments, which may indicate an increase in understanding of a particular content or skill area.

Long-Term Outcomes

Long-term outcomes are changes that can be observed for an extended period after the intervention or program has ended (Alter & Egan, 1997). Also termed final outcomes, long-term outcomes are defined as "changes achieved or maintained as of a specified point in the follow up process after services have been completed—that is, at the point of final output" (Kettner et al., 2017, p. 156). Long-term outcomes are typically more difficult to measure as they often require tracking clients after they have discontinued program services and are not in regular contact with program staff and administrators. Even if some sort of measurement is taken at a longer interval after participation in the program, it may be difficult to attribute continuing outcomes to the intervention as there may be factors in addition to the intervention that either impede or assist the maintenance of positive change. This sort of thing is readily seen in substance abuse treatment, where after clients are exposed to treatment, they return to the community where they may experience influences that either cause them to relapse, such as coming into contact with substance-using peers, or factors that reinforce continued abstinence, such as participation in community-based self-help groups.

Implementation

Once a program has been designed, and the above mentioned elements planned out, and funding obtained, the program needs to be implemented. Here, the role of organizational leaders is critical as it will be these individuals who will guide program staff in implementing the designed intervention in a manner consistent with the mission of the organization.

Schram (1997) specified a five-step process that translates program goals and objectives into action, which involves specifying tasks; delegating tasks and building a decision-making structure; sequencing tasks and deciding on time schedules; creating a resource bank; and establishing task groups, work roles, and communication channels.

Specifying tasks involves breaking tasks down into smaller, more manageable components—more minute units of work that can then be more easily parceled out to discrete staff members. It involves breaking down the major tasks of implementation into more specific, interconnected components that can then be assigned to those who are best able to move these program elements forward to completion.

Delegating tasks and building a decision-making structure involves, first, identifying the key people who are best suited to perform the specific tasks that have been identified, and then developing mechanisms for holding them accountable for task achievement. In order to accomplish this plan, clear decision-making structures need to be created. These decision-making structures need to be formalized for, as Schram (1997) indicates, a "covert or informal structure . . . can be confusing and demoralizing" (p. 138).

The third step in the implementation process, *sequencing tasks and deciding on time schedules*, consists of developing a specific plan for task achievement and identifying the exact time frames in which they are to be completed. Useful tools for this step exist called task–time flowcharts, such as PERT and Gantt charts. PERT stands for Program Evaluation Review Technique, while Gantt charts are named for business planner Henry Gantt, who developed his technique in the early 20th century (Schram, 1997). These charts help create guidelines for task achievement. They "tie together the work that needs to be accomplished, the personnel available to do it, and the deadlines for completion" (Schram, 1997, p. 145). An example of a Gantt chart is reproduced in Figure 15.3.

The fourth step in the implementation process described by Schram (1997) is *creating a resource bank*, which refers to "the people, agencies and objects that might provide goods, services, labor and advice" (1997, p. 146). In addition to directly identifying such resources, agency leaders will also need to help program staff identify and mobilize the resources to which they have access in order to achieve the goal of successful program implementation. One way to identify resources is to develop a resource analysis that looks at the individual tasks or activities to be accomplished and examines the resources needed, resources already possessed by the organization's staff, where additional needed resources may be located, and ways to make do without resources that cannot be located (Schram, 1997). Of course, funding is a primary resource that is absolutely necessary in this process, and good program implementation should always involve clear attention to this crucial resource.

The final step in the program implementation process, according to Schram (1997), involves *establishing task groups, work roles, and communication channels*. Task groups are a useful way of moving forward the identified activities that together encompass program implementation. Clearly focused task groups provide particular advantages that bring together multiple skills, energy, and division of labor of group members (Schram, 1997). In order to maximize the effectiveness of this implementation strategy, it is necessary to clearly define the work roles of group members, as well as establish "an appropriate reward structure to encourage independence" (Schram, 1997, p. 156). Communication is also essential, for clear communication between task group members is essential in order for the group to function effectively. However facilitated,

Task	Unit/Person Responsible	Month 1	Month 2	Month 3	Month 4	Month 5	Month 6	Month 7	Month 8	Month 9	Month 10	Month 11	Month 12
Task #1: Sub-Task A Sub-Task B Sub-Task C Sub-Task D													
Task #2: Sub-Task A													
Task #3: Sub-Task A Sub-Task B Sub-Task C													
Task #4													
Task #5													
Task #6													
Task #7													
Task #8													
Task #9													
Task #10													

FIGURE 15.3 Gantt chart.

task groups are an important vehicle with which to put program activities into practice, and thus their establishment is appropriately conceptualized as an important step in the program implementation.

As part of the process of program implementation, it is important that ongoing monitoring of the achievement of program tasks, activities, and milestones be tracked and data on these elements collected to demonstrate achievements. Monitoring has been defined as "the extent to which a program is implemented as designed and serves its intended target group" (Kettner et al., 2017, p. 194). Monitoring provides valuable feedback to program designers and agency leaders regarding the degree to which program tasks and activities are being completed in the time frames specified. To the extent that completion is not occurring, program managers can take action to bring the achievement of tasks and the delivery of program components into line with the initial design. Monitoring also provides data that demonstrates the degree to which the program is being implemented as designed, which is an important part of evaluation.

Evaluation

Box 15.4 displays the competencies/behaviors in this section. The evaluation of programs is essential to determining if, in fact, they are achieving their desired outcomes, and evaluation involves the application of "social science techniques to determining the workings and effectiveness of human [service] programs" (Kettner et al., 2017, p. 195). But evaluation is also more than that. At its core, evaluation requires analysis and reflection on the part of program designers and agency leaders of relevant data both on program implementation processes and the concrete, demonstrable results they produce for target populations on the identified issue. Good program evaluation addresses both, because it is critical to document that a program was implemented as designed in order to be able to attribute the observed changes in those served that intervention. Thus, program evaluation typically focuses on two areas: process and outcome.

BOX 15.4

NETWORK FOR SOCIAL WORK MANAGEMENT COMPETENCIES AND PRACTICE BEHAVIORS 18 AND COUNCIL ON SOCIAL WORK EDUCATION PRACTICE BEHAVIOR 7

Designs and develops effective programs (Network for Social Work Management Competencies 18). Practice Behaviors:

- Develops and enforces procedures for collecting, reporting, and analyzing data to measure program quality and achievement of defined outcomes (18.3).

CSWE Competency 7—Assess Individuals, Families, Groups, Organizations, and Communities
   Social workers

- 7.4 Select appropriate intervention strategies based on the assessment, research knowledge, and values and preferences of clients and constituencies.

CSWE, Council on Social Work Education.

Process Evaluation

Process evaluations focus on the achievement of process objectives, that is, the means used to achieve the intended results. Here, data are gathered on the units of service delivered, whether it be counseling sessions, amount of food provided, or other form of benefit. Process evaluations look at how the program was implemented and the specific tasks and activities performed as part of service delivery. Process evaluations provide feedback on the program, tracking specifically if it was implemented in a manner consistent with the design (Grinnell, Gabor, & Unrau, 2016; Schram, 1997). While these data, as noted previously, are ideally also collected during implementation and used for monitoring purposes, at the end of an intervention the same data are used to ascertain if a program was implemented as intended and thus provide information on the extent to which process objectives were met.

Outcome Evaluation

Outcome evaluations assess the degree to which the intended program outcomes were achieved or not (Grinnell et al., 2016). Thus, these evaluations are concerned with gathering data on the actual results—the anticipated change in quality of life of members of the target population which has been achieved as a result of the operation of the program. This process involves examining outcome measures and assessing the amount of change or number of program participants who exhibit a particular degree of change. These evaluations generate information, or feedback, for an organization's stakeholders, which can then be used to inform future changes in service delivery.

Feedback Mechanisms: Program Redesign and Organizational Survival

The program evaluation process should provide feedback that can be used by program designers and agency leaders to modify, adjust, and enhance services. Feedback that emerges from the evaluation process can be used to inform program redesign and, ultimately, contribute to organizational survival (Schram, 1997). Information generated by process and outcome evaluations can lead to informed decisions by agency leaders regarding how services can more effectively be delivered. The deliberate use of such feedback can not only enhance programmatic effectiveness but also allow human service organizations to respond in a nimbler manner to frequently shifting environmental, and funding, contexts.

SUMMARY

This chapter has examined the program design process, from needs assessment through program evaluation, and the feedback it generates to inform program redesign. Several concepts of need were presented and a description of how these could be assessed offered. Logic modeling was discussed as a technique that can be used to inform effective program design. Elements of good program design were described, and the program implementation process was examined. Finally, the evaluation of program process and outcomes was reviewed, followed by discussion on how the evalutation can be used to improve and enhance program and organizational performance.

ACTIVITIES

1. Using the logic model template provided in Figure 15.2, identify a problem or need and the goals of a programmatic intervention to address the problem or need. Detail the program objectives and the short-term results and long-term outcomes to be achieved in addressing the identified problem.

2. Describe the process of implementation of a program. How would an agency leader specify tasks; delegate these tasks and build a decision-making structure; sequence tasks and decide on time schedules; create a resource bank; and establish task groups, work roles, and communication channels to implement the program?

3. In thinking about sequencing tasks and deciding on time schedules for a program, prepare a PERT or Gannt chart to identify the timelines for achieving the identified tasks.

4. Discuss why monitoring provides important feedback that agency leaders can use to adjust programs as they are being implemented. How does the use of this information lead to more effective service delivery and potentially to more robust programmatic outcomes?

REFERENCES

Alter, C., & Egan, M. (1997). Logic modeling: A tool for teaching critical thinking in social work practice. *Journal of Social Work Education, 33*(1), 85–102. doi:10.1080/10437797.1997.10778855

Bradshaw, J. (1972, March). The concept of social need. *New Society, 30*, 640–643.

Bradshaw, J. (2013). A taxonomy of social need. In R. A. Cookson, R. Sainsbury, & C. Glendinning *Jonathan Bradshaw on social policy: Selected writings 1972–2011* (pp. 1–11). England: University of York.

Gil, D. G. (2013). *Confronting injustice and oppression: Concepts and strategies for social workers.* New York, NY: Columbia University Press.

Grinnell, R. M., Gabor, P. A., & Unrau, Y. A. (2016). *Program evaluation for social workers: Foundations of evidence-based programs* (7th ed.). New York, NY: Oxford University Press.

Hardina, D. (2002). *Analytic skills for community organization practice.* New York, NY: Columbia University Press.

Howlett, M., Mukherjee, I., & Rayner, J. (2014). The elements of effective program design: A two-level analysis. *Politics and Governance, 2*(2), 1–12. doi:10.17645/pag.v2i2.23

Kettner, P. M., Moroney, R. M., & Martin, L. M. (2017). *Designing and managing programs: An effectiveness-based approach.* Los Angeles, CA: Sage.

Kretzmann, J. P., & McKnight, J. L. (1993). *Building communities from the inside out: A path toward finding and mobilizing a community's assets*. Chicago, IL: ACTA Publications.

Martin, L. M., & Kettner, P. M. (2010). *Measuring the performance of human service programs*. Thousand Oaks, CA: Sage.

National Association of Social Workers. (2008). *Code of ethics of the National Association of Social Workers*. Washington, DC: Author.

Saleeby, D. (1997). *The strengths perspective in social work practice* (2nd ed.). New York, NY: Longman.

Schram, B. (1997). *Creating small scale social programs: Planning, implementation and evaluation*. Thousand Oaks, CA: Sage.

Sherraden, M. (1991). *Assets and the poor: A new American welfare policy*. Armonk, MY: M.E. Sharpe.

Sousa, J. (2010). Program-logic model. In A. J. Mills (Ed.), *Encyclopedia of case study research*. Thousand Oaks, CA: Sage.

CHAPTER 16

STRATEGIC RESOURCE DEVELOPMENT IN A SOCIAL WORK ENVIRONMENT

CHAPTER OBJECTIVES

- Applying the components and elements of a case statement.
- Recognizing and employing the characteristics of a solid development plan.
- Analyzing the myths of fundraising.
- Understanding what inspires giving.
- Creating strong systems of stewardship with donors.
- Employing strategies for successful fundraising.
- Understanding the elements of successful grant writing.
- Creating research centers.
- Approaching foundations for funding.

INTRODUCTION

Throughout this chapter we discuss strategic resource development. Strategic resource development entails creating a case statement, which is a description of your organization including its mission and goals and explains the rationale for why the agency needs financial support. A case statement also provides information to prospective donors about why you are seeking funds, how the donated funds will be allocated, and how the donation will help to achieve specific strategic objectives, while also identifying who exactly will benefit from these services. Successful funding strategies are discussed with examples from programs that have successfully raised funds.

Organizations, particularly academic institutions, create research centers to advance opportunities for faculty to engage in creative activities and to provide a service to the community (i.e., program evaluations of local organizations). By conducting research, the knowledge and evidence-based findings related to specific populations in need further contribute to the professional community. Finally, this chapter examines how to be successful in grant writing. The competencies that are addressed throughout this chapter are listed in Box 16.1.

BOX 16.1

COMPETENCIES AND PRACTICE BEHAVIORS ADDRESSED IN THIS CHAPTER

Fundraising: identifies and applies for new and recurring funding while ensuring accountability with existing funding systems (Network for Social Work Management Competencies 16). Practice Behaviors:

- Creates a culture of philanthropy that engages the organization's governing body, employees, volunteers, and actual and potential donors (16.1).
- Works closely with public and private funding sources to ensure positive relations and confidence in the organization (16.2).
- Develops and implements a successful fundraising plan which includes a diverse funding mix and utilizes a strong marketing focus (16.3).
- Establishes strong systems of stewardship with donors/funders (16.4).
- Seeks partnerships with other programs funded under federal/state/local authorities and other interest groups (16.5).
- Maintains active awareness of and pursues potential grant and funding sources in local, regional, or national community (16.6).
- Demonstrates innovative approaches to resource development at all levels of the organization (16.7).

Box 16.2 displays the competencies/behaviors in this section.

BOX 16.2

NETWORK FOR SOCIAL WORK MANAGEMENT COMPETENCIES AND PRACTICE BEHAVIORS 16

Fundraising: identifies and applies for new and recurring funding while ensuring accountability with existing funding systems (Network for Social Work Management Competencies 16). Practice Behaviors:

- Creates a culture of philanthropy that engages the organization's governing body, employees, volunteers, and actual and potential donors (16.1).

Creating a culture of philanthropy takes time and requires engaging with everyone involved in an organization, including the governing body, employees, volunteers, and actual and potential donors. The organization and its employees need to understand the importance of planned giving and fundraising so that they will be committed and motivated to the cause. Some organizations require that board members play an active role in fundraising and donating, starting with the board members themselves making annual contributions or personally raising a certain amount each year; some organizations even require board members to donate a set amount each year as a prerequisite to being on the board, a set amount that should take into consideration the income of the member. Board donations can range from $50 a year to $1,000,000. Donor amounts will vary, from both board members and other donors, and so will their attitudes about their contributions. Some people want to see their name in lights, others do not want anyone to know they gave, and others yet want to honor someone else with their donation.

All board members should play active roles in fundraising. Suggested roles include the following:

- Making an annual financial commitment so that 100% of the board participates (note this in the case statement material).
- Reviewing lists of potential donors and helping to identify and open doors to donors.
- Hosting and attending donor events.
- Helping to cultivate potential donors in person, at events, or by email.
- Thanking major gift donors.
- Possibly attending meetings with potential donors and soliciting for funding.
- Committing to the process of fundraising for the organization.

Staff also need to play an important role in managing fundraising activities and follow-up actions. Staff should

- Maintain information in a database system such as Excel and create lists and reports.
- Process all gifts, acknowledgements, and so on.
- Help plan and execute donor events.
- Help with public relations activities.
- Organize meetings with major donors.
- Supervise grant writing and consultants' work.
- Support board members in their fundraising-related roles.

In academic institutions, approaching the faculty to donate to the school will engage them in and create a philanthropic culture. Building a culture of giving for the faculty and alumni is important because they represent the school, and if they are shown to give, others from outside the university will also give. The objective is to obtain a high participation rate; do not worry about the amount of money they give. Approach the current graduating class and ask for donations or get your advisory board to offer a match of some kind. As you think about the ways you can create fundraising opportunities, answer the questions in Box 16.3.

BOX 16.3

COMPETENCY-BASED QUESTIONS

Answer these questions:

1. How does your organizational mission get communicated?
2. How do people get socialized in the culture, and purpose, of the work?
3. What moves and motivates people to want to engage in the work?
4. And what engages communities to want to help support the work?

Also important in fundraising is working closely with both the private and public sectors. See Box 16.4 which displays the competencies/behaviors in this section.

BOX 16.4

NETWORK FOR SOCIAL WORK MANAGEMENT COMPETENCIES AND PRACTICE BEHAVIORS 16

Fundraising: identifies and applies for new and recurring funding while ensuring accountability with existing funding systems (Network for Social Work Management Competencies 16). Practice Behaviors:

- Works closely with public and private funding sources to ensure positive relations and confidence in the organization (16.2).

Establishing relationships with local and state funding sources is a prerequisite to successful fundraising. Meeting at least annually with the executive directors of said agencies and sharing the importance of your organization's mission and goals and how obtaining their support will benefit both the funder's organization and the community is a good first step. Sharing your marketing material with both public and private funders through emails, events, and news advertisements is also recommended. Once your organization has obtained funding from a source, provide the funder with ongoing reports on how the funding is being used and the positive impacts the donation is making on the community or university.

BOX 16.5

NETWORK FOR SOCIAL WORK MANAGEMENT COMPETENCIES AND PRACTICE BEHAVIORS 16

Fundraising: identifies and applies for new and recurring funding while ensuring accountability with existing funding systems (Network for Social Work Management Competencies 16). Practice Behaviors:

- Develops and implements a successful fundraising plan which includes a diverse funding mix and utilizes a strong marketing focus (16.3).

Box 16.5 cites a fundraising plan—but how is one created? A necessary first step in developing a successful fundraising plan is to create a "case statement." Case statements lay the foundation for describing the program and why financial support is needed. A certain skill base is needed to develop a case statement. According to Holgate (2006), there are several skills needed to develop a case statement. Table 16.1 identifies and describes these skills.

If you or your staff do not possess these skills, we suggest you hire someone to write your case statement and/or your case stories of students and clients. Use a good creative writer who can tell the story. In a university, sources could be the public relations office or creative writing students. An agency could contract out for this service.

Case statements need to include a number of components that describe key aspects of the organization. Table 16.2 provides a list of the key components and further explanation for each component.

TABLE 16.1 **Skills Needed to Develop a Case Statement**

SKILLS NEEDED TO DEVELOP A CASE STATEMENT	FURTHER EXPLANATION
Good writing, verbal and presentation communication skills.	The case statement must be very concise, specific, and well written. The person that presents it must be able to communicate it well.
Desire to help others	The person(s) must strongly believe in the purpose of the case statement and its ability to help others once implemented.
Ability to build rapport	Person(s) must be able to work well with other people both inside and outside the organization.
Feel secure in including all relevant parties	By including representation from all units, everyone will believe they are a part of the plan.
Maintain optimism and belief in possibilities	Optimism will breed success.
Motivation in producing results will provide meaning in your life	Your motivation will inspire staff to work harder and when funds are forthcoming everyone will feel that their work has meaning.
Belief in positive principles such as fairness, kindness, dignity, charity, integrity, honesty, quality service and patience (Covey, 1991).	Using these funds, the organization will produce positive outcomes that will impact the lives of staff and clients.

SOURCE: Holgate, R. L. (2006). *Developing and marketing a case statement: Developing a case statement.* National Association of Deans and Directors of Schools of Social Work, Spring Meeting, February 17. Chicago Hyatt Regency, Chicago, IL.

TABLE 16.2 **Components in a Case Statement**

COMPONENTS OF CASE STATEMENTS	FURTHER EXPLANATION
Vision and mission statements	These statements should be from the strategic plan or current organizational plan. If you are raising money to train more social workers to work with elders, you need to tie this objective in with your organization's vision and mission.
A brief history	The history should be about your school or program, how it started, where it is located, and future plans. Make it short.
Stress the strengths	For the strengths of the program, be positive; this is a glass half full statement. People want to be associated with a winner.
Objectives of the specific project/campaign	Why is your organization asking for funds? Be concrete. People want to know how their money will be used.
Listing/discussion of the strategies/projects to achieve the objectives and the time table	A brief presentation of tables that display objectives and time lines.
A description of the budget, facilities, staff, ongoing evaluation, etc., required to carry out the strategic/projects	A budget overview along with a short list of operational facilities and key staff functions will provide funders with context. Also process and outcome measures that have been obtained will instill faith in the likelihood of success.

(continued)

TABLE 16.2 **Components in a Case Statement** *(Continued)*

COMPONENTS OF CASE STATEMENTS	FURTHER EXPLANATION
Who are the constituents that will benefit from the services offered	Describe in detail the demographics and needs of the people that will benefit from the funds provided.
Compelling reasons to contribute	Tell how your contribution will impact people or programs.
Why the service area requires this change in type of project/program or new project/program	State how conditions have changed, how your organization will deal with these changes, and why funding is needed to provide the best service in this new environment.

SOURCE: Galowich, R. J. (2006). *Developing and marketing a case statement: Those pesky case statements—What are they all about anyway?* National Association of Deans and Directors of Schools of Social Work, Spring Meeting, February 17. Chicago Hyatt Regency, Chicago, IL.

According to Galowich (2006), case statements must contain certain elements to be successful. Table 16.3 provides a list of key elements that should be in all case statements, along with further explanation of why.

TABLE 16.3 **Key Elements in Case Statements**

KEY ELEMENTS IN CASE STATEMENTS	FURTHER EXPLANATION
Justify and explain the institution, its programs, and its needs.	A case statement must meet the organization's mission and goals. Needs are usually the result of a problem. Do research to identify the problem and then identify solutions. Identify the recognized leaders of the program(s) and use stories from the people served by the organization.
Win the reader with [the institution's] vision that is supported by strong leadership and responsible management.	The vision statement should be clear and easy to understand. Make sure everyone knows and understands the case statement and that it is supported by all levels of leadership and management.
Present the institution so that it stands out from all others in the eyes of the reader.	State what is unique about your institution. You may have a unique program that does not exist elsewhere, or there are distinctive components of your program. You may have faculty or staff who are well known and respected in the community.
Be forward thinking, positive, and present clear, concise, vital and accurate facts and statistics.	The case statement should be focused on the future. All information and data should be easily understood and factual, with documentation if necessary.
Carefully lay out the fundraising plan.	Your donors need to know how you will spend their money and how it will impact the program.
Be a carefully explained plan for the future so as to invite investment.	If people invest in the plan they will have the opportunity to help someone else; you need to advertise how investors helped the program and clients. The plan should help you tell the program's story.

SOURCE: Galowich, R. J. (2006). *Developing and marketing a case statement: Those pesky case statements—What are they all about anyway?* National Association of Deans and Directors of Schools of Social Work, Spring Meeting, February 17. Chicago Hyatt Regency, Chicago, IL.

Table 16.4 provides a list in sequential order of key elements that will define your case statement. Examples of each element are also included.

TABLE 16.4 **Key Components and Elements of a Case Statement With Examples**

KEY COMPONENTS AND ELEMENTS OF A CASE STATEMENT	EXAMPLES
Write a vision and mission statement that is clear and easy to understand.	**Social Work Department Vision**—Social work promotes the personal and social development of people in their communities based on the values of social, economic, and environmental justice; civil and human rights; democracy; and full access to education, social, economic, and political participation. **Social Work Department Mission**—The Social Work Department graduates competent and compassionate agents of change who, guided by professional knowledge, skills, and values, are prepared to practice ethically on multiple system levels, to translate research into practice, and to provide leadership in the profession and in their communities.
Describe how this case statement will meet the organization's vision, mission, and goals.	Achieving the vision, mission, and goals requires additional funding support as state funding has decreased 5% every year for the last 10 years.
Present a brief history of your program, how it started, where you are, where you want to be, and what you still need.	The BSW program started in 1982, the MSW in 1988, and the DSW in 2018. All programs have high demand, have expanded recently, and could expand more with additional financial support.
Stress the strengths of the program and why it is successful. Be positive. People want to be associated with a winner.	According to a recent self-study report from the national accrediting organization, the program strengths include a strong faculty, diverse student body, excellent adjuncts, and superior leadership of the program head. According to a social work research article, the MSW program is the fourth hardest to get into in the country. The DSW program started its first class with 18 students, making it one of the largest doctoral social work programs in the country.
Identify the leaders of this case statement and program.	The members of the department management committee are the leaders of this case statement.
State what is unique about your institution. Explain why it is different from other similar programs. You may have a unique program that does not exist elsewhere. Identify faculty and/or staff who are well known and respected in the community.	The university has a high percentage of students graduating who are first-time university graduates in their family. Unique features of all programs: The BSW program offers several specialized courses in Elders, Child Welfare, and Addictions. The MSW program offers four specialized focus areas and a weekend cohort program in mental health and addictions. The DSW program is the only one in New England and offers a base in clinical, management, and teaching with the opportunity to specialize in each of these areas also. Faculty are on the following boards in the community:
Focus on the future. All information and data should be easily understood and factual with documentation if necessary.	The BSW and MSW programs plan to update their curricula to make it current and future-focused. The potential for growth in all program areas can be easily attained (add number of qualified students who apply each year and are denied entrance).

(continued)

TABLE 16.4 **Key Components and Elements of a Case Statement With Examples** *(Continued)*

KEY COMPONENTS AND ELEMENTS OF A CASE STATEMENT	EXAMPLES
List the objectives of the current campaign and the strategies/projects to achieve the objectives and the time table. Be concrete; people want to know how their money will be used.	Current objectives include the following: Increase scholarships—by five a year. Add an Endowed Chair in one of the specialty areas—two within five years. Expand the number of students in the MSW Elders specialization from six a year to 12. Expand field placements in agencies that do not have MSW supervisors by paying MSWs to provide supervision—five a year for next three years.
Describe why the service area requires this change in type of project/program or new project/program. State how conditions have changed and how your organization will deal with these changes.	The population is aging rapidly and the program needs to recruit more students into aging specializations. The tuition goes up each year and students need financial support. So recruiting students with scholarships to serve the elderly is the strategy we plan to employ.
State who are the constituents that will benefit from the services offered?	Students who are state residents will benefit from this program and an expansion of field placements to more agencies will serve more state residents.
Provide compelling reasons to contribute.	You will be helping students obtain a degree, many of whom will more than likely be the first person in their family to have a college degree.
Provide your donors with examples of how you will spend their money, how their money will impact the program.	Funding will be spent on student scholarships, expansion of service in field agencies, and creating an endowed chair.
Provide a description of the budget, facilities, staff, ongoing evaluation, etc., required to carry out the strategies/projects.	The budget for the program includes set costs for faculty and staff salaries and fringe benefits in the amount of $ . . . There is funding for four part-time graduate assistants and one student worker. The program has its own building and faculty receive computer upgrades every three years from a state-funded program. The program provides data on the achievement of student learning outcomes on its website [link: . . .].
Identify who is helping you raise all money. Include board members, staff, etc. If a person knows someone else on your list, he or she may give. Put together a list of all those involved in the campaign.	The program's management team is involved in fundraising as are all board members. The list of board members is provided in the appendices.
Add miscellaneous program information as appropriate, including information on the successes of key staff and/or their backgrounds.	Bios for the management team are in the appendices.

BSW, bachelor of social work; DSW, doctorate of social work; MSW, master of social work.

Table 16.5 can be used to build a case statement for your organization. Simply add information pertinent to your program in the right column corresponding to each key element.

TABLE 16.5 **Competency-Based Practice Exercise: Key Components and Elements of a Case Statement Practice**

KEY COMPONENTS AND ELEMENTS OF A CASE STATEMENT	ADD YOUR CASE STATEMENT COMPONENTS AND ELEMENTS
Write a vision and mission statement that is clear and easy to understand.	
Describe how this case statement will meet the organization's vision, mission, and goals.	
Present a brief history of your program, how it started, where you are, where you want to be, and what you still need.	
Stress the strengths of the program and why it is successful. Be positive. People want to be associated with a winner.	
Identify the leaders of this case statement and program.	
State what is unique about your institution. Explain why your program is different or unique from other similar programs. Identify faculty and/or staff who are well known and respected in the community.	
Focus on the future. All information and data should be easily understood and factual, with documentation if necessary.	
List the objectives of the current campaign and the strategies/projects to achieve the objectives and the timetable. Be concrete; people want to know how their money is being used.	
Describe why the service area requires this change in type of project/program or new project/program. State how conditions have changed and how your organization will deal with these changes.	
State who are the constituents that will benefit from the services offered.	
Provide compelling reasons to contribute.	
Provide your donors with examples of how you will spend their money, how their money will impact the program.	
Provide a description of the budget, facilities, staff, ongoing evaluation, etc., required to carry out the strategies/projects.	

(continued)

TABLE 16.5 **Competency-Based Practice Exercise: Key Components and Elements of a Case Statement Practice** *(Continued)*

KEY COMPONENTS AND ELEMENTS OF A CASE STATEMENT	ADD YOUR CASE STATEMENT COMPONENTS AND ELEMENTS
Identify who is helping you raise money. Include board members, staff, etc. If a person knows someone else on your list, they may give. Put together a list of all those involved in the campaign.	
Add miscellaneous program information as appropriate, including information on the successes of key staff and/or their backgrounds.	

Holgate (2006) provided an argument about the importance of case statements and how to effectively use them for maximum gain. Developing a case statement will enhance your development advantage. However, a written case statement is only the beginning. Table 16.6 lists four concurrent actions that will provide rewards as you go forward with your fundraising plan.

TABLE 16.6 **Steps Concurrent With Developing a Case Statement**

CONCURRENT STEPS IN DEVELOPING CASE STATEMENTS	FURTHER EXPLANATION
Identify the characteristics of a solid program.	A description of how and why the program is successful will go a long way in increasing support.
Make the case statement a donor-focused fundraising plan.	The focus should be on donors, particularly individual donors, who might have some connection to the program or the service through family or friends.
Use the case statement as a measure of success.	Achieving fundraising goals that results in these funds used as proposed, demonstrates a successful and authentic program.
Identify challenges and rewards.	There are many ups and downs during fundraising efforts. These should be discussed with staff to identify possible solutions to improve performance. The rewards are better services and program outcomes. You also should reward those that do well in the fundraising effort.

SOURCE: Holgate, R. L. (2006). *Developing and marketing a case statement: Developing a case statement.* National Association of Deans and Directors of Schools of Social Work, Spring Meeting, February 17. Chicago Hyatt Regency, Chicago, IL.

Case statements should provide supporting documents, just in case anyone asks. Table 16.7 provides a list of supporting documents and further explanation as to why these should be available if needed.

According to Holgate (2006), there are several key characteristics of a solid development plan. Table 16.8 lays out these characteristics, explains why they are important, and provides further explanation for each.

TABLE 16.7 **Case Statement Supporting Documents**

SUPPORT DOCUMENTS	FURTHER EXPLANATION
Listing of the board of trustees, committees, advisory boards, and staff.	Who is helping you raise money? If a person knows someone else on your list, they may give. Put together a list of all those involved in the campaign.
Recent audited financial statement and "eye popping" statistics and/or facts.	These documents can be used for a variety of purposes, including grant proposals.
Miscellaneous program information as appropriate.	Information on the successes of key staff and/or their backgrounds. Success stories of clients.

SOURCE: Galowich, R. J. (2006). *Developing and marketing a case statement: Those pesky case statements—What are they all about anyway?* National Association of Deans and Directors of Schools of Social Work, Spring Meeting, February 17. Chicago Hyatt Regency, Chicago, IL.

TABLE 16.8 **Characteristics of a Solid Development Program**

CHARACTERISTICS OF A SOLID DEVELOPMENT PROGRAM	FURTHER EXPLANATION
Donor-centric—focus as donors as people.	Develop solid relationships with donors. Appeal to people's instincts, beliefs, and history.
Focused • Shared vision, goals, direction • Clear priorities and plan • Results integrated	Look at and measure success.
Integrates across team	Build and engage support of organizational members. Each donor's beliefs are shaped by all of the experiences they have had; every single person in your program can shape a person's beliefs about the program, either positively or negatively.
Creative	Creative approaches will set you apart from competitors, plus donors respond to creative asks.
Responsive	When people ask for things, they expect answers; even if you do not know the answer, give them one.
Consistent	Maintain continuous engagement with current and future prospects.
Forward-looking	Provide inspiration for a donor: this is where we want to go, come with us. Need to be writing the case for the future. Rewards are sometimes far in the future, so it may be hard to focus on the present.
Evaluate the program	Articulate successful outcomes and add to market plan.

SOURCE: Holgate, R. L. (2006). *Developing and marketing a case statement: Developing a case statement.* National Association of Deans and Directors of Schools of Social Work, Spring Meeting, February 17. Chicago Hyatt Regency, Chicago, IL

There are several reasons to use a case statement. Table 16.9 provides several purposes and further explanation for why these purposes are important.

TABLE 16.9 **Case Statements Uses**

PURPOSES OF CASE STATEMENTS	FURTHER EXPLANATION
As an internal document to help resolve and focus planning and policies into a written statement that interprets the institution externally.	Planning and policies will change over time, so documentation that relates to funding needs to be kept up to date for internal and external uses.
In a shortened form (prospectus) it can be used to help test the market prior to conducting major fundraising.	Develop a prospectus that lays out a plan in three to four pages, test it, and then develop the case statement. How do you test it? Conduct focus groups of homogenous people, or conduct face-to-face interviews with donors, leadership in the community, potential donors, and corporate or family foundations. Plan to go back to these people for funds later. A short prospectus will test both the market for gifts and the purpose of the case statement. If you are in a larger organization, obtain permission from your institutional fundraising office to contact your alumni or past donors. Another source of funding are the members of other boards of directors and donors of social service agencies. Most organizations publish annual reports, which list their donors.
To rally leadership around policy, planning, and the sales story.	Will help leadership all be on the same page so that communication with the community identifies the purpose of the organization and what it is attempting to accomplish.
As a key tool in securing campaign leadership as well as quality staff.	Leadership and staff will come on board if they know exactly what the plan is and the importance of obtaining funding.
As the major support document when soliciting large annual, capital, and special gifts.	A document that is consistently used will ensure organizational uniqueness.
As a reference tool for future publications.	You can borrow language from this document for newsletters and in many other ways.
To raise your national and international reputation.	Advertise success, particularly obtaining large gifts, through email lists your organization participates in. For social workers it would be NADD, BPD, and CSWE, where the announcement of a multimillion-dollar gift certainly gets everyone's attention.

Baccalaureate Program Director; CSWE, Council on Social Work Education; NADD, National Association of Deans and Directors.

SOURCE: Galowich, R. J. (2006). *Developing and marketing a case statement: Those pesky case statements—What are they all about anyway?* National Association of Deans and Directors of Schools of Social Work, Spring Meeting, February 17. Chicago Hyatt Regency, Chicago, IL.

Now what should you do once you have packaged all the contents of the case statement? Use it! But first you should consider the following steps:

- Take the show on the road and actually hand the document out to people. It tells your story.

- For schools or programs that cannot promote their own case statements because the university or larger organization already has one, add the goals and objectives of your program to the larger document.

- Identify fundraising goals. In a university the funds will be used for scholarships and program support for student services. In an agency the funds will be used for client services.

- Tell people how you plan to use the money.

- Tell stories about what the money has accomplished; use personal quotes from people such as students receiving scholarships and clients receiving services for their loved ones.

- Identify your program's strengths:

    - For example, this is the only program to offer BSW, MSW and DSW programs in the state and region.

    - List the number of students, the number of hours students work in field internships, and the total number of dollars that labor provides the community, along with a list of all the agencies.

    - Does the university or agency have something in its mission that you support that serves the public good?

    - Address a key issue such as serving the elders, or those addicted. Funders will not want to pay your debt or salaries; they prefer to support services that really help people, such as scholarships (academia) or food (agency that serves the poor).

The message is if we have the money, here is what we can do.

According to Holgate (2006), there are five myths about fundraising that can curtail fundraising efforts. Table 16.10 presents these five myths along with the actual reality about giving.

TABLE 16.10 **Five Myths About Fundraising**

FUNDRAISING MYTH	REALITY AND STRATEGIES
Myth 1: It is our job to convince people to give.	Your job is to direct people who give to you. • $240 billion in charitable giving in 2003. • 84% of college educated people make gifts. • 91% with postgraduate study give (The Center on Philanthropy at Indiana University, 2004). • Focus on graduates of college programs.
Myth 2: Most gifts come from foundations and corporations.	• Individual gifts comprise 75% of total giving, $21.6 billion in bequests, 9% of total giving (The Center on Philanthropy at Indiana University, 2004). • Put people on a list so they have you on their list. Update alumni and donor list yearly.

(continued)

TABLE 16.10 **Five Myths About Fundraising** *(Continued)*

FUNDRAISING MYTH	REALITY AND STRATEGIES
Myth 3: All we need are a few really big gifts.	• $1 million donors begin with small gifts. • Gave first gift within 4 years of graduation. Usually give multiple gifts each year. • Most gifts are small gifts that sometimes turn into big gifts. Once a person starts giving and sees that the gift is put to good use, they may then give more.
Myth 4: People give us what we ask for.	• Giving is highly personal. • Match of interests and timing. • Yes and no can mean yes, no, or maybe. • Most people will not give what you ask for. They will give based on their current circumstances, which may change over time, and, once they start giving, they may be more generous at a later date when their circumstances change, e.g., their tax situation, inheritance, and increased income as they age.
Myth 5: Giving is a rational decision.	• Emotion, experience, and case influence donors. • Philanthropy is very personal. • Donor motivations vary. • It may take time to find the right donor—don't be discouraged. • Appeal to donors' emotions.

SOURCE: Holgate, R. L. (2006). *Developing and marketing a case statement: Developing a case statement.* National Association of Deans and Directors of Schools of Social Work, Spring Meeting, February 17. Chicago Hyatt Regency, Chicago, IL.

The philanthropic relationship lifecycle begins with engagement, leads to commitment, and then leads to stewardship, which engages donors even more. According to Holgate (2006) giving inspires more giving. Box 16.6 states that consistent small donors can give large amounts over time.

BOX 16.6

GIVING INSPIRES GIVING

Gifts come from the heart. The heart follows gifts:

- Consistent donors give 50% more during their lifetimes (get a person to give every year).
- Most $1 million–plus donors began with small gifts.
- Significant bequests come from consistent donors of modest gifts (you can get $100,000 or more bequests from people that gave only $5 or $10 a year, many are ending their lives with enormous estates; even your own faculty can give bequests).

SOURCE: Holgate, R. L. (2006). *Developing and marketing a case statement: Developing a case statement.* National Association of Deans and Directors of Schools of Social Work, Spring Meeting, February 17. Chicago Hyatt Regency, Chicago, IL.

According to Holgate (2006), there is a three-tier level of giving:

- Annual giving through the mail, phone, or electronic devices
- Major gifts resulting from personal visits and volunteer solicitation
- Principal gifts that result from contacts from your president or CEO, trustees, and deans or directors. To obtain principal gifts, start with five people and connect with them, visiting them regularly.

Raising funds requires a lot of time, so think about your time and the individual attention you need to give to some people. Table 16.11 lists how to prioritize fundraising activities from high to low along with steps to take at each level and finishes with follow-up activities.

TABLE 16.11 Prioritizing Activities

LEVEL OR PRIORITY	STEPS	FOLLOW-UP
High	Move to solicitation	Be persistent
Medium	Heavy cultivation	Contact frequently
Low	Newer prospects	Contact a few times and try to obtain a small donation

SOURCE: Holgate, R. L. (2006). *Developing and marketing a case statement: Developing a case statement*. National Association of Deans and Directors of Schools of Social Work, Spring Meeting, February 17. Chicago Hyatt Regency, Chicago, IL.

For fundraising activities to be successful you need to build relationships and create a natural flow, so there are back-and-forth communications. You may have to write to people every month to say, "I thought you might be interested in this," or "I will be in town for an event you may be attending also." Holgate (2006) suggested the need to focus on critical development responsibility by using quantitative and qualitative measures; these are displayed in Table 16.12.

TABLE 16.12 Critical Development Responsibility by Quantitative and Qualitative Measures

CRITICAL DEVELOPMENT RESPONSIBILITY	FURTHER EXPLANATION AND EXAMPLES
Clarify objectives	Identify objectives that are most important.
Define pool	Identify past, current, and potential donors, and how pool could be expanded.
Prioritize	Who to contact in order of likely donation.
Strategize	Create an overall plan to contact donors.
Communicate	Who and how to communicate with donors, and what information should be used.
Track Progress	Build database by names/contacts, dates, amount given, dates, when to contact again, and who should contact donor, and update it regularly.

(continued)

TABLE 16.12 **Critical Development Responsibility by Quantitative and Qualitative Measures** *(Continued)*

CRITICAL DEVELOPMENT RESPONSIBILITY	FURTHER EXPLANATION AND EXAMPLES
Quantitative Measures	**Further Explanation and Examples**
Contacts: Visits, phone calls, letters, email	Add to database contact method and track contact events.
Events, other initiatives	Plan your events in advance and take into consideration holiday and religious calendars.
Proposals	Maintain a standardized document that is updated yearly and could be used for a variety of purposes, including grant proposals.
Stewardship	Who contacts whom and who is ultimately in charge.
Dollars raised	Track quantity by funding cycle, maybe quarters.
Participation rates	Percent and amount of donors contacted who gave, percent and amount of funding coming from new donors yearly, percent and amount of staff who gave.
Qualitative Measures	**Further Explanation and Examples**
Regular discussion of what is happening in our relationships	How often you meet with donors and what they say about intent to give.
Assessment of quality, frequency, continuity	Assess yearly methods to contact donors, how frequently and from year to year.

SOURCE: Holgate, R. L. (2006). *Developing and marketing a case statement: Developing a case statement.* National Association of Deans and Directors of Schools of Social Work, Spring Meeting, February 17. Chicago Hyatt Regency, Chicago, IL.

According to Holgate (2006), there are several questions you should ask yourself about your fundraising strategies. One is what has been your personal experience in giving money? Table 16.13 provides five questions, each on self-help, for effective strategies and food for thought and conversation.

TABLE 16.13 **Competency-Based Exercise: Self-Help for Effective Strategies**

SELF-HELP FOR EFFECTIVE STRATEGIES	THINK OF YOUR CURRENT STRATEGIES AND ANSWER THE FOLLOWING QUESTIONS
Does your strategy deepen a prospect's relationship with your institution?	
Does your strategy increase knowledge of your prospect's interests?	
Does your strategy result in more information about a prospect's financial ability?	
Does your strategy lead to a gift?	

(continued)

TABLE 16.13 **Competency-Based Exercise: Self-Help for Effective Strategies** *(Continued)*

SELF-HELP FOR EFFECTIVE STRATEGIES	THINK OF YOUR CURRENT STRATEGIES AND ANSWER THE FOLLOWING QUESTIONS
Do you talk too much and not listen to donors enough?	
Food for Thought and Conversation	**Think of When You Gave Money for a Cause and Answer the Following Questions**
What is the most satisfying gift you have ever made to an institution?	
How does it feel to be asked for a gift? (think about yourself, why do you give when someone asks)	
What do you expect after you have made a gift? (cannot be fast enough, just call a person and thank them)	
What has been most rewarding for you as a volunteer? (we depend on volunteers for a variety of reasons, volunteers are our best advocates, can make suggestions on avenues we can use)	
What advice would you give to help us work better with donors and volunteers?	

SOURCE: Holgate, R. L. (2006). *Developing and marketing a case statement: Developing a case statement.* National Association of Deans and Directors of Schools of Social Work, Spring Meeting, February 17. Chicago Hyatt Regency, Chicago, IL.

There are a number of challenges that you will experience raising funds. Doing so takes a lot of time and can be a full-time job. You must be very flexible when working with potential donors. If they cannot meet you when you want, meet with them on their schedule. Remember to try to meet goals on schedule. You may need more resources than projected to achieve your goals. You will have disappointments; do not let them get you down. Finally, display and maintain discipline in your work and relationships.

Some donors may come across as difficult. Think about the questions in Box 16.7.

BOX 16.7

COMPETENCY-BASED CASE QUESTIONS ABOUT DIFFICULT DONORS

Case Questions

1. How do you work with difficult potential givers (those that take up a lot of time and want to give to a type of program that you cannot really create or implement)?
   Suggestion: You may have to stop talking to them. The way the donor wants to control the gift can be inappropriate.
   What else can you do in this situation?

(continued)

BOX 16.7 *(Continued)*

2. What if donors have specific demands for how the funds are to be used?
   Suggestion: Do not promise things to which you cannot commit.
   What else can you do in this situation?

However, despite all the time and effort fundraising can require, there can be many rewards and opportunities once a system of resource development has been established. Rewards can include the following:

- Connecting with and recognizing people.
- Succeeding in building a culture of philanthropy (e.g., start a senior class gift).
- Celebrating success (have a celebration to honor the most important donors).
- Recognizing continued commitment (think of ways to celebrate and acknowledge people).
- Increasing engagement (building lifelong relationships).

Strategies

According to Stanesa (2006), to maintain a successful fundraising effort you need to execute at every level of the school or agency; you need to get everyone involved. If a new building is needed, make a case for bricks and mortar, but you will need a good justification. Some major donors are willing to give large donations, especially if you name a building after them. However, most donors want their gift to go directly to people in need, not program administration. There are several process steps in successful fundraising (Stanesa, 2006). Box 16.8 lists steps to maintain a successful fundraising effort.

BOX 16.8

STEPS IN A SUCCESSFUL FUNDRAISING EFFORT

- Conduct a communications audit, including a review of all messages going out. Where does your admissions statement or program description appear? What are you saying about the school or agency, who is on your message lists, what you are sending them, who are you trying to reach and why?
- Review web, print, and email; how do different groups want to communicate?
- Do some research; ask people what they think.
- Create statistics about current space and program needs. For academic programs make available data on field placements, where students intern, and the number of hours donated for public service. For agencies, how many clients are served each year?
- Gather information from key constituencies. Have a consulting firm conduct interviews: what do people know about the school or program, why do they give? Ask alumni what are their perceptions of the school, what do people in their region of the country think of us.

(continued)

BOX 16.8 *(Continued)*

- Do focus groups with students and clients. Why did they come here?
- Schedule one-on-one visits with foundation heads.
- Develop a communication strategy to support your giving program. Develop a consistent message that goes out.

Another strategy is to create a cabinet of people, or task force, who are mostly not social workers. Expanding in such a way can give you more networks in the community. According to Stanesa (2006), *mission, context,* and *branding* are crucial for a plan to succeed. See Box 16.9 for more information.

BOX 16.9

COMPETENCY-BASED QUESTIONS: IMPORTANCE OF MISSION, CONTEXT, AND BRANDING

Answer these questions within the context of your organization.
Does the *mission* explicitly state why the program exists? Positioning is the key to that frame of reference.

- How do we differentiate ourselves based on our unique place?
- What do we offer, what do we provide, and what program services do we provide?
- What are the benefits (degree for students, intangibles such as the need for people to have their name on a building)?

What is the current *context*?

- What is happening in our current environment?
- What are the needs of key constituencies?
- Are we meeting needs and how do we know?
- Are there opportunities to meet unmet needs?
- What is our sustainable competitive advantage?
- Are there big system changes that may impact us?
- What are the political changes that shape our work?

Branding should start with differentiating your program.

- What is special and unique about us?
- What do we define as our unique benefits and for whom?
- Why do students or clients choose our program? Survey incoming students.
- How do we validate what it is we say about ourselves?
- What evidence do we have that we impact the community? Find the stories and tell them.
- What are the ways we integrate teaching, research, and service? For example, a student does an internship in a field of practice, and an alumnus may be working in that area.

(continued)

BOX 16.9 (Continued)

- ▩ What areas have we impacted and engaged?
- ▩ How would we help donors key into areas that interest them?

Major Gifts and Stewardship

As stated previously, individuals provide the majority of funding in the gift-giving and fundraising world. In the following section, we discuss marketing, motivation, capacity, opportunity, and stewardship. Box 16.10 displays the competencies/behaviors in this section.

BOX 16.10

NETWORK FOR SOCIAL WORK MANAGEMENT COMPETENCIES AND PRACTICE BEHAVIORS 16

Fundraising: identifies and applies for new and recurring funding while ensuring accountability with existing funding systems (Network for Social Work Management Competencies 16). Practice Behaviors:

- ▩ Establishes strong systems of stewardship with donors/funders (16.4).

Establishing strong systems of stewardship with donors and funders requires creative strategies applied in a variety of settings. Although most of the following examples apply to universities, they can also be used in public agency fundraising.

Marketing: Luck is the residue of preparation plus effort. You cannot separate fundraising from marketing. You are selling your school, vision, and profession. To be successful in fundraising, developing a good marketing campaign is critical. According to Edwards (Edwards, 2006), motivation, capacity, and opportunity are three keys to marketing and working with donors. Marketing and fundraising go hand in hand.

Motivation: Why should someone with money give it to your school? You have to motivate them. Develop relationships. Do not raise money to fund the school of social work. Fund what the school does rather than what it is. A famous basketball player gave $1 million to a social work program because his mother was on the board and he was interested in funding things that would strengthen families.

Capacity: Find people who have money. Nonprofits have fundraising events that provide food and entertainment at low costs in the hopes of attracting major donors. There are organizations that will do wealth screenings for your locality, which can be used to identify potential top donors. You can also use annual reports of other nonprofits, ideally with like-minded, similar services, to identify potential donors who might be interested in supporting your services. Additionally, organizations need to maximize the use of the board to identify potential donors.

Opportunity: Provide people with the opportunity to give. Use the right people, right time, and place. Develop relationships over a period of time. Most people do not give because they are not asked. Have lunch with a potential donor and ask for a donation—but pick up tab for lunch. If you do get a gift, it is not the end but the beginning. People may make an even bigger gift later if you treat them right (stewardship). For a big campaign you need to have at least three prospects to get one big gift. For major campaigns one's focus should be on major gifts, not small donors (such as attempts to do small parties with alumni to raise funds).

Stewardship means supporting the relationship so it lasts. Steps to take to support stewardship include the following:

- Conduct research to determine the capacity of the most important potential donors, or current donors that have given to your organization. Sometimes you can find out how much they have given to other organizations through researching annual reports of other organizations or advertisements, and then determine what they are comfortable giving. For example, if they gave $100,000 to another organization, you could ask big; if they gave $25,000, do not ask for $100,000.

- Encouraging major donors to attend cultivation events where they can inspire other potential donors.

- Give donors the amount of public recognition appropriate for their giving level and according to their wishes.

- Staff should enter in the donor database exactly how donors want their names(s) to appear in public lists, their interests, what they think about your organization, what other organizations do they give to, foundations or trusts associated with the donor, and how much they give to you and other organizations.

- With the donor's permission, submit a photo of the donor to the local newspaper or appropriate website.

- Consider sponsoring a wine and cheese party for top donors.

- Each donor is different, as is every stone on a beach. How does each want to be communicated with, and so on? (Shrewsbury, 2018).

You spend just as much time on the small events as you do getting $1 million from a rich donor. Sometimes, you will spend a lot of time with a potential donor, and you cannot be sure that that person will donate. But meeting with that person may pay off someday. Also talk to people who have an interest in social issues and social problems. Other strategies include convincing faculty members or employees to help raise funds; determining short-term goals to ready a big campaign; creating a base of individual donors (recent alumni that give gifts on an individual basis); creating a database of donors who are in a high-income category as they can make large gifts; sponsoring a dinner for top-end donors; and making the point that it is not about the size of the gift but the participation.

Another action strategy is to create a donor file for each person. Besides documenting the amount donated, track frequency. Describe the donor's connection to the program and why they have given. This file should also contain articles on the person and social scene events she or he has attended. Google your donors and potential donors, such as your alumni. You can find interesting material about the potential donor that may help you make a connection. Prior to meeting with the potential donor, review all of this information in the donor file. And if you receive money from a new donor, start a file on them.

Box 16.11 displays the competencies/behaviors in this section.

BOX 16.11

NETWORK FOR SOCIAL WORK MANAGEMENT COMPETENCIES AND PRACTICE BEHAVIORS 16

Fundraising: identifies and applies for new and recurring funding while ensuring accountability with existing funding systems (Network for Social Work Management Competencies 16). Practice Behaviors:

- Seeks partnerships with other programs funded under federal/state/local authorities and other interest groups. (16.5)

The best vehicle for building partnerships is to determine local needs and the type of area (urban–rural, liberal–conservation, low- or high-income area), faculty strengths and research interests, and possible collaborations with local, regional, and state organizations, including government agencies. Types of federal collaborations could include Title IV-E and/or Title XIX Medicaid for education and training in child welfare, including adoption and foster parent training, social work internships, evaluation, and research. State and local agencies are frequently in need of program evaluations and will contract out for such services. Faculty are always interested in undertaking evaluation projects, especially if they can be paid. Students can also be involved in these activities by directly working with faculty or through internship placements.

Collaborative agreements with other organizations can also be used to obtain funding from state, local, and federal sources and/or foundations. Work can be in the spirit of collaboration, affiliations, or legal/contractual partnerships established between organizations (e.g., BSW program across all state universities).

BOX 16.12

NETWORK FOR SOCIAL WORK MANAGEMENT COMPETENCIES AND PRACTICE BEHAVIORS 16

Fundraising: identifies and applies for new and recurring funding while ensuring accountability with existing funding systems (Network for Social Work Management Competencies 16). Practice Behaviors:

- Maintains active awareness of and pursues potential grant and funding sources in local, regional, or national community. (16.6)

Building Research Capacity and Developing a Center: Beginning Steps

Box 16.12 displays the competencies/behaviors in this section. In order to obtain grants, organizations are best served by establishing a research center. Research can vary by type of initiation, either agency-initiated (practice-oriented research/program evaluation and policy research) or investigator-initiated, federally funded or foundation-funded research. Research center models can also differ depending on their focus (specific, generic, research funding), types of research, number and types of faculty involvement, and staffing. To become involved in research, several factors should be considered, including the interests of the faculty and staff; the accessibility of research subjects; whether you can respond to community requests or needs; and what is in the interest and experience of the director (McRoy & White, 2005).

An example of a mission statement of a research center (The Center for Social Work Research, The School of Social Work, The University of Texas at Austin) follows, along with some examples of the types of research projects conducted by this center.

Mission: To initiate, facilitate, and promote interdisciplinary research on social work topics. Examples of types of research projects can be found in Box 16.13.

BOX 16.13

RESEARCH CENTER PROJECT EXAMPLES

- Child Welfare
- Cultural Diversity
- Domestic, Sexual, and Community Violence
- Families, Children, and Youth
- Gerontology
- Organizations
- Mental Health and Healthcare
- Social Work Education
- Substance Abuse
- Welfare

Putting together the components to build research capacity requires several simultaneous steps including hiring a research director, strategic planning, obtaining faculty buy-in, starting a doctoral program, focusing on faculty support in the pre- and postaward stages, obtaining higher-level organizational support, and support for staff training (Zlotnik et al., 2006). Box 16.14 lists a range of action steps that will make a difference in starting up a research center.

BOX 16.14

ACTION STEPS TO START A RESEARCH CENTER

- Obtain faculty buy-in and support.
- Adjust workload of faculty working on grants.
- Create infrastructure to support the center including support staff, senior research point person, technical assistance for faculty, internal reviewers, and external relationships to build capacity.
- Develop a plan for the role of the research director.
- Begin center discussion about focus, e.g., applied research to support community organization.

(continued)

BOX 16.14 *(Continued)*

- Address multiple issues at one time, as it will not be a linear process.
- Win support of central administration.
- Plan and launch a doctoral program.
- Hire students to work in the center.
- Hire copyeditor to review grants.
- Differentiate roles of business management staff to support grant management activities.
- Determine impact on faculty's research career.
- Determine the value of the research for the school and university.
- Determine the value of the faculty to the school.
- Consider the importance of the topics to address social ills.
- Develop a multiyear plan.
- Distinguish research from training, consultation, and program development activities. HOWEVER, build research opportunities from these other activities.
- Develop research mentorship strategies.
- Create research partnerships with community agencies—examine models such as Casey Family Programs or Casey Family Services.
- Call a retreat early on—explore norms and expectations including "levels of scholarship expected," vision to develop a "future" orientation.
- Establish that indirect cost return will be shared between the university and the school's centers.
- Readjust workload.
- Integrate doctoral students into centers and research.
- Set goals for minimum number of abstracts to CSWE and SSWR.
- Create center with a focus on relevant issues.
- Get federal grant representatives to come and present on future topics and policy, procedures, and infrastructure development.
- Establish the role of the dean—be a mentor, find new resources, talk to donors.

CSWE, Council on Social Work Education; SSWR, Society for Social Work and Research.

Building a Research Agenda

Zlotnik et al. (2006) has suggested that when a leader or manager starts a new job, he or she might consider developing and implementing a research agenda through a restructuring of existing centers and the development of new centers, linking faculty, and implementing projects.

As for what the current hot topics that research centers might consider, developing a research center with a focus on one or more of the Social Work Grand Challenges would be a good start. The Social Work Grand Challenges are in Box 16.15.

BOX 16.15

SOCIAL WORK GRAND CHALLENGES

- Grand Challenge 1—Maximize Every Person's Productive Potential
- Grand Challenge 2—Prevent Behavioral Problems in Youth
- Grand Challenge 3—Reduce Isolation and Loneliness
- Grand Challenge 4—Foster Safe Families
- Grand Challenge 5—End Homelessness
- Grand Challenge 6—Improve Health for All
- Grand Challenge 7—Reduce Incarceration
- Grand Challenge 8—Strengthen Financial Security
- Grand Challenge 9—End Racial Injustice
- Grand Challenge 10—Protect the Human Environment
- Grand Challenge 11—Promote Social and Economic Participation
- Grand Challenge 12—Harness Technology for Social Good

Research centers provide a range of helpful attributes, including dissemination of information on grants; helping faculty submit proposals (budget preparation; institutional review board [IRBs]; interfacing with university office of accounting; and copying, editing, proofing, etc.); and ongoing accounting assistance. However, research centers do create issues that need to be managed. Issues include maintaining sustainable funding to retain staff; matching faculty and funding opportunities; staffing issues (hiring, evaluating performance, etc.); and incentivizing faculty to conduct research.

Research centers usually create institutes which have a particular focus depending on issues and circumstances. Activities and tasks of centers can vary, but several core requirements are the following:

- Oversight and coordination of center activities
- Staff supervision
- Liaison with funding agencies
- Problem solving
- Accounting services
- Budget preparation
- Personnel
- Travel
- Interfacing with administrative personnel at the university
- Identifying funding sources
- Coordinating research presentation series

- Creating an annual newsletter
- Developing proposals
- Tracking/monitoring IRB proposals
- Collaborating with other units at the university

Issues that can arise include the following:

- Appropriate attention to expertise on specific populations
- Culturally competent research
- Interdisciplinary research
- Need for appropriate technical staff, including statisticians
- Need for grant specialists
- Balance between teaching and research

When starting up a research center, one major issue is determining the chief administrative officer. Should the executive be a research administrator, director, or an associate dean for research? There is a need for both administrative tasks and the promotion of scholarship among faculty. Administrative tasks can include budgeting, filling out the correct forms, getting grants through the system, linking to IRB and the sponsored programs office, monitoring funding opportunities, conducting internal review, mentoring, providing statistical expertise, offering consultation, and sponsoring brown bag research lunches, and so on.

How do you readjust the workload of faculty working on grants? In regard to the IRB process, place a faculty member from your program on the university IRB and have one of your doctoral students take the lead on assisting and submitting IRB forms. IRB forms usually just require copying content from the proposal into the appropriate locations in the IRB forms for more than half the IRB form content.

The Business Side of Research Centers

Once a research center has been established, the goal is to sustain it. Maintaining the business side of a center is very important. Zlotnik et al. (2006) has suggested that, to maintain research activities and contracts, it is important for the dean to make sure that context, policy, and practice are upheld, including what controls might exist in the university to approach foundations; what percentage of indirect charges accrues to the university, the unit, and to the principal investigator; and to realize that indirect charges can be negotiable with a foundation. Business issues, both pre- and postaward, are important. Preaward activities include support for consultation and help, seeking corporate and foundation funds, and knowing what exists in terms of business support in the school and university. Postaward activities include growing business operations, developing and monitoring budgets, working with university administrators, completing projects, producing reports, and circulating findings. Things to think about when leveraging research funds include building research capacity and creating, augmenting, or enhancing centers and research capacities in social work education programs. See Box 16.16 for more competency-based questions on research centers.

BOX 16.16

COMPETENCY-BASED QUESTIONS ON RESEARCH CENTER CAPACITY BUILDING AND EXTERNAL FUNDING

Centers and capacity-building possibilities—Infrastructure

- Do you have an associate dean or director of research?
- Is there someone designated to be responsible for mentoring, proposal review, organizing research improvement activities, supporting writing groups, sending faculty information on funding opportunities, etc.?
- Do you have statistics and methods expertise and/or consultation available for proposal development and research implementation?
- Are both senior and junior faculty engaged?
- Is a research center at the school level or the college level for schools embedded within a college? (What might be advantages or disadvantages of such a model? What are the interdisciplinary, financial, etc., benefits and challenges?])
- Are students involved in the center activities?
- Is the center staffed? At what level? What kind of expertise is needed?
- Are tenure track faculty part of the center or is it developed separately?
- Do you have established mechanisms for boilerplate materials to get grants out the door?
- Do you have a regular working relationship with the IRB and/or the office of sponsored research or the VP for research, etc., at your university?
- Does the center engage a range of faculty?
- Is the center interdisciplinary?
- Do you collaborate with other disciplines and departments, and/or community agencies?
- Is the impetus from the community, from higher-ups, from the school of social work, or from individual faculty?
- Have you received higher-level support at your university to assist in building research capacity?
- Is there the opportunity to buy out faculty time for grant development?
- What incentives are there for faculty to seek external funds?
- Does the university have specific rules to establish a "research center"?
- Do you distinguish between a research center and more topical centers that might do training, program development, and evaluation?

External funding

- Does indirect funding come back to the school, and if so, how is it used in research enhancement?
- Is specific funding coming from foundations or local, state or federal government?
- How stable is the funding source when launching a center?
- How sustainable is the funding?
- Do you plan to (need to) access external funds to build research capacity?

(continued)

BOX 16.16 *(Continued)*

- Do you have faculty who are investigators on federal grants where the principal investigator is outside of social work or outside of your university? How does that work? What is the advantage or disadvantage?
- Do you have someone who can be help with budget preparation?
- Is there a link between training contracts and development of research capacity?

Areas of research

- If you have created centers, are they topic specific?
- Does your school have a particular area of expertise and strength that has been used to marshal external resources?

IRB, institutional review board.

Building Research Capacity and Funding Without a Center: One Step at a Time

Developing a research center in some universities might be extremely complex. However, there are multiple steps a dean, director, or chairperson can take to enhance research efforts, including developing a doctoral program (it will enhance the school's position in the university and open interdisciplinary opportunities); creating a director's position; providing seed money; dedicating space, mentoring, and encouraging cross-disciplinary linkages; connecting with IRB and sponsored programs; using indirect funds as seed money to support faculty research training; encouraging a faculty member to be appointed to the university IRB committee; reducing faculty teaching loads to allow time for research; and hiring an experienced research faculty member who can help mentor other faculty in their research efforts (Zlotnik et al., 2006). There are several challenges to be overcome, including understanding that faculty needs will exceed resources that are available initially, so seek greater support for faculty; well-written proposals do not always get funded, so do not give up; support staff will need training for grant submissions; although the budget is increased through external funding, it is very soft money so take that into consideration when hiring and expanding operations and build in supports for technological assistance and hardware and software purchases.

GRANTS

Strategies for Effective Writing

The first step in effective grant writing is to carefully review the request for proposal (RFP) and then decide whether or not you, your organization, or specific program qualify to apply for the grant. Part of deciding whether or not to apply for the grant will also require you to consider the deadline for submission; since grant proposals usually require a fairly extensive process of compiling information, you want to ensure that you have adequate time to complete the process. You will also need to assess the potential likelihood of being awarded the grant and thus should conduct a cost-benefits analysis of pursuing the RFP. Furthermore, you will have to identify key persons who will be working on gathering information requested in the RFP, writing the grant, and monitoring the deadline for submission. Consider questions in advance such as will it require that multiple people write different sections, depending on their areas of expertise? Who will be responsible for reviewing the final draft, and how much time will they need to do so?

Common Pitfalls in Writing Proposals

Some common pitfalls in grant writing include providing too much general material and not enough of the right material. Grant writers need to be proficient in their succinct writing skills. Typically, the RFP outlines strict page limitations, thus one must learn the art of saying more with less. Another pitfall is not creating and maintaining boilerplate historical information and data about your programs that can be easily accessed and incorporated as the grant criteria may indicate. Finally, you must address all of the points or questions that are outlined in the RFP, again in a clear and concise manner.

Preparing a Grant Budget

Preparing grant budgets requires that you collaborate with the business office to develop the budget proposal. Traditionally, grant proposals require an additional budget narrative to describe what exactly is in the budget and the rationale for each budget item. As mentioned previously, the requirements outlined in the RFP should be followed precisely.

The Collaborative Process

Grants sometimes require collaboration with community providers, key community leaders, or key community organizations. Letters of support are also frequently required. Collaboration may include internal departments, particularly in large organizations that provide a continuum of diverse services. In universities, there may be a need to have interdisciplinary collaborations with other departments in order to effectively respond to all of the needs and requirements delineated in the grant criteria.

The Submission Process

Acknowledge the grant submission deadline date and determine if it is feasible to complete a proposal by that date. Grant writing teams frequently use the deadline date and work backward from that date to create benchmarks for assessing progress and keeping on task for the submission date. Be sure to discuss the deadline date with the signatories of the grant in advance and inquire about how much time is needed for them to review the proposal; then be sure to include that date as part of your benchmark dates. There are multiple forms and documents that will likely require signatures, and creating a task list can help to keep this process organized. Finally, you will need to understand the process of submission, that is, via email, an electronic portal, and so on. Be sure to explore and familiarize yourself with the electronic platforms that will be used for the submission process prior to the due date so that you can proactively troubleshoot any technical issues.

Working With the Grant Office After Submission

If your organization is not awarded the grant, it is in your and your organization's best interest to contact the grant program officer to inquire about your grant proposal score and aspects that might be improved for future submissions.

Grant Management: Managing the Grant Post Award

Presumably you have identified people that will work on the grant implementation during your proposal period, but once you are awarded the grant you will need to verify that they are still available and able to commit the amount of time they originally agreed to. If you have stated in the grant that you will be hiring new staff, you need to begin the hiring process, which can sometimes be problematic because of a tight time frame (i.e., you received notice that you are awarded the grant, but must have the program implemented within a specific—usually fast—time frame). You may have to refine job descriptions for the project team, post the position, and so on, expdiently.

Next you will need to create an implementation plan. As discussed in Chapter 15, Gantt and Program Evaluation Review Technique (PERT) charts, along with other forms of project management charts, can be helpful for planning the implementation stages and designing ongoing systems for monitoring the implementation progress and outcomes. If you are awarded the grant, there will be a number of reporting tasks, such as payments, reimbursements including salaries, and overhead costs. At times, you will need to negotiate with the funder for the acceptable percentage of indirect costs. Prior to the end of each funding cycle it is advisable to meet with the business or grants office to ensure that all invoices were submitted, processed, and paid within a timely manner. Note that many grants have strict reporting guidelines for when invoices must be submitted, and these need to be followed in order to comply with requirements. Additional reports include quarterly and annual progress reports as well as end of grant reports that specifically outline how the funds were spent and the measurable outcomes that were achieved.

Data and Measure Outcomes

Based on the criteria outlined in the RFP, combined with the purpose of the grant, you will need to develop both qualitative and quantitative outcome measures. Therefore, your organization or program must identify and gather data to evaluate and report on these outcomes. It is prudent to develop data collection procedures that are inherent to daily functioning rather than drastically altering your system of data collection, unless there is cogent reason to do so (i.e., use your current system, or make minor changes/additions to it).

Sustainability

The proposal should contain a plan for sustainability of the project after the initial funding has stopped. Grant funders want to see that the program or project will have lasting effects and are often more drawn to proposals that outline continuation funding plans. Box 16.17 displays the competencies/behaviors in this section.

BOX 16.17

NETWORK FOR SOCIAL WORK MANAGEMENT COMPETENCIES AND PRACTICE BEHAVIORS 16

Fundraising: identifies and applies for new and recurring funding while ensuring accountability with existing funding systems (Network for Social Work Management Competencies 16). Practice Behaviors:

- Demonstrates innovative approaches to resources development at all levels of the organization (16.7).

Investing in resource development is expensive and usually considered an extra benefit in the organizational chart. The old saying "you have to spend money to make money" is not considered by most organizations as practical. Social work academic programs have not invested in development efforts. A survey of the National Association of Deans and Directors (NADD) of graduate social work programs membership ($N = 102$ or 54% responded) on development issues found that most schools did not invest much in capital campaigns, staff, or an office (Adams, Flynn, Edwards, Vaughan, & Tebb, 2006).

■   Only 15% had led a capital campaign, and only 58% of them had set fundraising targets.

■   61% had development officers.

   ■   52% were full-time development officers, and 21% had less than 25% full time equivalent (FTE).

   ■   Less than half, 46%, had an office at their school of social work.

The same survey asked: Who pays for the development officer?

■   The Vice President's Office paid for 57%.

■   Another 30% were paid by the Vice President of Advancement and the Social Work Dean and the position reports to both.

■   The Dean of Social Work pays for only 13% of the development officers.

One recommendation is to obtain academic release time for a faculty member to engage in development if you do not have a development position.

SUCCESSFUL FUNDRAISING STRATEGIES

For programs that put a major effort into fundraising, it can consume a lot of time from the director's daily activities, possibly from one-quarter to half of the time. According to Adams et al. (2006), one should regard fundraising as a mechanism for implementing ideas and advancement. Do not think of it as raising money. Sell ideas to advance the profession, and have a large goal. We sometimes set our sights much too low. Set up a development operation. Consider creating both types of resource generation programs, one is institutional fundraising (person who raises funds for building, scholarships, etc.). Contrast that with fundraising done for research development. Talk to your alumni, wealthy donors, and work on an individual cultivation.

Encourage social work alumni to put the school in their wills and make sure they designate the school of social work. Also encourage donors to consider donating stocks and/or appreciated stock, they can donate the stock and retain the income.

Consider targeting undergraduate alumni, because at a lot of institutions the undergraduates give at a much higher rate (50% at University of Southern California [USC] compared with 17% for graduate students) (Adams, et al., 2006).

Create a board of wealthy people if possible. Recruiting from a wide range of fields of both private businesses and public organizations provides varied perspectives and access to greater wealth. To find these people attend local events, particularly those attended by wealthy people.

Most people have had personal tragedies that may help them connect to your program.

If you are successful, consider creating endowed professorships, providing professorships to some faculty, and, if you are really successful, building a new building and name it after the person who provided most of the funding for it. Develop relationships with programs from other countries and recruit students from high ranking families. Large corporations may also donate from these countries. One goal is to develop a network of friends. Get to know the board of trustees of the larger corporations as they may propose people to donate.

One former dean (Adams et al., 2006) recommends becoming involved in athletic programs. Go to women's coaches and have a school social work night at basketball games. Offer to serve as an honorary coach. Auction off things at sporting events and give out tickets to other events at pregame dinners, and so on. When attempting to recruit donors, do not take things personally; no may mean no to a particular thing at that time, but a yes may come later.

To involve faculty, establish an internal faculty development committee that helps prioritize goals and objectives (Adams et al., 2006).

Tebb (Adams et al., 2006) recommends creating a partnership with your development officer; you want the university to realize you need a plan. Formulize a plan with the development office and then met at least once a week with the development officer. Invite the development officer to retreats, parties, and events for your program. Put together an advisory board that includes attorneys, business people, and media along, with some social workers who will help promote social work with non–social workers. When successful, set up an agency head discretionary fund. This fund allows you to stay in the black, as most universities have not had a raise in operating funds for many years.

To set up a campaign organization, put cochairs in place for the campaign. Pick cochairs who have given in the past and someone from a well-connected family. It will help marketing if you can say that your faculty and staff have given 100% to the campaign and that your alumni have increased donations.

Another option is to look to alumni of the larger university who are not graduates of your program, they might be interested in social work for many reasons.

SUMMARY

This chapter addressed ways for leaders to use strategic resources development and provided information on how to create case statements. Developing case statements is critical because they are correlated with how organizations attract potential donors. This chapter reviewed ways to fundraise and appeal to potential donors, and also examined the steps of grant writing and creating research centers.

ACTIVITIES

1. Develop three strategies for fundraising using the suggestions from this chapter.

2. If you have a research center in your organization, identify how you might expand it based on additional topic areas, and identify potential funding sources for expansion.

3. Evaluate your current research center to determine its cost-effectiveness.

4. If you do not have a research center, identify topic areas that could be included in such a center. Discuss possible strategies in your organization to create a center.

RESOURCES

Some sources of federal funding include the following agencies:

- Department of Health and Human Services (HHS)
- National Institutes of Health (NIH)
- National Institute of Mental Health (NIMH)
- Centers for Disease Control and Prevention (CDC)

- National Institute on Drug Abuse (NIDA)
- Agency for Healthcare Research and Quality (AHRQ)
- Health Resources and Services Administration (HRSA)
- National Institute of Justice (NIJ)
- Department of Defense (DoD)
- Department of Education (DoED)
- Department of Housing and Urban Development, Veterans Administration (VA)
- National Science Foundation (NSF)
- Substance Abuse and Mental Health Services Administration (SAMHSA)
- National Institute of Child Health and Human Development (NICHD)
- National Institute on Alcohol Abuse and Alcoholism (NIAAA)

Also state and local public and private agencies, and national, regional, and local foundations, such as the Hartford Foundation, Robert Wood Johnson Foundation (RWJF), American Cancer Society, and so on.

Journal articles of interest for establishing research centers include:

Nutter, R. W., & Hudson, J. (1997). A survey of social work research centers. *Research on Social Work Practice, 7*(2). 239–262.

Wodarski, J. S. (1995). Guidelines for building research centers in schools of social work. *Research on Social Work Practice, 5*(3). 383–398.

REFERENCES

Adams, I., Flynn, M., Edwards, R., Vaughan, P., & Tebb, S., (2006). *Innovations exchange on development strategies.* Paper presented at the National Association of Deans and Directors Conference, Chicago, IL.

Covey, S. R. (1991). *Principle-centered leadership.* New York, NY: Summit Books.

Edwards, R. (2006). *Innovations Exchange on Development Strategies.* National Association of Deans and Directors of Schools of Social Work, Spring Meeting, February 16. Chicago Hyatt Regency, Chicago, IL.

Galowich, R. J. (2006). *Developing and marketing a case statement: Those pesky case statements—What are they all about anyway?* National Association of Deans and Directors of Schools of Social Work, Spring Meeting, February 17. Chicago Hyatt Regency, Chicago, IL.

Holgate, R. L. (2006). *Developing and marketing a case statement: Developing a case statement.* National Association of Deans and Directors of Schools of Social Work, Spring Meeting, February 17. Chicago Hyatt Regency, Chicago, IL.

McRoy, R., & White, B., *Research infrastructure models, NADD research plenary.* Paper presented the National Association of Deans and Directors Conference, San Antonio, TX.

Shrewsbury, S. (2018). *The new haven farms: The MG process. Power Point Presentation.* New Haven, CT: Vineyard Consulting.

Stanesa, J. (2006). *Developing and marketing a case statement: Fundraising strategies.* National Association of Deans and Directors of Schools of Social Work, Spring Meeting, February 17. Chicago Hyatt Regency, Chicago, IL.

The Center on Philanthropy at Indiana University. (2004). *Giving USA.* Indianapolis, IN.

Zlotnik, J., Zabora, J., Vroom, P., Middleton, J., Korr, W., & Davidson, K. (2006). *Leveraging funds and infrastructure enhancements for research centers.* National Association of Deans and Directors of Schools of Social Work, Fall Meeting, October 7. Hilton Savannah DeSoto. Savannah, GA.

PART 4

COMMUNITY COLLABORATION

CHAPTER 17

COMMUNITY COLLABORATION FOR SOCIAL WORKERS

CHAPTER OBJECTIVES

- Analyzing the task environment of an agency or institution to improve organizational effectiveness.
- Creating collaborative relationships with complementary agencies, institutions, and community groups to enhance the delivery of services.
- Evaluating opportunities for community partnerships and collaborations.
- Understanding the process of building policy advocacy coalitions.

INTRODUCTION

In order to enhance the delivery of services, human service organizations must build relationships with complementary agencies, institutions, and community groups. In this process, agencies must not only establish community collaborations to obtain needed resources but also effectively meet the needs of the client population they are serving.

This chapter covers the Network for Social Work Management Competencies and Practice Behaviors shown in Box 17.1.

BOX 17.1

NETWORK FOR SOCIAL WORK MANAGEMENT COMPETENCIES AND PRACTICE BEHAVIORS COVERED IN THIS CHAPTER

Possesses analytical and critical thinking skills that promote organizational growth (Network for Social Work Management Competencies 3). Practice Behaviors:

- Conceptualizes innovative partnerships to maximize agency resources (3.10).

Develops and manages both internal and external stakeholder relationships (Network for Social Work Management Competencies 6). Practice Behaviors:

- Successfully advocates at the national, state, and local levels for the organization, its clients, and for issues promoting social justice for vulnerable populations (6.4).

Builds relationships with complementary agencies, institutions, and community groups to enhance the delivery of services (Network for Social Work Management Competencies 21).
Practice Behaviors:

- Establishes partnerships and alliances with businesses, institutions of higher learning, local educational agencies, childcare centers, health and human services, employment and job training centers, boards, and other agencies to assess needs, enhance program resources, and improve services to service users (21.1).

- Collaborates with other health and human services organizations to better serve clients in ways that work toward the enhancement of client well-being and the achievement of the organizational mission (21.2).

- Identifies opportunities for partnerships, acquisitions and mergers, where applicable, which promote the achievement of the organizational mission and the well-being of clients served (21.3).

- Effectively manages policy advocacy coalitions dedicated to issues of social justice and client well-being (21.4).

CSWE Competency 3—Advance Human Rights and Social, Economic, and Environmental Justice

- 3.2 Engage in practices that advance social, economic, and environmental justice.

CSWE Competency 5—Engage in Policy Practice
Social workers

- 5.1 Identify social policy at the local, state, and federal levels that impacts well-being, service delivery, and access to social services.

CSWE Competency 8—Intervene With Individuals, Families, Groups, Organizations, and Communities
Social workers

- 8.3 Use interprofessional collaboration as appropriate to achieve beneficial practice outcomes.

- 8.4 Negotiate, mediate, and advocate with and on behalf of diverse clients and constituencies.

CSWE, Council on Social Work Education.

BACKGROUND: GENERAL AND TASK ENVIRONMENTS

BOX 17.2

NETWORK FOR SOCIAL WORK MANAGEMENT COMPETENCIES AND PRACTICE BEHAVIORS 21 AND COUNCIL ON SOCIAL WORK EDUCATION PRACTICE BEHAVIORS 8

Builds relationships with complementary agencies, institutions, and community groups to enhance the delivery of services (Network for Social Work Management Competencies 21). Practice Behaviors:

- Establishes partnerships and alliances with businesses, institutions of higher learning, local educational agencies, childcare centers, health and human services, employment and job training centers, boards, and other agencies to assess needs, enhance program resources, and improve services to service users (21.1).

CSWE Competency 8—Intervene With Individuals, Families, Groups, Organizations, and Communities
  Social workers

- 8.3 Use interprofessional collaboration as appropriate to achieve beneficial practice outcomes.

- 8.4 Negotiate, mediate, and advocate with and on behalf of diverse clients and constituencies.

CSWE, Council on Social Work Education.

Box 17.2 dictates that social workers must establish partnerships and alliances within the community. A useful framework for understanding the interface between a social service agency and the community in which it operates was offered by Yeheskel Hasenfeld. Hasenfeld (1983) posited that human service organizations were influenced by, and interacted with, two important aspects of the external environment: the general environment and the task environment. This framework can also be generalized to other organizations, such as university departments.

General Environment

The general environment consists of conditions that an individual agency could not, generally, immediately change—such as demographics, economics, political factors, culture, and technology (Hasenfeld, 1983). These aspects of the general environment "define the range of opportunities, constraints and options available" to an agency. Thus, demographics will impact the extent of the social problems with which an agency must deal. Broader economic conditions may expand or constrict the resources available. The political and legal conditions present in any particular period will impact this environment as well. Prevailing cultural and value systems will make certain kinds of services acceptable and possible in some contexts; it may limit their feasibility in others. And technology, broadly defined, will impact the range of services that may be provided. The functions of an agency can also be impacted by new techniques and service delivery mechanisms that develop in the broader society.

However, as a rule, these broader external factors are not readily amenable to the agency's immediate influence. Long-term change is certainly possible, but, at any one point in time, these factors in the general environment are experienced by the individual human service agencies as a given. In interacting with this broader general environment, organizations should seek to establish a particular domain in which they can most effectively operate, the organizational domain.

Organizational Domain

Hasenfeld (1983) defined the organizational domain as "the claims that the organization stakes out for itself in terms of human problems or needs covered, population served and services rendered" (p. 60). Determining the organizational domain is the first step to defining the task environment of an organization. Thus, as agencies establish a mission they are, in effect, defining an organizational domain in which they operate. To do this, they directly interface with the task environment. As an organization attempts to define its domain, it needs to obtain resources from a constellation of entities that constitute this task environment. Thus, in order for any agency to operate, it needs to interact and collaborate with these elements.

Task Environment

The task environment, then, consists of several sectors with which a human service organization needs to interact to define its domain and fulfill its mission. These sectors include providers of fiscal resources, providers of legitimation and authority, providers of clients, providers of complementary services, consumers/recipients of an organization's services, and competing organizations.

Depending on the particular agency, providers of fiscal resources might include government, private foundations, corporations, third-party payments, and fees for service from recipients. Providers of legitimation and authority, for public agencies might include federal, state, and local legislation. These providers may include organizations, churches, accrediting bodies, and professional associations in the case of private human service organizations. Providers of clients include other organizations that may interact with an organization's clientele, or the clients themselves. Providers of complementary services consist of other agencies or organizations "whose activities are needed by an organization to assure successful client services" (Hasenfeld, 1983, p. 61). Consumers and recipients of an organization's products refer to those individuals who receive services and the social networks of which they are part. Finally, competing organizations include those entities in the same organizational domain who may vie for similar clients, resources, and so on.

It is important to note that these categories are not mutually exclusive; that is, a single organization or agency may fall into one or more of these groupings. Providers of financial resources, for example, may also perform a legitimation function in relation to a particular organization. This cross-grouping is particularly the case with public sector agencies where federal, state, and, in some cases, local governments may provide resources but are also the source of the organization's legitimate authority to operate in its organizational domain.

Universities can also be examined with regard to their task environment (see Figure 17.1). The providers of fiscal resources at public universities typically include federal and state governments, students and their families, and private foundations. Organizations providing legitimation and authority include state governments and accrediting bodies. Providers of clients, that is, students, include secondary schools and other universities, as well as self-referral by students themselves. Organizations that provide complementary services include organizations that provide internship opportunities for students. Consumers of a university's "product," that is, graduates, can include other universities if further education is being pursued, and, of course, an array of employers. In the case of the field of social work, for example, the consumers are human service organizations. Competing organizations are other universities, or perhaps educational or training programs that offer pathways to a particular occupation.

This framework, then, can be used to examine those aspects of the task environment with which an organization must interface in order to perform its functions and establish its organizational

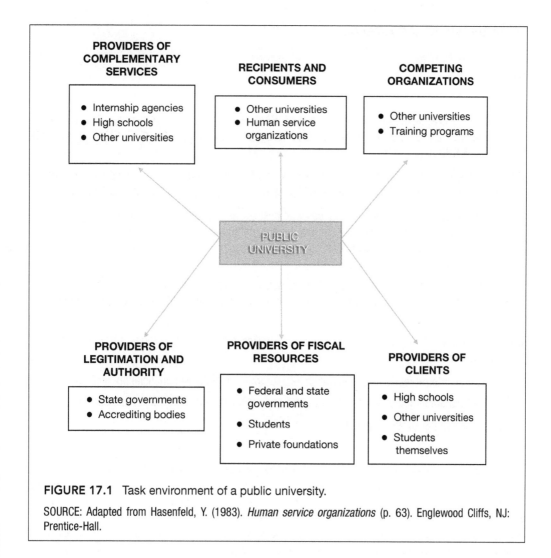

FIGURE 17.1 Task environment of a public university.

SOURCE: Adapted from Hasenfeld, Y. (1983). *Human service organizations* (p. 63). Englewood Cliffs, NJ: Prentice-Hall.

domain. It can be used to look at the aspects of this environment with which an organization may need to establish partnerships and alliances, or develop other forms of collaboration.

Another way to think of agency–community relations employs the concept of stakeholders. Sample and Austin (2013) divided the stakeholders of a nonprofit human service organization into two distinct categories—primary and secondary stakeholders. *Primary stakeholders* are groups like board members, staff, and clients who "play an active role in the governance, leadership, management, and/or service provision" (p. 688). These individuals and groups are largely internal to the agency, although some, such as agency executive directors, may also perform external functions. *Secondary stakeholders*, in contrast, consist of "those individuals and group representatives who . . . are not generally involved in organizational operations or governance and are not service recipients" (p. 688). They provide support and legitimation for agency activities in the community, and typically consist of funders, policy makers, competitors, and collaborators (Sample & Austin, 2013). Thus, many elements of the task environment described previously constitute the secondary stakeholders of human service organizations and are therefore elements an agency should consider when relating to the broader community.

Partnerships and Alliances

BOX 17.3

NETWORK FOR SOCIAL WORK MANAGEMENT COMPETENCIES AND PRACTICE BEHAVIORS 21 AND COUNCIL ON SOCIAL WORK EDUCATION PRACTICE BEHAVIORS 8

Builds relationships with complementary agencies, institutions, and community groups to enhance the delivery of services (Network for Social Work Management Competencies 21). Practice Behaviors:

- Establishes partnerships and alliances with businesses, institutions of higher learning, local educational agencies, childcare centers, health and human services, employment and job training centers, boards, and other agencies to assess needs, enhance program resources, and improve services to service users (21.1).

- Identifies opportunities for partnerships, acquisitions and mergers, where applicable, that promote the achievement of the organizational mission and the well-being of clients served (21.3).

CSWE Competency 8—Intervene With Individuals, Families, Groups, Organizations, and Communities Social workers

- 8.3 Use interprofessional collaboration as appropriate to achieve beneficial practice outcomes.

- 8.4 Negotiate, mediate, and advocate with and on behalf of diverse clients and constituencies.

CSWE, Council on Social Work Education.

Identifying opportunities for and establishing partnerships is key, as shown in Box 17.3. Perhaps the most important organizations with which it is necessary to forge partnerships and alliances are those that can provide financial resources to the agency. Without good contacts and relations with both current and potential funding organizations, it will be challenging for an agency to effectively fulfill its mission. To work with government organizations necessitates human service agencies in the public sector develop a government relations strategy. Typically, public agencies, which are part of the executive branch of government, operate a government relations office (sometimes referred to as government affairs) to interact with the legislative branch of government, which controls the funding for these agencies. Similarly, private nonprofit agencies must forge close relations with their funding organizations, both governmental and nongovernmental. Private nonprofits, ideally, will maintain robust lobbying efforts, either alone or in concert with organizations in similar service domains. Outreach to foundations and businesses is essential as these organizations can also provide funding for organizational operation.

Beyond maintaining relations with funders, agencies must consider other elements of the task environment. Sanctioning or legitimating bodies—including, where applicable, professional organizations—are other entities with which social service agencies must interact (Hardcastle, Powers, & Wenocur, 2011). Many private sector healthcare agencies, for example, are accredited by the Joint Commission on Accreditation of Healthcare Organizations. In social work education, the Council on Social Work Education performs this function. Interacting with these sanctioning bodies is a crucial function for agency leaders to perform. These bodies provide human service organizations with the authority to operate in their area of practice. In the case of universities, they provide critical legitimation for the quality of the education they offer.

Another important group of entities with which agencies must form partnerships and alliances is providers of complementary services. These are organizations that serve the same general clientele and therefore have a similar interest in promoting a more robust financing of services in this area. Similarly, in some instances, an organization may ally with competing organizations—groups which sometimes may work at cross-purposes when recruiting clients, but may have similar organizational interests in expanding the funding available to serve their populations.

Of course, those elements of an agency's task environment that control multiple resources are likely the most critical entities with which to form partnerships and alliances. In the case of a private nonprofit that contracts with a governmental agency to provide services to its client population that governmental agency might not only be a provider of financial resources and a source of legitimacy but may also be the primary provider of clients for the agency.

Some of the organizations with which agencies can establish partnerships include institutions of higher learning, local educational agencies, childcare centers, health and human services, employment and job training centers, boards, and other agencies. These alliances or partnerships can be used to assess needs, enhance program resources, and improve services to those assisted by the agency.

Collaboration With Other Health and Human Services Organizations

Box 17.4 displays the competencies/behaviors in this section.

BOX 17.4

NETWORK FOR SOCIAL WORK MANAGEMENT COMPETENCIES AND PRACTICE BEHAVIORS 3 AND 21

Possesses analytical and critical thinking skills that promote organizational growth (Network for Social Work Management Compentencies 3). Practice Behaviors:

- Conceptualizes innovative partnerships to maximize agency resources (3.10).

Builds relationships with complementary agencies, institutions, and community groups to enhance the delivery of services (Network for Social Work Management Competencies 21). Practice Behaviors:

- Collaborates with other health and human services organizations to better serve clients in ways that work toward the enhancement of client well-being and the achievement of the organizational mission (21.2).

Collaboration, then, is essential if agencies are to serve clients in ways that enhance client well-being and achieve the organizational mission. Facilitating such collaboration, however, is often not the most immediate priority of social service agencies. Often, the needs of primary stakeholders, those within the agency's immediate day-to-day environment, take priority and external relations and collaborations are accorded a lesser focus. Awareness of this tension, however, is the first step to addressing it. As Sample and Austin (2013) noted, agency leadership needs to "balance their accountability for meeting the needs and expectations of their primary stakeholders (e.g. clients and staff) while maintaining the ability to manage the pressures that secondary stakeholders (e.g. funders and policymakers) place on them" (pp. 692–693). They described a balancing process where the input of both constituencies is solicited in agency operation. An important aspect of the community-building process they described involves "taking into account how these voices differ in defining the goals and outcome objectives" of the agency (p. 693).

One approach developed to facilitate this balancing process in internal agency operations is the "maximum feasible participation" concept that has structured the design of community action programs since the 1960s (Levitan, 1969). The essence of this idea is to involve service recipients in the planning and directing of antipoverty programs. While it was a specific provision of the legislation that initiated the so-called "War on Poverty," the principles that it established about community collaboration within social agencies reverberate to this day. Within community action programs, the concept has taken the form of what is termed the "tripartite structure" of community action agency boards, the idea that one-third of the appointed members of these governing boards are selected by elected political leaders and therefore represent the "public"; a second-third are nominated by private organizations and therefore represent the larger community; and the third are selected by organizations composed of, or representing, the poor population that is to be served by these agencies. The last element, the inclusion of those served by the agencies on agency boards, was an important innovation. While not necessarily implemented in this specific manner in other human service organizations, this conscious attempt to represent different sectors of the task environment is a sound way to operationalize community input into an organization's internal operations. This kind of intra-agency community collaboration, then, is a critical aspect of achieving the mission and goals of the organization with respect to the client population served. Effective collaboration that incorporates as wide an array of internal and external actors as possible will enhance an organization's overall effectiveness.

Box 17.5 provides an example of how nonprofit organizations can collaborate with task environments.

BOX 17.5

COMPETENCY-BASED CASE: COLLABORATING WITH THE TASK ENVIRONMENT OF A PRIVATE NONPROFIT

A private nonprofit organization that provides residential and home-based services has noticed a surge in referrals from the state department seeking to place children diagnosed with neurodevelopmental disorders who are "stuck" in local EDs. Children with neurodevelopmental disorders have increasingly been seen in the ED due to acute crises, however, they are not clinically appropriate to admit to the inpatient psychiatric floor (and even if they were, there is a significant bed shortage), although the acuity of the presenting problems is preventing them from being discharged from the ED. Upon meeting with the children and their guardians, the team of residential clinicians begins to identify a pattern that many of the caregivers are extremely overwhelmed and exhausted. Some of the children attempt to elope from their family homes in the early morning hours and as a result parents/caregivers must sleep in shifts, while others are highly aggressive or self-injurious so that siblings are negatively affected and caregivers are beyond exhausted. The families and caregivers are dedicated, loving, and completely emotionally distraught. They do not want the child in the ED or in a residential placement, but they need more support than what is available to them in the community and covered by third-party payers.

The agency identified a common need, that being that family members needed planned respite and a way to divert children from the ED. There were several reasons for this common need, one being that the hospital environment is counterintuitive for youths with neurodevelopmental disorders; it is overstimulating and deviates from the predictable and structured routine they are accustomed to and in need of. Furthermore, the ED is an extremely costly holding environment. The organization, therefore, worked at the state level and collaborated with legitimating bodies and the task environment to purpose a respite program for children diagnosed with neurodevelopmental disorders. The program was designed to provide brief treatment, stabilization, and planned and emergency respite for children and families. The aim of the program was to provide more suitable services and prevent the utilization of ED services. The organization was able to collaborate with the legitimizing body and task environment to create a cost-effective program that would meet the unique needs of children and families.

ED, emergency department.

Box 17.6 provides an example of how mental health organizations can collaborate with task environments.

BOX 17.6

COMPETENCY-BASED CASE: COLLABORATING WITH THE TASK ENVIRONMENT OF A MENTAL HEALTH AGENCY

Two inpatient psychiatric units in an urban community identify a need for a step-down program to successfully discharge patients with chronic and severe mental illness. Over the past year the affiliated hospitals have recognized that patients with chronic and severe mental illnesses have had a number of repeat hospitalizations shortly after being discharged. Additionally, the hospitals recognized that the family members, with whom the patients are residing, consistently reported that they were not ready to have the patient return to the home. While the patients may no longer be meeting criteria to remain at an inpatient level of care, they were in need of transitional support, or a step-down level of care, prior to returning to their community homes. The hospitals collaborated with the state department of mental health to discuss the need. The state department of mental health then invited nonprofit organizations to work in collaboration with the department and the hospital to develop a step-down program that would help patients to transition back to the community, while decreasing the length of stays in the hospital. A program was developed where the nonprofit clinical teams would meet with the inpatient clinical teams to identify and prescreen patients, and then accept patients into the program for a brief transition period. While clients were at the step-down program, the social workers would work with both clients and family members, or other support networks, to coordinate services and resources that could enhance the likeliness of successful community living, and thus decrease recurrent hospitalizations.

Agencies can also engage in a purposeful manner with their secondary stakeholders. One way to do this is to utilize a technique Austin (2002) termed "managing out." This process involves intentionally networking with internal and external stakeholders. It involves "reaching out to people inside and outside the agency" (p. 35). Thus, collaboration can take a more interagency form and involve seeking to establish formal partnerships with secondary stakeholders.

Box 17.7 offers an example of how an organization facilitated collaboration to bring about a change directly impacting how clients were served.

BOX 17.7

COMPETENCY-BASED CASE: FACILITATING COLLABORATION TO BRING ABOUT A CHANGE

A private organization that serves youths diagnosed with autism spectrum disorder is licensed by the state division of children and families, also the organization's primary funder. However, the organization also receives referrals and provides care to youth who are served and funded under the state division of developmental services. Both state departments have service regulations that the organization must comply with. However, there are several regulations that are incongruent. One area in particular that drastically differs entails the regulations embedded in the medication certification rules. The organization, therefore, had to train staff to be medication certified in two different programs. The incongruities that

(continued)

BOX 17.7 (Continued)

existed raised significant concerns about the impact on clients. Moreover, it became apparent that the two state departments were unaware of the regulation differences that existed. Senior managers at the organization determined that it was necessary to bring the two divisions together and explain the dilemma they faced due to the incongruities. Eventually both divisions developed a plan to modify and merge the medication certification regulations so that there were no longer any discrepancies.

Identifying Opportunities for Partnerships

External partnerships are an opportunity to engage with the broader community and expand the circle of collaboration. As Austin (2002) described it, partnering is one of the key functions in "managing out," one that involves the "governance of human service organizations in a community, such as working with governing boards and inter-agency advisory boards . . . and monitoring changing community needs and building partnerships with a wide variety of institutions and individuals" (p. 44).

The development of external partnerships can be effectively facilitated through the building of relationships. Networking and relationship building can, and should, be supplemented with outreach activities such as arranging public speaking engagements with secondary stakeholder groups and other organizations in the community. In addition, other forms of public relations, focused on educating the broader community about the agency's work, should be used as well. These community and media relations have been identified as "one of the most neglected areas of human service administration" (Austin, 2002, p. 44). By engaging in planned, concerted outreach efforts, relationships with the broader community can be strengthened and expanded, and opportunities for more formal partnerships explored.

In forming partnerships with external or secondary stakeholders, various elements of the political–economic environment can be mobilized. Brager and Holloway (1978), in their classic analysis of organizational change, described these elements as "significant actors." These are "individuals or groups who are important to an organization because of their interest in its services and who have the potential or actual ability to influence the organization's direction" (p. 52). These actors include what they term "superordinates" as well as users and providers of services. Superordinates are entities "with responsibility for overseeing the organization's functioning," which are typically either public or private organizations that control funding or provide the authority under which agencies operate (Brager & Holloway, 1978, p. 52). Provider groups include unions and/or professional associations with whom agencies must contend, which can influence the practices within and outside of such organizations. Users of services are also an important constituency with which an agency must interact. These service users can be important external allies in advancing the organization's goals, but they can also impede those goals. To the greater extent that agencies are able to partner with these elements of the external environment, they will improve their effectiveness in achieving their goals. One way in which this process can be facilitated is through the establishment of various collective bodies that will allow agencies to formally ally with other groups and organizations operating in the same arena. There are several forms of this collectivism, including the use of coalitions to influence the policy environment.

Policy Advocacy Coalitions

Box 17.8 displays the competencies/behaviors in this section.

BOX 17.8

NETWORK FOR SOCIAL WORK MANAGEMENT COMPETENCIES AND PRACTICE BEHAVIORS 6 AND 21 AND COUNCIL ON SOCIAL WORK EDUCATION PRACTICE BEHAVIORS 3 AND 5

Builds relationships with complementary agencies, institutions, and community groups to enhance the delivery of services (Network for Social Work Management Competencies 21). Practice Behaviors:

- Effectively manages policy advocacy coalitions dedicated to issues of social justice and client well-being (21.4).

Develops and manages both internal and external stakeholder relationships (Network for Social Work Management Competencies 6). Practice Behaviors:

- Successfully advocates at the national, state, and local levels for the organization, its clients, and for issues promoting social justice for vulnerable populations (6.4).

CSWE Competency 3—Advance Human Rights and Social, Economic, and Environmental Justice

- 3.2 Engage in practices that advance social, economic, and environmental justice.

CSWE Competency 5—Engage in Policy Practice
  Social workers

- 5.1 Identify social policy at the local, state, and federal levels that impacts well-being, service delivery, and access to social services.

CSWE, Council on Social Work Education.

One important aspect of community collaboration concerns policy advocacy, where individuals and/or human service organizations come together to influence policy development. Policy advocacy is a critical component of the work that agencies do in the area of community collaboration. Policy advocacy refers to "practice that aims to help relatively powerless groups . . . improve their resources and opportunities" (Jansson, 2014, p. 1). Typically, policy advocacy is done through collective efforts that seek to impact policy in ways that will redistribute resources to these groups, and, in so doing, create a more economically and socially just society consistent with the values expressed in Section 6 of the National Association of Social Workers (NASW) Code of Ethics (NASW, 2008).

A useful vehicle that human service organizations may use to develop the power necessary to influence the policymaking process is the creation of a coalition. Coalitions are "complex interorganizational entities that require partners to commit to collaborative efforts toward a specific goal" (Misrahi, Rosenthal, & Ivery, 2013, p. 383). They have been described as "organizations of organizations" that are formed by members—who are, in this case, human service agencies—to augment their power and, thus, the likelihood of achieving their policy objectives. Organized, collective decision-making processes are a crucial factor in their operations, for they are intended to reflect the shared perspectives and goals of their members (Misrahi & Rosenthal, 2008). Building coalitions is a power-expansion strategy. By bringing together a wider array of organizational actors, a coalition increases the relative power they can harness to influence the decisions of policy makers. This coalescing of agencies helps increase the likelihood of achieving the goals of a policy change effort.

In thinking about an episode of policy change, it is useful to consider what Homan (2008) termed the "power–issue relationship." Generally, power and the issue should be in rough proportion to one another; that is, the issue should not be too big relative to the ability of the group to accomplish its objectives relative to the issue. The base of power commanded by those seeking change must be larger than the issue to be addressed. If it is not, two related approaches are available. The first is to partialize the issue; that is, to break the goals down into smaller elements and then pursue those components one at a time. Often, "this is done by breaking the goal down into its sequential steps" (Homan, 2008). The second approach is to expand the social change organization's base of power. Coalition building is one way to achieve this expansion.

The creation of coalitions may be informed by a conceptual framework developed by Misrahi and Rosenthal (2008), consisting of four parts (p. 473). The first element, *conditions*, concerns the political and economic context, which includes the resources available, the urgency of the issue, and the political feasibility of achieving desired change. Second, *commitment* refers to the value-based dedication of a core group of individuals who are invested in the change, as well as an understanding of the pragmatic realities faced by the organization as it pursues its social change objectives. The third element, *contributions*, consists of resources, ideology, and power. Resources include intangible sources such "as expertise, information and contacts" (p. 474). Ideology refers to the clear ideological purpose underlying the coalition's work, whereas power is the collective strength created by organizations coming together to achieve a shared purpose. The final element, *competence*, refers to the coalition's ability to mobilize its resources to achieve its identified social change goals.

Coalitions are not, however, the only method of promoting community collaboration to achieve shared goals. Additional mechanisms include networks, alliances, and task groups.

Box 17.9 describes a coalition that aims to raise awareness and act on issues that impact persons diagnosed with autism.

BOX 17.9

COMPETENCY-BASED CASE: AUTISM ACTION COALITION

An autism action coalition is comprised of a group of individuals, families, organizations, and policy makers. The aim of the coalition is to increase awareness about autism and to advocate and act on issues that will affect individuals and families living with autism. The mission of the coalition is to support and improve access to services and quality care for all individuals who are affected by ASDs.

Organizations that serve persons affected by ASD may be involved in the coalition for a number of reasons. It allows them to partner with other community providers to enhance a continuum of care for persons living with ASD. The forum can offer information about policy and practice issues, and the members can unite to advocate at the legislative office on behalf of the clients they serve. Advocacy may include recruiting family members of or individuals living with ASD to share their stories with policy makers, which can provide compelling evidence to reject or support a piece of legislation that will impact access to services.

ASD, autism spectrum disorder.

▨ Other Mechanisms for Community Collaboration

Networks are another approach to forging connections with the broader community. They involve both interpersonal and interorganizational dimensions. Networks are typically looser and less formalized relationships that rely, essentially, on contacts and exchange mechanisms. One definition suggests that networks are "social arrangements of peoples, groups, organizations, or other social units that interact and engage in exchanges to achieve their purposes" (Hardcastle et al., 2011, p. 273). They can be used to stimulate action on a particular task (Rubin & Rubin, 2008). These more fluid social connections between people and organizations, however, can still be utilized to build connections to the broader community, and, in so doing, advance the goals of the organizations with which one is associated.

Alliances, as Rubin and Rubin (2008) pointed out, are "organizations that work together on a single focused task" (p. 369). Although they are perhaps more formalized than networks, they are not as durable or long-lasting as coalitions. Because they are task-focused, they tend to disband once the goal on which they are working is accomplished.

A third mechanism is the task or working group, which brings together individual organizations to share information on a particular problem but then work separately to achieve the identified goal (Rubin & Rubin, 2008). In using this approach with community groups, the emphasis is placed on mobilizing individuals, building capacity, and organizing social change strategies (Toseland & Rivas, 2008). Mobilizing focuses on raising consciousness to promote action, where the goal is to get people to work toward community improvement. Capacity building focuses on developing the abilities and skills for group members. Social action involves intentional, participatory efforts to alleviate problems.

Box 17.10 provides several examples of networks in the human service field.

BOX 17.10

EXAMPLES OF NETWORKS

- ▨ Network for Social Work Management
- ▨ National Jobs for All Network
- ▨ NADD of Graduate Programs
- ▨ BPD
- ▨ National Association of Social Workers state chapters
- ▨ Human Services Network
- ▨ Child Welfare League of America

There are also a variety of special interest networks such as the LGBTQIA Community, Autism Speaks, Special Olympics state chapters, and many more.

BPD, Baccalaureate Program Directors; NADD, National Association of Deans and Directors; LGBTQIA, lesbian, gay, bisexual, transgender, queer or questioning, intersex, and asexual or allied.

SUMMARY

This chapter has addressed relevant community collaboration concepts such as the importance of engaging with the organizational domain and task environment with which an agency must interact. It has also presented various ways in which agencies can interface with and influence elements of the task environment by forming partnerships, networks and collaboratives.

The importance of using coalition building as a strategy of policy change has been emphasized. If appropriately implemented, these tools will enable organizations to better engage with the broader communities within which they are embedded, and through doing this, more effectively achieve their organizational goals.

Whatever community collaboration strategies or approaches are utilized to achieve organizational goals, they are an important facet of agency leadership with which social work practitioners must be familiar. Ultimately, the attainment of greater competency in community outreach and collaboration strategies, such as those described in this chapter, will enable agency leaders to improve the delivery of social welfare services to the populations they serve.

ACTIVITIES

1. Describe an agency's task environment (use your place of employment, internship, or some other agency). Describe three ways of improving relationships with this agency's task environment.

2. List the primary and secondary stakeholders of your organization. How does this knowledge enable agency leaders to better understand and interact with internal and external agency constituencies?

3. Discuss the process of "managing out" identified by Austin. How can this process be used to build networks which will strengthen the organization?

4. How can the formation of a coalition allow an organization to more effectively address an imbalance in a power–issue relationship?

REFERENCES

Austin, M. J. (2002). *Managing out: The community practice dimensions of effective agency management. Journal of Community Practice, 10*(4), 33–48. doi:10.1300/J125v10n04_03

Brager, G., & Holloway, S. (1978). *Changing human service organizations: Politics and practice.* New York: Free Press.

Hardcastle, D., Powers, P., & Wenocur, S. (2011). *Community practice: Theories and skills for social workers* (3rd ed.). New York, NY: Oxford University Press.

Hasenfeld, Y. (1983). *Human service organizations.* Englewood Cliffs, NJ: Prentice-Hall.

Homan, M. S. (2008). *Promoting community change: Making it happen in the real world* (4th ed.). Belmont, CA: Brooks-Cole.

Jansson, B. (2014). *Becoming an effective policy advocate: From policy practice to social justice* (7th ed.). Belmont, CA: Brooks-Cole.

Levitan, S. A. (1969). *The great society's poor law: A new approach to poverty.* Baltimore, MD: Johns Hopkins University Press.

Misrahi, T., & Rosenthal, B. B. (2008). Complexities of coalition building: Leaders' successes, strategies, struggles and solutions. In J. Rothman (Ed.), *Strategies of community intervention* (7th ed.). Peosta, IA: Eddie Bowers.

Misrahi, T., Rosenthal, B. B., & Ivery, J. (2013). Coalitions, collaborations and partnerships: Inter-organizational approaches to social change. In M. Weil, M. Reisch, & M. L. Ohmer (Eds.), *The handbook of community practice* (2nd ed.). Thousand Oaks, CA: Sage.

National Association of Social Workers. (2008). *Code of ethics of the National Association of Social Workers.* Washington, DC: Author.

Rubin, H. J., & Rubin, I. S. (2008). Community organizing and development (4th ed.). Boston, MA: Pearson Education, Inc.

Sample, M., & Austin, M. J. (2013). The role of human service nonprofits in promoting community building. In M. Weil, M. Reisch, & M. L. Ohmer (Eds.), *The handbook of community practice* (2nd ed.). Thousand Oaks, CA: Sage.

Toseland, R., & Rivas, R. (2008). Task groups: specialized methods. In J. Rothman (Ed.), *Strategies of community intervention* (7th ed.). Peosta, IA: Eddie Bowers.

PART 5

SUPPLEMENTAL MATERIAL

CHAPTER 18

BOOK OUTLINE BY PARTS AND DOMAINS FROM THE NSWM AND THE CSWE COMPETENCIES AND PRACTICE BEHAVIORS BY CHAPTERS

Part 1: Executive Leadership in Social Work

This part of the book provides information on leadership and management theory and practices with the intent of developing effective leaders in social work, social work higher education, and human service organizations. Readers are provided the opportunity to both learn about different leadership and management styles, including their own style, and then to practice specific leadership and management skills. In addition, readers will learn about promoting organizational vision, employing effective cross-cultural and multigenerational practices, facilitating innovative changes, advocating for social justice, using effective communication skills and best time management practices, making meetings productive, using problem-solving and decision-making techniques, managing the organizational functions, developing and motivating staff, and promoting lifelong learning practices.

DOMAIN: EXECUTIVE LEADERSHIP

- Interpersonal skills (Competency 2)
- Analytical and critical thinking skills (Competency 3)
- Professional behavior (Competency 4)
- Cross-cultural understanding (Competency 5)
- Maintains stakeholder relationships (Competency 6)
- Facilitates innovative changes (Competency 7)
- Advocates for social justice (Competency 8)
- Communication skills (Competency 9)

- **Decision making (Competency10)**
- **Promotes lifelong learning practices (Competency 11)**

Chapter 1: Leadership and Management Theory in Social Work

Competencies and Practice Behaviors Addressed in This Chapter
Possesses interpersonal skills that support viability and positive functioning of the organization (Network for Social Work Management Competencies 2). Practice Behaviors:

- Demonstrates the ability to assume different leadership styles as appropriate to the situation (2.3).
- Possesses strong skills in emotional intelligence, self-awareness, self-mastery, and so on (2.4).
- Is able to inspire confidence in others and form positive relationships easily (2.5).
- Is able to inspire confidence in others, both internally and externally (2.6).
- Demonstrates commitment to the work of the agency (2.7).
- Demonstrates and communicates deep knowledge about the work of the agency, using current performance data to discuss successes and challenges (2.8).

Advocates for public policy change and social justice at national, state, and local levels (Network for Social Work Management Competencies 8). Practice Behaviors:

- Strategically disseminates information about unmet needs and program accomplishments (8.1).
- Participates in professional organizations and industry groups that advocate for client social justice, equity, and fairness (8.2).

Council on Social Work Education (CSWE) Competency 1—Demonstrate Ethical and Professional Behavior

- 1.2 Use reflection and self-regulation to manage personal values and maintain professionalism in practice situations.

CSWE Competency 2—Engage Diversity and Difference in Practice

- 2.1 Apply and communicate understanding of the importance of diversity and difference in shaping life experiences in practice at the micro-, mezzo-, and macroevels.
- 2.2 Present themselves as learners and engage clients and constituencies as experts of their own experiences.
- 2.3 Apply self-awareness and self-regulation to manage the influence of personal biases and values in working with diverse clients and constituencies.

CSWE Competency 6—Engage With Individuals, Groups, Organizations, and Communities

- 6.1 Apply knowledge of human behavior and the social environment, person-in-environment, and other multidisciplinary theoretical frameworks to engage with clients and constituencies.
- 6.2 Use empathy, reflection, and interpersonal skills to effectively engage diverse clients and constituencies.

Chapter 2: Best Leadership and Management Practices in Social Work

Competencies and Practice Behaviors Addressed in This Chapter
Possesses analytical and critical thinking skills that promote organizational growth (Network for Social Work Management Competencies 3). Practice Behaviors:

- Manages ambiguous and complex organizational situations (3.7).

Advocates for public policy change and social justice at national, state, and local levels (Network for Social Work Management Competencies 8). Practice Behaviors:

- Advocates for an organizational culture that recognizes and rewards professionalism, quality customer service; employee engagement and empowerment, programs, and policies that further social justice; and efforts to achieve diversity in customers, employees, and ideas (8.6).

Models appropriate professional behavior and encourages other staff members to act in a professional manner (Network for Social Work Management Competencies 4). Practice Behaviors:

- Engages in and promotes ethical conduct (4.1).
- Protects the integrity and reputation of the organization (4.2).
- Creates and supports an organizational culture that values professionalism, service, and ethical conduct (4.3)
- Displays the ability to carry on effectively in the face of adversity, ambiguity, uncertainty, and anxiety (4.5).
- Demonstrates the ability not to be "consumed" by executive responsibilities and helps others to achieve the balance and maintain a sense of humor and perspective (4.7).

Initiates and facilitates innovate change processes (Network for Social Work Management Competencies 7). Practice Behaviors:

- Remains current on trends and identifies shifts that require an innovative response (7.1).
- Presents innovations to appropriate decision makers and stakeholders and makes decisions that are aligned with their feedback (7.2).
- Assists staff with implementing positive change and supports risk taking (7.3).
- Supports innovative practices to improve program-related issues and services (7.4).

CSWE Competency 1—Demonstrate Ethical and Professional Behavior

- 1.2 Use reflection and self-regulation to manage personal values and maintain professionalism in practice situations.
- 1.3 Demonstrate professional demeanor in behavior; appearance; and oral, written, and electronic communication.

CSWE Competency 2—Engage Diversity and Difference in Practice

- 2.1 Apply and communicate understanding of the importance of diversity and difference in shaping life experiences in practice at the micro-, mezzo-, and macrolevels.
- 2.2 Present themselves as learners and engage clients and constituencies as experts of their own experiences.

      2.3 Apply self-awareness and self-regulation to manage the influence of personal biases and values in working with diverse clients and constituencies.

CSWE Competency 6—Engage With Individuals, Families, Groups, Organizations, and Communities

      6.2 Use empathy, reflection, and interpersonal skills to effectively engage diverse clients and constituencies.

Chapter 3: Effective Communication and Marketing the Organization for Social Workers

Competencies and Practice Behaviors Addressed in This Chapter
Develops and manages both internal and external stakeholder relationships (Network for Social Work Management Competencies 6). Practice Behaviors:

      Communicates effectively to multiple constituencies, through various means and media, the mission, vision, and values of the organization along with organizational programs, policies, and performance so as to promote organizational transparency and enhance support and understanding from internal and external constituencies (6.2).

Advocates for public policy change and social justice at national, state and local levels (Network for Social Work Management Competencies 8). Practice Behaviors:

      When appropriate and in line with organizational mission, promotes their organization as a well-recognized advocate on public policy issues (8.4).

Demonstrates effective interpersonal and communication skills (Network for Social Work Management Competencies 9). Practice Behaviors:

      Is able to articulate the mission and vision of the organization both orally and in writing to staff of the agency (9.1).

      Is able to articulate the mission and vision of the agency to those outside the agency to ensure understanding of the work of the organization (9.2).

      Ensures that all written and oral communication in the agency is carefully planned and articulated so that it is clear in its message and sensitive to the various audiences that receive it (9.3).

      Manages communication in conflict and crisis situations in a competent and sensitive manner (9.4).

      Engages in emotionally intelligent communications with all stakeholders (9.5).

Marketing and public relations: engages in proactive communication about the agency's products and services (Network for Social Work Management Competencies 17). Practice Behaviors:

      Consistently establishes and maintains positive external relationships with key organizational constituencies such as the media, public governance bodies, actual and potential donors, the business community, professional and service organizations, and the public at large (17.1).

      Builds and conveys to multiple constituencies an organizational brand that reflects competence, integrity, and superior client/customer and community service (17.2).

      Develops and implements a successful marketing plan that dovetails with the fundraising activities of the organization (17.3).

- Ensures that the work of the agency is featured in various public relations venues to build and maintain visibility, access, and credibility and to ensure maximum usage of program resources (17.4).

- Develops clear guidelines for managing interactions with the press to ensure client confidentiality and accurate representation of agency performance (17.5).

- Maximizes the use of electronic media to communicate the work of the organization and deepens the public's understanding of the mission (17.6).

Chapter 4: Making Meetings Productive and Working With Groups for Social Workers

Competencies and Practice Behaviors Addressed in This Chapter
Models appropriate professional behavior and encourages other staff members to act in a professional manner (Network for Social Work Management Competencies 4). Practice Behaviors:

- Demonstrates the ability not to be "consumed" by executive responsibilities and helps others to achieve the balance and maintain a sense of humor and perspective (4.7).

Manages diversity and cross-cultural understanding (Network for Social Work Management Competencies 5). Practice Behaviors:

- Seeks input from all levels of staff, listens attentively, demonstrates fairness and consistency, and conveys information fully and clearly (5.4).

- Invites different perspectives to all client-related and management discussions within the organization (5.5).

- Encourages and allows opportunities for staff to confer and present issues and problems affecting program-related services (5.6).

Demonstrates effective interpersonal and communication skills (Network for Social Work Management Competencies 9). Practice Behaviors:

- Manages communication in conflict and crisis situations in a competent and sensitive manner (9.4).

Encourages active involvement of all staff and stakeholders in decision-making processes (Network for Social Work Management Competencies 10). Practice Behaviors:

- Shows evidence of stakeholder buy-in through such means as meetings or representative groups, and program surveys to the community (10.2).

Displays the ability to work with people and institutions to achieve creative compromises and "win–win" solutions (10.6).

Chapter 5: Problem Solving and Decision Making in Social Work

Competencies and Practice Behaviors Addressed in This Chapter
Establishes, promotes, and anchors the vision, philosophy, goals, objectives, and values of the organization (Network for Social Work Management Competencies 1). Practice Behaviors:

- Demonstrates the manner in which the vision, philosophy, and values are applied in making organizational decisions (1.6).

Possess analytical and critical thinking skills that promote organizational growth (Network for Social Work Management Competencies 3). Practice Behaviors:

- Understands and makes use of historical and current data to inform decision making about the agency (3.4).
- Demonstrates strong critical-thinking and problem-solving skills (3.6).

Initiates and facilitates innovative change processes (Network for Social Work Management Competencies 7). Practice Behaviors:

- Presents innovations to appropriate decision makers and stakeholders and makes decisions that are aligned with their feedback (7.2).

Encourages active involvement of all staff and stakeholders in decision-making processes (Network for Social Work Management Competencies 10). Practice Behaviors:

- Provides opportunities for internal and external stakeholders to give feedback before significant program changes are implemented (10.1).
- Shows evidence of stakeholder buy-in through such means as meetings or representative groups, and program surveys to the community (10.2).
- Delegates authority and decision making to appropriate entities and supports their decisions (10.3).
- Uses collaborative teams and other strategies to identify outcomes, design programs, share intervention strategies, conduct assessments, analyze results, and adjust intervention processes (10.4).
- Encourages consumers and underrepresented stakeholders to actively participate in decision-making processes (10.5).
- Displays the ability to work with people and institutions to achieve creative compromises and "win–win" solutions (10.6).

CSWE Competency 1—Demonstrate Ethical and Professional Behavior

Social workers

- 1.1 Make ethical decisions by applying the standards of the National Association of Social Workers (NASW) Code of Ethics, relevant laws and regulations, models for ethical decision making, ethical conduct of research, and additional codes of ethics as appropriate to context.

Chapter 6: Developing and Motivating Staff in Social Work

Competencies and Practice Behaviors Addressed in This Chapter
Possesses interpersonal skills that support viability and positive functioning of the organization (Network for Social Work Management Competencies 2). Practice Behaviors:

- Recognizes the value of optimizing the human potential of staff and ensures that the organization develops healthy and productive practices that develop staff in all ways (2.9).
- Demonstrates the ability to assemble a leadership team of individuals whose skills and abilities supplement one's own and to be a "team player" (2.10).

Models appropriate professional behavior and encourages other staff members to act in a professional manner (Network for Social Work Management Competencies 4). Practice Behaviors:

- Encourages staff to become involved in the identification and planning of their own professional development (4.4).

- Encourages staff to engage in a variety of activities including inquiry research, workshops, institutes, and observation/feedback (e.g., peer coaching and mentoring) (4.6).

Manages diversity and cross-cultural understanding (Network for Social Work Management Competencies 5). Practice Behaviors:

- Provides opportunities for staff to learn about different groups to enhance their practice, and encourages open discussion about issues to promote sensitivity (5.2).

- Seeks to employ a diverse workforce to align with clients served by the organization (5.3).

Plans, promotes, and models lifelong learning practices (Network for Social Work Management Competencies 11). Practice Behaviors:

- Positions the organization as a "learning organization," providing ongoing opportunities for all staff to receive professional development to assure quality service delivery (11.1).

- Ensures that the organization offers competent and regular supervision to staff at all levels of the organization (11.2).

- Whenever possible, offers staff an opportunity to learn from experts, as well as make presentations themselves, at outside conferences and meetings (11.6).

- Whenever possible, allows staff to take classes or work on advanced degrees with support of the agency. If agency funds are not available, flexibility in scheduling or other nonmonetary support should be offered to support learning (11.7).

CSWE Competency 6—Engage With Individuals, Families, Groups, Organizations, and Communities

- 6.2 Use empathy, reflection, and interpersonal skills to effectively engage diverse clients and constituencies.

Chapter 7: Professional Development in Leadership and Management in Social Work

Competencies and Practice Behaviors Addressed in This Chapter
Plans, promotes, and models lifelong learning practices (Network for Social Work Management Competencies 11). Practice Behaviors:

- Assumes a mentorship role for less experienced managers (11.3).

- Keeps up-to-date with research on instructional practices, management, and leadership, as well as on effective practices in professional development, and shares those practices with staff (11.4).

- Engages in a variety of activities to foster the manager's own learning, such as participating in collegial networking and subscribing to journals and LISTSERVs (11.5).

- Demonstrates self-confidence in leading the organization, capitalizing on his or her own strengths and compensating for his or her own limitations (11.8).

Chapter 8: Managing the Organizational Functions for Social Workers

Competencies and Practice Behaviors Addressed in This Chapter

Possesses interpersonal skills that support viability and positive functioning of the organization (Network for Social Work Management Competencies 2). Practice Behaviors:

- Establishes and maintains an organizational culture that recognizes and rewards professionalism, quality customer service, employee engagement and empowerment, and programs and services that further social justice (2.1).
- Inspires the workforce to move beyond cynicism and complacency, and perform and produce in a superior manner (2.2).

Possesses analytical and critical thinking skills that promote organizational growth (Network for Social Work Management Competencies 3). Practice Behaviors:

- Demonstrates a working knowledge of budget and finance, human resources, communication and marketing, applications of information technology, fundraising, and external relations; and an understanding or "feel" for the core work of the organization (3.1).
- Demonstrates an entrepreneurial spirit and attitude (3.2).
- Demonstrates strong skills in turning around dysfunctional organizations (3.5).

Models appropriate professional behavior and encourages other staff members to act in a professional manner (Network for Social Work Management Competencies 4).

- Engages in and promotes ethical conduct (4.1).
- Protects the integrity and reputation of the organization (4.2).
- Creates and supports an organizational culture that values professionalism, service, and ethical conduct (4.3).

Manages diversity and cross-cultural understanding (Network for Social Work Management Competencies 5). Practice Behaviors:

- Publicly acknowledges the diversity of the staff and clients and creates a climate that celebrates the differences (5.1).
- Seeks input from all levels of staff, listens attentively, demonstrates fairness and consistency, and conveys information fully and clearly (5.4).
- Invites different perspectives to all client-related and management discussions within the organization (5.5).
- Encourages and allows opportunities for staff to confer and present issues and problems affecting program-related services (5.6).
- Takes steps necessary to assure that all services provided by the organization are culturally competent (5.7).

Develops and manages both internal and external stakeholder relationships (Network for Social Work Management Competencies 6). Practice Behaviors:

- Consistently and effectively motivates governance body members, employees, volunteers, clients, and other key constituencies to work toward achieving the organizational mission (6.1).

Part 2: Resource Management Practices in Social Work

This part of the book covers how to effectively manage human resources, the budget and other financial resources, and information technology and social media. In addition, organizational accountability is presented including transparency, governance, and fiduciary responsibility.

DOMAIN: RESOURCE MANAGEMENT

- Effectively manages human resources (Competency 12)
- Effectively manages and oversees the budget and other financial resources (Competency 13)
- Ensures transparency, protection, and accountability (Competency 14)
- Manages all aspects of information technology (Competency 15)

Chapter 9: Accountability in Social Work

Competencies and Practice Behaviors Addressed in This Chapter:
Establishes and maintains a system of internal controls to ensure transparency, protection, and accountability for the use of organizational resources (Network for Social Work Management Competencies 14). Practice Behaviors:

- Prepares and manages organizational budgets in a manner that maximizes utilization of available funds for client service and complies with requirements of funders (14.1).
- Develops and implements a system of internal controls that adequately safeguards the resources of the organization (14.2).
- Demonstrates effective actions to protect the organization and its employees from liability by both managing and ensuring risks incurred within the scope of discharging established responsibilities (14.3).
- Assures the maintenance of financial records that comply with generally accepted accounting standards (14.4).
- Assures the appropriate safety, maintenance, protection, and utilization of other organizational resources, such as facilities and equipment (14.5).
- Helps design and manage a process of succession planning to assure the organizational continuity of executive, professional, and service leadership (14.6).
- Establishes strong systems of accountability for revenues received from various sources (14.7).

Advocates for public policy change and social justice at national, state, and local levels (Network for Social Work Management Competencies 8). Practice Behaviors:

- Challenges broad regulatory expectations and advocates for efficient and well-tailored policies with potential to impact clients' welfare (8.5).

Manages risk and legal affairs (Network for Social Work Management Competencies 19). Practice Behaviors:

- Protects the agency from undue risk by ensuring that appropriate policies and procedures exist in all areas of operation (19.1).

- Establishes systems of monitoring all areas of the organization where there may be potential risk (e.g., client services, record keeping, accounting, purchasing) (19.2).
- Ensures adherence to all laws, regulations, contracts, and legal agreements (19.3).

CSWE Competency 5—Engage in Policy Practice

Social workers

- 5.2 Assess how social welfare and economic policies impact the delivery of and access to social services.
- 5.3 Apply critical thinking to analyze, formulate, and advocate for policies that advance human rights and social, economic, and environmental justice.

CSWE Competency 8—Intervene With Individuals, Families, Groups, Organizations, and Communities

Social workers

- 8.5 Facilitate effective transitions and endings that advance mutually agreed-on goals..

Chapter 10: Human Resource Functions in a Social Work Environment

Competencies and Practice Behaviors Addressed in This Chapter
Manages diversity and cross-cultural understanding (Network for Social Work Management Competencies 5). Practice Behaviors:

- Seeks to employ a diverse workforce to align with clients served by the organization (5.3).

Effectively manages human resources (Network for Social Work Management Competencies 12). Practice Behaviors:

- Designs and manages the workplace to ensure a positive and supportive culture and climate for staff and clients (12.1).
- Designs and manages employee relations policies and practices that are fair, adhere to law, and are implemented in a consistent manner (12.2).
- Supervises recruitment, hiring, training, performance assessment, and promotion/termination based on established criteria (12.3).
- Creates, maintains, and fosters a discrimination- and harassment-free work environment for employees, clients, and general public (12.4).
- Successfully recruits and retains a diversity of employees to reflect the communities and constituencies served by the organization (12.5).
- In settings with Civil Service and Unions, works within existing systems to ensure that the most qualified employees are selected to carry out agency responsibilities (12.6).

Chapter 11: Supervising Staff in a Social Work Environment

Competencies and Practice Behaviors Addressed in This Chapter
Plans, promotes, and models lifelong learning practices (Network for Social Work Management Competencies 11). Practice Behaviors:

- Ensures that the organization offers competent and regular supervision to staff at all levels of the organization (11.2).

Effectively manages human resources (Network for Social Work Management Competencies 12). Practice Behaviors:

- Designs and manages the workplace to ensure a positive and supportive culture and climate for staff and clients (12.1).

- Designs and manages employee relations policies and practices that are fair, adhere to law, and are implemented in a consistent manner (12.2).

- Supervises recruitment, hiring, training, performance assessment, and promotion/termination based on established criteria (12.3).

Demonstrates effective interpersonal and communication skills (Network for Social Work Management Competencies 9). Practice Behaviors:

- Manages communication in conflict and crisis situations in a competent and sensitive manner (9.4).

CSWE Competency 1—Demonstrate Ethical and Professional Behavior

- 1.5 Use supervision and consultation to guide professional judgment and behavior.

Chapter 12: Management Information Systems and Managing Technology for Social Work Environments

Competencies and Practice Behaviors Addressed in This Chapter
Manages all aspects of information technology (Network for Social Work Management Competencies 15). Practice Behaviors:

- Identifies and utilizes technology resources to enhance the organization's process (15.1).

- Uses resources to promote the effective use of technology for clients and staff (15.2).

- Remains current with developments in technology and upgrades the organization accordingly (15.3).

- Encourages adaptation of technology for service tracking and for other purposes that enhance efficiency and quality (15.4).

CSWE Competency 1—Demonstrate Ethical and Professional Behavior

- 1.4 Use technology ethically and appropriately to facilitate practice outcomes.

CSWE Competency 4—Engage in Practice-informed Research and Research-informed Practice

Social workers

- 4.1 Use practice experience and theory to inform scientific inquiry and research.

CSWE Competency 7—Assess Individuals, Families, Groups, Organizations, and Communities

Social workers

- 7.1 Collect and organize data, and apply critical thinking to interpret information from clients and constituencies.

CSWE Competency 8—Intervene With Individuals, Families, Groups, Organizations, and Communities

Social workers

- 8.1 Critically choose and implement interventions to achieve practice goals and enhance capacities of clients and constituencies.

■ *Chapter 13: Financial Management in Social Work*

Competencies and Practice Behaviors Addressed in This Chapter
Possesses analytical and critical thinking skills that promote organizational growth (Network for Social Work Management Competencies 3). Practice Behaviors:

■ Makes creative use of agency resources to serve the needs of diverse clients (3.3).

Effectively manages and oversees the budget and other financial resources to support the organization's/program's mission and goals and to foster continuous program improvement and accountability (Network for Social Work Management Competencies 13). Practice Behaviors:

■ Manages utilization of resources to ensure that they are in line with the organization's mission and goals (13.1).

■ Ensures that expenditures are allowed and appropriate and that allocated funds are available throughout the fiscal year (13.2).

■ Monitors revenue and expenditures at regular intervals to ensure that budget assumptions are consistent with anticipated income and expenses (13.3).

■ Ensures that financial activities are consistent with organizational policies and are sufficiently documented for audit (13.4).

■ Oversees equitable allocation of funds based on such indicators as visits, outcomes, and historical precedent (13.5).

Monitors expenditures to ensure that operating units have sufficient resources to offer quality services, using dashboards and other visual tools to link expenditures to outcomes (13.6).

Part 3: Strategic Management and Administrative Skills for Organizational Growth and Success in a Social Work Environment

This part of the book provides the knowledge base and theory from which to develop advanced administrative skills that are critical to organizational growth and survival. These skills include fundraising, marketing and public relations, designing and developing effective programs, managing risk and legal affairs, and strategic planning and leadership challenges in social work education.

DOMAIN: STRATEGIC MANAGEMENT

■ **Promotes vision, goals, and objectives (Competency 1)**

■ **Fundraisers (Competency 16)**

■ **Marketing and public relations (Competency 17)**

■ **Designs and develops effective programs (Competency 18)**

■ **Manages risk and legal affairs (Competency 19)**

■ **Ensures strategic planning (Competency 20)**

Chapter 14: Strategic Planning in a Social Work Environment

Competencies and Practice Behaviors Addressed in This Chapter

Ensures strategic planning (Network for Social Work Management Competencies 20). Practice Behaviors:

- Understands the organization's relationship to its environment, the emerging internal and external forces affecting the organization, and the ability to position the organization within that environment for future and current success (20.1).

- Directs staff effectively in identifying areas of future growth and development in all areas of agency operations to be used in a strategic planning process (20.2).

- Demonstrates competence in the ability to orchestrate and support an inclusive and organization-wide strategic planning process designed to position the organization for success in achieving its mission in the mid- and long-term future (20.3).

- Constructs or directs the construction of an adequate business plan that details the pathway, timelines, and accountability for the accomplishment of identified strategic objectives (20.4).

Establishes, promotes, and anchors the vision, philosophy, goals, objectives, and values of the organization (Network for Social Work Management Competencies 1). Practice Behaviors:

- Creates, communicates, and anchors a vision for the organization (1.1).

- Works to ensure that all programs align with the overall organizational mission (1.2).

- Reviews the mission periodically to determine its relevance to client and community needs (1.3).

- Works closely with management staff to establish benchmarks to show alignment with vision, mission, philosophy, and goals (1.4).

- Identifies potential organizational drift from vision, mission, philosophy, and goals (1.5).

Possesses analytical and critical thinking skills that promote organizational growth (Network for Social Work Management Competencies 3). Practice Behaviors:

- Monitors economic and political trends, shifts in trends, values, and mores (3.8).

- Displays keen skills in strategic thinking (3.9).

Develops and manages both internal and external stakeholder relationships (Network for Social Work Management Competencies 6). Practice Behaviors:

- Plans, thinks, and acts strategically in concert with key stakeholders to position, evolve, and change the organization to assure success in the current and future environments (6.3).

CSWE Competency 5—Engage in Policy Practice

Social workers

- 5.2 Assess how social welfare and economic policies impact the delivery of and access to social services.

CSWE Competency 6—Engage With Individuals, Families, Groups, Organizations, and Communities

Social workers

- 6.1 Apply knowledge of human behavior and the social environment, person-in-environment, and other multidisciplinary theoretical frameworks to engage with clients and constituencies.

CSWE Competency 7—Assess Individuals, Families, Groups, Organizations, and Communities

Social workers

- 7.4 Select appropriate intervention strategies based on the assessment, research knowledge, and values and preferences of clients and constituencies.

CSWE Competency 8—Intervene With Individuals, Families, Groups, Organizations, and Communities

Social workers

- 8.1 Critically choose and implement interventions to achieve practice goals and enhance capacities of clients and constituencies
- 8.5 Facilitate effective transitions and endings that advance mutually agreed-on goals.

CSWE Competency 9—Evaluate Practice With Individuals, Families, Groups, Organizations, and Communities

Social workers

- 9.1 Select and use appropriate methods for evaluation of outcomes.
- 9.3 Critically analyze, monitor, and evaluate intervention and program processes and outcomes.

Chapter 15: Designing and Assessing Programs for Social Work

Competencies and Practice Behaviors Addressed in This Chapter
Designs and develops effective programs (Network for Social Work Management Competencies 18). Practice Behaviors:

- Guides program staff in designing and implementing interventions consistent with the mission of the organization that respect all types of clients from diverse circumstances (18.1).
- Supports and assists staff in planning evidence-based programs, based on performance standards, assessments, client data, research on effective practice, community, and user needs, demographics, resources, and economic and technological trends (18.2).
- Develops and enforces procedures for collecting, reporting, and analyzing data to measure program quality and achievement of defined outcomes (18.3).

CSWE Competency 4—Engage in Practice-informed Research and Research-informed Practice

Social workers

- 4.2 Apply critical thinking to engage in analysis of quantitative and qualitative research methods and research findings.
- 4.3 Use and translate research evidence to inform and improve practice, policy, and service delivery.

CSWE Competency 7—Assess Individuals, Families, Groups, Organizations, and Communities

Social workers

- 7.2 Apply knowledge of human behavior and the social environment, person-in-environment, and other multidisciplinary theoretical frameworks in the analysis of assessment data from clients and constituencies.

- 7.3 Develop mutually agreed-on intervention goals and objectives based on the critical assessment of strengths, needs, and challenges within clients and constituencies.

- 7.4 Select appropriate intervention strategies based on the assessment, research knowledge, and values and preferences of clients and constituencies.

CSWE Competency 8—Intervene With Individuals, Families, Groups, Organizations, and Communities

Social workers

- 8.2 Apply knowledge of human behavior and the social environment, person-in-environment, and other multidisciplinary theoretical frameworks in interventions with clients and constituencies.

CSWE Competency 9—Evaluate Practice With Individuals, Families, Groups, Organizations, and Communities

Social workers

- 9.2 Apply knowledge of human behavior and the social environment, person-in-environment, and other multidisciplinary theoretical frameworks in the evaluation of outcomes.

Chapter 16: Strategic Resource Development in a Social Work Environment

Competencies and Practice Behaviors Addressed in This Chapter
Fundraising: identifies and applies for new and recurring funding while ensuring accountability with existing funding systems (Network for Social Work Management Competencies 16). Practice Behaviors

- Creates a culture of philanthropy that engages the organization's governing body, employees, volunteers, and actual and potential donors (16.1).

- Works closely with public and private funding sources to ensure positive relations and confidence in the organization (16.2).

- Develops and implements a successful fundraising plan which includes a diverse funding mix and utilizes a strong marketing focus (16.3).

- Establishes strong systems of stewardship with donors/funders (16.4).

- Seeks partnerships with other programs funded under federal/state/local authorities and other interest groups (16.5).

- Maintains active awareness of and pursues potential grant and funding sources in local, regional, or national community (16.6).

- Demonstrates innovative approaches to resources development at all levels of the organization (16.7).

Part 4: COMMUNITY COLLABORATION

This part of the book covers the final domain from the Network for Social Work Management: community collaboration. Topics include building relationships to enhance program resources and service delivery, improving the likelihood of achieving organizational mission and better client well-being, and how to effectively manage policy advocacy coalitions to improve organizational function and client well-being.

DOMAIN: COMMUNITY COLLABORATION

- **Builds relationships with complementary agencies, institutions, and community groups and is an amalgamation of all the skills needed in social work management that are employed at the senior level.**

Chapter 17: Community Collaboration for Social Workers

Competencies and Practice Behaviors Addressed in This Chapter
Possesses analytical and critical thinking skills that promote organizational growth (Network for Social Work Management Competencies 3). Practice Behaviors:

- Conceptualizes innovative partnerships to maximize agency resources (3.10).

Develops and manages both internal and external stakeholder relationships (Network for Social Work Management Competencies 6). Practice Behaviors:

- Successfully advocates at the national, state, and local levels for the organization, its clients, and for issues promoting social justice for vulnerable populations (6.4).

Builds relationships with complementary agencies, institutions, and community groups to enhance the delivery of services (Network for Social Work Management Competencies 21). Practice Behaviors:

- Establishes partnerships and alliances with businesses, institutions of higher learning, local educational agencies, childcare centers, health and human services, employment and job training centers, boards, and other agencies to assess needs, enhance program resources, and improve services to service users (21.1).
- Collaborates with other health and human services organizations to better serve clients in ways that work toward the enhancement of client well-being and the achievement of the organizational mission (21.2).
- Identifies opportunities for partnerships, acquisitions and mergers, where applicable, that promote the achievement of the organizational mission and the well-being of clients served (21.3).
- Effectively manages policy advocacy coalitions dedicated to issues of social justice and client well-being (21.4).

CSWE Competency 3—Advance Human Rights and Social, Economic, and Environmental Justice

- 3.2 Engage in practices that advance social, economic, and environmental justice.

CSWE Competency 5—Engage in Policy Practice

Social workers

- 5.1 Identify social policy at the local, state, and federal level that impacts well-being, service delivery, and access to social services.

CSWE Competency 8—Intervene With Individuals, Families, Groups, Organizations, and Communities

Social workers

- 8.3 Use interprofessional collaboration as appropriate to achieve beneficial practice outcomes.
- 8.4 Negotiate, mediate, and advocate with and on behalf of diverse clients and constituencies.

CHAPTER 19

THE NETWORK FOR SOCIAL WORK MANAGEMENT HUMAN SERVICES MANAGEMENT COMPETENCIES AND PRACTICE BEHAVIORS

1. *ESTABLISHES, PROMOTES, AND ANCHORS THE VISION, PHILOSOPHY, GOALS, OBJECTIVES, AND VALUES OF THE ORGANIZATION*

   - Creates, communicates, and anchors a vision for the organization (1.1).

   - Works to ensure that all programs align with the overall organizational mission (1.2).

   - Reviews the mission periodically to determine its relevance to client and community needs (1.3).

   - Works closely with management staff to establish benchmarks to show alignment with vision, mission, philosophy, and goals (1.4).

   - Identifies potential organizational drift from vision, mission, philosophy, and goals (1.5).

   - Demonstrates the manner in which the vision, philosophy, and values are applied in making organizational decisions (1.6).

2. *POSSESSES INTERPERSONAL SKILLS THAT SUPPORT THE VIABILITY AND POSITIVE FUNCTIONING OF THE ORGANIZATION*

   - Establishes and maintains an organizational culture that recognizes and rewards professionalism, quality customer service, employee engagement and empowerment, and programs and services that further social justice (2.1).

   - Inspires the workforce to move beyond cynicism and complacency, and perform and produce in a superior manner (2.2).

   - Demonstrates the ability to assume different leadership styles as appropriate to the situation (2.3).

- Possesses strong skills in emotional intelligence, self-awareness, self-mastery, and so on (2.4).
- Is able to find common ground with others and form positive relationships easily (2.5).
- Is able to inspire confidence in others, both internally and externally (2.6).
- Demonstrates commitment to the work of the agency (2.7).
- Demonstrates and communicates deep knowledge about the work of the agency, using current performance data to discuss successes and challenges (2.8).
- Recognizes the value of optimizing the human potential of staff and ensures that the organization develops healthy and productive practices that develop staff in all ways (2.9).
- Demonstrates the ability to assemble a leadership team of individuals whose skills and abilities supplement one's own and to be a "team player" (2.10).

3. *POSSESSES ANALYTICAL AND CRITICAL THINKING SKILLS THAT PROMOTE ORGANIZATIONAL GROWTH*

- Demonstrates a working knowledge of budget and finance, human resources, communication and marketing, applications of information technology, fundraising, and external relations; and an understanding or "feel" for the core work of the organization (3.1).
- Demonstrates an entrepreneurial spirit and attitude (3.2).
- Makes creative use of agency resources to serve the needs of diverse clients (3.3).
- Understands and makes use of historical and current data to inform decision making about the agency (3.4).
- Demonstrates strong skills in turning around dysfunctional organizations (3.5).
- Demonstrates strong critical-thinking and problem-solving skills (3.6).
- Manages ambiguous and complex organizational situations (3.7).
- Monitors economic and political trends, shifts in trends, values, and mores (3.8).
- Displays keen skills in strategic thinking (3.9).
- Conceptualizes innovative partnerships to maximize agency resources (3.10).

4. *MODELS APPROPRIATE PROFESSIONAL BEHAVIOR AND ENCOURAGES OTHER STAFF MEMBERS TO ACT IN A PROFESSIONAL MANNER*

- Engages in and promotes ethical conduct (4.1).
- Protects the integrity and reputation of the organization (4.2).
- Creates and supports an organizational culture that values professionalism, service, and ethical conduct (4.3).
- Encourages staff to become involved in the identification and planning of their own professional development (4.4).
- Displays the ability to carry on effectively in the face of adversity, ambiguity, uncertainly, and anxiety (4.5).
- Encourages staff to engage in a variety of activities including inquiry research, workshops, institutes, and observation/feedback (e.g., peer coaching and mentoring) (4.6).

     ■   Demonstrates the ability not to be "consumed" by executive responsibilities and helps others to achieve the balance and maintain a sense of humor and perspective (4.7).

5. *MANAGES DIVERSITY AND CROSS-CULTURAL UNDERSTANDING*

     ■   Publicly acknowledges the diversity of the staff and clients and creates a climate that celebrates the differences (5.1).

     ■   Provides opportunities for staff to learn about different groups to enhance their practice, and encourages open discussion about issues to promote sensitivity (5.2).

     ■   Seeks to employ a diverse workforce to align with clients served by the organization (5.3).

     ■   Seeks input from all levels of staff, listens attentively, demonstrates fairness and consistency, and conveys information fully and clearly (5.4).

     ■   Invites different perspectives to all client-related and management discussions within the organization (5.5).

     ■   Encourages and allows opportunities for staff to confer and present issues and problems affecting program-related services (5.6).

     ■   Takes steps necessary to assure that all services provided by the organization are culturally competent (5.7).

6. *DEVELOPS AND MANAGES BOTH INTERNAL AND EXTERNAL STAKEHOLDER RELATIONSHIPS*

     ■   Consistently and effectively motivates governance body members, employees, volunteers, clients, and other key constituencies to work toward achieving the organizational mission (6.1).

     ■   Communicates effectively to multiple constituencies, through various means and media, the mission, vision, and values of the organization along with organizational programs, policies, and performance so as to promote organizational transparency and enhance support and understanding from internal and external constituencies (6.2).

     ■   Plans, thinks, and acts strategically in concert with key stakeholders to position, evolve, and change the organization to assure success in the current and future environments (6.3).

     ■   Successfully advocates at the national, state, and local levels for the organization, its clients, and for issues promoting social justice for vulnerable populations (6.4).

7. *INITIATES AND FACILITATES INNOVATIVE CHANGE PROCESSES*

     ■   Remains current on trends and identifies shifts that require an innovative response (7.1).

     ■   Presents innovations to appropriate decision makers and stakeholders and makes decisions that are aligned with their feedback (7.2).

     ■   Assists staff with implementing positive change and supports risk taking (7.3).

     ■   Supports innovative practices to improve program-related issues and services (7.4).

8. *ADVOCATES FOR PUBLIC POLICY CHANGE AND SOCIAL JUSTICE AT NATIONAL, STATE, AND LOCAL LEVELS*

- Strategically disseminates information about unmet needs and program accomplishments (8.1).

- Participates in professional organizations and industry groups that advocate for client social justice, equity, and fairness (8.2).

- Engages and encourages staff and client/customers to be active advocates for social justice issues (8.3).

- When appropriate and in line with organizational mission, promotes their organization as a well-recognized advocate on public policy topics (8.4).

- Challenges broad regulatory expectations and advocates for efficient and well-tailored policies with potential to impact clients' welfare (8.5).

- Advocates for an organizational culture that recognizes and rewards professionalism; quality customer service; employee engagement and empowerment, programs, and policies that further social justice; and efforts to achieve diversity in customers, employees, and ideas (8.6).

9. *DEMONSTRATES EFFECTIVE INTERPERSONAL AND COMMUNICATION SKILLS*

- Is able to articulate the mission and vision of the organization both orally and in writing to staff of the agency (9.1).

- Is able to articulate the mission and vision of the agency to those outside the agency to ensure understanding of the work of the organization (9.2).

- Ensures that all written and oral communication in the agency is carefully planned and articulated so that it is clear in its message and sensitive to the various audiences that receive it (9.3).

- Manages communication in conflict and crisis situations in a competent and sensitive manner (9.4).

- Engages in emotionally intelligent communications with all stakeholders (9.5).

10. *ENCOURAGES ACTIVE INVOLVEMENT OF ALL STAFF AND STAKEHOLDERS IN DECISION-MAKING PROCESSES*

- Provides opportunities for internal and external stakeholders to give feedback before significant program changes are implemented (10.1).

- Shows evidence of stakeholder buy-in through such means as meetings of representative groups, and program surveys to the community (10.2).

- Delegates authority and decision making to appropriate entities and supports their decisions (10.3).

- Uses collaborative teams and other strategies to identify outcomes, design programs, share intervention strategies, conduct assessments, analyze results, and adjust intervention processes (10.4).

- Encourages consumers and underrepresented stakeholders to actively participate in decision-making processes (10.5).

- Displays the ability to work with people and institutions to achieve creative compromises and "win–win" solutions (10.6).

11.   *PLANS, PROMOTES, AND MODELS LIFELONG LEARNING PRACTICES*

- Positions the organization as a "learning organization," providing ongoing opportunities for all staff to receive professional development to assure quality service delivery (11.1).

- Ensures that the organization offers competent and regular supervision to staff at all levels of the organization (11.2).

- Assumes a mentorship role for less experienced managers (11.3).

- Keeps up-to-date with research on instructional practices, management, and leadership, as well as on effective practices in professional development, and shares those practices with staff (11.4).

- Engages in a variety of activities to foster the manager's own learning, such as participating in collegial networking and subscribing to journals and LISTSERVs(11.5).

- Whenever possible, offers staff an opportunity to learn from experts, as well as make presentations themselves, at outside conferences and meetings (11.6).

- Whenever possible, allows staff to take classes or work on advanced degrees with support of the agency. If agency funds are not available, flexibility in scheduling or other nonmonetary support should be offered to support learning (11.7).

- Demonstrates self-confidence in leading the organization, capitalizing on his or her own strengths and compensating for his or her own limitations. (11.8).

12.   *EFFECTIVELY MANAGES HUMAN RESOURCES*

- Designs and manages the workplace to ensure a positive and supportive culture and climate for staff and clients (12.1).

- Designs and manages employee relations policies and practices that are fair, adhere to law, and are implemented in a consistent manner (12.2).

- Supervises recruitment, hiring, training, performance assessment, and promotion/termination based on established criteria (12.3).

- Creates, maintains, and fosters a discrimination- and harassment-free work environment for employees, clients, and the general public (12.4).

- Successfully recruits and retains a diversity of employees to reflect the communities and constituencies served by the organization (12.5).

- In settings with Civil Service and Unions, works within existing systems to ensure that the most qualified employees are selected to carry out agency responsibilities (12.6).

13.   *EFFECTIVELY MANAGES AND OVERSEES THE BUDGET AND OTHER FINANCIAL RESOURCES TO SUPPORT THE ORGANIZATION'S/PROGRAM'S MISSION AND GOALS AND TO FOSTER CONTINUOUS PROGRAM IMPROVEMENT AND ACCOUNTABILITY*

- Manages utilization of resources to ensure that they are in line with the organization's mission and goals (13.1).

- Ensures that expenditures are allowed and appropriate and that allocated funds are available throughout the fiscal year (13.2).

- Monitors revenue and expenditures at regular intervals to ensure that budget assumptions are consistent with anticipated income and expenses (13.3).

- Ensures that financial activities are consistent with organizational policies and are sufficiently documented for audit (13.4).
- Oversees equitable allocation of funds based on such indicators as visits, outcomes, and historical precedent (13.5).
- Monitors expenditures to ensure that operating units have sufficient resources to offer quality services, using dashboards and other visual tools to link expenditures to outcomes (13.6).

14. *ESTABLISHES AND MAINTAINS A SYSTEM OF INTERNAL CONTROLS TO ENSURE TRANSPARENCY, PROTECTION, AND ACCOUNTABILITY FOR THE USE OF ORGANIZATIONAL RESOURCES*

- Prepares and manages organizational budgets in a manner that maximizes utilization of available funds for client service and complies with requirements of funders (14.1).
- Develops and implements a system of internal controls that adequately safeguards the resources of the organization (14.2).
- Demonstrates effective actions to protect the organization and its employees from liability by both managing and ensuring risks incurred within the scope of discharging established responsibilities (14.3).
- Assures the maintenance of financial records that comply with generally accepted accounting standards (14.4).
- Assures the appropriate safety, maintenance, protection, and utilization of other organizational resources, such as facilities and equipment (14.5).
- Helps design and manage a process of succession planning to assure the organizational continuity of executive, professional, and service leadership (14.6).
- Establishes strong systems of accountability for revenues received from various sources (14.7).

15. *MANAGES ALL ASPECTS OF INFORMATION TECHNOLOGY*

- Identifies and utilizes technology resources to enhance the organization's process (15.1).
- Uses resources to promote the effective use of technology for clients and staff (15.2).
- Remains current with developments in technology and upgrades the organization accordingly (15.3).
- Encourages adaptation of technology for service tracking and for other purposes that enhance efficiency and quality (15.4).

16. *FUNDRAISING: IDENTIFIES AND APPLIES FOR NEW AND RECURRING FUNDING WHILE ENSURING ACCOUNTAILITY WITH EXISTING FUNDING SYSTEMS*

- Creates a culture of philanthropy that engages the organization's governing body, employees, volunteers, and actual and potential donors (16.1).
- Works closely with public and private funding sources to ensure positive relations and confidence in the organization (16.2).
- Develops and implements a successful fundraising plan which includes a diverse funding mix and utilizes a strong marketing focus (16.3).

- Establishes strong systems of stewardship with donors/funders (16.4).

- Seeks partnerships with other programs funded under federal/state/local authorities and other interest groups (16.5).

- Maintains active awareness of and pursues potential grant and funding sources in local, regional, or national community (16.6).

- Demonstrates innovative approaches to resources development at all levels of the organization (16.7).

17. *MARKETING AND PUBLIC RELATIONS: ENGAGES IN PROACTIVE COMMUNICATION ABOUT THE AGENCY'S PRODUCTS AND SERVICES*

- Consistently establishes and maintains positive external relationships with key organizational constituencies such as the media, public governance bodies, actual and potential donors, the business community, professional and service organizations, and the public at large (17.1).

- Builds and conveys to multiple constituencies an organizational brand that reflects competence, integrity, and superior client/customer and community service (17.2).

- Develops and implements a successful marketing plan that dovetails with the fundraising activities of the organization (17.3).

- Ensures that the work of the agency is featured in various public relations venues to build and maintain visibility, access, and credibility and to ensure maximum usage of program resources (17.4).

- Develops clear guidelines for managing interactions with the press to ensure client confidentiality and accurate representation of agency performance (17.5).

- Maximizes the use of electronic media to communicate the work of the organization and deepens the public's understanding of the mission (17.6).

18. *DESIGNS AND DEVELOPS EFFECTIVE PROGRAMS*

- Guides program staff in designing and implementing interventions consistent with the mission of the organization that respect all types of clients from diverse circumstances (18.1).

- Supports and assists staff in planning evidence-based programs, based on performance standards, assessments, client data, research on effective practice, community, and user needs, demographics, resources, and economic and technological trends (18.2).

- Develops and enforces procedures for collecting, reporting, and analyzing data to measure program quality and achievement of defined outcomes (18.3).

19. *MANAGES RISK AND LEGAL AFFAIRS*

- Protects the agency from undue risk by ensuring that appropriate policies and procedures exist in all areas of operation (19.1).

- Establishes systems of monitoring all areas of the organization where there may be potential risk (e.g., client services, record keeping, accounting, purchasing) (19.2).

- Ensures adherence to all laws, regulations, contracts, and legal agreements (19.3).

20. *ENSURES STRATEGIC PLANNING*

- Understands the organization's relationship to its environment, the emerging internal and external forces affecting the organization, and the ability to position the organization within that environment for future and correct success (20.1).

- Directs staff effectively in identifying areas of future growth and development in all areas of agency operations to be used in a strategic planning process (20.2).

- Demonstrates competence in the ability to orchestrate and support an inclusive and organization-wide strategic planning process designed to position the organization for success in achieving its mission in the mid- and long-term future (20.3).

- Constructs or directs the construction of an adequate business plan that details the pathway, timelines, and accountability for the accomplishment of identified strategic objectives (20.4).

21. *BUILDS RELATIONSHIPS WITH COMPLEMENTARY AGENCIES, INSTITUTIONS, AND COMMUNITY GROUPS TO ENHANCE THE DELIVERY OF SERVICES*

- Establishes partnerships and alliances with businesses, institutions of higher learning, local educational agencies, childcare centers, health and human services, employment and job training centers, boards, and other agencies to assess needs, enhance program resources, and improve services to service users (21.1).

- Collaborates with other health and human services organizations to better serve clients in ways that work toward the enhancement of client well-being and the achievement of the organizational mission (21.2).

- Identifies opportunities for partnerships, acquisitions and mergers, where applicable, that promote the achievement of the organizational mission and the well-being of clients served (21.3).

- Effectively manages policy advocacy coalitions dedicated to issues of social justice and client well-being (21.4).

CHAPTER 20

THE COUNCIL ON SOCIAL WORK EDUCATION COMPETENCIES

Competency 1: Demonstrate Ethical and Professional Behavior

Social workers understand the value base of the profession and its ethical standards, as well as relevant laws and regulations that may impact practice at the micro-, mezzo-, and macrolevels. Social workers understand frameworks of ethical decision making and how to apply principles of critical thinking to those frameworks in practice, research, and policy arenas. Social workers recognize personal values and the distinction between personal and professional values. They also understand how their personal experiences and affective reactions influence their professional judgment and behavior. Social workers understand the profession's history, its mission, and the roles and responsibilities of the profession. Social workers also understand the role of other professions when engaged in interprofessional teams. Social workers recognize the importance of lifelong learning and are committed to continually updating their skills to ensure they are relevant and effective. Social workers also understand emerging forms of technology and the ethical use of technology in social work practice. Social workers:

    1.1   Make ethical decisions by applying the standards of the National Association of Social Workers (NASW) Code of Ethics, relevant laws and regulations, models for ethical decision making, ethical conduct of research, and additional codes of ethics as appropriate to context.

    1.2   Use reflection and self-regulation to manage personal values and maintain professionalism in practice situations.

    1.3   Demonstrate professional demeanor in behavior; appearance; and oral, written, and electronic communication.

    1.4   Use technology ethically and appropriately to facilitate practice outcomes.

    1.5   Use supervision and consultation to guide professional judgment and behavior.

SOURCE: The content of Chapter 20 used with permission from Educational Policy and Accreditation Standards for Baccalaureate and Master's Social Work Programs, Copyright © 2015 Council on Social Work Education.

Competency 2: Engage Diversity and Difference in Practice

Social workers understand how diversity and difference characterize and shape the human experience and are critical to the formation of identity. The dimensions of diversity are understood as the intersectionality of multiple factors including but not limited to age, class, color, culture, disability and ability, ethnicity, gender, gender identity and expression, immigration status, marital status, political ideology, race, religion/spirituality, sex, sexual orientation, and tribal sovereign status. Social workers understand that, as a consequence of difference, a person's life experiences may include oppression, poverty, marginalization, and alienation as well as privilege, power, and acclaim. Social workers also understand the forms and mechanisms of oppression and discrimination and recognize the extent to which a culture's structures and values, including social, economic, political, and cultural exclusions, may oppress, marginalize, alienate, or create privilege and power. Social workers:

2.1   Apply and communicate understanding of the importance of diversity and difference in shaping life experiences in practice at the micro-, mezzo-, and macrolevels.

2.2   Present themselves as learners and engage clients and constituencies as experts of their own experiences.

2.3   Apply self-awareness and self-regulation to manage the influence of personal biases and values in working with diverse clients and constituencies.

Competency 3: Advance Human Rights and Social, Economic, and Environmental Justice

Social workers understand that every person regardless of position in society has fundamental human rights such as freedom, safety, privacy, an adequate standard of living, healthcare, and education. Social workers understand the global interconnections of oppression and human rights violations, and are knowledgeable about theories of human need and social justice and strategies to promote social and economic justice and human rights. Social workers understand strategies designed to eliminate oppressive structural barriers to ensure that social goods, rights, and responsibilities are distributed equitably and that civil, political, environmental, economic, social, and cultural human rights are protected. Social workers:

3.1   Apply their understanding of social, economic, and environmental justice to advocate for human rights at the individual and system levels.

3.2   Engage in practices that advance social, economic, and environmental justice.

Competency 4: Engage in Practice-Informed Research and Research-Informed Practice

Social workers understand quantitative and qualitative research methods and their respective roles in advancing a science of social work and in evaluating their practice. Social workers know the principles of logic, scientific inquiry, and culturally informed and ethical approaches to building knowledge. Social workers understand that evidence that informs practice derives from multidisciplinary sources and multiple ways of knowing. They also understand the processes for translating research findings into effective practice. Social workers:

4.1 Use practice experience and theory to inform scientific inquiry and research.

4.2 Apply critical thinking to engage in analysis of quantitative and qualitative research methods and research findings.

4.3 Use and translate research evidence to inform and improve practice, policy, and service delivery.

Competency 5: Engage in Policy Practice

Social workers understand that human rights and social justice, as well as social welfare and services, are mediated by policy and its implementation at the federal, state, and local levels. Social workers understand the history and current structures of social policies and services, the role of policy in service delivery, and the role of practice in policy development. Social workers understand their role in policy development and implementation within their practice settings at the micro-, mezzo-, and macrolevels and they actively engage in policy practice to effect change within those settings. Social workers recognize and understand the historical, social, cultural, economic, organizational, environmental, and global influences that affect social policy. They are also knowledgeable about policy formulation, analysis, implementation, and evaluation. Social workers:

5.1 Identify social policy at the local, state, and federal levels that impact well-being, service delivery, and access to social services.

5.2 Assess how social welfare and economic policies impact the delivery of and access to social services.

5.3 Apply critical thinking to analyze, formulate, and advocate for policies that advance human rights and social, economic, and environmental justice.

Competency 6: Engage With Individuals, Families, Groups, Organizations, and Communities

Social workers understand that engagement is an ongoing component of the dynamic and inter-active process of social work practice with, and on behalf of, diverse individuals, families, groups, organizations, and communities. Social workers value the importance of human relationships. Social workers understand theories of human behavior and the social environment, and critically evaluate and apply this knowledge to facilitate engagement with clients and constituencies, including individuals, families, groups, organizations, and communities. Social workers understand strategies to engage diverse clients and constituencies to advance practice effectiveness.

Social workers understand how their personal experiences and affective reactions may impact their ability to effectively engage with diverse clients and constituencies. Social workers value principles of relationship-building and interprofessional collaboration to facilitate engagement with clients, constituencies, and other professionals as appropriate. Social workers:

6.1 Apply knowledge of human behavior and the social environment, person-in-environment, and other multidisciplinary theoretical frameworks to engage with clients and constituencies.

6.2 Use empathy, reflection, and interpersonal skills to effectively engage diverse clients and constituencies.

Competency 7: Assess Individuals, Families, Groups, Organizations, and Communities

Social workers understand that assessment is an ongoing component of the dynamic and inter-active process of social work practice with, and on behalf of, diverse individuals, families, groups, organizations, and communities. Social workers understand theories of human behavior and the social environment, and critically evaluate and apply this knowledge in the assessment of diverse clients and constituencies, including individuals, families, groups, organizations, and communities. Social workers understand methods of assessment with diverse clients and constituencies to advance practice effectiveness. Social workers recognize the implications of the larger practice context in the assessment process and value the importance of interprofessional collaboration in this process. Social workers understand how their personal experiences and affective reactions may affect their assessment and decision making. Social workers:

    7.1   Collect and organize data, and apply critical thinking to interpret information from clients and constituencies.

    7.2   Apply knowledge of human behavior and the social environment, person-in-environment, and other multidisciplinary theoretical frameworks in the analysis of assessment data from clients and constituencies.

    7.3   Develop mutually agreed-on intervention goals and objectives based on the critical assessment of strengths, needs, and challenges within clients and constituencies.

    7.4   Select appropriate intervention strategies based on the assessment, research knowledge, and values and preferences of clients and constituencies.

Competency 8: Intervene With Individuals, Families, Groups, Organizations, and Communities

Social workers understand that intervention is an ongoing component of the dynamic and interactive process of social work practice with, and on behalf of, diverse individuals, families, groups, organizations, and communities. Social workers are knowledgeable about evidence-informed interventions to achieve the goals of clients and constituencies, including individuals, families, groups, organizations, and communities. Social workers understand theories of human behavior and the social environment, and critically evaluate and apply this knowledge to effectively intervene with clients and constituencies. Social workers understand methods of identifying, analyzing, and implementing evidence-informed interventions to achieve client and constituency goals. Social workers value the importance of interprofessional teamwork and communication in interventions, recognizing that beneficial outcomes may require interdisciplinary, interprofessional, and interorganizational collaboration. Social workers:

    8.1   Critically choose and implement interventions to achieve practice goals and enhance capacities of clients and constituencies.

    8.2   Apply knowledge of human behavior and the social environment, person-in-environment, and other multidisciplinary theoretical frameworks in interventions with clients and constituencies.

    8.3   Use interprofessional collaboration as appropriate to achieve beneficial practice outcomes.

    8.4   Negotiate, mediate, and advocate with and on behalf of diverse clients and constituencies.

    8.5   Facilitate effective transitions and endings that advance mutually agreed-on goals.

Competency 9: Evaluate Practice With Individuals, Families, Groups, Organizations, and Communities

Social workers understand that evaluation is an ongoing component of the dynamic and interactive process of social work practice with, and on behalf of, diverse individuals, families, groups, organizations, and communities. Social workers recognize the importance of evaluating processes and outcomes to advance practice, policy, and service delivery effectiveness. Social workers understand theories of human behavior and the social environment, and critically evaluate and apply this knowledge in evaluating outcomes. Social workers understand qualitative and quantitative methods for evaluating outcomes and practice effectiveness. Social workers:

9.1   Select and use appropriate methods for evaluation of outcomes.

9.2   Apply knowledge of human behavior and the social environment, person-in-environment, and other multidisciplinary theoretical frameworks in the evaluation of outcomes.

9.3   Critically analyze, monitor, and evaluate intervention and program processes and outcomes.

9.4   Apply evaluation findings to improve practice effectiveness at the micro-, mezzo-, and macrolevels.

INDEX

AA legislation. *See* Affirmative Action legislation
accountability, 257–260
    consequential, 251
    procedural, 251
accounts-based reporting, 371
action-oriented behaviors, 7
administrative supervision, 325
ADT. *See* attention deficit trait
advertising academic positions, through marketing, 268–269
affiliative leadership style, 14, 91
Affirmative Action (AA) legislation, 266
ageism, 342
agency
    community, 224
    promotion process for, 282–285
    task environment, 483
    unionized, 282
agency-community relations, 481
AIM approach. *See* all-inclusive multicultural approach
all-inclusive multicultural (AIM) approach, 188
altruism, 91
Americans with Disabilities Act, 341
annual financial audit, 249
"Area of Responsibility Calendar by Month," 215–217
assessment
    performance, 277–279
    process and outcome, 276–277
assignments
    delegating, aspects of, 326–329
    tasking, 39–40
attention deficit trait (ADT), 203
    management, 204
    organize for, 204
attributional bias, 17
audits, 375
authoritative leadership style, 14
autism action coalition, 488
autocratic leadership style, 13–14
autonomous motivation, 22
autonomy, 178, 196
    SCARF model, 169

baby boomers, 171–173
    as leaders, 172
    managers, 172
Bandura model of social cognitive learning, 200
Bandura theory, 200
behaviors
    action-oriented, 7
    ideal, 223
    of leaders, 33
    of managers, 33
    professional, 223
benchmarks establishment, 417
bias
    attributional, 17
    reexamining and changing hiring, 285–286
board members roles, 443
budgetary oversight, 374–375
budgets, 369
    grant, preparing, 369
    organizational, preparing and managing, 243–245
    preparing, 245–248
business plan, 420–421
    goals, 421
    legal structure, 421
    marketing plan, 421
    mission statement, 421
    service field, 421
    target market, 421
    vision, 421

campus interviews, 271
candidates
    interviews, 272–273
    inviting, to campus/agency, 271–272
    need to know about the program, 272–273
    negotiations, 276
    presentations, 271–272
    selection of final, 276
    thinning the pool of, 269–271
    wooing on-site/at work location, 272
capacity, 460
capital investments, 243–244

case statements
    components and elements of, 447–450
    components in, 445–446
    development, 444, 445, 450
    elements in, 446
    purposes of, 452
    supporting documents, 451
CEC. *See* continuing education credits
CEO. *See* chief executive officer
certainty, SCARF model, 169
CFO. *See* chief financial officer
change management, 45–46
charismatic leadership style, 11
chief executive officer (CEO), 242, 255
chief financial officer (CFO), 245
civil service and union environments, 286
COA. *See* Council on Accreditation
coaching leadership style, 16
coercive leadership style, 15
collaborative agreements, 462
collaborative process, 469
colorblind approach to organizational
    diversity, 187
commensalism, 33
committee
    decision making, 240
    personnel, 267–268
communication
    barriers to good, 278
    director, 77
    effective, 170, 176
    electronic, 42
    expectations, 229
    good, 38
    leaders need to exude transparent, 37–38
    leadership, 42
    and marketing, 234
    skills, 74–75
    strengthening relations and effective, 230
    style concepts, 62–63
    with superiors, 77–79
communication management
    in conflict situations, 64–67
    in crisis situations, 63–64
communicators
    effective, 38, 42
    leaders as strong, 38
community agency, 224
community collaborations, 477
    general environment, 479–480
    with health and human services
        organizations, 483–486
    identifying opportunities for
        partnerships, 486
    mechanisms for, 489
    organizational domain, 480

    partnerships and alliances, 482–483
    policy advocacy coalitions, 487–488
    task environment, 480–481
competencies, 165
competent services, cultural, 233
complacency
    culture of, 227
    cynicism and, 225–232
compliance committee, 251–252
compliance standards, 248, 252
confidence
    leadership, 201, 202
    in times of stress, 203
confident leaders, 202, 203
confidentiality
    ethical dilemmas of, 325
    in supervision, 325
conflict
    handling, 70–74
    strategies for managing, 67–70
consequential accountability, 251
contingency rewards system, 10
continuing education credits (CEC), 342
core values, 405–406
    academic values, 406
cost centers, 370–371
    reallocating resources between, 370
Council on Accreditation (COA), 250
Council on Social Work Education (CSWE),
    250–251, 264, 268, 269, 274, 316, 359, 390,
    452, 482
Council on Social Work Education competencies,
    3, 4–6, 12–13, 19, 35, 41, 51, 121, 164–165,
    184, 241, 248, 257, 320, 324, 350–351,
    357–358, 361, 390–391, 394–395, 396–397,
    416–417, 419, 428–429, 433, 438, 478–479,
    482, 487, 491
    advance human rights and social, economic,
        and environmental justice, 520
    assess individuals, families, groups,
        organizations, and communities, 522
    demonstrate ethical and professional
        behavior, 519
    engage diversity and difference in
        practice, 520
    engage in policy practice, 519
    engage in practice-informed research and
        research-informed practice, 520–521
    engage with individuals, families, groups,
        organizations, and communities, 521
    evaluate practice with individuals, families,
        groups, organizations, and
        communities, 523
    intervene with individuals, families,
        groups, organizations, and
        communities, 522

creating a resource ban (Schram), 436
credible leaders, 320
crisis de-escalation techniques, 253
critical thinking, 339
CSWE. *See* Council on Social Work Education
cultural competent services, 233
culture
    of complacency, 227
    organizational, 223
    workplace to ensure a positive and
        supportive, 265
curriculum delivery options, 272
customer service, ensuring quality, 224
customized learning, 196
cutbacks
    approaches to, 379
    responses to, 380
cynicism
    and complacency, 225–235
    deal with, 226–227
    workplace, 226

DA. *See* decision analysis
DCFID, 364
debriefing meetings, 184
decision analysis (DA), 145–149
    bit and piece, 150–151
    short-form, 149–150
decision makers, 180
decision making, 280
    approaches to, 125–127
    committee, 240
    decision analysis (DA), 145–149
    group, 129
    guidelines for, 130–135
    individual versus group, 127–130
    MIS use for planning and, 357–358
    pitfalls of, 157–159
    potential problem analysis
        (PPA), 152–155
    problem analysis (PA), 139–142
    situation appraisal (SA), 136–138
    stages of, 136
    taxonomy of comprehension, 121–125
    for various approaches, 157
decision making model, optimizing, 131
decision model, 129
Delphi method, 128
democratic leadership style, 14
desired future, 391–392
destructive employees, handling, 339–340
dilemmas of keeping good people, 329–331
directing meetings, 103
direction giving, 176
director communication, 77

discipline, 279
    progressive, 334–338
disciplining supervisees, 335
discourse, reflective, 321
discrimination, 283–285, 342
    and harassment, 283–284
distributive leadership, 50
diversity
    employees, management, 341–343
    and harassment, 284
    in hiring, 267
    multicultural approach to, 188
    organizational, 187
    workforce, 187, 285
Doctor of Social Work (DSW) program, 227
DSW program. *See* Doctor of Social Work program

EAP. *See* employee assistance program
EBT techniques, 351
educational innovations, 165
Educational Policy and Accreditation Standards
    (EPAS), 199
educational supervision, 322, 328
EEO. *See* Equal Employment Opportunity
effective communication, 176
    ground rules for, 61–62
    skills, 55
effective communicators, 38, 42
effective interpersonal skills, 57–79
effective presentations, 60–61
    effective workspace, 208–210
    gathering essential tools, 310
    managing workflow, 209–210
    setting up a filing system, 209
effective writing, strategies for, 468–469
EI. *See* emotional intelligence
electronic communication, 42
elevator speech, 59, 60
    purpose of, 60
email handling, 213–214
emotional integration, in supervision, 323
emotional intelligence (EI), 7, 23, 323
    inherent aspect of, 22
    in leadership and management
        practice, 19–20
emotional maturity, 197
emotional regulation, 44
emotions, positive, 204
empathetic supervisors, 322–323
empathic language, 177
empathic leaders, 21
empathic supervision, 322–323
empathy
    exuding, 322
    in leadership, 21

employee assistance program (EAP), 339
employee transfers
    demotion of, 335
    dismissal of, 335
employees
    dealing with legally protected, 340–343
    discipline, 279
    diversity management, 341–343
    engaging and empowering, 224
    handling incompetent and destructive,
        339–340
    motivation, 168–177
employment agency, 280
empowering supervisees, 326
empowering team members, 180
entrepreneurial mind-set leaders, 222
environmental influences, 368
environmental stressors, 323
EPAS. *See* Educational Policy and Accreditation
    Standards
Equal Employment Opportunity (EEO), 266
    EEO Act of 1972, 266
    laws, 341
Equal Pay Act, 341
equity, 266–267
erroneous stereotypes, 284
establishing task groups, work roles, and
    communication channel (Schram), 436
ethical behaviors, 324
ethical decisions, 324
ethical supervision, 324–326
executive leadership, 255
exemplary leadership style, 11–12
exemplary practice, 323–324
external controls, 248–249
external networking, 199
exuding empathy, 322

face-to-face communication, 171
facilitator, ostentatious group, 167
faculty
    supporting established, 281–282
    tenure and promotion process, 281–282
fairness, SCARF model, 169
Faraca v. Clements, 266
federal and state regulations, 257
federal collaborations, 462
feedback
    formal, 332–333
    informal, 333–334
    vague, 334
finance committee, 249
financial audits, 249
financial transparency, 242, 375

fiscal year, 245
fixed assets, 375
fixed mind-set, 328
fluid feedback, 333
formal education, dearth of, 199
formal feedback, 332–333
formal performance evaluations, 331, 332
fundraising, 455
    effort, 458–459
    strategies, 471–472
fundraising activities, 455
    board members roles in, 443
    staff roles in, 443

Gantt chart, 402, 425, 426, 436, 437
Generational Rapport Competencies (Espinoza and
    Ukleja), 173
generation X leaders, 172
generation X managers, 172
Gen Xers, 171, 173, 174
gifts and stewardship, 460–462
goals, mission statement and, 410
good communication, 38
good leaders, 21, 24, 36, 38, 203
good managers, 24
grant, 468–471
    budget preparation, 469
    management, 470
    post award, 470
    purpose of, 470
    sustainability, 470, 471
grant-funded programs, 243
grant office, working with, 469
group supervision, 321
group work, mutual aid process in, 167
groups, working with, 90–91
GROW model, 184, 186
growth-oriented environment, 265

harassment
    discrimination and, 283
    diversity and, 283, 284
    workplace, 284
Health Insurance Portability and Accountability
    Act (HIPAA), 359
hiring, 273–277
human resources (HR), 234
    issues, 264
    role, 268
human services, business-oriented approach, 321

ideal behaviors, 223
idealization, 423

idealized design, 423–424
      desired properties of the unit, 423
idealized influence, 10
idealized planning process, 424
idealized redesign, 424–425
IM. *See* instant messaging
immediate terminations, 279
imposter syndrome, 194
in-person communication, 171
inactive approach, 392
incentive plans, 179
incentive programs, 179
incompetence, 339
incompetent employees, handling, 339–340
informal feedback, 333–334
informal performance evaluations, 332
informal recognition, 22
informal social contacts, with mangers/peers, 284
information technology (IT), 351, 352, 354
inspirational motivation, 10
instant messaging (IM), 213–214
intellectual stimulation, 11
interactional justice, 21
internal controls, 248–250
internal environment, SWOT, 398
internal networking, 199
interpersonal skills, 4
interview questions, 270
intrinsic motivation, 180, 181, 200

JCAHO. *See* Joint Commission on Accreditation of
      Healthcare Organizations
job description, creating, 268
Joint Commission on Accreditation of Healthcare
      Organizations (JCAHO), 250, 482

language
      empathic, 177
      meaning-making, 177
LCSW. *See* licensed clinical social worker
leaders
      at agencies, 257
      baby boomers as, 172
      budget and finance, 234
      chasing the tail, 228
      communication and marketing, 234
      confident, 202, 203
      development, 192
      diversity management, 232–233
      empathic, 21
      entrepreneurial mind-set, 222
      external relations, 235
      focus on organizational culture, 36–37
      fundraising, 235

generation X, 172
generational characteristics, 172
good, 21, 38, 203
and human resource, 234
influential in preventing cynicism and
      complacency, 225
management information system (MIS)
      programs, 234–235
millennials, 172
mindful, 206
motivation, 229
multiple skills for, 234–235
need to exude transparent communication,
      37–38
noninstituted decisions, 228
perception of favorites, 228
in perpetual state of reflection, 38–39
planning to achieve goals, 210–212
role, 222, 224
role modeling, 231–232
as strong communicators, 38
task-oriented, 21
transformational, 21
understanding the core of the
      organization, 235
visionary, 23
leadership, 9–10
      communication, 42
      communication strategies for working
            with groups, 75–76
      conceptualizing, 50
      confidence, 201–202
      development training programs, 199
      distributive, 50
      empathy in, 21
      executive, 255
      moving up in, 193–194, 204
      social change model (SCM) of, 50
      styles, 5–6, 10–25
      styles and traits, 5
      tasks in meetings, 93–117
      training for social work students, 199
      traits, styles, and philosophies, 5–10
      transition to, 191
      versus management, 36–44
leadership and management, 3–4, 34, 41, 43
      blending, 8–9
      distinguishing, 6–9
      overlays, 45–52
      role of emotional intelligence
            in, 19–20
leadership styles, 10–25
      affiliative, 14, 91
      authoritative, 14
      autocratic, 13–14

leadership styles, (cont.)
    charismatic, 11
    coaching, 16
    coercive, 15
    democratic, 14
    differences in, 16–18
    for different settings, 106–108
    exemplary, 11–12
    pacesetting, 15
    servant, 12–13
    transactional, 10
    transformational, 10–11
learning, customized, 196
lesbian, gay, bisexual, trans, queer, intersex, asexual (LGBTQIA) community, 342
liability, 240
    protecting the organization and employees from, 250–252
licensed clinical social worker (LCSW), 245
Linkert scales, 332
liquid assets, 375
logic planning model, designing, 431–432

management information systems (MIS), 350, 352
    decision, 352
    planning and implementation phases, 355–357
    program, 234, 350–354
    for social service organizations, 355
    software during the vetting process, 353
    use for planning and decision making, 357–358
Management Supervisory Development Program, 157
managers
    at agencies, 257
    baby boomers, 172
    in "flow," 39
    generational characteristics, 172
    generation X, 172
    good, 21, 24, 38, 203
    influential in preventing cynicism and complacency, 225
    informal social contacts with, 284
    millennials, 172
    multiple skills for, 234–235
    planning to achieve goals, 210–212
    role, 222, 224
    role modeling, 231–232
marketing, 460
    advertising academic positions through, 268–269
    communication and, 234
    and public relations, 79–87

maturity, emotional, 197
meaning-making language, 177
meetings, 89
    appropriate, 97
    checklist for planning, 109–115
    conducting/participating in, 98–102
    controlling, 104–106
    directing, 103–104
    following up on, 108
    good discussion at, 101
    leadership tasks in, 93–116
    making meetings productive, 92–93
    measurable, 96–97
    organizing, 97–98
    outcome–purpose–objectives of, 96
    preparation for, 93–96
    results-oriented, 96
    sample agenda, 99
    setting the purpose or objectives of, 96–97
    successful, 90
    traps in planning and conducting, 115–117
mentees, 197–199
mentor, 197, 280
    good, 197–199
mentoring
    approaches to, 196–197
    benefits of, 195–196
mentorship, 197
    benefits of, 192
    impact, 194–195
millennials leaders, 172
millennials managers, 172
mindful leaders, 206
mind-set, fixed, 328
MIS. See management information systems
MIS programs. See management information systems; program
mission statement, 400, 407–410
    academic, 407–408
    and goals, 410–412
    social work department, 408–409
mission/values, clarifying, 401
MLT. See motivating language theory
motivating language theory (MLT), 176
motivation, 460
    autonomous, 22
    employee, 168–177
    factors of, 168
    generational differences and similarities of, 171–177
    inspirational, 10
    intrinsic, 181
mutual aid process, in group work, 167

National Association of Deans and Directors (NADD), 199
National Association of Social Workers (NASW), 429
    Code of Ethics, 487
need-based programs, 178
Network for Social Work Management (NSWM), 19, 199, 264, 403, 417, 489
    competencies, 3, 4–6, 12–13, 19, 23–24, 34–36, 45, 47–50, 56–58, 60, 63, 74, 79–80, 86, 90, 94, 100, 101, 104, 120–121, 125, 127–128, 130, 136, 157, 164–165, 168, 180, 184, 192, 194, 198, 200, 222–223, 225, 231–234, 241–242, 248, 257–259, 264–267, 273, 284, 286, 320, 322, 325, 331, 334, 340, 350, 351, 357–358, 361–363, 368–369, 374, 376, 390–391, 394–397, 404, 417–420, 428–429, 433, 438, 442, 444, 460, 462, 470, 478–479, 482–483, 487
networking
    external, 199
    internal, 199
    professional, 199
next actions list, 216
NGT. See Nominal Group Technique
Nominal Group Technique (NGT), 138
nonprofit organizations (NPO), 21, 22, 56, 80, 242, 243
NPO. See nonprofit organizations
NSWM. See Network for Social Work Management

objectives, 414–417
Occupational Safety and Health Administration (OSHA) standards, 252, 253
OJT. See on-the-job-training
on-the-job-training (OJT), 193, 195, 196
operating costs, funding for, 244
opportunity, 460–461
optimism, 226
optimizing decision-making model, 131
organization, budget, 367, 369
organizational budgets, preparing and managing, 243–245
organizational camps, 228
organizational culture, 223
    leaders focus on, 36–37
    management, 46–52
organizational diversity, 187
organizational domain, community collaborations, 480
organizational dysfunction, 227–229
    chasing the tail, 228
    culture of complacency, 227

lack of clear direction, 229
    noninstituted decisions, 228
    operating in crisis mode, 229
    organizational camps, 228
    perception of favorites, 228
    stale state, 228
organizational equilibrium, 256
organizational functions, 222, 240
organizational justice, 21
organizational policies, 259
organizational procedures, 258–260
organizational process, using technology to enhance, 351–364
organizational tables, 240
organizational transitions, 225
OSHA standards. See Occupational Safety and Health Administration standards
ostentatious group facilitator, 167

pacesetting leadership style, 15
patient-centered supervision, 322, 328
PBB. See performance-based budgeting
PE. See performance evaluations
peers
    informal social contacts with, 284
    supervision, 321
performance assessments, 277–279
    conducting, 278
    criteria for, 278
    interviews, 278
performance counseling interview, objectives of, 277
performance evaluations (PE), 331–335
    formal, 332–333
    informal, 333–334
    systems and documents for, 331–332
performance improvement committees, 242
performance-based budgeting (PBB), 371–374
    advantages, 373
    characteristics, 373
    implementing, 372
    purpose of, 372
personal competence, 20–22
personal development, 200–202
personal list of ground rules, 68
personality clashes, 40
personnel committee, 271, 272, 276, 277
    establishing, 267–268
    hiring committees, 267
PERT. See Program Evaluation Review Technique
philanthropic culture, 443
physical management training (PMT), 253, 254
physical work environment, 272
PMT. See physical management training

policies and procedures (P&P) manual, 259
policy advocacy coalitions, 487–488
positive emotions, 204
positive performance management (PPM), 277
positive work environment, 180
positive workplace environment, 265
potential problem analysis (PPA), 152–155
        implementation of, 155
power-issue relationship, 488
PPA. *See* potential problem analysis
PPM. *See* positive performance management
preactive approach, 392
Pregnancy Act, 341
primary stakeholders, 481
proactive approach, 392
problem analysis (PA), decision making, 139–142
        people problems and, 142–145
        primary purpose of, 155–156
        short form, 155–156
procedural accountability, 251
process-centered supervision, 322, 324
procrastination, 214
productivity, enhancing, 208
professional behavior, 223
professional development, 200–202
professional networking, 199
professionalism, rewarding, 223–224
professor-level appointments, 268
program design process, 429–439
        comparative need, 430–431
        elements of good design, 433–435
        evaluation, 437–439
        expressed need, 430
        felt need, 430
        implementation, 436–437
        logic planning model designing, 431–432
        needs/resources assessments, 430–431
        normative need, 430
        outcome evaluation, 438
        process evaluation, 438
        program redesign and organizational
                survival, 438–439
program design process, elements of good
        design, 433
        activities/resources, 434–435
        goals and objectives, 434
        long-term outcomes, 435
        needs/resource assessment, 433–434
        outcomes, 435
        outputs, 435
        short-term results, 435
Program Evaluation Review Technique (PERT), 436
program logic model, 431
progressive discipline, 334–338

projects list, 215
promotions, 279–280
        process for agencies, 282
psychological and task-oriented adjustment, 255
psychological contracts, 172
public relations, marketing and, 79–87

quality customer service, ensuring, 224

reactive approach, 392
recognition, 180
        primed model, 127
recruitment, 267–269
reflective discourse, 321
regulation, emotional, 44
relatedness, SCARF model, 169
relationship management, 23
request for proposal (RFP), 468
research agenda, 464–466
research center
        business side of, 466–468
        development, 468
        establishment, 462
retention, 329
retrenchment planning, 376–382
        implications of, 381–382
reward
        designing and allocating, 178–181
        professionalism, 223–224
        programs, 178
RFP. *See* request for proposal
root cause analysis, 184

safety committee, 253
safety, assuring the appropriate, 252–254
SCARF
        domains, 204
        model, 169
SCM. *See* social change model (SCM)
secondary stakeholders, 481
self-awareness, 20–23
self-care, 206
self-determination theory, 22
self-efficacy, 200
self-identity, 172
self-leadership, 255
self-management, 20–23
self-motivation, 22
self-perception, 194
self-reflection, 42–43
self-regulation, 42–43
servant leadership style, 12–13
service-delivery standards, 248

service-related tasks, 243
sexism, 342
short term problem solving, 184
situation appraisal (SA), decision making, 136–138
skills
    development, 180
    effective communication, 55, 57–79
    effective interpersonal, 57–79
    interpersonal, 4
    managerial, 203–214
Skype interview questions, 270
social awareness, 23
social change model (SCM) of leadership, 50
social cognitive learning, Bandura model of, 200
social cognitive learning theory, 200
social competence, 23–25
social justice, programs and services for, 224
social role theory, 16–18
social service
    agency, 285, 329
    sector, 46
social work
    clinicians, 194
    education, 482
    leaders, 243, 257, 367–370, 374
    leadership, 199
    managers, 243, 257, 367–370, 374
    practice, 165
    profession, 178, 239, 350, 360
    skills, 18–19
    supervision in, 321
    technology in, 350
socioeconomic climate, 321
solid development program, 451
sometime/maybe list, 217
staff
    anxiety, 240
    diversity management, 341–343
    engaging, 41, 43
    performance evaluations, 277
    roles in fundraising, 443
    training and development, 181–188
stakeholder mapping, 401
stale state, 228
status, SCARF model, 169
stereotypes, erroneous, 284
stewardship, gifts and, 460–462
stimulation, intellectual, 11
strategic planning process, 389–390
    abbreviated, 403
    action framework (Gantt chart) for, 425–426
    action framework creation, 402–403
    alternative futures, development, 399
    composite scenario creation, 400
    establishment, 393–394

    in general, 391–393
    implementation of, 418–421
    initial agreement on, 395
    logical future of the system, 398
    mandates, 396
    model, 395
    organization of the future, 400–402
    perceived situation, developing
        projections, 396–398
    realizing change, 403
    strategic goals and strategies, 402
    strategic issues, identifying, 399–400
    updating and keeping current, 419–420
strategic resource development, 441
strategy statement, mastering, 58–60
strengths, weaknesses, opportunities, and
    threats (SWOT)
    components of, 398
    internal environment, 398
stress
    confidence in times of, 203
    secondary, 204
stressors, environmental, 323
submission process, 469
successful teams, characteristics of, 167
succession planning, 254–256
superiors
    communication with, 77–79
    successfully deal with, 78
supervision
    administrative, 325
    confidentiality in, 325
    educational, 322, 328
    emotional integration in, 323
    empathic, 322–323
    ethical, 324–325
    good, identifying elements
        of, 322–326
    group, 321
    modality of, 321
    patient-centered, 322, 328
    peer, 321
    process-centered, 322, 324
    process-oriented methods of, 322
    in social work, 321
    supportive, 322
    therapist-centered, 322, 324
supervisors, 320
    empathetic, 322, 323
    empowerment, 326
    exemplary practice, 323–324
    human resources management, 330
    multiple roles of, 321–322
    progressive discipline, 334–338
supportive supervision, 322

task-oriented adjustments, 255
task-oriented leaders, 21
tasking assignments, 39–40
tax-exempt organizations, 242
team commitment, 168
team members, to participate in decisions, 180
team players, 165
teamwork, 240
technology as changing, 360–361
technology resources
    billing, 359
    client/patient portal, 360
    compiling data, 359–360
    compliance, 359
    cost savings, 358
    funding, 358
    identifying, 352–354
    reliability of data, 363–364
    technology to maximize, 358–364
    utilizing, 354–355
    validity of data, 361–363
telephone interview questions, 270
TERA. *See* tribe, expectation, rank, and autonomy
terminations, 279–280
    immediate, 279
therapist-centered supervision, 322–324
thinkers, visionary, 39, 321
thinking, critical, 339
times of stress, confidence in, 203
time wasters, avoid, 213–214
to-do list, 216, 217
training, 277
transactional leadership style, 10
transformational leaders, 21
transformational leadership style, 10–11
transitions
    organizational, 225
    periods, 225

transparency, 242–256
    financial, 242
transparent communication, 37–38
tribe, expectation, rank, and autonomy (TERA), 196

unionized agencies, 282
unscheduled tasks list, 217

vague feedback, 334
vision statement, 404–405
visionary leader, 23
visionary thinkers, 39, 321
Vroom-Jago decision model, 128, 159

waiting-for list, 217
wasters, avoid time, 213–214
whistleblower policy, 242
work environments, 67, 180, 188, 252, 392
workforce diversity, 187, 285
working with groups, 90–91
workplace, 165
    cynicism, 226
    diversity in, 187
    to ensure a positive and supportive
        culture, 265
    handling incompetency and destruction
        in, 339
    harassment, 284
workspace, effective, organizing an, 208–210
writing
    effective, strategies for, 468–469
    proposals, pitfalls in, 469